*The Broadview Anthology of*

# BRITISH LITERATURE

### The Twentieth Century and Beyond:
### Volume 6B, From 1945 to the Twenty-First Century

The Broadview Anthology of British Literature

*The Broadview Anthology of*

# BRITISH LITERATURE

## The Twentieth Century and Beyond:
## Volume 6B, From 1945 to the Twenty-First Century

### GENERAL EDITORS

Joseph Black, University of Massachusetts
Leonard Conolly, Trent University
Kate Flint, Rutgers University
Isobel Grundy, University of Alberta
Don LePan, Broadview Press
Roy Liuzza, University of Tennessee
Jerome J. McGann, University of Virginia
Anne Lake Prescott, Barnard College
Barry V. Qualls, Rutgers University
Claire Waters, University of California, Davis

broadview press

LIBRARY AND ARCHIVES CANADA CATALOGUING IN PUBLICATION

The Broadview anthology of British literature / general editors, Joseph Black ... [et al].

Includes bibliographical references and index.
Contents: v.1. The Medieval period. —v.2. The Renaissance and the early seventeenth century. —v. 3. The Restoration and the eighteenth century.—v.4. The age of romanticism.—v.5. The Victorian era.—v.6A. The twentieth century and beyond: from 1900 to World War II.—v.6B. The twentieth century and beyond: from 1945 to the twenty-first century.

ISBN 1-55111-609-x (v.1), —ISBN 1-55111-610-3 (v.2), —ISBN 1-55111-611-1 (v.3), —ISBN 1-55111-612-x (v.4),—ISBN 1-55111-613-8 (v.5),—ISBN 978-1-55111-923-6 (v.6A),—ISBN 978-1-55111-924-3 (v.6B)

1. English literature.  I. Black, Joseph Laurence, 1962–

PR1109.B77   2006                    820.8                    C2006-900091-3

Broadview Press is an independent, international publishing house, incorporated in 1985. Broadview believes in shared ownership, both with its employees and with the general public; since the year 2000 Broadview shares have traded publicly on the Toronto Venture Exchange under the symbol BDP.

We welcome comments and suggestions regarding any aspect of our publications—please feel free to contact us at the addresses below or at broadview@broadviewpress.com.

*North America*
PO Box 1243,
Peterborough, Ontario
Canada K9J 7H5

2215 Kenmore Ave.,
Buffalo, NY, USA 14207
Tel: (705) 743-8990;
Fax: (705) 743-8353
email: customerservice@broadviewpress.com

*UK, Ireland, and continental Europe*
NBN International
Estover Road
Plymouth
UK PL6 7PY
Tel: +44 (0) 1752 202301;
Fax: +44 (0) 1752 202331;
Fax Order Line: +44 (0) 1752 202333;
Cust Ser: enquiries@nbninternational.com
Orders: orders@nbninternational.com

*Australia and New Zealand*
UNIREPS,
University of New South Wales
Sydney, NSW, 2052
Australia
Tel: 61 2 9664 0999;
Fax: 61 2 9664 5420
email: info.press@unsw.edu.au

www. broadviewpress.com
Broadview Press acknowledges the financial support of the Government of Canada through the Book Publishing Industry Development Program (BPIDP) for our publishing activities.

Cover design by Lisa Brawn
PRINTED IN CANADA

# CONTRIBUTING EDITORS AND WRITERS

MANAGING EDITOR — Don LePan
EDITORIAL COORDINATOR — Jennifer McCue
DEVELOPMENTAL EDITOR — Laura Cardiff
ASSISTANT DEVELOPMENTAL EDITOR — Melissa Goertzen
GENERAL ACADEMIC AND TEXTUAL EDITORS — Colleen Franklin, Morgan Rooney
DESIGN COORDINATOR — Kathryn Brownsey

## CONTRIBUTING EDITORS

Katherine O. Acheson
Sandra Bell
Emily Bernhard Jackson
Joseph Black
Robert Boenig
Michael Calabrese
Laura Cardiff
Noel Chevalier
Mita Choudhury
Thomas J. Collins
Leonard Conolly
Dianne Dugaw
Michael Faletra
Christina Fitzgerald
Stephen Glosecki

Amanda Goldrick-Jones
John Holmes
Michael Keefer
Scott Kleinman
Gary Kuchar
Don LePan
Roy Liuzza
Marie Loughlin
D.L. Macdonald
Anne McWhir
Tobias Menely
David Oakleaf
Jude Polsky
Anne Lake Prescott
Joyce Rappaport

Herbert Rosengarten
Jason Rudy
Peter Sabor
Janice Schroeder
Geoffrey Sill
Emily Steiner
David Swain
Andrew Taylor
Peggy Thompson
Fred Waage
Craig Walker
Claire Waters
James Winny

## CONTRIBUTING WRITERS

Laura Cardiff
Jude Polsky
Victoria Abboud
Steven Alvarez
Balaka Basu
Lopamudra Basu
Jane Beal
Rachel Beatty
Jennifer Beauvais
Rachel Bennett
Emily Bernhard Jackson
Rebecca Blasco
Julie Brennan
Andrew Bretz
Emily Cargan
Mia Chen
Adrienne Eastwood
Wendy Eberle-Sinatra
Peter Enman
Jamie Ferguson

Louise Geddes
Alina Gharabegian
Jane Grove
Isobel Grundy
Dorothy Hadfield
Camille Isaacs
Erik Isford
Andrea Jones
Stephanie King
Don LePan
Anna Lepine
John McIntyre
Susan McNeil-Bindon
Pia Mukherji
Carrie Nartkler
Byron Nelson
Kenna Olsen
Seamus O'Malley
Kendra O'Neal Smith
Allisandra Paschkowiak

Laura Pellerine
Jason Rudy
Anne Salo
Janice Schroeder
Karen Selesky
Carrie Shanafelt
Nicole Shukin
James Soderholm
Anne Sorbie
Martha Stoddard-Holmes
Jenna Stook
Candace Taylor
Yevgeniya Traps
David van Belle
Shari Watling
Matthew Williams
bj Wray
Nicole Zylstra

LAYOUT AND TYPESETTING

Kathryn Brownsey          Susan Chamberlain

ILLUSTRATION FORMATTING AND ASSISTANCE

Cheryl Baldwin          Lisa Brawn

PRODUCTION COORDINATORS

Barbara Conolly          Leonard Conolly          Judith Earnshaw

PERMISSIONS COORDINATORS

Emily Cargan          Katie Dole          Jennifer Elsayed
Chris Griffin          Amy Nimegeer

PROOFREADERS

Jennifer Bingham          Lynn Fraser          Lynn Neufeld
Martin Boyne          Anne Hodgetts          Morgan Rooney
Lucy Conolly          Amy Neufeld          Kerry Taylor

EDITORIAL ADVISORS

Rachel Ablow, University of Rochester
Joan Beal, University of Sheffield
Donald Beecher, Carleton University
Rita Bode, Trent University
Susan Brown, University of Guelph
Catherine Burroughs, Wells College
Elizabeth Campbell, Oregon State University
Margaret Case, Ohio Northern University
William Christmas, San Francisco State
    University
Nancy Cirillo, University of Illinois, Chicago
Angelo Costanzo, Professor Emeritus,
    Shippensburg University
David Cowart, University of South Carolina
Alex Dick, University of British Columbia
Len Diepeveen, Dalhousie University
Daniel Fischlin, University of Guelph
Robert Forman, St. John's University
Barbara Gates, University of Delaware
Chris Gordon-Craig, University of Alberta
Stephen Guy-Bray, University of British
    Columbia
Elizabeth Hodgson, University of British
    Columbia

John Holmes, University of Reading
Peter Jeffrey, Princeton University
Michael Keefer, University of Guelph
Gordon Kipling, University of California,
    Los Angeles
William Liston, Ball State University
Peter Mallios, University of Maryland
Kirsteen McCue, University of Glasgow
Rod Michell, Thompson Rivers University
Byron Nelson, West Virginia University
Michael North, University of California,
    Los Angeles
Anna C. Patchias, formerly of the University of
    Virginia, Charlottesville
Alex Pettit, University of Northern Texas
John Pollock, San Jose State University
Jason Rudy, University of Maryland
Carol Senf, Georgia Tech
Sharon Smulders, Mount Royal College
Marni Stanley, Malaspina University-College
Goran Stanivukovic, St. Mary's University
Roderick Watson, University of Stirling
Julian Yates, University of Delaware

# CONTENTS

**VOLUME 6B, From 1945 to the Twenty-First Century**

## APPENDICES

## A FRESH APPROACH

To those with some awareness of the abundance of fresh material and lively debate in the field of English Studies in recent generations, it may seem surprising that this abundance has not been more fully reflected in the number of available anthologies. Thirty years ago there were two comprehensive anthologies designed for courses surveying British Literature: *The Norton Anthology of English Literature* and one alternative. In recent years there have been still two choices available—the *Norton* and one alternative. Over that time span *The Longman Anthology of British Literature* replaced *The Oxford Anthology of English Literature* in the role of "alternative," but there has been no expansion in range of available choices to match the expansion of content and of approach that has characterized the discipline itself. The number of available handbooks and guides to writing has multiplied steadily (to the point where there are literally hundreds of available choices), while the number of comprehensive anthologies of British literature has remained at two.

For those of us who have been working for the past three years on *The Broadview Anthology of British Literature*, it is not difficult to understand why. The very expansion of the discipline has made the task of assembling and editing an anthology that fully and vibrantly reflects the ways in which the British literary tradition is studied and taught an extraordinarily daunting one. The sheer amount of work involved is enormous, but so too is the amount of expertise that needs to be called on. With that background very much in mind, we have charted a new course in the preparation of *The Broadview Anthology of British Literature*. Rather than dividing up the work among a relatively small number of academics, and asking each of them to handle on their own the work of choosing, annotating, and preparing introductions to texts in their own areas of specialization, we have involved a large number of contributors in the process (as the pages following the

title page to this volume attest), and encouraged a high degree of collaboration at every level. First and foremost have been the distinguished academics who have served as our General Editors for the project, but in all there have literally been hundreds of people involved at various stages in researching, drafting headnotes or annotations, reviewing material, editing material, and finally carrying out the work of designing and typesetting the texts and other materials. That approach has allowed us to draw on a diverse range of talent, and to prepare a large anthology with unusual speed. It has also facilitated the maintenance of a high degree of consistency. Material has been reviewed and revised in-house at Broadview, by outside editors (chief among them Colleen Franklin, an academic with a wide-ranging background and also a superb copy editor), by a variety of academics with an extraordinarily diverse range of backgrounds and academic specialities, and by our team of General Editors for the project as a whole. The aim has been not only to ensure accuracy but also to make sure that the same standards are applied throughout the anthology to matters such as extent and coverage in author introductions, level of annotation, tone of writing, and student accessibility.

Our General Editors have throughout taken the lead in the process of making selections for the anthology. Along the way we have been guided by several core principles. We have endeavored to provide a selection that is broadly representative, while also being mindful of the importance of choosing texts that have the capacity to engage readers' interest today. We have for the most part made it a policy to include long works in their entirety or not at all; readers will find complete in these pages works such as *Utopia*, *Confessions of an English Opium Eater*, *In Memoriam* and *A Room of One's Own* that are often excerpted in other anthologies. Where inexpensive editions of works are available in our series of paperback Broadview Editions, we have often decided to omit them here, on the grounds that those wishing to teach one or more such works may easily order them in a combination package with the anthology; on these grounds we have decided against including *Frankenstein*, *Pride and Prejudice*, or *Heart of Darkness*. (For both Mary Shelley and Jane Austen we have made exceptions to our general policy regarding excerpts, however, including selections from *The Last Man* to represent Shelley and the first four chapters of *Pride and Prejudice*, together with a complete shorter work, *Lady Susan*, to represent Austen.)

Any discussion of what is distinctive about *The Broadview Anthology of British Literature* must focus above all on the contents. In every volume of the anthology there is material that is distinctive and fresh–including not only selections by lesser-known writers but also less familiar selections from canonical writers. The anthology takes a fresh approach too to a great many canonical texts. The first volume of the anthology includes not only Roy Liuzza's translation of *Beowulf* (widely acclaimed as the most engaging and reliable translation available), but also new translations by Liuzza of many other works of Old English poetry and prose. Also included in the first volume of the anthology are a new verse translation of *Judith* by Stephen Glosecki, and new translations by Claire Waters of several of the *Lais* of Marie de France. The second volume includes *King Lear* not only in the full Folio version but also with three key scenes from the Quarto version; readers are thus invited to engage firsthand with the question of how textual issues may substantially affect larger issues of meaning. And so on through all six volumes.

In a number of these cases the distinctive form of the anthology facilitates the presentation of content in an engaging and practical fashion. Notably, the adoption of a two-column format allows for some translations (the Marie de France *Lais*, the James Winny translation of *Sir Gawain and the Green Knight*) to be presented in parallel column format alongside the original texts, allowing readers to experience something of the flavor of the original, while providing convenient access to an accessible translation. Similarly, scenes from the Quarto version of *King Lear* are presented alongside the comparable sections of the Folio text, and passages from four translations of the Bible are laid out parallel to each other for ready comparison.

The large trim-size, two-column format also allows for greater flexibility in the presentation of visual materials. Throughout we have aimed to make this an anthology that is fully alive to the connections between literary and visual culture, from the discussion of the CHI-RHO page of the Lindisfarne Gospels in the first volume of the anthology (and the accompanying color illustration) to the inclusion in Volume 6 of a number of selections (including Graham Greene's "The Basement Room," Hanif Kureishi's "My Son the Fanatic," Tom Stoppard's "Professional Foul," and several skits from "Monty Python's Flying Circus") that may be discussed in connection with film or television versions. Along the way appear several full-page illustrations from the Ellesmere manuscript of Chaucer's *Canterbury Tales* and illustrations to a wide variety of other works, from *Robinson Crusoe* and *Gulliver's Travels* to *A Christmas Carol* and *The Road to Wigan Pier*.

## CONTEXTUAL MATERIALS

Visual materials are also an important component of the background materials that form an important part of the anthology. These materials are presented in two ways. Several "Contexts" sections on particular topics or themes appear in each volume of the anthology, presented independent of any particular text or author. These include broadly based groupings of material on such topics as "Religion and Spiritual Life," "Print Culture," "India and the Orient," "The Abolition of Slavery," "The New Art of Photography," and "The End of Empire." The groups of "In Context" materials each relate to a particular text or author. They range from the genealogical tables provided as a supplement to *Beowulf*; to materials on "The Eighteenth-Century Sexual Imagination" (presented in conjunction with Haywood's *Fantomina*); to a selection of materials relating to the Peterloo massacre (presented in conjunction with Percy Shelley's "The Mask of Anarchy"); to materials on "'The Vilest Scramble for Loot' in Central Africa" (presented in conjunction with Conrad's "An Outpost of Progress"). For the most part these contextual materials are, as the word suggests, included with a view to setting texts in their broader literary, historical, and cultural contexts; in some cases, however, the materials included in "Contexts" sections are themselves literary works of a high order. The autobiographical account by Eliza M. of nineteenth-century life in Cape Town, for example (included in the section in Volume 5 on "Race and Empire"), is as remarkable for its literary qualities as it is for the light it sheds on the realities of colonial life. In the inclusion of texts such as these, as well as in other ways, the anthology aims to encourage readers to explore the boundaries of the literary and the non-literary, and the issue of what constitutes a "literary text."

## WOMEN'S PLACE

A central element of the broadening of the canon of British literature in recent generations has of course been a great increase in the attention paid to texts by women writers. As one might expect from a publisher that has played an important role in making neglected works by women writers widely available, this anthology reflects the broadening of the canon quantitatively, by including a substantially larger number of women writers than have earlier anthologies of British literature. But it also reflects this broadening in other ways. In many anthologies of literature (anthologies of British literature, to be sure, but also anthologies of literature of a variety of other sorts) women writers are set somewhat apart, referenced in introductions and headnotes only in relation to issues of gender, and treated as important only for the fact of their being women writers. *The Broadview Anthology* strenuously resists such segregation; while women writers are of course discussed in relation to gender issues, their texts are also presented and discussed alongside those by men in a wide variety of other contexts, including seventeenth-century religious and political controversies, the abolitionist movement and World War I pacifism. Texts by women writers are front and center in the discussion of the development of realism in nineteenth-century fiction. And when it comes to the twentieth century, both Virginia Woolf and Dorothy Richardson are included alongside James Joyce as practitioners of groundbreaking modernist narrative techniques.

## "BRITISH," "ENGLISH," "IRISH," "SCOTTISH," "WELSH," "OTHER"

The broadening of English Studies, in conjunction with the expansion and subsequent contraction of British power and influence around the world, has considerably complicated the issue of exactly how inclusive anthologies should be. In several respects this anthology (like its two main competitors) is significantly more inclusive than its title suggests, including a number of non-British writers whose works connect in important ways with the traditions of British literature. We have endeavored first of all to portray the fluid and multilingual reality of the medieval period through the inclusion not only of works in Old and Middle English but also, where other cultures interacted with the nascent "English" language and "British" culture, works in Latin, in French, and in Welsh. In later periods the word "British" becomes deeply problematic in different respects, but on balance we have preferred it to the only obvious alternative, "English." There are several objections to the latter in this context. Perhaps most obviously, "English" excludes authors or texts not only from Ireland but also from Scotland and from Wales, both of which retain to this day cultures quite distinct from that of the English. "English literature," of course, may also be taken to mean "literature written in English," but since the anthology does not cover *all* literature written in English (most obviously in excluding American literature), the ambiguity would not in this case be helpful.

The inclusion of Irish writers presents a related but even more tangled set of issues. At the beginning of the period covered by the six volumes of this anthology we find works, such as the *Book of Kells*, that may have been created in what is now England, in what is now Scotland, in what is now Ireland—or in some combination of these. Through most of the seventeenth, eighteenth, and nineteenth centuries almost the whole of Ireland was under British control—but for the most part unwillingly. In the period covered in the last of the six volumes Ireland was partitioned, with Northern Ireland becoming a part of the United Kingdom and the

Republic of Ireland declared independent of Britain on 6 December 1921. Less than two months earlier, James Joyce had completed *Ulysses*, which was first published as a complete work the following year (in Paris, not in Britain). It would be obviously absurd to regard Joyce as a British writer up to just before the publication of *Ulysses*, and an Irish writer thereafter. And arguably he and other Irish writers should never be regarded as British, whatever the politics of the day. If on no other grounds than their overwhelming influence on and connection to the body of literature written in the British Isles, however, we have included Irish writers—among them Swift, Sheridan, Wilde, Shaw, Beckett, Bowen, Muldoon, and Heaney as well as Joyce —throughout this anthology. We have also endeavored to give a real sense in the introductions to the six volumes of the anthology, in the headnotes to individual authors, and in the annotations to the texts themselves, of the ways in which the histories and the cultures of England, Ireland, Scotland and Wales, much as they interact with one another, are also distinct.

Also included in this anthology are texts by writers from areas that are far removed geographically from the British Isles but that are or have been British possessions. Writers such as Mary Rowlandson, Olaudah Equiano, and Phillis Wheatley are included, as they spent all or most of their lives living in what were then British colonial possessions. Writers who came of age in an independent United States, on the other hand, are not included, unless (like T.S. Eliot) they subsequently put down roots in Britain and became important British literary figures. Substantial grey areas, of course, surround such issues. One might well argue, for example, that Henry James merits inclusion in an anthology of British literature, or that W.H. Auden and Thom Gunn are more American poets than British ones. But the chosen subject matter of James's work has traditionally been considered to mark him as having remained an American writer, despite having spent almost two-thirds of his life in England. And both Auden and Gunn so clearly made a mark in Britain before crossing the Atlantic that it would seem odd to exclude them from these pages on the grounds of their having lived the greater part of their adult lives in America. One of our competitors includes Sylvia Plath in their anthology of

British literature; Plath lived in England for only five of her thirty years, though, and her poetry is generally agreed to have more in common with the traditions of Lowell, Merwin and Sexton than with the currents of British poetry in the 1950s and '60s.

As a broad principle, we have been open to the inclusion of twentieth and twenty-first century work in English not only by writers from the British Isles but also by writers from British possessions overseas, and by writers from countries that were once British possessions and have remained a part of the British Commonwealth. In such cases we have often chosen selections that relate in one way or another to the tradition of British literature and the British colonial legacy. Of the Judith Wright poems included here, several relate to her coming to terms with the British colonial legacy in Australia; similarly, both the Margaret Atwood and the Alice Munro selections include work in which these Canadian authors attempt to recreate imaginatively the experience of British emigrants to Canada in the nineteenth century; the Chinua Achebe story in the anthology concerns the divide between British colonial culture and traditional Nigerian culture; and so on. For convenience we have also grouped most of the post-World War II non-British authors together, following the "Contexts: The End of Empire" section. (Other than that, the table of contents for the anthology is arranged chronologically according to the birthdate of each author.)

THE HISTORY OF LANGUAGE, AND OF PRINT CULTURE

Among the liveliest discussions we had at meetings of our General Editors were those concerning the issue of whether or not to bring spelling and punctuation into accord with present-day practice. We finally decided that, in the interests of making the anthology accessible to the introductory student, we should *in most cases* bring spelling and punctuation in line with present-day practice. An important exception has been made for works in which modernizing spelling and punctuation would alter the meaning or the aural and metrical qualities. In practice this means that works before the late sixteenth century tend to be presented either in their original form or in translation, whereas later texts tend to have spelling and punctuation modernized. But where spelling and punctuation choices in later texts are known (or believed on reliable authority) to represent conscious choice on the part of the author rather than simply the common practice of the time, we have in those cases, too, made an exception and retained the original spelling and punctuation. (Among these are texts by Edmund Spenser, by William Cowper, by William Blake, John Clare, and several other poets of the Romantic era, by George Bernard Shaw, and by contemporary figures such as Linton Kwesi Johnson.)

Beyond this, we all agreed that we should provide for readers a real sense of the development of the language and of print culture. To that end we have included in each volume examples of texts in their original form—in some cases through the use of pages shown in facsimile, in others by providing short passages in which spelling and punctuation have not been modernized. A list of these appears near the beginning of each volume of the anthology.

We have also included a section of the history of the language as part of the introduction to each volume. And throughout the anthology we include materials—visual as well as textual—relating to the history of print culture.

## A Dynamic and Flexible Anthology

Almost all major book publishing projects nowadays are accompanied by an adjunct website, and most large-scale anthologies are accompanied by websites that provide additional background materials in electronic form. The website component of this anthology, on the other hand, is precisely that—a *component* of the anthology itself. The notion of a website of this sort grew organically out of the process of trying to winnow down the contents of the anthology to a manageable level—the point at which all the material to be included would fit within the covers of bound books that would not be overwhelmingly heavy. And we simply could not do it. After we had made a very substantial round of cuts we were still faced with a table of contents in which each volume was at least 200 or 300 pages longer than our agreed-upon maximum. Our solution was not to try to

cut anything more, but rather to select a range of material to be made available in a website component of the anthology. This material is in every way produced according to the same high standards of the material in the bound books; the editorial standards, the procedures for annotation, the author introductions, and the page design and layout—all are the same. The texts on the web, in short, are not "extra" materials; they are an integral part of the full anthology. In accordance with that principle, we have been careful to include a wide range of texts by lesser-known writers within the bound books, and a number of texts by canonical writers within the web component of the anthology.

The latter may be used in a variety of ways. Most obviously, readings from the web component are available to any purchaser of the book. Instructors who adopt *The Broadview Anthology of British Literature* as a course text are also granted permission to reproduce any web material for which Broadview holds copyright in a supplementary coursepack. An alternative for instructors who want to "create their own" anthology is to provide the publisher with a list of desired table of contents; Broadview will then make available to students through their university bookstore a custom-made coursepack with precisely those materials included. Other options are available too. Volumes of the anthology itself may of course be shrink-wrapped together at special prices in any desired combination. They may also (for a modest additional charge) be combined in a shrink-wrapped package with one or more of the over 200 volumes in the Broadview Editions series.

We anticipate that over the years the web-based component of the anthology will continue to grow—every year there will be a greater choice of web-based texts in the anthology. And every year too we anticipate additional web "extras" (discussed below). But we never foresee a day when the web will be the only option; we expect physical books always to remain central to Broadview's approach to publishing.

## The Broadview List

One of the reasons we have been able to bring a project of this sort to fruition in such a relatively short time is that we have been able to draw on the resources of the full Broadview list: the many titles in the Broadview Editions series, and also the considerable range of other Broadview anthologies. As the contributors' pages and the permissions acknowledgments pages indicate, a number of Broadview authors have acted as contributing editors to this volume, providing material from other volumes that has been adapted to suit the needs of the present anthology; we gratefully acknowledge their contribution.

As it has turned out, the number of cases where we have been able to draw on the resources of the Broadview list in the full sense, using in these pages texts and annotations in very much the same form in which they appear elsewhere, has been relatively small; whether because of an issue such as the level of textual modernization or one of style of annotation, we have more often than not ended up deciding that the requirements of this anthology were such that we could not use material from another Broadview source as-is. But even in these cases we often owe a debt of gratitude to the many academics who have edited outstanding editions and anthologies for Broadview. For even where we have not drawn directly from them, we have often been inspired by them— inspired to think of a wider range of texts as possibilities than we might otherwise have done, inspired to think of contextual materials in places where we might otherwise not have looked, inspired by the freshness of approach that so many of these titles exemplify.

## EDITORIAL PROCEDURES AND CONVENTIONS, APPARATUS

The in-house set of editorial guidelines for *The Broadview Anthology of British Literature* now runs to over 40 pages, covering everything from conventions for the spacing of marginal notes, to the use of small caps for the abbreviations CE and BCE, to the approach we have adopted to references in author headnotes to name changes. Perhaps the most important core principle in the introductions to the various volumes, in the headnotes for each author, in the introductions in "Contexts" sections, and in annotations throughout the anthology, is to endeavor to provide a sufficient amount of information to enable students to read and interpret these texts, but without making evaluative judgements or imposing particular interpretations. In practice that is all a good deal more challenging than it sounds; it is often extremely difficult to describe why a particular author is considered to be important without using language that verges on the interpretive or the evaluative. But it is fine line that we have all agreed is worth trying to walk; we hope that readers will find that the anthology achieves an appropriate balance.

ANNOTATION:   It is also often difficult to make judgments as to where it is appropriate to provide an explanatory annotation for a word or phrase. Our policy as been to annotate where we feel it likely that most first- or second-year students are likely to have difficulty understanding the denotative meaning. (We have made it a practice not to provide notes discussing connotative meanings.) But in practice the vocabularies and levels of verbal facility of first- and second-year students may vary enormously, both from institution to institution and within any given college or university class. On the whole, we provide somewhat more annotation than our competitors, and somewhat less interpretation. Again, we hope that readers will find that the anthology has struck a appropriate balance.

THE ETHICS AND POLITICS OF ANNOTATION:   On one issue regarding annotation we have felt that principles are involved that go beyond the pedagogical. Most anthologies of British literature allow many words or phrases of a racist, sexist, anti-Semitic, or homophobic nature either to pass entirely without comment, or to be glossed with apologist comments that leave the impression that such comments were excusable in the past, and may even be unobjectionable in the present. Where derogatory comments about Jewish people and money-lending are concerned, for example, anthologies often leave the impression that money-lending was a pretty unsavory practice that Jewish people entered by choice; it has been all too rare to provide readers with any sense of the degree to which English society consistently discriminated against Jews, expelling them entirely for several centuries, requiring them to wear physical marks identifying their Jewish status, prohibiting them from entering most professions, and so on. *The Broadview*

*Anthology* endeavors in such cases, first of all, not to allow such words and phrases to pass without comment; and second, to gloss without glossing over.

DATES:  We make it a practice to include the date when a work was first made public, whether publication in print or, in the case of dramatic works, made public through the first performance of the play. Where that date is known to differ substantially from the date of composition, a note to this effect is included in parentheses. With medieval works, where there is no equivalent to the "publication" of later eras, where texts often vary greatly from one manuscript copy to another, and where knowledge as to date of original composition is usually imprecise, the date that appears at the end of each work is an estimate of the date of the work's origin in the written form included in the anthology. Earlier oral or written versions are of course in some cases real possibilities.

TEXTS:  Where translations appear in this anthology, a note at the bottom of the first page indicates what translation is being used. Similar notes also address overall textual issues where choice of copy text is particularly significant. Reliable editions of all works are listed in the bibliography for the anthology, which is included as part of the website component rather than in the bound books, to facilitate ready revision. (In addition to information as to reliable editions, the bibliography provides for each author and for each of the six periods a select lists of important or useful historical and critical works.) Copyright information for texts not in the public domain, however, is provided within the bound books in a section listing Permissions Acknowledgments.

INTRODUCTIONS:  In addition to the introductory headnotes for each author included in the anthology, each "Contexts" section includes a substantial introduction, and each volume includes an introduction to the period as a whole. These introductions to the six volumes of the anthology endeavor to provide a sense not only of the broad picture of literary developments in the period, but also of the historical, social, and political background, and of the cultural climate. Readers should be cautioned that, while there is inevitably some overlap between information presented here and information presented in the author headnotes, an effort has been made to avoid such repetition as much as possible; the general introduction to each period should thus be read in conjunction with the author headnotes. The general introductions aim not only to provide an overview of ways in which texts and authors included in these pages may connect with one another, but also to give readers a sense of connection with a range of other writers and texts of the period.

READING POETRY:  For much of the glossary and for the "Reading Poetry" section that appears as part of the appendices to each volume we have drawn on the superb material prepared by Herbert Rosengarten and Amanda Goldrick-Jones for *The Broadview Anthology of Poetry*; this section provides a concise but comprehensive introduction to the study of poetry. It includes discussions of diction, imagery, poetic figures, and various poetic forms, as well as offering an introduction to prosody.

MAPS:  Also appearing within each of the bound books are maps especially prepared for this anthology, including, for each volume, a map of Britain showing towns and features of relevance during the pertinent period; a map showing the counties of Britain and of Ireland; maps both of the London area and of the inner city; and world maps indicating the locations of some of the significant places referenced in the anthology, and for later volumes showing the extent of Britain's overseas territories.

GLOSSARY:  Some other anthologies of British literature include both glossaries of terms and essays introducing students to various political and religious categories in British history. Similar information is included in *The Broadview Anthology of British Literature*, but we have adopted a more integrated approach, including political and religious terms along with literary ones in a convenient general glossary. While we recognize that "googling" for information of this sort is often the student's first resort (and we recognize too the value of searching the web for the wealth of background reference information available there), we also recognize that information culled from the Internet is often far from reliable; it is our intent, through this glossary, through our introductions and headnotes, and through the wealth of accessible annotation in the anthology, to provide as part of the anthology a reliable core of information in the most convenient and accessible form possible.

OTHER MATERIALS: A chart of Monarchs and Prime Ministers is also provided within these pages. A range of other adjunct materials may be accessed through *The Broadview Anthology of British Literature* website. "Texts and Contexts" charts for each volume provide a convenient parallel reference guide to the dates of literary texts and historical developments. "Money in Britain" provides a thumbnail sketch of the world of pounds, shillings, and pence, together with a handy guide to estimating the current equivalents of monetary values from earlier eras. And the website offers, too, a variety of aids for the student and the instructor. An up-to-date list of these appears on the site.

# ACKNOWLEDGMENTS

The names of those on the Editorial Board that shaped this anthology appear on the title page, and those of the many who contributed directly to the writing, editing, and production of the project on the following two pages. Special acknowledgment should go to Jennifer McCue, who as Editorial Coordinator has been instrumental in tying together all the vast threads of this project and in making it a reality; to Laura Cardiff and Jude Polsky, who have carried larger loads than any others in drafting introductory materials and annotations, and who have done so with great skill and unfailing grace; to Kathryn Brownsey, who has been responsible for design and typesetting, and has continued to do a superb job and to maintain her good spirits even when faced with near-impossible demands; to Colleen Franklin, for the range of her scholarship as well as for her keen eye as our primary copy editor for the entire project; to Emily Cargan, Jennifer Elsayed and Amy Nimegeer who have together done superb work on the vast job of clearing permissions for the anthology; and to Michelle Lobkowicz and Anna Del Col, who have ably and enthusiastically taken the lead with marketing matters.

The academic members of the Advisory Editorial Board and all of us in-house at Broadview owe an enormous debt of gratitude to the hundreds of academics who have offered assistance at various stages of this project. In particular we would like to express our appreciation and our thanks to the following:

Rachel Ablow, University of Rochester
Bryan Alexander, Middlebury College
Sharon Alker, Whitman College
James Allard, Brock University
Laurel Amtower, San Diego State University
Rob Anderson, Oakland University
Christopher Armitage, University of North Carolina, Chapel Hill
Clinton Atchley, Henderson State University
John Baird, University of Toronto
William Baker, Northern Illinois University
Karen Bamford, Mount Allison University
John Batchelor, University of Newcastle
Lynn Batten, University of California, Los Angeles
Alexandra Bennett, Northern Illinois University
John Beynon, California State University, Fresno
Robert E. Bjork, Arizona State University
Rita Bode, Trent University
Robert Boenig, Texas A & M University
Rick Bowers, University of Alberta
David Brewer, Ohio State University

William Brewer, Appalachian State University
Susan Brown, University of Guelph
Sylvia Brown, University of Alberta
Sheila Burgar, University of Victoria
Catherine Burroughs, Wells College
Rebecca Bushnell, University of Pennsylvania
Michael Calabrese, California State University
Elizabeth Campbell, Oregon State University
Cynthia Caywood, University of San Diego
Jane Chance, Rice University
Ranita Chatterjee, California State University, Northridge
Nancy Cirillo, University of Illinois, Chicago
Eric Clarke, University of Pittsburgh
Jeanne Clegg, University of Aquila, Italy
Thomas J. Collins, University of Western Ontario
Kevin Cope, Louisiana State University
David Cowart, University of South Carolina
Catherine Craft-Fairchild, University of St. Thomas
Carol Davison, University of Windsor
Alex Dick, University of British Columbia

Len Diepeveen, Dalhousie University
Mary Dockray-Miller, Lesley College
Frank Donoghue, Ohio State University
Chris Downs, Saint James School
Julie Early, University of Alabama, Huntsville
Siân Echard, University of British Columbia
Garrett Epp, University of Alberta
Daniel Fischlin, University of Guelph
Verlyn Flieger, University of Maryland
Robert Forman, St. John's University
Lorcan Fox, University of British Columbia
Roberta Frank, Yale University
Jeff Franklin, University of Colorado, Denver
Maria Frawley, George Washington University
Mark Fulk, Buffalo State College
Andrew Galloway, Cornell University
Michael Gamer, University of Pennsylvania
Barbara Gates, University of Delaware
Daniel Gonzalez, University of New Orleans
Jan Gorak, University of Denver
Chris Gordon-Craig, University of Alberta
Ann-Barbara Graff, Georgia Tech University
Michael Griffin, formerly of Southern Illinois
    University
Elisabeth Gruner, University of Richmond
Stephen Guy-Bray, University of British Columbia
Ruth Haber, Worcester State College
Dorothy Hadfield, University of Guelph
Margaret Hadley, University of Calgary
Robert Hampson, Royal Holloway University of
    London
Michael Hanly, Washington State University
Lila Harper, Central Washington State University
Joseph Harris, Harvard University
Anthony Harrison, North Carolina State University
Douglas Hayes, Winona State University
Jennifer Hellwarth, Allegheny University
Peter Herman, San Diego State University
Kathy Hickock, Iowa State University
John Hill, US Naval Academy
Thomas Hill, Cornell University
Elizabeth Hodgson, University of British Columbia
Joseph Hornsby, University of Alabama
Scott Howard, University of Denver
Tara Hyland-Russell, St. Mary's College

Catherine Innes-Parker, University of Prince Edward
    Island
Jacqueline Jenkins, University of Calgary
John Johansen, University of Alberta
Richard Juang, Susquehanna University
Michael Keefer, University of Guelph
Sarah Keefer, Trent University
Jon Kertzer, University of Calgary
Helen Killoran, Ohio University
Gordon Kipling, University of California, Los Angeles
Anne Klinck, University of New Brunswick
Elizabeth Kraft, University of Georgia
Mary Kramer, University of Massachusetts, Lowell
Linda Leeds, Bellevue Community College
Mary Elizabeth Leighton, University of Victoria
William Liston, Ball State University
Sharon Locy, Loyola Marymount University
Ross MacKay, Malaspina University-College
Peter Mallios, University of Maryland
Arnold Markley, Penn State University
Pamela McCallum, University of Calgary
Kristen McDermott, Central Michigan University
John McGowan, University of North Carolina
Thomas McLean, University of Otago, New Zealand
Susan McNeill-Bindon, University of Alberta
Rod Michell, Thompson Rivers University
Kitty Millett, San Francisco State University
Richard Moll, University of Western Ontario
Monique Morgan, McGill University
Lucy Morrison, Salisbury University
Byron Nelson, West Virginia University
Carolyn Nelson, West Virginia University
Claudia Nelson, Southwest Texas State University
Holly Faith Nelson, Trinity Western University
John Niles, University of Wisconsin, Madison
Michael North, University of California, Los Angeles
Mary Anne Nunn, Central Connecticut State University
David Oakleaf, University of Calgary
Tamara O'Callaghan, Northern Kentucky University
Karen Odden, Assistant Editor for *Victorian Literature
    and Culture* (formerly of University of Wisconsin,
    Milwaukee)
Erika Olbricht, Pepperdine University
Patrick O'Malley, Georgetown University
Patricia O'Neill, Hamilton College

Delilah Orr, Fort Lewis College
Cynthia Patton, Emporia State University
Russell Perkin, St. Mary's University
Marjorie G. Perloff, Stanford University
Summer Pervez, University of Ottawa
John Peters, University of North Texas
Alexander Pettit, University of North Texas
Jennifer Phegley, The University of Missouri,
    Kansas City
John Pollock, San Jose State University
Mary Poovey, New York University
Gautam Premnath, University of Massachusetts, Boston
Regina Psaki, University of Oregon
Katherine Quinsey, University of Windsor
Geoff Rector, University of Ottawa
Margaret Reeves, Atkinson College, York University
Cedric Reverand, University of Wyoming
Gerry Richman, Suffolk University
David Robinson, University of Arizona
Laura Rotunno, Pennsylvania State University, Altoona
Nicholas Ruddick, University of Regina
Jason Rudy, University of Maryland
Donelle Ruwe, Northern Arizona University
Michelle Sauer, Minot State University
SueAnn Schatz, Lock Haven University of Pennsylvania
Dan Schierenbeck, Central Missouri State University
Norbert Schürer, California State University,
    Long Beach
David Seed, University of Liverpool
Karen Selesky, University College of the Fraser Valley
Carol Senf, Georgia Tech University
Judith Slagle, East Tennessee State University
Sharon Smulders, Mount Royal College
Malinda Snow, Georgia State University
Goran Stanivukovic, St. Mary's University
Richard Stein, University of Oregon

Eric Sterling, Auburn University Montgomery
James Stokes, University of Wisconsin, Stevens Point
Mary-Ann Stouck, Simon Fraser University
Nathaniel Strout, Hamilton College
Lisa Surridge, University of Victoria
Beth Sutton-Ramspeck, Ohio State University
Nanora Sweet, University of Missouri, St. Louis
Dana Symons, Simon Fraser University
Andrew Taylor, University of Ottawa
Elizabeth Teare, University of Dayton
Doug Thorpe, University of Saskatchewan
Jane Toswell, University of Western Ontario
Kim Trainor, University of British Columbia
Herbert Tucker, University of Virginia
John Tucker, University of Victoria
Mark Turner, King's College, University of London
Eleanor Ty, Wilfrid Laurier University
Deborah Tyler-Bennett, Loughborough University
Kirsten Uszkalo, University of Alberta
Lisa Vargo, University of Saskatchewan
Gina Luria Walker, New School, New York City
Kim Walker, Victoria University of Wellington
Miriam Wallace, New College of Florida
Hayden Ward, West Virginia State University
Ruth Wehlau, Queen's University
Lynn Wells, University of Regina
Chris Willis, Birkbeck University of London
Lisa Wilson, SUNY College at Potsdam
Anne Windholz, Augustana College
Susan Wolfson, Princeton University
Kenneth Womack, Pennsylvania State University
Carolyn Woodward, University of New Mexico
Julia Wright, Wilfrid Laurier University
Julian Yates, University of Delaware
Arlene Young, University of Manitoba
Lisa Zeitz, University of Western Ontario

# History of the Language and of Print Culture

In an effort to provide for readers a direct sense of the development of the language and of print culture, examples of texts in their original form, of illustrations, and of other materials related to book culture have been provided in each volume. A list of these within the present volume, arranged chronologically, appears below. An overview of developments in the history of language during the first half of the century appears on pages lxiii to lxiv; material on developments in the history of language since World War II appears on pages 621, 628-29, and 631-33; and a "Contexts" section on "Power, Politics, and the Book" appears as part of the website component of the anthology.

Cover, 1994 Broadview edition of Wilkie Collins's *The Evil Genius*, p. 625.

Cover of Kazuo Ishiguro's *Never Let Me Go*, color insert pages.

# THE LATE TWENTIETH CENTURY AND BEYOND: FROM 1945 TO THE TWENTY-FIRST CENTURY

## THE END OF THE WAR AND THE COMING OF THE WELFARE STATE

Winston Churchill had inspired the nation—many said saved the nation—in the dark days of 1940, and remained over the following five years, by all accounts, one of the greatest war leaders in British history. Yet in 1945, the electorate unceremoniously dumped him and the Conservative party from office, and installed the Labour Party under Clement Attlee in its place. Much as people were grateful to Churchill for his leadership in the war effort, he was seen very much as war leader and a figure of the past at a time at which people felt strongly that they had fought not so much to preserve the world of the past as for their right to make a better world.[1] All too clearly, voters had seen that Churchill's fondest wish at the end of the war was to return to the peacetime Britain of earlier days—a Britain with a vast Empire abroad and a rigid class system at home. Unlike the Prime Minister, at war's end the British people were increasingly seeing Imperial possessions as a drain on the nation's scarce resources, and the class system as an impediment to prosperity and an affront to notions of equality. With remarkably little fanfare, the old British world of masters and servants had already largely disappeared, but its husk still gave shape to many social attitudes; it remained almost impossibly difficult to "get ahead" if one came from a working-class background and had the "wrong accent," one could never be fully accepted in many social milieus if one's background was "in trade," and so on.

---

[1] Churchill might still have been elected had it not been for his veer to the extreme ideological right during the course of the campaign. Apparently strongly influenced by having read F. A. Hayek's polemic against socialism, in his speech on 4 June 1945 Churchill likened Britain's Labour Party to Hitler's secret police, suggesting that no Labour government "could afford to allow free expression of public discontent.... They would have to fall back on some sort of Gestapo." That speech is excerpted in a "Contexts" section elsewhere in this volume.

Quite aside from the issue of increasingly anachronistic social attitudes, the working class and the lower middle class continued to face great obstacles simply in their daily physical existence. For many, conditions at the end of World War II were little better than they had been at the end of World War I; with its calls to redistribute wealth and to engage the forces of government throughout the economy on behalf of general good, Labour represented a real change. And unquestionably, the various measures enacted by the Attlee government (many of them following on the recommendations of the 1942 and 1944 Reports to Parliament of William Beveridge) made Britain a much fairer society than she had been at any time previously in her history. The new initiatives included the establishment of the National Health Service and the National Insurance Act, which provided a measure of protection against poverty resulting from unemployment—or indeed from any other source.

If British life became more egalitarian during the Attlee years, however, much of what was being shared was still hardship. In a fifty-years-on retrospective, Doug Saunders memorably summarized the situation in postwar Britain:

> Food rationing during the war was bad. After the war it was terrible. Posters were put up reading "Eat Less Bread: Eat Potatoes Instead." Then, in the spring of 1946, those posters went down: there was no bread at all.... Coal supplies were cut back to almost nil, so that in the winter of 1947, the coldest in British history, people were ordered not to heat their homes.... If the economies and buildings and cities were fractured, even worse damage was done to families. About four million children had been shipped away from their parents to unknown locations and with almost no contact, for years. Children and parents alike returned from the war to find things utterly different.... Susan Goodman, who was ten years old at the end of the war, had

lived in the countryside, with her mother in London and her father in the armed forces. She recalls the moment when "this man got off the train—he was very tall and very yellow. He came up and said, 'Hello Sue, I'm Daddy,' and I put out my hand and said 'How do you do.' It was not auspicious."

Even into the 1950s, food and fuel shortages persisted—and as the hardships continued, people grew as tired of Attlee and Labour as they had been of Churchill and the Conservatives in 1945. With the 1950 election Churchill was returned to office, and he presided over a period of relative calm from 1950 to 1955. In terms of the ideological direction of the nation, however, it was the election of 1945 that had represented the great turning point. From the late 1940s through to the late 1970s, periods of Labour rule (first under Attlee, later under Prime Ministers Harold Wilson and James Callaghan) alternated with periods of Conservative rule (first under Churchill again, later under Prime Ministers Harold Macmillan and Edward Heath). Under Labour, the growth of what came to be known as the "welfare state" was fostered, while under the Conservatives, the social activism of Labour was eschewed—but even while the Conservatives were in power, little attempt was made to dismantle the structures through which Labour was attempting to reshape British society; for thirty years the domestic agenda for Britain remained one of building a more egalitarian society.

If the political shape of the 1950s, 1960s, and 1970s in Britain has something of a unity to it, the same cannot be said for the shape of its economic and cultural life over that period. Britain recovered far more slowly economically after World War II than did North America and many other parts of the world. The 1950s in North America are thought of as years of contentment in the midst of robust economic growth. Not so in Britain; for many, through much of that decade British life remained dreary and unsatisfying. The major literary movement of the era—the writings of the so-called "angry young men"—represented a reaction against the dreariness and lack of opportunity that characterized so much of British life. John Osborne's play *Look Back in Anger* (1956), which depicted the struggles of the rebellious Jimmy Porter,

Wartime rationing in Montreal, 1942. Unlike in Britain, hardships on the home front ended soon after the war in countries such as Canada and Australia.

The "London fog" for which the city became famous in the nineteenth and twentieth centuries was primarily created by air pollution. From December 1953 to March 1954, conditions became worse than ever, and there were more than 12,000 smog-related deaths. Since the 1950s air (and water) quality in London has improved dramatically as a result of anti-pollution measures.

became the touchstone in discussions of the movement, but works of prose fiction such as John Braine's *Room at the Top* (1957) and Alan Sillitoe's *Saturday Night and Sunday Morning* (1958) and *The Loneliness of the Long Distance Runner* (1959), which also dealt with the conflicts and resentments of young working-class or lower middle-class males struggling to get on in society, had almost as great an impact.

Two other writers—Kingsley Amis and Philip Larkin—were initially often mentioned in the same breath as Osborne and Sillitoe, but even in the 1950s these two were on quite different literary paths, and in the 1960s and 1970s, their work diverged even further both from that of angry young men and from each other's (though the two remained lifelong friends). With *Lucky Jim* (1954), a social satire about class distinctions, romantic bungling, and university life, Amis achieved literary celebrity at an early age. His subsequent novels were written in a similar vein—social satire bordering on farce—but as the years went on, the humor was tinged more with bitterness than with insight, and was discolored by misogyny. Larkin, too, tried his hand early on in his career with social satire— *A Girl in Winter* (1947) being the more notable of his two novels—but with Larkin, the satire was more gentle, and did not sit entirely at ease with his evident aim of achieving a high degree of psychological realism. It was as a poet that Larkin made a lasting mark; poetry turned out to be the perfect medium for his unique variety of psychological understanding, his sometimes wry biting wit, and his bleak honesty about old age and death. Like Amis, Larkin had his share of bitter and misogynist feelings (as his posthumously-published letters revealed), but these are far less obtrusive in his work than they are in that of Amis, and where Amis's work became more coarse and superficial over the years, Larkin's became more varied, more resonant, and more memorable. In its subject matter but also in its form, Larkin's poetry was quite out of step with the vast majority of British poetry published in the second half of the twentieth century; almost all his poems are built on a foundation of accentual syllabic meter, and most have a regular rhyme scheme. Yet they found a remarkably large audience; his final book, *High Windows*, made some British best seller lists in 1974.

Increasingly, critics and literary historians are coming to regard Larkin as the most important British poet of the second half of the twentieth century.

Another quite different group of writers might with equal appropriateness be described as "angry young men": those who emigrated to Britain from her overseas possessions. Particularly prominent were immigrants from the Caribbean; large numbers were recruited from Jamaica, Trinidad, and other Caribbean islands in the decade following World War II to help rebuild Britain's bombed-out cities. Though they made a real contribution to that rebuilding, they were often treated as second-class citizens, discriminated against in virtually every public sphere; the reaction was a series of race riots, beginning in the late 1950s.

The Caribbean-led wave of immigration in the post-war years was the beginning of a movement that would transform Britain demographically and culturally. Amongst their number were many of the founding voices of what would become known as post-colonial literature, including Samuel Selvon, George Lamming, and Derek Walcott. From the beginning, they wrote largely in opposition to (rather than within) British literary traditions; this was the beginning of the literary movement that Salman Rushdie memorably characterized a few decades later with the phrase, "The Empire writes back."

The important women writers from this period were far less angry in their work than their male counterparts —though doubtless they had at least as much cause to be. The novels of Iris Murdoch, of Muriel Spark, and of Doris Lessing work with vastly different settings and story materials, ranging from the story of the life of a school mistress at a girls' boarding school in Spark's *The Prime of Miss Jean Brodie* to a philosophically tinged exploration of faith and moral imagination in Iris Murdoch's *The Bell* (1958) to an evocation of the gritty edges of colonial existence in Southern Rhodesia in Lessing's *The Grass is Singing* (1950). Almost all are written in the vein of social or psychological realism— and most have something of an ethos of stoicism in the face of adversity. As a character in Murdoch's *Under the Net* (1954) puts it, "one must just blunder on. Truth lies in blundering on."

## THE END OF EMPIRE

If in the generation following World War II, the Conservatives came to accept many of the egalitarian social principles in which Labour believed, they also came to accept that the old approach to Empire was no longer workable. Britain's stature as a world power suffered serious damage during the Suez crisis of 1956, when it attempted unsuccessfully to block the nationalization by Egypt of the Suez Canal, and it suffered as well in the face of increasing resistance to Imperial rule in British colonies. (Perhaps most notably, the Mau Mau rebellion in East Africa of 1952–56 showed to what extent a relatively small uprising could destabilize colonial rule, inspiring brutal reprisals and widespread fear). By the early 1960s the die was cast; as a "Contexts" section on "The End of Empire" elsewhere in this anthology documents, Harold Macmillan's 1960 "Wind of Change" speech signaled Britain's intention to grant independence to virtually all of its remaining colonies, in Asia and the Caribbean as well as in Africa.

The HMS *Antelope* under attack during the Falklands War, 1982. One case in which the British forcibly resisted efforts to wrest a colonial possession from their control was that of the Falkland Islands off the coast of Argentina, to which Argentina also laid claim. When the Argentinian Armed Forces invaded in April 1982, Margaret Thatcher's government declared war. By early June, the British had retaken the Islands, and on June 14, Argentina surrendered. Before the war Thatcher had been deeply unpopular; in its wake her popularity soared, and in 1983 she was re-elected in a landslide.

Independence in a significant number of these nations also meant majority rule by blacks, which was anathema to many white settlers. In some new nations, independence was followed by an exodus of whites, while in Rhodesia, the government of Ian Smith unilaterally declared independence from Britain in order to maintain the white minority's privileged position and prevent majority rule. Most nations joined Britain in refusing to recognize Smith's regime and imposing sanctions against it, but it was not until 1980, after a ten-year guerrilla war, that the people of Rhodesia—renamed Zimbabwe—established a state based on the principles of majority rule. By 1980, then, all of Britain's former colonial possessions in Africa were independent, as were most in Asia and the Caribbean; the only remnants of the British Empire were a scattering of small territories such as Hong Kong, Gibraltar, the Falkland Islands off the coast of Argentina, and several Caribbean islands.

Doris Lessing was one of many post-war writers to focus in their fiction on the failings of colonialism. A few years before her novels and stories of southern Africa began to appear, Alan Paton's *Cry the Beloved Country* (1948), a simple and emotionally powerful tale of the hardships suffered by black South Africans under white rule, had achieved enormous success. At first such hardships were recounted for a wide audience only in novels by white writers. In the 1960s and 1970s, however, a new generation of writers of color emerged, and were rapidly accorded a place in the first rank of writing in English. Among the most important of these are V.S. Naipaul, whose major works include novels set in India (*A House for Mr. Biswas*, 1962), in Africa (*A Bend in the River*, 1979), and in his native Trinidad (*Miguel Street*, 1959); the Nigerian playwright Wole Soyinka, awarded the Nobel Prize for Literature in 1986; the Nigerian novelist Chinua Achebe, whose novels of struggle, corruption and loss in the post-colonial era (*Things Fall Apart* [1958] most notable among them) have taken on iconic status; the Trinidadian poet Derek Walcott; and the Kenyan novelist Ngũgĩ wa Thiong'o.

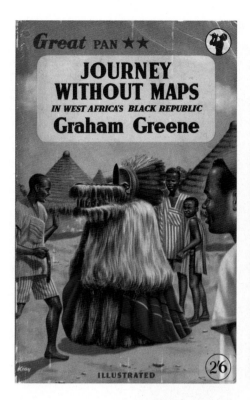

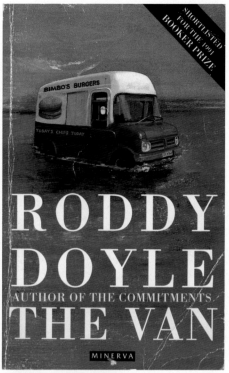

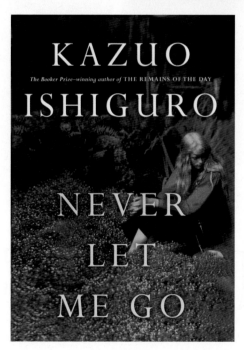

A sampling of book covers: Graham Greene's *Journey Without Maps* (1936; Pan paperback edition, 1948), Roddy Doyle's *The Van* (1991; Minerva paperback edition, 1992), and Kazuo Ishiguro's *Never Let Me Go* (2005). The image on the Ishiguro cover is "Christina," from a famous 1912–13 series of photographs by Lieutenant-Colonel Mervyn O'Gorman of his daughters, whom he photographed both in autochrome color and in black and white, sometimes on a beach near their Dorset home, sometimes (as here) in a garden setting.

Poster, The Beatles London Palladium Royal Command Performance, 1963. The Royal Variety Performance (also known as the Royal Command Performance) is a gala variety show held every year, the proceeds of which go to charity. When The Beatles performed at the show on 4 November 1963, the audience included the Queen Mother, Princess Margaret, and Lord Snowdon, but not the Queen. As the group was about to play their hit song "Twist and Shout," John Lennon made a request: "Will the people in the cheaper seats clap their hands? And the rest of you, if you'll just rattle your jewelry."

David Hockney, *My Mother, Bolton Abbey, Yorkshire*, 1982. Painter and photographer David Hockney (b. 1937) has long maintained his reputation as one of Britain's leading visual artists. Hockney initially created controversy with his open homosexuality, and in recent years he has incited debate with his views on art history, arguing strenuously that the old Masters employed camera-like techniques in order to achieve realistic effects. A native of Bradford, Hockney has lived largely in California since the 1970s.

Peel Square, Bradford, c. 1995. From the
1950s onwards many immigrants from Asia
have settled in Bradford.

Notting Hill Carnival, Notting Hill, London, 1979. The Carnival was started in 1964
to celebrate Caribbean culture within Britain.

One of the most important vehicles with which African writing was brought to the attention of the rest of the world was the African Writers Series, launched by the UK publisher Heinemann in 1962 at the instigation of Alan Hill and initially under the general editorship of Chinua Achebe. By the end of 1969, the year that *Political Spider: Stories from Black Orpheus* was published, the series had grown to 82 titles, including Achebe's *Things Fall Apart* and *Arrow of God*; *Weep Not Child* and *A Grain of Wheat* by "James Ngugi" (Ngũgĩ wa Thiong'o); and Wole Soyinka's *The Interpreters*.

All of these authors deal pointedly with issues of colonialism and post-colonialism in their work. It is Ngugi, however, who has raised most pointedly the issue of the ways in which politics and literature connect also with language. Ngugi's early novels—including *A River Between* (1965), a novel about young people grappling with the conventions of tribal life in a world in which almost no one speaks English—were written in English, and Ngugi established a worldwide reputation as an English novelist. In midlife, he decided both for personal and political reasons to write instead in his first language, Kikuyu; he argues persuasively in *Decolonizing the Mind* (1986) that English is inherently tainted by the culture of the colonizer: "language has a dual character; it is both a means of communication and a carrier of culture." The debate over this issue involved many of the leading writers in Britain's former colonies; Achebe and Soyinka were among those who decided to write some works in English, others in their first language. Even those who chose to write in English, however, no longer felt obliged to adopt the "correct" English of the English themselves; whether through the use of idioms, of non-standard syntax, or of local dialects and rhythms of speech, they have extended the linguistic range of literature in English.

While the 1960s and '70s saw an explosion of literature in English in nations newly independent from Britain, these decades also ushered in a new vibrancy and maturity in the literatures of Canada and Australia, which had long been formally independent from Britain but had retained into the 1950s a pervasive sense of Great Britain as "the mother country." By the 60s and 70s both nations were beginning to define themselves as much in terms with their relationship with the United States (and, in the case of Australia, with Asian countries) as they did in connection with their old relationship towards Britain. Here and there the work of important Canadian and Australian authors such as Margaret Atwood, P.K. Page, and Judith Wright illuminated the old connections with Britain, but just as often the work of these writers—like that of other major Australian and Canadian authors such as Patrick White (winner of the Nobel Prize in 1973), Les Murray, Peter Carey, Alice Munro, Carol Shields, and Michael Ondaatje—bears few traces of a British connection. Increasingly, indeed, literature in English had started to become more broadly international. Ondaatje, for example, has shown himself to be as comfortable writing about Italy and North Africa in World War II (in his Booker Prize-winning novel *The English Patient*) as he has writing about his native Sri Lanka and Canada.

Rohinton Mistry has lived in Canada since he was 23, but he continues to set his major works—most notably his novel *A Fine Balance* (1996)—in his native India.

### FROM THE 1960S TO CENTURY'S END

Within Britain, the 1960s and '70s were also a time of cultural explosion—though here literature may be said to have shared the stage with other forms of cultural expression, most notably popular music. The music of The Beatles and The Rolling Stones played a central part in defining "the swinging '60s," but these groups were part of a much broader movement as a large generation of young people sought—through long hair, the lively clothing styles of Carnaby Street, and a new-found sexual freedom—to reject the values of their parents' generation.

Ironically, the most lasting literary reflections of this memorable cultural moment may not be in any literary expression of exuberance from the 1960s, but in detached and faintly critical after-the-fact poems on the subject by Larkin, such as "Annus Mirabilis":

> Sexual intercourse began
> In nineteen sixty-three
> (which was rather late for me)—
> Between the end of the *Chatterley* ban
> And the Beatles' first LP.

The comic novels of Amis and of David Lodge (notably *Changing Places*, 1975) also give some sense of the cultural moment. But several of the most important figures of British literature of these years maintained a considerable distance between their own work and the cultural ferment of the times. Lawrence Durrell com-

In a controversial award, the Beatles were appointed MBEs (Members of the British Empire) in 1965. Even more controversially, John Lennon commented in March of the following year that the group was "more popular than Jesus."

*Lord of the Flies* has sold exceptionally well ever since its publication in 1954—including to high schools. This still from Peter Brook's 1963 film version of *Lord of the Flies* was also used as a cover image for the "educational edition" of the book the same year.

pleted the last of his series of evocative novels of the Anglo-Egyptian world, *The Alexandria Quartet*, in 1960; Anthony Powell continued to publish novels in his unique sequence *A Dance to the Music of Time*; and William Golding, who had burst onto the literary scene in 1954 with *Lord of the Flies*, a horrific depiction of young boys forced to create a society for themselves, continued to publish novelistic explorations of the psyche and of ethical questions.

One of the most important poetic voices to emerge in Britain in the 1960s and '70s also maintained a certain distance from the cultural mainstream; the focus of Ted Hughes's work remained largely on the natural world, and on the ways in which humans might connect to that world on a primal level. Doris Lessing, however, with the publication of her novel *The Golden Notebook* (1962), most certainly did connect with the mainstream of social and cultural change. Along with the non-fiction work *The Female Eunuch* by the Australian Germaine Greer, *The Golden Notebook* became a touchstone for women as they realized the extent to which they had been suppressed by the patriarchal structures and attitudes of society.

Committed as politicians had been to egalitarianism from the 1940s through to the 1970s, they had been largely unable to loosen the control that the British upper-class and upper middle-class continued to exert over key elements of British society. Perhaps the most egregious expression of this control was the connection that continued to exist between the best jobs and the old established universities. In almost all professions, preference continued to be given to graduates of Oxford and Cambridge. Though the Education Act of 1944 had put forward measures to increase the number of working-class students at British universities, many of the old attitudes persisted.

Ironically, it may have been a Conservative rather than a Labour government that challenged the old ethos most successfully. Margaret Thatcher (Prime Minister from 1979 to 1990), represented a very different brand of Conservatism from that of Winston Churchill and earlier Conservatives, much as she admired him and shared some of the old notions of Britain as a power in world affairs. A grocer's daughter, she stood in her own way as firmly against the restrictions of a hierarchical class structure as did her political opponents. But whereas Labour had sought to achieve equity by creating a welfare state, Thatcher aimed to do so by bringing the universities to heel, creating a sense of empowerment among the working-class and lower middle-class—and dismantling much of the welfare state in order to lower taxes. Thatcher succeeded in changing a great many British attitudes over the eleven years she held power, but in the course of doing so she fiercely divided the nation.

The 18 years of Conservative party government in Britain from 1979 to 1997—for the most part under Thatcher as Prime Minister—was a period in which government support for culture was cut back. In a series of moves that paralleled developments in the United States under Ronald Reagan, Thatcher attacked the foundations of the welfare state and conveyed a sense that Britain's cultural identity was to be expressed through fiercely defending the last remnants of Empire (she led a war against Argentina over the Falkland Islands in 1982) and in resisting integration with continental Europe rather than in fostering cultural expression through literature, music, and the visual arts. Ironically, this period saw perhaps the greatest flowering of British literature since the first decades of the twentieth century. Novelists were especially prominent, with Margaret Drabble, A.S. Byatt, Ian McEwan, Martin Amis, Graham Swift, and Jeannette Winterson all creating impressive bodies of work. Ironically, too, literature in Britain experienced a cultural broadening that stands in direct contrast to the narrowness of Thatcher's cultural focus. Britain itself was increasingly becoming a multi-cultural society with the continuing influx of immigrants from former British possessions; more and more, that diversity began to shape the British literary scene. Among the major figures of British literature during this period are Salman Rushdie, a novelist with a Pakistani family background whose works—from *Midnight's Children* (1980) and *Shame* (1983) to *Shalimar's Clown* (2005)—explore the cultures of India and Pakistan as much as they do that of Britain; Vikram Seth, another novelist whose major works (most notable among them *A Suitable Boy*, 1993) are set in India; Zadie Smith, who burst onto the literary scene in 2000 with a wide-ranging novel of post-colonial communities in England, *White Teeth*; and Nagasaki-born Kazuo Ishiguro, whose Japanese heritage informs much of his work but who has lived in Britain since the age of six.

Ishiguro's best known work, *The Remains of the Day* (1989), recounts the story of a British butler in a country house where collaborators with the Nazi regime are holding secret meetings; the novel has been widely acclaimed as among the most fully rounded fictional expressions of life under the old British class system, and of the stifling of human feeling under the sense of reserve that formed an integral part of that system. Much of Ishiguro's other work is set in the world of post-war Japan (*A Pale View of Hills*, 1982) and/or in dreamlike worlds that resist identification with fixed geographical or temporal locations (*The Unconsoled*, 1995). In his acclaimed novel *Never Let Me Go* (2005), young people are prepared for a mysterious fate at a boarding school in an English countryside where the precise geographical setting remains vague, and the temporal setting in an unspecified future even more so.

Like the literatures of Canada and Australia, that of Britain in the late twentieth and early twenty-first centuries was often more difficult to place. The diversity of British writing also came to be expressed during this period through an unrestricted openness regarding sexual orientation. Whereas leading writers such as W.H. Auden in the 1930s and Tom Gunn in the 1950s had left Britain for America in large part because American cities such as New York and San Francisco were then far more accepting of homosexuality than was London (let alone any other part of the British Isles), in the 1980s and 1990s gay and lesbian writers such as Hanif Kureishi and Jeannette Winterson remained in Britain and became central figures of London's literary culture. And in the twenty-first century, Carol Ann Duffy came to be acknowledged as a leading poetic voice in Britain.

Diversity of form and style also became increasingly characteristic of British literature in the 1980s and 1990s. Poets such as Geoffrey Hill carried on something

akin to the Modernist tradition, while poets such as Tony Harrison infused their work with powerful political content; poets such as Alice Oswald revived and extended traditions of English nature poetry; and a range of other poets (including Grace Nichols, Moniza Alvi, and Linton Kwesi Johnson) gave full expression to the new Britain. Women poets came to the fore as never before, in Ireland as well as in Britain, with Eavan Boland and Maedbh McGuckian particularly highly regarded. (A fuller discussion of these and other developments of the period appears elsewhere in this volume as an introduction to "Directions in Late Twentieth- and Early Twenty-First Century Poetry.")

The 1980s and 1990s may in some respects be characterized as the era of postmodernism in British literary culture; *postmodern* is a notoriously slippery term, however, and one worth pausing over. The most fruitful avenue of approach may be to look at Modernism and postmodernism side by side. In some ways postmodernism represents a reaction to Modernism, in others an extension of it—and in many ways the history of the one parallels that of the other. As Modernism had been the leading artistic and intellectual movement of the second and third decades of the twentieth century, so was postmodernism during the century's final two decades—at least in literature and the visual arts. Both Modernism and postmodernism may be said to have begun in France—Modernism with poets such as Arthur Rimbaud and Stephane Mallarmé and the Post-Impressionist and Cubist painters, post-modernism with philosophers such as Jacques Derrida and Michel Foucault. Modernism had at its core a rejection of traditional artistic forms and a tendency towards fragmentation of meaning as well as of form. The breaking down of the image in poetry and in painting was accompanied by extensive theorizing—by Mallarmé and the French Symbolists, by Ezra Pound and the Imagists, by the Italian Futurists, and by various others. Postmodernism was even more deeply colored by theory; indeed, it may be said to have begun at the "meta" level of theorizing rather than at the level of practice. It is notoriously resistant to definition—indeed, resistance to fixed definitions is itself a characteristic of postmodernism. Like Modernism, postmodernism embraces difficulty and distrusts the simple and straightforward. More broadly, postmodernism is characterized by a rejection of absolute truth or value, of closed systems, of grand unified narratives. As the French social philosopher Jean Baudrillard put it in 1987, "truth is what we should rid ourselves of as fast as possible and pass it on to somebody else. As with illnesses, it's the only way to be cured of it. He who hangs on to truth has lost."

Graham Law's edition of Wilkie Collins's *The Evil Genius*, one of the series-launching batch of four Broadview Literary Texts published in 1994. Even as English Studies focused to an unprecedented degree in the 1980s and '90s on literary theory, the discipline was also becoming increasingly aware of the importance of historicizing literary works—understanding them first of all in the cultural context out of which they emerged. An important related publishing venture was the launch of the Broadview series (later renamed Broadview Editions), which includes within each volume appendices of relevant historical and cultural documents.

As a style of discourse rather than a philosophical system, postmodernist theory dominated the academic study of literature in British and North American universities through much of the 1980s and 1990s. Postmodernism never came to dominate literature itself during that period to anything like the same degree, but the 1980s and 1990s fictions of Rushdie, Byatt, Ishiguro, Winterson, and Will Self, among others, often played with reality and illusion in ways that could be broadly characterized as postmodern. Works such as Byatt's novel *Possession* (1990) and Winterson's *Written on the Body* (1992), for example, display a willingness to combine different styles or forms in a single work—just as in architecture the postmodernist spirit embodies a willingness to borrow from seemingly disparate styles in designing a single structure.

One of the main thrusts of Modernism had been to apprehend consciousness directly in its often-chaotic progression. The main thrust of postmodernism, by contrast, was one of analysis more than of direct apprehension; the characteristic spirit of postmodernism is one of *self*-consciousness, of a highly attuned awareness to the problematized state of the writer, artist, or theorist as observer. Often that awareness encompasses a playfulness with regard to time—as famously expressed, for example, in the opening lines of Rushdie's Booker Prize-winning novel *Midnight's Children* (1980): "I was born in the city of Bombay ... once upon a time. No, that won't do, there's no getting away from the date."

British drama, which was influenced both by Modernism and by postmodernism, experienced great success throughout most of the second half of the twentieth century, and the beginning of the twenty-first. Major figures such as Harold Pinter and Tom Stoppard followed on from the work of Samuel Beckett in the attention that they paid to life's absurdity. In his most important plays, Pinter's focus was on personal and family relationships, whereas Stoppard's was on surprising conjunctions of circumstance and large ideas. In the groundbreaking *Rosencrantz and Guildenstern Are Dead* (1967), for example, he rewrote Shakespeare's *Hamlet* from the point of view of two of its most minor characters; in *Arcadia* (1993), which takes place both in the present and in the early years of the nineteenth century, he brought together ideas about eighteenth-century formal gardens, the science of Isaac Newton, and the life of Byron. Other leading dramatists of the period extended the frontiers of British drama in a variety of other directions. David Hare combined elements of realism with an often larger-than-life framework in plays such as *Plenty* (1978); Caryl Churchill experimented broadly with form in plays such as *Cloud Nine* (1979) and *Top Girls* (1982)—the latter informed both by an ear for dialogue closely attuned to the realities of contemporary Britain and by Churchill's strong feminist convictions; Alan Ayckbourn displayed a talent for farce in the extraordinary tour-de-force *The Norman Conquests*, and a deep sense, as well, of the ways in which the apparently meaningless surface details of life relate to its sad undertones; and Michael Frayn created works ranging from farce as broad as that of Ayckbourn (as in *Noises Off*, 1982) to large scale dramas of ideas (such as *Copenhagen*, 1998) as ambitious as those of Stoppard.

As British literature underwent these changes in the last few decades of the twentieth century, so too did it expand to embrace a range of new modes of expression. In the 1940s and 1950s, Graham Greene had been a rarity among major British writers in his willingness to write screenplays for films based on his works. By the end of the century, however, "crossover" writing of this sort had become common with Harold Pinter, Tom Stoppard, Hanif Kureishi, Neil Jordan, and Irvine Welsh among those who had written screenplays based on their novels or plays. Many also wrote for television; indeed, some of the finest drama of the era—including Stoppard's remarkable comedy *Professional Foul* (1977) on the conjunction of language philosophy and football (i.e., British soccer)—was written for the BBC. Some regularly scheduled British television programs may also lay claim to being among the more important works of the second half of the twentieth century. The comedy sketches of *Monty Python's Flying Circus* invented a new form of absurdist comedy in the early 1970s; the twelve episodes of *Fawlty Towers* (1975) set what some argued to be entirely new standards of farce; and the many episodes of *Yes, Minister* and its sequel *Yes, Prime Minister* introduced a new brand of cynical and yet warmly human comedy about the workings of British politics. Arguably, more recent television programs such as *The Office* (2001–02) have reached an equally high standard of comedy.

### IRELAND, SCOTLAND, WALES

The establishment of the Republic of Ireland in 1949 did not bring enduring peace to the island. With the six Ulster counties of Northern Ireland remaining a part of the United Kingdom of Great Britain and Northern Ireland, there was ongoing tension and, beginning in the late 1960s, almost recurrent violence over the status of Northern Ireland. The conflict came to be referred to as "The Troubles." A cycle of violence and repression continued, into the 1990s, as the Irish Republican Army (IRA) launched attacks on targets in England as well as in Northern Ireland, and the police and the British army launched repeated crackdowns, often involving considerable brutality. Staunchly Protestant Northern Irish politicians (the Reverend Ian Paisley most prominent among them) vowed "no surrender" to those who sought a compromise solution with Ireland and the Catholic minority in Northern Ireland.

In the late 1970s and early 1980s, a series of hunger strikes by IRA prisoners under British internment heightened tensions still further, and even after an Anglo-Irish agreement in 1985, periodic ceasefires brought only temporary cessations of conflict. In 1997, however, the IRA was persuaded to declare a ceasefire that showed promise of holding, and its political arm, Sinn Fein, joined in the multilateral Stormont talks aimed at finding a lasting solution. On 10 April 1998, an agreement was finally signed by the British and Irish governments. The Belfast Agreement (or "Good Friday Agreement") was endorsed by the major political parties of Ireland and of Northern Ireland, and in separate referendums by the electorates of both Ireland and Northern Ireland. Among the key provisions of the agreement were a commitment by all involved to an exclusively peaceful and democratic approach to change; abandonment by the Republic of its territorial claim to Northern Ireland; acceptance of the principle that the citizens of Northern Ireland had the right to determine by majority vote their constitutional future (in other words, partition was formally accepted, but so was the possibility that the Northern Irish could one day vote to

A gaping hole in front of the Grand Hotel in Brighton, site of the Conservative Party's conference in October 1980, was the result of an IRA bomb. Five were killed and many others injured; Prime Minister Thatcher was in her suite at the hotel when the explosion occurred, but was unharmed. An IRA statement acknowledged that Thatcher had been a target; "Today we were unlucky, but remember—we only have to be lucky once: you will have to be lucky always."

Nobel Peace Prize for their efforts.

Perhaps as important to the evolution of late twentieth- and early twenty-first-century Ireland as the coming of peace have been a precipitous decline of religious authority over Irish life and an extraordinary economic boom that has transformed the economy, particularly of the Irish Republic. Ireland has been slower than other Roman-Catholic-dominated societies of Europe (such as France, Italy, and Spain) to distance itself from the more socially conservative pronouncements of the papacy; not until 1995 was divorce permitted under Irish law, and it remains illegal to obtain an abortion in Ireland. But over the past generation, Ireland has steadily become a more secular society. Over the course of a remarkably brief period in the 1980s and 1990s it also went from being one of the poorest countries in Europe to one of the wealthiest and most dynamic. Changed attitudes, a highly educated workforce, and programs to encourage particular sectors of high-tech industry wrought an extraordinary economic transformation.

Perhaps not surprisingly, given these circumstances, one of the most engaging literary treatments in all of English literature of the transformative effects of capitalism on the human psyche emerged from this period of economic and cultural change in Ireland. Dublin novelist Roddy Doyle's *The Van* (1991) deals with a variety of business start-up—a fish-and-chip van—that is at the opposite end of the economic spectrum from the high-tech businesses that were the well-publicized stars of Ireland's economic transformation. But in the tragicomic microcosm that Doyle creates, he captures with deep understanding the ways in which energy, imagination, and heartlessness fuse together in the heated environment in which businesses grow. (Doyle's distinguished body of work includes two trilogies, among them the Barrytown trilogy of which *The Van* forms a part, as well as his 1993 Booker Prize-winning novel of childhood, *Paddy Clarke Ha Ha Ha*.)

join the Republic); and provision for a Northern Ireland Assembly to which additional power would devolve from the British government (still leaving Northern Ireland as part of the United Kingdom). Troubles of one sort or another remained in both Ireland and Northern Ireland, but "The Troubles" ended with the 1998 agreement; leaders on both sides were awarded the

The Irish contribution to the literature of the English-speaking world was scarcely less in the late twentieth century than it had been in the extraordinary period 1890–1960—the period of Oscar Wilde, George Bernard Shaw, J.M. Synge, W.B. Yeats, James Joyce, and Samuel Beckett. Interestingly, a disproportionate number of the important Irish writers of the late twentieth and early twenty-first centuries are poets of Northern Irish background—among them Seamus Heaney, Derek Mahon, Medbh McGuckian, Paul Muldoon, and Tom Paulin. (It is important to note here that Heaney and others on this list self-identify as Irish, not as Northern Irish.) The list of important Irish writers in this period, however, includes writers in all genres and regions, from the short story writer William Trevor, whose early years in a Protestant family in County Cork provided him with a unique perspective; to the acclaimed poet and Dubliner Eavan Boland; to the fiction-writer and film-maker Neil Jordan, a native of County Sligo in the northwest of Ireland, whose *The Crying Game* (1992) remains among the most memorable depictions of "The Troubles"; to the novelist Edna O'Brien, whose reaction against her childhood in what she later described as the "enclosed, fervid, and bigoted" atmosphere of the 1930s in a small village in County Clare colored much of her later fiction; to the novelist and Belfast native (in later life, Canadian citizen) Brian Moore; to the novelist, journalist, and Wexford native John Banville, whose *The Sea* (2005) was awarded the Booker Prize; and to Dublin dramatist and film-maker Conor McPherson, whose plays *The Weir* (1997) and *Shining City* (2004) explore the worlds of the living and the dead, and the ways in which Ireland continues to be possessed by its past.

Discontent with the dominant role played by England within Great Britain was a constant throughout the twentieth century in both Wales and Scotland, though in neither case was there a history of violence. In 1997 Tony Blair's Labour Party included in its election platform a commitment to devolution—a granting of power by the central government to proposed regional governments in Scotland and Wales. (Unlike the allocation of powers in a federal system, the granting of power under a system of devolution may be reversed; ultimate authority continues to reside with the central government.) Labour was elected with a solid majority, and devolution was approved in Scottish and Welsh referendums in the autumn of 1997; elections for the new Scottish Parliament and Welsh National assembly were held in May 1999, and since then the two regional governments have assumed a variety of responsibilities in such areas as health, housing, education, and culture.

A number of important British writers in the second half of the twentieth century were either Scottish or Welsh, including the Scottish novelist Muriel Spark, the Scottish poet Edwin Muir, and the Welsh poets Dylan Thomas and Gwyneth Lewis. Concern over the preservation of local language has been a constant both in Scotland and in Wales. The language known as Gaelic in Scotland, where it is the traditional language of the Highlands, is in its Irish variant referred to simply as Irish; on both sides of the Irish Sea it was long under pressure from English, but it was substantially revived in both Scotland and Ireland over the course of the twentieth century. In Ireland, both Irish and English are official languages, and approximately 100,000 are able to speak and 300,000 able to read Irish; in Scotland, there were in the late twentieth century approximately 80,000 able to speak Gaelic. Lowland Scots, on the other hand, is a variant of English—a very substantially different dialect from that spoken by most in England, but still a related tongue. It, too, was considered to be threatened by "Standard English," but determined efforts were made in the twentieth century to maintain its vitality. In the early twentieth century, the poet and political activist Hugh MacDiarmid (1892–1978) played a leading role in such efforts. A founder in 1928 of the National Party of Scotland, MacDiarmid worked to revive many of the words he found in John Jamieson's 1808 *Etymological Dictionary of the Scottish Language*, and enjoyed considerable success in reviving Scots as a language of poetry. And in the late twentieth and early twenty-first centuries, Lowland Scots has remained very much alive, in literature as well as in speech. Such is the case, for example, with the Edinburgh dialect that is reproduced by the novelist and film-maker Irvine Welsh in *Trainspotting* (novel 1993; film screenplay 1996): "Johnny wis a junky as well as a dealer. Ye hud tae go a wee bit further up the ladder before ye found a dealer whae didnae use."

Like Gaelic/Irish, Welsh is a language quite distinct from English. From the time of Henry VIII until the second half of the twentieth century, the Welsh language had been in more or less steady decline. Henry VIII had united England and Wales and forbidden the use of Welsh for official purposes with the 1536 Statute of Wales and the 1542 Acts of Union. In 1962, however, as a central element in the budding Welsh nationalist movement, a Welsh Language Society (Cymdeithas yr Iaith Gymraeg) was formed, and in 1967 its protests prompted the British Government to pass the Welsh Language Act, assigning equal status within Wales to Welsh and English—and declaring Wales to be no longer an official part of England. Since then the teaching of Welsh has been made an integral part of the educational system, and public agencies are obliged to offer bilingual service. It is now estimated that over 500,000 people in Wales are bilingual in Welsh and English, with the percentage of the population speaking the language increasing for the first time in over a century. In 2005 Gwyneth Lewis, who writes both in English and in Welsh, was named Wales's first Poet Laureate.

## THE NEW MILLENNIUM

Through the era of Conservative government under Thatcher and John Major, Britain remained deeply divided politically—over cultural politics and issues such as immigration policy; over to what extent Britain should be a free market economy or a social democratic one; and over foreign affairs. With the coming to power of Tony Blair and "New Labour," as the Labour Party began to style itself in 1994, a new era dawned in British politics. Blair had blunted the power of the unions within his own party, and the party now blended its long-standing commitment to social justice with a commitment to economic enterprise and to modernity that had been sorely lacking in the Labour Party for the previous generation or more. At century's end, long-divisive issues such as the racial composition of Britain and the conflict in Northern Ireland seemed well on the way to being resolved. Constitutional reforms had included not only the devolution of considerable power to new assemblies in Scotland and Wales but also a phasing-out of the hereditary peerage; no longer would one be able to inherit a seat in the House of Lords. Class divisions had receded, and Britons expressed a fresh confidence and a fresh sense of unity. The British seemed to have finally come to terms with their place in the world—a position of far less importance than that which they had held a century earlier, but one that no longer forced them to carry the economic and moral baggage of imperialism. It was also a position of surprising strength economically—particularly in the south of England, with London consolidating its position as one of the great financial centers of the world. Britain seemed to be in the forefront culturally, too. In the visual arts and in fashion, London held a central place, with publicity generating an annual furor over the awarding of the Turner Prize for best work by a British artist under the age of 50, and with brashly controversial artists such as Damien Hirst, Chris Ofili, and Gillian Wearing and celebrity collectors such as advertising mogul Charles Saatchi driving a culture of "Sensation" (to echo the name of the highly controversial 1997 and 2000 exhibitions from the Saatchi Collection in London and Brooklyn, respectively). London also laid claim to be the literary center of the world. "Rule, Britannia" had been Britain's defining song at its Imperial zenith; "Cool Britannia" was the term now coined to define Britain. During the millennium celebrations of 2000, Britain was as confident, as united, and as prosperous as she had been at any time since the great celebrations over the Diamond Jubilee of Queen Victoria, 100 years before Tony Blair, New Labour, and "Cool Britannia."

The sky over Britain at the millennium was far from cloudless, however, and in the early years of the twenty-first century many have perceived Britain's problems as standing out in bolder relief than her triumphs. In the first few years of the twentieth century the British people—the *English* people, especially—were stereotypically thought of as a people of civility and self-restraint, adherence to religion and religious propriety, and modesty that verged on prudery. In the first few years of the twenty-first century the stereotype of the British—again, the *English*, especially—included the behavior of the "lager louts" that went on nightly rampages in city centers; the lowest rates of church attendance in Europe; drunken hooliganism among soccer fans, displayed since the 1970s at matches across Europe as well as at home; and poverty-stricken and largely racially defined ghettos in post-industrial towns such as Leeds—areas which, as the suicide bombings on the London transport system in 2005 made painfully clear, could become breeding grounds for terrorism. According to social critics such as Theodore Dalrymple in works such as *Life at the Bottom* (2002), the lack of civility commonly associated with an alienated underclass was becoming more and more pervasive throughout all Britain, fueled by a "radical egotism" that had taken root in the new cultural freedom of the 1960s and that had become more and more strongly tainted during the late 1970s and the Thatcher years by materialism and uncaring individualism.

Grafted onto concern over these domestic issues was a broad concern over the place of a new Britain in a changed world. Was Britain's appropriate role that of aggressive ally of an increasingly bellicose United States? Could intervention in other nations' affairs, on either humanitarian or strategic grounds, be readily justified in a world in which concerns about terrorism, about human rights, and about the potential for a world-wide clash of cultures were coming to the fore? The participation by Prime Minister Tony Blair's government in the early twentieth-century wars in Afghanistan and Iraq provided powerful fuel for these debates.

These troubled aspects of British life are memorably represented in the literature of the late twentieth and early twenty-first centuries. The hooliganism that began to plague England in the late 1960s and 1970s was foreshadowed in Anthony Burgess's novel *A Clockwork Orange* (1962), in which the protagonist, fifteen-year old Alex DeLarge, leads a gang that commits a variety of violent crimes purely for the "kick" it gives them. The early fiction of Ian McEwan—perhaps most notably his first novel, *The Cement Garden* (1978)—depicts the grim plight of young people fending for themselves in the bleakness of a post-industrial landscape. The occasion for Tony Harrison's wide-ranging long poem *v* (1985) was the graffiti left on gravestones by Leeds United soccer hooligans; in a cemetery above the ground where "Leeds United play but disappoint their fans week after week," the fans "spray words on tombstones, pissed on beer":

> Subsidence makes the obelisks all list.
> One leaning left's marked FUCK, one right's
>     marked SHIT
> sprayed by some peeved supporter who was pissed....

In some cases the graffiti is football-related as well as foul-mouthed:

> Or, more expansively, there's LEEDS v.
> the opponent of last week, this week, or next,
> and a repertoire of blunt four-letter curses
> on the team or race that makes the sprayer vexed.

And, Harrison suggests, there is a wider resonance to these oppositions:

> These Vs are all the versuses of life
> From LEEDS v. DERBY, Black/White
> and (as I've known to my cost) man v. wife,
> Communist v. Fascist, Left v. Right,
>
> Class v. class as bitter as before,
> the unending violence of US and THEM …

Hanif Kureishi's *My Son the Fanatic* (both a short story and a screenplay for a film, 1997) depicts the violent radicalization in Britain of Islamic youth as a reaction to what they see as the hypocrisy and decadence of their fathers' assimilated Britishness. Caryl Churchill's work—notably her short apocalyptic play *Far Away* (2000)—presents a world in which individuals abandon responsibility for one another, and in which the possibility of wider and wider conflict (not only nations or civilizations at war with one another, but also the human at war with the non-human environment) is beginning to seem increasingly real. And Ian MacEwan's celebrated novel *Saturday* (2005) captures much of the ambivalence towards violence that at the time was coming to seem a part of British life—violence both on the streets of Britain and overseas. That novel, which concerns a surgeon who becomes terrorized by violent criminals and is provoked to violent response, is set against a backdrop of looming military conflict in Iraq. Asked if he is "for the war," the beleaguered surgeon Henry Perowne replies, "I'm not for any war. But this one could be the lesser evil. In five years' time we'll know."

In a the space of a few hours in 2005 Britain experienced the extremes of jubilation and anguish as four coordinated terrorist attacks by suicide bombers (three of them British born) shook the London Transport system less than 24 hours after London had been announced as the surprise winner in the competition to host the 2012 Summer Olympics. Those experiences may perhaps be set beside each other as symbolic of the powerful grounds for both optimism and pessimism in Britain. Will the lively spirit that animated Britain culturally and economically at the beginning of the millennium continue to flourish and expand, with the 2012 London Olympics as a centerpiece? Or will the shadows that have been cast across modern Britain lengthen and darken? On the future of Britain itself and of its role in the world, the jury is surely still out—and it is far from certain that "in five years' time we'll know." But there can be no doubt of the continuing vitality of British literature as we move further into the twenty-first century.

### THE HISTORY OF THE ENGLISH LANGUAGE

Perhaps the most extraordinary feature of English language in the late twentieth and early twenty-first century has been the pace of its growth—growth in its size and communicative capacity, but also in the extent to which it is spoken around the world. The two phenomena are now closely linked. Linguist Paul Payack of Global Language Monitor has estimated that English likely passed the one million word mark in 2006. (By comparison, the number of words in Old English was less than 60,000.) As in the first half of the twentieth century, much of that growth comes from new scientific coinages. But much of it is now also coming from "Chinglish" (Chinese-English) or "Hinglish" (Hindi-English) words, or other dual-language coinages. "Torunbusiness," for example, draws both on English and on the Mandarin word meaning *operating*; it means *open*, with reference to a business during opening hours.

In the twenty-year period 1947–67, almost all of Britain's former colonies became independent. Recognising the importance of English as a world-wide means of communication, most retained some official status for the English language. When India became independent in 1947, Hindi was declared the official language, English an "associate official language." In many new nations, English was accorded equal status with one or more other languages; thus in Malawi English and Chichewa are the official languages, in Swaziland, English and Swazi. In former colonies such as Nigeria and Zambia, where many local languages are spoken in different areas of the country, English was declared the *only* official language.

The speaking of English acquired a different coloring as it became the world's lingua franca, not only in the proliferation of accents but also in the timing of speech, and in the use of pitch rather than stress to mark "strong" syllables. English as it is spoken in Britain, the United States, Canada, Australia, and New Zealand remains a strongly inflected, stress-timed language; in other words, speakers typically stress certain syllables much more strongly than others, and vary the speed of speech in order to make the elapsed time between stresses more nearly equal. In other regions, however, where most people's first language is syllable- rather than stress-timed, and where pitch rather than stress marks "accented" syllables, those habits tend to be carried over into local habits of English pronunciation.

Inevitably, very substantial differences have arisen as well in the conventions of grammar and usage in different areas of the world. In the most extreme cases—as in Jamaica and several other Caribbean nations, pidgin and Creole forms of English that have become independent languages are more widely spoken than English itself. Elsewhere, conventions of spoken and of written English very different from those of "Standard English" have come to be broadly received as acceptable variants. In India "He is working here, isn't it?" or "I am not very much pleased" are generally regarded as entirely acceptable local usage. Indian Prime Minister Manmohan Singh put the matter clearly in a 2005 speech at Oxford University (excerpted in the "Contexts" section on "The End of Empire" elsewhere in this volume):

> Of course, people here may not recognise the language we speak, but let me assure you that it *is* English! In indigenising English, as so many people have done in so many nations across the world, we have made the language our own. Our choice of prepositions may not always be the Queen's English; we might occasionally split the infinitive; and we may drop an article here and add an extra one there. I am sure everyone will agree, however, that English has been enriched by Indian creativity. ...

Some of the most important changes in the English language in the second half of the twentieth century stemmed from the growing realization that the language had a systemic bias towards the male. In a landmark case referred to Britain by the Canadian courts, the Privy Council ruled in 1929 that the word *person* could not legally be taken to refer only to men. But could the word *man* be taken in an unbiased fashion to mean *human being*? To many, such usages seemed unproblematic—until they started to be brought up short by usages such as "the gestation period of the elephant is eleven months; that of man is nine months." From the 1970s onward it came to be more and more widely understood that *man* and *mankind* would always carry with them a whiff of malenesss, and thus could never fully and fairly represent all of humanity. Similarly the use of *he* to stand for both males and females has come to be widely criticised—and widely replaced, whether by "he or she" or simply by the use of plural constructions ("students … they" rather than "a student … he" ); gender-specific nouns have largely been superceded by gender-neutral alternatives (*police officer* for *policeman*, *server* for *waitress*); and patronizing gender terms ("the girls in the office") have largely fallen into disuse. Such change did not occur without a struggle, however. For many decades, those who ventured to suggest gender-neutral alternatives to the general practice were subjected to the sort of ridicule that H.W. Fowler and F.G. Fowler (authors of *Modern English Usage* and for most of the twentieth century considered the leading arbiters of proper English usage) aimed at one S. Ferrier in *The King's English* (1906, 1931; issued without further revision in paperback, 1962). Existing habit or convention was in such cases often the only "argument" advanced against principles of fairness:

> *He, his, him* may generally be allowed to stand for the common gender; the particular aversion to them shown by Miss Ferrier in the examples [quoted by the Fowlers] may be referred to her sex; and, ungallant as it may seem, we shall probably persist in refusing women their due here as stubbornly as Englishmen continue to offend the Scots by saying *England* instead of *Britain*.

One of the visible manifestations of changes in attitudes in the late twentieth century was the radical shift in the meaning of certain words and expressions relating to sexual behavior and sexual orientation. At mid-century *queer* was both an adjective meaning strange and a "descriptive" term with derogatory implications, used casually and openly by heterosexuals to denote homosexuals; in the 1970s it had come to be acknowledged as an offensive word that should be avoided; in the 1980s and 1990s it was claimed by the gay and lesbian community, many of whom began to self-identify as queer. In the academic community queer theory grew up as a sub-discipline of literary theory and criticism. *Gay,* which until mid-century had meant *merry* or *given to merriment,* began in the 1970s to replace *queer* as a colloquial designator—but one that carried positive rather than negative connotations. (Towards the end of the century, however, those positive associations began to be eroded somewhat, as heterosexual youth began to use *gay* in a derogatory fashion.)

Terms relating to heterosexual relationships were often also unstable. A noteworthy example is *making love,* which until the 1950s referred to the process of courting, emphatically not including the act of sexual intercourse. In the early 1960s, the meaning of the phrase quickly shifted, so that by the 1970s, the *only* commonly used denotation of *to make love* was *to have sex.* That was one of many examples of an increasingly overt sexualization of the language. In the case of a number of words that in the early twentieth century could carry either a sexual or a non-sexual meaning (e.g., *intercourse, ejaculate*), the sexual meaning had completely crowded out the non-sexual one by the end of the 1960s.

The twentieth century also saw a great change in the use of obscenities. In 1914, the utterance on stage of the phrase "not bloody likely" caused an uproar during the first English performance of Bernard Shaw's *Pygmalion.* Over the first half of the century, other swear words gradually made their way into print ("d— it all," for example, eventually gave way to "damn it all"). As the Christian religion held less and less sway over Britain in the second half of the century, so the sharp shock of swear words with religious referents was rubbed smooth, and stronger and stronger sexual terms came to replace them. In the world of literary publishing the publication of Philip Larkin's "This Be The Verse" in 1974 ("They fuck you up, your mum and dad") was something of a watershed. For some time after that, most reputable newspapers and magazines resisted the appearance of "the f-word" in their pages, but in last few years of the twentieth century and the early twenty-first that, too, has changed. In 2006, even the eminently respectable British newsmagazine *The Economist* found it acceptable to use such language in the course of quoting others; here is how their report in their 25–31 March 2006 issue on the state of Iraq three years after the 2003 invasion by American and British troops concluded: "On a toilet-wall in an American airbase in Western Iraq an American soldier has scrawled his own summary analysis: 'We came, we wasted a year of our lives. At least we got the fuckers to vote.'" In 1903—even in 1953 or 1963—such language in a respectable publication would have been entirely unimaginable.

The 41-storey tower universally known as "The Gherkin," which houses offices of the insurance company Swiss Re, has quickly become one of London's most recognizable structures. Designed by the prominent British architect Sir Norman Foster, it officially opened on 27 April 2004. The previous day Foster chanced to discover that Sir Christopher Wren, designer of St. Paul's Cathedral, had sketched plans for a similar structure more than 300 years earlier.

*London's Millennium Bridge* (above). The Bridge, the first new river crossing since the Tower Bridge opened in 1894, was designed jointly by Foster and Partners and Sir Anthony Caro. It opened on 10 June 2000 but had to be closed three days later due to unexpectedly strong swaying. Since its re-opening on 22 February 2002 it has proved enormously popular. To the north is St. Paul's Cathedral, to the south the Tate Modern gallery. The Tate Modern opened on 12 May 2000 in a building that had previously served as the Battersea Power Station. It now houses the Tate's collection of twentieth- and twenty-first century art; the original Tate Gallery in Chelsea, now renamed Tate Britain, houses the gallery's main collection.

# Leonora Carrington
## *b. 1917*

Surrealist painter and writer Leonora Carrington developed her unique artistic vision in the midst of the Surrealist Group of painters in Paris, a group whose credo was "the imaginary becomes real." In her fiction, as in her painting, Carrington blends the magical with the everyday in such a matter-of-fact manner that, if anything, it is the elements of the real world that seem the more preposterous of the two.

Carrington was born in 1917 in Chorley, Lancashire. As a child and adolescent, she attended a variety of schools, where teachers complained of her lack of interest and participation. Her real interest lay in painting and drawing, an interest she initially pursued through study with Amedee Ozenfant at London's Chelsea School of Art, where a fellow pupil also introduced her to surrealist artist Max Ernst. Carrington traveled with Ernst to the south of France and to Paris, where they began to move in a circle of fellow surrealist painters, including Marcel Duchamp, André Breton, Peggy Guggenheim, and Paul Eluard.

Here Carrington participated in surrealist exhibitions and began to write short stories, which Ernst often illustrated. Her first collection, *La Dame ovale* (*The Oval Lady*), was published in 1939. Its stories are shaped in part by Carrington's choice to write in French, a language in which she was not fluent. As a result, her narratives rely heavily on colloquialisms, clichés, and awkward phrases translated directly from English, but the limitations the language imposed upon her may also have helped to free her from any concerns about rationalism; the actions and events of her stories are largely dictated by the vocabulary she had available. Her simple narrative style also contributes to her narrators' tone of seemingly naive credulity, which heightens the surreal effects of her already strange plots.

At the beginning of World War II, Ernst (a German citizen) was imprisoned in France, and Carrington fled to Spain, where she suffered a mental breakdown and was committed to a psychiatric institution. Her examination of this experience, as set out in her autobiographical *Down Below* (1972), provides a glimpse into both the suffering and the artistic development that this breakdown brought about. Since this time her work has relied more heavily on dream imagery and fantasy, delving frequently into the realm of the subconscious. After her release, Carrington traveled to Portugal, where she met Mexican cultural attaché Renato Leduc, whom she married and followed to Mexico. Carrington and Leduc divorced shortly thereafter, and Carrington then married photographer and Hungarian refuge Chiqui Weisz, with whom she raised two sons.

Mexican culture made a tremendous impression on Carrington, who was shocked by the dark, threatening elements that seemed to permeate its religion, history, and folk beliefs. In particular, she viewed Mexico's history of human sacrifice and the apparent cruelty of its traditional gods with a sense of horror. This view of Mexican culture is evident in Carrington's paintings, which one critic aptly described as "gently menacing."

Exhibits of Carrington's art have been held in Paris, New York City, and Mexico. She has also sculptured, designed stage sets and costumes, and written plays, including *Penelope* (1957) and *"Opus*

*Sinistrus"* (1974). Her short stories have been collected in *The House of Fear: Notes from Down Below* (1988) and *"The Seventh Horse" and Other Tales* (1988). Her fiction often explores a dichotomy between male and female forces—the first of which she sees as aggressive, hierarchical, and destructive, and the second as creative, altruistic, intuitive, and spontaneous. In her 1976 novel *The Hearing Trumpet* (first published in French as *Le Cornet acoustique*, 1974), she provides a creative example of a world that is regenerated by being literally turned upside down: the heroine and her friends are a group of elderly women who preside over the earth's change of its axis. For Carrington, who was an important figure in the early days of the women's liberation movement in Mexico, this dichotomy between male and female forces is not just a matter for artistic exploration, but one for political concern. "If women remain passive," she says, "I think there is very little hope for the survival of life on this earth."

Some readers have found *The Hearing Trumpet* and Carrington's second novel, *The Stone Door* (*La Porte de pierre*), 1977, difficult to follow as they leap from one image to the next in a series of truncated narratives. But for many of readers, the odd characters, mystical journeys, undeniable whimsicality, and dry, witty tone make her works among the most enjoyable of the twentieth century.

⌘⌘⌘

## The Debutante

When I was a debutante, I often went to the zoo. I went so often that I knew the animals better than I knew girls of my own age. Indeed it was in order to get away from people that I found myself at the zoo every day. The animal I got to know best was a young hyena. She knew me too. She was very intelligent. I taught her French, and she, in return, taught me her language. In this way we passed many pleasant hours.

My mother was arranging a ball in my honour on the first of May. During this time I was in a state of great distress for whole nights. I've always detested balls, especially when they are given in my honour.

On the morning of the first of May 1934, very early, I went to visit the hyena.

"What a bloody nuisance," I said to her. "I've got to go to my ball tonight."

"You're very lucky," she said. "I'd love to go. I don't know how to dance, but at least I could make small talk."

"There'll be a great many different things to eat," I told her. "I've seen truckloads of food delivered to our house."

"And you're complaining," replied the hyena, disgusted. "Just think of me, I eat once a day, and you can't imagine what a heap of bloody rubbish I'm given."

I had an audacious idea, and I almost laughed. "All you have to do is to go instead of me!"

"We don't resemble each other enough, otherwise I'd gladly go," said the hyena rather sadly.

"Listen," I said. "No one sees too well in the evening light. If you disguise yourself, nobody will notice you in the crowd. Besides, we're practically the same size. You're my only friend, I beg you to do this for me."

She thought this over, and I knew that she really wanted to accept.

"Done," she said all of a sudden.

There weren't many keepers about, it was so early in the morning. I opened the cage quickly, and in a very few moments we were out in the street. I hailed a taxi; at home, everybody was still in bed. In my room I brought out the dress I was to wear that evening. It was a little long, and the hyena found it difficult to walk in my high-heeled shoes. I found some gloves to hide her hands, which were too hairy to look like mine. By the time the sun was shining into my room, she was able to make her way around the room several times, walking more or less upright. We were so busy that my mother almost opened the door to say good morning before the hyena had hidden under my bed.

"There's a bad smell in your room," my mother said, opening the window. "You must have a scented bath before tonight, with my new bath salts."

"Certainly," I said.

She didn't stay long. I think the smell was too much for her.

"Don't be late for breakfast," she said and left the room.

The greatest difficulty was to find a way of disguising the hyena's face. We spent hours and hours looking for a way, but she always rejected my suggestions. At last she said, "I think I've found the answer. Have you got a maid?"

"Yes," I said, puzzled.

"There you are then. Ring for your maid, and when she comes in we'll pounce upon her and tear off her face. I'll wear her face tonight instead of mine."

"It's not practical," I said. "She'll probably die if she hasn't got a face. Somebody will certainly find the corpse, and we'll be put in prison."

"I'm hungry enough to eat her," the hyena replied.

"And the bones?"

"As well," she said. "So, it's on?"

"Only if you promise to kill her before tearing off her face. It'll hurt her too much otherwise."

"All right. It's all the same to me."

Not without a certain amount of nervousness I rang for Mary, my maid. I certainly wouldn't have done it if I didn't hate having to go to a ball so much. When Mary came in I turned to the wall so as not to see. I must admit it didn't take long. A brief cry, and it was over. While the hyena was eating, I looked out the window. A few minutes later she said, "I can't eat any more. Her two feet are left over still, but if you have a little bag, I'll eat them later in the day."

"You'll find a bag embroidered with fleurs-de-lis in the cupboard. Empty out the handkerchiefs you'll find inside, and take it." She did as I suggested. Then she said, "Turn round now and look how beautiful I am."

In front of the mirror, the hyena was admiring herself in Mary's face. She had nibbled very neatly all around the face so that what was left was exactly what was needed.

"You've certainly done that very well," I said.

Towards evening, when the hyena was all dressed up, she declared, "I really feel in tip-top form. I have a feeling that I shall be a great success this evening."

When we had heard the music from downstairs for quite some time, I said to her, "Go on down now, and remember, don't stand next to my mother. She's bound to realise that it isn't me. Apart from her I don't know anybody. Best of luck." I kissed her as I left her, but she did smell very strong.

Night fell. Tired by the day's emotions, I took a book and sat down by the open window, giving myself up to peace and quiet. I remember that I was reading *Gulliver's Travels* by Jonathan Swift. About an hour later, I noticed the first signs of trouble. A bat flew in at the window, uttering little cries. I am terribly afraid of bats. I hid behind a chair, my teeth chattering. I had hardly gone down on my knees when the sound of beating wings was overcome by a great noise at my door. My mother entered, pale with rage.

"We'd just sat down at table," she said, "when that thing sitting in your place got up and shouted, 'So I smell a bit strong, what? Well, I don't eat cakes!' Whereupon it tore off its face and ate it. And with one great bound, disappeared through the window."

—1939

# Doris Lessing
## *b. 1919*

Often controversial, Doris Lessing's body of work spans six decades and several different genres. She was one of the first white writers to detail the mistreatment of blacks in Southern Africa, which resulted in her being declared a prohibited alien, both in her native Southern Rhodesia and in apartheid South Africa, in 1956. Her work examines clashes of cultures, racial inequality, and women's place in the world. Largely self-educated, she often includes elements of her own history and reflections on the "fragility of happiness" in her work.

Lessing was born in Persia to British parents Emily Maude Tayler, a nurse, and Alfred Cook Tayler, a bank clerk. Her father had had a leg amputated; her mother was the nurse who had tended him in the hospital while he recovered. Her father suffered from shell shock and often recounted stories of the atrocities of war to Lessing in her childhood and adolescence, so much so that she often referred to herself as "a child of war." In 1925, the family moved to Southern Rhodesia (now Zimbabwe) to take up farming. The enterprise proved unsuccessful, leaving the family in genteel poverty and Lessing with a survivalist ethic and a sense of practicality. Lessing's mother regularly sent away to England for books for Lessing and her younger brother. Isolated on the farm, Lessing was introduced to the writings of Charles Dickens, Rudyard Kipling, and D.H. Lawrence; later she would read Stendhal, Leo Tolstoy, and Fyodor Dostoevsky. She attended boarding schools in the capital, Salisbury (now Harare), but hated the experience, cherishing only the libraries that provided her with a wider assortment of books. Lessing would eventually drop out of school at 14; she later commented that "unhappy childhoods seem to produce fiction writers."

Lessing left home at 15 to become a nursemaid to a family in Salisbury. She found this boring and would compose poems in her head while minding the baby. Her employer did, however, introduce her to new books. It was during this period that she started writing in earnest, and she had two short stories published in magazines in South Africa. At the age of 19 she married; Lessing and her husband would eventually have two children, but the marriage did not last, not least because Lessing could not stand what felt to her like a life of hypocrisy. During this time, whites in southern Africa often lived in privilege at the expense of the blacks who were their servants; Lessing's outrage at the treatment of blacks would become an important theme in her work.

She became involved with the local Communists and their Left Book Club. While she was a committed member of the group, she was not motivated purely by politics: "the reason I became one was because the local Reds were the only people that ever read anything." It was while she was working with the Communists that she met and married her second husband, Gottfried Lessing, with whom she would have her third child. She eventually became disillusioned with the Communists after World War II, and would sever her relationship with them in 1954. Lessing continued to write and publish during this time, primarily poems and short stories. She also started work on what would become her first published book, *The Grass Is Singing*, a novel that depicts the racism and small-town claustrophobia of southern Africa under white rule; the protagonist mistreats and then has an affair with her black servant, and is eventually murdered by him. The novel was published in 1950 after Lessing had moved to England with her young son. From this point on, she would support herself with her writing.

She next began work on her *Children of Violence* series (1951–59), a multi-volume *bildungsroman* of her heroine Martha Quest. The series traces Quest's journey from Southern Rhodesia to England. *Children of Violence* includes *Martha Quest, A Proper Marriage,* and *A Ripple from the Storm,* which Lessing says is her most autobiographical work. In 1962 she published what remains her most famous work, *The Golden Notebook.* The novel examines the crisis of a novelist's life by interspersing pages from her notebooks into the narrative, thereby showing the multiple selves of a contemporary woman. The protagonist, Ann Wulf, attempts to live an honest life, free of the hypocrisy of her generation, and the novel was widely hailed by feminists. Lessing later asserted, however, that it had never been her intention that *The Golden Notebook* be labelled a feminist text.

The breadth of Lessing's literary output has been considerable. Some of her more popular novels include *The Memoirs of a Survivor, The Good Terrorist,* and *The Fifth Child.* She won the Somerset Maugham Award in 1956 and the W.H. Smith Award in 1986, and in 2002 she was awarded the David Cohen Literature Prize in recognition of her lifetime achievement. In the 1970s and 1980s she wrote a science-fiction series, *Canopus in Argos: Archives.* A lifelong interest in cats has led to two books, and she has even written a libretto for an opera. She has also written two volumes of an autobiography, one of which won the James Tait Black Prize for best biography in 1995. In speaking of her long career, she has said that being a writer has allowed her a certain freedom and that the writing process "takes the raw, the individual, the uncriticized, the unexamined, into the realm of the general."

⌘ ⌘ ⌘

## To Room Nineteen

This is a story, I suppose, about a failure in intelligence: the Rawlingses' marriage was grounded in intelligence.

They were older when they married than most of their married friends: in their well-seasoned late twenties. Both had had a number of affairs, sweet rather than bitter; and when they fell in love—for they did fall in love—had known each other for some time. They joked that they had saved each other "for the real thing." That they had waited so long (but not too long) for this real thing was to them a proof of their sensible discrimination. A good many of their friends had married young, and now (they felt) probably regretted lost opportunities; while others, still unmarried, seemed to them arid, self-doubting, and likely to make desperate or romantic marriages.

Not only they, but others, felt they were well matched: their friends' delight was an additional proof of their happiness. They had played the same roles, male and female, in this group or set, if such a wide, loosely connected, constantly changing constellation of people could be called a set. They had both become, by virtue of their moderation, their humour, and their abstinence from painful experience, people to whom others came for advice. They could be, and were, relied on. It was one of those cases of a man and a woman linking themselves whom no one else had ever thought of linking, probably because of their similarities. But then everyone exclaimed: Of course! How right! How was it we never thought of it before!

And so they married amid general rejoicing, and because of their foresight and their sense for what was probable, nothing was a surprise to them.

Both had well-paid jobs. Matthew was a sub-editor on a large London newspaper, and Susan worked in an advertising firm. He was not the stuff of which editors or publicized journalists are made, but he was much more than "a sub-editor," being one of the essential background people who in fact steady, inspire and make possible the people in the limelight. He was content with this position. Susan had a talent for commercial drawing. She was humorous about the advertisements she was responsible for, but she did not feel strongly about them one way or the other.

Both, before they married, had had pleasant flats, but they felt it unwise to base a marriage on either flat, because it might seem like a submission of personality on the part of the one whose flat it was not. They moved into a new flat in South Kensington on the clear understanding that when their marriage had settled down (a process they knew would not take long, and was in fact more a humorous concession to popular wisdom than what was due to themselves) they would buy a house and start a family.

And this is what happened. They lived in their charming flat for two years, giving parties and going to them, being a popular young married couple, and then Susan became pregnant, she gave up her job, and they bought a house in Richmond. It was typical of this couple that they had a son first, then a daughter, then twins, son and daughter. Everything right, appropriate, and what everyone would wish for, if they could choose. But people did feel these two had chosen; this balanced and sensible family was no more than what was due to them because of their infallible sense for *choosing* right.

And so they lived with their four children in their gardened house in Richmond and were happy. They had everything they had wanted and had planned for.

*And yet ...*

Well, even this was expected, that there must be a certain flatness ...

Yes, yes, of course, it was natural they sometimes felt like this. Like what?

Their life seemed to be like a snake biting its tail. Matthew's job for the sake of Susan, children, house, and garden—which caravanserai[1] needed a well-paid job to maintain it. And Susan's practical intelligence for the sake of Matthew, the children, the house and the garden—which unit would have collapsed in a week without her.

But there was no point about which either could say: "For the sake of *this* is all the rest." Children? But children can't be a centre of life and a reason for being. They can be a thousand things that are delightful, interesting, satisfying, but they can't be a wellspring to live from. Or they shouldn't be. Susan and Matthew knew that well enough.

Matthew's job? Ridiculous. It was an interesting job, but scarcely a reason for living. Matthew took pride in doing it well; but he could hardly be expected to be proud of the newspaper: the newspaper he read, *his* newspaper, was not the one he worked for.

Their love for each other? Well, that was nearest it. If this wasn't a centre, what was? Yes, it was around this point, their love, that the whole extraordinary structure revolved. For extraordinary it certainly was. Both Susan and Matthew had moments of thinking so, of looking in secret disbelief at this thing they had created: marriage, four children, big house, garden, charwomen,[2] friends, cars ... and this *thing*, this entity, all of it had come into existence, been blown into being out of nowhere, because Susan loved Matthew and Matthew loved Susan. Extraordinary. So that was the central point, the wellspring.

And if one felt that it simply was not strong enough, important enough, to support it all, well whose fault was that? Certainly neither Susan's nor Matthew's. It was in the nature of things. And they sensibly blamed neither themselves nor each other.

On the contrary, they used their intelligence to preserve what they had created from a painful and explosive world: they looked around them, and took lessons. All around them, marriages collapsing, or breaking, or rubbing along (even worse, they felt). They must not make the same mistakes, they must not.

They had avoided the pitfall so many of their friends had fallen into—of buying a house in the country *for the sake of the children*; so that the husband became a weekend husband, a weekend father, and the wife always careful not to ask what went on in the town flat which they called (in joke) a bachelor flat. No, Matthew was a full-time husband, a full-time father, and at nights, in the big married bed in the big married bedroom (which had an attractive view of the river) they lay

[1] *caravanserai* Large inn, found in eastern countries, at which caravans stay.

[2] *charwomen* Cleaning women.

beside each other talking and he told her about his day, and what he had done, and whom he had met; and she told him about her day (not as interesting, but that was not her fault) for both knew of the hidden resentments and deprivations of the woman who has lived her own life—and above all, has earned her own living—and is now dependent on a husband for outside interests and money.

Nor did Susan make the mistake of taking a job for the sake of her independence, which she might very well have done, since her old firm, missing her qualities of humour, balance, and sense, invited her often to go back. Children needed their mother to a certain age, that both parents knew and agreed on; and when these four healthy wisely brought-up children were of the right age, Susan would work again, because she knew, and so did he, what happened to women of fifty at the height of their energy and ability, with grown-up children who no longer needed their full devotion.

So here was this couple, testing their marriage, looking after it, treating it like a small boat full of helpless people in a very stormy sea. Well, of course, so it was … The storms of the world were bad, but not too close—which is not to say they were selfishly felt: Susan and Matthew were both well-informed and responsible people. And the inner storms and quicksands were understood and charted. So everything was all right. Everything was in order. Yes, things were under control.

So what did it matter if they felt dry, flat? People like themselves, fed on a hundred books (psychological, anthropological, sociological) could scarcely be unprepared for the dry, controlled wistfulness which is the distinguishing mark of the intelligent marriage. Two people, endowed with education, with discrimination, with judgment, linked together voluntarily from their will to be happy together and to be of use to others—one sees them everywhere, one knows them, one even is that thing oneself: sadness because so much is after all so little. These two, unsurprised, turned towards each other with even more courtesy and gentle love: this was life, that two people, no matter how carefully chosen, could not be everything to each other. In fact, even to say so, to think in such a way, was banal, they were ashamed to do it.

It was banal, too, when one night Matthew came home late and confessed he had been to a party, taken a girl home and slept with her. Susan forgave him, of course. Except that forgiveness is hardly the word. Understanding, yes. But if you understand something, you don't forgive it, you are the thing itself: forgiveness is for what you *don't* understand. Nor had he *confessed*—what sort of word is that?

The whole thing was not important. After all, years ago they had joked: Of course I'm not going to be faithful to you, no one can be faithful to one other person for a whole lifetime. (And there was the word *faithful*—stupid, all these words, stupid, belonging to a savage old world.) But the incident left both of them irritable. Strange, but they were both bad-tempered, annoyed. There was something unassimilable about it.

Making love splendidly after he had come home that night, both had felt that the idea that Myra Jenkins, a pretty girl met at a party, could be even relevant was ridiculous. They had loved each other for over a decade, would love each other for years more. Who, then, was Myra Jenkins?

Except, thought Susan, unaccountably bad-tempered, she was (is?) the first. In ten years. So either the ten years' fidelity was not important, or she isn't. (No, no, there is something wrong with this way of thinking, there must be.) But if she isn't important, presumably it wasn't important either when Matthew and I first went to bed with each other that afternoon whose delight even now (like a very long shadow at sundown) lays a long, wand-like finger over us. (Why did I say sundown?) Well, if what we felt that afternoon was not important, nothing is important, because if it hadn't been for what we felt, we wouldn't be Mr. and Mrs. Rawlings with four children, etc., etc. The whole thing is *absurd*—for him to have come home and told me was absurd. For him not to have told me was absurd. For me to care, or for that matter not to care, is absurd … and who is Myra Jenkins? Why, no one at all.

There was only one thing to do, and of course these sensible people did it: they put the thing behind them, and consciously, knowing what they were doing, moved forward into a different phase of their marriage, giving thanks for past good fortune as they did so.

For it was inevitable that the handsome, blond, attractive, manly man, Matthew Rawlings, should be at times tempted (oh, what a word!) by the attractive girls at parties she could not attend because of the four children; and that sometimes he would succumb (a word even more repulsive, if possible) and that she, a good-looking woman in the big well-tended garden at Richmond, would sometimes be pierced as by an arrow from the sky with bitterness. Except that bitterness was not in order, it was out of court. Did the casual girls touch the marriage? They did not. Rather it was they who knew defeat because of the handsome Matthew Rawlings's marriage body and soul to Susan Rawlings.

In that case why did Susan feel (though luckily not for longer than a few seconds at a time) as if life had become a desert, and that nothing mattered, and that her children were not her own?

Meanwhile her intelligence continued to assert that all was well. What if her Matthew did have an occasional sweet afternoon, the odd affair? For she knew quite well, except in her moments of aridity, that they were very happy, that the affairs were not important.

Perhaps that was the trouble? It was in the nature of things that the adventures and delights could no longer be hers, because of the four children and the big house that needed so much attention. But perhaps she was secretly wishing, and even knowing that she did, that the wildness and the beauty could be his. But he was married to her. She was married to him. They were married inextricably. And therefore the gods could not strike him with the real magic, not really. Well, was it Susan's fault that after he came home from an adventure he looked harassed rather than fulfilled? (In fact, that was how she knew he had been *unfaithful*, because of his sullen air, and his glances at her, similar to hers at him: What is it that I share with this person that shields all delight from me?) But none of it by anybody's fault. (But what did they feel ought to be somebody's fault?) Nobody's fault, nothing to be at fault, no one to blame, no one to offer or to take it ... and nothing wrong, either, except that Matthew never was really struck, as he wanted to be, by joy; and that Susan was more and more often threatened by emptiness. (It was usually in the garden that she was invaded by this feeling; she was coming to avoid the garden, unless the children or

Matthew were with her.) There was no need to use the dramatic words, unfaithful, forgive, and the rest: intelligence forbade them. Intelligence barred, too, quarrelling, sulking, anger, silences of withdrawal, accusations and tears. Above all, intelligence forbids tears.

A high price has to be paid for the happy marriage with the four healthy children in the large white gardened house.

And they were paying it, willingly, knowing what they were doing. When they lay side by side or breast to breast in the big civilized bedroom overlooking the wild sullied river, they laughed, often, for no particular reason; but they knew it was really because of these two small people, Susan and Matthew, supporting such an edifice on their intelligent love. The laugh comforted them; it saved them both, though from what, they did not know.

They were now both fortyish. The older children, boy and girl, were ten and eight, at school. The twins, six, were still at home. Susan did not have nurses or girls to help her: childhood is short; and she did not regret the hard work. Often enough she was bored, since small children can be boring; she was often very tired; but she regretted nothing. In another decade, she would turn herself back into being a woman with a life of her own.

Soon the twins would go to school, and they would be away from home from nine until four. These hours, so Susan saw it, would be the preparation for her own slow emancipation away from the role of hub-of-the-family into woman-with-her-own-life. She was already planning for the hours of freedom when all the children would be "off her hands." That was the phrase used by Matthew and by Susan and by their friends, for the moment when the youngest child went off to school. "They'll be off your hands, darling Susan, and you'll have time to yourself." So said Matthew, the intelligent husband, who had often enough commended and consoled Susan, standing by her in spirit during the years when her soul was not her own, as she said, but her children's.

What it amounted to was that Susan saw herself as she had been at twenty-eight, unmarried; and then again somewhere about fifty, blossoming from the root of what she had been twenty years before. As if the essential Susan were in abeyance, as if she were in cold storage. Matthew said something like this to Susan one night; and she agreed that it was true—she did feel something like that. What, then, was this essential Susan? She did not know. Put like that it sounded ridiculous, and she did not really feel it. Anyway, they had a long discussion about the whole thing before going off to sleep in each other's arms.

So the twins went off to their school, two bright affectionate children who had no problems about it, since their older brother and sister had trodden this path so successfully before them. And now Susan was going to be alone in the big house, every day of the school term, except for the daily woman who came in to clean.

It was now, for the first time in this marriage, that something happened which neither of them had foreseen.

This is what happened. She returned, at nine-thirty, from taking the twins to the school by car, looking forward to seven blissful hours of freedom. On the first morning she was simply restless, worrying about the twins "naturally enough" since this was their first day away at school. She was hardly able to contain herself until they came back. Which they did happily, excited by the world of school, looking forward to the next day. And the next day Susan took them, dropped them, came back, and found herself reluctant to enter her big and beautiful home because it was as if something was waiting for her there that she did not wish to confront. Sensibly, however, she parked the car in the garage, entered the house, spoke to Mrs. Parkes the daily woman about her duties, and went up to her bedroom. She was possessed by a fever which drove her out again, downstairs, into the kitchen, where Mrs. Parkes was making cake and did not need her, and into the garden. There she sat on a bench, and tried to calm herself, looking at trees, at a brown glimpse of the river. But she was filled with tension, like a panic, as if an enemy was in the garden with her. She spoke to herself severely, thus: All this is quite natural. First, I spent twelve years of my adult life working, *living my own life*. Then I married, and from the moment I became pregnant for the first time I signed myself over, so to speak, to other people. To the children. Not for one moment in twelve years have I been alone, had time to myself. So now I have to learn to be myself again. That's all.

And she went indoors to help Mrs. Parkes cook and clean, and found some sewing to do for the children. She kept herself occupied every day. At the end of the first term she understood she felt two contrary emotions. First: secret astonishment and dismay that during those weeks when the house was empty of children she had in fact been more occupied (had been careful to keep herself occupied) than ever she had been when the children were around her needing her continual attention. Second that now she knew the house would be full of them, and for five weeks, she resented the fact she would never be alone. She was already looking back at those hours of sewing, cooking (but by herself), as at a lost freedom which would not be hers for five long weeks. And the two months of term which would succeed the five weeks stretched alluringly open to her—freedom. But what freedom—when in fact she had been so careful *not* to be free of small duties during the last weeks? She looked at herself, Susan Rawlings, sitting in a big chair by the window in the bedroom, sewing shirts or dresses, which she might just as well have bought. She saw herself making cakes for hours at a time in the big family kitchen; yet usually she bought cakes. What she saw was a woman alone, that was true, but she had not felt alone. For instance, Mrs. Parkes was always somewhere in the house. And she did not like being in the garden at all, because of the closeness there of the enemy—irritation, restlessness, emptiness, whatever it was, which keeping her hands occupied made less dangerous for some reason.

Susan did not tell Matthew of these thoughts. They were not sensible. She did not recognize herself in them. What should she say to her dear friend and husband Matthew? "When I go into the garden, that is, if the children are not there, I feel as if there is an enemy there waiting to invade me." "What enemy, Susan darling?" "Well I don't know, really …" "Perhaps you should see a doctor?"

No, clearly this conversation should not take place. The holidays began and Susan welcomed them. Four children, lively, energetic, intelligent, demanding; she was never, not for a moment of her day, alone. If she was in a room, they would be in the next room, or waiting for her to do something for them; or it would soon be time for lunch or tea, or to take one of them to the dentist. Something to do: five weeks of it, thank goodness.

On the fourth day of these so welcome holidays, she found she was storming with anger at the twins, two shrinking beautiful children who (and this is what checked her) stood hand in hand looking at her with sheer dismayed disbelief. This was their calm mother, shouting at them. And what for? They had come to her with some game, some bit of nonsense. They looked at each other, moved closer for support, and went off hand in hand, leaving Susan holding on to the windowsill of the living room, breathing deep, feeling sick. She went to lie down, telling the older children she had a headache. She heard the boy Harry telling the little ones: "It's all right, Mother's got a headache." She heard that *It's all right* with pain.

That night she said to her husband: "Today I shouted at the twins, quite unfairly." She sounded miserable, and he said gently: "Well, what of it?"

"It's more of an adjustment than I thought, their going to school."

"But Susie, Susie darling ..." For she was crouched weeping on the bed. He comforted her: "Susan, what is all this about? You shouted at them? What of it? If you shouted at them fifty times a day it wouldn't be more than the little devils deserve." But she wouldn't laugh. She wept. Soon he comforted her with his body. She became calm. Calm, she wondered what was wrong with her, and why she should mind so much that she might, just once, have behaved unjustly with the children. What did it matter? They had forgotten it all long ago; Mother had a headache and everything was all right.

It was a long time later that Susan understood that that night, when she had wept and Matthew had driven the misery out of her with his big solid body, was the last time, ever in their married life, that they had been—to use their mutual language—with each other. And even that was a lie, because she had not told him of her real fears at all.

The five weeks passed, and Susan was in control of herself, and good and kind, and she looked forward to the holidays with a mixture of fear and longing. She did not know what to expect. She took the twins off to school (the elder children took themselves to school) and she returned to the house determined to face the

enemy wherever he was, in the house, or the garden or—where?

She was again restless, she was possessed by restlessness. She cooked and sewed and worked as before, day after day, while Mrs. Parkes remonstrated: "Mrs. Rawlings, what's the need for it? I can do that, it's what you pay me for."

And it was so irrational that she checked herself. She would put the car into the garage, go up to her bedroom, and sit, hands in her lap, forcing herself to be quiet. She listened to Mrs. Parkes moving around the house. She looked out into the garden and saw the branches shake the trees. She sat defeating the enemy, restlessness. Emptiness. She ought to be thinking about her life, about herself. But she did not. Or perhaps she could not. As soon as she forced her mind to think about Susan (for what else did she want to be alone for?) it skipped off to thoughts of butter or school clothes. Or it thought of Mrs. Parkes. She realized that she sat listening for the movements of the cleaning woman, following her every turn, bend, thought. She followed her in her mind from kitchen to bathroom, from table to oven, and it was as if the duster, the cleaning cloth, the saucepan, were in her own hand. She would hear herself saying: No, not like that, don't put that there ... Yet she did not give a damn what Mrs. Parkes did, or if she did it at all. Yet she could not prevent herself from being conscious of her, every minute. Yes, this was what was wrong with her: she needed, when she was alone, to be really alone, with no one near. She could not endure the knowledge that in ten minutes or in half an hour Mrs. Parkes would call up the stairs: "Mrs. Rawlings, there's no silver polish. Madam, we're out of flour."

So she left the house and went to sit in the garden where she was screened from the house by trees. She waited for the demon to appear and claim her, but he did not.

She was keeping him off, because she had not, after all, come to an end of arranging herself.

She was planning how to be somewhere where Mrs. Parkes would not come after her with a cup of tea, or a demand to be allowed to telephone (always irritating since Susan did not care who she telephoned or how often), or just a nice talk about something. Yes, she needed a place, or a state of affairs, where it would not be necessary to keep reminding herself: In ten minutes I must telephone Matthew about … and at half past three I must leave early for the children because the car needs cleaning. And at ten o'clock tomorrow I must remember … She was possessed with resentment that the seven hours of freedom in every day (during weekdays in the school term) were not free, that never, not for one second, ever, was she free from the pressure of time, from having to remember this or that. She could never forget herself; never really let herself go into forgetfulness.

Resentment. It was poisoning her. (She looked at this emotion and thought it was absurd. Yet she felt it.) She was a prisoner. (She looked at this thought too, and it was no good telling herself it was a ridiculous one.) She must tell Matthew—but what? She was filled with emotions that were utterly ridiculous, that she despised, yet that nevertheless she was feeling so strongly she could not shake them off.

The school holidays came round, and this time they were for nearly two months, and she behaved with a conscious controlled decency that nearly drove her crazy. She would lock herself in the bathroom, and sit on the edge of the bath, breathing deep, trying to let go into some kind of calm. Or she went up into the spare room, usually empty, where no one would expect her to be. She heard the children calling "Mother, Mother," and kept silent, feeling guilty. Or she went to the very end of the garden, by herself, and looked at the slow-moving brown river; she looked at the river and closed her eyes and breathed slow and deep, taking it into her being, into her veins.

Then she returned to the family, wife and mother, smiling and responsible, feeling as if the pressure of these people—four lively children and her husband—were a painful pressure on the surface of her skin, a hand pressing on her brain. She did not once break down into irritation during these holidays, but it was like living out a prison sentence, and when the children went back to school, she sat on a white stone seat near the flowing river, and she thought: It is not even a year since the twins went to school, since *they were off my hands* (What on earth did I think I meant when I used that stupid phrase?) and yet I'm a different person. I'm simply not myself. I don't understand it.

Yet she had to understand it. For she knew that this structure—big white house, on which the mortgage still cost four hundred a year, a husband, so good and kind and insightful, four children, all doing so nicely, and the garden where she sat, and Mrs. Parkes the cleaning woman—all this depended on her, and yet she could not understand why, or even what it was she contributed to it.

She said to Matthew in their bedroom: "I think there must be something wrong with me."

And he said: "Surely not, Susan? You look marvellous—you're as lovely as ever."

She looked at the handsome blond man, with his clear, intelligent, blue-eyed face, and thought: Why is it I can't tell him? Why not? And she said: "I need to be alone more than I am."

At which he swung his slow blue gaze at her, and she saw what she had been dreading: Incredulity. Disbelief. And fear. An incredulous blue stare from a stranger who was her husband, as close to her as her own breath.

He said: "But the children are at school and off your hands."

She said to herself: I've got to force myself to say: Yes, but do you realize that I never feel free? There's never a moment I can say to myself: There's nothing I have to remind myself about, nothing I have to do in half an hour, or an hour, or two hours …

But she said: "I don't feel well."

He said: "Perhaps you need a holiday."

She said, appalled: "But not without you, surely?" For she could not imagine herself going off without him. Yet that was what he meant. Seeing her face, he laughed, and opened his arms, and she went into them, thinking: Yes, yes, but why can't I say it? And what is it I have to say?

She tried to tell him, about never being free. And he listened and said: "But Susan, what sort of freedom can you possibly want—short of being dead! Am I ever free? I go to the office, and I have to be there at ten—all right, half past ten, sometimes. And I have to do this or that, don't I? Then I've got to come home at a certain time—I don't mean it, you know I don't—but if I'm not going to be back home at six I telephone you. When can I ever say to myself: I have nothing to be responsible for in the next six hours?"

Susan, hearing this, was remorseful. Because it was true. The good marriage, the house, the children, depended just as much on his voluntary bondage as it did on hers. But why did he not feel bound? Why didn't he chafe and become restless? No, there was something really wrong with her and this proved it.

And that word *bondage*—why had she used it? She had never felt marriage, or the children, as bondage. Neither had he, or surely they wouldn't be together lying in each other's arms content after twelve years of marriage.

No, her state (whatever it was) was irrelevant, nothing to do with her real good life with her family. She had to accept the fact that after all, she was an irrational person and to live with it. Some people had to live with crippled arms, or stammers, or being deaf. She would have to live knowing she was subject to a state of mind she could not own.

Nevertheless, as a result of this conversation with her husband, there was a new regime next holidays.

The spare room at the top of the house now had a cardboard sign saying: PRIVATE! DO NOT DISTURB! on it. (This sign had been drawn in coloured chalks by the children, after a discussion between the parents in which it was decided that was psychologically the right thing.) The family and Mrs. Parkes knew this was "Mother's Room" and that she was entitled to her privacy. Many serious conversations took place between Matthew and the children about not taking Mother for granted. Susan overheard the first, between father and Harry, the older boy, and was surprised at her irritation over it. Surely she could have a room somewhere in that big house and retire into it without such a fuss being made? Without it being so solemnly discussed? Why couldn't she simply have announced: "I'm going to fit out the little top room for myself, and when I'm in it I'm not to be disturbed for anything short of fire"? Just that, and finished, instead of long earnest discussions. When she heard Harry and Matthew explaining it to the twins with Mrs. Parkes coming in—"Yes, well, a family sometimes gets on top of a woman"—she had to go right away to the bottom of the garden until the devils of exasperation had finished their dance in her blood.

But now there was a room, and she could go there when she liked, she used it seldom; she felt even more

caged there than in her bedroom. One day she had gone up there after a lunch for ten children she had cooked and served because Mrs. Parkes was not there, and had sat alone for a while looking into the garden. She saw the children stream out from the kitchen and stand looking up at the window where she sat behind the curtains. They were all—her children and their friends—discussing Mother's Room. A few minutes later, the chase of children in some game came pounding up the stairs, but ended as abruptly as if they had fallen over a ravine, so sudden was the silence. They had remembered she was there, and had gone silent in a great gale of "Hush! Shhhhhh! Quiet, you'll disturb her …" And they went tiptoeing downstairs like criminal conspirators. When she came down to make tea for them, they all apologized. The twins put their arms around her, from front and back, making a human cage of loving limbs, and promised it would never occur again. "We forgot, Mummy, we forgot all about it!"

What it amounted to was that Mother's Room, and her need for privacy, had become a valuable lesson in respect for other people's rights. Quite soon Susan was going up to the room only because it was a lesson it was a pity to drop. Then she took sewing up there, and the children and Mrs. Parkes came in and out: it had become another family room.

She sighed, and smiled, and resigned herself—she made jokes at her own expense with Matthew over the room. That is, she did from the self she liked, she respected. But at the same time, something inside her howled with impatience, with rage … And she was frightened. One day she found herself kneeling by her bed and praying: "Dear God, keep it away from me, keep him away from me." She meant the devil, for she now thought of it, not caring if she were irrational, as some sort of demon. She imagined him, or it, as a youngish man, or perhaps a middle-aged man pretending to be young. Or a man young-looking from immaturity? At any rate, she saw the young-looking face which, when she drew closer, had dry lines about mouth and eyes. He was thinnish, meagre in build. And he had a reddish complexion, and ginger hair. That was he—a gingery, energetic man, and he wore a reddish hairy jacket, unpleasant to the touch.

Well, one day she saw him. She was standing at the

bottom of the garden, watching the river ebb past, when she raised her eyes and saw this person, or being, sitting on the white stone bench. He was looking at her, and grinning. In his hand was a long crooked stick, which he had picked off the ground, or broken off the tree above him. He was absent-mindedly, out of an absent-minded or freakish impulse of spite, using the stick to stir around in the coils of a blindworm or a grass snake (or some kind of snake-like creature; it was whitish and unhealthy to look at, unpleasant). The snake was twisting about, flinging its coils from side to side in a kind of dance of protest against the teasing prodding stick.

Susan looked at him thinking: Who is the stranger? What is he doing in our garden? Then she recognized the man around whom her terrors had crystallized. As she did so, he vanished. She made herself walk over to the bench. A shadow from a branch lay across thin emerald grass, moving jerkily over its roughness, and she could see why she had taken it for a snake, lashing and twisting. She went back to the house thinking: Right, then, so I've seen him with my own eyes, so I'm not crazy after all—there *is* a danger because I've seen him. He is lurking in the garden and sometimes even in the house, and he wants *to get into me and to take me over.*

She dreamed of having a room or a place, anywhere, where she could go and sit, by herself, no one knowing where she was.

Once, near Victoria,[1] she found herself outside a news agent that had Rooms to Let advertised. She decided to rent a room, telling no one. Sometimes she could take the train in from Richmond and sit alone in it for an hour or two. Yet how could she? A room would cost three or four pounds a week, and she earned no money, and how could she explain to Matthew that she needed such a sum? What for? It did not occur to her that she was taking it for granted she wasn't going to tell him about the room.

Well, it was out of the question, having a room; yet she knew she must.

One day, when a school term was well established, and none of the children had measles or other ailments, and everything seemed in order, she did the shopping early, explained to Mrs. Parkes she was meeting an old school friend, took the train to Victoria, searched until she found a small quiet hotel, and asked for a room for the day. They did not let rooms by the day, the manageress said, looking doubtful, since Susan so obviously was not the kind of woman who needed a room for unrespectable reasons. Susan made a long explanation about not being well, being unable to shop without frequent rests for lying down. At last she was allowed to rent the room provided she paid a full night's price for it. She was taken up by the manageress and a maid, both concerned over the state of her health … which must be pretty bad if, living at Richmond (she had signed her name and address in the register), she needed a shelter at Victoria.

The room was ordinary and anonymous, and was just what Susan needed. She put a shilling in the gas fire, and sat, eyes shut, in a dingy armchair with her back to a dingy window. She was alone. She was alone. She was alone. She could feel pressures lifting off her. First the sounds of traffic came very loud; then they seemed to vanish; she might even have slept a little. A knock on the door: it was Miss Townsend the manageress, bringing her a cup of tea with her own hands, so concerned was she over Susan's long silence and possible illness.

Miss Townsend was a lonely woman of fifty, running this hotel with all the rectitude expected of her, and she sensed in Susan the possibility of understanding companionship. She stayed to talk. Susan found herself in the middle of a fantastic story about her illness, which got more and more improbable as she tried to make it tally with the large house at Richmond, well-off husband, and four children. Suppose she said instead: Miss Townsend, I'm here in your hotel because I need to be alone for a few hours, above all *alone and with no one knowing where I am.* She said it mentally, and saw, mentally, the look that would inevitably come on Miss Townsend's elderly maiden's face. "Miss Townsend, my four children and my husband are driving me insane, do you understand that? Yes, I can see from the gleam of hysteria in your eyes that comes from loneliness controlled but only just contained that I've got everything in the world you've ever longed for. Well, Miss Townsend, I don't want any of it. You can have it, Miss Townsend. I wish I was absolutely alone in the world,

---

[1] *Victoria*   I.e., Victoria Station, in London.

like you. Miss Townsend, I'm besieged by seven devils, Miss Townsend, Miss Townsend, let me stay here in your hotel where the devils can't get me …" Instead of saying all this, she described her anæmia, agreed to try Miss Townsend's remedy for it, which was raw liver, minced, between whole-meal bread, and said yes, perhaps it would be better if she stayed at home and let a friend do shopping for her. She paid her bill and left the hotel, defeated.

At home Mrs. Parkes said she didn't really like it, no, not really, when Mrs. Rawlings was away from nine in the morning until five. The teacher had telephoned from school to say Joan's teeth were paining her, and she hadn't known what to say; and what was she to make for the children's tea, Mrs. Rawlings hadn't said.

All this was nonsense, of course, Mrs. Parkes's complaint was that Susan had withdrawn herself spiritually, leaving the burden of the big house on her.

Susan looked back at her day of "freedom" which had resulted in her becoming a friend to the lonely Miss Townsend, and in Mrs. Parkes's remonstrances. Yet she remembered the short blissful hour of being alone, really alone. She was determined to arrange her life, no matter what it cost, so that she could have that solitude more often. An absolute solitude, where no one knew her or cared about her.

But how? She thought of saying to her old employer: I want to back you up in a story with Matthew that I am doing part-time work for you. The truth is that … but she would have to tell him a lie too, and which lie? She could not say: I want to sit by myself three or four times a week in a rented room. And besides, he knew Matthew, and she could not really ask him to tell lies on her behalf, apart from his being bound to think it meant a lover.

Suppose she really took a part-time job, which she could get through fast and efficiently, leaving time for herself. What job? Addressing envelopes? Canvassing?

And there was Mrs. Parkes, working widow, who knew exactly what she was prepared to give to the house, who knew by instinct when her mistress withdrew in spirit from her responsibilities. Mrs. Parkes was one of the servers of this world, but she needed someone to serve. She had to have Mrs. Rawlings, her madam, at the top of the house or in the garden, so that she could come and get support from her: "Yes, the bread's not what it was when I was a girl … Yes, Harry's got a wonderful appetite, I wonder where he puts it all … Yes, it's lucky the twins are so much of a size, they can wear each other's shoes, that's a saving in these hard times … Yes, the cherry jam from Switzerland is not a patch on the jam from Poland, and three times the price …" And so on. That sort of talk Mrs. Parkes must have, every day, or she would leave, not knowing herself why she left.

Susan Rawlings, thinking these thoughts, found that she was prowling through the great thicketed garden like a wild cat; she was walking up the stairs, down the stairs, through the rooms, into the garden, along the brown running river, back, up through the house, down again … It was a wonder Mrs. Parkes did not think it strange. But on the contrary, Mrs. Rawlings could do what she liked, she could stand on her head if she wanted, provided she was *there*. Susan Rawlings prowled and muttered through her house, hating Mrs. Parkes, hating poor Miss Townsend, dreaming of her hour of solitude in the dingy respectability of Miss Townsend's hotel bedroom, and she knew quite well she was mad. Yes, she was mad.

She said to Matthew that she must have a holiday. Matthew agreed with her. This was not as things had been once—how they had talked in each other's arms in the marriage bed. He had, she knew, diagnosed her finally as *unreasonable*. She had become someone outside himself that he had to manage. They were living side by side in this house like two tolerably friendly strangers.

Having told Mrs. Parkes, or rather, asked for her permission, she went off on a walking holiday in Wales. She chose the remotest place she knew of. Every morning the children telephoned her before they went off to school, to encourage and support her, just as they had over Mother's Room. Every evening she telephoned them, spoke to each child in turn, and then to Matthew. Mrs. Parkes, given permission to telephone for instructions or advice, did so every day at lunchtime. When, as happened three times, Mrs. Rawlings was out on the mountainside, Mrs. Parkes asked that she should ring back at such and such a time, for she would not be happy in what she was doing without Mrs. Rawlings's blessing.

Susan prowled over wild country with the telephone wire holding her to her duty like a leash. The next time she must telephone, or wait to be telephoned, nailed her to her cross. The mountains themselves seemed trammelled by her unfreedom. Everywhere on the mountains, where she met no one at all, from breakfast time to dusk, excepting sheep, or a shepherd, she came face to face with her own craziness which might attack her in the broadest valleys, so that they seemed too small; or on a mountaintop from which she could see a hundred other mountains and valleys, so that they seemed too low, too small, with the sky pressing down too close. She would stand gazing at a hillside brilliant with ferns and bracken, jewelled with running water, and see nothing but her devil, who lifted inhuman eyes at her from where he leaned negligently on a rock, switching at his ugly yellow boots with a leafy twig.

She returned to her home and family, with the Welsh emptiness at the back of her mind like a promise of freedom.

She told her husband she wanted to have an *au pair* girl.

They were in their bedroom, it was late at night, the children slept. He sat, shirted and slippered, in a chair by the window, looking out. She sat brushing her hair and watching him in the mirror. A time-hallowed scene in the connubial bedroom. He said nothing, while she heard the arguments coming into his mind, only to be rejected because every one was *reasonable*.

"It seems strange to get one now, after all, the children are in school most of the day. Surely the time for you to have help was when you were stuck with them day and night. Why don't you ask Mrs. Parkes to cook for you? She's even offered to—I can understand if you are tired of cooking for six people. But you know that an *au pair* girl means all kinds of problems, it's not like having an ordinary char in during the day ..."

Finally he said carefully: "Are you thinking of going back to work?"

"No," she said, "no, not really." She made herself sound vague, rather stupid. She went on brushing her black hair and peering at herself so as to be oblivious of the short uneasy glances her Matthew kept giving her. "Do you think we can't afford it?" she went on vaguely,

not at all the old efficient Susan who knew exactly what they could afford.

"It's not that," he said, looking out of the window at dark trees, so as not to look at her. Meanwhile she examined a round, candid, pleasant face with clear dark brows and clear grey eyes. A sensible face. She brushed thick healthy black hair and thought: Yet that's the reflection of a madwoman. How very strange! Much more to the point if what looked back at me was the gingery green-eyed demon with his dry meagre smile ... Why wasn't Matthew agreeing? After all, what else could he do? She was breaking her part of the bargain and there was no way of forcing her to keep it: that her spirit, her soul, should live in this house, so that the people in it could grow like plants in water, and Mrs. Parkes remain content in their service. In return for this, he would be a good loving husband, and responsible towards the children. Well, nothing like this had been true of either of them for a long time. He did his duty, perfunctorily; she did not even pretend to do hers. And he had become like other husbands, with his real life in his work and the people he met there, and very likely a serious affair. All this was her fault.

At last he drew heavy curtains, blotting out the trees, and turned to force her attention: "Susan, are you really sure we need a girl?" But she would not meet his appeal at all. She was running the brush over her hair again and again, lifting fine black clouds in a small hiss of electricity. She was peering in and smiling as if she were amused at the clinging hissing hair that followed the brush.

"Yes, I think it would be a good idea on the whole," she said, with the cunning of a madwoman evading the real point.

In the mirror she could see her Matthew lying on his back, his hands behind his head, staring upwards, his face sad and hard. She felt her heart (the old heart of Susan Rawlings) soften and call out to him. But she set it to be indifferent.

He said: "Susan, the children?" It was an appeal that *almost* reached her. He opened his arms, lifting them from where they had lain by his sides, palms up, empty. She had only to run across and fling herself into them, onto his hard, warm chest, and melt into herself, into Susan. But she could not. She would not see his lifted arms. She said vaguely: "Well, surely it'll be even better for them? We'll get a French or a German girl and they'll learn the language."

In the dark she lay beside him, feeling frozen, a stranger. She felt as if Susan had been spirited away. She disliked very much this woman who lay here, cold and indifferent beside a suffering man, but she could not change her.

Next morning she set about getting a girl, and very soon came Sophie Traub from Hamburg, a girl of twenty, laughing, healthy, blue-eyed, intending to learn English. Indeed, she already spoke a good deal. In return for a room—"Mother's Room"—and her food, she undertook to do some light cooking, and to be with the children when Mrs. Rawlings asked. She was an intelligent girl and understood perfectly what was needed. Susan said: "I go off sometimes, for the morning or for the day—well, sometimes the children run home from school, or they ring up, or a teacher rings up. I should be here, really. And there's the daily woman …" And Sophie laughed her deep fruity *Fräulein*'s laugh, showed her fine white teeth and her dimples, and said: "You want some person to play mistress of the house sometimes, not so?"

"Yes, that is just so," said Susan, a bit dry, despite herself, thinking in secret fear how easy it was, how much nearer to the end she was than she thought. Healthy Fräulein Traub's instant understanding of their position proved this to be true.

The *au pair* girl, because of her own common sense, or (as Susan said to herself with her new inward shudder) because she had been *chosen* so well by Susan, was a success with everyone, the children liking her, Mrs. Parkes forgetting almost at once that she was German, and Matthew finding her "nice to have around the house." For he was now taking things as they came, from the surface of life, withdrawn both as a husband and a father from the household.

One day Susan saw how Sophie and Mrs. Parkes were talking and laughing in the kitchen, and she announced that she would be away until teatime. She knew exactly where to go and what she must look for. She took the District Line to South Kensington, changed to the Circle, got off at Paddington, and walked around looking at the smaller hotels until she was satisfied with one which had FRED'S HOTEL painted on windowpanes that needed cleaning. The façade was a faded shiny yellow, like unhealthy skin. A door at the end of a passage said she must knock; she did, and Fred appeared. He was not at all attractive, not in any way, being fattish, and rundown, and wearing a tasteless striped suit. He had small sharp eyes in a white creased face, and was quite prepared to let Mrs. Jones (she chose the farcical name deliberately, staring him out) have a room three days a week from ten until six. Provided of course that she paid in advance each time she came? Susan produced fifteen shillings (no price had been set by him) and held it out, still fixing him with a bold unblinking challenge she had not known until then she could use at will. Looking at her still, he took up a ten-shilling note from her palm between thumb and forefinger, fingered it, then shuffled up two half crowns, held out his own palm with these bits of money displayed thereon, and let his gaze lower broodingly at them. They were standing in the passage, a red-shaded light above, bare boards beneath, and a strong smell of floor polish rising about them. He shot his gaze up at her over the still-extended palm, and smiled as if to say: What do you take me for? "I shan't," said Susan, "be using this room for the purposes of making money." He still waited. She added another five shillings, at which he nodded and said: "You pay, and I ask no questions." "Good," said Susan. He now went past her to the stairs, and there waited a moment; the light from the street door being in her eyes, she lost sight of him momentarily. Then she saw a sober-suited, white-faced, white-balding little man trotting up the stairs like a waiter, and she went after him. They proceeded in utter silence up the stairs of this house where no questions were asked—Fred's Hotel, which could afford the freedom for its visitors that poor Miss Townsend's hotel could not. The room was hideous. It had a single window, with thin green brocade curtains, a three-quarter bed that had a cheap green satin bedspread on it, a fireplace with a gas fire and a shilling meter by it, a chest of drawers, and a green wicker armchair.

"Thank you," said Susan, knowing that Fred (if this was Fred, and not George, or Herbert or Charlie) was looking at her, not so much with curiosity, an emotion he would not own to, for professional reasons, but with a philosophical sense of what was appropriate. Having taken her money and shown her up and agreed to everything, he was clearly disapproving of her for coming here. She did not belong here at all, so his look said. (But she knew, already, how very much she did belong; the room had been waiting for her to join it.) "Would you have me called at five o'clock, please?" and he nodded and went downstairs.

It was twelve in the morning. She was free. She sat in the armchair, she simply sat, she closed her eyes and sat and let herself be alone. She was alone and no one knew where she was. When a knock came on the door she was annoyed, and prepared to show it, but it was Fred himself, it was five o'clock and he was calling her as ordered. He flicked his sharp little eyes over the room—bed, first. It was undisturbed. She might never have been in the room at all. She thanked him, said she would be returning the day after tomorrow, and left. She was back home in time to cook supper, to put the children to bed, to cook a second supper for her husband and herself later. And to welcome Sophie back from the pictures where she had gone with a friend. All these things she did cheerfully, willingly. But she was thinking all the time of the hotel room, she was longing for it with her whole being.

Three times a week. She arrived promptly at ten, looked Fred in the eyes, gave him twenty shillings, followed him up the stairs, went into the room, and shut the door on him with gentle firmness. For Fred, disapproving of her being here at all, was quite ready to let friendship, or at least acquaintanceship, follow his disapproval, if only she would let him. But he was content to go off on her dismissing nod, with the twenty shillings in his hand.

She sat in the armchair and shut her eyes.

What did she *do* in the room? Why, nothing at all. From the chair, when it had rested her, she went to the window, stretching her arms, smiling, treasuring her anonymity, to look out. She was no longer Susan Rawlings, mother of four, wife of Matthew, employer of Mrs. Parkes and of Sophie Traub, with these and those relations with friends, schoolteachers, tradesmen. She no longer was mistress of the big white house and garden, owning clothes suitable for this and that activity or occasion. She was Mrs. Jones, and she was alone, and she had no past and no future. Here I am, she thought, after all these years of being married and having children and playing those roles of responsibility—and I'm just the same. Yet there have been times I thought that nothing existed of me except the roles that went with being Mrs. Matthew Rawlings. Yes, here I am, and if I never saw any of my family again, here I would still be … how very strange that is! And she leaned on the sill, and looked into the street, loving the men and women who passed, because she did not know them. She looked at the downtrodden buildings over the street, and at the sky, wet and dingy, or sometimes blue, and she felt she had never seen buildings or sky before. And then she went back to the chair, empty, her mind a blank. Sometimes she talked aloud, saying nothing—an exclamation, meaningless, followed by a comment about the floral pattern on the thin rug, or a stain on the green satin coverlet. For the most part, she wool-gathered—what word is there for it?—brooded, wandered, simply went dark, feeling emptiness run deliriously through her veins like the movement of her blood.

This room had become more her own than the house she lived in. One morning she found Fred taking her a flight higher than usual. She stopped, refusing to go up, and demanded her usual room, Number 19. "Well, you'll have to wait half an hour then," he said. Willingly she descended to the dark disinfectant-smelling hall, and sat waiting until the two, man and woman, came down the stairs, giving her swift indifferent glances before they hurried out into the street, separating at the door. She went up to the room, *her* room, which they had just vacated. It was no less hers, though the windows were set wide open, and a maid was straightening the bed as she came in.

After these days of solitude, it was both easy to play her part as mother and wife, and difficult—because it was so easy, she felt an impostor. She felt as if her shell moved here, with her family, answering to Mummy, Mother, Susan, Mrs. Rawlings. She was surprised no one saw through her, that she wasn't turned out of doors, as a fake. On the contrary, it seemed the children loved her more; Matthew and she "got on" pleasantly, and Mrs. Parkes was happy in her work under (for the most part, it must be confessed) Sophie Traub. At night she lay beside her husband, and they made love again, apparently just as they used to, when they were really married. But she, Susan, or the being who answered so readily and improbably to the name of Susan, was not there; she was in Fred's Hotel, in Paddington, waiting for the easing hours of solitude to begin.

Soon she made a new arrangement with Fred and with Sophie. It was for five days a week. As for the money, five pounds, she simply asked Matthew for it. She saw that she was not even frightened he might ask what for; he would give it to her, she knew that, and yet it was terrifying it could be so, for this close couple, these partners, had once known the destination of every shilling they must spend. He agreed to give her five pounds a week. She asked for just so much, not a penny more. He sounded indifferent about it. It was as if he were paying her, she thought: *paying her off*—yes, that was it. Terror came back for a moment, when she understood this, but she stilled it; things had gone too far for that. Now, every week, on Sunday nights, he gave her five pounds, turning away from her before their eyes could meet on the transaction. As for Sophie Traub, she was to be somewhere in or near the house until six at night, after which she was free. She was not to cook, or to clean, she was simply to be there. So she gardened or sewed, and asked friends in, being a person who was bound to have a lot of friends. If the children were sick, she nursed them. If teachers telephoned, she answered them sensibly. For the five daytimes in the school week, she was altogether the mistress of the house.

One night in the bedroom, Matthew asked: "Susan, I don't want to interfere—don't think that, please—but are you sure you are well?"

She was brushing her hair at the mirror. She made two more strokes on either side of her head, before she replied: "Yes, dear, I am sure I am well."

He was again lying on his back, his big blond head on his hands, his elbows angled up and part-concealing his face. He said: "Then Susan, I have to ask you this question, though you must understand, I'm not putting any sort of pressure on you." (Susan heard the word pressure with dismay, because this was inevitable, of course she could not go on like this.) "Are things going to go on like this?"

"Well," she said, going vague and bright and idiotic again, so as to escape: "Well, I don't see why not."

He was jerking his elbows up and down, in annoyance or in pain, and, looking at him, she saw he had got thin, even gaunt; and restless angry movements were not what she remembered of him. He said: "Do you want a divorce, is that it?"

At this, Susan only with the greatest difficulty stopped herself from laughing; she could hear the bright bubbling laughter she *would* have emitted, had she let herself. He could only mean one thing: she had a lover, and that was why she spent her days in London, as lost to him as if she had vanished to another continent.

Then the small panic set in again; she understood that he hoped she did have a lover, he was begging her to say so, because otherwise it would be too terrifying.

She thought this out, as she brushed her hair, watching the fine black stuff fly up to make its little clouds of electricity, hiss, hiss, hiss. Behind her head, across the room, was a blue wall. She realized she was absorbed in watching the black hair making shapes against the blue. She should be answering him. "Do *you* want a divorce, Matthew?"

He said: "That surely isn't the point, is it?"

"You brought it up, I didn't," she said, brightly, suppressing meaningless tinkling laughter.

Next day she asked Fred: "Have enquiries been made for me?"

He hesitated, and she said: "I've been coming here a year now. I've made no trouble, and you've been paid every day. I have a right to be told."

"As a matter of fact, Mrs. Jones, a man did come asking."

"A man from a detective agency?"

"Well, he could have been, couldn't he?"

"I was asking you … well, what did you tell him?"

"I told him a Mrs. Jones came every weekday from ten until five or six and stayed in Number 19 by herself."

"Describing me?"

"Well, Mrs. Jones, I had no alternative. Put yourself in my place."

"By rights I should deduct what that man gave you for the information."

He raised shocked eyes; she was not the sort of person to make jokes like this! Then he chose to laugh; a pinkish wet slit appeared across his white crinkled face;

his eyes positively begged her to laugh, otherwise he might lose some money. She remained grave, looking at him.

He stopped laughing and said: "You want to go up now?"—returning to the familiarity, the comradeship, of the country where no questions are asked, on which (and he knew it) she depended completely.

She went up to sit in her wicker chair. But it was not the same. Her husband had searched her out. (The world had searched her out.) The pressures were on her. She was here with his connivance. He might walk in at any moment, here, into Room 19. She imagined the report from the detective agency: "A woman calling herself Mrs. Jones, fitting the description of your wife (etc., etc., etc.), stays alone all day in Room No. 19. She insists on this room, waits for it if it is engaged. As far as the proprietor knows, she receives no visitors there, male or female." A report something on these lines, Matthew must have received.

Well of course he was right: things couldn't go on like this. He had put an end to it all simply by sending the detective after her.

She tried to shrink herself back into the shelter of the room, a snail pecked out of its shell and trying to squirm back. But the peace of the room had gone. She was trying consciously to revive it, trying to let go into the dark creative trance (or whatever it was) that she had found there. It was no use, yet she craved for it, she was as ill as a suddenly deprived addict.

Several times she returned to the room, to look for herself there, but instead she found the unnamed spirit of restlessness, a prickling fevered hunger for movement, an irritable self-consciousness that made her brain feel as if it had coloured lights going on and off inside it. Instead of the soft dark that had been the room's air, were now waiting for her demons that made her dash blindly about, muttering words of hate; she was impelling herself from point to point like a moth dashing itself against a windowpane, sliding to the bottom, fluttering off on broken wings, then crashing into the invisible barrier again. And again and again. Soon she was exhausted, and she told Fred that for a while she would not be needing the room, she was going on holiday. Home she went, to the big white house by the river. The middle of a weekday, and she felt guilty at

returning to her own home when not expected. She stood unseen, looking in at the kitchen window. Mrs. Parkes, wearing a discarded floral overall of Susan's, was stooping to slide something into the oven. Sophie, arms folded, was leaning her back against a cupboard and laughing at some joke made by a girl not seen before by Susan—a dark foreign girl, Sophie's visitor. In an armchair Molly, one of the twins, lay curled, sucking her thumb and watching the grownups. She must have some sickness, to be kept from school. The child's listless face, the dark circles under her eyes, hurt Susan; Molly was looking at the three grownups working and talking in exactly the same way Susan looked at the four through the kitchen window: she was remote, shut off from them.

But then, just as Susan imagined herself going in, picking up the little girl, and sitting in an armchair with her, stroking her probably heated forehead, Sophie did just that; she had been standing on one leg, the other knee flexed, its foot set against the wall. Now she let her foot in its ribbon-tied red shoe slide down the wall, stood solid on two feet, clapping her hands before and behind her, and sang a couple of lines in German, so that the child lifted her heavy eyes at her and began to smile. Then she walked, or rather skipped, over to the child, swung her up, and let her fall into her lap at the same moment she sat herself. She said: "Hopla! Hopla! Molly …" and began stroking the dark untidy young head that Molly laid on her shoulder for comfort.

*Well*… Susan blinked the tears of farewell out of her eyes, and went quietly up the house to her bedroom. There she sat looking at the river through the trees. She felt at peace, but in a way that was new to her. She had no desire to move, to talk, to do anything at all. The devils that had haunted the house, the garden, were not there; but she knew it was because her soul was in Room 19 in Fred's Hotel; she was not really here at all. It was a sensation that should have been frightening: to sit at her own bedroom window, listening to Sophie's rich young voice sing German nursery songs to her child, listening to Mrs. Parkes clatter and move below, and to know that all this had nothing to do with her; she was already out of it.

Later, she made herself go down and say she was home; it was unfair to be here unannounced. She took lunch with Mrs. Parkes, Sophie, Sophie's Italian friend Maria, and her daughter Molly, and felt like a visitor.

A few days later, at bedtime, Matthew said: "Here's your five pounds," and pushed them over to her. Yet he must have known she had not been leaving the house at all.

She shook her head, gave it back to him, and said, in explanation, not in accusation: "As soon as you knew where I was, there was no point."

He nodded, not looking at her. He was turned away from her, thinking, she knew, how best to handle this wife who terrified him.

He said: "I wasn't trying to … it's just that I was worried."

"Yes I know."

"I must confess that I was beginning to wonder …"

"You thought I had a lover?"

"Yes, I am afraid I did."

She knew that he wished she had. She sat wondering how to say: "For a year now I've been spending all my days in a very sordid hotel room. It's the place where I'm happy. In fact, without it I don't exist." She heard herself saying this, and understood how terrified he was that she might. So instead she said: "Well, perhaps you're not far wrong."

Probably Matthew would think the hotel proprietor lied; he would want to think so.

"Well," he said, and she could hear his voice spring up, so to speak, with relief: "in that case I must confess I've got a bit of an affair on myself."

She said, detached and interested: "Really? Who is she?" and saw Matthew's startled look because of this reaction.

"It's Phil. Phil Hunt."

She had known Phil Hunt well in the old unmarried days. She was thinking: No, she won't do, she's too neurotic and difficult. She's never been happy yet. Sophie's much better. Well Matthew will see that himself, as sensible as he is.

This line of thought went on in silence, while she said aloud:

"It's no point telling you about mine, because you don't know him."

Quick, quick, invent, she thought. Remember how you invented all that nonsense for Miss Townsend.

She began slowly, careful not to contradict herself: "His name is Michael"—(*Michael What?*)— "Michael Plant." (What a silly name!) "He's rather like you—in looks, I mean." And indeed, she could imagine herself being touched by no one but Matthew himself. "He's a publisher." (Really? Why?) "He's got a wife already and two children."

She brought out this fantasy, proud of herself.

Matthew said: "Are you two thinking of marrying?"

She said, before she could stop herself: "Good God, *no!*"

She realized, if Matthew wanted to marry Phil Hunt, that this was too emphatic, but apparently it was alright, for his voice sounded relieved as he said: "It is a bit impossible to imagine oneself married to anyone else, isn't it?" With which he pulled her to him, so that her head lay on his shoulder. She turned her face into the dark of his flesh, and listened to the blood pounding through her ears saying: I am alone, I am alone, I am alone.

In the morning Susan lay in bed while he dressed.

He had been thinking things out in the night, because now he said: "Susan, why don't we make a foursome?"

Of course, she said to herself, of course he would be bound to say that. If one is sensible, if one is reasonable, if one never allows oneself a base thought or an envious emotion, naturally one says: Let's make a foursome!

"Why not?" she said.

"We could all meet for lunch. I mean, it's ridiculous, you sneaking off to filthy hotels, and me staying late at the office, and all the lies everyone has to tell."

What on earth did I say his name was?—she panicked, then said: "I think it's a good idea, but Michael is away at the moment. When he comes back though—and I'm sure you two would like each other."

"He's away, is he? So that's why you've been …" Her husband put his hand to the knot of his tie in a gesture of male coquetry she would not before have associated with him; and he bent to kiss her cheek with the expression that goes with the words: Oh you naughty little puss! And she felt its answering look, naughty and coy, come onto her face.

Inside she was dissolving in horror at them both, at how far they had both sunk from honesty of emotion.

So now she was saddled with a lover, and he had a mistress! How ordinary, how reassuring, how jolly! And now they would make a foursome of it, and go about to theatres and restaurants.

After all, the Rawlingses could well afford that sort of thing, and presumably the publisher Michael Plant could afford to do himself and his mistress quite well. No, there was nothing to stop the four of them developing the most intricate relationship of civilized tolerance, all enveloped in a charming afterglow of autumnal passion. Perhaps they would all go off on holidays together? She had known people who did. Or perhaps Matthew would draw the line there? Why should he, though, if he was capable of talking about "foursomes" at all?

She lay in the empty bedroom, listening to the car drive off with Matthew in it, off to work. Then she heard the children clattering off to school to the accompaniment of Sophie's cheerfully ringing voice. She slid down into the hollow of the bed, for shelter against her own irrelevance. And she stretched out her hand to the hollow where her husband's body had lain, but found no comfort there: he was not her husband. She curled herself up in a small tight ball under the clothes; she could stay here all day, all week, indeed, all her life.

But in a few days she must produce Michael Plant, and—but how? She must presumably find some agreeable man prepared to impersonate a publisher called Michael Plant. And in return for which she would— what? Well, for one thing they would make love. The idea made her want to cry with sheer exhaustion. Oh no, she had finished with all that—the proof of it was that the words "make love," or even imagining it, trying hard to revive no more than the pleasures of sensuality, let alone affection, or love, made her want to run away and hide from the sheer effort of the thing … Good Lord, why make love at all? Why make love with anyone? Or if you are going to make love, what does it matter who with? Why shouldn't she simply walk into the street, pick up a man and have a roaring sexual affair with him? Why not? Or even with Fred? What difference did it make?

But she had let herself in for it—an interminable stretch of time with a lover, called Michael, as part of a gallant civilized foursome. Well, she could not, and would not.

She got up, dressed, went down to find Mrs. Parkes, and asked her for the loan of a pound, since Matthew, she said, had forgotten to leave her money. She exchanged with Mrs. Parkes variations on the theme that husbands are all the same, they don't think, and without saying a word to Sophie, whose voice could be heard upstairs from the telephone, walked to the underground, travelled to South Kensington, changed to the Inner Circle, got out at Paddington, and walked to Fred's Hotel. There she told Fred that she wasn't going on holiday after all, she needed the room. She would have to wait an hour, Fred said. She went to a busy tearoom-cum-restaurant around the corner, and sat watching the people flow in and out the door that kept swinging open and shut, watched them mingle and merge and separate, felt her being flow into them, into their movement. When the hour was up she left a half crown for her pot of tea, and left the place without looking back at it, just as she had left her house, the big, beautiful white house, without another look, but silently dedicating it to Sophie. She returned to Fred, received the key of No. 19, now free, and ascended the grimy stairs slowly, letting floor after floor fall away below her, keeping her eyes lifted, so that floor after floor descended jerkily to her level of vision, and fell away out of sight.

No. 19 was the same. She saw everything with an acute, narrow, checking glance: the cheap shine of the satin spread, which had been replaced carelessly after the two bodies had finished their convulsions under it; a trace of powder on the glass that topped the chest of drawers; an intense green shade in a fold of the curtain. She stood at the window, looking down, watching people pass and pass and pass until her mind went dark from the constant movement. Then she sat in the wicker chair, letting herself go slack. But she had to be careful, because she did not want, today, to be surprised by Fred's knock at five o'clock.

The demons were not here. They had gone forever, because she was buying her freedom from them. She was slipping already into the dark fructifying dream that seemed to caress her inwardly, like the movement of her blood … but she had to think about Matthew first. Should she write a letter for the coroner? But what should she say? She would like to leave him with the look on his face she had seen this morning—banal, admittedly, but at least confidently healthy. Well, that was impossible, one did not look like that with a wife dead from suicide. But how to leave him believing she was dying because of a man—because of the fascinating publisher Michael Plant? Oh, how ridiculous! How absurd! How humiliating! But she decided not to trouble about it, simply not to think about the living. If he wanted to believe she had a lover, he would believe it. And he *did* want to believe it. Even when he had found out that there was no publisher in London called Michael Plant, he would think: Oh poor Susan, she was afraid to give me his real name.

And what did it matter whether he married Phil Hunt or Sophie? Though it ought to be Sophie who was already the mother of those children … and what hypocrisy to sit here worrying about the children, when she was going to leave them because she had not got the energy to stay.

She had about four hours. She spent them delightfully, darkly, sweetly, letting herself slide gently, gently, to the edge of the river. Then, with hardly a break in her consciousness, she got up, pushed the thin rug against the door, made sure the windows were tight shut, put two shillings in the meter, and turned on the gas. For the first time since she had been in the room she lay on the hard bed that smelled stale, that smelled of sweat and sex.

She lay on her back on the green satin cover, but her legs were chilly. She got up, found a blanket folded into the bottom of the chest of drawers, and carefully covered her legs with it. She was quite content lying there, listening to the faint soft hiss of the gas that poured into the room, into her lungs, into her brain, as she drifted off into the dark river.

—1978

## from *The Golden Notebook*

### from "INTRODUCTION" TO THE 1971 EDITION

The theme of "breakdown," that sometimes when people "crack up" it is a way of self-healing, of the inner self's dismissing false dichotomies and divisions, has of course been written about by other people, as well as by me, since then. But this is where,[1] apart from the odd short story, I first wrote about it. Here it is rougher, more close to experience, before experience has shaped itself into thought and pattern—more valuable perhaps because it is rawer material.

But nobody so much as noticed this central theme, because the book was instantly belittled, by friendly reviewers as well as by hostile ones, as being about the sex war, or was claimed by women as a useful weapon in the sex war.

I have been in a false position ever since, for the last thing I have wanted to do was to refuse to support women.

To get the subject of Women's Liberation over with—I support it, of course, because women are second-class citizens, as they are saying energetically and competently in many countries. It can be said that they are succeeding, if only to the extent they are being seriously listened to. All kinds of people previously hostile or indifferent say: "I support their aims but I don't like their shrill voices and their nasty ill-mannered ways." This is an inevitable and easily recognizable stage in every revolutionary movement: reformers must expect to be disowned by those who are only too happy to enjoy what has been won for them. I don't think that Women's Liberation will change much though—not because there is anything wrong with its aims, but because it is already clear that the whole world is being shaken into a new pattern by the cataclysms we are living through; probably by the time we are through, if we do get through at all, the aims of Women's Liberation will look very small and quaint.

But this novel was not a trumpet for Women's Liberation. It described many female emotions of aggression, hostility, resentment.

---

[1]  *this is where*  In *The Golden Notebook*.

It put them into print. Apparently what many women were thinking, feeling, experiencing, came as a great surprise. Instantly a lot of very ancient weapons were unleashed, the main ones, as usual, being on the theme of "She is unfeminine," "She is a man-hater." This particular reflex seems indestructible. Men—and many women, said that the suffragettes were defeminized, masculine, brutalized. There is no record I have read of any society anywhere when women demanded more than nature offers them that does not also describe this reaction from men—and some women. A lot of women were angry about *The Golden Notebook*. What women will say to other women, grumbling in their kitchens and complaining and gossiping or what they make clear in their masochism, is often the last thing they will say aloud—a man may overhear. Women are the cowards they are because they have been semi-slaves for so long. The number of women prepared to stand up for what they really think, feel, experience with a man they are in love with is still small. Most women will still run like little dogs with stones thrown at them when a man says: You are unfeminine, aggressive, you are unmanning me. It is my belief that any woman who marries, or takes seriously in any way at all, a man who uses this threat, deserves everything she gets. For such a man is a bully, does not know anything about the world he lives in, or about its history—men and women have taken infinite numbers of roles in the past, and do now, in different societies. So he is ignorant, or fearful about

being out of step—a coward ... I write all these remarks with exactly the same feeling as if I were writing a letter to post into the distant past: I am so sure that everything we now take for granted is going to be utterly swept away in the next decade.

(So why write novels? Indeed, why! I suppose we have to go on living *as if* ...)

Some books are not read in the right way because they have skipped a stage of opinion, assume a crystallization of information in society which has not yet taken place. This book was written as if the attitudes that have been created by the Women's Liberation movements already existed. It came out first ten years ago, in 1962. If it were coming out now for the first time it might be read, and not merely reacted to; things have changed very fast. Certain hypocrisies have gone. For instance, ten, or even five, years ago—it has been a sexually contumacious[1] time—novels and plays were being plentifully written by men furiously critical of women—particularly from the States but also in this country—portrayed as bullies and betrayers, but particularly as underminers and sappers. But these attitudes in male writers were taken for granted, accepted as sound philosophical bases, as quite normal, certainly not as woman-hating, aggressive or neurotic. It still goes on, of course—but things are better, there is no doubt of it.

—1971

---

[1]    *contumacious*   Rebellious.

# DYLAN THOMAS
## 1914 – 1953

The fiery career of Dylan Thomas left a burning after-image on the poetic retina of the English-speaking world in the mid-twentieth century. Thomas was a rollicking, even raucous, fixture in the taverns of London's Soho-Fitzrovia district, but he also haunted the rural hills and seashores of Wales, where he sought to articulate, through the tumbling power of his words, his sense that life and death were rolled together in nature's driving "green fuse."

Born in Swansea, Wales, Dylan Thomas grew up speaking English; his mother, Florence Hannah Williams, and his father, D.J. Thomas, chose the Anglicized urban world of Swansea over their Welsh roots. Thomas's father was a schoolteacher at Swansea Grammar School, which Dylan Thomas attended and where he proved to be far from a prize pupil. However, from an early age Dylan Thomas was writing poems whose images, rhythms and rhymes would soon be romanticized as "dark-rooted" and "atavistic" by critics who located his passionate verse in Celtic tradition. Yet if Thomas tapped into Welsh imagery, by the age of 15 he was more consciously modeling himself after the French symbolist poet Arthur Rimbaud, even calling himself "the Rimbaud of Cwmdonkin Drive." What attracted Thomas to poets such as Rimbaud and Keats was not only their iconoclasm, but also the fact that they had died young. Thomas regularly cut classes to pore over his own poetry, and launched into a habit of boisterous drinking that was destined to make his career as tragically brief as those of his idols.

In 1933, when Thomas was only 18 years old, the *New English Weekly* published an astonishing poem, his "And Death Shall Have No Dominion." When Thomas's *18 Poems* was published the following year, the strange and disturbing power of his verse woke up London's literary establishment. The cool, controlled style of T.S. Eliot, which conditioned poetic attitudes well into the 1950s, appeared subdued next to the chaotic heat generated by what one critic calls Thomas's "belligerent syntax." For a time, Thomas was labeled a Surrealist and a Dadaist, labels that framed his poetry as a jumble of random signs and erotic images startled out of a Freudian unconscious. Thomas initially exploited the cultural mileage that these early associations gave him, but when his reputation grew sturdier he was careful to distinguish his work from the Surrealists', and to avow that Freud had never been a direct influence. *18 Poems* won Thomas many admirers, including Edith Sitwell, a tireless champion of the curly-haired, Anglo-Welsh "cherub" who churned out formidable verse. "And Death Shall Have No Dominion" was included in his next volume, *25 Poems* (1936), which was also well received. *The Map of Love* (1939) failed to excite much critical acclaim, but with the postwar publication of *Deaths and Entrances* (1946) Thomas won over both the literati and the general public with the lilting rhythms and fresh imagery of poems such as "Fern Hill."

By this time, Thomas had become notorious as an indefatigable carouser, constantly appealing to friends for money and adored by women who wanted to "save" him from his excesses. In 1937, he met Caitlin Macnamara and entered into a stormy marriage that somehow survived an endless stream of creditors, mad bouts of drinking, and mutual infidelities. Caitlin bore Thomas three children.

During the Second World War, Thomas avoided military service on the grounds of poor health, instead finding employment writing film and radio scripts for Strand Films and the BBC. While Thomas remains best known for his early poetry, some critics contend that he was a better playwright and prose writer than poet. The autobiographical stories compiled in *Portrait of the Artist as a Young Dog* (1940) and the posthumously published *Adventures in the Skin Trade* (1955) feature prose that is by turns humorous, raw, and risqué. In his 1945 BBC broadcast "Quite Early One Morning," Thomas's love of place, his fine ear for dialogue, his comic wit and his unforgettable voice fused in a narrative of everyday life in New Quay which endeared him to radio audiences. Around the same time in America, Thomas's poetry was inspiring an almost devotional following with the publications of *The World I Breathe* (1939), *New Poems* (1943), and *Selected Writings* (1946).

For Thomas, the meaning of a word was by no means fixed. As with "Wales," which he savoured as if it were a "gobstopper of magical properties, ringing the word like a bell, making it rise and fall, whisper and thunder like the Welsh sea," Thomas was fascinated by the earthy taste, cadence, and physical horseplay inspired by language. He held that poetry was quintessentially the spoken word, and was meant to be read out loud. In a booming voice that detonated the energy stored in language, Thomas performed radio broadcasts and poetry readings throughout the 1940s and the early 50s – performances that were hugely popular both in Europe and in North America. In 1950 he traveled to New York, where the poet John Malcolm Brinnin had arranged a taxing, but lucrative, schedule of public readings and talks. (The lucre, as usual, quickly evaporated.) Whether reciting his own poetry or favorite poems by Auden, Hardy, and Sitwell. Thomas retained the ability to enthrall a crowd with his magnetic voice and his wildboy antics. His reputation preceded him across the American midwest, and on to San Francisco and Vancouver.

Some critics hold that in the last years of his life Thomas was running on empty, producing only strained works that tried to simulate the tremendous effect captured in his earliest poetry. Others see his writing mature in later works such as "Poem in October" (1945) and the radio drama *Under Milk Wood* (1954). Only a few years before Thomas's final, fatal trip to the United States, he and his family moved into The Boat House in Laugharne, Wales. His stay at The Boat House was to prove the last time Thomas would immerse himself in the landscape of the Welsh shoreline, where he had so often glimpsed the cycle that seemed to him to turn living and dying into almost indistinguishable forces. The respite was short-lived: on a third trip to New York in 1953, Thomas set out on a punishing drinking spree and died, as he had always imagined he would, before reaching the age of 40.

⌘ ⌘ ⌘

## The Force That Through the Green Fuse Drives the Flower

The force that through the green fuse drives the
　　flower
Drives my green age; that blasts the roots of trees
Is my destroyer.
And I am dumb to tell the crooked rose
5　My youth is bent by the same wintry fever.

The force that drives the water through the rocks
Drives my red blood; that dries the mouthing streams
Turns mine to wax.
And I am dumb to mouth unto my veins
10　How at the mountain spring the same mouth sucks.

The hand that whirls the water in the pool[1]
Stirs the quicksand; that ropes the blowing wind

---

[1] *hand ... pool*  See John 5.4.

Hauls my shroud sail.
And I am dumb to tell the hanging man
15   How of my clay is made the hangman's lime.[1]

The lips of time leech to the fountain head;
Love drips and gathers, but the fallen blood
Shall calm her sores.
And I am dumb to tell a weather's wind
20   How time has ticked a heaven round the stars.

And I am dumb to tell the lover's tomb
How at my sheet goes the same crooked worm.
—1933

## Fern Hill

Now as I was young and easy under the apple boughs
      About the lilting house and happy as the grass was
         green,
      The night above the dingle[2] starry,
         Time let me hail and climb
5        Golden in the heydays of his eyes,
And honoured among wagons I was prince of the
      apple towns
And once below a time I lordly had the trees and leaves
         Trail with daisies and barley
         Down the rivers of the windfall light.

10   And as I was green and carefree, famous among the barns
      About the happy yard and singing as the farm was home,
         In the sun that is young once only,
            Time let me play and be
            Golden in the mercy of his means,
15   And green and golden I was huntsman and herdsman,
         the calves
      Sang to my horn, the foxes on the hills barked clear
         and cold,
            And the sabbath rang slowly
            In the pebbles of the holy streams.

All the sun long it was running, it was lovely, the hay
20   Fields high as the house, the tunes from the chimneys,
            it was air
         And playing, lovely and watery
            And fire green as grass.
      And nightly under the simple stars
As I rode to sleep the owls were bearing the farm away,
25   All the moon long I heard, blessed among stables, the
            nightjars[3]
      Flying with the ricks,° and the horses      haystacks
            Flashing into the dark.

And then to awake, and the farm, like a wanderer white
With the dew, come back, the cock on his shoulder:
            it was all
30       Shining, it was Adam and maiden,
            The sky gathered again
            And the sun grew round that very day.
So it must have been after the birth of the simple light
In the first, spinning place, the spellbound horses
            walking warm
35       Out of the whinnying green stable
            On to the fields of praise.

And honoured among foxes and pheasants by the gay
      house
Under the new made clouds and happy as the heart
      was long,
      In the sun born over and over,
40         I ran my heedless ways,
         My wishes raced through the house high hay
And nothing I cared, at my sky blue trades,[4] that time
      allows
In all his tuneful turning so few and such morning songs
      Before the children green and golden
45         Follow him out of grace,

Nothing I cared, in the lamb white days, that time
      would take me
Up to the swallow thronged loft by the shadow of my
      hand,
      In the moon that is always rising,
         Nor that riding to sleep

----

[1]   *lime*   Mineral used to speed up decomposition.
[2]   *dingle*   Wooded dell.
[3]   *nightjars*   Nocturnal birds.
[4]   *trades*   Occupations.

50 I should hear him fly with the high fields
And wake to the farm forever fled from the childless land.
Oh as I was young and easy in the mercy of his means,
   Time held me green and dying
 Though I sang in my chains like the sea.
—1946

## Do Not Go Gentle Into That Good Night

Do not go gentle into that good night,
Old age should burn and rave at close of day;
Rage, rage against the dying of the light.

Though wise men at their end know dark is right,
5 Because their words had forked no lightning they
Do not go gentle into that good night.

Good men, the last wave by, crying how bright
Their frail deeds might have danced in a green bay,
Rage, rage against the dying of the light.

10 Wild men who caught and sang the sun in flight,
And learn, too late, they grieved it on its way,
Do not go gentle into that good night.

Grave men, near death, who see with blinding sight
Blind eyes could blaze like meteors and be gay,
15 Rage, rage against the dying of the light.

And you, my father, there on the sad height,
Curse, bless, me now with your fierce tears, I pray.
Do not go gentle into that good night.
Rage, rage against the dying of the light.
—1951

## A Refusal To Mourn The Death, By Fire, Of A Child In London

Never until the mankind making
 Bird beast and flower
Fathering and all humbling darkness
Tells with silence the last light breaking
5 And the still hour
Is come of the sea tumbling in harness

And I must enter again the round
Zion[1] of the water bead
And the synagogue of the ear of corn
10 Shall I let pray the shadow of a sound
Or sow my salt seed
In the least valley of sackcloth to mourn

The majesty and burning of the child's death.
I shall not murder
15 The mankind of her going with a grave truth
Nor blaspheme down the stations of the breath
With any further
Elegy of innocence and youth.

Deep with the first dead lies London's daughter,
20 Robed in the long friends,
The grains beyond age, the dark veins of her mother,
Secret by the unmourning water
Of the riding Thames.[2]
After the first death, there is no other.
—1946

---

[1] *Zion*  Hill in Jerusalem, previous center of Jewish worship; by
extension, the house of God.

[2] *Thames*  River in London.

# Judith Wright

## 1915 – 2000

Australian poet Judith Wright has been credited with being one of the first poets to express the realities of the Australian experience in her writing. She was a dominant figure in that nation's literature and criticism for many years and was the first Australian to win the Queen's Gold Medal for Poetry (1992). She was also known as one of the country's most political poets, and later in her life she became a leading environmentalist and campaigner for Aboriginal land rights. Wright believed that poets can play a significant role in the formation or alteration of a nation's consciousness; as a result, much of her poetry seeks to bridge the gap she perceives between Australian society and the land upon which it is founded, with its troubling colonial history.

Wright knew from an early age that she wanted to be a poet. Born near Armidale, New South Wales, she was raised on her family's sheep station and educated at home until the death of her mother in 1927, when she was sent to New England Girls' School. Wright was already composing poetry while at school, and from school she went immediately to the University of Sydney, where she took courses in English, philosophy, history, and psychology—all of which she believed would help her obtain insights into the society she sought to portray.

Wright's first collection of verse, *The Moving Image*, appeared in 1946. The poems in it gave strong expression to Wright's feelings of personal attachment to the land. They center on concrete references to Australian plant and animal life—the sorts of detail that had previously been all but absent from Australian poetry. In Wright's hands, such references are often invested with symbolic importance as the relationship between people and nature is explored. This first collection was quickly followed by a second, *Woman to Man* (1949). Several poems from this collection, including the collection's title poem and "Woman to Child," were seen as breaking new ground and expressing a distinctly female view of the world, of sexuality, and of relationships.

Wright did not limit her writing to poetry; she published a history of her pioneering ancestors, entitled *The Generations of Men*, in 1959, and in 1965 she cemented her reputation as a literary critic with her collection of essays, *Preoccupations in Australian Poetry*. In 1966 she released *The Nature of Love*, a volume of short stories, and after the birth of her daughter, Meredith, she wrote a series of acclaimed children's books. During these year she was also a frequent lecturer at various Australian universities, and in 1975 she collected her addresses and speeches in *Because I Was Invited*.

In 1979 Wright and her husband, the philosopher Jack McKinney, moved to a remote property near the heritage town of Braidwood—a location that became the subject of many of her later poems. This later work continues to explore many of Wright's familiar themes, but it often takes a more didactic and pessimistic tone. Earlier poems such as "At Cooloola" (1955) had expressed a degree of tension between society and the natural world. The voices in her later work are less lyrical and rely more on the rhythms of direct speech, as Wright protests her society's exploitation of resources. Poems such as the famous "Australia 1970" (1970) show her despair at the prospect of ecological disaster.

Wright's later work was often compared unfavorably to what had come before. Increasingly she turned to activism and political protest as a means of directly confronting the problems around her. She became a dedicated campaigner against nuclear power and wanton development, was involved in a successful battle to stop oil drilling on the Great Barrier Reef, and protested against sand mining on Frasier Island. In the 1960s she helped found the Wildlife Preservation Society of Queensland. She also became a vocal supporter of Aboriginal rights. Her book *The Cry for the Dead* (1981) details the treatment of Aboriginal people by settlers in Queensland from the 1840s to the 1920s.

Wright's last publication was *Half a Lifetime*, an autobiography of her life until the 1960s that was published in 2000. She died in June of the same year, and her ashes were scattered around the cemetery on Tamborine Mountain, near a strip of rainforest she had owned. At her request, this land was donated to the state to be preserved as a national park.

⌘ ⌘ ⌘

## Woman to Man

The eyeless labourer in the night,
   the selfless, shapeless seed I hold,
builds for its resurrection day—
silent and swift and deep from sight
5  foresees the unimagined light.

This is no child with a child's face;
this has no name to name it by:
yet you and I have known it well.
This is our hunter and our chase,
10  the third who lay in our embrace.

This is the strength that your arm knows,
the arc of flesh that is my breast,
the precise crystals of our eyes.
This is the blood's wild tree that grows
15  the intricate and folded rose.

This is the maker and the made;
this is the question and reply;
the blind head butting at the dark,
the blaze of light along the blade.
20  Oh hold me, for I am afraid.
    —1949

## The Bull

In the olive darkness of the sally-trees
  silently moved the air from night to day.
The summer-grass was thick with honey-daisies
where he, a curled god, a red Jupiter,[1]
5  heavy with power among his women lay.

But summer's bubble-sound of sweet creek-water
dwindles and is silent; the seeding grasses
grow harsh, and wind and frost in the black sallies
roughen the sleek-haired slopes. Seek him out, then,
10  the angry god betrayed, whose godhead passes,

and down the hillsides drive him from his mob.
What enemy steals his strength— what rival steals
his mastered cows? His thunders powerless,
the red storm of his body shrunk with fear,
15  runs the great bull, the dogs upon his heels.
    —1949

---

[1] *Jupiter*  Roman equivalent of the Greek God Zeus, ruler of the gods, who disguised himself as a bull when he raped Europa.

## Woman to Child

You who were darkness warmed my flesh
where out of darkness rose the seed.
Then all a world I made in me;
all the world you hear and see
5   hung upon my dreaming blood.

There moved the multitudinous stars,
and coloured birds and fishes moved.
There swam the sliding continents.
All time lay rolled in me, and sense,
10   and love that knew not its beloved.

O node and focus of the world;
I hold you deep within that well
you shall escape and not escape—
that mirrors still your sleeping shape;
15   that nurtures still your crescent cell.

I wither and you break from me;
yet though you dance in living light
I am the earth, I am the root,
I am the stem that fed the fruit,
20   the link that joins you to the night.
—1949

## At Cooloola

The blue crane fishing in Cooloola's twilight
has fished there longer than our centuries.
He is the certain heir of lake and evening,
and he will wear their colour till he dies,

5   but I'm a stranger, come of a conquering people.
I cannot share his calm, who watch his lake,
being unloved by all my eyes delight in,
and made uneasy, for an old murder's sake.

Those dark-skinned people who once named Cooloola
10   knew that no land is lost or won by wars,
for earth is spirit: the invader's feet will tangle
in nets there and his blood be thinned by fears.

Riding at noon and ninety years ago,
my grandfather was beckoned by a ghost—
15   a black accoutred warrior armed for fighting,
who sank into bare plain, as now into time past.

White shores of sand, plumed reed and paperbark,[1]
clear heavenly levels frequented by crane and swan—
I know that we are justified only by love,
20   but oppressed by arrogant guilt, have room for none.

And walking on clean sand among the prints
of bird and animal, I am challenged by a driftwood spear
thrust from the water; and, like my grandfather,
must quiet a heart accused by its own fear.
—1955

## Sports Field

Naked all night the field
breathed its dew until
the great gold ball of day
sprang up from the dark hill.

5   Now as the children come
the field and they are met.
Their day is measured and marked,
its lanes and tapes are set;

and the children gilt by the sun
10   shoulder one another;
crouch at the marks to run,
and spring, and run together—

the children pledged and matched,
and built to win or lose,
15   who grow, while no one watches,
the selves in their sidelong eyes.

The watchers love them in vain.
What's real here is the field,
the starter's gun, the lane,
20   the ball dropped or held;

[1] *paperbark*  Term for several kinds of Australian trees that are distinguished by flaky layers of pale, paper-thin bark.

and set towards the future
they run like running water,
for only the pride of winning,
the pain the losers suffer,

25   till the day's great golden ball
that no one ever catches,
drops; and at its fall
runners and watchers

pick up their pride and pain
30   won out of the measured field
and turn away again
while the star-dewed night comes cold.

So pride and pain are fastened
into the heart's future,
35   while naked and perilous
the night and the field glitter.
—1969

## Two Dreamtimes

*(For Kath Walker, now Oodgeroo Noonuccal)*

Kathy my sister with the torn heart,
I don't know how to thank you
for your dreamtime stories of joy and grief
written on paperbark.[1]

5   You were one of the dark children
I wasn't allowed to play with—
riverbank campers, the wrong colour
(I couldn't turn you white.)

So it was late I met you,
10   late I began to know
they hadn't told me the land I loved
was taken out of your hands.

Sitting all night at my kitchen table
with a cry and a song in your voice,
15   your eyes were full of the dying children,
the blank-eyed taken women,

the sullen looks of the men who sold them
for rum to forget the selling;
the hard rational white faces
20   with eyes that forget the past.

With a knifeblade flash in your black eyes
that always long to be blacker,
your Spanish-Koori[2] face
of a fighter and singer,

25   arms over your breast folding
your sorrow in to hold it,
you brought me to you some of the way
and came the rest to meet me;

over the desert of red sand
30   came from your lost country
to where I stand with all my fathers,
their guilt and righteousness.

Over the rum your voice sang
the tales of an old people,
35   their dreaming buried, the place forgotten …
We too have lost our dreaming.

We the robbers, robbed in turn,
selling this land on hire-purchase;[3]
what's stolen once is stolen again
40   even before we know it.

If we are sisters, it's in this—
our grief for a lost country,
the place we dreamed in long ago,
poisoned now and crumbling.

45   Let us go back to that far time,
I riding the cleared hills,
plucking blue leaves for their eucalypt scent,
hearing the call of the plover,

---

[1] *paperbark* Term for several kinds of Australian trees that are distinguished by flaky layers of pale, paper-thin bark.

[2] *Koori* Name that Aboriginal people of Tasmania, Victoria, and New South Wales use to identify themselves; the term is also used widely to denote an indigenous person.

[3] *hire-purchase* System of payment by which an item that is rented or hired becomes the property of the hirer.

in a land I thought was mine for life.
50  I mourn it as you mourn
the ripped length of the island beaches,
the drained paperbark swamps.

The easy Eden-dreamtime then
in a country of birds and trees
55  made me your shadow-sister, child,
dark girl I couldn't play with.

But we are grown to a changed world;
over the drinks at night
we can exchange our separate griefs,
60  but yours and mine are different.

A knife's between us. My righteous kin
still have cruel faces.
Neither you nor I can win them,
though we meet in secret kindness.

65  I am born of the conquerors,
you of the persecuted.
Raped by rum and an alien law,
progress and economics,

are you and I and a once-loved land
70  peopled by tribes and trees;
doomed by traders and stock-exchanges,
bought by faceless strangers.

And you and I are bought and sold,
our songs and stories too,
75  though quoted low in a falling market
(publishers shake their heads at poets).

Time that we shared for a little while,
telling sad tales of women
(black or white at a different price)
80  meant much and little to us.

My shadow-sister, I sing to you
from my place with my righteous kin,
to where you stand with the Koori dead,
"Trust none—not even poets."

85  The knife's between us. I turn it round,
the handle to your side,

the weapon made from your country's bones.
I have no right to take it.

But both of us die as our dreamtime dies.
90  I don't know what to give you
for your gay stories, your sad eyes,
but that, and a poem, sister.
—1973

## from *A Human Pattern: Selected Poems*

### "FOREWORD"

For many years, a notion has been around that poetry is dying, if not dead. It hasn't died, and unless a dislike generated in school and university days prevails, it won't die.

But it is certainly in danger, just as the earth itself is in danger, from the philosophies generated by greed. Materialism, positivism, and behaviourism are foes of both poetry and the survival of the earth. They have ruled during my lifetime; but I think they are on the way out.

Poems, like all literature, are written from within a social, historical, and personal context and bearing. The poems in this selection emerged from my own life, from the early days of World War II when fear, loss, displacement, and destruction filled lives in Australia as elsewhere, to today when we are in even greater peril of losing the very world we live in, through the results of ignorance, greed, and immensely increased power. These poems were written in these times and, along with my own search for wholeness, their themes are dominated by the way I saw those influences.

And the plight of the peoples who had lived here before us for so many thousands of years, and whose care for this country left us the fertility and beauty our times are now laying waste, runs as an undercurrent through the book.

I think poetry should be treated, not as a lofty art separated from life, but as a way of seeing and expressing not just the personal view, but the whole context of the writer's times. For me, it has been a way of searching for understanding of my own life and of what was happening to me and around me.
—1989

# P.K. PAGE
*b. 1916*

Patricia Kathleen Page has long been recognized as one of Canada's leading poets. She has been awarded several honorary degrees, is a Companion of the Order of Canada (1999), and in 2002 received the Queen's Golden Jubilee Medal. Since her début on the literary scene in the 1930s she has produced a body of work that comprises over twenty books—including several collections of poetry, an autobiography, short fiction, a novel, and three children's stories. Her second collection of poetry, *The Metal and the Flower* (1954), won the Governor General's Award for Poetry in 1954, and *Planet Earth* (2002) was shortlisted for the 2003 Griffin Poetry Prize. Page is also a respected artist whose paintings and drawings have been displayed in art galleries internationally.

Page was born in Swanage, England, on 23 November 1916. The daughter of a Canadian army officer, she moved frequently. Her family left England for Canada in 1919 and lived in several cities before settling temporarily in Montreal in 1941. There she met poets Patrick Anderson, Neufville Shaw, F.R. Scott, and A.M. Klein, with whom she helped to produce the influential literary magazine *Preview* (1942–45).

Page published widely in *Preview* and elsewhere before her first collection, *As Ten As Twenty* appeared in 1946. Many of these early poems, such as "The Stenographers," show the influence of the left-leaning *Preview* group in their depiction of the dehumanizing effects of social institutions. However, the density of images and symbols in Page's writing moves even her most polemical poems beyond social realism. Other poems in this first collection (for example, "The Landlady") anticipate her later work in their focus on the inner lives of individuals and on the theme of visual perception.

In 1950, while working as a scriptwriter for the National Film Board in Ottawa, Page met and married William Arthur Irwin, then commissioner of the Board. Page's itinerant lifestyle continued when Irwin entered the diplomatic service: a three-year assignment in Australia was followed by postings to Brazil and Mexico. In Brazil, Page found herself rendered mute by the language barrier and was unable to write poetry. She turned instead to drawing and painting, displaying her work under the name P.K. Irwin. Some of her art appears in her memoir of these years, *Brazilian Journal* (1987).

Since returning to Canada permanently in 1964, Page has continued to work as both a writer and an artist, producing a body of work that is startling in its diversity and fecundity. Page has been nourished by such diverse literary sources as the British poets John Donne and W.B. Yeats; continental writers Rainer Maria Rilke and Federico García Lorca; and the Persian poets of the twelfth and fifteenth centuries who wrote within the traditions of the Sufi philosophy. Page frequently pays tribute to these sources: her seventh poetry collection, *Hologram* (1994), for example, is composed of a series of glosas; in this form, made popular by Spanish Renaissance poets, each poem is inspired by and composed around a quatrain written by another poet.

Whatever their influence, Page's poems often share a common goal. A visionary poet, she sees poets as dreamers who strive to access a larger, mystical realm that lies beyond ordinary life: "At times I seem to be attempting to copy exactly something which exists in a dimension where worldly senses are inadequate." In poems such as "After Rain" (1967), everyday objects and occurrences—when viewed from unusual perspectives—provide insight into this other dimension. This is also true of her later poems, although in general Page's writing has become sparser, less "clotted with images" (a phrase she has used to describe her early poems), and more personal.

Page has been settled in Victoria, British Columbia, since her husband's retirement in 1964. While she no longer travels to the extent she once did, her poems continue to have a global reach. In Toronto in 2000 an orchestra, two choirs, and three soloists performed Derek Holman's millennial oratorio *The Invisible Reality*, which was based on eight of Page's poems. In 2001 her poem "Planet Earth" (a glosa for Pablo Neruda) was broadcast by satellite and read at over 200 locations worldwide—including sites considered "international ground," such as the top of Mount Everest and Casey, Antarctica—when the United Nations selected it for their celebratory program "Year of Dialogue Among Civilizations Through Poetry."

⌘⌘⌘

## The Stenographers

After the brief bivouac of Sunday,
    their eyes, in the forced march of Monday to
        Saturday,
hoist the white flag, flutter in the snow-storm of paper,
haul it down and crack in the mid-sun of temper.

5  In the pause between the first draft and the carbon
they glimpse the smooth hours when they were
        children—
the ride in the ice-cart, the ice-man's name,
the end of the route and the long walk home;

remember the sea where floats at high tide
10  were sea marrows growing on the scatter-green vine
or spools of grey toffee, or wasps' nests on water;
remember the sand and the leaves of the country.

Bell rings and they go and the voice draws their pencil
like a sled across snow; when its runners are frozen
15  rope snaps and the voice then is pulling no burden
but runs like a dog on the winter of paper.

Their climates are winter and summer—no wind
for the kites of their hearts—no wind for a flight;
a breeze at the most, to tumble them over
20  and leave them like rubbish—the boy-friends of blood.

In the inch of the noon as they move they are stagnant.
The terrible calm of the noon is their anguish;
the lip of the counter, the shapes of the straws
like icicles breaking their tongues, are invaders.

25  Their beds are their oceans—salt water of weeping
the waves that they know—the tide before sleep;
and fighting to drown they assemble their sheep
in columns and watch them leap desks for their fences
and stare at them with their own mirror-worn faces.

30  In the felt of the morning the calico-minded,
sufficiently starched, insert papers, hit keys,
efficient and sure as their adding machines;
yet they weep in the vault, they are taut as net curtains
stretched upon frames. In their eyes I have seen
35  the pin men of madness in marathon trim
race round the track of the stadium pupil.
—1946

## The Landlady

Through sepia air the boarders come and go,
    impersonal as trains. Pass silently
the craving silence swallowing her speech;
click doors like shutters on her camera eye.

5   Because of her their lives become exact:
their entrances and exits are designed;
phone calls are cryptic. Oh, her ticklish ears
advance and fall back stunned.

Nothing is unprepared. They hold the walls
10  about them as they weep or laugh. Each face
is dialled to zero publicly. She peers
stippled with curious flesh;

pads on the patient landing like a pulse,
unlocks their keyholes with the wire of sight,
15  searches their rooms for clues when they are out,
pricks when they come home late.

Wonders when they are quiet, jumps when they move,
dreams that they dope or drink, trembles to know
the traffic of their brains, jaywalks their street
20  in clumsy shoes.

Yet knows them better than their closest friends:
their cupboards and the secrets of their drawers,
their books, their private mail, their photographs
are theirs and hers.

25  Knows when they wash, how frequently their clothes
go to the cleaners, what they like to eat,
their curvature of health, but even so
is not content.

And like a lover must know all, all, all.
30  Prays she may catch them unprepared at last
and palm the dreadful riddle of their skulls—
hoping the worst.
—1946

## Ecce Homo[1]

London had time to idle in galleries then.
We went together to the gallery in Leicester Square,

Epstein was showing there.
On the way you said
5  "Polygamy should be legalized … monogamy is dead."
A wind of birds interrupted your words.
"Talking of birds," you said,
"we tarred and feathered his Rima.[2]
No … not I… but my race.
10  We are a queer people,
inarticulate and yet…
Ah! here is the place."

We entered the gallery
but what I remember most
15  was my unexpected entry
into the door of my mind
with Rima as my host,
saying, as you had said,
"Monogamy is dead."

20  People had never spoken like that before.
It had always been,
"Lovely weather we're having."
Or, at the most,
"I wish I hadn't read
25  that awful book by Cronin, it's obscene.
*Hatter's Castle* it's called …
I shouldn't read it."
Never dreaming a swift awakening was what I needed.

We entered the little room where *Ecce Homo* stood,
30  but it was bare to me.
I was away with Rima, discussing polygamy.
And then I felt your hand
tighten upon my arm
and heard you say in alarm,
35  "To understand,
Christ must be forgotten.
this is the mighty God. The God begotten
straight from the minds of the prophets,
straight from their fearful minds.
40  This is the God of plagues,

---

1  *Ecce Homo* Latin: behold the man. Title of a sculpture by Jacob Epstein (1880–1959) which Page had seen on display in the Leicester Gallery in London.

2  *Rima* Title of a sculpture by Jacob Epstein that depicts W.H. Hudson's famous character Rima, the bird-girl from his novel *Green Mansions* (1904). The sculpture, a memorial to Hudson, has been defaced with paint since being erected in London's Hyde Park.

not the Christ who died
for love of humanity—the beautiful gentle Boy,
humorous, sunny-eyed.
Before you look," you said,
45  "remember, remember it is not Christ," you said.

*Ecce Homo* (1925), by Jacob Epstein.

I looked and the little room was filled with might,
with the might of fear in stone,
immense and shackled.
The flesh that covered the bone
50  seemed bone itself,
terrible, holy… you could not take a breath—
the Man, deformed, thick-hipped,
the God of Death,
in a little room in a gallery in Leicester Square,
55  silently standing there.

"There is much we do not know,"
you turned to me.
(Behold the Man, Rima, polygamy!)
"I think we should find somewhere nice and quiet for tea.
60  To think," you said.

I nodded my head. "To think," I said.
And like a young tree I put out a timid shoot
and prayed for the day, the wonderful day when it bore
its fruit.
65  And suddenly we were out in the air again.

London had time to idle in galleries then.
—1946

## Stories of Snow

Those in the vegetable rain retain
an area behind their sprouting eyes
held soft and rounded with the dream of snow
precious and reminiscent as those globes—
5   souvenir of some never nether land—
which hold their snowstorms circular, complete,
high in a tall and teakwood cabinet.

In countries where the leaves are large as hands
where flowers protrude their fleshy chins
10  and call their colours
an imaginary snowstorm sometimes falls
among the lilies.
And in the early morning one will waken
to think the glowing linen of his pillow
15  a northern drift, will find himself mistaken
and lie back weeping.
And there the story shifts from head to head,
of how, in Holland, from their feather beds
hunters arise and part the flakes and go
20  forth to the frozen lakes in search of swans—
the snow light falling white along their guns,
their breath in plumes.
While tethered in the wind like sleeping gulls
ice boats await the raising of their wings
25  to skim the electric ice at such a speed
they leap jet strips of naked water,
and how these flying, sailing hunters feel
air in their mouths as terrible as ether.
And on the story runs that even drinks
30  in that white landscape dare to be no colour;
how, flasked and water clear, the liquor slips
silver against the hunters' moving hips.

And of the swan in death these dreamers tell
of its last flight and how it falls, a plummet,
35  pierced by the freezing bullet
and how three feathers, loosened by the shot,
descend like snow upon it.
While hunters plunge their fingers in its down
deep as a drift, and dive their hands
40  up to the neck of the wrist
in that warm metamorphosis of snow
as gentle as the sort that woodsmen know
who, lost in the white circle, fall at last
and dream their way to death.

45  And stories of this kind are often told
in countries where great flowers bar the roads
with reds and blues which seal the route to snow
as if, in telling, raconteurs unlock
the colour with its complement and go
50  through to the area behind the eyes
where silent, unrefractive whiteness lies.
—1946

## Young Girls

Nothing, not even fear of punishment
can stop the giggle in a girl.
Oh mothers' trim
shapes on the chesterfield cannot dispel
5  their lolloping fatness.
Adolescence tumbles about in them
on cinder schoolyard or behind the expensive gates.

See them in class like porpoises
with smiles and tears
10  loosed from the same subterranean faucet; some
find individual adventure in
the obtuse angle, some in a phrase
that leaps like a smaller fish from a sea of words.
But most, deep in their daze, dawdle and roll,
15  their little breasts like wounds beneath their clothes.

A shoal of them in a room makes it a pool.
How can one teacher keep the water out,
or, being adult, find the springs and taps

of their tempers and tortures?
20  Who on a field filled with their female cries
can reel them in on a line of words
or land them neatly in a net?
On the dry ground they goggle, flounder, flap.

Too much weeping in them and unfamiliar blood
25  has set them perilously afloat.
Not divers these—but as if the waters rose in flood—
making them partially amphibious
and always drowning a little and hearing bells;
until the day the shore line wavers less,
30  and caught and swung on the bright hooks of their sex,
earth becomes home, their natural element.
—1954

## After Rain

The snails have made a garden of green lace:
broderie anglaise[1] from the cabbages,
chantilly[2] from the choux-fleurs,[3] tiny veils—
I see already that I lift the blind
5  upon a woman's wardrobe of the mind.

Such female whimsy floats about me like
a kind of tulle, a flimsy mesh,
while feet in gum boots pace the rectangles—
garden abstracted, geometry awash—
10  an unknown theorem argued in green ink,
dropped in the bath.
Euclid[4] in glorious chlorophyll, half drunk.

I none too sober slipping in the mud
where rigged with guys of rain
15  the clothes-reel gauche
as the rangey skeleton of some

---

[1]  *broderie anglaise*  Open embroidery on linen or cambric, generally consisting of outlines of various sized holes arranged to make floral or geometrical patterns.

[2]  *chantilly*  Delicate French lace, named after the town in Northern France where it is made.

[3]  *choux-fleurs*  French: cauliflowers.

[4]  *Euclid*  Greek mathematician who developed the principles of geometry in the third century BCE.

gaunt delicate spidery mute
is pitched as if
listening;
20  while hung from one thin rib
a silver web—
its infant, skeletal, diminutive,
now sagged with sequins, pulled ellipsoid,
glistening.

25  I suffer shame in all these images.
The garden is primeval, Giovanni
in soggy denim squelches by my hub
over his ruin,
shakes a doleful head.
30  But he so beautiful and diademmed,[1]
his long Italian hands so wrung with rain
I find his ache exists beyond my rim
and almost weep to see a broken man
made subject to my whim.

35  O choir him, birds, and let him come to rest
within this beauty as one rests in love,
till pears upon the bough
encrusted with
small snails as pale as pearls
40  hang golden in
a heart that knows tears are a part of love.

And choir me too to keep my heart a size
larger than seeing, unseduced by each
bright glimpse of beauty striking like a bell,
45  so that the whole may toll,
its meaning shine
clear of the myriad images that still—
do what I will—encumber its pure line.
—1967

## Nursing Home

Old women will not enter paradise.
They will be made young and beautiful first.
                 MOHAMMED

---

[1] *diademmed* Crowned with a diadem or ornamental band worn
around the head as a symbol of honor or glory.

Where have they gone
5  the inhabitants of these bodies?
    (I think of hermit crabs'
    dry jerking passage over shifting beaches)

Tennis champions
barely able to move
10  ancient scholars
mindless as newts
pulling themselves along
with sticks and handrails
moving decrepit
15  directionless
in wheelchairs
stopping without reason
reasoning with
demonic
20  private logic

Old men, old women
Which are which?
Trembling, teetering, dribbling, calling

Some still peer out through their eyes
25  The sharpened points of their gaze
engage me, probe

One sings unending "Jingle Bells"
Their failing strengths
surge in monstrous energies:
30  "NURSE HELP"
barked like a dog
"My father will see you are
amply rewarded"
"TAKE ME OUT"

35  Who yelled?
What mouth
allowed that metal out?

They sit like parsnips
boiled potatoes
40  propped, inert
Do they feel vegetable?
Mineral?

Cold stone?
Dense slumbering stone?
45 Pellets of lead?

Sedatives mineralize
Even the nurses
are white and obdurate
as onyx
50      (I know this place
        this grey and mineral kingdom
        its mineral animals
        its static hours
        I have been trapped
55      in a dying mineral
        my half life had more digits
        than I could count
        myself mineral
        muted, caught
60      in mineral immensities
        the vegetation as enduring
        as plastic flowers)
There are no words for it
there are no words

65 "I am Josephine Maria Plumtree
killed a dog
That's my identity
You take a saw—a little saw
and cut away the jaw
70 Josephine Maria Plumtree
killed a dog"

"NURSE HELP
I want a knife to cut these strings"

Where are they going
75 these voyagers?

Who steers?
—1974

from *"Address At Simon Fraser"*[1]

*Written in Victoria, B.C., during the heavy snow-fall of February 1990, which brought to mind the even colder winter of 1989.*

… How can a city dweller visualize
a world unpavemented, unstreetlamped? or
imagine how the constellations shine
as night ingathers earth and sets alight
5  the topaz pole star pulsing in the north—
front runner of vast galaxies that stretch
clustered in patterns like huge honeycombs.
The jury's out on this, and who am I,
neither astronomer nor scientist,
10 to venture an informed opinion? Yet
the mere idea of honeycombing space
so matches with some image in my head
that when I read the story in the press
I shouted "snap," and saw, as in a flash,
15 the whole hexagonal geometry.

And how can youngsters who have never seen
a seed by slow degrees become a shoot,
conceptualize, except in their own loins,
"the force that through the green fuse drives the flower"?[2]
20 A city boy I know won't eat a pear
picked from a green, unsanitary tree,
balks at the thought of it, prefers the bland
and un-sunripened, supermarket fruit
refrigerated, plastic-wrapped, germ-free.
25 Is he the symbol of an age that's lost
its evolutionary memory?

But to get back to art, for there my heart
is, there—beyond materiality,
beyond the buy-and-sell, beyond the want
30 embedded in us, and beyond desire—
resides the magic greed has cancelled out.
If we'll but give it time, a work of art

---

[1] *Simon Fraser*   Simon Fraser University, British Columbia, Canada.
[2] *the force … flower*   Title and first line of a 1934 poem by Dylan Thomas.

"can rap and knock and enter in our souls"[1]
and re-align us—all our molecules—
35    to make us whole again. A work of art,
could, "had we but world enough and time,"[2]
portray for us—all Paradise apart—
"the face (we) had / before the world was made,"[3]
or, to compound the image, vivify
40    Plato's invisible reality.[4]

But is there time enough? This turning world
we call our home, or *notre pays*[5]—could
become inimical to humankind—
humanunkind as cummings[6] might have said—
45    in fewer years than I have walked this earth.

So, what is there to tell you? Only this.
"Imagination is the star in man."[7]
Read woman, if you wish. And though we are
trapped in the body of an animal,
50    we're half angelic, and our angel ear,
which hears the music of the spheres, can hear
the planet's message, dark, admonishing,
as the archaic torso of Apollo
admonished Rilke, "you must change your life."[8]

---

[1] *can rap ... souls* Cf. Robert Browning, "Bishop Blougram's Apology" (1855).

[2] *had we ... time* From Andrew Marvell's "To His Coy Mistress" (1681): "Had we but world enough, and time, / This coyness, Lady, were no crime" (lines 1–2).

[3] *the face ... made* Cf. W.B. Yeats, "Before the World Was Made" (1933), lines 7–8: "I'm looking for the face I had / Before the world was made."

[4] *Plato's invisible reality* Reference to Greek philosopher Plato (428?–348? BCE) and his concept of the "realm of Forms," in which Forms are abstract entities that form the basis of true reality (as opposed to the realm of experience).

[5] *notre pays* French: our country.

[6] *cummings* American poet e.e. cummings (1894–1962).

[7] *Imagination ... man* Quotation attributed to Austrian physician and toxicologist Theophrastus Paracelsus (1493–1541).

[8] *as the archaic ... life* Reference to German poet Rainer Maria Rilke's poem "Archaic Torso of Apollo" (1908) that detailed his reaction to an ancient statue of Apollo (discovered at Miletus), the Greek god of poetry, music, and the sun. See lines 13–14: "for there is no place on this stone, / that does not see you. You must change your life."

Art and the planet tell us. Change your life.
55    —1991

## Planet Earth

*It has to be spread out, the skin of this planet,*
*has to be ironed, the sea in its whiteness;*
*and the hands keep on moving,*
smoothing the holy surfaces.
        "In Praise of Ironing," PABLO NERUDA[9]

It has to be loved the way a laundress loves her linens,
    the way she moves her hands caressing the fine
        muslins
knowing their warp and woof,
like a lover coaxing, or a mother praising.
5    It has to be loved as if it were embroidered
with flowers and birds and two joined hearts upon it.
It has to be stretched and stroked.
It has to be celebrated.
O this great beloved world and all the creatures in it.
10    *It has to be spread out, the skin of this planet.*

The trees must be washed, and the grasses and mosses.
They have to be polished as if made of green brass.
The rivers and little streams with their hidden cresses
and pale-coloured pebbles
15    and their fool's gold
must be washed and starched or shined into brightness,
the sheets of lake water
smoothed with the hand
and the foam of the oceans pressed into neatness.
20    *It has to be ironed, the sea in its whiteness.*

and pleated and goffered,[10] the flower-blue sea
the protean, wine-dark, grey, green, sea
with its metres of satin and bolts of brocade.
And sky—such an O! overhead—night and day
25    must be burnished and rubbed
by hands that are loving
so the blue blazons forth

---

[9] *Pablo Neruda* Chilean poet and Nobel prizewinner (1904–73).

[10] *geoffered* Decorated with repeated patterns of indentation (usually referring to pages of a book).

and the stars keep on shining
within and above
30    *and the hands keep on moving.*

It has to be made bright, the skin of this planet
till it shines in the sun like gold leaf.
Archangels then will attend to its metals
and polish the rods of its rain.
35    Seraphim will stop singing hosannas
to shower it with blessings and blisses and praises
and, newly in love,
we must draw it and paint it
our pencils and brushes and loving caresses
40    *smoothing the holy surfaces.*
        —1994

### Calgary[1]

Calgary. The twenties. Cold, and the sweet
melt of chinooks.[2] A musical weather.
World rippling and running. World
watery with flutes. And woodwinds.
5    The wonder of water in that icy world.
The magic of melt. And the grief of it. Tears—
heart's hurt? heart's help?

This was the wilderness: western Canada.
Tomahawk country—teepees, coyotes,
10    cayuses and lariats.[3] The land that Ontario[4]
looked down its nose at. Nevertheless
we thought it civilized. Civilized? Semi.

Remittance men,[5] ranchers—friends of my family—
public school failures, penniless outcasts,
15    bigoted bachelors with British accents.
But in my classroom, Canadian voices—
hard r's and flat a's, a prairie language
—were teaching me tolerance, telling me something.
This vocal chasm divided my childhood.
20    Talking across it, a tightrope talker
corrected at home, corrected in classrooms:
*wawteh, wadder*—the wryness of words!

Such my preparation for a life of paradox—
a borderland being, barely belonging,
25    one on the outskirts, over the perimeter.
        —2005

---

1    *Calgary*    City in the Canadian prairie province of Alberta.
2    *chinooks*    Warm, dry winds.
3    *cayuses*    Ponies; *lariats*    Ropes used to lasso cattle.
4    *Ontario*    Province in central Canada.
5    *Remittance men*    Emigrants assisted by money sent from home.

# PENELOPE FITZGERALD
## *1916 – 2000*

In 1996 British writer Penelope Fitzgerald was awarded the Heywood Hill Prize for a lifetime achievement in literature—a remarkable accomplishment, considering that she did not begin writing until the age of 60. Biographer, novelist, short-story writer, and (with her posthumous collection *Afterlife*) essayist, Fitzgerald was almost an instant success as an author—*The New York Times Book Review* called her work "the best argument ... for a publishing career begun late in life." Fitzgerald is reminiscent of Jane Austen in her use of social comedy, irony, and a precise, matter-of-

fact style, yet her philosophical examinations of human behavior and relationships also often elevate her fiction to the realm of the metaphysical.

Fitzgerald was born in December 1916 in the town of Lincoln in the English Midlands. She grew up in a scholarly and spiritual family—her father was an editor of *Punch* magazine; two of her uncles were Anglican priests, and one of them wrote detective fiction; her grandfathers on both sides were bishops. Fitzgerald attended Somerville College, Oxford, where she studied under J.R.R. Tolkien. After graduating she held miscellaneous positions, many of which later provided material for her novels. During the war she was employed as a sound assistant at the BBC (the setting for her second novel, *Human Voices* [1980]). In the 1960s she taught child actors at a theater school (the basis of her 1982 novel *At Freddie's*). She worked in a bookshop (as does the protagonist in *The Bookshop* [1978]) and, like the characters in *Offshore* (1979), lived temporarily on a houseboat at Battersea, near London.

Fitzgerald started her writing career as a biographer, publishing her life of Pre-Raphaelite painter Edward Burne-Jones in 1975, and following it two years later with *The Knox Brothers*, a history of her father and his four brothers. These are both highly regarded, as is her life of poet Charlotte Mew, published in 1984. It was the final illness of her husband, who died of cancer in 1976, that prompted Fitzgerald to turn to fiction. She read her first novel, *The Golden Child* (1977), aloud to him as a means of entertainment. Set in an unnamed London museum, the novel is a murder mystery inspired by her visit to the British Museum's Tutankhamun exhibit.

With her Booker Prize-winning *Offshore*, Fitzgerald "had finished writing about the things in my own life, which I wanted to write about," and decided to "launch out." Accordingly her following four novels are set as far away as Moscow, Italy, and Germany and reach as far back as the sixteenth century. An admirer of Walter Scott's ability to mix historical and fictional characters, Fitzgerald made use of this tactic in her later novels. Italian political theorist Antonio Gramsci makes an appearance in *Innocence* (1986), as do eighteenth-century German writers Fichte, Goethe, and Schlegel in *The Blue Flower* (1995).

Fitzgerald's fiction is distinctive in its brevity (her novels are usually less than 200 pages) and in the powers of selectivity and compression she demonstrates. With precise observations she sums up her characters in a few words. In these tightly woven, elliptical novels, setting, time span, and plot are restricted, much of the key action takes place behind the scenes, and conflicts are rarely resolved. Fitzgerald creates compelling dramas out of the seemingly accidental or commonplace—in a passing incident characters fall in or out of love, throw their lives away, or change for the better. The realm of her fiction is largely cerebral: she is a critic of manners and morals whose aim was to study the motives driving her characters.

Though she observes her characters with an unwavering critical gaze, Fitzgerald treats them all, no matter what their faults, with compassion. Fitzgerald said her writing, rather than being fueled by aesthetic or political concerns, was informed by her spiritual beliefs. She believed that in imagining the joys and sufferings of others she had remained true to her "deepest convictions, I mean to the courage of those who are born to be defeated, the weaknesses of the strong, and the tragedy of misunderstandings and missed opportunities which I have done my best to treat as comedy, for otherwise how can we manage to bear it?"

Fitzgerald died in the year 2000, aged 84.

⌘ ⌘ ⌘

## The Axe

You will recall that when the planned redundancies became necessary as the result of the discouraging trading figures shown by this small firm—in contrast, so I gather from the Company reports, with several of your other enterprises—you personally deputed to me the task of "speaking" to those who were to be asked to leave. It was suggested to me that if they were asked to resign in order to avoid the unpleasantness of being given their cards, it might be unnecessary for the firm to offer any compensation. Having glanced personally through my staff sheets, you underlined the names of four people, the first being that of my clerical assistant, W. S. Singlebury. Your actual words to me were that he seemed fairly old and could probably be frightened into taking a powder.[1] You were speaking to me in your "democratic" style.

From this point on I feel able to write more freely, it being well understood, at office-managerial level, that you do not read more than the first two sentences of any given report. You believe that anything which cannot be put into two sentences is not worth attending to, a piece of wisdom which you usually attribute to the late Lord Beaverbrook.[2]

As I question whether you have ever seen Singlebury, with whom this report is mainly concerned, it may be helpful to describe him. He worked for the Company for many more years than myself, and his attendance record was excellent. On Mondays, Wednesdays and Fridays, he wore a blue suit and a green knitted garment with a front zip. On Tuesdays and Thursdays he wore a pair of grey trousers of man-made material which he called "my flannels," and a fawn cardigan. The cardigan was omitted in summer. He had, however, one distinguishing feature, very light blue eyes, with a defensive expression, as though apologizing for something which he felt guilty about, but could not put right. The fact is that he was getting old. Getting old is, of course, a crime of which we grow more guilty every day.

Singlebury had no wife or dependants, and was by no means a communicative man. His room is, or was, a kind of cubby-hole adjoining mine—you have to go through it to get into my room—and it was always kept very neat. About his "things" he did show some mild emotion. They had to be ranged in a certain pattern in respect to his in and out trays, and Singlebury stayed behind for two or three minutes every evening to do this. He also managed to retain every year the complimentary desk calendar sent to us by Dino's, the Italian cafe on the corner. Singlebury was in fact the only one of my personnel who was always quite certain of the date. To this too his attitude was apologetic. His phrase was, "I'm afraid it's Tuesday."

---

[1] *taking a powder* Leaving.

[2] *Lord Beaverbrook* William Maxwell Aitken (1879–1964), Canadian businessman and newspaper magnate, made 1st Baron Beaverbrook in 1917.

His work, as was freely admitted, was his life, but the nature of his duties—though they included the post-book and the addressograph—was rather hard to define, having grown round him with the years. I can only say that after he left, I was surprised myself to discover how much he had had to do.

Oddly connected in my mind with the matter of the redundancies is the irritation of the damp in the office this summer and the peculiar smell (not the ordinary smell of damp), emphasized by the sudden appearance of representatives of a firm of damp eliminators who had not been sent for by me, nor is there any record of my having done so. These people simply vanished at the end of the day and have not returned. Another firm, to whom I applied as a result of frequent complaints by the female staff, have answered my letters but have so far failed to call.

Singlebury remained unaffected by the smell. Joining, very much against his usual habit, in one of the too frequent discussions of the subject, he said that he knew what it was; it was the smell of disappointment. For an awkward moment I thought he must have found out by some means that he was going to be asked to go, but he went on to explain that in 1942 the whole building had been requisitioned by the Admiralty and that relatives had been allowed to wait or queue there in the hope of getting news of those missing at sea. The repeated disappointment of these women, Singlebury said, must have permeated the building like a corrosive gas. All this was very unlike him. I made it a point not to encourage anything morbid. Singlebury was quite insistent, and added, as though by way of proof, that the lino in the corridors was Admiralty issue and had not been renewed since 1942 either. I was astonished to realize that he had been working in the building for so many years before the present tenancy. I realized that he must be considerably older than he had given us to understand. This, of course, will mean that there are wrong entries on his cards.

The actual notification to the redundant staff passed off rather better, in a way, than I had anticipated. By that time everyone in the office seemed inexplicably conversant with the details, and several of them in fact had gone far beyond their terms of reference, young Patel, for instance, who openly admits that he will be leaving us as soon as he can get a better job, taking me aside and telling me that to such a man as Singlebury dismissal would be like death. Dismissal is not the right word, I said. But death is, Patel replied. Singlebury himself, however, took it very quietly. Even when I raised the question of the Company's Early Retirement pension scheme, which I could not pretend was over-generous, he said very little. He was generally felt to be in a state of shock. The two girls whom you asked me to speak to were quite unaffected, having already found themselves employments as hostesses at the Dolphinarium near here. Mrs. Horrocks, of Filing, on the other hand, *did* protest, and was so offensive on the question of severance pay that I was obliged to agree to refer it to a higher level. I consider this as one of the hardest day's work that I have ever done for the Company.

Just before his month's notice (if we are to call it that) was up, Singlebury, to my great surprise, asked me to come home with him one evening for a meal. In all the past years the idea of his having a home, still less asking anyone back to it, had never arisen, and I did not at all want to go there now. I felt sure, too, that he would want to reopen the matter of compensation, and only a quite unjustified feeling of guilt made me accept. We took an Underground together after work, travelling in the late rush-hour to Clapham North, and walked some distance in the rain. His place, when we eventually got to it, seemed particularly inconvenient, the entrance being through a small cleaner's shop. It consisted of one room and a shared toilet on the half-landing. The room itself was tidy, arranged, so it struck me, much on the lines of his cubby-hole, but the window was shut and it was oppressively stuffy. This is where I bury myself, said Singlebury.

There were no cooking arrangements and he left me there while he went down to fetch us something ready to eat from the Steakorama next to the cleaner's. In his absence I took the opportunity to examine his room, though of course not in an inquisitive or prying manner. I was struck by the fact that none of his small store of stationery had been brought home from the office. He returned with two steaks wrapped in aluminium foil, evidently a special treat in my honour, and afterwards he went out on to the landing and made cocoa, a drink which I had not tasted for more than thirty years. The evening dragged rather. In the course of conversation it turned out that Singlebury was fond of reading. There were in fact several issues of a colour-printed encyclopaedia which he had been collecting as it came out, but unfortunately it had ceased publication after the seventh part. Reading is my hobby, he said. I pointed out that a hobby was rather something that one did with one's hands or in the open air—a relief from the work of the brain. Oh, I don't accept that distinction, Singlebury said. The mind and the body are the same. Well, one cannot deny the connection, I replied. Fear, for example, releases adrenalin, which directly affects the nerves. I don't mean connection, I mean identity, Singlebury said, the mind is the blood. Nonsense, I said, you might just as well tell me that the blood is the mind. It stands to reason that the blood can't think.

I was right, after all, in thinking that he would refer to the matter of the redundancy. This was not till he was seeing me off at the bus-stop, when for a moment he turned his grey, exposed-looking face away from me and said that he did not see how he could manage if he really had to go. He stood there like someone who has "tried to give satisfaction"—he even used this phrase, saying that if the expression were not redolent of a bygone age, he would like to feel he had given satisfaction. Fortunately we had not long to wait for the 45 bus.

At the expiry of the month the staff gave a small tea-party for those who were leaving. I cannot describe this occasion as a success.

The following Monday I missed Singlebury as a familiar presence and also, as mentioned above, because I had never quite realized how much work he had been taking upon himself. As a direct consequence of losing him I found myself having to stay late—not altogether unwillingly, since although following general instructions I have discouraged overtime, the extra pay in my own case would be instrumental in making ends meet. Meanwhile Singlebury's desk had not been cleared —that is, of the trays, pencil-sharpener and complimentary calendar which were, of course, office property. The feeling that he would come back—not like Mrs. Horrocks, who has rung up and called round incessantly—but simply come back to work out of habit and through not knowing what else to do, was very strong,

without being openly mentioned. I myself half expected and dreaded it, and I had mentally prepared two or three lines of argument in order to persuade him, if he *did* come, not to try it again. Nothing happened, however, and on the Thursday I personally removed the "things" from the cubby-hole into my own room.

Meanwhile in order to dispel certain quite unfounded rumours I thought it best to issue a notice for general circulation, pointing out that if Mr. Singlebury should turn out to have taken any unwise step, and if in consequence any inquiry should be necessary, we should be the first to hear about it from the police. I dictated this to our only permanent typist, who immediately said, oh, he would never do that. He would never cause any unpleasantness like bringing police into the place, he'd do all he could to avoid that. I did not encourage any further discussion, but I asked my wife, who is very used to social work, to call round at Singlebury's place in Clapham North and find out how he was. She did not have very much luck. The people in the cleaner's shop knew, or thought they knew, that he was away, but they had not been sufficiently interested to ask where he was going.

On Friday young Patel said he would be leaving, as the damp and the smell were affecting his health. The damp is certainly not drying out in this seasonally warm weather.

I also, as you know, received another invitation on the Friday, at very short notice, in fact no notice at all; I was told to come to your house in Suffolk Park Gardens that evening for drinks. I was not unduly elated, having been asked once before after I had done rather an awkward small job for you. In our Company, justice must not only be done, it must be seen not to be done. The food was quite nice; it came from your Caterers Grade 3. I spent most of the evening talking to Ted Hollow, one of the area sales-managers. I did not expect to be introduced to your wife, nor was I. Towards the end of the evening you spoke to me for three minutes in the small room with a green marble floor and matching wallpaper leading to the ground-floor toilets. You asked me if everything was all right, to which I replied, all right for whom? You said that nobody's fault was nobody's funeral. I said that I had tried to give satisfaction. Passing on towards the washbasins, you told me with seeming cordiality to be careful and watch it when I had had mixed drinks.

I would describe my feeling at this point as resentment, and I cannot identify exactly the moment when it passed into unease. I do know that I was acutely uneasy as I crossed the hall and saw two of your domestic staff, a man and a woman, holding my coat, which I had left in the lobby, and apparently trying to brush it. Your domestic staff all appear to be of foreign extraction and I personally feel sorry for them and do not grudge them a smile at the oddly assorted guests. Then I saw they were not smiling at my coat but that they seemed to be examining their fingers and looking at me earnestly and silently, and the collar or shoulders of my coat was covered with blood. As I came up to them, although they were still both absolutely silent, the illusion or impression passed, and I put on my coat and left the house in what I hope was a normal manner.

I now come to the present time. The feeling of uneasiness which I have described as making itself felt in your house has not diminished during this past weekend, and partly to take my mind off it and partly for the reasons I have given, I decided to work over-time again tonight, Monday the twenty-third. This was in spite of the fact that the damp smell had become almost a stench, as of something putrid, which must have affected my nerves to some extent, because when I went out to get something to eat at Dino's I left the lights on, both in my own office and in the entrance hall. I mean that for the first time since I began to work for the Company I left them on deliberately. As I walked to the corner I looked back and saw the two solitary lights looking somewhat forlorn in contrast to the glitter of the Arab-American Mutual Loan Corporation opposite. After my meal I felt absolutely reluctant to go back to the building, and wished then that I had not given way to the impulse to leave the lights on, but since I had done so and they must be turned off, I had no choice.

As I stood in the empty hallway I could hear the numerous creakings, settlings and faint tickings of an old building, possibly associated with the plumbing system. The lifts for reasons of economy do not operate after 6:30 p.m., so I began to walk up the stairs. After one flight I felt a strong creeping tension in the nerves of the back such as any of us feel when there is danger

from behind; one might say that the body was thinking for itself on these occasions. I did not look round, but simply continued upwards as rapidly as I could. At the third floor I paused, and could hear footsteps coming patiently up behind me. This was not a surprise; I had been expecting them all evening.

Just at the door of my own office, or rather of the cubby-hole, for I have to pass through that, I turned, and saw at the end of the dim corridor what I had also expected, Singlebury, advancing towards me with his unmistakable shuffling step. My first reaction was a kind of bewilderment as to why he, who had been such an excellent timekeeper, so regular day by day, should become a creature of the night. He was wearing the blue suit. This I could make out by its familiar outline, but it was not till he came halfway down the corridor towards me, and reached the patch of light falling through the window from the street, that I saw that he was not himself—I mean that his head was nodding or rather swivelling irregularly from side to side. It crossed my mind that Singlebury was drunk. I had never known him drunk or indeed seen him take anything to drink, even at the office Christmas party, but one cannot estimate the effect that trouble will have upon a man. I began to think what steps I should take in this situation. I turned on the light in his cubby-hole as I went through and waited at the entrance of my own office. As he appeared in the outer doorway I saw that I had not been correct about the reason for the odd movement of the head. The throat was cut from ear to ear so that the head was nearly severed from the shoulders. It was this which had given the impression of nodding, or rather, lolling. As he walked into his cubby-hole Singlebury raised both hands and tried to steady the head as though conscious that something was wrong. The eyes were thickly filmed over, as one sees in the carcasses in a butcher's shop.

I shut and locked my door, and not wishing to give way to nausea, or to lose all control of myself, I sat down at my desk. My work was waiting for me as I had left it —it was the file on the matter of the damp elimination—and, there not being anything else to do, I tried to look through it. On the other side of the door I could hear Singlebury sit down also, and then try the drawers of the table, evidently looking for the "things" without which he could not start work. After the drawers had been tried, one after another, several times, there was almost total silence.

The present position is that I am locked in my own office and would not, no matter what you offered me, indeed I could not, go out through the cubby-hole and pass what is sitting at the desk. The early cleaners will not be here for seven hours and forty-five minutes. I have passed the time so far as best I could in writing this report. One consideration strikes me. If what I have next door is a visitant which should not be walking but buried in the earth, then its wound cannot bleed, and there will be no stream of blood moving slowly under the whole width of the communicating door. However I am sitting at the moment with my back to the door, so that, without turning round, I have no means of telling whether it has done so or not.

—1975

# Graham Greene

## *1904 – 1991*

Whether their protagonists are secret agents, priests, detectives, military officers, or gentlemen, the novels of Graham Greene are almost invariably "parables of the damned." Built on themes of political intrigue, treachery, deception, guilt, and ultimately failure, Greene's stories transport readers to troubled and exotic locations—Liberia, Haiti, Vietnam, and the Belgian Congo, for example—places where sides must be taken and loyalties tested in extreme situations. Characters in "Greeneland" (a term coined by Arthur Calder-Marshall) must often make a difficult choice between allegiance to a country or loyalty to an individual; complex moral decisions are the heart of the matter in a typical Greene story.

Greene was raised in a family in which several members worked in various capacities as secret agents, and his own life played out much like the plot of one of his novels. He grew up in Berkhamsted, Hertfordshire, the fourth of six children born to Marion Raymond, a cousin of the writer Robert Louis Stevenson, and Charles Henry Greene, headmaster of Berkhamsted School. Unfortunately for him, Greene was educated at his father's school; he was tormented by his classmates and torn between filial loyalty and faithfulness to his peers. Greene went on to attend Balliol College, Oxford, where he studied history and became a writer and editor for *The Oxford Outlook*. While at university he published his first book, *Babbling April* (1925), a collection of poems. There he also met his future wife, Vivienne Dayrell-Browning, who wrote to him correcting his use of a Catholic term in one of his articles for the school paper. Greene subsequently took an interest in Catholicism and was baptized in 1926; the couple married in 1927 and had two children. Greene was incapable of remaining a family man, however; he had many affairs, separated from Vivienne in 1948, and would say in later life that, much as he was "very fond of" his son and daughter, "my books are my children."

After graduation Greene became a subeditor at the *Nottingham Journal* and later worked for *The Times* in London (1926–30). In 1929 Greene published his first novel, *The Man Within*, which received both public and critical acclaim; this success enabled him to secure a three-book contract and quit his job at *The Times*. The next two novels met with less success, whereupon Greene decided to write the first of what he came to call his "entertainments," a name intended to distinguish them from his more serious novels. *Stamboul Train* (1932, entitled *Orient Express* in the United States), was indeed a commercial success, and spawned the first of many films based on his books. In 1935 Greene began reviewing books and then films for *The Spectator*, eventually becoming known as one of the most brilliant film critics of his time. (As Greene discovered, however, the world of criticism was not without its perils; an article he wrote on Shirley Temple in 1937 landed him in a nasty lawsuit and created a fiasco at *Night and Day*, the short-lived magazine in which the review appeared.)

In the mid-1930s Greene began the extensive peregrinations that eventually led people to speculate about his involvement in espionage. Whether traveling to Germany (1934), Liberia (an excursion he documented in 1936's *Journey without Maps*), Mexico (the scene of *The Power and the Glory*, 1940), Vietnam (*The Quiet American*, 1955), or Cuba (*Our Man in Havana*, 1958), Greene always seemed to be followed closely by political intrigue. He admitted to being on staff at the SIS (Secret Intelligence Service) during World War II, first stationed in Sierra Leone and later working for counter intelligence under the direction of Kim Philby (who ultimately defected to the Soviet Union after being unmasked as a double agent). Although Greene was never formally accused of being a double agent himself, he maintained a friendship with the Soviet spy, even writing the preface to Philby's memoirs. Greene did flirt with Communism for much of his life and met with various communist leaders, including Fidel Castro and Ho Chi Minh; he also publicly vilified the United States and its foreign policy, prompting controversy about his own allegiances. His politically conservative friend Evelyn Waugh, however, had no doubts as to his true loyalties: "He is a great one for practical jokes. I think also he is a secret agent on our side and all his buttering up of the Russians is 'cover.'"

Although Greene's creative focus remained first and foremost on his novels, he also tried his hand at playwriting, at screenwriting, and at short fiction. His short story "The Basement Room" (1935, subsequently made into a film with Greene's collaboration on the screenplay) is unusual among his work in the degree to which it focuses on the world of the child, but in its gritty detail and its themes of sinfulness, loyalty, and betrayal, it is of a piece with the mainstream of his work.

Greene's plots often involve political intrigue, but many consider his books on Catholic themes written in the 1940s and early 1950s to be his best work. His first such book was *Brighton Rock* (1938)—a dark novel styled by Greene "an entertainment"—in which a priest speaks of "the appalling strangeness of the mercy of God." Questions of mercy, grace, and damnation rise again and again in his later novels, especially in the three that established his international reputation: *The Power and the Glory* (1940), *The Heart of the Matter* (1948), and *The End of the Affair* (1951). In a 1948 review of *The Heart of the Matter*, George Orwell criticized what he took to be one implication of the novel—that there is more virtue in being an "erring Catholic" than a "virtuous pagan." In Orwell's view, Greene appeared "to share the idea, which has been floating around ever since Baudelaire, that there is something rather distingué in being damned; Hell is a sort of high-class nightclub, entry to which is reserved for Catholics only."

Orwell's suspicion of Greene has been shared by many academic critics, but it has remained a minority view. Greene won numerous major awards—including the John Dos Passos (Madrid) and Jerusalem Prizes, honorary degrees from Cambridge and Oxford, the Order of Merit, and numerous international arts and letters awards—and many thought he would win the Nobel Prize. (It was often speculated that his life of political intrigue kept him from winning.) Greene published two volumes of his autobiography, *A Sort of Life* (1971) and *Ways of Escape* (1980), and just before his death in 1991 in Switzerland he gave approval to Norman Sherry to complete his biography. The priest at his funeral, apparently reluctant to commit himself too precisely in view of the numerous stories about Greene's checkered past, said: "My faith tells me that he is now with God, or on the way there."

⌘⌘⌘

## The Basement Room

### 1

When the front door had shut the two of them out and the butler Baines had turned back into the dark and heavy hall, Philip began to live. He stood in front of the nursery door, listening until he heard the engine of the taxi die out along the street. His parents were safely gone for a fortnight's[1] holiday; he was "between nurses," one dismissed and the other not arrived; he was alone in the great Belgravia[2] house with

---

[1] *fortnight* Two weeks.

[2] *Belgravia* Fashionable area of London.

Baines and Mrs. Baines.

He could go anywhere, even through the green baize door[1] to the pantry or down the stairs to the basement living-room. He felt a happy stranger in his home because he could go into any room and all the rooms were empty.

You could only guess who had once occupied them: the rack of pipes in the smoking-room beside the elephant tusks, the carved wood tobacco jar; in the bedroom the pink hangings and the pale perfumes and three-quarter finished jars of cream which Mrs. Baines had not yet cleared away for her own use; the high glaze on the never-opened piano in the drawing-room, the china clock, the silly little tables and the silver. But here Mrs. Baines was already busy, pulling down the curtains, covering the chairs in dust-sheets.

"Be off out of here, Master Philip," and she looked at him with her peevish eyes, while she moved round, getting everything in order, meticulous and loveless and doing her duty.

Philip Lane went downstairs and pushed at the baize door; he looked into the pantry, but Baines was not there, then he set foot for the first time on the stairs to the basement. Again he had the sense: this is life. All his seven nursery years vibrated with the strange, the new experience. His crowded brain was like a city which feels the earth tremble at a distant earthquake shock. He was apprehensive, but he was happier than he had ever been. Everything was more important than before.

Baines was reading a newspaper in his shirt-sleeves. He said, "Come in, Phil, and make yourself at home. Wait a moment and I'll do the honours," and going to a white cleaned cupboard he brought out a bottle of ginger-beer and half a Dundee cake. "Half past eleven in the morning," Baines said. "It's opening time, my boy," and he cut the cake and poured out the ginger-beer. He was more genial than Philip had ever known him, more at ease, a man in his own home.

"Shall I call Mrs. Baines?" Philip asked, and he was glad when Baines said no. She was busy. She liked to be busy, so why interfere with her pleasure?

"A spot of drink at half past eleven," Baines said, pouring himself out a glass of ginger-beer, "gives an appetite for chop and does no man any harm."

"A chop?" Philip asked.

"Old Coasters,"[2] Baines said, "they call all food chop."

"But it's not a chop?"

"Well, it might be, you know, if cooked with palm oil. And then some paw-paw[3] to follow."

Philip looked out of the basement window at the dry stone yard, the ash-can and the legs going up and down the railings.

"Was it hot there?"

"Ah, you never felt such heat. Not a nice heat, mind, like you get in the park on a day like this. Wet," Baines said, "corruption." He cut himself a slice of cake. "Smelling of rot," Baines said, rolling his eyes round the small basement room, from clean cupboard to clean cupboard, the sense of bareness, of nowhere to hide a man's secrets. With an air of regret for something lost he took a long draught of ginger-beer.

"Why did father live out there?"

"It was his job," Baines said, "same as this is mine now. And it was mine then too. It was a man's job. You wouldn't believe it now, but I've had forty niggers[4] under me, doing what I told them to."

"Why did you leave?"

"I married Mrs. Baines."

Philip took the slice of Dundee cake in his hand and munched it round the room. He felt very old, independent and judicial; he was aware that Baines was talking to him as man to man. He never called him Master Philip as Mrs. Baines did, who was servile when she was not authoritative.

Baines had seen the world; he had seen beyond the railings. He sat there over his ginger pop with the resigned dignity of an exile; Baines didn't complain; he had chosen his fate, and if his fate was Mrs. Baines he had only himself to blame.

---

[1] *green baize door*  In substantial English houses, a cloth-covered (green baize) door separates the living quarters of the family from the service rooms.

[2] *Coasters*  Residents of West Africa who are of European origin.

[3] *paw-paw*  Papaya.

[4] *niggers*  By the 1930s the word "nigger" was increasingly recognized as an unacceptably derogatory term in much of British society, but it was still in common use.

But today—the house was almost empty and Mrs. Baines was upstairs and there was nothing to do—he allowed himself a little acidity.

"I'd go back tomorrow if I had the chance."

"Did you ever shoot a nigger?"

"I never had any call to shoot," Baines said. "Of course I carried a gun. But you didn't need to treat them bad. That just made them stupid. Why," Baines said, bowing his thin grey hair with embarrassment over the ginger pop, "I loved some of those damned niggers. I couldn't help loving them. There they'd be laughing, holding hands; they like to touch each other; it made them feel fine to know the other fellow was around. It didn't mean anything we could understand; two of them would go about all day without loosing hold, grown men; but it wasn't love; it didn't mean anything we could understand."

"Eating between meals," Mrs. Baines said. "What would your mother say, Master Philip?"

She came down the steep stairs to the basement, her hands full of pots of cream and salve, tubes of grease and paste. "You oughtn't to encourage him, Baines," she said, sitting down in a wicker armchair and screwing up her small ill-humored eyes at the Coty lipstick, Pond's cream, the Leichner rouge and Cyclax powder and Elizabeth Arden astringent.

She threw them one by one into the wastepaper basket. She saved only the cold cream. "Tell the boy stories," she said. "Go along to the nursery, Master Philip, while I get lunch."

Philip climbed the stairs to the baize door. He heard Mrs. Baines's voice like the voice in a nightmare when the small Price light has guttered in the saucer and the curtains move; it was sharp and shrill and full of malice, louder than people ought to speak, exposed.

"Sick to death of your ways, Baines, spoiling the boy. Time you did some work about the house," but he couldn't hear what Baines said in reply. He pushed open the baize door, came up like a small earth animal in his grey flannel shorts into a wash of sunlight on a parquet floor,[1] the gleam of mirrors dusted and polished and beautified by Mrs. Baines.

Something broke downstairs, and Philip sadly mounted the stairs to the nursery. He pitied Baines; it occurred to him how happily they could live together in the empty house if Mrs. Baines were called away. He didn't want to play with his Meccano sets;[2] he wouldn't take out his train or his soldiers; he sat at the table with his chin on his hands: this is life; and suddenly he felt responsible for Baines, as if he were the master of the house and Baines an aging servant who deserved to be cared for. There was not much one could do; he decided at least to be good.

He was not surprised when Mrs. Baines was agreeable at lunch; he was used to her changes. Now it was "another helping of meat, Master Philip," or "Master Philip, a little more of this nice pudding." It was a pudding he liked, Queen's pudding with a perfect meringue, but he wouldn't eat a second helping lest she might count that a victory. She was the kind of woman who thought that any injustice could be counterbalanced by something good to eat.

She was sour, but she liked making sweet things; one never had to complain of a lack of jam or plums; she ate well herself and added soft sugar to the meringue and the strawberry jam. The half-light through the basement window set the motes moving above her pale hair like dust as she sifted the sugar, and Baines crouched over his plate saying nothing.

Again Philip felt responsibility. Baines had looked forward to this, and Baines was disappointed: everything was being spoilt. The sensation of disappointment was one which Philip could share; he could understand better than anyone this grief, something hoped for not happening, something promised not fulfilled, something exciting which turned dull. "Baines," he said, "will you take me for a walk this afternoon?"

"No," Mrs. Baines said, "no. That he won't. Not with all the silver to clean."

"There's a fortnight to do it in," Baines said.

"Work first, pleasure afterward."

Mrs. Baines helped herself to some more meringue.

Baines put down his spoon and fork and pushed his plate away. "Blast," he said.

"Temper," Mrs. Baines said, "temper. Don't you go breaking any more things, Baines, and I won't have you swearing in front of the boy. Master Philip, if you've finished you can get down."

---

[1] *parquet floor*   Patterned wood floor.

[2] *Meccano sets*   Construction toy.

She skinned the rest of the meringue off the pudding.

"I want to go for a walk," Philip said.

"You'll go and have a rest."

"I want to go for a walk."

"Master Philip," Mrs. Baines said. She got up from the table, leaving her meringue unfinished, and came towards him, thin, menacing, dusty in the basement room. "Master Philip, you just do as you're told." She took him by the arm and squeezed it; she watched him with a joyless passionate glitter and above her head the feet of typists trudged back to the Victoria offices after the lunch interval.

"Why shouldn't I go for a walk?"

But he weakened; he was scared and ashamed of being scared. This was life; a strange passion he couldn't understand moving in the basement room. He saw a small pile of broken glass swept into a corner by the wastepaper basket. He looked at Baines for help and only intercepted hate; the sad hopeless hate of something behind bars.

"Why shouldn't I?" he repeated.

"Master Philip," Mrs. Baines said, "you've got to do as you're told. You mustn't think just because your father's away there's nobody here to —"

"You wouldn't dare," Philip cried, and was startled by Baines's low interjection:

"There's nothing she wouldn't dare."

"I hate you," Philip said to Mrs. Baines. He pulled away from her and ran to the door, but she was there before him; she was old, but she was quick.

"Master Philip," she said, "you'll say you're sorry." She stood in front of the door quivering with excitement. "What would your father do if he heard you say that?"

She put a hand out to seize him, dry and white with constant soda, the nails cut to the quick, but he backed away and put the table between them, and suddenly to his surprise she smiled; she became again as servile as she had been arrogant. "Get along with you, Master Philip," she said with glee, "I see I'm going to have my hands full till your father and mother come back."

She left the door unguarded and when he passed her she slapped him playfully. "I've got too much to do today to trouble about you. I haven't covered half the chairs," and suddenly even the upper part of the house became unbearable to him as he thought of Mrs. Baines moving around shrouding the sofas, laying out the dust-sheets.

So he wouldn't go upstairs to get his cap but walked straight out across the shining hall into the street, and again, as he looked this way and looked that way, it was life he was in the middle of.

## 2

The pink sugar cakes in the window on a paper doily, the ham, the slab of mauve sausage, the wasps driving like small torpedoes across the pane caught Philip's attention. His feet were tired by pavements; he had been afraid to cross the road, had simply walked first in one direction, then in the other. He was nearly home now; the square was at the end of the street; this was a shabby outpost of Pimlico,[1] and he smudged the pane with his nose looking for sweets, and saw between the cakes and ham a different Baines. He hardly recognized the bulbous eyes, the bald forehead. This was a happy, bold, and buccaneering Baines, even though it was, when you looked closer, a desperate Baines.

Philip had never seen the girl, but he remembered Baines had a niece. She was thin and drawn, and she wore a white mackintosh;[2] she meant nothing to Philip; she belonged to a world about which he knew nothing at all. He couldn't make up stories about her, as he could make them up about withered Sir Hubert Reed, the Permanent Secretary, about Mrs. Wince-Dudley, who came once a year from Penstanley in Suffolk with a green umbrella and an enormous black handbag, as he could make them up about the upper servants in all the houses where he went to tea and games. She just didn't belong. He thought of mermaids and Undine,[3] but she didn't belong there either, nor to the adventures of Emil, nor to the Bastables.[4] She sat there looking at an iced pink cake in the detachment and mystery of the completely disinherited, looking at the half-used pots of

[1] *Pimlico* Place of resort in suburban London, formerly celebrated for its cakes.

[2] *mackintosh* Lightweight raincoat.

[3] *Undine* Female water spirits.

[4] *Emil... Bastables* Erich Kastner's adventures of Emil and Edith Nesbit's Bastable books are children's classics.

powder which Baines had set out on the marble-topped table between them.

Baines was urging, hoping, entreating, commanding, and the girl looked at the tea and the china pots and cried. Baines passed his handkerchief across the table, but she wouldn't wipe her eyes; she screwed it in her palm and let the tears run down, wouldn't do anything, wouldn't speak, would only put up a silent resistance to what she dreaded and wanted and refused to listen to at any price. The two brains battled over the tea-cups loving each other, and there came to Philip outside, beyond the ham and wasps and dusty Pimlico pane, a confused indication of the struggle.

He was inquisitive and he didn't understand and he wanted to know. He went and stood in the doorway to see better, he was less sheltered than he had ever been; other people's lives for the first time touched and pressed and moulded. He would never escape that scene. In a week he had forgotten it, but it conditioned his career, the long austerity of his life; when he was dying, rich and alone, it was said that he asked: "Who is she?" Baines had won; he was cocky and the girl was happy. She wiped her face, she opened a pot of powder, and their fingers touched across the table. It occurred to Philip that it might be amusing to imitate Mrs. Baines's voice and to call "Baines" to him from the door.

His voice shriveled them; you couldn't describe it in any other way, it made them smaller, they weren't together any more. Baines was the first to recover and trace the voice, but that didn't make things as they were. The sawdust was spilled out of the afternoon; nothing you did could mend it, and Philip was scared. "I didn't mean…" He wanted to say that he loved Baines, that he had only wanted to laugh at Mrs. Baines. But he had discovered you couldn't laugh at Mrs. Baines. She wasn't Sir Hubert Reed, who used steel nibs and carried a pen-wiper in his pocket; she wasn't Mrs. Wince-Dudley; she was darkness when the night-light went out in a draft; she was the frozen blocks of earth he had seen one winter in a graveyard when someone said, "They need an electric drill"; she was the flowers gone bad and smelling in the little closet room at Penstanley. There was nothing to laugh about. You had to endure her when she was there and forget about her quickly when she was away, suppress the thought of her, ram it down

deep.

Baines said, "It's only Phil," beckoned him in and gave him the pink iced cake the girl hadn't eaten, but the afternoon was broken, the cake was like dry bread in the throat. The girl left them at once: she even forgot to take the powder. Like a blunt icicle in her white mackintosh she stood in the doorway with her back to them, then melted into the afternoon.

"Who is she?" Philip asked. "Is she your niece?"

"Oh, yes," Baines said, "that's who she is; she's my niece," and poured the last drops of water onto the coarse black leaves in the teapot.

"May as well have another cup," Baines said.

"The cup that cheers," he said hopelessly, watching the bitter black fluid drain out of the spout.

"Have a glass of ginger pop, Phil?"

"I'm sorry. I'm sorry, Baines."

"It's not your fault, Phil. Why, I could really believe it wasn't you at all, but her. She creeps in everywhere." He fished two leaves out of his cup and laid them on the back of his hand, a thin soft flake and a hard stalk. He beat them with his hand: "Today," and the stalk detached itself, "tomorrow, Wednesday, Thursday, Friday, Saturday, Sunday," but the flake wouldn't come, stayed where it was, drying under his blows, with a resistance you wouldn't believe it to possess. "The tough one wins," Baines said.

He got up and paid the bill and out they went into the street. Baines said, "I don't ask you to say what isn't true. But you needn't actually *tell* Mrs. Baines you met us here."

"Of course not," Philip said, and catching something of Sir Hubert Reed's manner, "I understand, Baines." But he didn't understand a thing; he was caught up in other people's darkness.

"It was stupid," Baines said. "So near home, but I hadn't time to think, you see. I'd got to see her."

"I haven't time to spare," Baines said. "I'm not young. I've got to see that she's all right."

"Of course you have, Baines."

"Mrs. Baines will get it out of you if she can."

"You can trust me, Baines," Philip said in a dry important Reed voice; and then, "Look out. She's at the window watching." And there indeed she was, looking up at them, between the lace curtains, from the basement room, speculating. "Need we go in, Baines?" Philip asked, cold lying heavy on his stomach like too much pudding; he clutched Baines's arm.

"Careful," Baines said softly, "careful."

"But need we go in, Baines? It's early. Take me for a walk in the park."

"Better not."

"But I'm frightened, Baines."

"You haven't any cause," Baines said. "Nothing's going to hurt you. You just run along upstairs to the nursery. I'll go down by the area and talk to Mrs. Baines." But he stood hesitating at the top of the stone steps pretending not to see her, where she watched between the curtains. "In at the front door, Phil, and up the stairs."

Philip didn't linger in the hall; he ran, slithering on the parquet Mrs. Baines had polished, to the stairs. Through the drawing-room doorway on the first floor he saw the draped chairs; even the china clock on the mantel was covered like a canary's cage. As he passed, it chimed the hour, muffled and secret under the duster. On the nursery table he found his supper laid out: a glass of milk and a piece of bread and butter, a sweet biscuit, and a little cold Queen's pudding without the meringue. He had no appetite; he strained his ears for Mrs. Baines's coming, for the sound of voices, but the basement held its secrets; the green baize door shut off that world. He drank the milk and ate the biscuit, but he didn't touch the rest, and presently he could hear the soft precise footfalls of Mrs. Baines on the stairs: she was a good servant, she walked softly; she was a determined woman, she walked precisely.

But she wasn't angry when she came in; she was ingratiating as she opened the night nursery door— "Did you have a good walk, Master Philip?"—pulled down the blinds, laid out his pajamas, came back to clear his supper. "I'm glad Baines found you. Your mother wouldn't have liked you being out alone." She examined the tray. "Not much appetite, have you, Master Philip? Why don't you try a little of this nice pudding? I'll bring you up some more jam for it."

"No, no, thank you, Mrs. Baines," Philip said.

"You ought to eat more," Mrs. Baines said. She sniffed round the room like a dog. "You didn't take any pots out of the wastepaper basket in the kitchen, did

you, Master Philip?"

"No," Philip said.

"Of course you wouldn't. I just wanted to make sure." She patted his shoulder and her fingers flashed to his lapel; she picked off a tiny crumb of pink sugar. "Oh, Master Philip," she said, "that's why you haven't any appetite. You've been buying sweet cakes. That's not what your pocket money's for."

"But I didn't," Philip said. "I didn't."

She tasted the sugar with the tip of her tongue.

"Don't tell lies to me, Master Philip. I won't stand for it any more than your father would."

"I didn't, I didn't," Philip said. "They gave it to me. I mean Baines," but she had pounced on the word "they." She had got what she wanted; there was no doubt about that, even when you didn't know what it was she wanted. Philip was angry and miserable and disappointed because he hadn't kept Baines's secret. Baines oughtn't to have trusted him; grown-up people should keep their own secrets, and yet here was Mrs. Baines immediately entrusting him with another.

"Let me tickle your palm and see if you can keep a secret." But he put his hand behind him; he wouldn't be touched. "It's a secret between us, Master Philip, that I know all about them. I suppose she was having tea with him," she speculated.

"Why shouldn't she?" he asked, the responsibility for Baines weighing on his spirit, the idea that he had got to keep her secret when he hadn't kept Baines's making him miserable with the unfairness of life. "She was nice."

"She was nice, was she?" Mrs. Baines said in a bitter voice he wasn't used to.

"And she's his niece."

"So that's what he said," Mrs. Baines struck softly back at him like the clock under the duster. She tried to be jocular. "The old scoundrel. Don't you tell him I know, Master Philip." She stood very still between the table and the door, thinking very hard, planning something. "Promise you won't tell. I'll give you that Meccano set, Master Philip…"

He turned his back on her; he wouldn't promise, but he wouldn't tell. He would have nothing to do with their secrets, the responsibilities they were determined to lay on him. He was only anxious to forget. He had received already a larger dose of life than he had bargained for, and he was scared. "A 2A Meccano set, Master Philip." He never opened his Meccano set again, never built anything, never created anything, died the old dilettante, sixty years later with nothing to show rather than preserve the memory of Mrs. Baines's malicious voice saying good night, her soft determined footfalls on the stairs to the basement, going down, going down.

### 3

The sun poured in between the curtains and Baines was beating a tattoo on a water-can. "Glory, glory," Baines said. He sat down on the end of the bed and said, "I beg to announce that Mrs. Baines has been called away. Her mother's dying. She won't be back until tomorrow."

"Why did you wake me up so early?" Philip complained. He watched Baines with uneasiness; he wasn't going to be drawn in; he'd learnt his lesson. It wasn't right for a man of Baines's age to be so merry. It made a grown person human in the same way that you were human. For if a grown-up could behave so childishly, you were liable to find yourself in their world. It was enough that it came at you in dreams: the witch at the corner, the man with a knife. So "It's very early," he whined, even though he loved Baines, even though he couldn't help being glad that Baines was happy. He was divided by the fear and the attraction of life.

"I want to make this a long day," Baines said. "This is the best time." He pulled the curtains back. "It's a bit misty. The cat's been out all night. There she is, sniffing round the area. They haven't taken in any milk at 59. Emma's shaking out the mats at 63." He said, "This was what I used to think about on the Coast: somebody shaking mats and the cat coming home. I can see it today," Baines said, "just as if I was still in Africa. Most days you don't notice what you've got. It's a good life if you don't weaken." He put a penny on the washstand. "When you've dressed, Phil, run and get a *Mail* from the barrow[1] at the corner. I'll be cooking the sausages."

"Sausages?"

"Sausages," Baines said. "We're going to celebrate today." He celebrated at breakfast, restless, cracking jokes, unaccountably merry and nervous. It was going to

be a long, long day, he kept on coming back to that: for years he had waited for a long day, he had sweated in the damp Coast heat, changed shirts, gone down with fever, lain between the blankets and sweated, all in the hope of this long day, the cat sniffing round the area, a bit of mist, the mats beaten at 63. He propped the *Mail* in front of the coffee-pot and read pieces aloud. He said, "Cora Down's been married for the fourth time." He was amused, but it wasn't his idea of a long day. His long day was the Park, watching the riders in the Row,[2] seeing Sir Arthur Stillwater pass beyond the rails ("He dined with us once in Bo; up from Freetown; he was governor there"), lunch at the Corner House for Philip's sake (he'd have preferred himself a glass of stout and some oysters at the York bar), the Zoo, the long bus ride home in the last summer light: the leaves in the Green Park were beginning to turn and the motors nuzzled out of Berkeley Street with the low sun gently glowing on their windscreens. Baines envied no one, not Cora Down, or Sir Arthur Stillwater, or Lord Sandale, who came out onto the steps of the Army and Navy[3] and then went back again—he hadn't anything to do and might as well look at another paper. "I said don't let me see you touch that black again." Baines had led a man's life; everyone on top of the bus pricked his ears when he told Philip all about it.

"Would you have shot him?" Philip asked, and Baines put his head back and tilted his dark respectable manservant's hat to a better angle as the bus swerved round the Artillery Memorial.

"I wouldn't have thought twice about it. I'd have shot to kill," he boasted, and the bowed figure went by, the steel helmet, the heavy cloak, the down-turned rifle and the folded hands.

"Have you got the revolver?"

"Of course I've got it," Baines said. "Don't I need it with all the burglaries there've been?" This was the Baines whom Philip loved: not Baines singing and carefree, but Baines responsible, Baines behind barriers, living his man's life.

All the buses streamed from Victoria like a convoy of aeroplanes to bring Baines home with honour. "Forty

---

[1]   *barrow*   Cart used by street vendors.

[2]   *Park ... Row*   The bridle path in Hyde Park, in London, is called "Rotten Row" (from "Route de Roi," French for "the King's Way").

[3]   *Army and Navy*   Club in London for British officers.

blacks under me," and there waiting near the area steps was the proper reward, love at lighting-up time.

"It's your niece," Philip said, recognizing the white mackintosh, but not the happy sleepy face. She frightened him like an unlucky number; he nearly told Baines what Mrs. Baines had said; but he didn't want to bother, he wanted to leave things alone.

"Why, so it is," Baines said. "I shouldn't wonder if she was going to have a bit of supper with us." But he said, they'd play a game, pretend they didn't know her, slip down the area steps, "and here," Baines said, "we are," lay the table, put out the cold sausages, a bottle of beer, a bottle of ginger pop, a flagon[1] of harvest burgundy. "Everyone his own drink," Baines said. "Run upstairs, Phil, and see if there's been a post."

Philip didn't like the empty house at dusk before the lights went on. He hurried. He wanted to be back with Baines. The hall lay there in quiet and shadow prepared to show him something he didn't want to see. Some letters rustled down and someone knocked. "Open in the name of the Republic." The tumbrils[2] rolled, the head bobbed in the bloody basket. Knock, knock, and the postman's footsteps going away. Philip gathered the letters. The slit in the door was like the grating in a jeweller's window. He remembered the policeman he had seen peer through. He had said to his nurse, "What's he doing?" and when she said, "He's seeing if everything's all right," his brain immediately filled with images of all that might be wrong. He ran to the baize door and the stairs. The girl was already there and Baines was kissing her. She leaned breathlessly against the dresser.

"Here's Emmy, Phil."

"There's a letter for you, Baines."

"Emmy," Baines said, "it's from her." But he wouldn't open it. "You bet she's coming back."

"We'll have supper, anyway," Emmy said. "She can't harm that."

"You don't know her," Baines said. "Nothing's safe. Damn it," he said, "I was a man once," and he opened the letter.

"Can I start?" Philip asked, but Baines didn't hear; he presented in his stillness an example of the importance grown-up people attached to the written word: you had to write your thanks, not wait and speak them, as if letters couldn't lie. But Philip knew better than that, sprawling his thanks across a page to Aunt Alice who had given him a teddy bear he was too old for. Letters could lie all right, but they made the lie permanent. They lay as evidence against you: they made you meaner than the spoken word.

"She's not coming back till tomorrow night," Baines said. He opened the bottles, he pulled up the chairs, he kissed Emmy again against the dresser.

"You oughtn't to, Emmy said, "with the boy here."

"He's got to learn," Baines said, "like the rest of us," and he helped Philip to three sausages. He only took one himself; he said he wasn't hungry, but when Emmy said she wasn't hungry either he stood over her and made her eat. He was timid and rough with her and made her drink the harvest burgundy because he said she needed building up; he wouldn't take no for an answer, but when he touched her his hands were light and clumsy too, as if he was afraid to damage something delicate and didn't know how to handle anything so light.

"This is better than milk and biscuits, eh?"

"Yes," Philip said, but he was scared, scared for Baines as much as for himself. He couldn't help wondering at every bite, at every draught of the ginger pop, what Mrs. Baines would say if she ever learnt of this meal; he couldn't imagine it, there was a depth of bitterness and rage in Mrs. Baines you couldn't sound. He said, "She won't be coming back tonight?" but you could tell by the way they immediately understood him that she wasn't really away at all; she was there in the basement with them, driving them to longer drinks and louder talk, biding her time for the right cutting word. Baines wasn't really happy; he was only watching happiness from close to instead of from far away.

"No," he said, "she'll not be back till late tomorrow." He couldn't keep his eyes off happiness. He'd played around as much as other men; he kept on reverting to the Coast as if to excuse himself for his innocence. He wouldn't have been so innocent if he'd lived his life in London, so innocent when it came to

---

[1] *flagon*  Flask.

[2] *tumbrils*  Carts used to carry prisoners to the guillotine during the French Revolution.

tenderness. "If it was you, Emmy," he said, looking at the white dresser, the scrubbed chairs, "this'd be like a home." Already the room was not quite so harsh; there was a little dust in corners, the silver needed a final polish, the morning's paper lay untidily on a chair.

"You'd better go to bed, Phil; it's been a long day."

They didn't leave him to find his own way up through the dark shrouded house; they went with him, turning on lights, touching each other's fingers on the switches. Floor after floor they drove the night back. They spoke softly among the covered chairs. They watched him undress, they didn't make him wash or clean his teeth, they saw him into bed and lit his night-light and left his door ajar. He could hear their voices on the stairs, friendly like the guests he heard at dinner-parties when they moved down the hall, saying good night. They belonged; wherever they were they made a home. He heard a door open and a clock strike, he heard their voices for a long while, so that he felt they were not far away and he was safe. The voices didn't dwindle, they simply went out, and he could be sure that they were still somewhere not far from him, silent together in one of the many empty rooms, growing sleepy together as he grew sleepy after the long day.

He just had time to sigh faintly with satisfaction, because this too perhaps had been life, before he slept and the inevitable terrors of sleep came round him: a man with a tricolour hat beat at the door on His Majesty's service, a bleeding head lay on the kitchen table in a basket, and the Siberian wolves crept closer. He was bound hand and foot and couldn't move; they leapt round him breathing heavily; he opened his eyes and Mrs. Baines was there, her grey untidy hair in threads over his face, her black hat askew. A loose hairpin fell on the pillow and one musty thread brushed his mouth. "Where are they?" she whispered. "Where are they?"

4

Philip watched her in terror. Mrs. Baines was out of breath as if she had been searching all the empty rooms, looking under loose covers.

With her untidy grey hair and her black dress buttoned to her throat, her gloves of black cotton, she was so like the witches of his dreams that he didn't dare to speak. There was a stale smell in her breath.

"She's here," Mrs. Baines said, "you can't deny she's here." Her face was simultaneously marked with cruelty and misery; she wanted to "do things" to people, but she suffered all the time. It would have done her good to scream, but she daren't do that: it would warn them. She came ingratiatingly back to the bed where Philip lay rigid on his back and whispered,

"I haven't forgotten the Meccano set. You shall have it tomorrow, Master Philip. We've got secrets together, haven't we? Just tell me where they are."

He couldn't speak. Fear held him as firmly as any nightmare. She said, "Tell Mrs. Baines, Master Philip. You love your Mrs. Baines, don't you?" That was too much; he couldn't speak, but he could move his mouth in terrified denial, wince away from her dusty image.

She whispered, coming closer to him, "Such deceit. I'll tell your father. I'll settle with you myself when I've found them. You'll smart; I'll see you smart." Then immediately she was still, listening. A board had creaked on the floor below, and a moment later, while she stooped listening above his bed, there came the whispers of two people who were happy and sleepy together after a long day. The night-light stood beside the mirror and Mrs. Baines could see there her own reflection, misery and cruelty wavering in the glass, age and dust and nothing to hope for. She sobbed without tears, a dry, breathless sound, but her cruelty was a kind of pride which kept her going; it was her best quality, she would have been merely pitiable without it. She went out of the door on tiptoe, feeling her way across the landing, going so softly down the stairs that no one behind a shut door could hear her. Then there was complete silence again; Philip could move; he raised his knees; he sat up in bed; he wanted to die. It wasn't fair, the walls were down again between his world and theirs, but this time it was something worse than merriment that the grown people made him share; a passion moved in the house he recognized but could not understand.

It wasn't fair, but he owed Baines everything: the Zoo, the ginger pop, the bus ride home. Even the supper called to his loyalty. But he was frightened; he was touching something he touched in dreams; the bleeding head, the wolves, the knock, knock, knock. Life fell on him with savagery, and you couldn't blame him if he never faced it again in sixty years. He got out of bed. Carefully from habit he put on his bedroom slippers and tiptoed to the door: it wasn't quite dark on the landing below because the curtains had been taken down for the cleaners and the light from the street washed in through the tall windows. Mrs. Baines had her hand on the glass door-knob; she was very carefully turning it; he screamed: "Baines, Baines."

Mrs. Baines turned and saw him cowering in his pajamas by the banisters; he was helpless, more helpless even than Baines, and cruelty grew at the sight of him and drove her up the stairs. The nightmare was on him again and he couldn't move; he hadn't any courage left, he couldn't even scream.

But the first cry brought Baines out of the best spare bedroom and he moved quicker than Mrs. Baines. She hadn't reached the top of the stairs before he'd caught her round the waist. She drove her black cotton gloves at his face and he bit her hand. He hadn't time to think, he fought her like a stranger, but she fought back with knowledgeable hate. She was going to teach them all and it didn't really matter whom she began with; they had all deceived her; but the old image in the glass was by her side, telling her she must be dignified, she wasn't young enough to yield her dignity; she could beat his face, but she mustn't bite; she could push, but she mustn't kick.

Age and dust and nothing to hope for were her handicaps. She went over the banisters in a flurry of black clothes and fell into the hall; she lay before the front door like a sack of coals which should have gone down the area into the basement. Philip saw; Emmy saw; she sat down suddenly in the doorway of the best spare bedroom with her eyes open as if she were too tired to stand any longer. Baines went slowly down into the hall.

It wasn't hard for Philip to escape; they'd forgotten him completely. He went down the back, the servants' stairs, because Mrs. Baines was in the hall. He didn't understand what she was doing lying there; like the pictures in a book no one had read to him, the things he didn't understand terrified him. The whole house had been turned over to the grown-up world; he wasn't safe in the night nursery; their passions had flooded in. The only thing he could do was to get away, by the back stairs, and up through the area, and never come back.

He didn't think of the cold, of the need for food and sleep; for an hour it would seem quite possible to escape from people for ever.

He was wearing pajamas and bedroom slippers when he came up into the square, but there was no one to see him. It was that hour of the evening in a residential district when everyone is at the theater or at home. He climbed over the iron railings into the little garden: the plane-trees spread their large pale palms between him and the sky. It might have been an illimitable forest into which he had escaped. He crouched behind a trunk and the wolves retreated; it seemed to him between the little iron seat and the tree-trunk that no one would ever find him again. A kind of embittered happiness and self-pity made him cry; he was lost; there wouldn't be any more secrets to keep; he surrendered responsibility once and for all. Let grown-up people keep to their world and he would keep to his, safe in the small garden between the plane-trees.

Presently the door of 48 opened and Baines looked this way and that; then he signaled with his hand and Emmy came; it was as if they were only just in time for a train, they hadn't a chance of saying goodbye. She went quickly by like a face at a window swept past the platform, pale and unhappy and not wanting to go. Baines went in again and shut the door; the light was lit in the basement, and a policeman walked round the square, looking into the areas. You could tell how many families were at home by the lights behind the first-floor curtains.

Philip explored the garden: it didn't take long: a twenty-yard square of bushes and plane-trees, two iron seats and a gravel path, a padlocked gate at either end, a scuffle of old leaves. But he couldn't stay: something stirred in the bushes and two illuminated eyes peered out at him like a Serbian wolf, and he thought how terrible it would be if Mrs. Baines found him there. He'd have no time to climb the railings; she'd seize him from behind.

He left the square at the unfashionable end and was immediately among the fish-and-chip shops, the little stationers selling *Bagatelle*,[1] among the accommodation addresses and the dingy hotels with open doors. There were few people about because the pubs were open, but

---

[1] *Bagatelle* Trifles; sundry items.

a blowsy woman carrying a parcel called out to him across the street and the commissionaire outside a cinema would have stopped him if he hadn't crossed the road. He went deeper: you could go farther and lose yourself more completely here than among the plane-trees. On the fringe of the square he was in danger of being stopped and taken back: it was obvious where he belonged; but as he went deeper he lost the marks of his origin. It was a warm night: any child in those free-living parts might be expected to play truant from bed. He found a kind of camaraderie even among grown-up people; he might have been a neighbour's child as he went quickly by, but they weren't going to tell on him, they'd been young once themselves. He picked up a protective coating of dust from the pavements, of smuts from the trains which passed along the backs in a spray of fire. Once he was caught in a knot of children running away from something or somebody, laughing as they ran; he was whirled with them round a turning[1] and abandoned, with a sticky fruit-drop in his hand.

He couldn't have been more lost, but he hadn't the stamina to keep on. At first he feared that someone would stop him; after an hour he hoped that someone would. He couldn't find his way back, and in any case he was afraid of arriving home alone; he was afraid of Mrs. Baines, more afraid than he had ever been. Baines was his friend, but something had happened which gave Mrs. Baines all the power. He began to loiter on purpose to be noticed, but no one noticed him. Families were having a last breather on the doorsteps, the refuse bins had been put out and bits of cabbage stalks soiled his slippers. The air was full of voices, but he was cut off; these people were strangers and would always now be strangers; they were marked by Mrs. Baines and he shied away from them into a deep class-consciousness. He had been afraid of policemen, but now he wanted one to take him home; even Mrs. Baines could do nothing against a policeman. He sidled past a constable who was directing traffic, but he was too busy to pay him any attention. Philip sat down against a wall and cried.

It hadn't occurred to him that that was the easiest way, that all you had to do was to surrender, to show you were beaten and accept kindness … It was lavished on him at once by two women and a pawnbroker.

Another policeman appeared, a young man with a sharp incredulous face. He looked as if he noted everything he saw in pocket-books and drew conclusions. A woman offered to see Philip home, but he didn't trust her: she wasn't a match for Mrs. Baines immobile in the hall. He wouldn't give his address; he said he was afraid to go home. He had his way; he got his protection. "I'll take him to the station," the policeman said, and holding him awkwardly by the hand (he wasn't married; he had his career to make) he led him round the corner, up the stone stairs into the little bare over-heated room where Justice lived.

5

Justice waited behind a wooden counter on a high stool; it wore a heavy mustache; it was kindly and had six children ("three of them nippers like yourself"); it wasn't really interested in Philip, but it pretended to be, it wrote the address down and sent a constable to fetch a glass of milk. But the young constable was interested; he had a nose for things.

"Your home's on the telephone, I suppose," Justice said. "We'll ring them up and say you are safe. They'll fetch you very soon. What's your name, sonny?"

"Philip."

"Your other name?"

"I haven't got another name." He didn't want to be fetched; he wanted to be taken home by someone who would impress even Mrs. Baines. The constable watched him, watched the way he drank the milk, watched him when he winced away from questions.

"What made you run away? Playing truant, eh?"

"I don't know."

"You oughtn't to do it, young fellow. Think how anxious your father and mother will be."

"They are away."

"Well, your nurse."

"I haven't got one."

"Who looks after you, then?" The question went home. Philip saw Mrs. Baines coming up the stairs at him, the heap of black cotton in the hall. He began to cry.

"Now, now, now," the sergeant said. He didn't know what to do; he wished his wife were with him; even a policewoman might have been useful.

---

[1]    *turning*  A curve in the street.

"Don't you think it's funny," the constable said, "that there hasn't been an inquiry?"

"They think he's tucked up in bed."

"You are scared, aren't you?" the constable said. "What scared you?"

"I don't know."

"Somebody hurt you?"

"No."

"He's had bad dreams," the sergeant said. "Thought the house was on fire, I expect. I've brought up six of them. Rose is due back. She'll take him home."

"I want to go home with you," Philip said; he tried to smile at the constable, but the deceit was immature and unsuccessful.

"I'd better go," the constable said. "There may be something wrong."

"Nonsense," the sergeant said. "It's a woman's job. Tact is what you need. Here's Rose. Pull up your stockings, Rose. You're a disgrace to the Force. I've got a job of work for you." Rose shambled in: black cotton stockings drooping over her boots, a gawky Girl Guide manner, a hoarse hostile voice. "More tarts, I suppose."

"No, you've got to see this young man home." She looked at him owlishly.

"I won't go with her," Philip said. He began to cry again. "I don't like her."

"More of that womanly charm, Rose," the sergeant said. The telephone rang on his desk. He lifted the receiver. "What? What's that?" he said. "Number 48? You've got a doctor?" He put his hand over the telephone mouth. "No wonder this nipper wasn't reported," he said. "They've been too busy. An accident. Woman slipped on the stairs."

"Serious?" the constable asked. The sergeant mouthed at him; you didn't mention the word death before a child (didn't he know? he had six of them), you made noises in the throat, you grimaced, a complicated shorthand for a word of only five letters anyway.

"You'd better go, after all," he said, "and make a report. The doctor's there."

Rose shambled from the stove; pink apply-dapply cheeks, loose stockings. She stuck her hands behind her. Her large morgue-like mouth was full of blackened teeth. "You told me to take him and now just because

something interesting… I don't expect justice from a man…"

"Who's at the house?" the constable asked.

"The butler."

"You don't think," the constable said, "he saw…"

"Trust me," the sergeant said. "I've brought up six. I know 'em through and through. You can't teach me anything about children."

"He seemed scared about something."

"Dreams," the sergeant said.

"What name?"

"Baines."

"This Mr. Baines," the constable said to Philip, "you like him, eh? He's good to you?" They were trying to get something out of him; he was suspicious of the whole roomful of them; he said "yes" without conviction because he was afraid at any moment of more responsibilities, more secrets.

"And Mrs. Baines?"

"Yes."

They consulted together by the desk. Rose was hoarsely aggrieved; she was like a female impersonator, she bore her womanhood with an unnatural emphasis even while she scorned it in her creased stockings and her weather-exposed face. The charcoal shifted in the stove; the room was over-heated in the mild late summer evening. A notice on the wall described a body found in the Thames, or rather the body's clothes: wool vest, wool pants, wool shirt with blue stripes, size ten boots, blue serge suit worn at the elbows, fifteen and a half celluloid collar. They couldn't find anything to say about the body, except its measurements, it was just an ordinary body.

"Come along," the constable said. He was interested, he was glad to be going, but he couldn't help being embarrassed by his company, a small boy in pajamas. His nose smelt something, he didn't know what, but he smarted at the sight of the amusement they caused: the pubs had closed and the streets were full again of men making as long a day of it as they could. He hurried through the less frequented streets, chose the darker pavements, wouldn't loiter, and Philip wanted more and more to loiter, pulling at his hand, dragging with his feet. He dreaded the sight of Mrs. Baines waiting in the hall: he knew now that she was dead. The sergeant's mouthing had conveyed that; but she wasn't buried, she wasn't out of sight: he was going to see a dead person in the hall when the door opened.

The light was on in the basement, and to his relief the constable made for the area steps. Perhaps he wouldn't have to see Mrs. Baines at all. The constable knocked on the door because it was too dark to see the bell, and Baines answered. He stood there in the doorway of the neat bright basement room and you could see the sad complacent plausible sentence he had prepared wither at the sight of Philip; he hadn't expected Philip to return like that in the policeman's company. He had to begin thinking all over again; he wasn't a deceptive man. If it hadn't been for Emmy he would have been quite ready to let the truth lead him where it would.

"Mr. Baines?" the constable asked.

He nodded; he hadn't found the right words; he was daunted by the shrewd knowing face, the sudden appearance of Philip there.

"This little boy from here?"

"Yes," Baines said. Philip could tell that there was a message he was trying to convey, but he shut his mind to it. He loved Baines, but Baines had involved him in secrets, in fears he didn't understand. That was what happened when you loved—you got involved; and Philip extricated himself from life, from love, from Baines.

"The doctor's here," Baines said. He nodded at the door, moistened his mouth, kept his eyes on Philip, begging for something like a dog you can't understand. "There's nothing to be done. She slipped on these stone basement stairs. I was in here. I heard her fall." He wouldn't look at the notebook, at the constable's spidery writing which got a terrible lot on one page.

"Did the boy see anything?"

"He can't have done. I thought he was in bed. Hadn't he better go up? It's a shocking thing. O," Baines said, losing control, "it's a shocking thing for a child."

"She's through there?" the constable asked.

"I haven't moved her an inch," Baines said.

"He'd better then —"

"Go up the area and through the hall," Baines said, and again he begged dumbly like a dog: one more secret,

keep this secret, do this for old Baines, he won't ask another.

"Come along," the constable said. "I'll see you up to bed. You're a gentleman. You must come in the proper way through the front door like the master should. Or will you go along with him, Mr. Baines, while I see the doctor?"

"Yes," Baines said, "I'll go." He came across the room to Philip, begging, begging, all the way with his old soft stupid expression: this is Baines, the old Coaster; what about a palm-oil chop, eh?; a man's life; forty niggers; never used a gun; I tell you I couldn't help loving them; it wasn't what we call love, nothing we could understand. The messages flickered out from the last posts at the border, imploring, beseeching, reminding; this is your old friend Baines; what about elevenses;[1] a glass of ginger pop won't do you any harm; sausages; a long day. But the wires were cut, the messages just faded out into the vacancy of the scrubbed room in which there had never been a place where a man could hide his secrets.

"Come along, Phil, it's bedtime. We'll just go up the steps…" Tap, tap, tap, at the telegraph; you may get through, you can't tell, somebody may mend the right wire. "And in at the front door."

"No," Philip said, "no. I won't go. You can't make me go. I'll fight. I won't see her."

The constable turned on them quickly. "What's that? Why won't you go?"

"She's in the hall," Philip said. "I know she's in the hall. And she's dead. I won't see her."

"You moved her then?" the constable said to Baines. "All the way down here? You've been lying, eh? That means you had to tidy up… Were you alone?"

"Emmy," Philip said, "Emmy." He wasn't going to keep any more secrets: he was going to finish once and for all with everything, with Baines and Mrs. Baines and the grown-up life beyond him. "It was all Emmy's fault," he protested with a quaver which reminded Baines that after all he was only a child; it had been hopeless to expect help there; he was a child; he didn't understand what it all meant; he couldn't read this shorthand of terror; he'd had a long day and he was

---

[1] *elevenses*  Light morning meal usually consisting of cake or bread and tea.

tired out. You could see him dropping asleep where he stood against the dresser, dropping back into the comfortable nursery peace. You couldn't blame him. When he woke in the morning, he'd hardly remember a thing.

"Out with it," the constable said, addressing Baines with professional ferocity, "who is she?" just as the old man sixty years later startled his secretary, his only watcher, asking, "Who is she? Who is she?" dropping lower and lower to death, passing on the way perhaps the image of Baines: Baines hopeless, Baines letting his head drop, Baines "coming clean."

—1936

## IN CONTEXT

### Reflections on Writing and Filmmaking

In the following excerpts Greene comments on how *The Basement Room* was brought to the screen in 1948 as *The Fallen Idol*, and on the forces that shaped his life as a writer.

### "Preface" to *The Fallen Idol* (1992)

*The Fallen Idol* unlike *The Third Man* was not written for the films. That is only one of many reasons why I prefer it. It was published as *The Basement Room* in 1935 and conceived on the cargo steamer on the way home from Liberia to relieve the tedium of the voyage. *The Fallen Idol* is, of course, a meaningless title for the original story printed here, and even for the film it always reminded me of the problem paintings of John Collier.[1] It was chosen by the distributors.

I was surprised when Carol Reed suggested that I should collaborate with him on a film of *The Basement Room* because it seemed to me that the subject was unfilmable—a murder committed by the most sympathetic character and an unhappy ending which would certainly have imperilled the £250,000 that films nowadays cost.

However, we went ahead, and in the conferences that ensued the story was quietly changed, so that the subject no longer concerned a small boy who unwittingly betrayed his best friend to the police, but dealt instead with a small boy who believed that his friend was a murderer and nearly procured his arrest by telling lies in his defence. I think this, especially with Reed's handling, was a good subject, but the reader must not be surprised by not finding it the subject of the original story.

Why was the scene changed to an Embassy? This was Reed's idea since we both felt that the large Belgravia house was already in these post-war years a period piece, and we did not want to make an historical film. I fought the solution for a while and then wholeheartedly concurred.

It is always difficult to remember which of us made which change in the original story except in certain details. For example, the cross-examination of the girl beside the bed that she had used with Baines was mine: the witty interruption of the man who came to wind the clock was Reed's. The snake was mine (I have always liked snakes), and for a short while it met with Reed's sympathetic opposition.

Of one thing about both these films I have complete certainty, that their success is due to Carol Reed, the only director I know with that particular warmth of human sympathy, the extraordinary feeling for the right face for the right part, the exactitude of cutting, and not least important the power of sympathizing with an author's worries and an ability to guide him.

---

[1]  *John Collier*  Portrait painter and illustrator (1850–1934).

from "Interview with Marie-Françoise Allain" (1983)

*"Divided loyalty" made its appearance between childhood and adolescence. What was there before?*

A state of happiness. My childhood was extremely peaceful until thirteen, when I was taken away from home and sent to boarding school. My father was still on hand, as he was our headmaster, but the contrast was all the sharper because I had always known him in a happy atmosphere within a large family. We were self-sufficient—six brothers and sisters and six cousins who lived only a few hundred yards away: so there were twelve of us children of varying ages.

At Berkhamsted the Greenes were very numerous. They represented practically one per cent of the population, for you had to allow not only for the dozen children and their four parents but also for several aunts. We didn't need anyone else....

*You desired solitude, but at the same time you mention this terrible sense of ostracism which afflicted you. Just what did you want?*

Solitude has never bothered me. I've done most of my travelling alone. Emotional loneliness didn't worry me either. I loved and admired my mother precisely because she never trespassed on my privacy.

There was probably some trauma when I was taken away from my family. I could scarcely stand my schoolfellows or children of my age. I had my sisters and my brothers, who were all I needed. Today I'm still very close to my younger sister and my younger brother.

*And your children?*

Well, not in that sense. I think my books are my children. I'm very fond of my son and daughter; but just as I didn't want my parents meddling in my private life, I don't want to intrude into theirs. I simply want to be there if they need me. The only period of enforced separation from my children was when they were small, during the war. I evacuated them to Oxford, while I was in London, then Sierra Leone, then London again. It had to be so; first London was under the Blitz, then the V.1's and the V.2's, and I was working for MI6[1] from 1941 to '44.

*Do you not feel guilty when you confess that your books are your children?*

Not in the least. Perhaps it's an unfortunate admission, but it's every writer's obsession, and it will out. I'm not a part-timer!

I'm sure I didn't initially make a conscious choice of isolation. I don't know what induced me to conceal from my parents the fact that I could read. It may have been an innate penchant for secrecy, or it may have been a very rational fear of their realizing that I was big enough to be thrown into the world of school. I was six or seven—very late for my age. I remember when I received an honorary degree at Cambridge, I met an old scholar who was receiving the same award with me—Dr. Dover Wilson, the greatest living authority on Shakespeare. He had known my parents; he turned to me and whispered, "To think that they were so worried about you because you were taking so long to learn to read!" I had managed to keep it a secret for a few months ... until the day when my mother gave me a book to pass the time on a train journey, and I kept it shut too obviously, fixing my eye with suspicious obstinacy on the cover with its colour illustration.

---

[1]   *MI6*   The Secret Intelligence Service.

Later, this impulse towards introversion would drive me to spend hours hiding on Berkhamsted Common. I was a past master in the art of playing truant. Banishment, whether enforced or voluntary, has certainly sparked the theme of escape in my books, as in *The Man Within* and even in my first, unpublished, novel which dealt with the black child of white parents, who was himself a black sheep. . . .

*Have your childhood and adolescence become determining factors for you as a writer?*

The Jesuits say, "Give me a child till he's sixteen, and he's mine for life." Everything that can happen to a person, I think, is determined in the first sixteen years of his life. The books I liked best in my childhood, those which really influenced me (I don't mean from a technical viewpoint) were not the works of Turgenev or Dostoyevsky, the great discoveries of one's adult life. I loved cloak-and-dagger novels, novels of adventure, and I believe that in a way it's adventure novels I'm writing today.

My marked inclination towards melodrama stems from that adolescent reading. I've only avoided melodrama in one or two books, *The End of the Affair* and *Travels with my Aunt*. By melodrama I mean a measure of violence in the action. I must still confess to a preference for authors now rated of secondary importance, Stanley Weyman, John Buchan, Rider Haggard. I always like to pay tribute to them. When I published my *Collected Essays*, in which I devoted several chapters to them, I was in a way discharging a debt, for it was they who instilled into me this passion for writing.

# PHILIP LARKIN
## 1922 – 1985

Although Philip Larkin published two novels in his lifetime as well as several other nonfiction works, his reputation as one of the most important figures in twentieth-century British literature rests on his poetry. His accessible style and straightforward language; the commentary he provided on Britain's changing post-war status; and above all the extraordinary skill with which he crafted poetic expressions of emotions widely shared (if not always expressed) made him one of the most popular poets of his time. Though often described as anti-social, Larkin was a witty conversationalist, and he maintained several relationships that spanned most of his adult life. His work is often (and

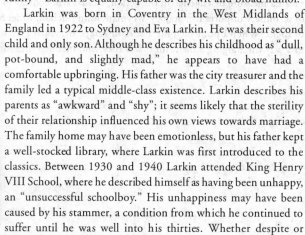

rightly) described as bleakly pessimistic, and frequently touches on themes of solitude and mortality. Yet his poems are also often funny—Larkin is equally capable of dry wit and broad humor.

Larkin was born in Coventry in the West Midlands of England in 1922 to Sydney and Eva Larkin. He was their second child and only son. Although he describes his childhood as "dull, pot-bound, and slightly mad," he appears to have had a comfortable upbringing. His father was the city treasurer and the family led a typical middle-class existence. Larkin describes his parents as "awkward" and "shy"; it seems likely that the sterility of their relationship influenced his own views towards marriage. The family home may have been emotionless, but his father kept a well-stocked library, where Larkin was first introduced to the classics. Between 1930 and 1940 Larkin attended King Henry VIII School, where he described himself as having been unhappy, an "unsuccessful schoolboy." His unhappiness may have been caused by his stammer, a condition from which he continued to suffer until he was well into his thirties. Whether despite or because of his unhappiness, Larkin did begin writing during this period; his first poem was published in the school paper, *The Coventrian*, in 1934, when he was 12.

In 1940, Larkin sent one of his poems to the literary magazine *The Listener*, which accepted and published "Ultimatum" in November of that year. In the same year he entered Oxford to study English, and the experience of university turned out to be a great stimulus for him in terms both of writing and of personal friendships. It was while he was at Oxford that he met Kingsley Amis, some years later to become famous as a novelist; the two remained fast friends for life. (Although they often showed each other their work in its early stages, it was a love of jazz above all that first drew them together.) Larkin developed in these years a distrust of the Modernist notion that twentieth-century literature should express the difficulties of twentieth-century life, and gained an appreciation for a plainer style of writing. He greatly admired W.H. Auden and W.B. Yeats, and tried for years to mimic Yeats's writing in particular.

Larkin graduated in 1943 and returned to his parents' house in Coventry that year, his poor eyesight making him ineligible to fight in World War II. After failing the civil service exam twice, Larkin answered an advertisement in the paper for a librarian in Wellington, Shropshire. He remained in the profession for the rest of his life, stating that "librarianship suits me." The solitude of the work as well as the regular hours gave him sufficient time to pursue his writing; during this period he produced his first volume of poetry, *The North Ship*, published at his own expense in 1945. It went largely unnoticed. The following two years produced Larkin's only novels, *Jill* in 1946 and *A Girl in Winter* in 1947. Larkin later described the novels as "over-sized poems"; their lack of success encouraged him to give up the form, and from that point onwards he concentrated on poetry. While in Shropshire Larkin also qualified professionally as a librarian; from 1955 until his death he worked as a librarian at the University of Hull.

In the 1950s Larkin began to be associated with a literary group known simply as "The Movement." Its members included Amis as well as Bruce Montgomery, Thom Gunn, and Donald Davie. They were all representatives of a new style of British writing that was anti-romantic, sardonic, and concerned with everyday British life. In Larkin's case, it was *The Less Deceived* (1955), and the poem "Church Going" in particular, that solidified his poetic reputation as an anti-romantic poet. With this volume Larkin shook off the influence of Yeats and established his own style and voice. Spare in their imagery, and typically with a strong but unobtrusive framework of rhythm and rhyme, the poems often chronicle the place of choice or fate in a person's life. Loneliness, misunderstanding, and deception are central themes in Larkin's work, and the aesthetic act often seemed his only bulwark against despair. "People say I'm very negative and I suppose I am," he admitted, "but the impulse for producing a poem is never negative; the most negative poem in the world is a very positive thing to have done."

*The Less Deceived* was followed by *The Whitsun Weddings* and *High Windows* in 1964 and 1974 respectively; the poems in these later collections are largely in the same vein as Larkin's earlier work but are less frequently ironic, more often directly revealing of emotion. Larkin also occasionally adopted a different voice in which the presence of rhyme is more obtrusive, the thoughts bluntly pointed, and the tone loudly sardonic. Two of the poems from *High Windows* written in this tone —"This Be The Verse" and "Annus Mirabilis"—caused something of a sensation on the book's publication, and have remained among the most often quoted of Larkin's poems.

In addition to his poetry, Larkin was engaged with other literary pursuits. From 1961 to 1971 he published a regular jazz column in *The Daily Telegraph*. Some of these columns were later reproduced in *All What Jazz*, published in 1970. He was editor of the *Oxford Book of Twentieth-Century Verse* (1973), and his nonfiction writing was collected in *Required Writing* (1983). Larkin won the Queen's Gold Medal for Poetry in 1965, was appointed a Companion of the British Empire in 1975, and received seven honorary doctorates. He was offered the position of British Poet Laureate in 1984, but turned it down because he did not want the media attention with which it was associated. Although Larkin had a number of romantic relationships, he never married, and once said that "two can live as stupidly as one." (The publication in 1992 of Larkin's *Selected Letters*, which contains derogatory language about women, as well as slurs against socialists and various racial groups, led many to attribute Larkin's views on marriage as much to his tendency towards misogyny as to his innate pessimism with regard to the human condition.) Larkin's poetic output was much reduced in the 1980s; his last major poem, "Aubade," was published in the *Times Literary Supplement* in 1977. Larkin was admitted to hospital in 1985, suffering from cancer, and had his esophagus removed. He died later that year.

⌘ ⌘ ⌘

## Days

What are days for?
  Days are where we live.
They come, they wake us
Time and time over.
5   They are to be happy in:
  Where can we live but days?

Ah, solving that question
Brings the priest and the doctor
In their long coats
10   Running over the fields.
  —1953

## Church Going

Once I am sure there's nothing going on
I step inside, letting the door thud shut.
Another church: matting, seats, and stone,
And little books; sprawlings of flowers, cut
5   For Sunday, brownish now; some brass and stuff
Up at the holy end; the small neat organ;
And a tense, musty, unignorable silence,
Brewed God knows how long. Hatless, I take off
My cycle-clips in awkward reverence,

10   Move forward, run my hand around the font.[1]
From where I stand, the roof looks almost new—
Cleaned, or restored? Someone would know: I don't.
Mounting the lectern, I peruse a few
Hectoring large-scale verses, and pronounce
15   "Here endeth" much more loudly than I'd meant.
The echoes snigger briefly. Back at the door
I sign the book, donate an Irish sixpence,
Reflect the place was not worth stopping for.

Yet stop I did: in fact I often do,
20   And always end much at a loss like this,
Wondering what to look for; wondering, too,
When churches fall completely out of use
What we shall turn them into, if we shall keep

A few cathedrals chronically on show,
25   Their parchment, plate and pyx[2] in locked cases,
And let the rest rent-free to rain and sheep.
Shall we avoid them as unlucky places?

Or, after dark, will dubious women come
To make their children touch a particular stone;
30   Pick simples° for a cancer; or on some          *medicinal herbs*
Advised night see walking a dead one?
Power of some sort or other will go on
In games, in riddles, seemingly at random;
But superstition, like belief, must die,
35   And what remains when disbelief has gone?
Grass, weedy pavement, brambles, buttress, sky,

A shape less recognisable each week,
A purpose more obscure. I wonder who
Will be the last, the very last, to seek
40   This place for what it was; one of the crew
That tap and jot and know what rood-lofts° were?   *church galleries*
Some ruin-bibber, randy for antique,
Or Christmas-addict, counting on a whiff
Of gown-and-bands and organ-pipes and myrrh?
45   Or will he be my representative,

Bored, uninformed, knowing the ghostly silt
Dispersed, yet tending to this cross of ground
Through suburb scrub because it held unspilt
So long and equably what since is found
50   Only in separation—marriage, and birth,
And death, and thoughts of these—for which was built
This special shell? For, though I've no idea
What this accoutred frowsty° barn is worth,          *stuffy*
It pleases me to stand in silence here;

55   A serious house on serious earth it is,
In whose blent air all our compulsions meet,
Are recognised, and robed as destinies.
And that much never can be obsolete,
Since someone will forever be surprising
60   A hunger in himself to be more serious,
And gravitating with it to this ground,

---

[1] *font* Baptismal receptacle.

[2] *pyx* Vessel in which the bread of the Eucharist is kept.

Which, he once heard, was proper to grow wise in,
If only that so many dead lie round.
—1954

## Talking in Bed

Talking in bed ought to be easiest,
Lying together there goes back so far,
An emblem of two people being honest.

Yet more and more time passes silently.
5    Outside, the wind's incomplete unrest
Builds and disperses clouds about the sky,

And dark towns heap up on the horizon.
None of this cares for us. Nothing shows why
At this unique distance from isolation

10   It becomes still more difficult to find
Words at once true and kind,
Or not untrue and not unkind.
—1960

## Dockery and Son

"Dockery was junior to you,
    Wasn't he?" said the Dean. "His son's here now."
Death-suited, visitant, I nod. "And do
You keep in touch with—" Or remember how
5    Black-gowned, unbreakfasted, and still half-tight
We used to stand before that desk, to give
"Our version" of "these incidents last night"?
I try the door of where I used to live:

Locked. The lawn spreads dazzlingly wide.
10   A known bell chimes. I catch my train, ignored.
Canal and clouds and colleges subside
Slowly from view. But Dockery, good Lord,
Anyone up[1] today must have been born
In '43, when I was twenty-one.

15   If he was younger, did he get this son
At nineteen, twenty? Was he that withdrawn

High-collared public[2]-schoolboy, sharing rooms
With Cartwright who was killed? Well, it just shows
How much ... How little ... Yawning, I suppose
20   I fell asleep, waking at the fumes
And furnace-glares of Sheffield, where I changed,[3]
And ate an awful pie, and walked along
The platform to its end to see the ranged
Joining and parting lines reflect a strong

25   Unhindered moon. To have no son, no wife,
No house or land still seemed quite natural.
Only a numbness registered the shock
Of finding out how much had gone of life,
How widely from the others. Dockery, now:
30   Only nineteen, he must have taken stock
Of what he wanted, and been capable
Of ... No, that's not the difference: rather, how

Convinced he was he should be added to!
Why did he think adding meant increase?
35   To me it was dilution. Where do these
Innate assumptions come from? Not from what
We think truest, or most want to do:
Those warp tight-shut, like doors. They're more a style
Our lives bring with them: habit for a while,
40   Suddenly they harden into all we've got

And how we got it; looked back on, they rear
Like sand-clouds, thick and close, embodying
For Dockery a son, for me nothing,
Nothing with all a son's harsh patronage.
45   Life is first boredom, then fear.
Whether or not we use it, it goes,

---

1   *Anyone up*   To refer to being "up" at Oxford or Cambridge was a common colloquialism for attending university in those towns. Both of these ancient universities are composed of many colleges.

2   *public*   In Britain the term "public school" came into use in the late sixteenth century to distinguish grammar schools operated by private individuals or church authorities from those open to a broader public. Such schools were (and are) fee-charging institutions attended overwhelmingly by privileged students; they are thus similar to *private* schools in such countries as the United States and Canada.

3   *Sheffield, where I changed*   Larkin, who attended Oxford University, was for most of his adult life a librarian at the University of Hull. When traveling between Oxford and Hull by train one would normally change trains at Sheffield.

And leaves what something hidden from us chose,
And age, and then the only end of age.
—1963

### Annus Mirabilis[1]

Sexual intercourse began
In nineteen sixty-three
(Which was rather late for me)—
Between the end of the *Chatterley* ban[2]
5    And the Beatles' first LP.

Up till then there'd only been
A sort of bargaining,
A wrangle for a ring,
A shame that started at sixteen
10    And spread to everything.

Then all at once the quarrel sank:
Everyone felt the same,
And every life became
A brilliant breaking of the bank,
15    A quite unlosable game.

So life was never better than
In nineteen sixty-three (Though just too late for me)—
Between the end of the *Chatterley* ban
And the Beatles' first LP.
—1967

### High Windows

When I see a couple of kids
And guess he's fucking her and she's
Taking pills or wearing a diaphragm,
I know this is paradise

5    Everyone old has dreamed of all their lives—
Bonds and gestures pushed to one side
Like an outdated combine harvester,
And everyone young going down the long slide

To happiness, endlessly. I wonder if
10    Anyone looked at me, forty years back,
And thought, *That'll be the life;*
*No God any more, or sweating in the dark*

*About hell and that, or having to hide*
*What you think of the priest. He*
15    *And his lot will all go down the long slide*
*Like free bloody birds.* And immediately

Rather than words comes the thought of high windows:
The sun-comprehending glass,
And beyond it, the deep blue air, that shows
20    Nothing, and is nowhere, and is endless.
—1967

### This Be The Verse

They fuck you up, your mum and dad.
They may not mean to, but they do.
They fill you with the faults they had
And add some extra, just for you.

5    But they were fucked up in their turn
By fools in old-style hats and coats,
Who half the time were soppy-stern
And half at one another's throats.

Man hands on misery to man.
10    It deepens like a coastal shelf.
Get out as early as you can,
And don't have any kids yourself.
—1971

---

1    *Annus Mirabilis*    Latin: wondrous year.

2    *the Chatterley ban*    D.H. Lawrence's novel *Lady Chatterley's Lover*
was banned in both the UK and USA on the grounds of obscenity;
it contained four-letter words and descriptions of sexual activity that
were, for the time, quite explicit. On 2 November 1960, Penguin
Books won an obscenity trial over the issue, and the ban was lifted
in the UK.

## Vers de Société[1]

My wife and I have asked a crowd of craps
To come and waste their time and ours; perhaps
You'd care to join us? In a pig's arse, friend.
Day comes to an end.
5   The gas fire breathes, the trees are darkly swayed.
And so Dear Warlock-Williams: I'm afraid—

Funny how hard it is to be alone.
I could spend half my evenings, if I wanted,
Holding a glass of washing sherry, canted°   *obliquely pushed*
10   Over to catch the drivel of some bitch
Who's read nothing but Which;[2]
Just think of all the spare time that has flown

Straight into nothingness by being filled
With forks and faces, rather than repaid
15   Under a lamp, hearing the noise of wind,
And looking out to see the moon thinned
To an air-sharpened blade.
A life, and yet how sternly it's instilled

All solitude is selfish. No one now
20   Believes the hermit with his gown and dish[3]
Talking to God (who's gone too); the big wish
Is to have people nice to you, which means
Doing it back somehow.
Virtue is social. Are, then, these routines

25   Playing at goodness, like going to church?
Something that bores us, something we don't do well
(Asking that ass about his fool research)
But try to feel, because, however crudely,
It shows us what should be?
30   Too subtle, that. Too decent, too. Oh hell,

Only the young can be alone freely.
The time is shorter now for company,

---

[1]   *Vers de Société*   Poem about social life.

[2]   *Which*   British consumer product testing magazine.

[3]   Followers of an important strain of hermitic Christianity in medieval Europe who wore gowns of sackcloth or rough material (intended to be uncomfortable) and held out their dishes to solicit alms from other Christians.

And sitting by a lamp more often brings
Not peace, but other things.
35   Beyond the light stand failure and remorse
Whispering Dear Warlock-Williams: Why, of course—
—1971

## The Old Fools

What do they think has happened, the old fools,
To make them like this? Do they somehow suppose
It's more grown-up when your mouth hangs open and
drools
And you keep on pissing yourself, and can't remember
5   Who called this morning? Or that, if they only chose,
They could alter things back to when they danced all night,
Or went to their wedding, or sloped arms some September?
Or do they fancy there's really been no change,
And they've always behaved as if they were crippled or
tight,
10   Or sat through days of thin continuous dreaming
Watching light move? If they don't (and they can't),
it's strange;
            Why aren't they screaming?

At death, you break up: the bits that were you
Start speeding away from each other for ever
15   With no one to see. It's only oblivion, true:
We had it before, but then it was going to end,
And was all the time merging with a unique endeavour
To bring to bloom the million-petalled flower
Of being here. Next time you can't pretend
20   There'll be anything else. And these are the first signs:
Not knowing how, not hearing who, the power
Of choosing gone. Their looks show that they're for it:
Ash hair, toad hands, prune face dried into lines—
            How can they ignore it?

25   Perhaps being old is having lighted rooms
Inside your head, and people in them, acting.
People you know, yet can't quite name; each looms
Like a deep loss restored, from known doors turning,
Setting down a lamp, smiling from a stair, extracting
30   A known book from the shelves; or sometimes only
The rooms themselves, chairs and a fire burning,

The blown bush at the window, or the sun's
Faint friendliness on the wall some lonely
Rain-ceased midsummer evening. That is where they
    live:
35 Not here and now, but where all happened once.
           This is why they give

An air of baffled absence, trying to be there
Yet being here. For the rooms grow farther, leaving
Incompetent cold, the constant wear and tear
40 Of taken breath, and them crouching below
Extinction's alp, the old fools, never perceiving
How near it is. This must be what keeps them quiet:
The peak that stays in view wherever we go
For them is rising ground. Can they never tell
45 What is dragging them back, and how it will end?
Not at night? Not when the strangers come? Never,
    throughout
The whole hideous inverted childhood? Well,
        We shall find out.

—1973

## Aubade [1]

I work all day, and get half-drunk at night.
Waking at four to soundless dark, I stare.
In time the curtain-edges will grow light.
Till then I see what's really always there:
5 Unresting death, a whole day nearer now,
Making all thought impossible but how
And where and when I shall myself die.
Arid interrogation: yet the dread
Of dying, and being dead,
10 Flashes afresh to hold and horrify.

The mind blanks at the glare. Not in remorse
—The good not done, the love not given, time
Torn off unused—nor wretchedly because
An only life can take so long to climb

15 Clear of its wrong beginnings, and may never;
But at the total emptiness for ever,
The sure extinction that we travel to
And shall be lost in always. Not to be here,
Not to be anywhere,
20 And soon; nothing more terrible, nothing more true.

This is a special way of being afraid
No trick dispels. Religion used to try,
That vast moth-eaten musical brocade
Created to pretend we never die,
25 And specious° stuff that says *No rational being*    *misleading*
*Can fear a thing it will not feel,* not seeing
That this is what we fear—no sight, no sound,
No touch or taste or smell, nothing to think with,
Nothing to love or link with,
30 The anaesthetic from which none come round.

And so it stays just on the edge of vision,
A small unfocused blur, a standing chill
That slows each impulse down to indecision.
Most things may never happen: this one will,
35 And realisation of it rages out
In furnace-fear when we are caught without
People or drink. Courage is no good:
It means not scaring others. Being brave
Lets no one off the grave.
40 Death is no different whined at than withstood.

Slowly light strengthens, and the room takes shape.
It stands plain as a wardrobe, what we know,
Have always known, know that we can't escape,
Yet can't accept. One side will have to go.
45 Meanwhile telephones crouch, getting ready to ring
In locked-up offices, and all the uncaring
Intricate rented world begins to rouse.
The sky is white as clay, with no sun.
Work has to be done.
50 Postmen like doctors go from house to house.
—1977

---

[1] *aubade* From the Old French "alba," an early morning song or poem, the motif of which is usually a call for lovers to wake before parting.

# ALAN SILLITOE
## b. 1928

Novelist Alan Sillitoe exploded onto the 1950s literary scene with his vivid portrayals of working-class life in his hometown of Nottingham. His views of the attitudes, perspectives, and conditions of the working class broke new ground in English fiction; it was said that his first work alone (*Saturday Night and Sunday Morning*, 1958) assured him a place in the history of the English novel. Sillitoe has since gone on to produce over 50 novels, as well as poems, children's books, travel fiction, essays, and an autobiography, *Life Without Armour* (1995). Like D.H. Lawrence, another Nottingham novelist to whom he is often compared, Sillitoe's fiction is compelling in the vitality of its characters, the authenticity of their dialogue and transcribed thoughts, and the intimately rendered details of their everyday lives.

Sillitoe was himself born into a poor, laboring family in 1928. He grew up during the Depression of the 1930s; his father was unemployed and he and his family often went hungry as they moved from one overcrowded slum house to another. Sillitoe left school at 14

to earn money at a variety of factory jobs before joining the Air Training Corps during World War II. In 1946 the Royal Air Force (RAF) posted him to Malaya as a wireless operator where, in order to endure the long shifts in his radio hut, he read extensively and began to experiment with writing stories. His voracious reading continued after he completed his post in Malaya, when he was diagnosed with tuberculosis and was bed-ridden for over a year while recovering. The reading he did during this time—including Homer, Joseph Conrad, James Joyce, Fyodor Dostoevsky, and Aldous Huxley—changed both his view of the world and his desire to make the Air Force his career.

In 1950 Sillitoe, discharged from the RAF, returned home to Nottingham determined to make a living as a writer. There he met the American poet Ruth Fainlight, whom he later married. In 1952 the couple decided to move to Majorca, where they could live cheaply on Sillitoe's RAF pension and pursue their separate writing careers. After several unsuccessful publication attempts, Sillitoe released his first novel, *Saturday Night and Sunday Morning*, in 1958.

With its belligerent, factory-working hero Arthur Seaton, *Saturday Night and Sunday Morning* was seen by critics and reviewers of the time as fitting into a then-current movement in British literature—referred to as the "Angry Young Man" phenomenon—that focused on working-class, strongly masculine heroes and their hostility towards social norms and institutions. Kingsley Amis's novel *Lucky Jim* (1954), John Osborne's play *Look Back in Anger* (1956), and John Braine's novel *Room at the Top* (1957) were three other works that helped to define the Angry Young Man genre. (The term was often used in ways that conflated the protagonist with the authors of the literary works.) At the time, the context of these works was shockingly visceral: fighting, drinking, swearing, sexual conquests, and manual labor were often foregrounded. These works gained a wide readership, less on account of the crudity of much of their story material, though, than as a result of their success in articulating a sense of futility, dissatisfaction, and impatience with tradition that was shared by much of Britain after the war.

In 1945 a Labour government had been elected with a majority in the House of Commons for the first time in British history. Many had assumed that this event signaled the beginning of a much-anticipated social revolution. But the slowness of the British economy to recover after the war limited the government's ability to fund new initiatives, class differences persisted, and life for too many remained a drab and depressing struggle. In this environment the violence and destruction depicted by the Angry Young Men, whose protagonists saw themselves as participants in a life-long battle between those with power and those without, had wide appeal. Many of their works were bestsellers, and several were also made into successful films, including Sillitoe's *Saturday Night and Sunday Morning* and the long short story *The Loneliness of the Long-Distance Runner* (1959). The latter work, set in a reformatory, concerns the seemingly unbridgeable gap between the lower classes and the rest of British society. Though they share many of the same ambitions and visions of glory, the lower-class boys in the story have been raised according to an opposing set of morals and values that no amount of schooling, punishment, or imprisonment will persuade them to renounce. Sillitoe shows the reform system as only further solidifying these class differences and rendering communication virtually impossible.

Though their work in the 1950s had much in common, the subsequent work of the Angry Young Men diverged widely. Sillitoe's fiction expanded out of its original working-class, male-centered, Nottingham confines; though he has continued occasionally to set his works in Nottingham, Sillitoe has also taken readers as far away as Malaysia and Algeria, and has written from the perspective of both male and female characters from diverse backgrounds and social classes. Many of his Nottingham novels explore the same family of characters, the Seatons, but Sillitoe has expanded his view of the family, documenting their changes through time and working towards his goal of an entire *comédie humaine* set in Nottingham. His novel *A Man of His Time* (2004) even blends biography and fiction as real members of Sillitoe's mother's family—examined in his biographical *Raw Material* (1972)—interact with the fictional Seatons.

Whatever the form or setting of his work, Sillitoe continues to explore the struggle of individuals to assert their identity in the face of an often-hostile world, and to dissect society as a whole through vivid portrayals of everyday people and daily events.

⌘⌘⌘

## The Loneliness of the Long-Distance Runner

As soon as I got to Borstal[1] they made me a long-distance cross-country runner. I suppose they thought I was just the build for it because I was long and skinny for my age (and still am) and in any case I didn't mind it much, to tell you the truth, because running had always been made much of in our family, especially running away from the police. I've always been a good runner, quick and with a big stride as well, the only trouble being that no matter how fast I run, and I did a very fair lick even though I do say so myself, it didn't stop me getting caught by the cops after that bakery job.

You might think it a bit rare, having long-distance cross-country runners in Borstal, thinking that the first thing a long-distance cross-country runner would do when they set him loose at them fields and woods would be to run as far away from the place as he could get on a bellyful of Borstal slumgullion[2]—but you're wrong,

---

[1]  *Borstal*  Reformatory for juvenile offenders. The term refers to the reformatory at Borstal where the methods used at British reformatories were first established.

[2]  *slumgullion*  Watery stew of meat and vegetables.

and I'll tell you why. The first thing is that them bastards over us aren't as daft as they most of the time look, and for another thing I'm not so daft as I would look if I tried to make a break for it on my long-distance running, because to abscond and then get caught is nothing but a mug's game, and I'm not falling for it. Cunning is what counts in this life, and even that you've got to use in the slyest way you can; I'm telling you straight: they're cunning, and I'm cunning. If only "them" and "us" had the same ideas we'd get on like a house on fire, but they don't see eye to eye with us and we don't see eye to eye with them, so that's how it stands and how it will always stand. The one fact is that all of us are cunning, and because of this there's no love lost between us. So the thing is that they know I won't try to get away from them: they sit there like spiders in that crumbly manor house, perched like jumped-up jackdaws on the roof, watching out over the drives and fields like German generals from the tops of tanks. And even when I jog-trot on behind a wood and they can't see me anymore they know my sweeping-brush head will bob along that hedge-top in an hour's time and that I'll report to the bloke on the gate. Because when on a raw and frosty morning I get up at five o'clock and stand shivering my belly off on the stone floor and all the rest still have another hour to snooze before the bells go, I slink downstairs through all the corridors to the big outside door with a permit running-card in my fist, I feel like the first and last man on the world, both at once, if you can believe what I'm trying to say. I feel like the first man because I've hardly got a stitch on and am sent against the frozen fields in a shimmy and shorts—even the first poor bastard dropped on to the earth in midwinter knew how to make a suit of leaves, or how to skin a pterodactyl for a topcoat. But there I am, frozen stiff, with nothing to get me warm except a couple of hours' long-distance running before breakfast, not even a slice of bread-and-sheepdip.[1] They're training me up fine for the big sports day when all the pig-faced snotty-nosed dukes and ladies—who can't add two and two together and would mess themselves like loonies if they didn't have slavies to beck-and-call—come and make speeches to us about sports being just the thing to get us

leading an honest life and keep our itching finger-ends off them shop locks and safe handles and hairgrips to open gas meters. They give us a bit of blue ribbon and a cup for a prize after we've shagged ourselves out running or jumping, like race horses, only we don't get so well looked-after as race horses, that's the only thing.

So there I am, standing in the doorway in shimmy and shorts, not even a dry crust in my guts, looking out at frosty flowers on the ground. I suppose you think this is enough to make me cry? Not likely. Just because I feel like the first bloke in the world wouldn't make me bawl. It makes me feel fifty times better than when I'm cooped up in that dormitory with three hundred others. No, it's sometimes when I stand there feeling like the last man in the world that I don't feel so good. I feel like the last man in the world because I think that all those three hundred sleepers behind me are dead. They sleep so well I think that every scruffy head's kicked the bucket in the night and I'm the only one left, and when I look out into the bushes and frozen ponds I have the feeling that it's going to get colder and colder until everything I can see, meaning my red arms as well, is going to be covered with a thousand miles of ice, all the earth, right up to the sky and over every bit of land and sea. So I try to kick this feeling out and act like I'm the first man on earth. And that makes me feel good, so as soon as I'm steamed up enough to get this feeling in me, I take a flying leap out of the doorway, and off I trot.

I'm in Essex. It's supposed to be a good Borstal, at least that's what the governor said to me when I got here from Nottingham. "We want to trust you while you are in this establishment," he said, smoothing out his newspaper with lily-white workless hands, while I read the big words upside down: *Daily Telegraph.* "If you play ball with us, we'll play ball with you." (Honest to God, you'd have thought it was going to be one long tennis match.) "We want hard honest work and we want good athletics," he said as well. "And if you give us both these things you can be sure we'll do right by you and send you back into the world an honest man." Well, I could have died laughing, especially when straight after this I hear the barking sergeant-major's voice calling me and two others to attention and marching us off like we was Grenadier Guards. And when the governor kept saying how "we" wanted you to do this, and "we"

---

[1] *sheepdip*  The fat and juice left in the pan after meat has been cooked, often soaked up with a piece of bread and eaten.

wanted you to do that, I kept looking round for the other blokes, wondering how many of them there was. Of course, I knew there were thousands of them, but as far as I knew only one was in the room. And there *are* thousands of them, all over the poxeaten country, in shops, offices, railway stations, cars, houses, pubs —In-law blokes like you and them, all on the watch for Outlaw blokes like me and us—and waiting to 'phone for the coppers as soon as we make a false move. And it'll always be there, I'll tell you that now, because I haven't finished making all my false moves yet, and I dare say I won't until I kick the bucket. If the In-laws are hoping to stop me making false moves they're wasting their time. They might as well stand me up against a wall and let fly with a dozen rifles. That's the only way they'll stop me, and a few million others. Because I've been doing a lot of thinking since coming here. They can spy on us all day to see if we're pulling our puddings and if we're working good or doing our "athletics" but they can't make an X-ray of our guts to find out what we're telling ourselves. I've been asking myself all sorts of questions, and thinking about my life up to now. And I like doing all this. It's a treat. It passes the time away and don't make Borstal seem half so bad as the boys in our street used to say it was. And this long-distance running lark is the best of all, because it makes me think so good that I learn things even better than when I'm on my bed at night. And apart from that, what with thinking so much while I'm running I'm getting to be one of the best runners in the Borstal. I can go my five miles round better than anybody else I know.

So as soon as I tell myself I'm the first man ever to be dropped into the world, and as soon as I take that first flying leap out into the frosty grass of an early morning when even birds haven't the heart to whistle, I get to thinking, and that's what I like. I go my rounds in a dream, turning at lane or footpath corners without knowing I'm turning, leaping brooks without knowing they're there, and shouting good morning to the early cow-milker without seeing him. It's a treat, being a long-distance runner, out in the world by yourself with not a soul to make you bad-tempered or tell you what to do or that there's a shop to break and enter a bit back from the next street. Sometimes I think that I've never

been so free as during that couple of hours when I'm trotting up the path out of the gates and turning by that bare-faced, big-bellied oak tree at the lane end. Everything's dead, but good, because it's dead before coming alive, not dead after being alive. That's how I look at it. Mind you, I often feel frozen stiff at first. I can't feel my hands or feet or flesh at all, like I'm a ghost who would-n't know the earth was under him if he didn't see it now and again through the mist. But even though some people would call this frost-pain suffering if they wrote about it to their mams in a letter, I don't, because I know that in half an hour I'm going to be warm, that by the time I get to the main road and am turning on to the wheatfield footpath by the bus stop I'm going to feel as hot as a potbellied stove and as happy as a dog with a tin tail.

It's a good life, I'm saying to myself, if you don't give in to coppers and Borstal-bosses and the rest of them bastard-faced In-laws. Trot-trot-trot. Puff-puff-puff. Slap-slap-slap go my feet on the hard soil. Swish-swish-swish as my arms and side catch the bare branches of a bush. For I'm seventeen now, and when they let me out of this—if I don't make a break and see that things turn out otherwise—they'll try to get me in the army, and what's the difference between the army and this place I'm in now? They can't kid me, the bastards. I've seen the barracks near where I live, and if there weren't swaddies[1] on guard outside with rifles you wouldn't know the difference between their high walls and the place I'm in now. Even though the swaddies come out at odd times a week for a pint of ale, so what? Don't I come out three mornings a week on my long-distance running, which is fifty times better than boozing. When they first said that I was to do my long-distance running without a guard pedalling beside me on a bike I couldn't believe it; but they called it a progressive and modern place, though they can't kid me because I know it's just like any other Borstal, going by the stories I've heard, except that they let me trot about like this. Borstal's Borstal no matter what they do; but anyway I moaned about it being a bit thick sending me out so early to run five miles on an empty stomach, until they talked me round to thinking it wasn't so bad—which I knew all the time—until they called me a good sport and patted

---

[1] *swaddies* Soldiers.

me on the back when I said I'd do it and that I'd try to win them the Borstal Blue Ribbon Prize Cup For Long Distance Cross Country Running (All England). And now the governor talks to me when he comes on his rounds, almost as he'd talk to his prize race horse, if he had one.

"All right, Smith?" he asks.

"Yes, sir," I answer.

He flicks his grey moustache: "How's the running coming along?"

"I've set myself to trot round the grounds after dinner just to keep my hand in, sir," I tell him.

The pot-bellied pop-eyed bastard gets pleased at this: "Good show. I know you'll get us that cup," he says.

And I swear under my breath: "Like boggery, I will." No, I won't get them that cup, even though the stupid tash-twitching[1] bastard has all his hopes in me. Because what does his barmy[2] hope mean? I ask myself. Trot-trot-trot, slap-slap-slap, over the stream and into the wood where it's almost dark and frosty-dew twigs sting my legs. It don't mean a bloody thing to me, only to him, and it means as much to him as it would mean to me if I picked up the racing paper and put my bet on a hoss I didn't know, had never seen, and didn't care a sod if I ever did see. That's what it means to him. And I'll lose that race, because I'm not a race horse at all, and I'll let him know it when I'm about to get out—if I don't sling my hook even before the race. By Christ I will. I'm a human being and I've got thoughts and secrets and bloody life inside me that he doesn't know is there, and he'll never know what's there because he's stupid. I suppose you'll laugh at this, me saying the governor's a stupid bastard when I know hardly how to write and he can read and write and add-up like a professor. But what I say is true right enough. He's stupid, and I'm not, because I can see further into the likes of him than he can see into the likes of me. Admitted, we're both cunning, but I'm more cunning and I'll win in the end even if I die in gaol at eighty-two, because I'll have more fun and fire out of my life than he'll ever get out of his. He's read a thousand books I suppose, and for all I know he might even have written

a few, but I know for a dead cert,[3] as sure as I'm sitting here, that what I'm scribbling down is worth a million to what he could ever scribble down. I don't care what anybody says, but that's the truth and can't be denied. I know when he talks to me and I look into his army mug[4] that I'm alive and he's dead. He's as dead as a doornail. If he ran ten yards he'd drop dead. If he got ten yards into what goes on in my guts he'd drop dead as well—with surprise. At the moment it's dead blokes like him as have the whip-hand over blokes like me, and I'm almost dead sure it'll always be like that, but even so, by Christ, I'd rather be like I am—always on the run and breaking into shops for a packet of fags[5] and a jar of jam—than have the whip-hand over somebody else and be dead from the toe nails up. Maybe as soon as you get the whip-hand over somebody you do go dead. By God, to say that last sentence has needed a few hundred miles of long-distance running. I could no more have said that at first than I could have took a million-pound note from my back pocket. But it's true, you know, now I think of it again, and has always been true, and always will be true, and I'm surer of it every time I see the governor open that door and say Goodmorning lads.

As I run and see my smoky breath going out into the air as if I had ten cigars stuck in different parts of my body I think more on the little speech the governor made when I first came. Honesty. Be honest. I laughed so much one morning I went ten minutes down in my timing because I had to stop and get rid of the stitch in my side. The governor was so worried when I got back late that he sent me to the doctor's for an X-ray and heart check. Be honest. It's like saying: Be dead, like me, and then you'll have no more pain of leaving your nice slummy house for Borstal or prison. Be honest and settle down in a cosy six pounds a week job. Well, even with all this long-distance running I haven't yet been able to decide what he means by this, although I'm just about beginning to—and I don't like what it means. Because after all my thinking I found that it adds up to something that can't be true about me, being born and brought up as I was. Because another thing people like the governor will never understand is that I *am* honest,

1 *tash* Moustache.
2 *barmy* Empty-headed.
3 *cert* Certainty.
4 *mug* Face.
5 *fags* Cigarettes.

that I've never been anything else but honest, and that I'll always be honest. Sounds funny. But it's true because I know what honest means according to me and he only knows what it means according to him: I think my honesty is the only sort in the world, and he thinks his is the only sort in the world as well. That's why this dirty great walled-up and fenced-up manor house in the middle of nowhere has been used to coop-up blokes like me. And if I had the whip-hand I wouldn't even bother to build a place like this to put all the cops, governors, posh whores, penpushers, army officers, Members of Parliament in; no, I'd stick them up against a wall and let them have it, like they'd have done with blokes like us years ago, that is, if they'd ever known what it means to be honest, which they don't and never will so help me God Almighty.

I was nearly eighteen months in Borstal before I thought about getting out. I can't tell you much about what it was like there because I haven't got the hang of describing buildings or saying how many crumby chairs and slatted windows make a room. Neither can I do much complaining, because to tell you the truth I didn't suffer in Borstal at all. I gave the same answer a pal of mine gave when someone asked him how much he hated it in the army. "I didn't hate it," he said. "They fed me, gave me a suit, and pocket-money, which was a bloody sight more than I ever got before, unless I worked myself to death for it, and most of the time they wouldn't let me work but sent me to the dole office twice a week." Well, that's more or less what I say. Borstal didn't hurt me in that respect, so since I've got no complaints I don't have to describe what they gave us to eat, what the dorms were like, or how they treated us. But in another way Borstal does something to me. No, it doesn't get my back up, because it's always been up, right from when I was born. What it does do is show me what they've been trying to frighten me with. They've got other things as well, like prison and, in the end, the rope. It's like me rushing up to thump a man and snatch the coat off his back when, suddenly, I pull up because he whips out a knife and lifts it to stick me like a pig if I come too close. That knife is Borstal, clink, the rope. But once you've seen the knife you learn a bit of un-armed combat. You have to, because you'll never get that sort of knife in your own hands, and this unarmed

combat doesn't amount to much. Still, there it is, and you keep on rushing up to this man, knife or not, hoping to get one of your hands on his wrist and the other on his elbow both at the same time, and press back until he drops the knife.

You see, by sending me to Borstal they've shown me the knife, and from now on I know something I didn't know before: that it's war between me and them. I always knew this, naturally, because I was in Remand Homes[1] as well and the boys there told me a lot about their brothers in Borstal, but it was only touch and go then, like kittens, like boxing-gloves, like dobbie.[2] But now that they've shown me the knife, whether I ever pinch another thing in my life again or not, I know who my enemies are and what war is. They can drop all the atom bombs they like for all I care: I'll never call it war and wear a soldier's uniform, because I'm in a different sort of war, that they think is child's play. The war they think is war is suicide, and those that go and get killed in war should be put in clink for attempted suicide because that's the feeling in blokes' minds when they rush to join up or let themselves be called up. I know, because I've thought how good it would be sometimes to do myself in and the easiest way to do it, it occurred to me, was to hope for a big war so's I could join up and get killed. But I got past that when I knew I already was in a war of my own, that I was born into one, that I grew up hearing the sound of "old soldiers" who'd been over the top at Dartmoor, half-killed at Lincoln,[3] trapped in no-man's-land at Borstal, that sounded louder than any Jerry[4] bombs. Government wars aren't my wars; they've got nowt[5] to do with me, because my own war's all that I'll ever be bothered about. I remember when I was fourteen and I went out into the country with three of my cousins, all about the same age, who later went to different Borstals, and then to different regiments, from which they soon deserted, and then to different gaols where they still are as far as I know. But anyway, we were all kids then, and wanted to go out to

---

[1] *Remand Homes*   Institutions to which children ages 8 to 14 were committed for detention.

[2] *dobbie*   A dotard, an imbecile.

[3] *Dartmoor ... Lincoln*   Jails.

[4] *Jerry*   German.

[5] *nowt*   Nothing.

the woods for a change, to get away from the roads of stinking hot tar one summer. We climbed over fences and went through fields, scrumping[1] a few sour apples on our way, until we saw the wood about a mile off. Up Colliers' Pad we heard another lot of kids talking in high-school voices behind a hedge. We crept up on them and peeped through the brambles, and saw they were eating a picnic, a real posh spread out of baskets and flasks and towels. There must have been about seven of them, lads and girls sent out by their mams and dads for the afternoon. So we went on our bellies through the hedge like crocodiles and surrounded them, and then dashed into the middle, scattering the fire and batting their tabs[2] and snatching up all there was to eat, then running off over Cherry Orchard fields into the wood, with a man chasing us who'd come up while we were ransacking their picnic. We got away all right, and had a good feed into the bargain, because we'd been clambed[3] to death and couldn't wait long enough to get our chops ripping into them thin lettuce and ham sandwiches and creamy cakes.

Well, I'll always feel during every bit of my life like those daft kids should have felt before we broke them up. But they never dreamed that what happened was going to happen, just like the governor of this Borstal who spouts to us about honesty and all that wappy stuff don't know a bloody thing, while I know every minute of my life that a big boot is always likely to smash any nice picnic I might be barmy and dishonest enough to make for myself. I admit that there've been times when I've thought of telling the governor all this so as to put him on his guard, but when I've got as close as seeing him I've changed my mind, thinking to let him either find out for himself or go through the same mill as I've gone through. I'm not hard-hearted (in fact I've helped a few blokes in my time with the odd quid,[4] lie, fag, or shelter from the rain when they've been on the run) but I'm boggered if I'm going to risk being put in the cells just for trying to give the governor a bit of advice he don't deserve. If my heart's soft I know the sort of people I'm going to save it for. And any advice I'd give

the governor wouldn't do him the least bit of good; it'd only trip him up sooner than if he wasn't told at all, which I suppose is what I want to happen. But for the time being I'll let things go on as they are, which is something else I've learned in the last year or two. (It's a good job I can only think of these things as fast as I can write with this stub of pencil that's clutched in my paw, otherwise I'd have dropped the whole thing weeks ago.)

By the time I'm half-way through my morning course, when after a frost-bitten dawn I can see a phlegmy bit of sunlight hanging from the bare twigs of beech and sycamore, and when I've measured my half-way mark by the short-cut scrimmage down the steep bush-covered bank and into the sunken lane, when still there's not a soul in sight and not a sound except the neighing of a piebald foal in a cottage stable that I can't see, I get to thinking the deepest and daftest of all. The governor would have a fit if he could see me sliding down the bank because I could break my neck or ankle, but I can't not do it because it's the only risk I take and the only excitement I ever get, flying flat-out like one of them pterodactyls from the "Lost World" I once heard on the wireless,[5] crazy like a cut-balled cockerel, scratching myself to bits and almost letting myself go but not quite. It's the most wonderful minute because there's not one thought or word or picture of anything in my head while I'm going down. I'm empty, as empty as I was before I was born, and I don't let myself go, I suppose, because whatever it is that's farthest down inside me don't want me to die or hurt myself bad. And it's daft to think deep, you know, because it gets you nowhere, though deep is what I am when I've passed this half-way mark because the long-distance run of an early morning makes me think that every run like this is a life—a little life, I know—but a life as full of misery and happiness and things happening as you can ever get really around yourself—and I remember that after a lot of these runs I thought that it didn't need much know-how to tell how a life was going to end once it had got well started. But as usual I was wrong, caught first by the cops and then by my own bad brain, I could never trust myself to fly scot-free over these traps, was always tripped up sooner or later no matter how many I got

---

[1] *scrumping* Stealing.

[2] *batting their tabs* Hitting their ears.

[3] *clambed* Starved.

[4] *quid* Slang for a pound of English money.

[5] *wireless* Radio.

over to the good without even knowing it. Looking back I suppose them big trees put their branches to their snouts and gave each other the wink, and there I was whizzing down the bank and not seeing a bloody thing.

2

I don't say to myself: "You shouldn't have done the job and then you'd have stayed away from Borstal"; no, what I ram into my runner-brain is that my luck had no right to scram just when I was on my way to making the coppers think I hadn't done the job after all. The time was autumn and the night foggy enough to set me and my mate Mike roaming the streets when we should have been rooted in front of the telly or stuck into a plush posh seat at the pictures, but I was restless after six weeks away from any sort of work, and well you might ask me why I'd been bone-idle for so long because normally I sweated my thin guts out on a milling-machine with the rest of them, but you see, my dad died from cancer of the throat, and mam collected a cool five hundred in insurance and benefits from the factory where he'd worked, "for your bereavement," they said, or words like that.

Now I believe, and my mam must have thought the same, that a wad of crisp blue-back fivers ain't a sight of good to a living soul unless they're flying out of your hand into some shopkeeper's till, and the shopkeeper is passing you tip-top things in exchange over the counter, so as soon as she got the money, mam took me and my five brothers and sisters out to town and got us dolled-up in new clothes. Then she ordered a twenty-one-inch telly, a new carpet because the old one was covered with blood from dad's dying and wouldn't wash out, and took a taxi home with bags of grub and a new fur coat. And do you know—you wain't believe me when I tell you—she'd still near three hundred left in her bulging handbag the next day, so how could any of us go to work after that? Poor old dad, he didn't get a look in,[1] and he was the one who'd done the suffering and dying for such a lot of lolly.[2]

Night after night we sat in front of the telly with a ham sandwich in one hand, a bar of chocolate in the other, and a bottle of lemonade between our boots,

while mam was with some fancy-man upstairs on the new bed she'd ordered, and I'd never known a family as happy as ours was in that couple of months when we'd got all the money we needed. And when the dough ran out I didn't think about anything much, but just roamed the streets—looking for another job, I told mam—hoping I suppose to get my hands on another five hundred nicker[3] so's the nice life we'd got used to could go on and on for ever. Because it's surprising how quick you can get used to a different life. To begin with, the adverts on the telly had shown us how much more there was in the world to buy than we'd ever dreamed of when we'd looked into shop windows but hadn't seen all there was to see because we didn't have the money to buy it with anyway. And the telly made all these things seem twenty times better than we'd ever thought they were. Even adverts at the cinema were cool and tame, because now we were seeing them in private at home. We used to cock our noses up at things in shops that didn't move, but suddenly we saw their real value because they jumped and glittered around the screen and had some pasty-faced tart going head over heels to get her nail-polished grabbers on to them or her lipstick lips over them, not like the crumby adverts you saw on posters or in newspapers as dead as doornails; these were flickering around loose, half-open packets and tins, making you think that all you had to do was finish opening them before they were yours, like seeing an unlocked safe through a shop window with the man gone away for a cup of tea without thinking to guard his lolly. The films they showed were good as well, in that way, because we couldn't get our eyes unglued from the cops chasing the robbers who had satchel-bags crammed with cash and looked like getting away to spend it—until the last moment. I always hoped they would end up free to blow the lot, and could never stop wanting to put my hand out, smash into the screen (it only looked a bit of rag-screen like at the pictures) and get the copper in a half-nelson so's he'd stop following the bloke with the money-bags. Even when he'd knocked off a couple of bank clerks I hoped he wouldn't get nabbed. In fact then I wished more than ever he wouldn't because it meant the hot-chair if he did, and I wouldn't wish that on anybody no matter what they'd

---

[1]  *a look in*  Any part of it.

[2]  *lolly*  Money.

[3]  *nicker*  Pounds.

done, because I'd read in a book where the hot-chair worn't a quick death at all, but that you just sat there scorching to death until you were dead. And it was when these cops were chasing the crooks that we played some good tricks with the telly, because when one of them opened his big gob to spout about getting their man I'd turn the sound down and see his mouth move like a goldfish or mackerel or a minnow mimicking what they were supposed to be acting—it was so funny the whole family nearly went into fits on the brand-new carpet that hadn't yet found its way to the bedroom. It was the best of all though when we did it to some Tory[1] telling us about how good his government was going to be if we kept on voting for them—their slack chops rolling, opening and bumbling, hands lifting to twitch moustaches and touching their buttonholes to make sure the flower hadn't wilted, so that you could see they didn't mean a word they said, especially with not a murmur coming out because we'd cut off the sound. When the governor of the Borstal first talked to me I was reminded of those times so much that I nearly killed myself trying not to laugh. Yes, we played so many good stunts on the box of tricks that mam used to call us the Telly Boys, we got so clever at it.

My pal Mike got let off with probation because it was his first job—anyway the first they ever knew about—and because they said he would never have done it if it hadn't been for me talking him into it. They said I was a menace to honest lads like Mike—hands in his pockets so that they looked stone-empty, head bent forward as if looking for half-crowns[2] to fill 'em with, a ripped jersey on and his hair falling into his eyes so that he could go up to women and ask them for a shilling because he was hungry—and that I was the brains behind the job, the guiding light when it came to making up anybody's mind, but I swear to God I worn't owt like that because really I ain't got no more brains than a gnat after hiding the money in the place I did. And I—being cranky like I am—got sent to Borstal because to tell you the honest truth I'd been to Remand Homes before—though that's another story and I suppose if ever I tell it it'll be just as boring as this one is. I was glad though that Mike got away with it, and I

only hope he always will, not like silly bastard me.

So on this foggy night we tore ourselves away from the telly and slammed the front door behind us, setting off up our wide street like slow tugs on a river that'd broken their hooters, for we didn't know where the housefronts began what with the perishing cold mist all around. I was snatched to death without an overcoat: mam had forgotten to buy me one in the scrummage of shopping, and by the time I thought to remind her of it the dough was all gone. So we whistled "The Teddy Boys Picnic" to keep us warm, and I told myself that I'd get a coat soon if it was the last thing I did. Mike said he thought the same about himself, adding that he'd also get some brand-new glasses with gold rims, to wear instead of the wire frames they'd given him at the school clinic years ago. He didn't twig[3] it was foggy at first and cleaned his glasses every time I pulled him back from a lamp-post or car, but when he saw the lights on Alfreton Road looking like octopus eyes he put them in his pocket and didn't wear them again until we did the job. We hadn't got two ha'pennies[4] between us, and though we weren't hungry we wished we'd got a bob[5] or two when we passed the fish and chip shops because the delicious sniffs of salt and vinegar and frying fat made our mouths water. I don't mind telling you we walked the town from one end to the other and if our eyes worn't glued to the ground looking for lost wallets and watches they was swivelling around house windows and shop doors in case we saw something easy and worth nipping into.

Neither of us said as much as this to each other, but I know for a fact that that was what we was thinking. What I don't know—and as sure as I sit here I know I'll never know—is which of us was the first bastard to latch his peepers on to that baker's backyard. Oh yes, it's all right me telling myself it was me, but the truth is that I've never known whether it was Mike or not, because I do know that I didn't see the open window until he stabbed me in the ribs and pointed it out. "See it?" he said.

"Yes," I told him, "so let's get cracking."

"But what about the wall though?" he whispered, looking a bit closer.

---

[1] *Tory*   Member of the Conservative party.

[2] *half-crowns*   Coins worth two shillings and sixpence.

[3] *twig*   Perceive, recognize.

[4] *ha'pennies*   Half-pennies, coins worth half the value of a penny.

[5] *bob*   Shilling.

"On your shoulders," I chipped in.

His eyes were already up there: "Will you be able to reach?" It was the only time he ever showed any life.

"Leave it to me," I said, ever-ready. "I can reach anywhere from your ham-hock shoulders."

Mike was a nipper compared to me, but underneath the scruffy draught-board jersey he wore were muscles as hard as iron, and you wouldn't think to see him walking down the street with glasses on and hands in pockets that he'd harm a fly, but I never liked to get on the wrong side of him in a fight because he's the sort that don't say a word for weeks on end—sits plugged in front of the telly, or reads a cowboy book, or just sleeps—when suddenly BIFF—half kills somebody for almost nothing at all, such as beating him in a race for the last Football Post on a Saturday night, pushing in before him at a bus stop, or bumping into him when he was day-dreaming about Dolly-on-the-Tub next door. I saw him set on a bloke once for no more than fixing him in a funny way with his eyes, and it turned out that the bloke was cockeyed but nobody knew it because he'd just that day come to live in our street. At other times none of these things would matter a bit, and I suppose the only reason why I was pals with him was because I didn't say much from one month's end to another either.

He puts his hands up in the air like he was being covered with a Gatling-Gun,[1] and moved to the wall like he was going to be mowed down, and I climbed up him like he was a stile or step-ladder, and there he stood, the palms of his upshot maulers flat and turned out so's I could step on 'em like they was the adjustable jack-spanner under a car, not a sound of a breath nor the shiver of a flinch coming from him. I lost no time in any case, took my coat from between my teeth, chucked it up to the glass-topped wall (where the glass worn't too sharp because the jags had been worn down by years of accidental stones) and was sitting astraddle before I knew where I was. Then down the other side, with my legs rammed up into my throat when I hit the ground, the crack coming about as hard as when you fall after a high parachute drop, that one of my mates told me was like jumping off a twelve-foot wall, which this must have been. Then I picked up my bits and pieces and opened the gate for Mike, who was still grinning and full of life because the hardest part of the job was already done. "I came, I broke, I entered," like that clever-dick Borstal song.

I didn't think about anything at all, as usual, because I never do when I'm busy, when I'm draining pipes, looting sacks, yaling locks, lifting latches, forcing my bony hands and lanky legs into making something move, hardly feeling my lungs going in-whiff and out-whaff, not realizing whether my mouth is clamped tight or gaping, whether I'm hungry, itching from scabies, or whether my flies are open and flashing dirty words like muck and spit into the late-night final fog. And when I don't know anything about all this then how can I honest-to-God say I think of anything at such times? When I'm wondering what's the best way to get a window open or how to force a door, how can I be thinking or have anything on my mind? That's what the four-eyed white-smocked bloke with the note-book couldn't understand when he asked me questions for days and days after I got to Borstal; and I couldn't explain it to him then like I'm writing it down now; and even if I'd been able to maybe he still wouldn't have caught on because I don't know whether I can under-stand it myself even at this moment, though I'm doing my best you can bet.

So before I knew where I was I was inside the baker's office watching Mike picking up that cash box after he'd struck a match to see where it was, wearing a tailor-made fifty-shilling grin on his square crew-cut nut as his paws closed over the box like he'd squash it to nothing. "Out," he suddenly said, shaking it so's it rattled. "Let's scram."

"Maybe there's some more," I said, pulling half a dozen drawers out of a rollertop desk.

"No," he said, like he'd already been twenty years in the game, "this is the lot," patting his tin box, "this is it."

I pulled out another few drawers, full of bills, books and letters. "How do you know, you loony sod?"

He barged past me like a bull at a gate. "Because I do."

Right or wrong, we'd both got to stick together and do the same thing. I looked at an ever-loving babe of a brand-new typewriter, but knew it was too traceable, so blew it a kiss, and went out after him. "Hang on," I said, pulling the door to, "we're in no hurry."

---

[1] *Gatling-Gun* Type of machine gun.

"Not much we aren't," he says over his shoulder.

"We've got months to splash the lolly," I whispered as we crossed the yard, "only don't let that gate creak too much or you'll have the narks tuning-in."

"You think I'm barmy?" he said, creaking the gate so that the whole street heard.

I don't know about Mike, but now I started to think of how we'd get back safe through the streets with that moneybox up my jumper. Because he'd clapped it into my hand as soon as we'd got to the main road, which might have meant that he'd started thinking as well, which only goes to show how you don't know what's in anybody else's mind unless you think about things yourself. But as far as my thinking went at that moment it wasn't up to much, only a bit of fright that wouldn't budge not even with a hot blow-lamp, about what we'd say if a copper asked us where we were off to with that hump in my guts.

"What is it?" he'd ask, and I'd say: "A growth." "What do you mean, a growth, my lad?" he'd say back, narky[1] like. I'd cough and clutch myself like I was in the most tripe-twisting pain in the world, and screw my eyes up like I was on my way to the hospital, and Mike would take my arm like he was the best pal I'd got. "Cancer," I'd manage to say to Narker, which would make his slow punch-drunk brain suspect a thing or two. "A lad of your age?" So I'd groan again, and hope to make him feel a real bully of a bastard, which would be impossible, but anyway: "It's in the family. Dad died of it last month, and I'll die of it next month by the feel of it." "What, did he have it in the guts?" "No, in the throat. But it's got me in the stomach." Groan and cough. "Well, you shouldn't be out like this if you've got cancer, you should be in the hospital." I'd get ratty now: "That's where I'm trying to go if only you'd let me and stop asking so many questions. Aren't I, Mike?" Grunt from Mike as he unslung his cosh.[2] Then just in time the copper would tell us to get on our way, kind and considerate all of a sudden, saying that the outpatient department of the hospital closes at twelve, so hadn't he better call us a taxi? He would if we liked, he says, and he'd pay for it as well. But we tell him not to bother, that he's a good bloke even if he is a copper, that

we know a short cut anyway. Then just as we're turning a corner he gets it into his big batchy[3] head that we're going the opposite way to the hospital, and calls us back. So we'd start to run ... if you can call all that thinking.

Up in my room Mike rips open that money-box with a hammer and chisel, and before we know where we are we've got seventy-eight pounds fifteen and fourpence ha'penny *each* lying all over my bed like tea spread out on Christmas Day: cake and trifle, salad and sandwiches, jam tarts and bars of chocolate: all shared and shared alike between Mike and me because we believed in equal work and equal pay, just like the comrades my dad was in until he couldn't do a stroke anymore and had no breath left to argue with. I thought how good it was that blokes like that poor baker didn't stash all his cash in one of the big marble-fronted banks that take up every corner of the town, how lucky for us that he didn't trust them no matter how many millions of tons of concrete or how many iron bars and boxes they were made of, or how many coppers kept their blue pop-eyed peepers glued on to them, how smashing it was that he believed in money-boxes when so many shopkeepers thought it old-fashioned and tried to be modern by using a bank, which wouldn't give a couple of sincere, honest, hardworking, conscientious blokes like Mike and me a chance.

Now you'd think, and I'd think, and anybody with a bit of imagination would think, that we'd done as clean a job as could ever be done, that, with the baker's shop being at least a mile from where we lived, and with not a soul having seen us, and what with the fog and the fact that we weren't more than five minutes in the place, that the coppers should never have been able to trace us. But then, you'd be wrong, I'd be wrong, and everybody else would be wrong, no matter how much imagination was diced out between us.

Even so, Mike and I didn't splash the money about, because that would have made people think straightaway that we'd latched on to something that didn't belong to us. Which wouldn't do at all, because even in a street like ours there are people who love to do a good turn for the coppers, though I never know why they do. Some people are so mean-gutted that even if they've only got tuppence more than you and they think you're the sort

---

[1] *narky*  Irritable, sarcastic.

[2] *cosh*  A weighted weapon or a stick.

[3] *botchy*  Silly, dotty.

that would take it if you have half the chance, they'd get you put inside if they saw you ripping lead out of a lavatory, even if it weren't their lavatory—just to keep their tuppence out of your reach. And so we didn't do anything to let on about how rich we were, nothing like going down town and coming back dressed in brand-new Teddy boy suits and carrying a set of skiffle-drums[1] like another pal of ours who'd done a factory office about six months before. No, we took the odd bobs and pennies out and folded the notes into bundles and stuffed them up the drainpipe outside the door in the backyard. "Nobody'll ever think of looking for it there," I said to Mike. "We'll keep it doggo[2] for a week or two, then take a few quid a week out till it's all gone. We might be thieving bastards, but we're not green."

Some days later a plain-clothes dick knocked at the door. And asked for me. I was still in bed, at eleven o'clock, and had to unroll myself from the comfortable black sheets when I heard mam calling me. "A man to see you," she said. "Hurry up, or he'll be gone."

I could hear her keeping him at the back door, nattering about how fine it had been but how it looked like rain since early this morning—and he didn't answer her except to snap out a snotty yes or no. I scrambled into my trousers and wondered why he'd come—knowing it was a copper because "a man to see you" always meant just that in our house—and if I'd had any idea that one had gone to Mike's house as well at the same time I'd have twigged it to be because of that hundred and fifty quid's worth of paper stuffed up the drainpipe outside the back door about ten inches away from that plain-clothed copper's boot, where mam still talked to him thinking she was doing me a favour, and I wishing to God she'd ask him in, though on second thoughts realizing that that would seem more suspicious than keeping him outside, because they know we hate their guts and smell a rat if they think we're trying to be nice to them. Mam wasn't born yesterday, I thought, thumping my way down the creaking stairs.

I'd seen him before: Borstal Bernard in nicky-hat, Remand Home Ronald in rowing-boat boots, Probation

Pete in a pit-prop mackintosh, three-months clink in collar and tie (all this out of a Borstal skiffle-ballad that my new mate made up, and I'd tell you it in full but it doesn't belong in this story), a 'tec[3] who'd never had as much in his pockets as that drainpipe had up its jackses. He was like Hitler in the face, right down to the paint-brush tash, except that being six-foot tall made him seem worse. But I straightened my shoulders to look into his illiterate blue eyes—like I always do with any copper.

Then he started asking me questions, and my mother from behind said: "He's never left that television set for the last three months, so you've got nowt on him, mate. You might as well look for somebody else, because you're wasting the rates you get out of my rent and the income-tax that comes out of my pay-packet standing there like that"—which was a laugh because she'd never paid either to my knowledge, and never would, I hoped.

"Well, you know where Papplewick Street is, don't you?" the copper asked me, taking no notice of mam.

"Ain't it off Alfreton Road?" I asked him back, helpful and bright.

"You know there's a baker's half-way down on the left-hand side, don't you?"

"Ain't it next door to a pub, then?" I wanted to know.

He answered me sharp: "No, it bloody well ain't." Coppers always lose their tempers as quick as this, and more often than not they gain nothing by it. "Then I don't know it," I told him, saved by the bell.

He slid his big boot round and round on the door-step. "Where were you last Friday night?" Back in the ring, but this was worse than a boxing match.

I didn't like him trying to accuse me of something he wasn't sure I'd done. "Was I at that baker's you mentioned? Or in the pub next door?"

"You'll get five years in Borstal if you don't give me a straight answer," he said, unbuttoning his mac[4] even though it was cold where he was standing.

"I was glued to the telly, like mam says," I swore blind. But he went on and on with his looney questions:

"Have you got a television?"

The things he asked wouldn't have taken in a kid of two, and what else could I say to the last one except: "Has the aerial fell down? Or would you like to

[1] *skiffle-drums*  Skiffle was a type of popular music in Britain in the 1950s. It was developed from American folk music and was primarily played on guitars and improvised percussion instruments.

[2] *doggo*  Hidden, quiet.

[3] *'tec*  Detective.

[4] *mac*  Mackintosh, i.e., raincoat.

come in and see it?"

He was liking me even less for saying that. "We know you weren't listening to the television set last Friday, and so do you, don't you?"

"P'raps not, but I was *looking* at it, because sometimes we turn the sound down for a bit of fun." I could hear mam laughing from the kitchen, and I hoped Mike's mam was doing the same if the cops had gone to him as well.

"We know you weren't in the house," he said, starting up again, cranking himself with the handle. They always say "We" "We," never "I" "I"—as if they feel braver and righter knowing there's a lot of them against only one.

"I've got witnesses," I said to him. "Mam for one. Her fancy-man, for two. Ain't that enough? I can get you a dozen more, or thirteen altogether, if it was a baker's that got robbed."

"I don't want no lies," he said, not catching on about the baker's dozen. Where do they scrape cops up from anyway?

"All I want is to get from you where you put that money." Don't get mad, I kept saying to myself, don't get mad—hearing mam setting out cups and saucers and putting the pan on the stove for bacon. I stood back and waved him inside like I was a butler. "Come and search the house. If you've got a warrant."

"Listen, my lad," he said, like the dirty bullying jumped-up bastard he was, "I don't want too much of your lip, because if we get you down to the Guildhall you'll get a few bruises and black-eyes for your trouble."

And I knew he wasn't kidding either, because I'd heard about all them sort of tricks. I hoped one day though that him and all his pals would be the ones to get the black-eyes and kicks; you never knew. It might come sooner than anybody thinks, like in Hungary.

"Tell me where the money is, and I'll get you off with probation."

"What money?" I asked him, because I'd heard that one before as well.

"You know what money."

"Do I look as though I'd know owt about money?" I said, pushing my fist through a hole in my shirt.

"The money that was pinched, that you know all about," he said. "You can't trick me, so it's no use

trying."

"Was it three-and-eightpence ha'penny?" I asked.

"You thieving young bastard. We'll teach you to steal money that doesn't belong to you."

I turned my head around: "Mam," I called out, "get my lawyer on the blower,[1] will you?"

"Clever, aren't you?" he said in a very unfriendly way, "but we won't rest until we clear all this up."

"Look," I pleaded, as if about to sob my socks off because he'd got me wrong, "it's all very well us talking like this, it's like a game almost, but I wish you'd tell me what it's all about, because honest-to-God I've just got out of bed and here you are at the door talking about me having pinched a lot of money, money that I don't know anything about."

He swung around now as if he'd trapped me, though I couldn't see why he might think so. "Who said anything about money? I didn't. What made you bring money into this little talk we're having?"

"It's you," I answered, thinking he was going barmy, and about to start foaming at the chops, "you've got money on the brain, like all policemen. Baker's shops as well."

He screwed his face up. "I want an answer from you: where's that money?"

But I was getting fed-up with all this. "I'll do a deal."

Judging by his flash-bulb face he thought he was suddenly on to a good thing. "What sort of a deal?"

So I told him: "I'll give you all the money I've got, one and fourpence ha'penny, if you stop this third-degree and let me go in and get my breakfast. Honest, I'm clambed to death. I ain't had a bite since yesterday. Can't you hear my guts rollin'?"

His jaw dropped, but on he went, pumping me for another half hour. A routine check-up, as they say on the pictures. But I knew I was winning on points.

Then he left, but came back in the afternoon to search the house. He didn't find a thing, not a French farthing. He asked me questions again and I didn't tell him anything except lies, lies, lies, because I can go on doing that forever without batting an eyelid. He'd got nothing on me and we both of us knew it, otherwise I'd have been down at the Guildhall in no time, but he kept on keeping on because I'd been in a Remand Home for

---

[1] *blower* Telephone.

a high-wall job before; and Mike was put through the same mill because all the local cops knew he was my best pal.

When it got dark me and Mike were in our parlour with a low light on and the telly off, Mike taking it easy in the rocking chair and me slouched out on the settee, both of us puffing a packet of Woods.[1] With the door bolted and curtains drawn we talked about the dough we'd crammed up the drainpipe. Mike thought we should take it out and both of us do a bunk to Skegness or Cleethorpes[2] for a good time in the arcades, living like lords in a boarding house near the pier, then at least we'd both have had a big beano before getting sent down.

"Listen, you daft bleeder," I said, "we aren't going to get caught at all, *and* we'll have a good time, later." We were so clever we didn't even go out to the pictures, though we wanted to.

In the morning old Hitler-face questioned me again, with one of his pals this time, and the next day they came, trying as hard as they could to get something out of me, but I didn't budge an inch. I know I'm showing off when I say this, but in me he'd met his match, and I'd never give in to questions no matter how long it was kept up. They searched the house a couple of times as well, which made me think they thought they really had something to go by, but I know now that they hadn't, and that it was all buckshee speculation. They turned the house upside down and inside out like an old sock, went from top to bottom and front to back but naturally didn't find a thing. The copper even poked his face up the front-room chimney (that hadn't been used or swept for years) and came down looking like Al Jolson[3] so that he had to swill himself clean at the scullery sink. They kept tapping and pottering around the big aspidistra plant that grandma had left to mam, lifting it up from the table to look under the cloth, putting it aside so's they could move the table and get at the boards under the rug—but the big headed stupid ignorant bastards never once thought of emptying the soil out of the plant pot, where they'd have found the crumpled-up money-box that we'd buried the night we did the job. I suppose it's still there, now I think about it, and I suppose mam wonders now and again why the plant don't prosper like it used to—as if it could with a fistful of thick black tin lapped around its guts.

The last time he knocked at our door was one wet morning at five minutes to nine and I was sleep-logged in my crumby bed as usual. Mam had gone to work that day so I shouted for him to hold on a bit, and then went down to see who it was. There he stood, six-feet tall and sopping wet, and for the first time in my life I did a spiteful thing I'll never forgive myself for: I didn't ask him to come in out of the rain, because I wanted him to get double pneumonia and die. I suppose he could have pushed by me and come in if he'd wanted, but maybe he'd got used to asking questions on the doorstep and didn't want to be put off by changing his ground even though it was raining. Not that I don't like being spiteful because of any barmy principle I've got, but this bit of spite, as it turned out, did me no good at all. I should have treated him as a brother I hadn't seen for twenty years and dragged him in for a cup of tea and a fag, told him about the picture I hadn't seen the night before, asked him how his wife was after her operation and whether they'd shaved her moustache off to make it, and then sent him happy and satisfied out by the front door. But no, I thought, let's see what he's got to say for himself now.

He stood a little to the side of the door, either because it was less wet there, or because he wanted to see me from a different angle, perhaps having found it monotonous to watch a bloke's face always telling lies from the same side. "You've been identified," he said, twitching raindrops from his tash. "A woman saw you and your mate yesterday and she swears blind you are the same chaps she saw going into that bakery."

I was dead sure he was still bluffing, because Mike and I hadn't even seen each other the day before, but I looked worried. "She's a menace then to innocent people, whoever she is, because the only bakery I've been in lately is the one up our street to get some cutbread on tick[4] for mam."

He didn't bite on this. "So now I want to know where the money is"—as if I hadn't answered him at all.

---

[1]   *Woods*   Woodbines, a brand of cheap cigarettes.

[2]   *Skegness or Cleethorpes*   Two popular but inelegant resorts on the east coast of England.

[3]   *Al Jolson*   An American vaudeville entertainer who performed in blackface.

[4]   *on tick*   On credit.

"I think mam took it to work this morning to get herself some tea in the canteen." Rain was splashing down so hard I thought he'd get washed away if he didn't come inside. But I wasn't much bothered, and went on: "I remember I put it in the telly-vase last night—it was my only one-and-three and I was saving it for a packet of tips this morning—and I nearly had a jibbering black fit just now when I saw it had gone. I was reckoning on it for getting me through today because I don't think life's worth living without a fag, do you?"

I was getting into my stride and began to feel good, twigging that this would be my last pack of lies, and that if I kept it up for long enough this time I'd have the bastards beat: Mike and me would be off to the coast in a few weeks time having the fun of our lives, playing at penny football and latching on to a couple of tarts that would give us all they were good for. "And this weather's no good for picking-up fag-ends in the street," I said, "because they'd be sopping wet. Course, I know you could dry 'em out near the fire, but it don't taste the same you know, all said and done. Rainwater does summat to 'em that don't bear thinkin' about: it turns 'em back into hoss-tods without the taste though."

I began to wonder, at the back of my brainless eyes, why old copper-lugs didn't pull me up sharp and say he hadn't got time to listen to all this, but he wasn't looking at me anymore, and all my thoughts about Skegness went bursting to smithereens in my sludgy loaf. I could have dropped into the earth when I saw what he'd fixed his eyes on.

He was looking at *it,* an ever-loving fiver, and I could only jabber: "The one thing is to have some real fags because new hoss-tods is always better than stuff that's been rained on and dried, and I know how you feel about not being able to find money because one-and-three's one-and-three in anybody's pocket, and naturally if I see it knocking around I'll get you on the blower tomorrow straightaway and tell you where you can find it."

I thought I'd go down in a fit: three green-backs as well had been washed down by the water, and more were following, lying flat at first after their fall, then getting tilted at the corners by wind and rainspots as if they were alive and wanted to get back into the dry snug drainpipe out of the terrible weather, and you can't

imagine how I wished they'd be able to. Old Hitler-face didn't know what to make of it but just kept staring down and down, and I thought I'd better keep on talking, though I knew it wasn't much good now.

"It's a fact, I know, that money's hard to come by and half-crowns don't get found on bus seats or in dustbins, and I didn't see any in bed last night because I'd 'ave known about it, wouldn't I? You can't sleep with things like that in the bed because they're too hard, and anyway at first they're…" It took Hitler-boy a long time to catch on; they were beginning to spread over the yard a bit, reinforced by the third colour of a ten-bob note, before his hand clamped itself on to my shoulder.

3

The pop-eyed potbellied governor said to a pop-eyed potbellied Member of Parliament who sat next to his pop-eyed potbellied whore of a wife that I was his only hope for getting the Borstal Blue Ribbon Prize Cup For Long Distance Cross Country Running (All England), which I was, and it set me laughing to myself inside, and I didn't say a word to any potbellied pop-eyed bastard that might give them real hope, though I knew the governor anyway took my quietness to mean he'd got that cup already stuck on the bookshelf in his office among the few other mildewed trophies.

"He might take up running in a sort of professional way when he gets out," and it wasn't until he'd said this and I'd heard it with my own flap-tabs that I realized it might be possible to do such a thing, run for money, trot for wages on piece work at a bob a puff rising bit by bit to a guinea a gasp and retiring through old age at thirty-two because of lace-curtain lungs, a football heart, and legs like varicose beanstalks. But I'd have a wife and car and get my grinning long-distance clock in the papers and have a smashing secretary to answer piles of letters sent by tarts who'd mob me when they saw who I was as I pushed my way into Woolworth's for a packet of razor blades and a cup of tea. It was something to think about all right, and sure enough the governor knew he'd got me when he said, turning to me as if I would at any rate have to be consulted about it all: "How does this matter strike you, then, Smith, my lad?" A line of potbellied pop-eyes gleamed at me and a row of goldfish mouths opened and wiggled gold teeth at me, so

I gave them the answer they wanted because I'd hold my trump card until later. "It'd suit me fine, sir," I said.

"Good lad. Good show. Right spirit. Splendid."

"Well," the governor said, "get that cup for us today and I'll do all I can for you. I'll get you trained so that you whack every man in the Free World." And I had a picture in my brain of me running and beating everybody in the world, leaving them all behind until only I was trot-trotting across a big wide moor alone, doing a marvellous speed as I ripped between boulders and reed-clumps, when suddenly: CRACK! CRACK!—bullets that can go faster than any man running, coming from a copper's rifle planted in a tree, winged me and split my gizzard in spite of my perfect running, and down I fell.

The potbellies expected me to say something else. "Thank you, sir," I said.

Told to go, I trotted down the pavilion steps, out on to the field because the big cross-country was about to begin and the two entries from Gunthorpe had fixed themselves early at the starting line and were ready to move off like white kangaroos. The sports ground looked a treat: with big tea-tents all round and flags flying and seats for families—empty because no mam or dad had known what opening day meant—and boys still running heats for the hundred yards, and lords and ladies walking from stall to stall, and the Borstal Boys Brass Band in blue uniforms; and up on the stands the brown jackets of Hucknall as well as our own grey blazers, and then the Gunthorpe lot with shirt sleeves rolled. The blue sky was full of sunshine and it couldn't have been a better day, and all of the big show was like something out of Ivanhoe[1] that we'd seen on the pictures a few days before.

"Come on, Smith," Roach the sports master called to me, "we don't want you to be late for the big race, eh? Although I dare say you'd catch them up if you were." The others catcalled and grunted at this, but I took no notice and placed myself between Gunthorpe and one of the Aylesham trusties, dropped on my knees and plucked a few grass blades to suck on the way round. So the big race it was, for them, watching from the grandstand under a fluttering Union Jack,[2] a race for the governor, that he had been waiting for, and I hoped

he and all the rest of his pop-eyed gang were busy placing big bets on me, hundred to one to win, all the money they had in their pockets, all the wages they were going to get for the next five years, and the more they placed the happier I'd be. Because here was a dead cert going to die on the big name they'd built for him, going to go down dying with laughter whether it choked him or not. My knees felt the cool soil pressing into them, and out of my eye's corner I saw Roach lift his hand. The Gunthorpe boy twitched before the signal was given; somebody cheered too soon; Medway bent forward; then the gun went, and I was away.

We went once around the field and then along a half-mile drive of elms, being cheered all the way, and I seemed to feel I was in the lead as we went out by the gate and into the lane, though I wasn't interested enough to find out. The five-mile course was marked by splashes of whitewash gleaming on gateposts and trunks and stiles and stones, and a boy with a waterbottle and bandage-box stood every half-mile waiting for those that dropped out or fainted. Over the first stile, without trying, I was still nearly in the lead but one; and if any of you want tips about running, never be in a hurry, and never let any of the other runners know you are in a hurry even if you are. You can always overtake on long-distance running without letting the others smell the hurry in you; and when you've used your craft like this to reach the two or three up front then you can do a big dash later that puts everybody else's hurry in the shade because you've not had to make haste up till then. I ran to a steady jog-trot rhythm, and soon it was so smooth that I forgot I was running, and I was hardly able to know that my legs were lifting and falling and my arms going in and out, and my lungs didn't seem to be working at all, and my heart stopped that wicked thumping I always get at the beginning of a run. Because you see I never race at all; I just run, and somehow I know that if I forget I'm racing and only jog-trot along until I don't know I'm running I always win the race. For when my eyes recognize that I'm getting near the end of the course—by seeing a stile or cottage corner—I put on a spurt, and such a fast big spurt it is because I feel that up till then I haven't been running and that I've used up no energy at all. And I've been able to do this because I've been thinking; and I wonder if I'm the only one in the running business with this system of forgetting that I'm running because I'm too busy thinking; and I wonder if any of the other lads are on to the same lark, though I know for a fact that they aren't. Off like the wind along the cobbled footpath and rutted lane, smoother than the flat grass track on the field and better for thinking because it's not too smooth, and I was in my element that afternoon knowing that nobody could beat me at running but intending to beat myself before the day was over. For when the governor talked to me of being honest when I first came in he didn't know what the word meant or he wouldn't have had me here in this race, trotting along in shimmy and shorts and sunshine. He'd have had me where I'd have had him if I'd been in his place: in a quarry breaking rocks until he broke his back. At least old Hitler-face the plain-clothes dick was honester than the governor, because he at any rate had had it in for me and I for him, and when my case was coming up in court a copper knocked at our front door at four o'clock in the morning and got my mother out of bed when she was paralytic tired, reminding her she had to be in court at dead on half past nine. It was the finest bit of spite I've ever heard of, but I would call it honest, the same as my mam's words were honest when she really told that copper what she thought of him and called him all the dirty names she'd ever heard of, which took her half an hour and woke the terrace up.

I trotted on along the edge of a field bordered by the sunken lane, smelling green grass and honeysuckle, and I felt as though I came from a long line of whippets trained to run on two legs, only I couldn't see a toy rabbit in front and there wasn't a collier's[1] cosh behind to make me keep up the pace. I passed the Gunthorpe runner whose shimmy was already black with sweat and I could just see the corner of the fenced-up copse in front where the only man I had to pass to win the race was going all out to gain the half-way mark. Then he turned into a tongue of trees and bushes where I couldn't see him anymore, and I couldn't see anybody, and I knew what the loneliness of the long-distance runner running across country felt like, realizing that as far as I was concerned this feeling was the only honesty and realness there was in the world and I knowing it would

be no different ever, no matter what I felt at odd times, and no matter what anybody else tried to tell me. The runner behind me must have been a long way off because it was so quiet, and there was even less noise and movement than there had been at five o'clock of a frosty winter morning. It was hard to understand, and all I knew was that you had to run, run, run, without knowing why you were running, but on you went through fields you didn't understand and into woods that made you afraid, over hills without knowing you'd been up and down, and shooting across streams that would have cut the heart out of you had you fallen into them. And the winning post was no end to it, even though crowds might be cheering you in, because on you had to go before you got your breath back, and the only time you stopped really was when you tripped over a tree trunk and broke your neck or fell into a disused well and stayed dead in the darkness forever. So I thought: they aren't going to get me on this racing lark, this running and trying to win, this jog-trotting for a bit of blue ribbon, because it's not the way to go on at all, though they swear blind that it is. You should think about nobody and go your own way, not on a course marked out for you by people holding mugs of water and bottles of iodine in case you fall and cut yourself so that they can pick you up—even if you want to stay where you are—and get you moving again.

On I went, out of the wood, passing the man leading without knowing I was going to do so. Flip-flap, flip-flap, jog-trot, jog-trot, crunchslap-crunchslap, across the middle of a broad field again, rhythmically running in my greyhound effortless fashion, knowing I had won the race though it wasn't half over, won it if I wanted it, could go on for ten or fifteen or twenty miles if I had to and drop dead at the finish of it, which would be the same, in the end, as living an honest life like the governor wanted me to. It amounted to: win the race and be honest, and on trot-trotting I went, having the time of my life, loving my progress because it did me good and set me thinking which by now I liked to do, but not caring at all when I remembered that I had to win this race as well as run it. One of the two, I had to win the race or run it, and I knew I could do both because my legs had carried me well in front—now coming to the short cut down the bramble bank and over the sunken

---

[1] *collier* Coal miner.

road—and would carry me further because they seemed made of electric cable and easily alive to keep on slapping at those ruts and roots, but I'm not going to win because the only way I'd see I came in first would be if winning meant that I was going to escape the coppers after doing the biggest bank job of my life, but winning means the exact opposite, no matter how they try to kill or kid me, means running right into their white-gloved wall-barred hands and grinning mugs and staying there for the rest of my natural long life of stone-breaking anyway, but stone-breaking in the way I want to do it and not in the way they tell me.

Another honest thought that comes is that I could swing left at the next hedge of the field, and under its cover beat my slow retreat away from the sports ground winning post. I could do three or six or a dozen miles across the turf like this and cut a few main roads behind me so's they'd never know which one I'd taken; and maybe on the last one when it got dark I could thumb a lorry-lift and get a free ride north with somebody who might not give me away. But no, I said I wasn't daft didn't I? I won't pull out with only six months left, and besides there's nothing I want to dodge and run away from; I only want a bit of my own back on the In-laws and Potbellies by letting them sit up there on their big posh seats and watch me lose this race, though as sure as God made me I know that when I do lose I'll get the dirtiest crap and kitchen jobs in the months to go before my time is up. I won't be worth a threpp'ny-bit[1] to anybody here, which will be all the thanks I get for being honest in the only way I know. For when the governor told me to be honest it was meant to be in his way not mine, and if I kept on being honest in the way he wanted and won my race for him he'd see I got the cushiest six months still left to run; but in my own way, well, it's not allowed, and if I find a way of doing it such as I've got now then I'll get what-for in every mean trick he can set his mind to. And if you look at it in my way, who can blame him? For this is war —and ain't I said so?—and when I hit him in the only place he knows he'll be sure to get his own back on me for not collaring that cup when his heart's been set for ages on seeing himself standing up at the end of the afternoon to clap me on the back as I take the cup from Lord Earwig or some such chinless wonder with a name like that. And so I'll hit him where it hurts a lot, and he'll do all he can to get his own back, tit for tat, though I'll enjoy it most because I'm hitting first, and because I planned it longer. I don't know why I think these thoughts are better than any I've ever had, but I do, and I don't care why. I suppose it took me a long time to get going on all this because I've had no time and peace in all my bandit life, and now my thoughts are coming pat and the only trouble is I often can't stop, even when my brain feels as if it's got cramp, frostbite and creeping paralysis all rolled into one and I have to give it a rest by slap-dashing down through the brambles of the sunken lane. And all this is another upper-cut I'm getting in first at people like the governor, to show how—if I can—his races are never won even though some bloke always comes unknowingly in first, how in the end the governor is going to be doomed while blokes like me will take the pickings of his roasted bones and dance like maniacs around his Borstal's ruins. And so this story's like the race and once again I won't bring off a winner to suit the governor; no, I'm being honest like he told me to, without him knowing what he means, though I don't suppose he'll ever come in with a story of his own, even if he reads this one of mine and knows who I'm talking about.

I've just come up out of the sunken lane, kneed and elbowed, thumped and bramble-scratched, and the race is two-thirds over, and a voice is going like a wireless in my mind saying that when you've had enough of feeling good like the first man on earth of a frosty morning, and you've known how it is to be taken bad like the last man on earth on a summer's afternoon, then you get at last to being like the only man on earth and don't give a bogger about either good or bad, but just trot on with your slippers slapping the good dry soil that at least would never do you a bad turn. Now the words are like coming from a crystal-set[2] that's broken down, and something's happening inside the shell-case of my guts that bothers me and I don't know why or what to blame it on, a grinding near my ticker as though a bag of rusty screws is loose inside me and I shake them up every time I trot forward. Now and again I break my rhythm to feel my left shoulder-blade by swinging a right hand across my chest as if to rub the knife away that has somehow

---

[1]    *threpp'ny-bit*   Three-pence coin.

[2]    *crystal-set*   Receiving set, used for listening to radio broadcasts.

got stuck there. But I know it's nothing to bother about, that more likely it's caused by too much thinking that now and again I take for worry. For sometimes I'm the greatest worrier in the world I think (as you twigged I'll bet from me having got this story out) which is funny anyway because my mam don't know the meaning of the word so I don't take after her; though dad had a hard time of worry all his life up to when he filled his bedroom with hot blood and kicked the bucket that morning when nobody was in the house. I'll never forget it, straight I won't, because I was the one that found him and I often wished I hadn't. Back from a session on the fruit-machines at the fish-and-chip shop, jingling my three-lemon loot to a nail-dead house, as soon as I got in I knew something was wrong, stood leaning my head against the cold mirror above the mantel-piece trying not to open my eyes and see my stone-cold clock —because I knew I'd gone as white as a piece of chalk since coming in as if I'd been got at by a Dracula-vampire and even my penny-pocket winnings kept quiet on purpose.

Gunthorpe nearly caught me up. Birds were singing from the briar hedge, and a couple of thrushies flew like lightning into some thorny bushes. Corn had grown high in the next field and would be cut down soon with scythes and mowers; but I never wanted to notice much while running in case it put me off my stroke, so by the haystack I decided to leave it all behind and put on such a spurt, in spite of nails in my guts, that before long I'd left both Gunthorpe and the birds a good way off; I wasn't far now from going into that last mile and a half like a knife through margarine, but the quietness I suddenly trotted into between two pickets was like opening my eyes underwater and looking at the pebbles on a stream bottom, reminding me again of going back that morning to the house in which my old man had croaked, which is funny because I hadn't thought about it at all since it happened and even then I didn't brood much on it. I wonder why? I suppose that since I started to think on these long-distance runs I'm liable to have anything crop up and pester at my tripes and innards, and now that I see my bloody dad behind each grass-blade in my barmy runner-brain I'm not so sure I like to think and that it's such a good thing after all. I choke my phlegm and keep on running anyway and curse the

Borstal-builders and their athletics—flappity-flap, slop-slop, crunchslap-crunchslap-crunchslap—who've maybe got their own back on me from the bright beginning by sliding magic-lantern[1] slides into my head that never stood a chance before. Only if I take whatever comes like this in my runner's stride can I keep on keeping on like my old self and beat them back; and now I've thought on this far I know I'll win, in the crunchslap end. So anyway after a bit I went upstairs one step at a time not thinking anything about how I should find dad and what I'd do when I did. But now I'm making up for it by going over the rotten life mam led him ever since I can remember, knocking-on with different men even when he was alive and fit and she not caring whether he knew it or not, and most of the time he wasn't so blind as she thought and cursed and roared and threatened to punch her tab, and I had to stand up to stop him even though I knew she deserved it. What a life for all of us. Well, I'm not grumbling, because if I did I might just as well win this bleeding race, which I'm not going to do, though if I don't lose speed I'll win it before I know where I am, and then where would I be?

Now I can hear the sportsground noise and music as I head back for the flags and the lead-in drive, the fresh new feel of underfoot gravel going against the iron muscles of my legs. I'm nowhere near puffed despite that bag of nails that rattles as much as ever, and I can still give a big last leap like gale-force wind if I want to, but everything is under control and I know now that there ain't another long-distance cross-country running runner in England to touch my speed and style. Our doddering bastard of a governor, our half-dead gan-grened gaffer is hollow like an empty petrol drum, and he wants me and my running life to give him glory, to put in him blood and throbbing veins he never had, wants his potbellied pals to be his witnesses as I gasp and stagger up to his winning post so's he can say: "My Borstal gets that cup, you see. I win my bet, because it pays to be honest and try to gain the prizes I offer to my lads, and they know it, have known it all along. They'll always be honest now, because I made them so." And his pals will think: "He trains his lads to live right, after all; he deserves a medal but we'll get him made a Sir"—and at this very moment as the birds come back

---

[1] *magic-lantern* Device used to display images.

to whistling I can tell myself I'll never care a sod what any of the chinless spineless In-laws think or say. They've seen me and they're cheering now and loud-speakers set around the field like elephant's ears are spreading out the big news that I'm well in the lead, and can't do anything else but stay there. But I'm still thinking of the Out-law death my dad died, telling the doctors to scat from the house when they wanted him to finish up in hospital (like a bleeding guinea-pig, he raved at them). He got up in bed to throw them out and even followed them down the stairs in his shirt though he was no more than skin and stick. They tried to tell him he'd want some drugs but he didn't fall for it, and only took the pain-killer that mam and I got from a herb-seller in the next street. It's not till now that I know what guts he had, and when I went into the room that morning he was lying on his stomach with the clothes thrown back, looking like a skinned rabbit, his grey head resting just on the edge of the bed, and on the floor must have been all the blood he'd had in his body, right from his toe-nails up, for nearly all of the lino[1] and carpet was covered in it, thin and pink.

And down the drive I went, carrying a heart blocked up like Boulder Dam across my arteries, the nail-bag clamped down tighter and tighter as though in a wood-work vice, yet with my feet like birdwings and arms like talons ready to fly across the field except that I didn't want to give anybody that much of a show, or win the race by accident. I smell the hot dry day now as I run towards the end, passing a mountain-heap of grass emptied from cans hooked on to the fronts of lawn-mowers pushed by my pals; I rip a piece of tree-bark with my fingers and stuff it in my mouth, chewing wood and dust and maybe maggots as I run until I'm nearly sick, yet swallowing what I can of it just the same because a little birdie whistled to me that I've got to go on living for at least a bloody sight longer yet but that for six months I'm not going to smell that grass or taste that dusty bark or trot this lovely path. I hate to have to say this but something bloody-well made me cry, and crying is a thing I haven't bloody-well done since I was a kid of two or three. Because I'm slowing down now for Gunthorpe to catch me up, and I'm doing it in a place just where the drive turns in to the sportsfield—

where they can see what I'm doing, especially the governor and his gang from the grandstand, and I'm going so slow I'm almost marking time. Those on the nearest seats haven't caught on yet to what's happening and are still cheering like mad ready for when I make that mark, and I keep on wondering when the bleeding hell Gunthorpe behind me is going to nip by on to the field because I can't hold this up all day, and I think Oh Christ it's just my rotten luck that Gunthorpe's dropped out and that I'll be here for half an hour before the next bloke comes up, but even so, I say, I won't budge, I won't go for that last hundred yards if I have to sit down cross-legged on the grass and have the governor and his chinless wonders pick me up and carry me there, which is against their rules so you can bet they'd never do it because they're not clever enough to break the rules— like I would be in their place—even though they are their own. No, I'll show him what honesty means if it's the last thing I do, though I'm sure he'll never under-stand because if he and all them like him did it'd mean they'd be on my side which is impossible. By God I'll stick this out like my dad stuck out his pain and kicked them doctors down the stairs: if he had guts for that then I've got guts for this and here I stay waiting for Gunthorpe or Aylesham to bash that turf and go right slap-up against that bit of clothes-line stretched across the winning post. As for me, the only time I'll hit that clothes-line will be when I'm dead and a comfortable coffin's been got ready on the other side. Until then I'm a long-distance runner, crossing country all on my own no matter how bad it feels.

The Essex boys were shouting themselves blue in the face telling me to get a move on, waving their arms, standing up and making as if to run at that rope them-selves because they were only a few yards to the side of it. You cranky lot, I thought, stuck at that winning post, and yet I knew they didn't mean what they were shout-ing, were really on my side and always would be, not able to keep their maulers to themselves, in and out of cop-shops and clink. And there they were now having the time of their lives letting themselves go in cheering me which made the governor think they were heart and soul on his side when he wouldn't have thought any such thing if he'd had a grain of sense. And I could hear the lords and ladies now from the grandstand, and could

---

[1] *lino* Linoleum.

see them standing up to wave me in: "Run!" they were shouting in their posh voices. "Run!" But I was deaf, daft and blind, and stood where I was, still tasting the bark in my mouth and still blubbing like a baby, blubbing now out of gladness that I'd got them beat at last.

Because I heard a roar and saw the Gunthorpe gang throwing their coats up in the air and I felt the pat-pat of feet on the drive behind me getting closer and closer and suddenly a smell of sweat and a pair of lungs on their last gasp passed me by and went swinging on towards that rope, all shagged out and rocking from side to side, grunting like a Zulu that didn't know any better, like the ghost of me at ninety when I'm heading for that fat upholstered coffin. I could have cheered him myself: "Go on, go on, get cracking. Knot yourself up on that piece of tape." But he was already there, and so I went on, trot-trotting after him until I got to the rope, and collapsed, with a murderous sounding roar going up through my ears while I was still on the wrong side of it. It's about time to stop; though don't think I'm not still running, because I am, one way or another. The governor at Borstal proved me right; he didn't respect my honesty at all; not that I expected him to, or tried to explain it to him, but if he's supposed to be educated then he should have more or less twigged it. He got his own back right enough, or thought he did, because he had me carting dustbins about every morning from the big full-working kitchen to the garden-bottoms where I had to empty them; and in the afternoon I spread out slops over spuds and carrots growing in the allotments. In the evenings I scrubbed floors, miles and miles of them. But it wasn't a bad life for six months, which was another thing he could never understand and would have made it grimmer if he could, and it was worth it when I look back on it, considering all the thinking I did, and the fact that the boys caught on to me losing the race on purpose and never had enough good words to say about me, or curses to throw out (to themselves) at the governor.

The work didn't break me; if anything it made me stronger in many ways, and the governor knew, when I left, that his spite had got him nowhere. For since leaving Borstal they tried to get me in the army, but I didn't pass the medical and I'll tell you why. No sooner was I out, after that final run and six-months hard, that I went down with pleurisy, which means as far as I'm concerned that I lost the governor's race all right, and won my own twice over, because I know for certain that if I hadn't raced my race I wouldn't have got this pleurisy, which keeps me out of khaki but doesn't stop me doing the sort of work my itchy fingers want to do. I'm out now and the heat's switched on again, but the rats haven't got me for the last big thing I pulled. I counted six hundred and twenty-eight pounds and am still living off it because I did the job all on my own, and after it I had the peace to write all this, and it'll be money enough to keep me going until I finish my plans for doing an even bigger snatch, something up my sleeve I wouldn't tell to a living soul. I worked out my systems and hiding-places while pushing scrubbing-brushes around them Borstal floors, planned my outward life of innocence and honest work, yet at the same time grew perfect in the razor-edges of my craft for what I knew I had to do once free; and what I'll do again if netted by the poaching coppers.

In the meantime (as they say in one or two books I've read since, useless though because all of them ended on a winning post and didn't teach me a thing) I'm going to give this story to a pal of mine and tell him that if I do get captured again by the coppers he can try and get it put into a book or something, because I'd like to see the governor's face when he reads it, if he does, which I don't suppose he will; even if he did read it though I don't think he'd know what it was all about. And if I don't get caught the bloke I give this story to will never give me away; he's lived in our terrace for as long as I can remember, and he's my pal. That I do know.

—1959

# IN CONTEXT

## "Angry Young Men"

The term "Angry Young Men," which came to be associated in the 1950s with a group that
included Alan Sillitoe, was taken from the title of a 1950 autobiography by Jimmy Porter.
The writer who came most strongly to exemplify the "Angry Young Men" in the public mind,
however, was John Osborne, whose play *Look Back In Anger* (1956) had a considerable
impact on British culture in the 1950s. The following selections from Osborne's own
autobiography, *A Better Class of Person* (1981), give some sense of the grimness of the
economic and social life of many Britons of the time, and of the bitterness this caused
amongst young people—young men in particular.

### from John Osborne, *A Better Class of Person: An Autobiography, Vol. 1: 1929–1956* (1981)

If the pebble-dash house in Clandon Close[1] was not exactly a dead-and-alive hole there was little
activity inside or around it. It led nowhere, a terminus of semi-detached inertia. The houses in and
around were a uniform standard, scattered in their ribbon millions all over England between the wars.
There were occasional attempts at exotic variations such as extra bow windows in odd places or patio-
type entrances which seemed to be useful for nothing but umbrellas. Bungalows, with concrete front
gardens, had a sort of jaunty independence, inhabited by a somewhat younger set, often without
children. My grandmother's house was not typical because it was the type itself. The hall was a small,
unusable area flanked on one side by a tiny lavatory and bathroom and on the right side by a room
which was usually called, for some reason, the Playroom. In most houses it was used as a cloakroom
or for storing old toys and golf clubs. A few self-important husbands might even call it the Study or
the Den, but there would be few books there, just *News Chronicle* give-away editions of Charles
Dickens or the Waverley novels[2] gathering dust behind the golf clubs.

Novels were read in other rooms, borrowed from the twopenny library in the Parade. Biographies
of statesmen or soldiers came from the public library. Few letters were written except at Christmas
and Easter, few dens contained a desk. Letter writing was a practice which was foreign to the people
who lived here. They were immune or indifferent to contact, past or present, as if they came from
nowhere and wanted to keep it that way. Routine was Stoneleigh's[3] altar, its liturgy Radio
Normandy,[4] its mother's milk a nice quiet hot drink as usual after yet another nice quiet evening.
Casual entertaining or informal hospitality were like tolerating a smell on the landing or a blocked-up
sink. Conviviality seldom went beyond planned visits from relatives. Whim or sudden impulse was
unthinkable and blasphemed against the very idea of the God Routine. The litany read: "I just have
to have my routine. If I don't have my routine I don't know where I am," or "Well, before we start
anything we've got to work out a routine." I think Routine. Therefore I am Routine.

---

[1]   *Clandon Close*   Located in the borough of Ealing in West London.

[2]   *Waverley novels*   Novels by Sir Walter Scott.

[3]   *Stoneleigh*   Town in eastern Surrey, close to the border of greater London.

[4]   *Radio Normandy*   English radio station that, for some years, also transmitted broadcasts from ten stations in
Europe.

Spontaneity was bad breath to them. Certainly Grandma Osborne's conviction of her son's wanton instability would only have been confirmed if she had seen my maternal grandmother sitting long into the night with my father, my grandfather swearing over the *Watch Tower* and the *News of the World*, eating eel pie and faggots,[1] drinking port and Guinness, disregarding time, health, and tomorrow. What little social contact took place in Stoneleigh was mostly on the station platform and from the high-fenced back gardens on summer Sundays, when the air was broken in the early afternoon by repeated cries of "Come on, it's getting cold; it's on the *table*," as if some sick or dying patient needed attention or the kiss of life. The few telephones, always beside the front door next to the coatstand in the hall, like an unwanted ornament or vacuum cleaner, can seldom have been used for idle conversation. Sited by the coldest draught with nowhere to sit, it was an instrument for discouraging communication, forbidding it in the interest of frugality of pocket and spirit, only to be used in the reporting of sickness, disaster, or death.

Apart from the offensive notion of outside interferences like casual friendly visits, there was a similar attitude to religion which was looked upon largely as an intrusion from outside, better kept out of the house, like a muddy dog which would mark the furniture with its paws. The nearest church was up in the shopping parade by the railway station and the Stoneleigh Hotel. I can't remember what denomination it was but it looked like a steepled garage, less assured than the Great West Road factory Papist style, so it was probably Non-Conformist, a religion more suited to Stoneleigh, itself no place for Sunday drunkenness and large families. I had no contact with church at all until we went to live in Ewell Village,[2] which had a reasonably ancient parish church where I became a choir member for a short time, purely for venal reasons. We were paid one and sixpence a week, plus funeral and wedding fees....

[The family] never got up later than seven o'clock, breakfast was eaten and washed up by eight-thirty. The only reason it was necessary to keep to these spartan hours in such an otherwise indolent household was in order to have an Early Dinner, which was essential to the living of a Proper Normal Life, supposedly in the interests of my cousin Tony. The God Routine had to be obeyed even if, as in their case, it was to countenance sloth rather than endeavour. Its Prime Hours were as fixed as Sext, Nones and Compline,[3] being Early Breakfast, Early Dinner, Early Tea, Early Supper and Early Bed. To have even considered Late Breakfast or Late Supper would have broken the rule of Grandma's enclosed order. I'm sure she never had either in her life. Had she been there she would certainly have made sure that the Last Supper was an Early one. Whatever the old man pretended to be doing he was back in time for dinner. By saying Dinner rather than Lunch, she did not, like my mother, categorize the rich and privileged as people who had Dinner at Night. She regarded them as Late instead of Early, staying up Too Late and eating Too Much. Their own Early Dinner would be ready at half-past twelve or a quarter to one at the latest and would be washed up by one-thirty.

It was then time for grandfather to go upstairs to bed for his afternoon sleep, where he would lie down on his own in his long underwear until it was time for him to come down and make the tea. Meanwhile, she would have her Rest. One was supposed to make as little noise as possible during this, although she affected to be indulgent about it. She would read out from the *South Wales and Newport Argus*, the only paper she ever read at length, mostly the names of those in the Births, Marriages and Deaths columns.

---

[1] *faggots*  Inexpensive viands similar to sausages but round in shape; made of chopped liver and lungs combined with gravy and held together with pieces of pig's intestinal membrane.

[2] *Ewell Village*  Located in eastern Surrey, just south of Stoneleigh.

[3] *Sext, Nones and Compline*  In the Catholic Church, services taking place at the sixth hour of the day (noon), the ninth hour of the day (3 p.m.), and at the end of the day, respectively.

Death received first attention. Birth announcements were a matter of counting months on fingers. A few marriages produced a sniff of respectful approval but most a sceptical intake of breath. It was as if almost everyone at home had committed some predictable foolishness, like the girlish mistake of her own marriage. My mother in one of her occasional prurient confidences told me that Auntie Annie, as Grandma Osborne was known, had only allowed Grandpa to touch her twice during their marriage. This was when they were both managing the King's Arms in Newport at the turn of the century, and she submitted herself to this unroutinelike ordeal solely after secret tippling while working behind the bar, a job she despised and held to be far beneath her. It rang true. Nancy was born in 1903. Grandpa Osborne, poor neutered old dog, was to die in 1941, going without his oats for thirty-eight years. I thought of them in their feather bed, of the old man lying upstairs alone every afternoon, Annie downstairs reading the *South Wales Argus*. What were his thoughts? Denied affection, sex, respect, even the work he shunned. Years later, George Devine[1] told me a story about his own father. George's uncle was dying when he confided to him that George's mother had only allowed his father to approach her once. "Only the once, George." The result was George. Innocent of calculation, his father would sometimes give her presents of flowers or chocolates. Her response was always the same: "Oh, I see. I know what you want. Well, you're *not* going to get it." I always used to call him "One shot George." ...

## PASSING LOOKS AT CHRISTMAS

I remember some Christmases very vividly and some not at all. My early Christmases were spent between Harbord Street and Clandon Close. Christmas Day in one and Boxing Day in the other. When I was twelve I was in a nursing home for sick boys. When I was twenty-one I was drinking evaporated milk and eating brown bread and peanut butter on a camp bed in a theatre on Hayling Island.

The highlight of Christmas at both houses was the Family Row. The common acrimony and bitterness of generations would claim its victims long before the Christmas wrappings had been thrown away. It was impossible not to be caught in some cross-fire or stray flack at some points during these festive manoeuvres. I would be attacked through my mother for her profligate spending on the new clothes I might be wearing. You could be made to feel very foolish indeed standing in your new jacket or trousers which suddenly seemed to sprout pound-note signs all over them.

The Osborne Row differed from the Grove Row but they had their similarities. With the Groves at Tottenham or Harbord Street the atmosphere would be violent, even physically, and thick with accumulated melodrama. Religion was a favourite launching pad, even though only Grandpa Grove and Auntie Queenie seemed to have any religious beliefs at all. The Osborne Family Rows, in spite of the fact that they were unheedingly Christian, were centred on the related subject of money. Their disputations were on wills, testaments, entails; who had been left out, what some loved one's real intentions had been and how subsequently thwarted after death.

The Osborne Family Row was more reticent, subtle, bitter and less likely forgotten. It was stage-managed by my grandmother, like a child who alone knows the rules of a new game so that it is assured of winning. About four o'clock on Boxing Day, the appetite for muscatels and almonds and Chinese figs would begin to pall. A dawdling disappointment hung in the air. Into this let-down lull, Grandma would make the first throw. The game was hers and the name of the game was money and property. The property was mostly of a very small kind: a reference to some diamond engagement rings foolishly pawned at the wrong time; pawn tickets lost or unredeemed; fur coats handed on to the wrong recipient; wills misinterpreted; wills wrongful; unintended; insurance policies not taken out

---

[1] *George Devine* British actor and theater director (1910–66).

or allowed to lapse; stocks withheld; shares pledged. Nothing was beyond recall or valuation. Even my father's notorious Lisbon hospital bills were itemized yet again.

Having started the game rolling, the old woman would sit back in her hymnal posture, the corners of her mouth tucked into a smile and wait for all the other players to make wrong moves. My mother said little and when she did was ruled out of order and, by implication, stupid. My father seemed to become whiter and thinner than ever, watching his mother as she sat back, her eyes half-closed like a smug fakir. I could swear she was singing in her head contentedly, "Say not the struggle naught availeth," or one of her favourite self-loving songs, which sucked up to the innocence of brave old age, like "When We Grow Too Old to Dream" or "Little Old Lady Passing By." She regarded these songs as some kind of personal tribute to her own geriatric divinity. They were only two of the many Battle Hymns praising a world made in the image of Grandma.

The Grove Family Rows were not masterminded but emerged from a port-wine haze of unsated disappointment. Grandma Grove was a stoic rather than an optimist. What the two families shared was the heart pumped from birth by misgiving. Not a proud misgiving of the spirit but a timid melancholy or dislike of joy, effort or courage: "I don't suppose it'll last."... "I knew it wouldn't last." ... "How do you know it'll work?" ... "But aren't you worried?" ... "Well, there's nothing we can do about it." ... "No use crying over it." ... "Can't expect too much, go too far, only get disappointed".

Disappointment was oxygen to them. Their motto might have been *ante coitum triste est*.[1] The Grove despond was all chaos, shouting, and tearful rebukes. Their battle cries were: "You've always had it easy."... "You didn't have to go out to work like I did when I was twelve." ... "You were always Dad's favourite."... "What about you and Mum then?"... "I've worked hard for everything I've ever had." The Osborne slough was full of sly casual strokes, all the more wounding to my mother because no one said openly what they meant, not about money and certainly not about property, but about emotional privilege, social advantage, hypocrisy, and religiosity against ordinary plain dealing. The Osbornes appeared to preserve calm while being more succinct and specific. Their bitterness and sense of having been cheated from birth were certainly deeper. If my mother tried to wade in to an Osborne Row she was soon made speechless by the cold stare of Grandma and the passing looks of amusement between her and Nancy as my mother mangled the language and mispronounced words and became confused at their silences. "Did you see that?" she'd say afterwards. "They were *passing looks*." She would flush through her flaking Tokalon powder, bite her nails and turn to my father for support, which seldom came.

For Boxing Day, Grandma Osborne had perfected a pumpkin trick which turned all the cold Christmas pudding and mince pies suddenly into funeral baked meats. She did it almost on the stroke of five and in one wand-like incantation. Lying back in the Hymnal position, she would close her eyes, smile her thin gruel of a smile and say, "Ah, well, there's *another* Christmas over." I dreaded the supreme satisfaction with which she laid the body of Christmas spirit to rest. In this one phrase she crushed the festive flower and the jubilant heart. On New Year's Eve she used less relish in confirming that there was little reason to feel good about the year passing and certainly less about the coming one.

Two days of bewilderment, betrayal, triumph, and, above all, irredeemable and incurable disappointment ended. My parents gathered up our presents. A redemptive after-battle calm settled over the sitting-room strewn with wrapping paper and ribbon. We shuffled out in near silence back to Stoneleigh Park Road and my father's whisky bottle. Another Christmas Over. And in the beginning God created Grandma. To her the Inferno was as unthinkable as Paradise.

---

[1]  *ante ... est*  Latin: Before copulation [everyone] is sad. A paraphrase of Aristotles's saying "Quod omne animal post coitum est triste" (After copulation every animal is sad).

# THOM GUNN
## 1929 – 2004

An Englishman who spent much of his life in San Francisco, Thom Gunn brought together the poetic and cultural influences of England with those of the United States. In doing so he made a career of combining opposing forces—with the effect of opening up the possibilities inherent in each. The result is a body of poetry that defies easy classification; with subjects that range from San Francisco street life to European history and from motorcycle gangs to King David, and forms that include traditional sonnets, free verse, and everything in between, Gunn's poetry displays exceptional diversity and great technical skill.

Photo Courtesy of the artist
Fergus Greer.

Gunn (whose full given name was Thomson, his mother's maiden name) was born in Gravesend, Kent, in 1929. His teenage years, which coincided with World War II, were spent in a boarding school in Hampshire, and before enrolling in Trinity College, Cambridge, he completed two years of national service in the army. At Cambridge he began almost immediately to make a name for himself as a poet, and his first collection, *Fighting Terms* (1954), was released shortly after his graduation.

In these poems Gunn made use of the elements he admired in the poetry he had studied: the traditional meters of Spenser, Milton, and Dante; Elizabethan and Jacobean poetic devices; the terseness of Ben Jonson's epigrams; and the extended metaphors and direct, personal address of Donne. Within these traditional forms were distinctly modern speakers who gave voice to a sense of solipsistic isolation. This unconventional use of elevated, archaic forms for "low" modern content was characteristic of what became Gunn's lifelong penchant for (as he termed it) "filtering some kind of subject matter through a form associated with its opposite." At the time this technique was associated by journalists and critics with the ideas and techniques of a group that they dubbed "the Movement." Described as an anti-literary revolution against the aristocratic pretensions of contemporary literature, the Movement was said to include writers Donald Davie, Kingsley Amis, and Philip Larkin, in addition to Gunn, though the later writing of all these authors dispelled any sense that they could be seen as a unified group.

Following the release of *Fighting Terms*, Gunn's partner, Mike Kitay (whom Gunn had met at Cambridge), relocated to California, and Gunn accepted a creative writing fellowship at Stanford University in order to accompany him. There he added William Carlos Williams, Thomas Hardy, and the Beat poets to his list of influences and began experimenting with less rigid forms and meters, as transitional collections such as *My Sad Captains* (1961) and *Passages of Joy* (1982) demonstrate. In the first of these, half the poems are in rhymed syllabic verse (rather than accentual-syllabic meter), a form that Gunn said was a step towards free verse. (In accentual-syllabic verse forms lines follow standard patterns of stressed and unstressed syllables, whereas in syllabic verse, lines have set numbers of syllables with no fixed pattern dictating which are stressed and which unstressed.) *Passages of Joy* mixes free verse and rhymed poetry and demonstrates Gunn's developing talent for using form as a means of controlling content, and as an important tool in examining experience. For more casual perceptions he relied on free verse, while strict meter forced him, as he said, to commit to "a particular kind of very taut emotion" and to delve deeper into his experiences. For example, many of the poems in his collection *Moly* (1971) arose from his experiences with LSD and other drugs, yet these are also the most rigidly iambic of his later poems—the formal structure was the only way to contain these "untenable experiences."

Gunn often used meter to underline the action of his poems, which frequently focus on physical motion—the flight of a bird, the crawling of a snail, the slight movement of a sleeping body. His descriptions are sufficiently lively to have provoked critic Yvor Winters, Gunn's teacher at Stanford, to describe much of Gunn's poetry as existing "on the narrow line between writing and skilful journalism." Within all the best of Gunn's poems, however, an emotional or spiritual change takes place such that the reader is given not only the sense of an experience, but also an increased understanding of that experience. While many of the poems in *Man With Night Sweats* (1992), for example, have been praised for showing the AIDS epidemic as seen from inside the San Francisco gay community, these poems are not merely descriptive: they use the context of AIDS to produce poems about mortality, change, and endurance.

*Boss Cupid* (2004) was Gunn's final collection; he died in 2004, at the age of 74. Among the most powerful pieces in this diverse final volume are the conversational "Gossip" sequence, the series of intense, first-person poems spoken by serial killer Jeffrey Dahmer, and a powerful third-person description of Gunn's mother's suicide, which had taken place nearly sixty years earlier. The variety of subjects and metrical forms makes this collection the crowning achievement of a poet who continually sought to defy definition. While many have seen Gunn's as a poetry of "tensions," Gunn himself preferred the word "continuities," having said that his life "insists on continuities—between America and England, between free verse and metre, between vision and everyday consciousness."

⌘⌘⌘

### The Wound

The huge wound in my head began to heal
About the beginning of the seventh week.
Its valleys darkened, its villages became still:
For joy I did not move and dared not speak,
5  Not doctors would cure it, but time, its patient skill.

And constantly my mind returned to Troy.
After I sailed the seas I fought in turn
On both sides, sharing even Helen's[1] joy
Of place, and growing up—to see Troy burn—
10  As Neoptolemus,[2] that stubborn boy.

I lay and rested as prescription said.
Manoeuvered with the Greeks, or sallied out

Each day with Hector.[3] Finally my bed
Became Achilles' tent, to which the lout
15  Thersites[4] came reporting numbers dead.

I was myself: subject to no man's breath:
My own commander was my enemy.
And while my belt hung up, sword in the sheath,
Thersites shambled in and breathlessly
20  Cackled about my friend Patroclus'[5] death.

---

[1] *Helen*  Wife of Menelaus. Her abduction by Paris of Troy brought about the Trojan War.

[2] *Neoptolemus*  Vengeful son of Achilles who slew Priam in the Trojan War.

[3] *Hector*  Courageous Trojan warrior and son of Priam who was killed by Achilles.

[4] *Thersites*  Greek soldier who, according to Homer, was extraordinarily vulgar and mean-spirited. He was eventually killed by Achilles after he mocked Achilles's sorrow at the Amazon queen Penthesilia's death.

[5] *Patroclus*  Close friend of Achilles who, when Achilles refused to continue fighting in the Trojan War, donned his armor and fought for him. When Patroclus was killed by Ajax, Achilles refused to bury his body for several days.

I called for armour, rose, and did not reel.
But, when I thought, rage at his noble pain
Flew to my head, and turning I could feel
My wound break open wide. Over again
25  I had to let those storm-lit valleys heal.
— 1953

## Tamer and Hawk

I thought I was so tough,
But gentled at your hands,
Cannot be quick enough
To fly for you and show
5  That when I go I go
At your commands.

Even in flight above
I am no longer free:
You seeled[1] me with your love,
10  I am blind to other birds—
The habit of your words
Has hooded me.

As formerly, I wheel
I hover and I twist,
15  But only want the feel,
In my possessive thought,
Of catcher and of caught
Upon your wrist.

You but half civilize,
20  Taming me in this way.
Through having only eyes
For you I fear to lose,
I lose to keep, and choose
Tamer as prey.
—1953

---

[1]  *seeled*  Part of the taming process in falconry, seeling requires the
tamer to stitch up the eyes of the hawk.

## To His Cynical Mistress

And love is then no more than a compromise?
An impermanent treaty waiting to be signed
By the two enemies?
—While the calculating Cupid feigning impartial blind
5  Drafts it, promising peace, both leaders wise
To his antics sign but secretly double their spies.

On each side is the ignorant animal nation
Jostling friendly in streets, enjoying in good faith
This celebration
10  Forgetting their enmity with cheers and drunken breath
But for them there has not been yet amalgamation:
The leaders calmly plot assassination.
—1958

## The Hug

It was your birthday, we had drunk and dined
Half of the night with our old friend
Who'd showed us in the end
To a bed I reached in one drunk stride.
5  Already I lay snug,
And drowsy with the wine dozed on one side.

I dozed, I slept. My sleep broke on a hug,
Suddenly, from behind,
In which the full lengths of our bodies pressed:
10  Your instep to my heel,
My shoulder-blades against your chest.
It was not sex, but I could feel
The whole strength of your body set,
Or braced, to mine,
15  And locking me to you
As if we were still twenty-two
When our grand passion had not yet
Become familial.
My quick sleep had deleted all
20  Of intervening time and place.
I only knew
The stay of your secure firm dry embrace.
—1992

## The Missing

Now as I watch the progress of the plague,
   The friends surrounding me fall sick, grow thin,
And drop away. Bared, is my shape less vague
—Sharply exposed and with a sculpted skin?

5  I do not like the statue's chill contour,
   Not nowadays. The warmth investing me
Led outward through mind, limb, feeling, and more
   In an involved increasing family.

Contact of friend led to another friend,
10  Supple entwinement through the living mass
Which for all that I knew might have no end,
   Image of an unlimited embrace.

I did not just feel ease, though comfortable:
   Aggressive as in some ideal of sport,

15  With ceaseless movement thrilling through the whole,
   Their push kept me as firm as their support.

But death—Their deaths have left me less defined:
   It was their pulsing presence made me clear.
I borrowed from it, I was unconfined,
20  Who tonight balance unsupported here,

Eyes glaring from raw marble, in a pose
   Languorously part-buried in the block,
Shins perfect and no calves, as if I froze
   Between potential and a finished work.

25  —Abandoned incomplete, shape of a shape,
   In which exact detail shows the more strange,
Trapped in unwholeness, I find no escape
   Back to the play of constant give and change.
        —1992 (WRITTEN AUGUST 1987)

# HAROLD PINTER
## b. 1930

One of the most prolific of contemporary British playwrights, Harold Pinter is also a study in contrasts. Raised in working-class surroundings during a period of intense economic hardship and social unrest, he seems, in his early work at least, to eschew a direct interest in the political. And although his plays reveal a deeply felt connection to the absurdist world of Samuel Beckett and to the existential anguish of writers such as Kafka, he is at the same time steadfastly devoted to the faithful reproduction of natural dialogue and everyday experience upon the stage. Often noted for his emphasis upon silence and on the language "that we don't hear," Pinter remains equally insistent upon the centrality of language—no matter how flawed—to human experience.

Born and educated in London's East End (his father was a tailor), Pinter came of age in the immediate aftermath of World War II. After briefly attending the Royal Academy of Dramatic Art in London, Pinter spent the next eight years acting in a variety of repertory companies in Ireland and England. His first breakthrough as a writer came in 1957 with *The Room*, a one-act play centered upon two commonplace characters sitting alone in a room, into which a series of ambiguously defined individuals intrude throughout the play's course. Lauded by the drama critic Harold Hobson for its ability to "make one doubt the comforting solidity of the earth," *The Room*, in its focus upon confinement and fragmented communication, signaled some of the major preoccupations of Pinter's work over the ensuing decades. Pinter followed the success of *The Room* with *The Dumb Waiter* and *The Birthday Party*, both of which appeared in 1958 and helped to establish his early reputation as a compelling voice within English theater of the mid-century. One of his more frequently staged plays, *The Birthday Party*, caused one critic to dub Pinter's style "the comedy of menace," a phrase that nicely captured his inheritance of, and departure from, received forms such as the "comedy of manners" so popular in the early part of the century. Faithful to the speech rhythms and dialects of Pinter's immediate surroundings, and punctuated by silences, one-way conversations, and frenetic interrogations, *The Birthday Party* underlines the persecuted, even tortured, existence of modern individuals whose lives are lived in secrecy and isolation. Words, like the silences between them, are neither transparent nor benign.

If early responses to *The Birthday Party* were mixed—its first London run came to a halt after only one week—this state of affairs would not last. Pinter's 1960 play *The Caretaker* won the *Evening Standard* Drama Award for that year and was trumpeted by reviewers in both England and the United States. More accolades followed, including the Shakespeare Prize in 1970 and a Tony Award for *The Homecoming* (1965), a play that both shocked and captivated audiences with its patently unromantic portrayal of a family mired in guilt, violence, and scandal. At the same time, Pinter turned his eye to other media and dramatic forms. *A Slight Ache*, a radio play commissioned by the BBC, and *Tea Party*, a television play broadcast across Europe in 1965, demonstrated just how well-suited Pinter's focus on modern alienated life was for these avenues of dramatic production and reception.

Throughout his career, Pinter has sustained his reputation as an innovator of inherited forms. In *Betrayal* (1978), a story involving age-old themes such as memory and deception is presented in reverse chronological order, giving new emphasis to Pinter's recurrent interests in defamiliarizing and destabilizing received notions of motivation, agency, and theatrical representation. His more recent work, beginning with *One for the Road* in 1984, has taken a more overtly political turn, concerning itself with such topical issues as totalitarianism, intellectual dissidence, and globalization. (Pinter has also become something of a political activist; in 2000, for example, he campaigned actively against the NATO bombing of Serbia.) But, even as Pinter has redefined both himself and the theatrical media in which he works, he has remained committed to an examination of the issues that have always dominated the lives of his characters: language, identity, violence, and the connections among them. Pinter's plays seek to uncover and expose the disquieting psychological and political realities that lie buried beneath the sounds and silences of everyday speech.

Pinter is also a successful actor and director, appearing, for example, in a 1992 revival of his own play *No Man's Land* (1975) as well as in other theater and film roles. In 2002, he was appointed a Companion of Honour, Britain's highest civilian award, and in 2005 he was awarded the Nobel Prize for literature.

⌘ ⌘ ⌘

## *The Homecoming*

### CHARACTERS

Max, *a man of seventy*
Lenny, *a man in his early thirties*
Sam, *a man of sixty-three*
Joey, *a man in his middle twenties*
Teddy, *a man in his middle thirties*
Ruth, *a woman in her early thirties*

(*Summer*
*An old house in North London.*
*A large room, extending the width of the stage.*
*The back wall, which contained the door, has been removed. A square arch shape remains. Beyond it, the hall. In the hall a staircase, ascending up left, well in view. The front door up right. A coatstand, hooks, etc.*
*In the room a window, right. Odd tables, chairs. Two large armchairs. A large sofa, left. Against the right wall a large sideboard, the upper half of which contains a mirror. Up left, a radiogram.*)[1]

### ACT 1

(*Evening.*)

(*Lenny is sitting on the sofa with a newspaper, a pencil in his hand. He wears a dark suit. He makes occasional marks on the back page. Max comes in, from the direction of the kitchen. He goes to sideboard, opens top drawer, rummages in it, closes it.*)

(*He wears an old cardigan and a cap, and carries a stick. He walks downstage, stands, looks about the room.*)

MAX.  What have you done with the scissors? (*Pause.*) I said I'm looking for the scissors. What have you done with them? (*Pause.*) Did you hear me? I want to cut something out of the paper.

5  LENNY.  I'm reading the paper.

MAX.  Not that paper. I haven't even read that paper. I'm talking about last Sunday's paper. I was just having a look at it in the kitchen. (*Pause.*) Do you hear what I'm saying? I'm talking to you! Where's the scissors?

10  LENNY.  (*Looking up, quietly.*) Why don't you shut up, you daft prat?[2]

(*Max lifts his stick and points it at him.*)

---

[1]  *radiogram*  Radio and a phonograph together in one cabinet.

[2]  *prat*  Slang: jerk, goof.

MAX.  Don't you talk to me like that. I'm warning you. (*He sits in large armchair.*) There's an advertisement in the paper about flannel vests. Cut price. Navy surplus. I could do with a few of them. (*Pause.*) I think I'll have a fag. Give me a fag. (*Pause.*) I just asked you to give me a cigarette. (*Pause.*) Look what I'm lumbered with. (*He takes a crumpled cigarette from his pocket.*) I'm getting old, my word of honour. (*He lights it.*) You think I wasn't a tearaway?[1] I could have taken care of you, twice over. I'm still strong. You ask your Uncle Sam what I was. But at the same time I always had a kind heart. Always. (*Pause.*) I used to knock about with a man called MacGregor. I called him Mac. You remember Mac? Eh? (*Pause.*) Huhh! We were two of the worst hated men in the West End of London. I tell you, I still got the scars. We'd walk into a place, the whole room'd stand up, they'd make way to let us pass. You never heard such silence. Mind you, he was a big man, he was over six foot tall. His family were all MacGregors, they came all the way from Aberdeen, but he was the only one they called Mac. (*Pause.*) He was very fond of your mother, Mac was. Very fond. He always had a good word for her. (*Pause.*) Mind you, she wasn't such a bad woman. Even though it made me sick just to look at her rotten stinking face, she wasn't such a bad bitch. I gave her the best bleeding years of my life, anyway.

LENNY.  Plug it, will you, you stupid sod, I'm trying to read the paper.

MAX.  Listen! I'll chop your spine off, you talk to me like that! You understand? Talking to your lousy filthy father like that!

LENNY.  You know what, you're getting demented. (*Pause.*) What do you think of Second Wind for the three-thirty?

MAX.  Where?

LENNY.  Sandown Park.[2]

MAX.  Don't stand a chance.

LENNY.  Sure he does.

MAX.  Not a chance.

LENNY.  He's the winner.

---

[1] *tearaway*  Hooligan.

[2] *Sandown Park*  Horse racing track fifteen miles southwest of London.

(*Lenny ticks the paper.*)

MAX.  He talks to me about horses. (*Pause.*) I used to live on the course. One of the loves of my life. Epsom?[3] I knew it like the back of my hand. I was one of the best-known faces down at the paddock. What a marvellous open-air life. (*Pause.*) He talks to me about horses. You only read their names in the papers. But I've stroked their manes, I've held them, I've calmed them down before a big race. I was the one they used to call for. Max, they'd say, there's a horse here, he's highly strung, you're the only man on the course who can calm him. It was true. I had a ... I had an instinctive under-standing of animals. I should have been a trainer. Many times I was offered the job—you know, a proper post, by the Duke of ... I forget his name ... one of the Dukes. But I had family obligations, my family needed me at home. (*Pause.*) The times I've watched those animals thundering past the post. What an experience. Mind you, I didn't lose, I made a few bob[4] out of it, and you know why? Because I always had the smell of a good horse. I could smell him. And not only the colts but the fillies. Because the fillies are more highly strung than the colts, they're more unreliable, did you know that? No, what do you know? Nothing. But I was always able to tell a good filly by one particular trick. I'd look her in the eye. You see? I'd stand in front of her and look her straight in the eye, it was a kind of hypnotism, and by the look deep down in her eye I could tell whether she was a stayer or not. It was a gift. I had a gift. (*Pause.*) And he talks to me about horses.

LENNY.  Dad, do you mind if I change the subject? (*Pause.*) I want to ask you something. The dinner we had before, what was the name of it? What do you call it? (*Pause.*) Why don't you buy a dog? You're a dog cook. Honest. You think you're cooking for a lot of dogs.

MAX.  If you don't like it get out.

LENNY.  I am going out. I'm going out to buy myself a proper dinner.

MAX.  Well, get out! What are you waiting for?

(*Lenny looks at him.*)

---

[3] *Epsom*  Racecourse at Epsom Downs, Surrey, U.K.

[4] *bob*  Shilling.

LENNY.  What did you say?

MAX.  I said shove off out of it, that's what I said.

LENNY.  You'll go before me, Dad, if you talk to me in that tone of voice.

95 MAX.  Will I, you bitch?

(*Max grips his stick.*)

LENNY.  Oh, Daddy, you're not going to use your stick on me, are you? Eh? Don't use your stick on me Daddy. No, please. It wasn't my fault, it was one of the others. I haven't done anything wrong, Dad, honest. Don't

100 clout me with that stick, Dad.

(*Silence.*)

(*Max sits hunched. Lenny reads the paper.*)

(*Sam comes in the front door. He wears a chauffeur's uniform.*)

(*He hangs his hat on a hook in the hall and comes into the room. He goes to a chair, sits in it and sighs.*)

Hullo, Uncle Sam.

SAM.  Hullo.

LENNY.  How are you, Uncle?

SAM.  Not bad. A bit tired.

105 LENNY.  Tired? I bet you're tired. Where you been?

SAM.  I've been to London Airport.

LENNY.  All the way up to London Airport? What, right up the M4?[1]

SAM.  Yes, all the way up there.

110 LENNY.  Tch, tch, tch. Well, I think you're entitled to be tired, Uncle.

SAM.  Well, it's the drivers.

LENNY.  I know. That's what I'm talking about. I'm talking about the drivers.

115 SAM.  Knocks you out.

(*Pause.*)

MAX.  I'm here, too, you know.

(*Sam looks at him.*)

I said I'm here, too. I'm sitting here.

SAM.  I know you're here. (*Pause.*) I took a Yankee out there today … to the Airport.

120 LENNY.  Oh, a Yankee, was it?

SAM.  Yes, I been with him all day. Picked him up at the Savoy[2] at half past twelve, took him to the Caprice[3] for his lunch. After lunch I picked him up again, took him down to a house in Eaton Square—he had to pay a visit to a friend there—and then round about tea-time I took

125 him right the way out to the Airport.

LENNY.  Had to catch a plane there, did he?

SAM.  Yes. Look what he gave me. He gave me a box of cigars.

(*Sam takes a box of cigars from his pocket.*)

130 MAX.  Come here. Let's have a look at them.

(*Sam shows Max the cigars. Max takes one from the box, pinches it and sniffs it.*)

It's a fair cigar.

SAM.  Want to try one?

(*Max and Sam light cigars.*)

You know what he said to me? He told me I was the best chauffeur he'd ever had. The best one.

135 MAX.  From what point of view?

SAM.  Eh?

MAX.  From what point of view?

LENNY.  From the point of view of his driving, Dad, and his general sense of courtesy, I should say.

140 MAX.  Thought you were a good driver, did he, Sam? Well, he gave you a first-class cigar.

SAM.  Yes, he thought I was the best he'd ever had. They all say that, you know. They won't have anyone else, they only ask for me. They say I'm the best chauffeur in

145 the firm.

LENNY.  I bet the other drivers tend to get jealous, don't they, Uncle?

SAM.  They do get jealous. They get very jealous.

MAX.  Why?

---

[1]  *M4*  Highway in the U.K.

[2]  *Savoy*  Famous London hotel.

[3]  *Caprice*  Le Caprice, a high-end London restaurant.

*(Pause.)*

150 SAM. I just told you.

MAX. No, I just can't get it clear, Sam. Why do the other drivers get jealous?

SAM. Because (a) I'm the best driver, and because … (b) … I don't take liberties. *(Pause.)* I don't press myself on
155 people, you see. These big businessmen, men of affairs, they don't want the driver jawing all the time, they like to sit in the back, have a bit of peace and quiet. After all, they're sitting in a Humber Super Snipe,[1] they can afford to relax. At the same time, though, this is what
160 really makes me special … I do know how to pass the time of day when required. *(Pause.)* For instance, I told this man today I was in the second world war. Not the first. I told him I was too young for the first. But I told him I fought in the second. *(Pause.)* So did he, it turned
165 out.

*(Lenny stands, goes to the mirror and straightens his tie.)*

LENNY. He was probably a colonel, or something, in the American Air Force.

SAM. Yes.

LENNY. Probably a navigator, or something like that, in
170 a Flying Fortress.[2] Now he's most likely a high executive in a worldwide group of aeronautical engineers.

SAM. Yes.

LENNY. Yes, I know the kind of man you're talking about.

*(Lenny goes out, turning to his right.)*

175 SAM. After all, I'm experienced. I was driving a dust cart at the age of nineteen. Then I was in long-distance haulage. I had ten years as a taxi-driver and I've had five as a private chauffeur.

MAX. It's funny you never got married, isn't it? A man
180 with all your gifts. *(Pause.)* Isn't it? A man like you?

SAM. There's still time.

MAX. Is there?

*(Pause.)*

SAM. You'd be surprised.

MAX. What you been doing, banging away at your lady
185 customers, have you?

SAM. Not me.

MAX. In the back of the Snipe? Been having a few crafty reefs[3] in a layby,[4] have you?

SAM. Not me.

190 MAX. On the back seat? What about the armrest, was it up or down?

SAM. I've never done that kind of thing in my car.

MAX. Above all that kind of thing, are you, Sam?

SAM. Too true.

195 MAX. Above having a good bang on the back seat, are you?

SAM. Yes, I leave that to others.

MAX. You leave it to others? What others? You paralysed prat!

200 SAM. I don't mess up my car! Or my … my boss's car! Like other people.

MAX. Other people? What other people? *(Pause.)* What other people?

*(Pause.)*

SAM. Other people.

*(Pause.)*

205 MAX. When you find the right girl, Sam, let your family know, don't forget, we'll give you a number one send-off, I promise you. You can bring her to live here, she can keep us all happy. We'd take it in turns to give her a walk round the park.

210 SAM. I wouldn't bring her here.

MAX. Sam, it's your decision. You're welcome to bring your bride here, to the place where you live, or on the other hand you can take a suite at the Dorchester.[5] It's entirely up to you.

215 SAM. I haven't got a bride.

---

[1] *Humber Super Snipe*  British luxury car.

[2] *Flying Fortress*  Boeing B-17 bomber, a mainstay of the American Air Force in World War II.

[3] *reefs*  Gropes.

[4] *layby*  Area beside a roadway in which vehicles may park without interfering with traffic.

[5] *Dorchester*  London luxury hotel.

(*Sam stands, goes to the sideboard, takes an apple from the bowl, bites into it.*)

Getting a bit peckish.[1]

(*He looks out of the window.*)

Never get a bride like you had, anyway. Nothing like your bride … going about these days. Like Jessie. (*Pause.*) After all, I escorted her once or twice, didn't I?
220  Drove her round once or twice in my cab. She was a charming woman. (*Pause.*) All the same, she was your wife. But still … they were some of the most delightful evenings I've ever had. Used to just drive her about. It was my pleasure.
225 MAX. (*Softly, closing his eyes.*) Christ.
SAM. I used to pull up at a stall and buy her a cup of coffee. She was a very nice companion to be with.

(*Silence.*)
(*Joey comes in the front door. He walks into the room, takes his jacket off, throws it on a chair and stands.*)
(*Silence.*)

JOEY. Feel a bit hungry.
SAM. Me, too.
230 MAX. Who do you think I am, your mother? Eh? Honest. They walk in here every time of the day and night like bloody animals. Go and find yourself a mother.

(*Lenny walks into the room, stands.*)

JOEY. I've been training down at the gym.
235 SAM. Yes, the boy's been working all day and training all night.
MAX. What do you want, you bitch? You spend all the day sitting on your arse at London Airport, buy yourself a jamroll. You expect me to sit here waiting to rush into
240  the kitchen the moment you step in the door? You've been living sixty-three years, why don't you learn to cook?
SAM. I can cook.
MAX. Well, go and cook!

---
[1] *peckish* Hungry.

(*Pause.*)
245 LENNY. What the boys want, Dad, is your own special brand of cooking, Dad. That's what the boys look forward to. The special understanding of food, you know, that you've got.
MAX. Stop calling me Dad. Just stop all that calling me
250 Dad, do you understand?
LENNY. But I'm your son. You used to tuck me up in bed every night. He tucked you up, too, didn't he, Joey? (*Pause.*) He used to like tucking up his sons.

(*Lenny turns and goes towards the front door.*)

MAX. Lenny.
255 LENNY. (*Turning.*) What?
MAX. I'll give you a proper tuck up one of these nights, son. You mark my word.

(*They look at each other.*)
(*Lenny opens the front door and goes out.*)
(*Silence.*)

JOEY. I've been training with Bobby Dodd. (*Pause.*) And I had a good go at the bag as well. (*Pause.*) I wasn't in
260 bad trim.
MAX. Boxing's a gentleman's game. (*Pause.*) I'll tell you what you've got to do. What you've got to do is you've got to learn how to defend yourself, and you've got to learn how to attack. That's your only trouble as a boxer.
265 You don't know how to defend yourself, and you don't know how to attack. (*Pause.*) Once you've mastered those arts you can go straight to the top. (*Pause.*)
JOEY. I've got a pretty good idea … of how to do that.

(*Joey looks round for his jacket, picks it up, goes out of the room and up the stairs.*)
(*Pause.*)

MAX. Sam … why don't you go, too, eh? Why don't
270 you just go upstairs? Leave me quiet. Leave me alone.
SAM. I want to make something clear about Jessie, Max. I want to. I do. When I took her out in the cab, round the town, I was taking care of her, for you. I was looking after her for you, when you were busy, wasn't I? I was

showing her the West End. (*Pause.*) You wouldn't have trusted any of your other brothers. You wouldn't have trusted Mac, would you? But you trusted me. I want to remind you. (*Pause.*) Old Mac died a few years ago, didn't he? Isn't he dead? (*Pause.*) He was a lousy stinking rotten loudmouth. A bastard uncouth sodding runt. Mind you, he was a good friend of yours. (*Pause.*)

MAX.   Eh, Sam …

SAM.   What?

MAX.   Why do I keep you here? You're just an old grub.

SAM.   Am I?

MAX.   You're a maggot.

SAM.   Oh yes?

MAX.   As soon as you stop paying your way here, I mean when you're too old to pay your way, you know what I'm going to do? I'm going to give you the boot.

SAM.   You are, eh?

MAX.   Sure. I mean, bring in the money and I'll put up with you. But when the firm gets rid of you—you can flake off.

SAM.   This is my house as well, you know. This was our mother's house.

MAX.   One lot after the other. One mess after the other.

SAM.   Our father's house.

MAX.   Look what I'm lumbered with. One cast-iron bunch of crap after another. One flow of stinking pus after another. (*Pause.*) Our father! I remember him. Don't worry. You kid yourself. He used to come over to me and look down at me. My old man did. He'd bend right over me, then he'd pick me up. I was only that big. Then he'd dandle me. Give me the bottle. Wipe me clean. Give me a smile. Pat me on the bum. Pass me around, pass me from hand to hand. Toss me up in the air. Catch me coming down. I remember my father.

(*Blackout.*)
(*Lights up.*)
(*Night.*)
(*Teddy and Ruth stand at the threshold of the room.*)
(*They are both well dressed in light summer suits and light raincoats.*)
(*Two suitcases are by their side.*)
(*They look at the room. Teddy tosses the key in his hand, smiles.*)

TEDDY.   Well, the key worked. (*Pause.*) They haven't changed the lock.

(*Pause.*)

RUTH.   No one's here.

TEDDY.   (*Looking up.*) They're asleep.

(*Pause.*)

RUTH.   Can I sit down?

TEDDY.   Of course.

RUTH.   I'm tired.

(*Pause.*)

TEDDY.   Then sit down. (*She does not move.*) That's my father's chair.

RUTH.   That one?

TEDDY.   (*Smiling.*) Yes, that's it. Shall I go up and see if my room's still there?

RUTH.   It can't have moved.

TEDDY.   No, I mean if my bed's still there.

RUTH.   Someone might be in it.

TEDDY.   No. They've got their own beds.

(*Pause.*)

RUTH.   Shouldn't you wake someone up? Tell them you're here?

TEDDY.   Not at this time of night. It's too late. (*Pause.*) Shall I go up?

(*He goes into the hall, looks up the stairs, comes back.*)

Why don't you sit down? (*Pause.*) I'll just go up … have a look.

(*He goes up the stairs, stealthily.*)
(*Ruth stands, then slowly walks across the room.*)
(*Teddy returns.*)

It's still there. My room. Empty. The bed's there. What are you doing?

*(She looks at him.)*

Blankets, no sheets. I'll find some sheets. I could hear
snores. Really. They're all still here, I think. They're all
335 snoring up there. Are you cold?

RUTH.  No.

TEDDY.  I'll make something to drink, if you like.
Something hot.

RUTH.  No, I don't want anything.

*(Teddy walks about.)*

340 TEDDY.  What do you think of the room? Big, isn't it?
It's a big house. I mean, it's a fine room, don't you
think? Actually there was a wall, across there … with a
door. We knocked it down … years ago … to make an
open living area. The structure wasn't affected, you see.
345 My mother was dead.

*(Ruth sits.)*

Tired?

RUTH.  Just a little.

TEDDY.  We can go to bed if you like. No point in
waking anyone up now. Just go to bed. See them all in
350 the morning … see my father in the morning …

*(Pause.)*

RUTH.  Do you want to stay?

TEDDY.  Stay? *(Pause.)* We've come to stay. We're bound
to stay … for a few days.

RUTH.  I think … the children … might be missing us.

355 TEDDY.  Don't be silly.

RUTH.  They might.

TEDDY.  Look, we'll be back in a few days, won't we?

*(He walks about the room.)*

Nothing's changed. Still the same. *(Pause.)* Still, he'll get
a surprise in the morning, won't he? The old man. I
360 think you'll like him very much. Honestly. He's a …
well, he's old, of course. Getting on. *(Pause.)* I was born
here, do you realize that?

RUTH.  I know.

*(Pause.)*

TEDDY.  Why don't you go to bed? I'll find some sheets.
365 I feel … wide awake, isn't it odd? I think I'll stay up for
a bit. Are you tired?

RUTH.  No.

TEDDY.  Go to bed. I'll show you the room.

RUTH.  No, I don't want to.

370 TEDDY.  You'll be perfectly all right up there without
me. Really you will. I mean, I won't be long. Look, it's
just up there. It's the first door on the landing. The
bathroom's right next door. You … need some rest, you
know. *(Pause.)* I just want to … walk about for a few
375 minutes. Do you mind?

RUTH.  Of course I don't.

TEDDY.  Well … Shall I show you the room?

RUTH.  No, I'm happy at the moment.

TEDDY.  You don't have to go to bed. I'm not saying you
380 have to. I mean, you can stay up with me. Perhaps I'll
make a cup of tea or something. The only thing is we
don't want to make too much noise, we don't want to
wake anyone up.

RUTH.  I'm not making any noise.

385 TEDDY.  I know you're not.

*(He goes to her.)*

*(Gently.)* Look, it's all right, really. I'm here. I mean …
I'm with you. There's no need to be nervous. Are you
nervous?

RUTH.  No.

390 TEDDY.  There's no need to be. *(Pause.)* They're very
warm people, really. Very warm. They're my family.
They're not ogres. *(Pause.)* Well, perhaps we should go
to bed. After all, we have to be up early, to see Dad.
Wouldn't be quite right if he found us in bed, I think.
395 *(He chuckles.)* Have to be up before six, come down, say
hullo.

*(Pause.)*

RUTH.  I think I'll have a breath of air.

TEDDY.  Air? *(Pause.)* What do you mean?

RUTH.  *(Standing.)* Just a stroll.

400 TEDDY. At this time of night? But we've … only just got here. We've got to go to bed.

RUTH. I just feel like some air.

TEDDY. But I'm going to bed.

RUTH. That's all right.

405 TEDDY. But what am I going to do? (*Pause.*) The last thing I want is a breath of air. Why do you want a breath of air?

RUTH. I just do.

TEDDY. But it's late.

410 RUTH. I won't go far. I'll come back.

(*Pause.*)

TEDDY. I'll wait up for you.

RUTH. Why?

TEDDY. I'm not going to bed without you.

RUTH. Can I have the key?

(*He gives it to her.*)

415 Why don't you go to bed?

(*He puts his arms on her shoulders and kisses her. They look at each other, briefly. She smiles.*)

I won't be long.

(*She goes out of the front door.*)
(*Teddy goes to the window, peers out after her, half turns from the window, stands, suddenly chews his knuckles. Lenny walks into the room from up left. He stands. He wears pyjamas and dressing-gown. He watches Teddy. Teddy turns and sees him.*)
(*Silence.*)

TEDDY. Hullo, Lenny.

LENNY. Hullo, Teddy.

(*Pause.*)

TEDDY. I didn't hear you come down the stairs.

420 LENNY. I didn't. (*Pause.*) I sleep down here now. Next door. I've got a kind of study, workroom cum[1] bedroom

─────────
[1] *cum* Latin: with.

next door now, you see.

TEDDY. Oh. Did I … wake you up?

LENNY. No. I just had an early night tonight. You know 425 how it is. Can't sleep. Keep waking up.

(*Pause.*)

TEDDY. How are you?

LENNY. Well, just sleeping a bit restlessly, that's all. Tonight, anyway.

TEDDY. Bad dreams?

430 LENNY. No, I wouldn't say I was dreaming. It's not exactly a dream. It's just that something keeps waking me up. Some kind of tick.

TEDDY. A tick?

LENNY. Yes.

435 TEDDY. Well, what is it?

LENNY. I don't know.

(*Pause.*)

TEDDY. Have you got a clock in your room?

LENNY. Yes.

TEDDY. Well, maybe it's the clock.

440 LENNY. Yes, could be, I suppose. (*Pause.*) Well, if it's the clock I'd better do something about it. Stifle it in some way, or something.

(*Pause.*)

TEDDY. I've just come back for a few days

LENNY. Oh yes? Have you?

(*Pause.*)

445 TEDDY. How's the old man?

LENNY. He's in the pink.

(*Pause.*)

TEDDY. I've been keeping well.

LENNY. Oh, have you? (*Pause.*) Staying the night then, are you?

450 TEDDY. Yes.

LENNY. Well, you can sleep in your old room.

TEDDY.  Yes, I've been up.
LENNY.  Yes, you can sleep there.

(*Lenny yawns.*)

Oh well.

455  TEDDY.  I'm going to bed.
LENNY.  Are you?
TEDDY.  Yes, I'll get some sleep.
LENNY.  Yes I'm going to bed, too.

(*Teddy picks up the cases.*)

I'll give you a hand.
460  TEDDY.  No, they're not heavy.

(*Teddy goes into the hall with the cases. Lenny turns out the
light in the room. The light in the hall remains on. Lenny
follows into the hall.*)

LENNY.  Nothing you want?
TEDDY.  Mmmm?
LENNY.  Nothing you might want, for the night? Glass of
water, anything like that?
465  TEDDY.  Any sheets anywhere?
LENNY.  In the sideboard in your room.
TEDDY.  Oh, good.
LENNY.  Friends of mine occasionally stay there, you
know, in your room, when they're passing through this
470  part of the world.

(*Lenny turns out the hall light and turns on the first
landing light.*)
(*Teddy begins to walk up the stairs.*)

TEDDY.  Well, I'll see you at breakfast, then.
LENNY.  Yes, that's it. Ta-ta.

(*Teddy goes upstairs. Lenny goes off left.*)
(*Silence.*)
(*The landing light goes out. Slight night light in the hall
and room. Lenny comes back into the room, goes to the
window and looks out. He leaves the window and turns on
a lamp. He is holding a small clock. He sits, places the clock
in front of him, lights a cigarette and sits. Ruth comes in*)

*the front door. She stands still. Lenny turns his head, smiles.
She walks slowly into the room.*)

LENNY.  Good evening.
RUTH.  Morning, I think.
475  LENNY.  You're right there. (*Pause.*) My name's Lenny.
What's yours?
RUTH.  Ruth.

(*She sits, puts her coat collar around her.*)

LENNY.  Cold?
RUTH.  No.
480  LENNY.  It's been a wonderful summer, hasn't it?
Remarkable. (*Pause.*) Would you like something?
Refreshment of some kind? An aperitif, anything like
that?
RUTH.  No, thanks.
485  LENNY.  I'm glad you said that. We haven't got a drink
in the house. Mind you, I'd soon get some in, if we had
a party or something like that. Some kind of celebration
... you know. (*Pause.*) You must be connected with my
brother in some way. The one who's been abroad.
490  RUTH.  I'm his wife.
LENNY.  Eh listen, I wonder if you can advise me. I've
been having a bit of a rough time with this clock. The
tick's been keeping me up. The trouble is I'm not all
that convinced it was the clock. I mean there are lots of
495  things which tick in the night, don't you find that? All
sorts of objects, which, in the day, you wouldn't call
anything else but commonplace. They give you no
trouble. But in the night any given one of a number of
them is liable to start letting out a bit of a tick. Whereas
500  you look at these objects in the day and they're just
commonplace. They're as quiet as mice during the
daytime. So ... all things being equal ... this question of
me saying it was the clock that woke me up, well, that
could very easily prove something of a false hypothesis.

(*He goes to the sideboard, pours from a jug into a glass,
takes the glass to Ruth.*)

505  Here you are. I bet you could do with this.
RUTH.  What is it?
LENNY.  Water.

(*She takes it, sips, places the glass on a small table by her chair. Lenny watches her.*)

Isn't it funny? I've got my pyjamas on and you're fully dressed.

(*He goes to the sideboard and pours another glass of water.*)

510 Mind if I have one? Yes, it's funny seeing my old brother again after all these years. It's just the sort of tonic my Dad needs, you know. He'll be chuffed[1] to his bollocks in the morning, when he sees his eldest son. I was surprised myself when I saw Teddy, you know. Old

515 Ted. I thought he was in America.
RUTH.  We're on a visit to Europe.
LENNY.  What, both of you?
RUTH.  Yes.
LENNY.  What, you sort of live with him over there, do

520 you?
RUTH.  We're married.
LENNY.  On a visit to Europe, eh? Seen much of it?
RUTH.  We've just come from Italy.
LENNY.  Oh, you went to Italy first, did you? And then

525 he brought you over here to meet the family, did he? Well, the old man'll be pleased to see you, I can tell you.
RUTH.  Good.
LENNY.  What did you say?
RUTH.  Good.

(*Pause.*)

530 LENNY.  Where'd you go to in Italy?
RUTH.  Venice.
LENNY.  Not dear old Venice? Eh? That's funny. You know, I've always had a feeling that if I'd been a soldier in the last war—say in the Italian campaign—I'd

535 probably have found myself in Venice. I've always had that feeling. The trouble was I was too young to serve, you see. I was only a child, I was too small, otherwise I've got a pretty shrewd idea I'd probably have gone through Venice. Yes, I'd almost certainly have gone

540 through it with my battalion. Do you mind if I hold your hand?
RUTH.  Why?

---

[1]  *chuffed*  Pleased.

LENNY.  Just a touch.

(*He stands and goes to her.*)

Just a tickle.
545 RUTH.  Why?

(*He looks down at her.*)

LENNY.  I'll tell you why.

(*Slight pause.*)

One night, not too long ago, one night down by the docks, I was standing alone under an arch, watching all the men jibbing the boom,[2] out in the harbour, and playing about with a yardarm, when a certain lady came

550 up to me and made me a certain proposal. This lady had been searching for me for days. She'd lost track of my whereabouts. However, the fact was she eventually caught up with me, and when she caught up with me she made me this certain proposal. Well, this proposal

555 wasn't entirely out of order and normally I would have subscribed to it. I mean I would have subscribed to it in the normal course of events. The only trouble was she was falling apart with the pox.[3] So I turned it down. Well, this lady was very insistent and started taking

560 liberties with me down under this arch, liberties which by any criterion I couldn't be expected to tolerate, the facts being what they were, so I clumped her one. It was on my mind at the time to do away with her, you know, to kill her, and the fact is, that as killings go, it would

565 have been a simple matter, nothing to it. Her chauffeur, who had located me for her, he'd popped round the corner to have a drink, which just left this lady and myself, you see, alone, standing underneath this arch, watching all the steamers steaming up, no one about, all

570 quiet on the Western Front, and there she was up against this wall—well, just sliding down the wall, following the blow I'd given her. Well, to sum up, everything was in my favour, for a killing. Don't worry about the chauffeur. The chauffeur would never have

575 spoken. He was an old friend of the family. But … in

---

[2]  *jibbing the boom*  Shifting a sail.

[3]  *the pox*  Venereal disease.

the end I thought ... Aaah, why go to all the bother ... you know, getting rid of the corpse and all that, getting yourself into a state of tension. So I just gave her another belt in the nose and a couple of turns of the
580  boot and sort of left it at that.

RUTH.   How did you know she was diseased?

LENNY.   How did I know? (*Pause.*) I decided she was.

(*Silence.*)

You and my brother are newly-weds, are you?

RUTH.   We've been married six years.

585  LENNY.   He's always been my favourite brother, old Teddy. Do you know that? And my goodness we are proud of him here, I can tell you. Doctor of Philosophy and all that ... leaves quite an impression. Of course, he's a very sensitive man, isn't he? Ted. Very. I've often
590  wished I was as sensitive as he is.

RUTH.   Have you?

LENNY.   Oh yes. Oh yes, very much so. I mean, I'm not saying I'm not sensitive. I am. I could just be a bit more so, that's all.

595  RUTH.   Could you?

LENNY.   Yes, just a bit more so, that's all. (*Pause.*) I mean, I am very sensitive to atmosphere, but I tend to get desensitized, if you know what I mean, when people make unreasonable demands on me. For instance, last
600  Christmas I decided to do a bit of snow-clearing for the Borough Council, because we had a heavy snow over here that year in Europe. I didn't have to do this snow-clearing—I mean I wasn't financially embarrassed in any way—it just appealed to me, it appealed to something
605  inside me. What I anticipated with a good deal of pleasure was the brisk cold bite in the air in the early morning. And I was right. I had to get my snowboots on and I had to stand on a corner, at about five-thirty in the morning, to wait for the lorry to pick me up, to take
610  me to the allotted area. Bloody freezing. Well, the lorry came, I jumped on the tailboard, headlights on, dipped, and off we went. Got there, shovels up, fags on, and off we went, deep into the December snow, hours before cockcrow. Well, that morning, while I was having my
615  mid-morning cup of tea in a neighbouring cafe, the shovel standing by my chair, an old lady approached me and asked me if I would give her a hand with her iron mangle.[1] Her brother-in-law, she said, had left it for her, but he'd left it in the wrong room, he'd left it in the
620  front room. Well, naturally, she wanted it in the back room. It was a present he'd given her, you see, a mangle, to iron out the washing. But he'd left it in the wrong-room, he'd left it in the front room, well that was a silly place to leave it, it couldn't stay there. So I took time off
625  to give her a hand. She only lived up the road. Well, the only trouble was when I got there I couldn't move this mangle. It must have weighed about half a ton. How this brother-in-law got it up there in the first place I can't even begin to envisage. So there I was, doing a bit
630  of shoulders on with the mangle, risking a rupture, and this old lady just standing there, waving me on, not even lifting a little finger to give me a helping hand. So after a few minutes I said to her, now look here, why don't you stuff this iron mangle up your arse? Anyway, I said,
635  they're out of date, you want to get a spin drier. I had a good mind to give her a workover there and then, but as I was feeling jubilant with the snow-clearing I just gave her a short-arm jab to the belly and jumped on a bus outside. Excuse me, shall I take this ashtray out of your
640  way?

RUTH.   It's not in my way.

LENNY.   It seems to be in the way of your glass. The glass was about to fall. Or the ashtray. I'm rather worried about the carpet. It's not me, it's my father. He's
645  obsessed with order and clarity. He doesn't like mess. So, as I don't believe you're smoking at the moment, I'm sure you won't object if I move the ashtray. (*He does so.*) And now perhaps I'll relieve you of your glass.

RUTH.   I haven't quite finished.

650  LENNY.   You've consumed quite enough, in my opinion.

RUTH.   No, I haven't.

LENNY.   Quite sufficient, in my own opinion.

RUTH.   Not in mine, Leonard.

(*Pause.*)

LENNY.   Don't call me that, please.

655  RUTH.   Why not?

LENNY.   That's the name my mother gave me. (*Pause.*) Just give me the glass.

RUTH.   No.

---

[1]  *mangle*  Laundry wringer.

(*Pause.*)

LENNY.  I'll take it, then.

660  RUTH.  If you take the glass … I'll take you.

(*Pause.*)

LENNY.  How about me taking the glass without you taking me?

RUTH.  Why don't I just take you?

(*Pause.*)

LENNY.  You're joking. (*Pause.*) You're in love, anyway,
665  with another man. You've had a secret liaison with another man. His family didn't even know. Then you come here without a word of warning and start to make trouble.

(*She picks up the glass and lifts it towards him.*)

RUTH.  Have a sip. Go on. Have a sip from my glass.

(*He is still.*)

670  Sit on my lap. Take a long cool sip.

(*She pats her lap. Pause.*)
(*She stands, moves to him with the glass.*)

Put your head back and open your mouth.

LENNY.  Take that glass away from me.

RUTH.  Lie on the floor. Go on. I'll pour it down your throat.

675  LENNY.  What are you doing, making me some kind of proposal?

(*She laughs shortly, drains the glass.*)

RUTH.  Oh, I was thirsty.

(*She smiles at him, puts the glass down, goes into the hall and up the stairs.*)
(*He follows into the hall and shouts up the stairs.*)

LENNY.  What was that supposed to be? Some kind of proposal?

(*Silence.*)
(*He comes back into the room, goes to his own glass, drains it.*)
(*A door slams upstairs.*)
(*The landing light goes on.*)
(*Max comes down the stairs, in pyjamas and cap. He comes into the room.*)

680  MAX.  What's going on here? You drunk?

(*He stares at Lenny.*)

What are you shouting about? You gone mad?

(*Lenny pours another glass of water.*)

Prancing about in the middle of the night shooting your head off. What are you, a raving lunatic?

LENNY.  I was thinking aloud.

685  MAX.  Is Joey down here? You been shouting at Joey?

LENNY.  Didn't you hear what I said, Dad? I said I was thinking aloud.

MAX.  You were thinking so loud you got me out of bed.

LENNY.  Look, why don't you just … pop off, eh?

690  MAX.  Pop off? He wakes me up in the middle of the night, I think we got burglars here, I think he's got a knife stuck in him, I come down here, he tells me to pop off.

(*Lenny sits down.*)

He was talking to someone. Who could he have been
695  talking to? They're all asleep. He was having a conversation with someone. He won't tell me who it was. He pretends he was thinking aloud. What are you doing, hiding someone here?

LENNY.  I was sleepwalking. Get out of it, leave me
700  alone, will you?

MAX.  I want an explanation, you understand? I asked you who you got hiding here.

(*Pause.*)

LENNY.   I'll tell you what, Dad, since you're in the mood
for a bit of a ... chat. I'll ask you a question. It's a
705   question I've been meaning to ask you for some time.
That night ... you know ... the night you got me ...
that night with Mum, what was it like? Eh? When I was
just a glint in your eye. What was it like? What was the
background to it? I mean, I want to know the real facts
710   about my background. I mean, for instance, is it a fact
that you had me in mind all the time, or is it a fact that
I was the last thing you had in mind? (*Pause.*) I'm only
asking this in a spirit of inquiry, you understand that,
don't you? I'm curious. And there's lots of people of my
715   age share that curiosity, you know that, Dad? They
often ruminate, sometimes singly, sometimes in groups,
about the true facts of that particular night—the night
they were made in the image of those two people *at it*.
It's a question long overdue, from my point of view, but
720   as we happen to be passing the time of day here tonight
I thought I'd pop it to you.

(*Pause.*)

MAX.   You'll drown in your own blood.
LENNY.   If you prefer to answer the question in writing
I've got no objection.

(*Max stands.*)

725   I should have asked my dear mother. Why didn't I ask
my dear mother? Now it's too late. She's passed over to
the other side.

(*Max spits at him.*)
(*Lenny looks down at the carpet.*)

Now look what you've done. I'll have to Hoover[1] that in
the morning, you know.

(*Max turns and walks up the stairs.*)
(*Lenny sits still.*)
(*Blackout.*)
(*Lights up.*)
(*Morning.*)
(*Joey in front of the mirror. He is doing some slow*

---

[1]   *Hoover* Vacuum.

*limbering-up exercises. He stops, combs his hair, carefully.*
*He then shadowboxes, heavily, watching himself in the*
*mirror.*)
(*Max comes in from up left.*)
(*Both Max and Joey are dressed. Max watches Joey in*
*silence.*)
(*Joey stops shadowboxing, picks up a newspaper and sits.*)
(*Silence.*)

730 MAX.   I hate this room. (*Pause.*) It's the kitchen I like.
It's nice in there. It's cosy. (*Pause.*) But I can't stay in
there. You know why? Because he's always washing up
in there, scraping the plates, driving me out of the
kitchen, that's why.
735 JOEY.   Why don't you bring your tea in here?
MAX.   I don't want to bring my tea in here. I hate it here.
I want to drink my tea in there.

(*He goes into the hall and looks towards the kitchen.*)

What's he doing in there?

(*He returns.*)

What's the time?
740 JOEY.   Half past six.
MAX.   Half past six. (*Pause.*) I'm going to see a game of
football this afternoon. You want to come? (*Pause.*) I'm
talking to you.
JOEY.   I'm training this afternoon. I'm doing six rounds
745   with Blackie.
MAX.   That's not till five o'clock. You've got time to see
a game of football before five o'clock. It's the first game
of the season.
JOEY.   No, I'm not going.
750 MAX.   Why not?

(*Pause.*)
(*Max goes into the hall.*)

Sam! Come here!

(*Max comes back into the room. Sam enters with a cloth.*)

SAM.   What?

MAX.  What are you doing in there?

SAM.  Washing up.

755 MAX.  What else?

SAM.  Getting rid of your leavings.

MAX.  Putting them in the bin, eh?

SAM.  Right in.

MAX.  What point you trying to prove?

760 SAM.  No point.

MAX.  Oh yes, you are. You resent making my breakfast, that's what it is, isn't it? That's why you bang round the kitchen like that, scraping the frying-pan, scraping all the leavings into the bin, scraping all the plates, scraping

765 all the tea out of the teapot … that's why you do that, every single stinking morning. I know. Listen, Sam. I want to say something to you. From my heart.

(*He moves closer.*)

I want you to get rid of these feelings of resentment you've got towards me. I wish I could understand them.

770 Honestly, have I ever given you cause? Never. When Dad died he said to me, Max, look after your brothers. That's exactly what he said to me.

SAM.  How could he say that when he was dead?

MAX.  What?

775 SAM.  How could he speak if he was dead?

(*Pause.*)

MAX.  Before he died, Sam. Just before. They were his last words. His last sacred words, Sammy. You think I'm joking? You think when my father spoke—on his deathbed—I wouldn't obey his words to the last letter?

780 You hear that, Joey? He'll stop at nothing. He's even prepared to spit on the memory of our Dad. What kind of a son were you, you wet wick? You spent half your time doing crossword puzzles! We took you into the butcher's shop, you couldn't even sweep the dust off the

785 floor. We took MacGregor into the shop, he could run the place by the end of a week. Well, I'll tell you one thing. I respected my father not only as a man but as a number one butcher! And to prove it I followed him into the shop. I learned to carve a carcass at his knee. I

790 commemorated his name in blood. I gave birth to three grown men! All on my own bat. What have you done?

(*Pause.*) What have you done? You tit!

SAM.  Do you want to finish the washing up? Look, here's the cloth.

795 MAX.  So try to get rid of these feelings of resentment, Sam.  After all, we are brothers.

SAM.  Do you want the cloth? Here you are. Take it.

(*Teddy and Ruth come down the stairs. They walk across the hall and stop just inside the room. The others turn and look at them. Joey stands. Teddy and Ruth are wearing dressing-gowns.*)
(*Silence.*)
(*Teddy smiles.*)

TEDDY.  Hullo … Dad … We overslept. (*Pause.*) What's for breakfast?

(*Silence.*)
(*Teddy chuckles.*)

800 Huh. We overslept.

(*Max turns to Sam.*)

MAX.  Did you know he was here?

SAM.  No.

(*Max turns to Joey.*)

MAX.  Did you know he was here? (*Pause.*) I asked you if you knew he was here.

805 JOEY.  No.

MAX.  Then who knew? (*Pause.*) Who knew? (*Pause.*) I didn't know.

TEDDY.  I was going to come down, Dad, I was going to … be here, when you came down. (*Pause.*) How are

810 you? (*Pause.*) Uh … look, I'd … like you to meet …

MAX.  How long you been in this house?

TEDDY.  All night.

MAX.  All night? I'm a laughing-stock. How did you get in?

815 TEDDY.  I had my key.

(*Max whistles and laughs.*)

MAX.  Who's this?

TEDDY.   I was just going to introduce you.

MAX.  Who asked you to bring tarts in here?

TEDDY.  Tarts?

820 MAX.  Who asked you to bring dirty tarts into this house?

TEDDY.  Listen, don't be silly

MAX.  You been here all night?

TEDDY.  Yes, we arrived from Venice

825 MAX.  We've had a smelly scrubber[1] in my house all night. We've had a stinking pox-ridden slut in my house all night.

TEDDY.  Stop it! What are you talking about?

MAX.  I haven't seen the bitch for six years, he comes

830 home without a word, he brings a filthy scrubber off the street, he shacks up in my house!

TEDDY.  She's my wife! We're married!

(*Pause.*)

MAX.  I've never had a whore under this roof before. Ever since your mother died. My word of honour. (*To*

835 *Joey.*) Have you ever had a whore here? Has Lenny ever had a whore here? They come back from America, they bring the slopbucket with them. They bring the bedpan with them. (*To Teddy.*) Take that disease away from me. Get her away from me.

840 TEDDY.  She's my wife.

MAX.  (*To Joey.*) Chuck them out. (*Pause.*) A Doctor of Philosophy, Sam, you want to meet a Doctor of Philosophy? (*To Joey.*) I said chuck them out. (*Pause.*) What's the matter? You deaf?

845 JOEY.  You're an old man. (*To Teddy.*) He's an old man.

(*Lenny walks into the room, in a dressing-gown. He stops. They all look round. Max turns back, hits Joey in the stomach with all his might. Joey contorts, staggers across the stage. Max, with the exertion of the blow, begins to collapse. His knees buckle. He clutches his stick. Sam moves forward to help him. Max hits him across the head with his stick, Sam sits, head in hands. Joey, hands pressed to his stomach, sinks down at the feet of Ruth. She looks down at him. Lenny and Teddy are still. Joey slowly stands. He is close to Ruth. He turns from Ruth, looks round at Max. Sam*

[1] *scrubber* Prostitute.

*clutches his head. Max breathes heavily, very slowly gets to his feet. Joey moves to him. They look at each other.*)
(*Silence.*)
(*Max moves past Joey, walks towards Ruth. He gestures with his stick.*)

MAX.  Miss.

(*Ruth walks towards him.*)

RUTH.  Yes?

(*He looks at her.*)

MAX.  You a mother?

RUTH.  Yes.

850 MAX.  How many you got?

RUTH.  Three.

(*He turns to Teddy.*)

MAX.  All yours, Ted? (*Pause.*) Teddy, why don't we have a nice cuddle and kiss, eh? Like the old days? What about a nice cuddle and kiss, eh?

855 TEDDY.  Come on, then.

(*Pause.*)

MAX.  You want to kiss your old father? Want a cuddle with your old father?

TEDDY.  Come on, then. (*Teddy moves a step towards him.*) Come on. (*Pause.*)

860 MAX.  You still love your old Dad, eh?

(*They face each other.*)

TEDDY.  Come on, Dad. I'm ready for the cuddle.

(*Max begins to chuckle, gurgling. He turns to the family and addresses them.*)

MAX.  He still loves his father!

(*Curtain.*)

ACT 2

(*Afternoon.*)

(*Max, Teddy, Lenny and Sam are about the stage, lighting cigars.*)

(*Joey comes in from up left with a coffee tray, followed by Ruth. He puts the tray down. Ruth hands coffee to all the men. She sits with her cup. Max smiles at her.*)

RUTH.    That was a very good lunch.

MAX.    I'm glad you liked it. (*To the others.*) Did you hear that? (*To Ruth.*) Well, I put my heart and soul into it, I can tell you. (*He sips.*) And this is a lovely cup of coffee.

5    RUTH.    I'm glad.

(*Pause.*)

MAX.    I've got the feeling you're a first-rate cook.

RUTH.    I'm not bad.

MAX.    No, I've got the feeling you're a number one cook. Am I right, Teddy?

10    TEDDY.    Yes, she's a very good cook.

(*Pause.*)

MAX.    Well, it's a long time since the whole family was together, eh? If only your mother was alive. Eh, what do you say, Sam? What would Jessie say if she was alive? Sitting here with her three sons. Three fine grown-up

15    lads. And a lovely daughter-in-law. The only shame is her grandchildren aren't here. She'd have petted them and cooed over them, wouldn't she, Sam? She'd have fussed over them and played with them, told them stories, tickled them—I tell you she'd have been

20    hysterical. (*To Ruth.*) Mind you, she taught those boys everything they know. She taught them all the morality they know. I'm telling you. Every single bit of the moral code they live by—was taught to them by their mother. And she had a heart to go with it. What a heart. Eh,

25    Sam? Listen, what's the use of beating round the bush? That woman was the backbone to this family. I mean, I was busy working twenty-four hours a day in the shop, I was going all over the country to find meat, I was making my way in the world, but I left a woman at

30    home with a will of iron, a heart of gold and a mind.

Right, Sam? (*Pause.*) What a mind. (*Pause.*) Mind you, I was a generous man to her. I never left her short of a few bob. I remember one year I entered into negotiations with a top-class group of butchers with

35    continental connections. I was going into association with them. I remember the night I came home, I kept quiet. First of all I gave Lenny a bath, then Teddy a bath, then Joey a bath. What fun we used to have in the bath, eh, boys? Then I came downstairs and I made

40    Jessie put her feet up on a pouffe[1]—what happened to that pouffe, I haven't seen it for years—she put her feet up on the pouffe and I said to her, Jessie, I think our ship is going to come home, I'm going to treat you to a couple of items, I'm going to buy you a dress in pale

45    corded blue silk, heavily encrusted in pearls, and for casual wear, a pair of pantaloons in lilac flowered taffeta. Then I gave her a drop of cherry brandy. I remember the boys came down, in their pyjamas, all their hair shining, their faces pink, it was before they started

50    shaving, and they knelt down at our feet, Jessie's and mine. I tell you, it was like Christmas.

(*Pause.*)

RUTH.    What happened to the group of butchers?

MAX.    The group? They turned out to be a bunch of criminals like everyone else. (*Pause.*) This is a lousy

55    cigar.

(*He stubs it out. He turns to Sam.*)

What time you going to work?

SAM.    Soon.

MAX.    You've got a job on this afternoon, haven't you?

SAM.    Yes, I know.

60    MAX.    What do you mean, you know? You'll be late. You'll lose your job. What are you trying to do, humiliate me?

SAM.    Don't worry about me.

MAX.    It makes the bile come up in my mouth. The

65    bile—you understand? (*To Ruth.*) I worked as a butcher all my life, using the chopper and the slab, the slab, you know what I mean, the chopper and the slab! To keep my family in luxury. Two families! My mother was

---

[1]    *pouffe*    Low padded seat.

bedridden, my brothers were all invalids. I had to earn
70  the money for the leading psychiatrists. I had to read
books! I had to study the disease, so that I could cope
with an emergency at every stage. A crippled family,
three bastard sons, a slutbitch of a wife—don't talk to
me about the pain of childbirth—I suffered the pain,
75  I've still got the pangs—when I give a little cough my
back collapses—and here I've got a lazy idle bugger of a
brother won't even get to work on time. The best
chauffeur in the world. All his life he's sat in the front
seat giving lovely hand signals. You call that work? This
80  man doesn't know his gearbox from his arse!

SAM.  You go and ask my customers! I'm the only one
they ever ask for.

MAX.  What do the other drivers do, sleep all day?

SAM.  I can only drive one car. They can't all have me at
85  the same time.

MAX.  Anyone could have you at the same time. You'd
bend over for half a dollar on Blackfriars Bridge.[1]

SAM.  Me!

MAX.  For two bob and a toffee apple.

90  SAM.  He's insulting me. He's insulting his brother. I'm
driving a man to Hampton Court[2] at four forty-five.

MAX.  Do you want to know who could drive?
MacGregor! MacGregor was a driver.

SAM.  Don't you believe it.

(*Max points his stick at Sam.*)

95  MAX.  He didn't even fight in the war. This man didn't
even fight in the bloody war!

SAM.  I did!

MAX.  Who did you kill?

(*Silence.*)

(*Sam gets up, goes to Ruth, shakes her hand and goes out of
the front door.*)

(*Max turns to Teddy.*)

Well, how you been keeping, son?

100  TEDDY.  I've been keeping very well, Dad.

MAX.  It's nice to have you with us, son.

---

[1]  *Blackfriars Bridge*  One of London's bridges over the Thames
River.

[2]  *Hampton Court*  Castle in Herefordshire.

TEDDY.  It's nice to be back, Dad.

(*Pause.*)

MAX.  You should have told me you were married,
Teddy. I'd have sent you a present. Where was the
105  wedding, in America?

TEDDY.  No. Here. The day before we left.

MAX.  Did you have a big function?

TEDDY.  No, there was no one there.

MAX.  You're mad. I'd have given you a white wedding.
110  We'd have had the cream of the cream here. I'd have
been only too glad to bear the expense, my word of
honour.

(*Pause.*)

TEDDY.  You were busy at the time. I didn't want to
bother you.

115  MAX.  But you're my own flesh and blood. You're my
first born. I'd have dropped everything. Sam would have
driven you to the reception in the Snipe, Lenny would
have been your best man, and then we'd have all seen
you off on the boat. I mean, you don't think I
120  disapprove of marriage, do you? Don't be daft. (*To
Ruth.*) I've been begging my two youngsters for years to
find a nice feminine girl with proper credentials—it
makes life worth living. (*To Teddy.*) Anyway, what's the
difference, you did it, you made a wonderful choice,
125  you've got a wonderful family, a marvellous career ... so
why don't we let bygones be bygones? (*Pause.*) You
know what I'm saying? I want you both to know that
you have my blessing.

TEDDY.  Thank you.

130  MAX.  Don't mention it. How many other houses in the
district have got a Doctor of Philosophy sitting down
drinking a cup of coffee?

(*Pause.*)

RUTH.  I'm sure Teddy's very happy ... to know that
you're pleased with me. (*Pause.*) I think he wondered
135  whether you would be pleased with me.

MAX.  But you're a charming woman.

(*Pause.*)

RUTH.  I was …
MAX.  What? (*Pause.*) What she say?

(*They all look at her.*)

RUTH.  I was … different … when I met Teddy … first.
140 TEDDY.  No you weren't. You were the same.
RUTH.  I wasn't.
MAX.  Who cares? Listen, live in the present, what are you
worrying about? I mean, don't forget the earth's about
five thousand million years old, at least. Who can afford
145 to live in the past?

(*Pause.*)

TEDDY.  She's a great help to me over there. She's a
wonderful wife and mother. She's a very popular
woman. She's got lots of friends. It's a great life, at the
University … you know … it's a very good life. We've
150 got a lovely house … we've got all … we've got
everything we want. It's a very stimulating environment.
(*Pause.*) My department … is highly successful. (*Pause.*)
We've got three boys, you know.
MAX.  All boys? Isn't that funny, eh? You've got three,
155 I've got three. You've got three nephews, Joey. Joey!
You're an uncle, do you hear? You could teach them
how to box.

(*Pause.*)

JOEY.  (*To Ruth.*) I'm a boxer. In the evenings, after
work. I'm in demolition in the daytime.
160 RUTH.  Oh?
JOEY.  Yes. I hope to be full time, when I get more bouts.
MAX.  (*To Lenny.*) He speaks so easily to his sister-in-
law, do you notice? That's because she's an intelligent
and sympathetic woman.

(*He leans to her.*)

165 Eh, tell me, do you think the children are missing their
mother?

(*She looks at him.*)

TEDDY.  Of course they are. They love her. We'll be
seeing them soon.

(*Pause.*)

LENNY.  (*To Teddy.*) Your cigar's gone out.
170 TEDDY.  Oh, yes.
LENNY.  Want a light?
TEDDY.  No. No. (*Pause.*) So has yours.
LENNY.  Oh, yes. (*Pause.*) Eh, Teddy, you haven't told us
much about your Doctorship of Philosophy. What do
175 you teach?
TEDDY.  Philosophy.
LENNY.  Well, I want to ask you something. Do you
detect a certain logical incoherence in the central
affirmations of Christian theism?
180 TEDDY.  That question doesn't fall within my province.
LENNY.  Well, look at it this way … you don't mind my
asking you some questions, do you?
TEDDY.  If they're within my province.
LENNY.  Well, look at it this way. How can the unknown
185 merit reverence? In other words, how can you revere
that of which you're ignorant? At the same time, it
would be ridiculous to propose that what we *know*
merits reverence. What we know merits any one of a
number of things, but it stands to reason reverence isn't
190 one of them. In other words, apart from the known and
the unknown, what else is there?

(*Pause.*)

TEDDY.  I'm afraid I'm the wrong person to ask.
LENNY.  But you're a philosopher. Come on, be frank.
What do you make of all this business of being and not-
195 being?
TEDDY.  What do you make of it?
LENNY.  Well, for instance, take a table. Philosophically
speaking. What is it?
TEDDY.  A table.
200 LENNY.  Ah. You mean it's nothing else but a table. Well,
some people would envy your certainty, wouldn't they,
Joey? For instance, I've got a couple of friends of mine,
we often sit round the Ritz Bar having a few liqueurs,

and they're always saying things like that, you know,
205 things like: Take a table, take it. All right, I say, *take* it,
*take* a table, but once you've taken it, what you going to
do with it? Once you've got hold of it, where you going
to take it?

MAX.   You'd probably sell it.

210 LENNY.   You wouldn't get much for it.

JOEY.   Chop it up for firewood.

(*Lenny looks at him and laughs.*)

RUTH.   Don't be too sure though. You've forgotten
something. Look at me. I ... move my leg. That's all it
is. But I wear ... underwear ... which moves with me
215 ... it ... captures your attention. Perhaps you
misinterpret. The action is simple. It's a leg ... moving.
My lips move. Why don't you restrict ... your
observations to that? Perhaps the fact that they move is
more significant ... than the words which come through
220 them. You must bear that ... possibility ... in mind.

(*Silence.*)

(*Teddy stands.*)

I was born quite near here. (*Pause.*) Then ... six years
ago, I went to America. (*Pause.*) It's all rock. And sand.
It stretches ... so far ... everywhere you look. And
there's lots of insects there. (*Pause.*) And there's lots of
225 insects there.

(*Silence. She is still. Max stands.*)

MAX.   Well, it's time to go to the gym. Time for your
workout, Joey.

LENNY.   (*Standing.*) I'll come with you.

(*Joey sits looking at Ruth.*)

MAX.   Joe.

(*Joey stands. The three go out. Teddy sits by Ruth, holds her
hand. She smiles at him.*)

(*Pause.*)

230 TEDDY.   I think we'll go back. Mmnn? (*Pause.*) Shall we

go home?

RUTH.   Why?

TEDDY.   Well, we were only here for a few days, weren't
we? We might as well ... cut it short, I think.

235 RUTH.   Why? Don't you like it here?

TEDDY.   Of course I do. But I'd like to go back and see
the boys now.

(*Pause.*)

RUTH.   Don't you like your family?

TEDDY.   Which family?

240 RUTH.   Your family here.

TEDDY.   Of course I like them. What are you talking
about?

(*Pause.*)

RUTH.   You don't like them as much as you thought you
did?

245 TEDDY.   Of course I do. Of course I ... like them. I
don't know what you're talking about. (*Pause.*) Listen.
You know what time of the day it is there now, do you?

RUTH.   What?

TEDDY.   It's morning. It's about eleven o'clock.

250 RUTH.   Is it?

TEDDY.   Yes, they're about six hours behind us ... I
mean ... behind the time here. The boys'll be at the
pool ... now ... swimming. Think of it. Morning over
there. Sun. We'll go anyway, mmnn? It's so clean there.

255 RUTH.   Clean.

TEDDY.   Yes.

RUTH.   Is it dirty here?

TEDDY.   No, of course not. But it's cleaner there.
(*Pause.*) Look, I just brought you back to meet the
260 family, didn't I? You've met them, we can go. The fall
semester will be starting soon.

RUTH.   You find it dirty here?

TEDDY.   I didn't say I found it dirty here. (*Pause.*) I
didn't say that. (*Pause.*)

265 Look. I'll go and pack. You rest for a while. Will you?
They won't be back for at least an hour. You can sleep.
Rest. Please.

(*She looks at him.*)

You can help me with my lectures when we get back. I'd
love that. I'd be so grateful for it, really. We can bathe
270 till October. You know that. Here, there's nowhere to
bathe, except the swimming bath down the road. You
know what it's like? It's like a urinal. A filthy urinal!
(*Pause.*) You liked Venice, didn't you? It was lovely,
wasn't it? You had a good week. I mean ... I took you
275 there. I can speak Italian.
RUTH.   But if I'd been a nurse in the Italian campaign I
would have been there before.

(*Pause.*)

TEDDY.   You just rest. I'll go and pack.

(*Teddy goes out and up the stairs. She closes her eyes, Lenny
appears from up left. He walks into the room and sits near
her. She opens her eyes.*)
(*Silence.*)

LENNY.   Well, the evenings are drawing in.
280 RUTH.   Yes, it's getting dark.

(*Pause.*)

LENNY.   Winter'll soon be upon us. Time to renew one's
wardrobe.

(*Pause.*)

RUTH.   That's a good thing to do.
LENNY.   What?

(*Pause.*)

285 RUTH.   I always ... (*Pause.*) Do you like clothes?
LENNY.   Oh, yes. Very fond of clothes.

(*Pause.*)

RUTH.   I'm fond ... (*Pause.*) What do you think of my
shoes?
LENNY.   They're very nice.
290 RUTH.   No, I can't get the ones I want over there.
LENNY.   Can't get them over there, eh?

RUTH.   No ... you don't get them there. (*Pause.*) I was
a model before I went away.
LENNY.   Hats? (*Pause.*) I bought a girl a hat once. We
295 saw it in a glass case, in a shop. I tell you what it had. It
had a bunch of daffodils on it, tied with a black satin
bow, and then it was covered with a cloche of black
veiling. A cloche. I'm telling you. She was made for it.
RUTH.   No ... I was a model for the body. A
300 photographic model for the body.
LENNY.   Indoor work?
RUTH.   That was before I had ... all my children.
(*Pause.*) No, not always indoors. (*Pause.*) Once or twice
we went to a place in the country, by train. Oh, six or
305 seven times. We used to pass a ... a large white water
tower. This place ... this house ... was very big ... the
trees ... there was a lake, you see ... we used to change
and walk down towards the lake ... we went down a
path ... on stones ... there were ... on this path. Oh,
310 just ... wait ... yes ... when we changed in the house we
had a drink. There was a cold buffet. (*Pause.*)
Sometimes we stayed in the house but ... most often ...
we walked down to the lake ... and did our modelling
there. (*Pause.*) Just before we went to America I went
315 down there. I walked from the station to the gate and
then I walked up the drive. There were lights on ... I
stood in the drive ... the house was very light.

(*Teddy comes down the stairs with the cases. He puts them
down, looks at Lenny.*)

TEDDY.   What have you been saying to her?

(*He goes to Ruth.*)

Here's your coat.

(*Lenny goes to the radiogram and puts on a record of slow
jazz.*)

320 RUTH.   Come on. Put it on.
LENNY.   (*To Ruth.*) What about one dance before you
go?
TEDDY.   We're going.
LENNY.   Just one.
325 TEDDY.   No. We're going.

LENNY.   Just one dance, with her brother-in-law, before she goes.

(*Lenny bends to her.*)

Madam?

(*Ruth stands. They dance, slowly. Teddy stands, with Ruth's coat. Max and Joey come in the front door and into the room. They stand. Lenny kisses Ruth. They stand, kissing.*)

JOEY.   Christ, she's wide open. (*Pause.*) She's a tart.
330     (*Pause.*) Old Lenny's got a tart in here.

(*Joey goes to them. He takes Ruth's arm. He smiles at Lenny. He sits with Ruth on the sofa, embraces and kisses her. He looks up at Lenny.*)

Just up my street.

(*He leans her back until she lies beneath him. He kisses her. He looks up at Teddy and Max.*)

It's better than a rubdown, this.

(*Lenny sits on the arm of the sofa. He caresses Ruth's hair as Joey embraces her. Max comes forward, looks at the cases.*)

MAX.   You going, Teddy? Already? (*Pause.*) Well, when you coming over again, eh? Look, next time you come
335     over, don't forget to let us know beforehand whether you're married or not. I'll always be glad to meet the wife. Honest. I'm telling you.

(*Joey lies heavily on Ruth. They are almost still. Lenny caresses her hair.*)

Listen, you think I don't know why you didn't tell me you were married? I know why. You were ashamed. You
340     thought I'd be annoyed because you married a woman beneath you. You should have known me better. I'm broadminded. I'm a broadminded man.

(*He peers to see Ruth's face under Joey, turns back to Teddy.*)

Mind you, she's a lovely girl. A beautiful woman. And a mother too. A mother of three. You've made a happy
345     woman out of her. It's something to be proud of. I mean, we're talking about a woman of quality. We're talking about a woman of feeling.

(*Joey and Ruth roll off the sofa on to the floor. Joey clasps her. Lenny moves to stand above them. He looks down on them. He touches Ruth gently with his foot. Ruth suddenly pushes Joey away. She stands up. Joey gets to his feet, stares at her.*)

RUTH.   I'd like something to eat. (*To Lenny.*) I'd like a drink. Did you get any drink?
350 LENNY.   We've got drink.
RUTH.   I'd like one, please.
LENNY.   What drink?
RUTH.   Whisky.
LENNY.   I've got it.

(*Pause.*)

355 RUTH.   Well, get it.

(*Lenny goes to the sideboard, takes out bottle and glasses. Joey moves towards her.*)

Put the record off.

(*He looks at her, turns, puts the record off.*)

I want something to eat.

(*Pause.*)

JOEY.   I can't cook. (*Pointing to Max.*) He's the cook.

(*Lenny brings her a glass of whisky.*)

LENNY.   Soda on the side?
360 RUTH.   What's this glass? I can't drink out of this. Haven't you got a tumbler?
LENNY.   Yes.

RUTH.  Well, put it in a tumbler.

(*He takes the glass back, pours whisky into a tumbler, brings it to her.*)

LENNY.   On the rocks? Or as it comes?

365  RUTH.  Rocks? What do you know about rocks?

LENNY.   We've got rocks. But they're frozen stiff in the fridge.

(*Ruth drinks. Lenny looks round at the others.*)

Drinks all round?

(*He goes to the sideboard and pours drinks. Joey moves closer to Ruth.*)

JOEY.   What food do you want?

(*Ruth walks round the room.*)

370  RUTH.  (*To Teddy.*) Has your family read your critical works?

MAX.   That's one thing I've never done. I've never read one of his critical works.

TEDDY.   You wouldn't understand them.

(*Lenny hands drinks all round.*)

375  JOEY.   What sort of food do you want? I'm not the cook, anyway.

LENNY.   Soda, Ted? Or as it comes?

TEDDY.   You wouldn't understand my works. You wouldn't have the faintest idea of what they were about.
380  You wouldn't appreciate the points of reference. You're way behind. All of you. There's no point in my sending you my works. You'd be lost. It's nothing to do with the question of intelligence. It's a way of being able to look at the world. It's a question of how far you can operate
385  on things and not in things. I mean it's a question of your capacity to ally the two, to relate the two, to balance the two. To see, to be able to *see*! I'm the one who can see. That's why I can write my critical works. Might do you good … have a look at them … see how
390  certain people can view … things … how certain people

can maintain … intellectual equilibrium. Intellectual equilibrium. You're just objects. You just … move about. I can observe it. I can see what you do. It's the same as I do. But you're lost in it. You won't get me
395  being … I won't be lost in it.

(*Blackout.*)
(*Lights up.*)
(*Evening.*)
(*Teddy sitting, in his coat, the cases by him.*)
(*Pause.*)

SAM.   Do you remember MacGregor, Teddy?

TEDDY.   Mac?

SAM.   Yes.

TEDDY.   Of course I do.

400  SAM.   What did you think of him? Did you take to him?

TEDDY.   Yes. I liked him. Why?

(*Pause.*)

SAM.   You know, you were always my favourite, of the lads. Always. (*Pause.*) When you wrote to me from America I was very touched, you know. I mean you'd
405  written to your father a few times but you'd never written to me. But then, when I got that letter from you … well, I was very touched. I never told him. I never told him I'd heard from you. (*Pause.*) (*Whispering.*) Teddy, shall I tell you something? You were always your
410  mother's favourite. She told me. It's true. You were always the … you were always the main object of her love. (*Pause.*) Why don't you stay for a couple more weeks, eh? We could have a few laughs.

(*Lenny comes in the front door and into the room.*)

LENNY.   Still here, Ted? You'll be late for your first
415  seminar.

(*He goes to the sideboard, opens it, peers in it, to the right and the left, stands.*)

Where's my cheese-roll? (*Pause.*) Someone's taken my cheese-roll. I left it there. (To Sam.) You been thieving?

TEDDY.   I took your cheese-roll, Lenny.

(*Silence.*)
(*Sam looks at them, picks up his hat and goes out of the front door.*)
(*Silence.*)

LENNY.    You took my cheese roll?
420  TEDDY.    Yes.
LENNY.    I made that roll myself. I cut it and put the butter on. I sliced a piece of cheese and put it in between. I put it on a plate and I put it in the sideboard. I did all that before I went out. Now I come back and
425  you've eaten it.
TEDDY.    Well, what are you going to do about it?
LENNY.    I'm waiting for you to apologize.
TEDDY.    But I took it deliberately, Lenny.
LENNY.    You mean you didn't stumble on it by mistake?
430  TEDDY.    No, I saw you put it there. I was hungry, so I ate it.

(*Pause.*)

LENNY.    Barefaced audacity. (*Pause.*) What led you to be so … vindictive against your own brother? I'm bowled over. (*Pause.*) Well, Ted, I would say this is something
435  approaching the naked truth, isn't it? It's a real cards on the table stunt. I mean, we're in the land of no holds barred now. Well, how else can you interpret it? To pinch your younger brother's specially made cheese roll when he's out doing a spot of work, that's not equivocal,
440  it's unequivocal. (*Pause.*) Mind you, I will say you do seem to have grown a bit sulky during the last six years. A bit sulky. A bit inner. A bit less forthcoming. It's funny, because I'd have thought that in the United States of America, I mean with the sun and all that, the
445  open spaces, on the old campus, in your position, lecturing, in the centre of all the intellectual life out there, on the old campus, all the social whirl, all the stimulation of it all, all your kids and all that, to have fun with, down by the pool, the Greyhound buses and
450  all that, tons of iced water, all the comfort of those Bermuda shorts and all that, on the old campus, no time of the day or night you can't get a cup of coffee or a Dutch gin, I'd have thought you'd have grown more forthcoming, not less. Because I want you to know that
455  you set a standard for us, Teddy. Your family looks up

to you, boy, and you know what it does? It does its best to follow the example you set. Because you're a great source of pride to us. That's why we were so glad to see you come back, to welcome you back to your birthplace.
460  That's why. (*Pause.*) No, listen, Ted, there's no question that we live a less rich life here than you do over there. We live a closer life. We're busy, of course. Joey's busy with his boxing, I'm busy with my occupation, Dad still plays a good game of poker, and he does the cooking as
465  well, well up to his old standard, and Uncle Sam's the best chauffeur in the firm. But nevertheless we do make up a unit, Teddy, and you're an integral part of it. When we all sit round the backyard having a quiet gander at the night sky, there's always an empty chair
470  standing in the circle, which is in fact yours. And so when you at length return to us, we do expect a bit of grace, a bit of je ne sais quoi, a bit of generosity of mind, a bit of liberality of spirit, to reassure us. We do expect that. But do we get it? Have we got it? Is that what
475  you've given us?

(*Pause.*)

TEDDY.    Yes.

(*Joey comes down the stairs and into the room, with a newspaper.*)

LENNY.    (*To Joey.*) How'd you get on?
JOEY.    Er … not bad.
LENNY.    What do you mean? (*Pause.*) What do you
480  mean?
JOEY.    Not bad.
LENNY.    I want to know what you *mean*—by not bad.
JOEY.    What's it got to do with you?
LENNY.    Joey, you tell your brother everything.

(*Pause.*)

485  JOEY.    I didn't get all the way.
LENNY.    You didn't get all the way? (*Pause.*) (*With emphasis.*) You didn't get all the way? But you've had her up there for two hours.
JOEY.    Well?
490  LENNY.    You didn't get all the way and you've had her up

there for two hours!
JOEY.  What about it?

(*Lenny moves closer to him.*)

LENNY.  What are you telling me?
JOEY.  What do you mean?
495 LENNY.  Are you telling me she's a tease? (*Pause.*) She's a tease! (*Pause.*) What do you think of that, Ted? Your wife turns out to be a tease. He's had her up there for two hours and he didn't go the whole hog.
JOEY.  I didn't say she was a tease.
500 LENNY.  Are you joking? It sounds like a tease to me, don't it to you, Ted?
TEDDY.  Perhaps he hasn't got the right touch.
LENNY.  Joey? Not the right touch? Don't be ridiculous. He's had more dolly than you've had cream cakes. He's
505 irresistible. He's one of the few and far between. Tell him about the last bird you had, Joey.

(*Pause.*)

JOEY.  What bird?
LENNY.  The last bird! When we stopped the car ...
JOEY.  Oh, that ... yes ... well, we were in Lenny's car
510 one night last week ...
LENNY.  The Alfa.
JOEY.  And er ... bowling down the road ...
LENNY.  Up near the Scrubs.[1]
JOEY.  Yes, up over by the Scrubs ...
515 LENNY.  We were doing a little survey of North Paddington.
JOEY.  And er ... it was pretty late, wasn't it?
LENNY.  Yes, it was late. Well?

(*Pause.*)

JOEY.  And then we ... well, by the kerb, we saw this
520 parked car ... with a couple of girls in it.
LENNY.  And their escorts.
JOEY.  Yes, there were two geezers in it. Anyway ... we got out ... and we told the ... two escorts ... to go away ... which they did ... and then we ... got the girls out
525 of the car ...

[1] *the Scrubs* Wormwood Scrubs Prison, London.

LENNY.  We didn't take them over the Scrubs.
JOEY.  Oh, no. Not over the Scrubs. Well, the police would have noticed us there ... you see. We took them over a bombed site.
530 LENNY.  Rubble. In the rubble.
JOEY.  Yes, plenty of rubble. (*Pause.*) Well ... you know ... then we had them.
LENNY.  You've missed out the best bit. He's missed out the best bit!
535 JOEY.  What bit?
LENNY.  (*To Teddy.*) His bird says to him, I don't mind, she says, but I've got to have some protection. I've got to have some contraceptive protection. I haven't got any contraceptive protection, old Joey says to her. In that
540 case I won't do it, she says. Yes you will, says Joey, never mind about the contraceptive protection.

(*Lenny laughs.*)

Even my bird laughed when she heard that. Yes, even she gave out a bit of a laugh. So you can't say old Joey isn't a bit of a knockout when he gets going, can you?
545 And here he is upstairs with your wife for two hours and he hasn't even been the whole hog. Well, your wife sounds like a bit of a tease to me, Ted. What do you make of it, Joey? You satisfied? Don't tell me you're satisfied without going the whole hog?

(*Pause.*)

550 JOEY.  I've been the whole hog plenty of times. Sometimes ... you can be happy ... and not go the whole hog. Now and again ... you can be happy ... without going any hog.

(*Lenny stares at him. Max and Sam come in the front door and into the room.*)

MAX.  Where's the whore? Still in bed? She'll make us all
555 animals.
LENNY.  The girl's a tease.
MAX.  What?
LENNY.  She's had Joey on a string.
MAX.  What do you mean?

560 TEDDY.  He had her up there for two hours and he didn't go the whole hog.

(*Pause.*)

MAX.  My Joey? She did that to my boy? (*Pause.*) To my youngest son? Tch, tch, tch, tch. How you feeling, son? Are you all right?

565 JOEY.  Sure I'm all right.

MAX.  (*To Teddy.*) Does she do that to you, too?

TEDDY.  No.

LENNY.  He gets the gravy.

MAX.  You think so?

570 JOEY.  No he don't.

(*Pause.*)

SAM.  He's her lawful husband. She's his lawful wife.

JOEY.  No he don't! He don't get no gravy! I'm telling you. I'm telling all of you. I'll kill the next man who says he gets the gravy.

575 MAX.  Joey … what are you getting so excited about? (*To Lenny.*) It's because he's frustrated. You see what happens?

JOEY.  Who is?

MAX.  Joey. No one's saying you're wrong. In fact
580 everyone's saying you're right.

(*Pause.*)
(*Max turns to the others.*)

You know something? Perhaps it's not a bad idea to have a woman in the house. Perhaps it's a good thing. Who knows? Maybe we should keep her. (*Pause.*) Maybe we'll ask her if she wants to stay. (*Pause.*)

585 TEDDY.  I'm afraid not, Dad. She's not well, and we've got to get home to the children.

MAX.  Not well? I told you, I'm used to looking after people who are not so well. Don't worry about that. Perhaps we'll keep her here.

(*Pause.*)

590 SAM.  Don't be silly.

MAX.  What's silly?

SAM.  You're talking rubbish.

MAX.  Me?

SAM.  She's got three children.

595 MAX.  She can have more! Here. If she's so keen.

TEDDY.  She doesn't want any more.

MAX.  What do you know about what she wants, eh, Ted?

TEDDY.  (*Smiling.*) The best thing for her is to come
600 home with me, Dad. Really. We're married, you know.

(*Max walks about the room, clicks his fingers.*)

MAX.  We'd have to pay her, of course. You realize that? We can't leave her walking about without any pocket money. She'll have to have a little allowance.

JOEY.  Of course we'll pay her. She's got to have some
605 money in her pocket.

MAX.  That's what I'm saying. You can't expect a woman to walk about without a few bob to spend on a pair of stockings.

(*Pause.*)

LENNY.  Where's the money going to come from?

610 MAX.  Well, how much is she worth? What we talking about, three figures?

LENNY.  I asked you where the money's going to come from. It'll be an extra mouth to feed. It'll be an extra body to clothe. You realize that?

615 JOEY.  I'll buy her clothes.

LENNY.  What with?

JOEY.  I'll put in a certain amount out of my wages.

MAX.  That's it. We'll pass the hat round. We'll make a donation. We're all grown-up people, we've got a sense
620 of responsibility. We'll all put a little in the hat. It's democratic.

LENNY.  It'll come to a few quid,[1] Dad. (*Pause.*) I mean, she's not a woman who likes walking around in second-hand goods. She's up to the latest fashion. You wouldn't
625 want her walking about in clothes which don't show her off at her best, would you?

MAX.  Lenny, do you mind if I make a little comment? It's not meant to be critical. But I think you're concentrating too much on the economic

---

[1] *quid*  Slang: one pound (i.e., English pound, a unit of currency).

630 considerations. There are other considerations. There are the human considerations. You understand what I mean? There are the human considerations. Don't forget them.

LENNY. I won't.

635 MAX. Well don't. (*Pause.*) Listen, we're bound to treat her in something approximating, at least, to the manner in which she's accustomed. After all, she's not someone off the street, she's my daughter-in-law!

JOEY. That's right.

640 MAX. There you are, you see. Joey'll donate, Sam'll donate.

(*Sam looks at him.*)

I'll put a few bob out of my pension, Lenny'll cough up. We're laughing. What about you, Ted? How much you going to put in the kitty?

645 TEDDY. I'm not putting anything in the kitty.

MAX. What? You won't even help to support your own wife? You lousy stinkpig. Your mother would drop dead if she heard you take that attitude.

LENNY. Eh, Dad.

(*Lenny walks forward.*)

650 I've got a better idea.

MAX. What?

LENNY. There's no need for us to go to all this expense. I know these women. Once they get started they ruin your budget. I've got a better idea. Why don't I take her

655 up with me to Greek Street?

(*Pause.*)

MAX. You mean put her on the game?[1] (*Pause.*) We'll put her on the game. That's a stroke of genius, that's a marvellous idea. You mean she can earn the money herself—on her back?

660 LENNY. Yes.

MAX. Wonderful. The only thing is, it'll have to be short hours. We don't want her out of the house all night.

LENNY. I can limit the hours.

MAX. How many?

665 LENNY. Four hours a night.

MAX. (*Dubiously.*) Is that enough?

LENNY. She'll bring in a good sum for four hours a night.

MAX. Well, you should know. After all, it's true, the last

670 thing we want to do is wear the girl out. She's going to have her obligations this end as well. Where you going to put her in Greek Street?

LENNY. It doesn't have to be right in Greek Street, Dad. I've got a number of flats all around that area.

675 MAX. You have? Well, what about me? Why don't you give me one?

LENNY. You're sexless.

JOEY. Eh, wait a minute, what's all this?

MAX. I know what Lenny's saying. Lenny's saying she

680 can pay her own way. What do you think, Teddy? That'll solve all our problems.

JOEY. Eh, wait a minute. I don't want to share her.

MAX. What did you say?

JOEY. I don't want to share her with a lot of yobs![2]

685 MAX. Yobs! You arrogant git![3] What arrogance. (*To Lenny.*) Will you be supplying her with yobs?

LENNY. I've got a very distinguished clientele, Joey. They're more distinguished than you'll ever be.

MAX. So you can count yourself lucky we're including

690 you in.

JOEY. I didn't think I was going to have to share her!

MAX. Well, you *are* going to have to share her! Otherwise she goes straight back to America. You understand? (*Pause.*) It's tricky enough as it is, without

695 you shoving your oar in. But there's something worrying me. Perhaps she's not so up to the mark. Eh? Teddy, you're the best judge. Do you think she'd be up to the mark? (*Pause.*) I mean what about all this teasing? Is she going to make a habit of it? That'll get us nowhere.

(*Pause.*)

700 TEDDY. It was just love play ... I suppose ... that's all I suppose it was.

MAX. Love play? Two bleeding hours? That's a bloody long time for love play!

---

[1] *on the game*  Slang: to work as a prostitute.

[2] *yobs*  Slang: louts.

[3] *git*  Slang: worthless person.

LENNY. I don't think we've got anything to worry about
705 on that score, Dad.
MAX. How do you know?
LENNY. I'm giving you a professional opinion.

(*Lenny goes to Teddy.*)

LENNY. Listen, Teddy, you could help us, actually. If I
were to send you some cards, over to America ... you
710 know, very nice ones, with a name on, and a telephone
number, very discreet, well, you could distribute them
... to various parties, who might be making a trip over
here. Of course, you'd get a little percentage out of it.
MAX. I mean, you needn't tell them she's your wife.
715 LENNY. No, we'd call her something else. Dolores, or
something.
MAX. Or Spanish Jacky.
LENNY. No, you've got to be reserved about it, Dad. We
could call her something nice ... like Cynthia ... or
720 Gillian.

(*Pause.*)

JOEY. Gillian.

(*Pause.*)

LENNY. No, what I mean, Teddy, you must know lots of
professors, heads of departments, men like that. They
pop over here for a week at the Savoy, they need
725 somewhere they can go to have a nice quiet poke.[1] And
of course you'd be in a position to give them inside
information.
MAX. Sure. You can give them proper data. I bet you
before two months we'd have a waiting list.
730 LENNY. You could be our representative in the States.
MAX. Of course. We're talking in international terms!
By the time we've finished Pan-American'll[2] give us a
discount.

(*Pause.*)

TEDDY. She'd get old ... very quickly.

---
[1]  *poke*  Slang: act of sexual intercourse.

[2]  *Pan-American*  A now-defunct commercial airline.

735 MAX. No ... not in this day and age! With the health
service?[3] Old! How could she get old? She'll have the
time of her life.

(*Ruth comes down the stairs, dressed. She comes into the
room. She smiles at the gathering, and sits.*)
(*Silence.*)

TEDDY. Ruth ... the family have invited you to stay, for
a little while longer. As a ... as a kind of guest. If you
740 like the idea I don't mind. We can manage very easily at
home ... until you come back.
RUTH. How very nice of them.

(*Pause.*)

MAX. It's an offer from our heart.
RUTH. It's very sweet of you.
745 MAX. Listen ... it would be our pleasure.

(*Pause.*)

RUTH. I think I'd be too much trouble.
MAX. Trouble? What are you talking about? What
trouble? Listen, I'll tell you something. Since poor Jessie
died, eh, Sam? we haven't had a woman in the house.
750 Not one. Inside this house. And I'll tell you why.
Because their mother's image was so dear any other
woman would have ... tarnished it. But you ... Ruth ...
you're not only lovely and beautiful, but you're kin.
You're kith. You belong here.

(*Pause.*)

755 RUTH. I'm very touched.
MAX. Of course you're touched. I'm touched.

(*Pause.*)

TEDDY. But Ruth, I should tell you ... that you'll have
to pull your weight a little, if you stay. Financially. My
father isn't very well off.
760 RUTH. (*To Max.*) Oh, I'm sorry.

---
[3]  *health service*  Government-run national healthcare plan.

MAX.  No, you'd just have to bring in a little, that's all.
A few pennies. Nothing much. It's just that we're
waiting for Joey to hit the top as a boxer. When Joey
hits the top … well …

(*Pause.*)

765 TEDDY.  Or you can come home with me.
LENNY.  We'd get you a flat.

(*Pause.*)

RUTH.  A flat?
LENNY.  Yes.
RUTH.  Where?
770 LENNY.  In town. (*Pause.*) But you'd live here, with us.
MAX.  Of course you would. This would be your home.
In the bosom of the family.
LENNY.  You'd just pop up to the flat a couple of hours
a night, that's all.
775 MAX.  Just a couple of hours, that's all. That's all.
LENNY.  And you make enough money to keep you
going here.

(*Pause.*)

RUTH.  How many rooms would this flat have?
LENNY.  Not many.
780 RUTH.  I would want at least three rooms and a
bathroom.
LENNY.  You wouldn't need three rooms and a
bathroom.
MAX.  She'd need a bathroom.
785 LENNY.  But not three rooms.

(*Pause.*)

RUTH.  Oh, I would. Really.
LENNY.  Two would do.
RUTH.  No. Two wouldn't be enough. (*Pause.*) I'd want
a dressing-room, a rest-room, and a bedroom.

(*Pause.*)

790 LENNY.  All right, we'll get you a flat with three rooms
and a bathroom.
RUTH.  With what kind of conveniences?
LENNY.  All conveniences.
RUTH.  A personal maid?
795 LENNY.  Of course. (*Pause.*) We'd finance you, to begin
with, and then, when you were established, you could
pay us back in instalments.
RUTH.  Oh, no, I wouldn't agree to that.
LENNY.  Oh, why not?
800 RUTH.  You would have to regard your original outlay
simply as a capital investment.

(*Pause.*)

LENNY.  I see. All right.
RUTH.  You'd supply my wardrobe, of course?
LENNY.  We'd supply everything. Everything you need.
805 RUTH.  I'd need an awful lot. Otherwise I wouldn't be
content.
LENNY.  You'd have everything.
RUTH.  I would naturally want to draw up an inventory
of everything I would need, which would require your
810 signature in the presence of witnesses.
LENNY.  Naturally.
RUTH.  All aspects of the agreement and conditions of
employment would have to be clarified to our mutual
satisfaction before we finalize the contract.
815 LENNY.  Of course.

(*Pause.*)

RUTH.  Well, it might prove a workable agreement.
LENNY.  I think so.
MAX.  And you'd have the whole of your daytime free, of
course. You could do a bit of cooking here if you
820 wanted to.
LENNY.  Make the beds.
MAX.  Scrub the place out a bit.
TEDDY.  Keep everyone company.

(*Sam comes forward.*)

SAM. (*In one breath.*) MacGregor had Jessie in the back
825 of my cab as I drove them along.

(*He croaks and collapses. He lies still. They all look at him.*)

MAX. What's he done? Dropped dead?
LENNY. Yes.
MAX. A corpse? A corpse on my floor? Get him out of here! Clear him out of here!

(*Joey bends over Sam.*)

830 JOEY. He's not dead.
LENNY. He probably was dead, for about thirty seconds.
MAX. He's not even dead!

(*Lenny looks down at Sam.*)

LENNY. Yes, there's still some breath there.
MAX. (*Pointing at Sam.*) You know what that man had?
835 LENNY. Has.
MAX. Has! A diseased imagination.

(*Pause.*)

RUTH. Yes, it sounds a very attractive idea.
MAX. Do you want to shake on it now, or do you want to leave it till later?
840 RUTH. Oh, we'll leave it till later.

(*Teddy stands. He looks down at Sam.*)

TEDDY. I was going to ask him to drive me to London Airport.

(*He goes to the cases, picks on up.*)

Well, I'll leave your case, Ruth. I'll just go up the road to the Underground.
845 MAX. Listen, if you go the other way, first left, first right, you remember, you might find a cab passing there.
TEDDY. Yes, I might do that.

MAX. Or you can take the tube[1] to Piccadilly Circus,
850 won't take you ten minutes, and pick up a cab from there out to the Airport.
TEDDY. Yes, I'll probably do that.
MAX. Mind you, they'll charge you double fare. They'll charge you for the return trip. It's over the six-mile
855 limit.
TEDDY. Yes. Well, bye-bye, Dad. Look after yourself.

(*They shake hands.*)

MAX. Thanks, son. Listen. I want to tell you something. It's been wonderful to see you.

(*Pause.*)

TEDDY. It's been wonderful to see you.
860 MAX. Do your boys know about me? Eh? Would they like to see a photo, do you think, of their grandfather?
TEDDY. I know they would.

(*Max brings out his wallet.*)

MAX. I've got one on me. I've got one here. Just a minute. Here you are. Will they like that one?
865 TEDDY. (*Taking it.*) They'll be thrilled.

(*He turns to Lenny.*)

Good-bye, Lenny.

(*They shake hands.*)

LENNY. Ta-ta, Ted. Good to see you. Have a good trip.
TEDDY. Bye-bye, Joey.

(*Joey does not move.*)

JOEY. Ta-ta.

(*Teddy goes to the front door.*)

870 RUTH. Eddie.

---

[1] *tube* Subway.

*(Teddy turns. Pause.)*

Don't become a stranger.

*(Teddy goes, shuts the front door. Silence.)*
*(The three men stand. Ruth sits relaxed on her chair. Sam lies still. Joey walks slowly across the room. He kneels at her chair. She touches his head, lightly. He puts his head in her lap. Max begins to move above them, backwards and forwards. Lenny stands still. Max turns to Lenny.)*

MAX.  I'm too old, I suppose. She thinks I'm an old man. *(Pause.)* I'm not such an old man. *(Pause.)* *(To Ruth.)* You think I'm too old for you? *(Pause.)* Listen. You
875  think you're just going to get that big slag[1] all the time? You think you're just going to have him … you're going to just have him all the time? You're going to have to work! You'll have to take them on, you understand? *(Pause.)* Does she realize that? *(Pause.)* Lenny, do you
880  think she understands … *(He begins to stammer.)* What … what … what … we're getting at? What … we've got

in mind? Do you think she's got it clear? *(Pause.)* I don't think she's got it clear. *(Pause.)* You understand what I mean? Listen, I've got a funny idea she'll do the dirty on
885  us, you want to bet? She'll use us, she'll make use of us, I can tell you! I can smell it! You want to bet? *(Pause.)* She won't … be adaptable!

*(He begins to groan, clutches his stick, falls on to his knees by the side of her chair. His body sags. The groaning stops. His body straightens. He looks at her, still kneeling.)*

I'm not an old man. *(Pause.)* Do you hear me?

*(He raises his face to her.)*

Kiss me.

*(She continues to touch Joey's head, lightly. Lenny stands, watching.)*

*(Curtain.)*

—1965

---

[1]  *slag*  Brute.

# TED HUGHES
## 1930 – 1998

When Ted Hughes was chosen to succeed Sir John Betjeman as England's Poet Laureate in 1984, a reporter in *The Times* described the selection as "a bit like appointing a grim young cow to replace a cuddly old teddy bear." Coming on the British literary scene in the 1950s, Hughes startled readers with his poetic voice. With bold metaphors and forceful rhythms, his poems paint grim, often violent, visions of human existence. At the same time, he celebrates the power of nature and attempts to reunite humanity with the natural world, using myth and folklore to explore alternative possibilities of spirituality.

Edward James Hughes was born in Mytholmroyd, a county in West Yorkshire, the landscape of which—with its valleys, cliffs, and surrounding moors—pervades much of his poetry. Hughes studied English literature for two years at Cambridge before switching to archaeology and anthropology in his final year of study—seeking to escape what he called "the terrible, suffocating, maternal octopus" of the English poetic tradition. In 1956 after graduating, Hughes met and married Sylvia Plath, an American student studying at Cambridge on a Fulbright Fellowship. The following year, having published some individual poems, Hughes released his first collection, *The Hawk in the Rain* (1957). The poems of this début—including "The Thought-Fox" and "Pike"—depict animals participating in a natural world from which humans are isolated by their intellect.

After teaching briefly in the United States, Hughes and Plath returned to England, where their two children were born and where Hughes published his second collection, *Lupercal* (1960). Hughes also began writing children's books and radio plays during this period. After Plath committed suicide in 1963, following the couple's separation, Hughes put his own poetry on hold to focus on editing and publishing his wife's poems and journals.

Hughes's return to poetry, *Wodwo* (1967), signaled a change in direction from his earlier work. An interest in anthropology began to color his work, as did a marked interest in occult, mythic, and folktale sources. The collection often features characters looking for meaning or identity through various belief systems—such as the mysterious wodwo figure in the collection's title poem, who seeks to know, "What am I?" The volume following, *Crow: From the Life and Songs of the Crow* (1970), created in collaboration with artist Leonard Baskin, presents a series of poems informed by Hughes's own mythology. These poems, which follow a crow from the genesis of the world until nuclear apocalypse, lay bare the brutality in nature, though with more humor than was present in his earlier work. Hughes said his goal in the Crow poems was to achieve a certain style consisting of "a super-simple and a super-ugly language which would in a way shed everything except just what he [Crow] wanted to say." Perhaps not surprisingly, this carrion-eating, graceless, self-serving protagonist (who became the main character of several subsequent works) brought charges of misanthropy and crudeness upon Hughes.

With *Crow* Hughes discovered his penchant for collaborative ventures, and more followed, including *Cave Birds* (1978), also with Leonard Baskin; *Remains of Elmet* (1979), in which he explores, with photographer Fay Godwin, the history of his native region from ancient to industrial times; and *River* (1983), which, accompanied by photographs by Peter Keen, provides a composite view of a river over the course of a year. Another of his later collections, *Moortown* (1979), documents his experiences dairy farming with Jack Orchard, the father of his second wife, Carol.

Though Hughes continued to publish volumes of new and collected poems, in his later years he devoted himself increasingly to judging competitions and performing readings—particularly for children—and became an active supporter of environmental and ecological causes. Hughes also turned to writing prose and to translating, publishing *Tales from Ovid* (1997), a collection of essays entitled *Winter Pollen* (1994), and his critical work on Shakespeare, *Shakespeare and the Goddess of Complete Being* (1992), which united his interest in the author with his passion for mythology.

In 1998 Hughes broke his thirty-year silence concerning his marriage with Plath and published *Birthday Letters*, a series of poems addressed to his dead wife. During the years following her death, Hughes had frequently been accused by some of Plath's admirers of "murdering" the female poet, and his surname was repeatedly defaced on her gravestone. Hughes's last collection had the effect of silencing, rather than reigniting, the expected opposition, and sales for the book have remained high since its publication.

Hughes was diagnosed with colon cancer in 1997 and died in 1998, two weeks after receiving the Order of Merit from Queen Elizabeth II. Hughes's unique vision of the natural world—and of humanity's place in it—has endured after his death, and his poetry remains widely read and studied. Of his continued popularity, British poet and critic Dick Davis explains, "He brings back to our suburban, centrally-heated and, above all, *safe* lives reports from an authentic frontier of reality and the imagination. His poems speak to us of a world that is constantly true in a way that we know our temporary comforts cannot be."

⌘ ⌘ ⌘

## The Thought-Fox

I imagine this midnight moment's forest:
Something else is alive
Beside the clock's loneliness
And this blank page where my fingers move.

5  Through the window I see no star:
Something more near
Though deeper within darkness
Is entering the loneliness:

Cold, delicately as the dark snow
10  A fox's nose touches twig, leaf;
Two eyes serve a movement, that now
And again now, and now, and now

Sets neat prints into the snow
Between trees, and warily a lame
15  Shadow lags by stump and in hollow
Of a body that is bold to come

Across clearings, an eye,
A widening deepening greenness,
Brilliantly, concentratedly,
20  Coming about its own business

Till, with a sudden sharp hot stink of fox,
It enters the dark hole of the head.
The window is starless still; the clock ticks,
The page is printed.

—1957

## Pike

Pike, three inches long, perfect
Pike in all parts, green tigering the gold.
Killers from the egg: the malevolent aged grin.
They dance on the surface among the flies.

5   Or move, stunned by their own grandeur,
Over a bed of emerald, silhouette
Of submarine delicacy and horror.
A hundred feet long in their world.

In ponds, under the heat-struck lily pads—
10  Gloom of their stillness:
Logged on last year's black leaves, watching upwards.
Or hung in an amber cavern of weeds

The jaws' hooked clamp and fangs
Not to be changed at this date;
15  A life subdued to its instrument;
The gills kneading quietly, and the pectorals.

Three we kept behind glass,
Jungled in weed: three inches, four,
And four and a half: fed fry to them—
20  Suddenly there were two. Finally one.

With a sag belly and the grin it was born with.
And indeed they spare nobody.
Two, six pounds each, over two feet long,
High and dry and dead in the willow-herb—

25  One jammed past its gills down the other's gullet:
The outside eye stared: as a vice locks—
The same iron in this eye
Though its film shrank in death.

A pond I fished, fifty yards across,
30  Whose lilies and muscular tench[1]
Had outlasted every visible stone
Of the monastery that planted them—

Stilled legendary depth:
It was as deep as England. It held
35  Pike too immense to stir, so immense and old
That past nightfall I dared not cast

But silently cast and fished
With the hair frozen on my head
For what might move, for what eye might move.
40  The still splashes on the dark pond,

Owls hushing the floating woods
Frail on my ear against the dream
Darkness beneath night's darkness had freed,
That rose slowly towards me, watching.
—1959

## Wodwo[2]

What am I? Nosing here, turning leaves over
Following a faint stain on the air to the river's edge
I enter water. What am I to split
The glassy grain of water looking upward I see the bed
5   Of the river above me upside down very clear
What am I doing here in mid-air? Why do I find
this frog so interesting as I inspect its most secret
interior and make it my own? Do these weeds
know me and name me to each other have they
10  seen me before, do I fit in their world? I seem
separate from the ground and not rooted but dropped
out of nothing casually I've no threads
fastening me to anything I can go anywhere
I seem to have been given the freedom
15  of this place what am I then? And picking
bits of bark off this rotten stump gives me
no pleasure and it's no use so why do I do it
me and doing that have coincided very queerly
But what shall I be called am I the first
20  have I an owner what shape am I what
shape am I am I huge if I go
to the end on this way past these trees and past these trees

---

[1] *tench*  Fish, like a carp.

[2] *Wodwo*  Middle English word, taken from *Sir Gawain and the Green Knight*, that means "an enemy in the forest," "a wild man of the woods," or (Hughes's own definition) "some sort of goblin creature."

till I get tired that's touching one wall of me
for the moment if I sit still how everything
25  stops to watch me I suppose I am the exact centre
but there's all this what is it roots
roots roots roots and here's the water
again very queer but I'll go on looking
—1967

## Theology

No, the serpent did not
Seduce Eve to the apple.
All that's simply
Corruption of the facts.

5  Adam ate the apple.
Eve ate Adam.
The serpent ate Eve.
This is the dark intestine.

The serpent, meanwhile,
10  Sleeps his meal off in Paradise—
Smiling to hear
God's querulous calling.
—1967

## A Childish Prank

Man's and woman's bodies lay without souls,
Dully gaping, foolishly staring, inert
On the flowers of Eden.
God pondered.

5  The problem was so great, it dragged him asleep.

Crow laughed.
He bit the Worm, God's only son,
Into two writhing halves.

He stuffed into man the tail half
10  With the wounded end hanging out.

He stuffed the head half headfirst into woman
And it crept in deeper and up
To peer out through her eyes
Calling its tail-half to join up quickly, quickly
15  Because O it was painful.

Man awoke being dragged across the grass.
Woman awoke to see him coming.
Neither knew what had happened.

God went on sleeping.

20  Crow went on laughing.
—1972

## The Seven Sorrows

The first sorrow of autumn
Is the slow goodbye
Of the garden who stands so long in the evening—

A brown poppy head,
5  The stalk of a lily,
And still cannot go.

The second sorrow
Is the empty feet
Of the pheasant who hangs from a hook with his
brothers.
10  The woodland of gold
Is folded in feathers
With its head in a bag.

And the third sorrow
Is the slow goodbye
15  Of the sun who has gathered the birds and who gathers
The minutes of evening,
The golden and holy
Ground of the picture.

The fourth sorrow
20  Is the pond gone black

Ruined and sunken the city of water—
The beetle's palace,
The catacombs
Of the dragonfly.

25 And the fifth sorrow
Is the slow goodbye
Of the woodland that quietly breaks up its camp.
One day it's gone. It has left only litter—
Firewood, tentpoles.

30 And the sixth sorrow
Is the fox's sorrow
The joy of the huntsman, the joy of the hounds,
The hooves that pound
Till earth closes her ear
35 To the fox's prayer.

And the seventh sorrow
Is the slow goodbye
Of the face with its wrinkles that looks through the
    window
As the year packs up
40 Like a tatty fairground
That came for the children.
    —1975

## Heptonstall Old Church[1]

A great bird landed here.

Its song drew men out of rock,
Living men out of bog and heather.

Its song put a light in the valleys
5 And harness on the long moors.

Heptonstall Old Church.

Its song brought a crystal from space
And set it in men's heads.

Then the bird died.

Its giant bones
10 Blackened and became a mystery.

The crystal in men's heads
Blackened and fell to pieces.

The valleys went out.
The moorland broke loose.
    —1979

---

[1] *Heptonstall Old Church*  The town of Heptonstall was three miles from Hughes's childhood home of Mytholmroyd, in West Yorkshire. The ruins of the "old church" (dating from the thirteenth century) stand beside the present church, constructed in 1854. The bodies of Sylvia Plath and of Hughes's parents are buried in its churchyard.

## You Hated Spain[1]

Spain frightened you. Spain
Where I felt at home. The blood-raw light,
The oiled anchovy faces, the African
Black edges to everything, frightened you.
5    Your schooling had somehow neglected Spain.
The wrought-iron grille, death and the Arab drum.
You did not know the language, your soul was empty
Of the signs, and the welding light
Made your blood shrivel. Bosch[2]
10   Held out a spidery hand and you took it
Timidly, a bobby-sox[3] American.
You saw right down to the Goya[4] funeral grin
And recognized it, and recoiled
As your poems winced into chill, as your panic
15   Clutched back towards college America.
So we sat as tourists at the bullfight
Watching bewildered bulls awkwardly butchered,
Seeing the grey-faced matador, at the barrier
Just below us, straightening his bent sword
20   And vomiting with fear. And the horn
That hid itself inside the blowfly belly
Of the toppled picador punctured
What was waiting for you. Spain
Was the land of your dreams: the dust-red cadaver
25   You dared not wake with, the puckering amputations
No literature course had glamorized.
The juju[5] land behind your African lips.
Spain was what you tried to wake up from
And could not. I see you, in moonlight,
30   Walking the empty wharf at Alicante[6]
Like a soul waiting for the ferry,

A new soul, still not understanding,
Thinking it is still your honeymoon
In the happy world, with your whole life waiting,
35   Happy, and all your poems still to be found.
—1998

## Daffodils

Remember how we[7] picked the daffodils?
Nobody else remembers, but I remember.
Your daughter came with her armfuls, eager and happy,
Helping the harvest. She has forgotten.
5    She cannot even remember you. And we sold them.
It sounds like sacrilege, but we sold them.
Were we so poor? Old Stoneman, the grocer,
Boss-eyed, his blood-pressure purpling to beetroot
(It was his last chance,
10   He would die in the same great freeze as you),
He persuaded us. Every Spring
He always bought them, sevenpence a dozen,
"A custom of the house."

Besides, we still weren't sure we wanted to own
15   Anything. Mainly we were hungry
To convert everything to profit.
Still nomads—still strangers
To our whole possession. The daffodils
Were incidental gilding of the deeds,
20   Treasure trove. They simply came,
And they kept on coming.
As if not from the sod but falling from heaven.
Our lives were still a raid on our own good luck.
We knew we'd live for ever. We had not learned
25   What a fleeting glance of the everlasting
Daffodils are. Never identified
The nuptial flight of the rarest ephemera—
Our own days!
                    We thought they were a windfall.
30   Never guessed they were a last blessing.
So we sold them. We worked at selling them
As if employed on somebody else's
Flower-farm. You bent at it
In the rain of that April—your last April.

---

[1]    *You Hated Spain*   Both this poem and "Daffodils" are from Hughes's collection *Birthday Letters*, the poems in which are all addressed to Sylvia Plath.

[2]    *Bosch*   Dutch painter Hieronymus Bosch (c. 1450–1516), whose works often depicted figures that were part human, part monster.

[3]    *bobby-sox*   I.e., adolescent. "Bobby-socks" were short socks, reaching just above the ankle, often worn by girls in their early teens in the 1950s and early 1960s.

[4]    *Goya*   Spanish painter Françisco de Goya (1746–1828), known for his grotesques.

[5]    *juju*   Possessing supernatural or magical powers.

[6]    *Alicante*   Port and tourist center in southeastern Spain.

[7]    *we*   I.e., Hughes and Sylvia Plath.

35 We bent there together, among the soft shrieks
Of their jostled stems, the wet shocks shaken
Of their girlish dance-frocks—
Fresh-opened dragonflies, wet and flimsy,
Opened too early.

40 We piled their frailty lights on a carpenter's bench,
Distributed leaves among the dozens—
Buckling blade-leaves, limber, groping for air, zinc-
      silvered—
Propped their raw butts in bucket water,
Their oval, meaty butts,
45 And sold them, sevenpence a bunch—

Wind-wounds, spasms from the dark earth,
With their odourless metals,
A flamy purification of the deep grave's stony cold
As if ice had a breath—

50 We sold them, to wither.
The crop thickened faster than we could thin it.
Finally, we were overwhelmed
And we lost our wedding-present scissors.

55 Every March since they have lifted again
Out of the same bulbs, the same
Baby-cries from the thaw,
Ballerinas too early for music, shiverers
In the draughty wings of the year.
On that same groundswell of memory, fluttering
60 They return to forget you stooping there
Behind the rainy curtains of a dark April,
Snipping their stems.

But somewhere your scissors remember.
Wherever they are.
65 Here somewhere, blades wide open,
April by April
Sinking deeper
Through the sod—an anchor, a cross of rust.
      —1998

# A.S. BYATT
## b. 1936

Occasionally given the seemingly contradictory tag "Victorian modernist," fiction-writer A.S. Byatt is known for intricate, self-referential, erudite, and deliberately intellectual work that spans the divide between Victorian realism and twentieth-century experimental fiction in striking fashion. She is also a compelling storyteller who revels in her art and who enjoys exploring the ways in which literature changes and informs our lives.

Byatt was born Antonia Susan Drabble in 1936 in Sheffield, England, the second daughter of judge and novelist John F. Drabble and teacher Kathleen Drabble. (Byatt's younger half-sister, Margaret, also became a renowned novelist.) Byatt was educated at a private school in York, where her mother was a teacher, and then at Newnham College, Cambridge; at Bryn Mawr, Pennsylvnia; and at Somerville College, Oxford. While completing her dissertation at Oxford (on seventeenth-century literature) Byatt worked simultaneously on her first novel, *The Shadow of the Sun* (1964). After graduating, Byatt taught first at the Central School of Art and Design in London and then as a lecturer in English and American Literature at University College, London. She has continued in the years since to work as a scholar and critic as well as a writer of fiction—and in the fiction itself academic figures abound, and theoretical and critical trends are frequent subjects of examination and satire.

While Byatt's first novel was well received, it was her second, *The Game* (1967), that established her reputation as an important novelist. Both her early novels show her struggle to combine the roles of academic and critic with that of novelist. With these early works she also established her characteristic focus on the creative process and the imagination.

With *The Virgin in the Garden* (1978) Byatt began a series of denser, more consciously experimental novels. *Virgin*, *Still Life* (1986), *Babel Tower* (1996), and *A Whistling Woman* (2002) all follow the life of a single heroine, Frederica Potter, as she attends Cambridge and becomes an academic. These narratives use realist techniques—such as highly developed, extensively psychologized characters, and detailed scenery and social setting—together with dense metaphor, allusion, and symbolism.

Byatt's 1990 novel *Possession: A Romance* established her reputation around the world. This Booker Prize-winning novel, which has since been made into a motion picture, draws parallels between a 1980s love affair involving Victorian academics and a love affair involving two Victorian authors. These two stories from two historical periods intertwine both historically and symbolically and are rendered in complex detail: Byatt invents complete poems, letters, and diary entries—supposedly written by the two Victorian authors—to be scrutinized by the academics.

Byatt published another major novel, *The Biographer's Tale*, in 2000. She has also written numerous collections of short stories, including *Sugar and Other Stories* (1987), *The Djinn in the Nightingale's Eye: Five Fairy Tales* (1994), and *Little Black Book of Stories* (2004). Her short fiction, like her novels, is characterized by interpenetrating genres and story lines, frequent toying with plot and point of view, rich description, and dense language. In the story reprinted here, "The July Ghost" (originally published in *Sugar*), Byatt's focus is perhaps less the ghostly apparition itself than the mental mechanisms of the female protagonist of the story—how she constructs and consciously cleaves to certain patterns of thought. As one reviewer commented in the *Los Angeles Times Book Review*, Byatt's works tend to be about "'ideas' rather than 'things,'" and these ideas are rarely simple ones. Byatt's works regularly tackle themes such as faith and doubt, good and evil, and the nature of social mores and of Western civilization. Byatt herself says, "perhaps the most important thing to say about my books is that they try to be about the life of the mind as well as of society and the relations between people. I admire—am excited by—intellectual curiosity of any kind (scientific, linguistic, psychological) and also by literature as a complicated, huge, interrelating pattern."

As a writer of richly patterned narratives that often yoke together ideas and story material in surprising combinations, Byatt has frequently been characterized as a postmodernist literary figure. Her academic and popular criticism, however—from the studies on Iris Murdoch and on William Wordsworth and Samuel Taylor Coleridge that she published early in her career to the criticism she has contributed in more recent times to leading newspapers—is generally direct and straightforward in its style. Her most recent critical volume is *Portraits in Fiction* (2001), an exploration of the connections between novels and paintings.

In both her fiction and her criticism Byatt has worked to redefine the relationship between contemporary fiction and the conventions of the past. The recipient of many awards, Byatt was appointed Dame Commander of the British Empire (DBE) in 1999. She lives in London.

⌘⌘⌘

## The July Ghost

"I think I must move out of where I'm living," he said. "I have this problem with my landlady."

He picked a long, bright hair off the back of her dress, so deftly that the act seemed simply considerate. He had been skilful at balancing glass, plate and cutlery, too. He had a look of dignified misery, like a dejected hawk. She was interested.

"What sort of problem? Amatory, financial, or domestic?"

"None of those, really. Well, not financial."

He turned the hair on his finger, examining it intently, not meeting her eye.

"Not financial. Can you tell me? I might know somewhere you could stay. I know a lot of people."

"You would." He smiled shyly. "It's not an easy problem to describe. There's just the two of us. I occupy the attics. Mostly."

He came to a stop. He was obviously reserved and secretive. But he was telling her something. This is usually attractive.

"Mostly?" Encouraging him.

"Oh, it's not like *that*. Well, not ... Shall we sit down?"

They moved across the party, which was a big party, on a hot day. He stopped and found a bottle and filled her glass. He had not needed to ask what she was drinking. They sat side by side on a sofa: he admired the brilliant poppies bold on her emerald dress, and her pretty sandals. She had come to London for the summer to work in the British Museum. She could really have managed with microfilm in Tucson for what little manuscript research was needed, but there was a dragging love affair to end. There is an age at which, however desperately happy one is in stolen moments, days, or weekends with one's married professor, one either prises him loose or cuts and runs. She had had a stab at both, and now considered she had successfully cut and run. So it was nice to be immediately appreciated. Problems are capable of solution. She said as much to him, turning her soft face to his ravaged one, swinging the long bright hair. It had begun a year ago, he told her in a rush, at another party actually; he had met this woman, the landlady in question, and had made, not immediately, a kind of *faux pas,* he now saw, and she had been very decent, all things considered, and so …

He had said, "I think I must move out of where I'm living." He had been quite wild, had nearly not come to the party, but could not go on drinking alone. The woman had considered him coolly and asked, "Why?" One could not, he said, go on in a place where one had once been blissfully happy, and was now miserable, however convenient the place. Convenient, that was, for work, and friends, and things that seemed, as he mentioned them, ashy and insubstantial compared to the memory and the hope of opening the door and finding Anne outside it, laughing and breathless, waiting to be told what he had read, or thought, or eaten, or felt that day. Someone I loved left, he told the woman. Reticent on that occasion too, he bit back the flurry of sentences about the total unexpectedness of it, the arriving back and finding only an envelope on a clean table, and spaces in the bookshelves, the record stack, the kitchen cupboard. It must have been planned for weeks, she must have been thinking it out while he rolled on her, while she poured wine for him, while … No, no. Vituperation is undignified and in this case what he felt was lower and worse than rage: just pure, child-like loss. "One ought not to mind places," he said to the woman. "But one does," she had said. "I know."

She had suggested to him that he could come and be her lodger, then; she had, she said, a lot of spare space going to waste, and her husband wasn't there much. "We've not had a lot to say to each other, lately." He could be quite self-contained, there was a kitchen and a bathroom in the attics; she wouldn't bother him. There was a large garden. It was possibly this that decided him: it was very hot, central London, the time of year when a man feels he would give anything to live in a room opening on to grass and trees, not a high flat in a dusty street. And if Anne came back, the door would be locked and mortice-locked.[1] He could stop thinking about Anne coming back. That was a decisive move:

Anne thought he wasn't decisive. He would live without Anne.

For some weeks after he moved in he had seen very little of the woman. They met on the stairs, and once she came up, on a hot Sunday, to tell him he must feel free to use the garden. He had offered to do some weeding and mowing and she had accepted. That was the weekend her husband came back, driving furiously up to the front door, running in, and calling in the empty hall, "Imogen, Imogen!" To which she had replied, uncharacteristically, by screaming hysterically. There was nothing in her husband, Noel's, appearance to warrant this reaction; their lodger, peering over the banister at the sound, had seen their upturned faces in the stairwell and watched hers settle into its usual prim and placid expression as he did so. Seeing Noel, a balding, fluffy-templed, stooping thirty-five or so, shabby corduroy suit, cotton polo neck, he realized he was now able to guess her age, as he had not been. She was a very neat woman, faded blonde, her hair in a knot on the back of her head, her legs long and slender, her eyes downcast. Mild was not quite the right word for her, though. She explained then that she had screamed because Noel had come home unexpectedly and startled her: she was sorry. It seemed a reasonable explanation. The extraordinary vehemence of the screaming was probably an echo in the stairwell. Noel seemed wholly downcast by it, all the same.

He had kept out of the way, that weekend, taking the stairs two at a time and lightly, feeling a little aggrieved, looking out of his kitchen window into the lovely, overgrown garden, that they were lurking indoors, wasting all the summer sun. At Sunday lunch-time he had heard the husband, Noel, shouting on the stairs.

"I can't go on, if you go on like that. I've done my best, I've tried to get through. Nothing will shift you, will it, you won't *try*, will you, you just go on and on. Well, I have my life to live, you can't throw a life away … can you?"

He had crept out again on to the dark upper landing and seen her standing, half-way down the stairs, quite still, watching Noel wave his arms and roar, or almost

---

[1] *mortice-locked*  Locked with a deadbolt.

roar, with a look of impassive patience, as though this nuisance must pass off. Noel swallowed and gasped; he turned his face up to her and said plaintively,

"You do see I can't stand it? I'll be in touch, shall I? You must want … you must need … you must…"

She didn't speak.

"If you need anything, you know where to get me."

"Yes."

"Oh, well…" said Noel, and went to the door. She watched him, from the stairs, until it was shut, and then came up again, step by step, as though it was an effort, a little, and went on coming, past her bedroom, to his landing, to come in and ask him, entirely naturally, please to use the garden if he wanted to, and please not to mind marital rows. She was sure he understood … things were difficult … Noel wouldn't be back for some time. He was a journalist: his work took him away a lot. Just as well. She committed herself to that "just as well." She was a very economical speaker.

So he took to sitting in the garden. It was a lovely place: a huge, hidden, walled south London garden, with old fruit trees at the end, a wildly waving disorderly buddleia, curving beds full of old roses, and a lawn of overgrown, dense rye-grass. Over the wall at the foot was the Common, with a footpath running behind all the gardens. She came out to the shed and helped him to assemble and oil the lawnmower, standing on the little path under the apple branches while he cut an experimental serpentine across her hay. Over the wall came the high sound of children's voices, and the thunk and thud of a football. He asked her how to raise the blades: he was not mechanically minded.

"The children get quite noisy," she said. "And dogs. I hope they don't bother you. There aren't many safe places for children, round here."

He replied truthfully that he never heard sounds that didn't concern him, when he was concentrating. When he'd got the lawn into shape, he was going to sit on it and do a lot of reading, try to get his mind in trim again, to write a paper on Hardy's poems, on their curiously archaic vocabulary.

"It isn't very far to the road on the other side, really," she said. "It just seems to be. The Common is an illusion of space, really. Just a spur of brambles and

gorse-bushes and bits of football pitch between two fast four-laned main roads. I hate London commons."

"There's a lovely smell, though, from the gorse and the wet grass. It's a pleasant illusion."

"No illusions are pleasant," she said, decisively, and went in. He wondered what she did with her time: apart from little shopping expeditions she seemed to be always in the house. He was sure that when he'd met her she'd been introduced as having some profession: vaguely literary, vaguely academic, like everyone he knew. Perhaps she wrote poetry in her north-facing living-room. He had no idea what it would be like. Women generally wrote emotional poetry, much nicer than men, as Kingsley Amis[1] has stated, but she seemed, despite her placid stillness, too spare and too fierce—grim?—for that. He remembered the screaming. Perhaps she wrote Plath[2]-like chants of violence. He didn't think that quite fitted the bill, either. Perhaps she was a freelance radio journalist. He didn't bother to ask anyone who might be a common acquaintance. During the whole year, he explained to the American at the party, he hadn't actually *discussed* her with anyone. Of course he wouldn't, she agreed vaguely and warmly. She knew he wouldn't. He didn't see why he shouldn't, in fact, but went on, for the time, with his narrative.

They had got to know each other a little better over the next few weeks, at least on the level of borrowing tea, or even sharing pots of it. The weather had got hotter. He had found an old-fashioned deck-chair, with faded striped canvas, in the shed, and had brushed it over and brought it out on to his mown lawn, where he sat writing a little, reading a little, getting up and pulling up a tuft of couch grass. He had been wrong about the children not bothering him: there was a succession of incursions by all sizes of children looking for all sizes of balls, which bounced to his feet, or crashed in the shrubs, or vanished in the herbaceous border, black and white footballs, beach-balls with concentric circles of primary colours, acid yellow tennis balls. The children came over the wall: black faces, brown faces, floppy long hair, shaven heads, respectable dotted sun-hats and

---

[1] *Kingsley Amis*  Sir Kingsley Amis (1922–95), a conservative English author, critic, and teacher.

[2] *Plath*  Sylvia Plath (1932–63), American poet and novelist.

camouflaged cotton army hats from Milletts. They came over easily, as though they were used to it, sandals, training shoes, a few bare toes, grubby sunburned legs, cotton skirts, jeans, football shorts. Sometimes, perched on the top, they saw him and gestured at the balls; one or two asked permission. Sometimes he threw a ball back, but was apt to knock down a few knobby little unripe apples or pears. There was a gate in the wall, under the fringing trees, which he once tried to open, spending time on rusty bolts only to discover that the lock was new and secure, and the key not in it.

The boy sitting in the tree did not seem to be looking for a ball. He was in a fork of the tree nearest the gate, swinging his legs, doing something to a knot in a frayed end of rope that was attached to the branch he sat on. He wore blue jeans and training shoes, and a brilliant tee shirt, striped in the colours of the spectrum, arranged in the right order, which the man on the grass found visually pleasing. He had rather long blond hair, falling over his eyes, so that his face was obscured.

"Hey, you. Do you think you ought to be up there? It might not be safe."

The boy looked up, grinned, and vanished monkey-like over the wall. He had a nice, frank grin, friendly, not cheeky.

He was there again, the next day, leaning back in the crook of the tree, arms crossed. He had on the same shirt and jeans. The man watched him, expecting him to move again, but he sat, immobile, smiling down pleasantly, and then staring up at the sky. The man read a little, looked up, saw him still there, and said,

"Have you lost anything?"

The child did not reply: after a moment he climbed down a little, swung along the branch hand over hand, dropped to the ground, raised an arm in salute, and was up over the usual route over the wall.

Two days later he was lying on his stomach on the edge of the lawn, out of the shade, this time in a white tee shirt with a pattern of blue ships and water-lines on it, his bare feet and legs stretched in the sun. He was chewing a grass stem, and studying the earth, as though watching for insects. The man said, "Hi, there," and the boy looked up, met his look with intensely blue eyes under long lashes, smiled with the same complete warmth and openness, and returned his look to the earth.

He felt reluctant to inform on the boy, who seemed so harmless and considerate: but when he met him walking out of the kitchen door, spoke to him, and got no answer but the gentle smile before the boy ran off towards the wall, he wondered if he should speak to his landlady. So he asked her, did she mind the children coming in the garden. She said no, children must look for balls, that was part of being children. He persisted—they sat there, too, and he had met one coming out of the house. He hadn't seemed to be doing any harm, the boy, but you couldn't tell. He thought she should know.

He was probably a friend of her son's, she said. She looked at him kindly and explained. Her son had run off the Common with some other children, two years ago, in the summer, in July, and had been killed on the road. More or less instantly, she had added drily, as though calculating that just *enough* information would preclude the need for further questions. He said he was sorry, very sorry, feeling to blame, which was ridiculous, and a little injured, because he had not known about her son, and might inadvertently have made a fool of himself with some casual reference whose ignorance would be embarrassing.

What was the boy like, she said. The one in the house? "I don't—talk to his friends. I find it painful. It could be Timmy, or Martin. They might have lost something, or want … "

He described the boy. Blond, about ten at a guess, he was not very good at children's ages, very blue eyes, slightly built, with a rainbow-striped tee shirt and blue jeans, mostly though not always—oh, and those football practice shoes, black and green. And the other tee shirt, with the ships and wavy lines. And an extraordinarily nice smile. A really *warm* smile. A nice-looking boy.

He was used to her being silent. But this silence went on and on and on. She was just staring into the garden. After a time, she said, in her precise conversational tone,

"The only thing I want, the only thing I want at all in this world, is to see that boy."

She stared at the garden and he stared with her, until the grass began to dance with empty light, and the edges of the shrubbery wavered. For a brief moment he shared the strain of not seeing the boy. Then she gave a little sigh, sat down, neatly as always, and passed out at his feet.

After this she became, for her, voluble. He didn't move her after she fainted, but sat patiently by her, until she stirred and sat up; then he fetched her some water, and would have gone away, but she talked.

"I'm too rational to see ghosts, I'm not someone who would see anything there was to see, I don't believe in an after-life, I don't see how anyone can, I always found a kind of satisfaction for myself in the idea that one just came to an end, to a sliced-off stop. But that was myself; I didn't think *he*—not *he*—I thought ghosts were—what people *wanted* to see, or were afraid to see … and after he died, the best hope I had, it sounds silly, was that I would go mad enough so that instead of waiting every day for him to come home from school and rattle the letter-box I might actually have the illusion of seeing or hearing him come in. Because I can't stop my body and mind waiting, every day, every day, I can't let go. And his bedroom, sometimes at night I go in, I think I might just for a moment forget he *wasn't* in there sleeping, I think I would pay almost anything—anything at all—for a moment of seeing him like I used to. In his pyjamas, with his—his—his hair … ruffled, and, his … you said, his … that *smile*.

"When it happened, they got Noel, and Noel came in and shouted my name, like he did the other day, that's why I screamed, because it—seemed the same—and then they said, he is dead, and I thought coolly, *is* dead, that will go on and on and on till the end of time, it's a continuous present tense, one thinks the most ridiculous things, there I was thinking about grammar, the verb to be, when it ends to be dead … And then I came out into the garden, and I half saw, in my mind's eye, a kind of ghost of his face, just the eyes and hair, coming towards me—like every day waiting for him to come home, the way you think of your son, with such pleasure, when he's—not there—and I—I thought—no, I won't *see* him, because he is dead, and I won't dream about him because he is dead, I'll be rational and practical and continue to live because one must, and there was Noel …

"I got it wrong, you see, I was so *sensible,* and then I was so shocked because I couldn't get to want anything—I couldn't *talk* to Noel—I—I—made Noel take away, destroy, all the photos, I—didn't dream, you can will not to dream, I didn't … visit a grave, flowers, there isn't any point. I was so sensible. Only my body wouldn't stop waiting and all it wants is to—to see that boy. *That* boy. That boy you—saw."

He did not say that he might have seen another boy, maybe even a boy who had been given the tee shirts and jeans afterwards. He did not say, though the idea crossed his mind, that maybe what he had seen was some kind of impression from her terrible desire to see a boy where nothing was. The boy had had nothing terrible, no aura of pain about him: he had been, his memory insisted, such a pleasant, courteous, self-contained boy, with his own purposes. And in fact the woman herself almost immediately raised the possibility that what he had seen was what she desired to see, a kind of mix-up of radio waves, like when you overheard police messages on the radio, or got BBC I on a switch that said ITV. She was thinking fast, and went on almost immediately to say that perhaps his sense of loss, his loss of Anne, which was what had led her to feel she could bear his presence in her house, was what had brought them—dare she say—near enough, for their wavelengths to mingle, perhaps, had made him susceptible … You mean, he had said, we are a kind of emotional vacuum, between us, that must be filled. Something like that, she had said, and had added, "But I don't believe in ghosts."

Anne, he thought, could not be a ghost, because she was elsewhere, with someone else, doing for someone else those little things she had done so gaily for him, tasty little suppers, bits of research, a sudden vase of unusual flowers, a new bold shirt, unlike his own cautious taste, but suiting him, suiting him. In a sense, Anne was worse lost because voluntarily absent, an absence that could not be loved because love was at an end, for Anne.

"I don't suppose you will, now," the woman was saying. "I think talking would probably stop any—

mixing of messages, if that's what it is, don't you? But—if—*if* he comes again"—and here for the first time her eyes were full of tears—"if—you must promise, you will *tell* me, you must promise."

He had promised, easily enough, because he was fairly sure she was right, the boy would not be seen again. But the next day he was on the lawn, nearer than ever, sitting on the grass beside the deck-chair, his arms clasping his bent, warm brown knees, the thick, pale hair glittering in the sun. He was wearing a football shirt, this time, Chelsea's colours. Sitting down in the deck-chair, the man could have put out a hand and touched him, but did not: it was not, it seemed, a possible gesture to make. But the boy looked up and smiled, with a pleasant complicity, as though they now understood each other very well. The man tried speech: he said, "It's nice to see you again," and the boy nodded acknowledgement of this remark, without speaking himself. This was the beginning of communication between them, or what the man supposed to be communication. He did not think of fetching the woman. He became aware that he was in some strange way *enjoying the boy's company.* His pleasant stillness—and he sat there all morning, occasionally lying back on the grass, occasionally staring thoughtfully at the house—was calming and comfortable. The man did quite a lot of work—wrote about three reasonable pages on Hardy's original air-blue gown—and looked up now and then to make sure the boy was still there and happy.

He went to report to the woman—as he had after all promised to do—that evening. She had obviously been waiting and hoping—her unnatural calm had given way to agitated pacing, and her eyes were dark and deeper in. At this point in the story he found in himself a necessity to bowdlerize[1] for the sympathetic American, as he had indeed already begun to do. He had mentioned only a child who had "seemed like" the woman's lost son, and he now ceased to mention the child at all, as an actor in the story, with the result that what the American woman heard was a tale of how he, the man, had become increasingly involved in the woman's solitary grief, how their two losses had become a kind of *folie à deux*[2] from which he could not extricate himself. What follows is not what he told the American girl, though it may be clear at which points the bowdlerized version coincided with what he really believed to have happened. There was a sense he could not at first analyse that it was improper to talk about the boy—not because he might not be believed; that did not come into it; but because something dreadful might happen.

"He sat on the lawn all morning. In a football shirt."

"Chelsea?"

"Chelsea."

"What did he do? Does he look happy? Did he speak?" Her desire to know was terrible.

"He doesn't speak. He didn't move much. He seemed—very calm. He stayed a long time."

"This is terrible. This is ludicrous. There *is no boy.*"

"No. But I saw him."

"Why you?"

"I don't know." A pause. "I do *like* him."

"He is—was—a most likeable boy."

Some days later he saw the boy running along the landing in the evening, wearing what might have been pyjamas, in peacock towelling, or might have been a track suit. Pyjamas, the woman stated confidently, when he told her: his new pyjamas. With white ribbed cuffs, weren't they? And a white polo neck? He corroborated this, watching her cry—she cried more easily now—finding her anxiety and disturbance very hard to bear. But it never occurred to him that it was possible to break his promise to tell her when he saw the boy. That was another curious imperative from some undefined authority.

They discussed clothes. If there were ghosts, how could they appear in clothes long burned, or rotted, or worn away by other people? You could imagine, they agreed, that something of a person might linger—as the Tibetans and others believe the soul lingers near the body before setting out on its long journey. But clothes? And in this case so many clothes? I must be seeing your memories, he told her, and she nodded fiercely, compressing her lips, agreeing that this was likely, adding, "I am too rational to go mad, so I seem to be putting it on

---

[1] *bowdlerize*   Alter so as to remove or modify indelicate words or passages.

[2] *folie à deux*   French: a madness shared by two.

you."

He tried a joke. "That isn't very kind to me, to imply that madness comes more easily to me."

"No, sensitivity. I am insensible. I was always a bit like that, and this made it worse. I am the *last* person to see any ghost that was trying to haunt me."

"We agreed it was your memories I saw."

"Yes. We agreed. That's rational. As rational as we can be, considering."

All the same, the brilliance of the boy's blue regard, his gravely smiling salutation in the garden next morning, did not seem like anyone's tortured memories of earlier happiness. The man spoke to him directly then:

"Is there anything I can *do* for you? Anything you want? Can I help you?"

The boy seemed to puzzle about this for a while, inclining his head as though hearing was difficult. Then he nodded, quickly and perhaps urgently, turned, and ran into the house, looking back to make sure he was followed. The man entered the living-room through the french windows, behind the running boy, who stopped for a moment in the centre of the room, with the man blinking behind him at the sudden transition from sunlight to comparative dark. The woman was sitting in an armchair, looking at nothing there. She often sat like that. She looked up, across the boy, at the man; and the boy, his face for the first time anxious, met the man's eyes again, asking, before he went out into the house.

"What is it? What is it? Have you seen him again? Why are you …?"

"He came in here. He went—out through the door."

"I didn't see him."

"No."

"Did he—oh, this is so *silly*—did he see me?"

He could not remember. He told the only truth he knew.

"He brought me in here."

"Oh, what can I do, what am I going to *do*? If I killed myself—I have thought of that—but the idea that I should be with him is an illusion I … this silly situation is the nearest I shall ever get. To him. He was *in here with me?*"

"Yes."

And she was crying again. Out in the garden he could see the boy, swinging agile on the apple branch.

He was not quite sure, looking back, when he had thought he had realized what the boy had wanted him to do. This was also, at the party, his worst piece of what he called bowdlerization, though in some sense it was clearly the opposite of bowdlerization. He told the American girl that he had come to the conclusion that it was the woman herself who had wanted it, though there was in fact, throughout, no sign of her wanting anything except to see the boy, as she said. The boy, bolder and more frequent, had appeared several nights running on the landing, wandering in and out of bathrooms and bedrooms, restlessly, a little agitated, questing almost, until it had "come to" the man that what he required was to be re-engendered, for him, the man, to give to his mother another child, into which he could peacefully vanish. The idea was so clear that it was like another imperative, though he did not have the courage to ask the child to confirm it. Possibly this was out of delicacy—the child was too young to be talked to about sex. Possibly there were other reasons. Possibly he was mistaken: the situation was making him hysterical, he felt action of some kind was required and must be possible. He could not spend the rest of the summer, the rest of his life, describing nonexistent tee shirts and blond smiles.

He could think of no sensible way of embarking on his venture, so in the end simply walked into her bedroom one night. She was lying there, reading; when she saw him her instinctive gesture was to hide, not her bare arms and throat, but her book. She seemed, in fact, quite unsurprised to see his pyjamaed figure, and, after she had recovered her coolness, brought out the book definitely and laid it on the bedspread.

"My new taste in illegitimate literature. I keep them in a box under the bed."

*Ena Twigg, Medium. The Infinite Hive. The Spirit World. Is There Life After Death?*

"Pathetic," she proffered.

He sat down delicately on the bed.

"Please, don't grieve so. Please, let yourself be comforted. Please … "

He put an arm round her. She shuddered. He pulled her closer. He asked why she had had only the one son, and she seemed to understand the purport of his question, for she tried, angular and chilly, to lean on him a little, she became apparently compliant. "No real reason," she assured him, no material reason. Just her husband's profession and lack of inclination: that covered it.

"Perhaps," he suggested, "if she would be comforted a little, perhaps she could hope, perhaps … "

For comfort then, she said, dolefully, and lay back, pushing Ena Twigg off the bed with one fierce gesture, then lying placidly. He got in beside her, put his arms round her, kissed her cold cheek, thought of Anne, of what was never to be again. Come on, he said to the woman, you must live, you must try to live, let us hold each other for comfort.

She hissed at him "Don't *talk*" between clenched teeth, so he stroked her lightly, over her nightdress, breasts and buttocks and long stiff legs, composed like an effigy on an Elizabethan tomb. She allowed this, trembling slightly, and then trembling violently: he took this to be a sign of some mixture of pleasure and pain, of the return of life to stone. He put a hand between her legs and she moved them heavily apart; he heaved himself over her and pushed, unsuccessfully. She was contorted and locked tight: frigid, he thought grimly, was not the word. *Rigor mortis,* his mind said to him, before she began to scream.

He was ridiculously cross about this. He jumped away and said quite rudely, "Shut up," and then ungraciously, "I'm sorry." She stopped screaming as suddenly as she had begun and made one of her painstaking economical explanations.

"Sex and death don't go. I can't afford to let go of my grip on myself. I hoped. What you hoped. It was a bad idea. I apologize."

"Oh, never mind," he said and rushed out again on to the landing, feeling foolish and almost in tears for warm, lovely Anne.

The child was on the landing, waiting. When the man saw him, he looked questioning, and then turned his face against the wall and leant there, rigid, his shoulders hunched, his hair hiding his expression. There was a similarity between woman and child. The man felt, for the first time, almost uncharitable towards the boy, and then felt something else.

"Look, I'm sorry. I tried. I did try. Please turn round."

Uncompromising, rigid, clenched back view.

"Oh well," said the man, and went into his bedroom.

So now, he said to the American woman at the party, I feel a fool, I feel embarrassed, I feel we are hurting, not helping each other, I feel it isn't a refuge. Of course you feel that, she said, of course you're right—it was temporarily necessary, it helped both of you, but you've got to live your life. Yes, he said, I've done my best, I've tried to get through, I have my life to live. Look, she said, I want to help, I really do, I have these wonderful friends I'm renting this flat from, why don't you come, just for a few days, just for a break, why don't you? They're real sympathetic people, you'd like them, I like them, you could get your emotions kind of straightened out. She'd probably be glad to see the back of you, she must feel as bad as you do, she's got to relate to her situation in her own way in the end. We all have.

He said he would think about it. He knew he had elected to tell the sympathetic American because he had sensed she would be—would offer—a way out. He had to get out. He took her home from the party and went back to his house and landlady without seeing her into her flat. They both knew that this reticence was promising—that he hadn't come in then, because he meant to come later. Her warmth and readiness were like sunshine, she was open. He did not know what to say to the woman.

In fact, she made it easy for him: she asked, briskly, if he now found it perhaps uncomfortable to stay, and he replied that he had felt he should move on, he was of so little use … Very well, she had agreed, and had added crisply that it had to be better for everyone if "all this" came to an end. He remembered the firmness with which she had told him that no illusions were pleasant. She was strong: too strong for her own good. It would take years to wear away that stony, closed, simply surviving insensibility. It was not his job. He would go. All the same, he felt bad.

He got out his suitcases and put some things in them. He went down to the garden, nervously, and put away the deck-chair. The garden was empty. There were no voices over the wall. The silence was thick and deadening. He wondered, knowing he would not see the boy again, if anyone else would do so, or if, now he was gone, no one would describe a tee shirt, a sandal, a smile, seen, remembered, or desired. He went slowly up to his room again.

The boy was sitting on his suitcase, arms crossed, face frowning and serious. He held the man's look for a long moment, and then the man went and sat on his bed. The boy continued to sit. The man found himself speaking.

"You do see I have to go? I've tried to get through. I can't get through. I'm no use to you, am I?"

The boy remained immobile, his head on one side, considering. The man stood up and walked towards him.

"Please. Let me go. What are we, in this house? A man and a woman and a child, and none of us can get through. You can't want that?"

He went as close as he dared. He had, he thought, the intention of putting his hand on or through the child. But could not bring himself to feel there was no boy. So he stood, and repeated,

"I can't get through. Do you want me to stay?"

Upon which, as he stood helplessly there, the boy turned on him again the brilliant, open, confiding, beautiful desired smile.

—1987

# PUBLIC VOICES:
# THE END OF EMPIRE AND
# A NEW BRITAIN

## *CONTEXTS*

This section brings together two groups of excerpts from speeches and public statements, several of which have become touchstones in discussions of the changes that Britain and her former possessions have undergone since the Second World War.

The first group comprises pieces relating to the end of the British Empire, and the transformation both of Britain's place in the world community and of that of its former colonies. The section opens with excerpts from a landmark speech made by Mahatma Gandhi in 1942, regarding the struggle for independence in India, and a statement in response from British representative Sir Stafford Cripps. Included in the website component of this section is a speech by Martin Luther King on the occasion of the independence of Ghana—the first of Britain's African possessions to become a sovereign state. Also included is the famous 1961 speech by British Prime Minister Harold Macmillan on the "wind of change" that brought independence to former British colonies throughout Africa.

The colonial and post-colonial experience has continued to inform much of the discourse in the academic study of literature in English in the late twentieth and early twenty-first centuries—and in political discussions too, the colonial legacy of Britain continues to be controversial. But as the twenty-first century unfolds, views of that legacy in the former British colonies and in Britain herself may finally be converging. For many years in Britain voices critical of the colonial past have been stronger than those defending or expressing affection for past imperial glory. In the former colonies—many of which have now been independent for close to half a century—the shaping force of colonialism continues to be acknowledged, but it is usually not treated as the sole determining factor for present-day political, economic, and cultural conditions. And when the colonial legacy is discussed, it is more and more often seen in a more complex way. Such is the case, for example, with the last of the speeches excerpted in this group, delivered by Indian Prime Minister Manmohan Singh at Oxford in 2005.

The second group of documents deals with socio-economic issues and the ideology of left and right. As World War II ended, the British remained united in their belief that Winston Churchill deserved much of the credit for the country's survival during the dark days of 1940, when London was being bombed daily and a Nazi invasion seemed imminent. But the war—while doing little to address economic inequality—had eroded support for social class distinctions of the sort that Churchill embodied; many felt a strong desire for a more egalitarian Britain. Many doubted too that the great war leader was well suited temperamentally to lead the country in peacetime—an impression that was solidified by Churchill's belligerence during the campaign of 1945 (the most striking example of which was the speech excerpted in this section, in which the Prime Minister likened his socialist opposition to the Nazis). With the end of the war came the election of a Labour Government, led by Clement Attlee, and a dramatic shift to the left for Britain; a key 1945 speech by Attlee in which he outlines the program for change is excerpted here.

The "wind of change" in Britain's overseas policies also had important implications at home. All political parties in postwar Britain were officially opposed to discrimination on the grounds of race, religion, or ethnic origin, but the country had a long history of such discrimination, and the prospect of unlimited numbers from British possessions overseas emigrating to "the mother country" made many in Britain uncomfortable. In 1965, the introduction by Harold Wilson's Labour government of a Race Relations Act was the first effort to ensure through the law that everyone would be treated equally within Britain; it made it a civil offense, for example, to refuse access to anyone on racial grounds to public places such as hotels, restaurants, and the public transit system. In 1968, the government proposed to broaden the list of such offences to cover employment and housing, but the proposal was met by a considerable backlash. The most vocal of the opponents of the government's proposal was Conservative Member of Parliament Enoch Powell, whose infamous "Rivers of Blood" speech is excerpted in the website component of this section. In the face of widespread fears over a "flood" of immigration (especially from newly independent Commonwealth countries), Immigration Minister James Callaghan withdrew what had been an automatic right for Commonwealth citizens with British passports to enter the country. But the government held firm on the expanded measures against racial discrimination, and the 1968 Race Relations Act became law in November of that year.

Though Powell's race-based arguments regarding immigrants and citizenship remain popular among some elements of the far right in Britain, they have never entered the mainstream of conservative thought, and have not been shared by a majority of British people. In the late 1970s, however, the pendulum of British opinion on many other socio-economic issues did swing dramatically to the right. The agenda of Labour governments dominated British politics from 1945 through to 1979, but by the late 1970s, the economy was beset by high inflation and increasing unemployment, and many were disenchanted both with some of the more extreme manifestations of the "welfare state" and with union influence in the workplace. The period between January and March 1979, in which a series of strikes by workers in key sectors (including health workers and garbage collectors) took place, was dubbed "the winter of discontent." The Conservative Party famously made its point with billboard advertisements showing workers in unemployment queues, along with the slogan "Labour's Not Working." The radical conservative Margaret Thatcher became Prime Minister on 4 June 1979. Her agenda of lowering taxes, privatizing nationalized industries and public services, and restricting the power of unions was highly controversial, but Thatcher stood firm; her 10 October 1980 speech ("The Lady's Not for Turning") is perhaps the best-known expression of her resolution in the face of opposition.

In the 1990s, the "Thatcherite revolution" had in turn run out of steam; the Conservative Party remained in power under John Major but was widely unpopular, and new Labour Party leader Tony Blair had revitalized that party, putting democratic reforms into place (whereas union leaders had previously been able to control blocks of votes, for example, now each party member held one vote), and bringing the party towards the center ideologically. Many of the priorities of Blair and his followers—such as improving educational standards and enacting constitutional reform regarding the House of Lords and the status of Scotland and Wales—were very different from the traditional agenda of the Labour Party, so much so that Blair re-christened the party "New Labour" and described his policies as representing a third way, different from either the old political left or the conservative right. In the 4 October 1994 speech excerpted below, Blair set out an agenda for New Labour.

The final selection included in the website component of this section is one that raises questions in relation both to the internal political and cultural life of Britain and to the place of Britain in the world. Under both Thatcher and Blair, the British governments established itself as the closest ally of the United States, and in that role went to war in Iraq alongside Americans in Iraq in 1991, in Afghanistan in 2002, and again in Iraq in 2003. In the speech excerpted here, Blair defends the latter action in the context of what he had come to believe was a changed world.

⌘ ⌘ ⌘

## The "Quit India" Movement

The Quit India Movement (in Hindi *Bharat Chhodo Andolan*) is remembered as a watershed moment in the struggle for Indian independence. Sir Stafford Cripps visited India in March 1942, hoping to placate those clamoring for independence from British rule and bringing an offer to form, at the conclusion of the war, a body responsible for drafting a constitution for an India that would be in large part independent; until then, he sought a pledge of full support in the war effort against the Axis powers —against Japan in particular. For Mohandas Gandhi (1869–1948), the revered leader who preached a doctrine of non-violent resistance to oppression, and for others who had long been struggling against British colonial rule and who had been let down in the past by British promises, this was not enough. Gandhi (who was given the honorific title "Mahatma," meaning "a revered, loved and respected person") brought before the Indian National Congress (on 14 July 1942) and the All India Congress Committee (on 8 August 1942) a resolution that came to be known as the "Quit India" resolution, demanding immediate independence from Britain and promising full-scale disobedience if the demand was not met. Gandhi's August 8 "Quit India" speech, excerpted below, is regarded as a landmark, as is the slogan he first introduced at this time and that became a rallying cry throughout India, "Do or Die" (in Hindi *Karenge Ya Marenge*).

When the British rejected the demands of the Indian Congress—Cripps's initial statement of response is excerpted below—hundreds of thousands followed Gandhi's call and joined in protest. In the short term the resistance movement was a failure; the British reacted swiftly and brutally, incarcerating the entire Congress leadership for the remainder of the war (though Gandhi himself was released on health grounds in 1944) and arresting over 100,000 people. In the longer term, however, the movement paved the way for independence following the war; on 15 August 1947, India officially became a sovereign nation.

## from Mohandas K. Gandhi, Speech to the All India Congress Committee, Bombay, 8 August 1942

Ours is not a drive for power, but purely a nonviolent fight for India's independence. In a violent struggle, a successful general has been often known to effect a military coup and to set up a dictatorship. But under the Congress scheme of things, essentially nonviolent as it is, there can be no room for dictatorship. A non-violent soldier of freedom will covet nothing for himself, he fights only for the freedom of his country. The Congress is unconcerned as to who will rule, when freedom is attained. The power, when it comes, will belong to the people of India, and it will be for them to decide to whom it should be entrusted....

There is the question of your attitude towards the British. I have noticed that there is hatred towards the British among the people. The people say they are disgusted with their behaviour. The people make no distinction between British imperialism and the British people. To them, the two are one. This hatred would even make them welcome the Japanese. It is most dangerous. It means that they will exchange one slavery for another. We must get rid of this feeling. Our quarrel is not with the British people; we fight their imperialism. The proposal for the withdrawal of British power did not come out of anger. It came to enable India to play its due part at the present critical juncture. It is not a happy position for a big country like India to be merely helping with money and material obtained willynilly from her while the United Nations are conducting the war. We cannot evoke the true spirit of sacrifice and valour, so long as we are not free. I know the British Government will not be able to withhold freedom from us, when we have made enough self-sacrifice. We must, therefore, purge ourselves of hatred. Speaking for myself, I can say that I have never felt any hatred. As a matter of fact, I feel myself to be a greater friend of the British now than ever before. One reason is that they are today in distress. My very friendship, therefore, demands that I should try to save them from their mistakes. As I view the situation, they are on the brink of an abyss. It, therefore, becomes my duty to warn them of their danger even though it may, for the time being, anger them to the point of cutting off the friendly hand that is stretched out to help them. People may laugh; nevertheless that is my claim. At a time when I may have to launch the biggest struggle of my life, I may not harbour hatred against anybody....

Every one of you should, from this moment onwards, consider yourself a free man or woman, and act as if you are free and are no longer under the heel of this imperialism.

It is not a make-believe that I am suggesting to you. It is the very essence of freedom. The bond of the slave is snapped the moment he considers himself to be a free being. He will plainly tell the master: "I was your bond slave till this moment, but I am a slave no longer. You may kill me if you like, but if you keep me alive, I wish to tell you that if you release me from the bondage, of your own accord, I will ask for nothing more from you. You used to feed and clothe me, though I could have provided food and clothing for myself by my labour. I hitherto depended on you instead of on God, for food and raiment. But God has now inspired me with an urge for freedom and I am today a free man, and will no longer depend on you."

You may take it from me that I am not going to strike a bargain with the Viceroy[1] for ministries and the like. I am not going to be satisfied with anything short of complete freedom. Maybe, he will propose the abolition of salt tax,[2] the drink evil, etc. But I will say, "Nothing less than freedom."

Here is a mantra,[3] a short one, that I give you. You may imprint it on your hearts and let every breath of yours give expression to it. The mantra is: "Do or Die." We shall either free India or die in the attempt; we shall not live to see the perpetuation of our slavery. Every true Congressman or woman will join the struggle with an inflexible determination not to remain alive to see the country in bondage and slavery. Let that be your

---

[1] *Viceroy*  Highest-ranking British official in Colonial India.

[2] *salt tax*  The British imperial government in India ruled that it was illegal for anyone but the British government to sell salt, thus ensuring that they had a monopoly. This monopoly became a chief point of protest for Gandhi in his famous Salt March to Dandi in 1930.

[3] *mantra*  Sacred words repeated in a prayer or incantation.

pledge. Keep jails out of your consideration. If the Government keeps me free, I will not put on the Government the strain of maintaining a large number of prisoners at a time when it is in trouble. Let every man and woman live every moment of his or her life hereafter in the consciousness that he or she eats or lives for achieving freedom and will die, if need be, to attain that goal. Take a pledge, with God and your own conscience as witness, that you will no longer rest till freedom is achieved and will be prepared to lay down your lives in the attempt to achieve it. He who loses his life will gain it; he who will seek to save it shall lose it. Freedom is not for the coward or the faint-hearted....

[The 8 August speech was made available to the press both in Hindi and in English. The excerpts above are from the part of the speech that was delivered in Hindi. Excerpts from the final portion of the speech, which was delivered in English, appear below.]

... Let me tell you that I do not regard England or for that matter America as free countries. They are free after their own fashion, free to hold in bondage coloured races of the earth. Are England and America fighting for the liberty of these races today? If not, do not ask me to wait until after the war. You shall not limit my concept of freedom. The English and American teachers, their history, their magnificent poetry have not said that you shall not broaden the interpretation of freedom. And according to my interpretation of that freedom I am constrained to say they are strangers to that freedom which their teachers and poets have described. If they will know the real freedom they should come to India. ...

I trust the whole of India today to launch upon a non-violent struggle. I trust because of my nature to rely upon the innate goodness of human nature which perceives the truth and prevails during the crisis as if by instinct. But even if I am deceived in this I shall not swerve. I shall not flinch. From its very inception the Congress based its policy on peaceful methods....

I want Englishmen, Europeans, and all the United Nations to examine in their hearts what crime had India committed in demanding Independence. I ask, is it right for you to distrust such an organization with all its background, tradition and record of over half a century and misrepresent its endeavours before all the world by every means at your command?… There is a chorus of disapproval and righteous protest all over the world against us. They say we are erring, the move is inopportune. I had great regard for British diplomacy, which has enabled them to hold the Empire so long. Now it stinks in my nostrils, and others have studied that diplomacy and are putting it into practice. They may succeed in getting, through these methods, world opinion on their side for a time; but India will speak against that world opinion. She will raise her voice against all the organized propaganda. I will speak against it. Even if all the United Nations opposes me, even if the whole of India forsakes me, I will say, "You are wrong. India will wrench with non-violence her liberty from unwilling hands." I will go ahead not for India's sake alone, but for the sake of the world. Even if my eyes close before there is freedom, non-violence will not end.…

I have pledged the Congress and the Congress will do or die.

## from Sir Stafford Cripps, Statement on India, 6 August 1942

Many hard comments have been made on my efforts in India from the side of the Congress party, yet I feel content in the deep conviction that the offer I travelled 22,000 miles to discuss with Indian leaders was a real contribution to a solution of our differences.

Concerning the attitude of the British Government there can be no doubt the Secretary of State for India made a statement last week which makes it plain that "His Majesty's Government stand firmly by the broad intentions of their offer in the draft declaration" which I took with me to India, and that they "reiterate their resolve to give the fullest opportunity for attainment by India of complete self-government."

It is, therefore, plain beyond doubt that Indian self-government is assured as soon as hostilities are over and it becomes possible to re-plan life in India upon a new basis. It is of no avail for protagonists of sectional interests in India to deny these simple facts. A promise

Gandhi, shown soon after Indian independence in 1947, accompanied by Lord and Lady Mountbatten.

has been made and that promise will be carried out.

Is it reasonable then for people of India, while hostilities are continuing, to demand some complete and fundamental constitutional change? Is it practical in the middle of a hard-fought war in which the United States, China, and Britain are exerting all their strength to protect the Eastern world from domination by Japan?

Gandhi has asked that the British Government should walk out of India and leave the Indian people to settle differences among themselves, even if it means chaos and confusion. What would this chaos and confusion actually mean? All government which is based on the existing constitution would immediately cease. There would be no Viceroy, no executive council, no legislative assembly, and no civil service with any legal authority.

The Governors of the provinces would cease to function; so would all the provincial governments and legislatures. There would be no authority to collect revenue and no money to pay for any government service. The police would cease to have any authority, courts of justice would no longer function, and there would be no laws and no order. The evil-minded could pillage the land, and disorder and crime could run riot.

In this chaos Gandhi proposes to set up a provisional government if he can, but as there would then be no electoral machinery and no law as to representation, it could at best be no more than a government nominated by themselves and such other leaders of Indian opinion as might be willing to work with him. Others might work against him and defy his provisional government.

Chaos in India at this moment would not affect India only. It would affect vitally the whole war against the Axis powers. Gandhi has more recently recognized the need for continuance of British, American and Chinese efforts in India and has suggested that these troops might remain by agreement with some new Indian Government.

But the difficulty of the situation does not lie in whether an agreement can be come to with an Indian Government, but whether in conditions of chaos and complete lack of law and order an Indian Government can establish itself, pass all the necessary laws, lay down a completely new Constitution, and get the agreement of all sections of Indian opinion so as to avoid an immediate civil war.

It was because of these difficulties, inherent in an attempt to change over control of a country so vast as India, that we have recognized that while the war lasts a complete change-over to an entirely new Constitution is impossible.

Apart altogether from our own vital interests, we cannot and must not desert those other nations who have already gone through so much tragedy and suffering to defeat the evil designs of the Axis powers. We have pledged ourselves, and of this the United Nations of the world are witness, to give the fullest opportunity for attainment of self-government by India as soon as hostilities are over. I repeat that that is beyond doubt….

No one will expect the British Government or the Government of India to give way to threats of violence, disorder and chaos; and, indeed, representatives of large sections of Indian opinion have expressly warned us that we must not do so.

We make no threats, but we must assert unequivocally our duty to India, to the great minority and to the United Nations to preserve law and order until hostilities cease, and we can then give, as we have promised, the fullest opportunity for attainment of self-government by the Indian people.

It is not yet too late for the Indian people to decide on rapid, ordered progress. I can assure them that the British people are as determined upon self-government for India as they are themselves. We ask the great masses of India to be patient a short time longer, while the cause of freedom is being fought out, not because we want to delay, but because the hard facts of war make a complete change impossible at the moment.

I sincerely hope we shall all of us face these difficult questions with calmness, sincerity and mutual trust, because I am convinced that if both peoples so exercise their will to solve our problems there need be no violence.

India has indeed a great and free future before her, in which she can make her special contribution to the well-being of mankind. The first and indispensable part of that contribution is to work with the United Nations for the defeat of fascism and of brutal aggression.

## from Harold Macmillan, Speech Made to the South Africa Parliament, 3 February 1960

By 1961, the British had clearly accepted, as British Prime Minister Harold Macmillan put it in the famous speech excerpted below, that the "wind of change" was blowing across Africa. South Africa, however, was a special case; since 1910, the Union of South Africa had held Dominion status similar to that of Canada and Australia, and Britain envisaged it playing an important part in the British Commonwealth. Since 1948, however, the country had been following increasingly harsh discriminatory policies under white supremacist National Party governments—policies that were entirely at odds with most developments elsewhere in Africa. In his "wind of change" speech, British Prime Minister Harold Macmillan gently suggested to South African legislators that history was not on the side of apartheid—and spoke of how he saw the position of African nations in the "Cold War" between the Western powers and the Communist bloc. South African Prime Minister Hendrik Verwoerd was not about to be swayed by the wind of change, however; in 1961 South Africa left the British Commonwealth, and it was not until 1994 that the country abandoned apartheid and became a democracy.

It is, as I have said, a special privilege for me to be here in 1960 when you are celebrating what I might call the golden wedding of the Union. At such a time it is natural and right that you should pause to take stock of your position, to look back at what you have achieved, to look forward to what lies ahead. In the fifty years of their nationhood the people of South Africa have built a strong economy founded upon a healthy agriculture and thriving and resilient industries.

No one could fail to be impressed with the immense material progress which has been achieved. That all this has been accomplished in so short a time is a striking testimony to the skill, energy and initiative of your people. We in Britain are proud of the contribution we have made to this remarkable achievement. Much of it has been financed by British capital....

As I have travelled around the Union I have found everywhere, as I expected, a deep preoccupation with what is happening in the rest of the African continent.

I understand and sympathise with your interests in these events, and your anxiety about them. Ever since the break up of the Roman Empire one of the constant facts of political life in Europe has been the emergence of independent nations. They have come into existence over the centuries in different forms, with different kinds of government, but all have been inspired by a deep, keen feeling of nationalism, which has grown as the nations have grown.

In the twentieth century, and especially since the end of the war, the processes which gave birth to the nation states of Europe have been repeated all over the world. We have seen the awakening of national consciousness in peoples who have for centuries lived in dependence upon some other power. Fifteen years ago this movement spread through Asia. Many countries there, of different races and civilisations, pressed their claim to an independent national life. Today the same thing is happening in Africa, and the most striking of all the impressions I have formed since I left London a month ago is of the strength of this African national consciousness. In different places it takes different forms, but it is happening everywhere. The wind of change is blowing through this continent, and whether we like it or not, this growth of national consciousness is a political fact. We must all accept it as a fact, and our national policies must take account of it.

Well, you understand this better than anyone. You are sprung from Europe, the home of nationalism, and here in Africa you have yourselves created a new nation. A new nation. Indeed in the history of our times yours will be recorded as the first of the African nationalisms. ...

As I have said, the growth of national consciousness in Africa is a political fact, and we must accept it as such. That means, I would judge, that we must come to terms with it. I sincerely believe that if we cannot do so we may imperil the precarious balance between the East and West on which the peace of the world depends. The world today is divided into three main groups. First there are what we call the Western Powers. You in South Africa and we in Britain belong to this group, together with our friends and allies in other parts of the Commonwealth. In the United States of America and in Europe we call it the Free World. Secondly there are the

Communists—Russia and her satellites in Europe and China whose population will rise by the end of the next ten years to the staggering total of 800 million. Thirdly, there are those parts of the world whose people are at present uncommitted either to Communism or to our Western ideas.

In this context we think first of Asia and then of Africa. As I see it the great issue in this second half of the twentieth century is whether the uncommitted peoples of Asia and Africa will swing to the East or to the West. Will they be drawn into the Communist camp? Or will the great experiments in self-government that are now being made in Asia and Africa, especially within the Commonwealth, prove so successful, and by their example so compelling, that the balance will come down in favour of freedom and order and justice?

The struggle is joined, and it is a struggle for the minds of men. What is now on trial is much more than our military strength or our diplomatic and administrative skill. It is our way of life. The uncommitted nations want to see before they choose.

## from Manmohan Singh, Acceptance Speech on the Occasion of the Awarding of the Degree of Doctor of Civil Law, Honoris Causa, Oxford University, 11 July 2005

In a surprise move, Manmohan Singh, a highly respected former Finance Minister, became the first Sikh Prime Minister of India in 2004, when the Congress Party leader, Italian-born Sonia Gandhi, declined to assume the post following her election victory. Singh's historic July 2005 speech at Oxford University was the first major address by an Indian Prime Minister to be devoted largely to acknowledging positive aspects of the British colonial legacy. When the text of the speech was released in India, it was strongly criticized by the opposition Janata Party. "Prime Minister Singh has insulted the sentiments of [millions of] proud Indians by lavishing praise on British colonial rule," spokesperson Muktar Abbas Naqvi was quoted as saying. "He owes an apology to the nation. ... The high praise showered on the British has insulted the freedom fighters who gave their lives to free India from British colonial rule."

I must at the outset express my deep sense of shock and anger at the terrorist attacks[1] in London. On behalf of the people of India and on my own behalf I convey my own sincere condolences to the families and friends of the deceased and those who have been injured. I also extend the sympathy and solidarity of the people of India with the people of the United Kingdom, in particular the citizens of London.

I arrived here in the United Kingdom after dealing with the aftermath of yet another terrorist attack in India.[2] It is clear once again that terrorism is a global threat. Terrorism anywhere is a threat to peace, freedom, human dignity and civilisation everywhere. Terrorism is cowardice aimed at the innocent people. It is fed on hatred and cynicism.

Every time terrorists strike anywhere all of us who believe in democracy and the rule of law must stand together and affirm our firm commitment to fight this scourge resolutely and unitedly. I sincerely hope that all of those who cherish and value open and free societies will join hands in the war against terrorism wherever it is fought. I wish the people of London well. I pray that their lives will soon return to normal and they can resume their celebrations for having been chosen the venue for the 2012 Olympics.[3]

This is an emotional moment for me. Oxford brings back many fond memories that I cherish. For this reason, as much as for the intrinsic value of the honour you bestow upon me, I am truly overwhelmed. I am grateful to you, Mr. Chancellor, and to your colleagues, for this honour. I have had the good fortune of receiving several honorary degrees. However, there can be nothing more valuable than receiving an honorary degree from one's own alma mater. To be so honoured by a university where one has burnt the proverbial midnight oil to earn a regular degree, is a most fulfilling experience. I thank you for it. This is a day I will truly cherish.

[1] *terrorist attacks*   On 7 July 2005 coordinated attacks on London's transportation system killed more than 50 people.

[2] *yet another terrorist attack in India*   Disputes over the territory of Kashmir resulted in tension and violence in India and Pakistan through 2004 and 2005. Separate incidents on 7 July and 8 July had resulted in 17 deaths in India.

[3] *celebrations ... Olympics*   On 6 July 2005, the International Olympic Committee announced that London would host the 2012 Olympics.

The world has changed beyond recognition since I was a student here.[1] Yet, some age-old problems endure. Developing countries have found a new voice, a new status and have acquired a new sense of confidence over the last few decades. As an Indian, I see a renewed sense of hope and purpose. This new optimism gives us Indians a sense of self-confidence and this shapes our world view today. It would be no exaggeration to suggest that the success of hundreds of young Indian students and professionals in universities like Oxford, and elsewhere across the world, has contributed to this renewed self-confidence of a new India.

The economics we learnt at Oxford in the 1950s was also marked by optimism about the economic prospects for the post-War and post-colonial world. But in the 1960s and 1970s, much of the focus of development economics shifted to concerns about the limits to growth. There was considerable doubt about the benefits of international trade for developing countries. I must confess that when I returned home to India, I was struck by the deep distrust of the world displayed by many of my countrymen. We were influenced by the legacy of our immediate past. Not just by the perceived negative consequences of British imperial rule, but also by the sense that we were left out in the cold by the Cold War.

There is no doubt that our grievance against the British Empire had a sound basis. As the painstaking statistical work of the Cambridge historian Angus Maddison has shown, India's share of world income collapsed from 22.6 per cent in 1700, almost equal to Europe's share of 23.3 per cent at that time, to as low as 3.8 per cent in 1952. Indeed, at the beginning of the 20th century, "the brightest jewel in the British Crown" was the poorest country in the world in terms of per capita income.

However, what is significant about the Indo-British relationship is the fact that despite the economic impact of colonial rule, the relationship between individual Indians and Britons, even at the time of our Independence, was relaxed and, I may even say, benign.

This was best exemplified by the exchange that Mahatma Gandhi[2] had here at Oxford in 1931 when he met members of the Raleigh Club and the Indian *Majlis*.[3] The Mahatma was in England then for the Round Table Conference[4] and during its recess, he spent two weekends at the home of A.D. Lindsay, the Master of Balliol. At this meeting, the Mahatma was asked: "How far would you cut India off from the Empire?" His reply was precise—"From the Empire, entirely; from the British nation not at all, if I want India to gain and not to grieve." He added, "The British Empire is an Empire only because of India. The Emperorship must go and I should love to be an equal partner with Britain, sharing her joys and sorrows. But it must be a partnership on equal terms."

This remarkable statement by the Mahatma has defined the basis of our relationship with Britain.

Jawaharlal Nehru[5] echoed this sentiment when he urged the Indian Constituent Assembly in 1949 to vote in favour of India's membership [in] the Commonwealth. Nehru set the tone for independent India's relations with its former master when he intervened in the Constituent Assembly's debate on India joining the Commonwealth and said: "I wanted the world to see that India did not lack faith in herself, and that India was prepared to co-operate even with those with whom she had been fighting in the past provided the basis of the co-operation today was honourable, that it was a free basis, a basis which would lead to the good not only of ourselves, but of the world also. That is to say, we would not deny that co-operation simply because in the past

---

[2]  *Mahatma Gandhi*  Mohandas Gandhi (1869–1948) was the revered leader of the movement for independence in India, and of the movement for non-violence worldwide.

[3]  *Raleigh Club*  British dining club for explorers and adventurers, later the Royal Geographical Society; *Majlis* Council; assembly for discussion.

[4]  *Round Table Conference*  The conference resulted in a March 1931 agreement between Gandhi and Lord Irwin, then the Viceroy of British India, according to the terms of which Gandhi would stop his campaign of civil disobedience, the British would not prosecute anyone for non-violent offences committed under the campaign, and the British would allow the Indian National Congress to participate in talks aimed at forming an Indian constitution.

[5]  *Jawaharlal Nehru*  Nehru (1889–1964) was the Prime Minister of India from independence in 1947 until 1964.

we had fought and thus carry on the trail of our past karma along with us. We have to wash out the past with all its evil." India and Britain set an example to the rest of the world in the way they sought to relate to each other, thanks to the wisdom and foresight of Mahatma Gandhi and Jawaharlal Nehru. When I became the Finance Minister of India in 1991, our Government launched the Indo-British Partnership Initiative. Our relationship had by then evolved to a stage where we had come to regard each other as partners. Today, there is no doubt in my mind that Britain and India are indeed partners and have much in common in their approach to a wide range of global issues.

What impelled the Mahatma to take such a positive view of Britain and the British people even as he challenged the Empire and colonial rule? It was, undoubtedly, his recognition of the elements of fair play that characterised so much of the ways of the British in India. Consider the fact that an important slogan of India's struggle for freedom was that "Self Government is more precious than Good Government." That, of course, is the essence of democracy. But the slogan suggests that even at the height of our campaign for freedom from colonial rule, we did not entirely reject the British claim to good governance. We merely asserted our natural right to self-governance.

Today, with the balance and perspective offered by the passage of time and the benefit of hindsight, it is possible for an Indian Prime Minister to assert that India's experience with Britain had its beneficial consequences too. Our notions of the rule of law, of a Constitutional government, of a free press, of a professional civil service, of modern universities and research laboratories have all been fashioned in the crucible where an age old civilisation met the dominant Empire of the day.

These are all elements which we still value and cherish. Our judiciary, our legal system, our bureaucracy and our police are all great institutions, derived from British-Indian administration, and they have served the country well. The idea of India as enshrined in our Constitution, with its emphasis on the principles of secularism, democracy, the rule of law and, above all, the equality of all human beings irrespective of caste, community, language or ethnicity, has deep roots in India's ancient civilisation. However, it is undeniable

that the founding fathers of our republic were also greatly influenced by the ideas associated with the age of enlightenment in Europe. Our Constitution remains a testimony to the enduring interplay between what is essentially Indian and what is very British in our intellectual heritage.

The idea of India as an inclusive and plural society draws on both these traditions. The success of our experiment of building a democracy within the framework of a multi-cultural, multi-ethnic, multi-lingual, and multi-religious society will encourage all societies to walk the path we have trodden. In this journey, both Britain and India have learnt from each other and have much to teach the world. This is perhaps the most enduring aspect of the Indo-British encounter. It used to be said that the sun never sets on the British Empire. I am afraid we were partly responsible for sending that adage out of fashion! But, if there is one phenomenon on which the sun cannot set, it is the world of the English-speaking people, in which the people of Indian origin are the single largest component.

Of all the legacies of the Raj,[1] none is more important than the English language and the modern school system. That is, if you leave out cricket! Of course, people here may not recognise the language we speak, but let me assure you that it is English! In indigenising English, as so many people have done in so many nations across the world, we have made the language our own. Our choice of prepositions may not always be the Queen's English; we might occasionally split the infinitive; and we may drop an article here and add an extra one there. I am sure everyone will agree, however, that English has been enriched by Indian creativity as well, and we have given you R.K. Narayan and Salman Rushdie.[2] Today, English in India is seen as just another Indian language.

No Indian has paid a more poetic and generous tribute to Britain for this inheritance than Gurudev Rabindranath Tagore.[3] In the opening lines of his *Gitanjali*, Gurudev says:

[1] *Raj*  British Raj, British rule in the Indian sub-continent.

[2] *R.K. Narayan and Salman Rushdie*  Narayan (1906–2001) and Rushdie (b. 1947) are both acclaimed writers of fiction.

[3] *Gurudev Rabindranath Tagore*  Tagore (1861–1941) was a Nobel Prize-winning poet.

The West has today opened its door.
There are treasures for us to take.
We will take and we will also give,
From the open shores of India's immense humanity.

To see the India-British relationship as one of "give and take," at the time when he first did so, was an act of courage and statesmanship. It was, however, also an act of great foresight. As we look back and also look ahead, it is clear that the Indo-British relationship is one of "give and take." The challenge before us today is to see how we can take this mutually beneficial relationship forward in an increasingly inter-dependent world....

I wish to end by returning to my alma mater. Oxford, since the 19th century, has been a centre for Sanskrit learning and the study of Indian culture. The Boden professorship in Sanskrit, and the Spalding professorship in Eastern Religions and Ethics, stand testimony to the university's commitment to India and Indian culture....

In the context of the study and preservation of Indian culture, I also wish to recall the contribution of another Oxonian, Lord Curzon,[1] about whose project to preserve and restore Indian monuments Jawaharlal Nehru said, "After every other Viceroy has been forgotten, Curzon will be remembered because he restored all that was beautiful in India."...

I always come back to the city of dreaming spires and of lost causes as a student. Mr. Chancellor, I am here this time in all humility as the representative of a great nation and a great people. I am beholden to you, Mr. Chancellor, and to my old university for the honour that I receive today. Thank you.

from Winston Churchill, Campaign Speech, 4 June 1945

This attack on the Labour Party was the first of four broadcasts Churchill made as Conservative Party leader during his election campaign of June 1945. The speech in general, and particularly his likening of the socialism of the Labour Party in Britain to the practices of the notoriously brutal Secret Police in Nazi Germany—the Gestapo—was widely seen as being in extremely poor taste, even by many Conservatives who approved of the substance of Churchill's view of socialism. The speech did serious damage to Churchill's reputation, and contributed to the Conservative loss to Labour in the election.

... My friends, I must tell you that a Socialist policy is abhorrent to the British ideas of freedom. Although it is now put forward in the main by people who have a good grounding in the Liberalism and Radicalism of the early part of this century, there can be no doubt that Socialism is inseparably interwoven with Totalitarianism and the abject worship of the State. It is not alone that property, in all its forms, is struck at, but liberty, in all its forms, is challenged by the fundamental conceptions of Socialism.

Look how even today they hunger for controls of every kind, as if these were delectable foods instead of wartime inflictions and monstrosities. There is to be one State to which all are to be obedient in every act of their lives. This State is to be the arch-employer, the arch-planner, the arch-administrator and ruler, and the arch-caucus-boss.

How is an ordinary citizen or subject of the King to stand up against this formidable machine, which, once it is in power, will prescribe for every one of them where they are to work; what they are to work at; where they may go and what they may say; what views they are to hold and within what limits they may express them; where their wives are to go to queue-up[2] for the State ration; and what education their children are to receive to mould their views of human liberty and conduct in the future?

A Socialist State once thoroughly completed in all its details and its aspects—and that is what I am speaking of—could not afford to suffer opposition. Here in old England, in Great Britain, of which old England forms no inconspicuous part, in this glorious Island, the cradle and citadel of free democracy throughout the world, we do not like to be regimented and ordered about and have every action of our lives prescribed for us. In fact

---

[1] *Lord Curzon*  George Nathaniel Curzon (1859–1925), Viceroy of India from 1899 to 1905, during which time he oversaw a restoration of the Taj Mahal.

[2] *queue-up*  Lineup.

we punish criminals by sending them to Wormwood Scrubs and Dartmoor,[1] where they get full employment, and whatever board and lodging is appointed by the Home Secretary.

Socialism is, in its essence, an attack not only upon British enterprise, but upon the right of the ordinary man or woman to breathe freely without having a harsh, clumsy, tyrannical hand clapped across their mouths and nostrils. ... I declare to you, from the bottom of my heart, that no Socialist system can be established without a political police. Many of those who are advocating Socialism or voting Socialist today will be horrified at this idea. That is because they are short-sighted, that is because they do not see where their theories are leading them.

No Socialist government conducting the entire life and industry of the country could afford to allow free, sharp, or violently worded expressions of public discontent. They would have to fall back on some form of *Gestapo*, no doubt very humanely directed in the first instance. And this would nip opinion in the bud; it would stop criticism as it reared its head, and it would gather all the power to the supreme party and the party leaders, rising like stately pinnacles above their vast bureaucracies of civil servants, no longer servants and no longer civil. And where would the ordinary simple folk—the common people, as they like to call them in America—where would they be, once this mighty organism had got them in its grip?

I stand for the sovereign freedom of the individual within the laws which freely elected Parliaments have freely passed. I stand for the rights of the ordinary man to say what he thinks of the government of the day, however powerful, and to turn them out, neck and crop, if he thinks he can better his temper or his home thereby, and if he can persuade enough others to vote with him.

But, you will say, look at what has been done in the war. Have not many of those evils which you have depicted been the constant companions of our daily life? It is quite true that the horrors of war do not end with the fighting-line. They spread far away to the base and the homeland, and everywhere people give up their rights and liberties for the common cause. But this is because the life of their country is in mortal peril, or for the sake of the cause of freedom in some other land. They give them freely as a sacrifice. It is quite true that the conditions of Socialism play a great part in wartime. We all submit to being ordered about to save our country. But when the war is over and the imminent danger to our existence is removed, we cast off these shackles and burdens which we imposed upon ourselves in times of dire and mortal peril, and quit the gloomy caverns of war and march out into the breezy fields, where the sun is shining and where all may walk joyfully in its warm and golden rays....

## from Clement Attlee, Speech on the King's Address, 16 August 1945

> Attlee was leader of the Labour Party for twenty years, and Prime Minister from 1945 to 1951—a time of sweeping change in which his government introduced the National Health Service, nationalized the Bank of England and a number of key industries (including the coal industry), and supported movement towards independence in Britain's colonial possessions. The speech excerpted below was Attlee's first major address to Parliament as Prime Minister.

... Yesterday we gave thanks for the final victory over all our enemies,[2] and the world is once more at peace. For the first time for almost six years, the Prime Minister can speak in this House without referring to war operations. Later we shall be taking an opportunity of thanking the Fighting Forces, but I think that before I deal with the general policy contained in the Gracious Speech from the Throne and with the speech of my Right Hon. Friend opposite,[3] which I thought showed him to be in most excellent form, there is a duty which I ought to take the earliest opportunity of performing. It may be that I shall be setting a precedent in doing so, but I have been looking through the speeches of Prime Ministers on these occasions, and I find there are many varieties. The surrender of Japan has brought to an end the greatest war in history, and a General Election,

---

[1]  *Wormwood Scrubs and Dartmoor*  British prisons.

[2]  *Yesterday ... enemies*  On 15 August 1945, Japan surrendered, effectively ending World War II.

[3]  *Right Hon. Friend opposite*  Attlee here refers to Churchill.

which took place at a time which was not of our seeking, has resulted in the Right Hon. Gentleman the Member for Woodford [Mr. Churchill] being on the Opposition benches at a time when the fruits of his long leadership of the nation in war are being garnered.

I think it is fitting that today I should pay a tribute to one of the main architects of our victory. However we may be divided politically in this House I believe I shall be expressing the views of the whole House in making acknowledgment here of the transcendent services rendered by the Right Hon. Gentleman to this country, to the Commonwealth and Empire, and to the world during his tenure of office as Prime Minister. During those years he was the leader of the country in war. We have seen in Fascist countries a detestable cult of leadership which has only been a cover for dictatorship, but there is a true leadership which means the expression by one man of the soul of a nation, and the translation of the common will into action. In the darkest and most dangerous hour of our history this nation found in my Right Hon. Friend the man who expressed supremely the courage and determination never to yield which animated all the men and women of this country. In undying phrases he crystallised the unspoken feeling of all. "Words only," it might be said, but words at great moments of history are deeds. We had more than words from the Right Hon. Gentleman. He radiated a stream of energy throughout the machinery of Government, indeed throughout the life of the nation. Many others shared in the work of organising and inspiring the nation in its great effort, but he set the pace. He was able to bring into cooperation men of very different political views and to win from them loyal service. At critical times, by his personal relationship with the heads of Allied States, he promoted the harmony and cooperation of all, and in the sphere of strategy his wide experience, grasp of essentials, his willingness to take necessary risks, were of the utmost value.

I had the honour to serve with the Right Hon. Gentleman in the War Cabinet throughout the whole of the Coalition Government from the days of Dunkirk[1]

to the surrender of Germany. There are many things on which we disagree, but I think it right to take this early occasion, before we turn to controversy, to express the gratitude and admiration for his leadership in war which we feel. His place in history is secure, and although he was no longer at the head of affairs when the Japanese surrendered and final victory came, this really was the outcome of plans made long before under his leadership.

History will link with the name of Winston Churchill that of another great leader of democracy, the late President Roosevelt.[2] The one is present with us here today; the other did not live to see victory, but his service to the cause of freedom this country can never forget. I should also wish at this hour to acknowledge the great contribution made by all the peoples of the British Commonwealth and Empire to this great victory, by all our Allies, the people of the United States of America, of Russia, of China, and by all others who fought against the common enemy. And perhaps above all I should like to emphasise that victory has come through the contributions of thousands and millions of ordinary men and women. In all the various spheres of activity it has been the steadfastness, courage, and sense of duty of the ordinary citizen that saved civilisation....

I want to say a few words, first of all, on the international situation.... We have to realise that in all the countries of Europe which have been overrun by Nazi Germany, and in the satellite countries, there are very difficult political problems to be settled. There are many governments today in Europe that rest on no sure foundation of popular election. It is really optimistic to expect the political life in those countries to settle down easily, quickly and smoothly. In many of them political life has never been easy and smooth even in the best of times of peace. It is our intention everywhere to help to secure that the will of the people shall prevail. We look forward with hope to the emergence of democratic governments based on free elections to take a part in building up the shattered framework of the European

---

[1] *days of Dunkirk* Allied armies in 1940 had retreated to a beachhead near the French village of Dunkirk. Though some 34,000 Allied soldiers died in the conflict around Dunkirk, it was considered

that the Allies secured the opportunity for later victory as they succeeded (with the help of a flotilla of fishing boats and other small craft) in evacuating most of their forces across the Channel to the relative safety of Britain.

[2] *President Roosevelt* Franklin D. Roosevelt (1882–1945), American President from 1933 to 1945.

polity. In this task we shall seek to render all the assistance in our power, in cooperation with our Allies, especially with our great Allies, the United States of America and Russia.

Clement Attlee, leader of the Labour Party, campaigning in London in 1945.

But it is necessary to realise that it is not only the political and social life of Europe that has been shattered. The economic situation is very grave. I fear there are many people in Europe who are going to be both cold and hungry this winter despite all that can be done. The reasons are obvious. While the damage done to the industries of the liberated countries has not been as great, I think, as we first feared, the damage to means of communication has been tremendous. Ports, railways, roads and bridges have been destroyed. There is a great shortage of railway rolling stock, a great shortage of lorries,[1] and we have to remember that in countries of advanced industrialisation accustomed to the free movement of supplies from one district to another,

there are bound to be local shortages and the general situation will be very difficult.... [S]hortages of coal, transport, food and raw materials tend to aggravate each other. We will do our best to help to remedy them, but as the Right Hon. Gentleman opposite said so well, we have been and still are cut to the bone at home. It is no use thinking this country has some great surplus it can pour into other countries. It cannot. We have cut ourselves very close indeed. While the end of the war with Japan will bring some assistance, it would be unwise to expect it will materially affect the position for some months....

I now turn to affairs at home, and, here again, I would like to say something on the general economic position that faces us. I do not think anybody is ignorant of the gravity of the problem. During these last six years, we have deliberately transformed our whole economic system for the single purpose of defeating the enemy in battle. The battle has been won, but the result of the means we had to adopt remains. On the one hand, the machinery of our economic life has been diverted from peace to war, and it is true that, since the end of the war with Germany, we have been making some start in the process of reconversion. The Right Hon. Gentleman said we were in a difficult position with the continuance of the Japanese war, for how long we did not know—a kind of twilight of reconstruction. Well, it is true that we can now move ahead without that war hanging over us, but it does not alter the fact that the transition is very difficult. We were organised as a war machine to fight the Japanese. That has come to an end, thank Heaven, much earlier than any had expected, but it will take time before the effects can be felt....

We have the inevitable consequences of a six years' war to grapple with, but it would be a great mistake for a Government to concern themselves only with short-term problems, pressing as these are. Before the war there was, in our view, much that was wrong in the economic and social conditions in this country. A new start is being made under new conditions. We must look ahead to the future and not be forever casting lingering glances back to a past which cannot be recaptured. We have to set about reconditioning the fabric of the economic life of the nation, in order that our economic resources can be fully utilised in the common interest.

---

[1] *lorries* Trucks.

We cannot afford to have ill-managed, ill-equipped, unprogressive industries.

It is our policy that the industries and services of this country shall make their maximum contribution to the public good. At the General Election we set very plainly before the electors our policy of bringing under public ownership some of the main factors in the economic life of this country. As has been pointed out in the Gracious Speech, we intend to bring the Bank of England under public ownership and to deal with the problem of the great basic industry of coal. During the whole of the interval between the two world wars, and many years before that, we have heard of the trouble in the coal industry, year by year, and it has had widespread repercussions on our national prosperity and on other industries. Commission after Commission, committee after committee has reported adversely on the structure and organisation. We intend, therefore, to bring this industry under public ownership as part of a wider scheme of converting the provision of fuel, light and power to the public service.

My Right Hon. Friend opposite[1] referred to the Trade Disputes Act of 1927,[2] which was imposed for the first time in the history of trade union legislation without any discussion with the trade unions. That has long rankled as an act of injustice in the minds of trade unionists. I rather thought my Right Hon. Friend was going to cite that in another part of his speech where he was talking about freedom. This has laid as an imposition on the right of free association, and has deprived great bodies of citizens of their rights of free association which they had enjoyed for many years without any abuse, so I shall enlist his support, as a libertarian, when we introduce the Bill in favour of this repeal. It may well be that we shall have to consider, after the lapse of years, other matters in connection with the relations of these great bodies to the State, but the first thing is to clear away this thing which has to a large extent poisoned the industrial life of this country....

Finally, we intend to introduce legislation which will complete and, I believe, improve the results of the postwar planning carried out in the Coalition Government, providing for a comprehensive scheme of industrial insurance, to extend and improve the existing insurance as part of the system of social security, and to expedite the setting up of a National Health Service.

I freely admit that the programme of work we have laid before this Parliament is heavy, but we are living in a time when great changes are due. The country will expect much from this House. I do not think it will be disappointed....

## from Margaret Thatcher, Speech to the Conservative Party Conference, Brighton, 10 October 1980

Opposition from the left to the capitalist policies enacted by Margaret Thatcher in her first year as Prime Minister was strong, and even in the Conservative Party some were starting to feel that she was trying to go too far too fast. Her defiant address at the party's annual conference is usually referred to as "The Lady's Not for Turning" speech. The phrase was a play on the title of a popular 1950s play by Christopher Fry, *The Lady's Not for Burning*.

Mr. Chairman, ladies and gentlemen, most of my Cabinet colleagues have started their speeches of reply by paying very well deserved tributes to their junior Ministers. At Number 10[3] I have no junior Ministers. There is just Denis[4] and me, and I could not do without him.

I am, however, very fortunate in having a marvellous deputy who is wonderful in all places at all times in all things—Willie Whitelaw.

At our party conference last year I said that the task in which the Government were engaged—to change the national attitude of mind—was the most challenging to face any British Administration since the war. Challenge is exhilarating. This week we Conservatives have been taking stock, discussing the achievements, the set-backs and the work that lies ahead as we enter our second parliamentary year....

It is sometimes said that because of our past we, as a people, expect too much and set our sights too high.

---

[1] *My ... opposite*  I.e., Winston Churchill.

[2] *Trade Disputes Act of 1927*  Law that banned civil servants from joining unions affiliated with the Trades Union Congress.

[3] *Number 10*  10 Downing Street, the official London residence of the British Prime Minister.

[4] *Denis*  I.e., Denis Thatcher, Margaret Thatcher's spouse.

That is not the way I see it. Rather it seems to me that throughout my life in politics our ambitions have steadily shrunk. Our response to disappointment has not been to lengthen our stride but to shorten the distance to be covered. But with confidence in ourselves and in our future what a nation we could be!

In its first seventeen months this Government have laid the foundations for recovery. We have undertaken a heavy load of legislation, a load we do not intend to repeat because we do not share the Socialist fantasy that achievement is measured by the number of laws you pass. But there was a formidable barricade of obstacles that we had to sweep aside. For a start, in his first Budget Geoffrey Howe[1] began ... incentives to stimulate the abilities and inventive genius of our people. Prosperity comes not from grand conferences of economists but by countless acts of personal self-confidence and self-reliance.

Under Geoffrey's stewardship, Britain has repaid $3,600 million of international debt, debt which had been run up by our predecessors. And we paid quite a lot of it before it was due. In the past twelve months Geoffrey has abolished exchange controls over which British Governments have dithered for decades. Our great enterprises are now free to seek opportunities overseas. This will help to secure our living standards long after North Sea oil has run out. This Government thinks about the future. We have made the first crucial changes in trade union law to remove the worst abuses of the closed shop, to restrict picketing to the place of work of the parties in dispute, and to encourage secret ballots.

Jim Prior has carried all these measures through with the support of the vast majority of trade union members....

Free competition in road passenger transport promises travellers a better deal. Michael Heseltine[2] has given to millions—yes, millions—of council tenants the right to buy their own homes. It was Anthony Eden[3] who

chose for us the goal of "a property-owning democracy." But for all the time that I have been in public affairs that has been beyond the reach of so many, who were denied the right to the most basic ownership of all—the homes in which they live. They wanted to buy. Many could afford to buy. But they happened to live under the jurisdiction of a Socialist council, which would not sell and did not believe in the independence that comes with ownership. Now Michael Heseltine has given them the chance to turn a dream into reality. And all this and a lot more in seventeen months.

The Left continues to refer with relish to the death of capitalism. Well, if this is the death of capitalism, I must say that it is quite a way to go.

But all this will avail us little unless we achieve our prime economic objective—the defeat of inflation. Inflation destroys nations and societies as surely as invading armies do. Inflation is the parent of unemployment. It is the unseen robber of those who have saved.

No policy which puts at risk the defeat of inflation—however great its short-term attraction—can be right. Our policy for the defeat of inflation is, in fact, traditional. It existed long before ... "monetarism"[4] became a convenient term of political invective. But some people talk as if control of the money supply was a revolutionary policy. Yet it was an essential condition for the recovery of much of continental Europe. Those countries knew what was required for economic stability. Previously, they had lived through rampant inflation; they knew that it led to suitcase money, massive unemployment and the breakdown of society itself. They determined never to go that way again.

Today, after many years of monetary self-discipline, they have stable, prosperous economies better able than ours to withstand the buffeting of world recession.

So at international conferences to discuss economic affairs many of my fellow Heads of Government find our policies not strange, unusual or revolutionary, but normal, sound and honest. And that is what they are. Their only question is: "Has Britain the courage and resolve to sustain the discipline for long enough to break through to success?"

Yes, Mr. Chairman, we have, and we shall. This

---

[1] *Geoffrey Howe* (b.1926) Chancellor of the Exchequer (the equivalent of the Treasury Secretary or the Minister of Finance in nations such as Canada and Australia) in Thatcher's government.

[2] *Michael Heseltine* (b. 1933) Secretary of State for the Environment from 1979 to 1983.

[3] *Anthony Eden* (1897–1977) Prime Minister of Britain from 1955 to 1957.

[4] *monetarism* School of economic thought emphasizing the importance to an economy of variations in money supply.

Government are determined to stay with the policy and see it through to its conclusion. That is what marks this administration as one of the truly radical ministries of post-war Britain....

Of course, our vision and our aims go far beyond the complex arguments of economics, but unless we get the economy right we shall deny our people the opportunity to share that vision and to see beyond the narrow horizons of economic necessity. Without a healthy economy we cannot have a healthy society. Without a healthy society the economy will not stay healthy for long.

But it is not the State that creates a healthy society. When the State grows too powerful people feel that they count for less and less. The State drains society, not only of its wealth but of initiative, of energy, the will to improve and innovate as well as to preserve what is best. Our aim is to let people feel that they count for more and more. If we cannot trust the deepest instincts of our people we should not be in politics at all. Some aspects of our present society really do offend those instincts.

Decent people do want to do a proper job at work, not to be restrained or intimidated from giving value for money. They believe that honesty should be respected, not derided. They see crime and violence as a threat not just to society but to their own orderly way of life. They want to be allowed to bring up their children in these beliefs, without the fear that their efforts will be daily frustrated in the name of progress or free expression. Indeed, that is what family life is all about.

There is not a generation gap in a happy and united family. People yearn to be able to rely on some generally accepted standards. Without them you have not got a society at all, you have purposeless anarchy. A healthy society is not created by its institutions, either. Great schools and universities do not make a great nation any more than great armies do. Only a great nation can create and involve great institutions—of learning, of healing, of scientific advance. And a great nation is the voluntary creation of its people—a people composed of men and women whose pride in themselves is founded on the knowledge of what they can give to a community of which they in turn can be proud.

If our people feel that they are part of a great nation and they are prepared to will the means to keep it great, a great nation we shall be, and shall remain. So, what

can stop us from achieving this? What then stands in our way? The prospect of another winter of discontent?[1] I suppose it might.

But I prefer to believe that certain lessons have been learnt from experience, that we are coming, slowly, painfully, to an autumn of understanding. And I hope that it will be followed by a winter of common sense. If it is not, we shall not be diverted from our course. To those waiting with bated breath for that favourite media catchphrase, the "U" turn,[2] I have only one thing to say. "You turn if you want to. The lady's not for turning." I say that not only to you but to our friends overseas and also to those who are not our friends.

In foreign affairs we have pursued our national interest robustly while remaining alive to the needs and interests of others. We have acted where our predecessors dithered and here I pay tribute to Lord Carrington.[3] When I think of our much-travelled Foreign Secretary I am reminded of the advert, you know the one I mean, about "The peer that reaches those foreign parts that other peers cannot reach."[4]

Long before we came into office, and therefore long before the invasion of Afghanistan,[5] I was pointing to the threat from the East. I was accused of scaremongering. But events have more than justified my words.

Soviet Marxism is ideologically, politically and morally bankrupt. But militarily the Soviet Union is a powerful and growing threat. Yet it was Mr. Kosygin[6]

---

[1] *winter of discontent*   See William Shakespeare, *Richard III*, 1.1.1–2. "Now is the winter of our discontent / Made glorious summer by this sun of York." Refers in this case to the winter of 1979, which was plagued by massive labor unrest. See the Introduction to this section.

[2] *the "U" turn*   Edward Heath's Conservative government (1970–1974) were accused of abandoning their free market policies when they were elected. This became known in the popular press as the Heath Government's "U-turn."

[3] *Lord Carrington*   Peter Alexander Rupert Carington (b.1919), Foreign Secretary in Thatcher's government, earned worldwide praise in 1979 for the central part he played in negotiating majority rule and an end to civil war in Rhodesia, the former colony of Britain that became Zimbabwe on 18 April 1980.

[4] *The peer ... reach*   A play on a famous advertisement for Heineken as the beer that "refreshes the parts other beers cannot reach."

[5] *invasion of Afghanistan*   Soviet troops entered Afghanistan in December 1979, beginning a nine-year period of occupation.

[6] *Mr. Kosygin*   Alexei Kosygin (1904–1980), Prime Minister of the Soviet Union from 1964 to 1980.

who said "No peace-loving country, no person of integrity, should remain indifferent when an aggressor holds human life and world opinion in insolent contempt." We agree. The British Government are not indifferent to the occupation of Afghanistan. We shall not allow it to be forgotten. Unless and until the Soviet troops are withdrawn other nations are bound to wonder which of them may be next. Of course there are those who say that by speaking out we are complicating East-West relations, that we are endangering détente.[1] But the real danger would lie in keeping silent. Detente is indivisible and it is a two-way process.

The Soviet Union cannot conduct wars by proxy in South-East Asia and Africa, foment[2] trouble in the Middle East and Caribbean and invade neighbouring countries and still expect to conduct business as usual. Unless detente is pursued by both sides it can be pursued by neither, and it is a delusion to suppose otherwise....

This afternoon I have tried to set before you some of my most deeply held convictions and beliefs. This Party, which I am privileged to serve, and this Government, which I am proud to lead, are engaged in the massive task of restoring confidence and stability to our people.

I have always known that that task was vital. Since last week it has become even more vital than ever. We close our Conference in the aftermath of that sinister Utopia unveiled at Blackpool.[3] Let Labour's Orwellian nightmare[4] of the Left be the spur for us to dedicate with a new urgency our every ounce of energy and moral strength to rebuild the fortunes of this free nation.

If we were to fail, that freedom could be imperilled. So let us resist the blandishments of the faint hearts; let us ignore the howls and threats of the extremists; let us stand together and do our duty, and we shall not fail.

---

[1] *détente* Process entailing various measures aimed at easing strained relations between the Soviet Union and its allies and the West.

[2] *foment* Incite.

[3] *sinister ... Blackpool* The 1980 Labour Party conference in Blackpool featured a shift in the party towards more radical policies such as nuclear disarmament, withdrawal from the European community, and mandatory re-selection of Parliamentary candidates.

[4] *Orwellian nightmare* Thatcher here alludes to *1984*, George Orwell's 1949 dystopian novel about life under a totalitarian regime.

Newly-elected Prime Minister Margaret Thatcher as she was moving into 10 Downing St. in 1979.

from Tony Blair, Speech to the Labour Party Conference, Blackpool, 4 October 1994

The speech excerpted below was Tony Blair's first Labour Party conference speech as party leader. He had been chosen to lead the party following the death of John Smith from a heart attack in May 1994. Smith, who had led the party for only two years, was 55. Blair enacted extensive reforms within the Labour Party, and became Prime Minister when he defeated the Conservatives (led by John Major) in the 1997 general election.

Today I set out my vision for our party and our country: what we are; where we stand; how we will govern. We meet in a spirit of hope, hope that change can come, hope that we can rid our country of this Tory Government—their broken promises, their failed policies, their discredited philosophy—and elect in its place a Labour Government for Britain.

We all remember where we were, and what we were doing, when we heard that John Smith had died. Together, one nation, all parties united in mourning, and in celebration of his integrity, his honesty and his decency. We were proud to know him and proud to be led by him. We will honour his memory best by ensuring the Party he loved becomes, once again, the Government of the country he loved.

We have begun our task. The people have already elected us to control 175 councils. In May we won over two and a half thousand new seats. We have won four by-elections this year, and three of our four new MPs are women. In the European elections we gained record numbers of seats. These were not opinion polls. They were elections. We are winning them.

We had our own election too. One million people took part in a leadership contest that was a tribute to our democracy, and from which we emerged with our unity and strength enhanced....

We are a Party proud of our international solidarity. I am delighted to welcome representatives here this afternoon from the government of the new Republic of South Africa.... We also congratulate our sister parties in Sweden, Australia, Denmark, and Holland on their recent election successes. And we wish every success to socialists and social democratic parties in Austria and Germany in their forthcoming elections. Fifty years ago, the British Labour government helped to form the United Nations. We will continue to work for it to be stronger, more cohesive and capable of bringing new order to a world no longer dominated by the Cold War. ... We live in a world where a quarter of its population lack drinking water and a fifth starve; where civil war in Rwanda[1] and elsewhere is rife. We should not forget those people. I can tell you overseas aid and develop-

ment will always be a central part of the Labour Party I lead....

The tide of ideas in British politics is at last on the turn. For the first time in a generation, it is the right-wing that appears lost and disillusioned. No longer believing in their own language, they turn to ours. Some are trying out "community." "Partnership." Even "fairness."...

To parents wanting their children to be taught in classrooms that are not crumbling, to students with qualifications but no university place, let us say, the Tories have failed you, we are on your side, your ambitions are our ambitions. To men and women who get up in the morning, and find the kitchen door smashed in, again ... the video gone, again ... to the pensioners who fear to go out of their homes, let us say the Tories have abused your trust, we are on your side—your concerns are our concerns. To the small businesses, pushed to the wall by greedy banks, employers burdened by government failure, ... to employees laid off [and] the thousands of others insecure in their jobs in every part of this county—let us say the Tories have forgotten you, but we will not. Your anxieties are our anxieties. To middle and lower income Britain, suffering the biggest tax rises in peacetime history, the Tories have betrayed you. We are back as the Party of the majority in British politics. Back to speak up for Britain. Back as the people's party.

Look at Britain fifteen years after Mrs Thatcher [first] stood on the steps of Downing Street.[2] Where there was discord, is there harmony? Where there was error, is there truth? Where there was doubt, is there faith? Where there was despair, is there hope? Harmony? When crime has more than doubled? Truth? When they won an election on lies about us and lies about what they would do? Faith? When politics is debased by their betrayal? Hope? When three million people are jobless, nearly six million on income support.... and one in three children grow up in poverty?...

It's time to take these Tories apart for what they have done to our country. Not because they lack compassion, though they do. But because they are the most feckless, irresponsible group of incompetents ever let

---

[1] *civil war in Rwanda*   The conflict that raged in the African country in 1994 has since come to be characterized in the first instance as attempted genocide rather than civil war; the Hutu majority, incited by officially sanctioned radio broadcasts, slaughtered some 800,000 civilians (almost all of them members of the Tutsi minority) over a two-month period. In response, a rebel army led by Tutsi exiles invaded from across the Ugandan border, and managed quickly to wrest control of the country from the old government. The international community was extremely slow and ineffective in responding to the crisis.

[2] *Downing Street*   10 Downing Street, the official London residence of the British Prime Minister.

loose in the Government of Britain. Their time is up. Their philosophy is done. Their experiment is over. Their failure is clear. It is time to go. And why are they incompetent? Not just because of the individuals. It is not this or that Minister that is to blame, it is an entire set of political values that is wrong. They fail because they fail to understand that a nation, like a community, must work together in order for the individuals within it to succeed. It is such a simple failing and yet it is fundamental.

Go and look at a company that is succeeding. It won't treat its workforce as servants but as partners. They will be motivated and trained and given a common purpose. Of course sweatshop conditions in the short-term can make do. But in the end they fail. The quality and commitment isn't there. It's the same with a country. It can be run on privilege and greed for a time; but in the end it fails. This is not theory. We have living proof of it. At the end of 15 years, we are taxing and spending more not to invest in future success but to pay for past failure. I don't mind paying taxes for education and health and the police. What I mind is paying them for unemployment, crime, and social squalor....

Tory economics is based on a view of the market that is crude, out of date, and inefficient. And their view of society is one of indifference, to shrug their shoulders and walk away. They think we choose between self-interest and the interests of society or the country as a whole. In reality, self-interest demands that we work together to achieve what we cannot do on our own. More and more I believe that though, of course, ability plays a great part in life, what most distinguishes those at the top from those at the bottom is their life-chances. So much talent is wasted. So much potential underdeveloped. I don't just mean the unemployed. I mean those who just have jobs, when they should have careers with prospects and a hope of advancement. We can learn from the family. The Tories have posed as the Party of the family for too long. They are no more the Party of the family than they are the Party of law and order. They have done more to undermine stable family life in this country than any other Government in memory. The Tory view of the family is the same as its view of the individual: you are on your own. But the essence of family life is that you are not on your own. You are in it together. Families work best when the members of it help and sustain each other. The same is true of communities and of nations. Community is not some piece of nostalgia. It means what we share. It means working together. It is about how we treat each other. So we teach our children to take pride in their school, their town, their country. We teach them self-respect; and we teach them respect for others too. We teach them self-support and self-improvement; and we teach them mutual support and mutual improvement too.

The Tories despise such principles. Their view is simple: let's just watch as the hospitals spring up, as the schools rise in green and pleasant playing fields. Let's just sit tight on this planet of miracles, where the free market builds business, trains employees, controls inflation, preserves demand, ensures everlasting growth....

Market forces cannot educate us or equip us for this world of rapid technological and economic change. We must do it together. We cannot buy our way to a safe society. We must work for it together. We cannot purchase an option on whether we grow old. We must plan for it together. We can't protect the ordinary against the abuse of power by leaving them to it; we must protect each other. That is our insight. A belief in society. Working together. Solidarity. Cooperation. Partnership. These are our words. This is my socialism. And we should stop apologising for using the word. It is not the socialism of Marx or state control. It is rooted in a straightforward view of society. In the understanding that the individual does best in a strong and decent community of people with principles and standards and common aims and values. We are the Party of the individual because we are the Party of community....

Mass unemployment is inconsistent with a civilised society. It is time to state clearly, in the words of the pioneering White Paper of 1944,[1] that it is the duty of government to maintain a high and stable level of employment. It is a responsibility we share as a society. That commitment—the goal of full employment—I reaffirm today.

---

[1] *White Paper of 1944*  Government document on unemployment that stated that maintenance of acceptable levels of employment is the responsibility of government.

It will take time. The means of doing it will change. But it must be done if this is to become a society of which everyone feels a part. Above all, we must conquer the weaknesses of our economy that hold our country back. It won't be done by state control. But it won't be done by market dogma. It can only be done by a dynamic market economy based on partnership between Government and industry, between employer and employee, and between public and private sector. Take investment in infrastructure. Only in Tory Britain could the Government have tried to build the Channel Tunnel without public investment. They even passed a law against it. In desperation they had to ask the taxpayer to fork out more than half the cost. Now it's up and running … trains speed through France at 185 miles per hour, through the tunnel at 85 miles per hour, and then go through Kent—at 47 miles per hour. The French got the high-speed link. We got the slow coach link. But then we've got the Tories.

Government must take the lead, and a Labour Government would do that. We would get public and private finance working together in transport in housing, in capital projects, in health and education. And if there are Treasury rules or antiquated concepts of public borrowing that hold us back, change them. That is what intelligent Government is for.

In technology, there is an information revolution under way. Fifty per cent of employees in Britain now work in information processing. In the next century, seventy per cent of wealth will be created in the information industries. And eighty per cent of all the information stored anywhere in the world is in English. Massive markets. Massive competitive advantage. But massive Tory failure. We should be investing in the new electronic superhighways—satellite and telecommunications technology that is the nerve centre of a new information economy—doing for the next century what roads and railways have done for this one. …

Small and medium-sized businesses will be the driving force of a new economy. The Tories have done nothing for them. Labour has put forward recently the most comprehensive programme for small business development seen in this country. Welcomed by small business. Active Government working in partnership.

Now, I hear people, some of them in our own party,

falling for the Tory attack that we have no policies. What nonsense. We have a huge body of policy which we are now developing. The difference is that we now have policies that win us votes rather than lose them.

Most of all, we need to train and educate our people. Education will be the passion of my Government. I know how important the education of my children is to me. I will not tolerate children going to run-down schools, with bad discipline, low standards, mediocre expectation or poor teachers, and nor should anyone else. If schools are bad, they should be made to be good. If teachers can't teach properly, they shouldn't be teaching at all. And if the Government can't see why education matters—then sack the Government and get one that does. …

With opportunity must come responsibility. For the Tories, the language of responsibility is what those at the top preach to the rest, whilst neglecting it themselves. But the left have undervalued the notion of responsibility and duty and it is time we understood how central it is to ourselves. Parents should have responsibility for their children. Fathers too. Companies to their employees and their community. Ministers to the truth. Citizens to each other. It is at the heart of our message about crime. The Labour Party is now the Party of Law and Order in Britain today. And quite right too. One in 50 crimes ever goes punished. Sentencing is haphazard. Victims are given short shrift. Meanwhile, the Home Secretary protests that he has been attacked, week after week, for being too tough. He's dreaming. He'd love to be attacked for being tough. He's attacked because he is long on rhetoric and short on policies that work. …

We need a new approach. One that is tough on crime, and tough on the causes of crime. Over the past year we have put forward a range of detailed programmes to fight crime. … The unemployed youngster has no right to steal your radio. But let's get just as serious about catching the people in the City[1] with an eye on your pension. This is where the Tories fall down.

Responsibility is a value shared. If it doesn't apply to everyone it ends up applying to no one. It applies to those who defraud the state of benefits. It applies to those who evade their taxes. And it also applies to those water, gas, electricity company bosses, running monop-

---

[1]  *the City*  London's financial district.

oly services at our expense, awarding themselves massive salaries, share options, perks, and pay-offs. They have responsibility too.... A society without responsibility is the enemy of the society built on merit and hard work. It creates an economy in which enterprise is just another word for the quick buck. The Thatcherites used to boast they were anti-establishment. But the trouble with them is that they never wanted to bust the establishment, just buy their way into it. And the new establishment is not a meritocracy,[1] but a power elite of money-shifters, middlemen and speculators—people whose self-interest will always come before the national or the public interest. If they are allowed to go on running the country in their interests, is it any wonder that it is not run in ours?...

It sticks in my gullet when I see Tory MPs, some of whom earn more for a half day's consultancy work than some of my constituents earn in a month, denounce our plans for a minimum wage. And it is also wrong that the taxpayer ends up paying more than a billion pounds on benefits to subsidise poverty pay. A minimum wage exists in every European country, in America too, for the simple reason that it makes social and economic sense. Of course the minimum wage should be set sensibly. And it will be, but there will be no retreat from its basic principle because it is right....

The Tories always complain that the welfare state costs too much. The answer is not just increasing benefits, adequate though those benefits should be. But the people on benefits need and deserve better. Not more benefits, but help in getting off benefits. Welfare should be about opportunity and security in a changing world. It is about helping people to move on and move up. Because the world has changed, the welfare state has to change with it. And we are the only people who can be trusted to change it, because we are the people who believe in it. The Tories will cut benefits and make poverty worse. We will put welfare to work. A nation at work not on benefits. That is our pledge....

If the Government are getting it right, as over Northern Ireland, we give credit. We welcome without reservation new hope beginning there. We pay tribute to our own government, the Irish government, Unionist and Nationalist opinion in the North for their efforts in the peace process....

People look to politicians for leadership. And leadership is about having the courage to say no as well as yes. Even this week I have heard people saying a Labour government must repeal all the Tory trade union laws. Now there is not a single person in this country who believes that to be realistic, or that we will do it. No one believes strike ballots should be abandoned. So why do we say it? We shouldn't, and I won't....

We have to change the rules of government and we will. We are putting forward the biggest programme of change to democracy ever proposed by a political party. Every citizen to be protected by fundamental rights that cannot be taken away by the state or their fellow citizens, enshrined in a Bill of Rights. Government will be brought closer to the people. We will legislate for a Scottish Parliament, an Assembly for Wales, in the first year of a Labour government. And the Tory quangos[2] will be brought back under proper democratic control. We will enact a Freedom of Information Act to attack secrecy wherever it exists, public or private sector. We will reform the House of Commons to make its working practices and its powers to investigate more effective, and to achieve through our Party the increase in the number of women MPs that we have talked about for so long. We will make history by ending the ancient and indefensible privilege of hereditary peers voting on the law of the land. We will tighten the rules of financing of political parties....

We have changed. We were right to change. Parties that do not change die, and this Party is a living movement not an historical monument. If the world changes, and we don't, then we become of no use to the world. Our principles cease being principles and just ossify[3] into dogma. We haven't changed to forget our principles, but to fulfil them. Not to lose our identity but to keep our relevance. Change is an important part of

---

[1] *meritocracy* System in which power or authority is allocated on the basis of merit (as opposed to wealth, social, class, or other criteria).

[2] *quangos* From "Quasi Autonomous Non-Governmental Organizations," administrative bodies that are outside the civil service but receive funding from, and have members appointed by, the government.

[3] *ossify* Harden.

gaining the nation's trust. We were right to introduce one member one vote last year and that change is done....

The British people are a great people. We have proud democratic traditions. We are a nation of tolerance, innovation, and creativity. We have an innate sense of fair play. We have a great history and culture. And when great challenges face us, as they have twice this century, we rise to them. But if we have a fault, it is that unless roused, we tend to let things be. We say "things could be worse" rather than "things should be better." And the Tories encourage this fault. They thrive on complacency. I say it is time we were roused. Let us be blunt. Our system of government has become outdated. Our economy has been weakened. Our people have been under-educated. Our welfare state and public services have been run down—and our society has been made more divided than at any time for 100 years.

But our politics need not be like this. Our country need not be like this. Ours is a project of national renewal, renewing our commitment as a nation, as a community of people in order to prepare and provide for ourselves in the new world we face. We must build a nation with pride in itself. A thriving community, rich in economic prosperity, secure in social justice, confident in political change. A land in which our children can bring up their children with a future to look forward to. That is our hope. Not just to promise change—but to achieve it. Our Party. New Labour. Our mission. New Britain. New Labour. New Britain.

# CHINUA ACHEBE
## b. 1930

Chinua Achebe gained international attention with the publication of his first novel, *Things Fall Apart* (1958); it has since attained the status of a modern classic, and has sold over ten million copies. *Things Fall Apart*, together with Achebe's subsequent novels, follows the course of Nigerian history from just before colonial rule until immediately after independence. Written from the perspective of the colonized Nigerians, these works record the trauma that resulted from Africa's experience with European rule and—without idealizing Nigerians—demonstrate the value, dignity, and beauty of a culture that was all but lost during colonial rule. Though Achebe's writing, whether short story, novel, or political essay, often focuses explicitly on his native country, he argues against a narrowly nationalistic approach and seeks what he calls "universal communication across racial and cultural boundaries as a means of fostering respect for all people."

Achebe was born Albert Chinualumoga Achebe in 1930 in eastern Nigeria. Both Achebe's parents were Christian converts, and his father was employed as a catechist for the Church Missionary Society. Achebe attended the prestigious Government College at Umuahia before enrolling in University College, Ibadan, a newly constituent college of the University of London. There Achebe decided to study literature, following a curriculum that mirrored that of the College's British parent school—with the sole addition of some writers thought relevant to African students, such as Joseph Conrad, H. Rider Haggard, and colonial administrators such as Joyce Cary (whose novel *Mister Johnson* had a profound influence on Achebe). The work of these writers, which frequently features stereotypical and racist depictions of African people, helped to persuade Achebe to write, and also determined his choice to write in English. Unlike many other African writers (such as Kenyan writer Ngũgĩ wa Thiongo) who choose to use their native language rather than that of their colonizers, Achebe feels that by writing in English he can more directly take issue with these colonial writers by replacing their portraits of the African with his own.

While in university, Achebe contributed several stories to the *University Herald*. These stories, published much later in *Girls at War and Other Stories* (1972), foreground the ways in which conflicts between modern and traditional values have been exacerbated by colonial contact. The traditional balance between material and spiritual aspects of society, and between a concern for self and for community, is typically disrupted, robbing subjects of a strong culture on which to rely. Achebe, himself educated in a system that favored all elements of the new, colonial order—whether cultural, religious, or academic—over those of traditional Biafran society, had to learn for himself much of the history of his people.

After graduating from university, Achebe married, started a family, and embarked on a twelve-year career as a producer for the Nigerian Broadcasting Corporation. Encouraged by literary critic Gilbert Phelps, one of his teachers at the BBC staff school, Achebe published *Things Fall Apart* in 1958. Much of what struck readers of this first novel was Achebe's ability to adapt the English language to his own goals in writing about Nigeria. He relies heavily on Ibo proverbs—which often highlight the themes of his works or help further characterization—and vernacular speech patterns, as well as on native imagery and folklore. In this way his English manages to convey the flavor of Nigerian experience, belief, and culture. In Achebe's view, "the price a world language must be prepared to pay is submission to many different kinds of use. The African writer should aim to use English in a way that brings out his message best. ... He should aim at fashioning out an English which is at once universal and able to carry his peculiar experience."

*No Longer at Ease* (1960), *Arrow of God* (1964), *A Man of the People* (1966), and *Anthills of the Savannah* (1987), Achebe's other novels, have also been highly acclaimed. Achebe's prescience has often been noted in his examinations of Nigeria's political situation. *A Man of the People*, for example, expressed Achebe's concern over what he identified as Nigeria's lack of strong leadership—a lack that led to Nigeria's first military coup in January 1966, the month of the novel's publication.

During the civil war that followed, Achebe traveled and spoke extensively on behalf of his people, who briefly formed the independent state of Biafra in 1967. Following the conclusion of civil war in 1970, Achebe continued his political activities while accepting various teaching posts at American schools. The poetry and essays written during this period are more overtly political than his earlier work. *Morning Yet on Creation Day* (1974) contains both literary and political essays; many of these have been reprinted in the collection *Hopes and Impediments* (1988), which opens with Achebe's controversial essay on Joseph Conrad's *Heart of Darkness*.

Achebe returned to work at the University of Nigeria in 1976, but after a serious car accident in 1990 he moved to the United States to recuperate, accepting a post at Bard College, New York. There he published a new collection of poems and essays, *Another Africa* (1997), and a memoir in the form of three essays, entitled *Home and Exile* (2000).

Throughout his career Achebe has insisted that his political actions and his literary pursuits are not two separate activities, but two ways of attempting to achieve the same end. He firmly believes that storytelling, far from being an idle pursuit, is a socially relevant form of political engagement. "Literature, whether handed down by word of mouth or in print, gives us a second handle on reality; enabling us to encounter in the safe manageable dimensions of make-believe the very same threats to integrity that may assail the psyche in real life; and at the same time providing through the self-discovery which it imparts, a veritable weapon for coping with these threats."

⌘⌘⌘

## The Sacrificial Egg

Julius Obi sat gazing at his typewriter. The fat Chief Clerk, his boss, was snoring at his table. Outside, the gatekeeper in his green uniform was sleeping at his post. You couldn't blame him; no customer had passed through the gate for nearly a week. There was an empty basket on the giant weighing machine. A few palm-kernels lay desolately in the dust around the machine. Only the flies remained in strength.

Julius went to the window that overlooked the great market on the bank of the River Niger. This market, though still called Nkwo, had long spilled over into Eke, Oye, and Afo with the coming of civilization and the growth of the town into the big palm-oil port. In spite of this encroachment, however, it was still busiest on its original Nkwo day, because the deity who had presided over it from antiquity still cast her spell only on her own day—let men in their greed spill over themselves. It was said that she appeared in the form of an old woman in the centre of the market just before cock-crow and waved her magic fan in the four directions of the earth—in front of her, behind her, to the right, and to the left—to draw to the market men and women from distant places. And they came bringing the produce of their lands—palm-oil and kernels, cola nuts, cassava, mats, baskets and earthenware pots; and took home many-coloured cloths, smoked fish, iron pots and plates. These were the forest peoples. The other half of the world who lived by the great rivers came down also—by canoe, bringing yams and fish. Sometimes it was a big canoe with a dozen or more people in it; sometimes it was a lone fisherman and his wife in a small vessel from the swift-flowing Anambara.[1] They moored their canoe on the bank and sold their fish, after much haggling. The woman then walked up the steep banks of the river to the heart of the market to buy salt and oil and, if the sales had been very good, even a length of cloth. And for her children at home she bought bean cakes and mai-mai[2] which the Igara women cooked. As evening approached, they took up their paddles again and paddled away, the water shimmering in the sunset and their canoe becoming smaller and smaller in the distance until it was just a dark crescent on the water's face and two dark bodies swaying forwards and backwards in it. Umuru then was the meeting place of the forest people who were called Igbo and the alien river folk whom the Igbo called Olu and beyond whom the world stretched in indefiniteness.

Julius Obi was not a native of Umuru. He had come like countless others from some bush village inland. Having passed his Standard Six in a mission school he had come to Umuru to work as a clerk in the offices of the all-powerful European trading company which bought palm-kernels at its own price and cloth and metalware, also at its own price. The offices were situated beside the famous market so that in his first two or three weeks Julius had to learn to work within its huge enveloping hum. Sometimes when the Chief Clerk was away he walked to the window and looked down on the vast anthill activity. Most of these people were not here yesterday, he thought, and yet the market had been just as full. There must be many, many people in the world to be able to fill the market day after day like this. Of course they say not all who came to the great market were real people. Janet's mother, Ma, had said so.

"Some of the beautiful young women you see squeezing through the crowds are not people like you or me but mammy-wota[3] who have their town in the depths of the river," she said. "You can always tell them, because they are beautiful with a beauty that is too perfect and too cold. You catch a glimpse of her with the tail of your eye, then you blink and look properly, but she has already vanished in the crowd."

Julius thought about these things as he now stood at the window looking down on the silent, empty market. Who would have believed that the great boisterous market could ever be quenched like this? But such was the strength of Kitikpa, the incarnate power of smallpox. Only he could drive away all those people and leave the market to the flies.

When Umuru was a little village, there was an agegrade[4] who swept its market-square every Nkwo day. But progress had turned it into a busy, sprawling, crowded and dirty river port, a no-man's-land where strangers outnumbered by far the sons of the soil, who could do nothing about it except shake their heads at this gross perversion of their prayer. For indeed they had prayed—who will blame them—for their town to grow and prosper. And it had grown. But there is good growth and there is bad growth. The belly does not bulge out only with food and drink; it might be the abominable disease which would end by sending its sufferer out of the house even before he was fully dead.

The strangers who came to Umuru came for trade and money, not in search of duties to perform, for they had those in plenty back home in their village which was real home.

And as if this did not suffice, the young sons and daughters of Umuru soil, encouraged by schools and churches were behaving no better than the strangers. They neglected all their old tasks and kept only the revelries.

Such was the state of the town when Kitikpa came to see it and to demand the sacrifice the inhabitants owed the gods of the soil. He came in confident knowledge of the terror he held over the people. He was an evil deity, and boasted it. Lest he be offended those he

---

[1] *Anambara* Anambara River, a south-flowing tributary of the River Niger.

[2] *mai-mai* Cakes made of beans, eggs, and chilies.

[3] *mammy-wota* River deities; legendary seductresses who bring wealth but no children.

[4] *agegrade* Member of a specific age set, a group of young men of similar ages who occupy different social roles, or perform different duties, at each stage of maturation.

killed were not killed but decorated, and no one dared weep for them. He put an end to the coming and going between neighbours and between villages. They said, "Kitikpa is in that village," and immediately it was cut off by its neighbours.

Julius was sad and worried because it was almost a week since he had seen Janet, the girl he was going to marry. Ma had explained to him very gently that he should no longer go to see them "until this thing is over, by the power of Jehovah." (Ma was a very devout Christian convert and one reason why she approved of Julius for her only daughter was that he sang in the choir of the CMS church.)

"You must keep to your rooms," she had said in hushed tones, for Kitikpa strictly forbade any noise or boisterousness. "You never know whom you might meet on the streets. That family has got it." She lowered her voice even more and pointed surreptitiously at the house across the road whose doorway was barred with a yellow palm-frond. "He has decorated one of them already and the rest were moved away today in a big government lorry."

Janet walked a short way with Julius and stopped; so he stopped too. They seemed to have nothing to say to each other yet they lingered on. Then she said goodnight and he said goodnight. And they shook hands, which was very odd, as though parting for the night were something new and grave.

He did not go straight home, because he wanted desperately to cling, even alone, to this strange parting. Being educated he was not afraid of whom he might meet, so he went to the bank of the river and just walked up and down it. He must have been there a long time because he was still there when the wooden gong of the night-mask sounded. He immediately set out for home, half-walking and half-running, for night-masks were not a matter of superstition; they were real. They chose the night for their revelry because like the bat's their ugliness was great.

In his hurry he stepped on something that broke with a slight liquid explosion. He stopped and peeped down at the footpath. The moon was not up yet but there was a faint light in the sky which showed that it would not be long delayed. In this half-light he saw that he had stepped on an egg offered in sacrifice. Someone oppressed by misfortune had brought the offering to the crossroads in the dusk. And he had stepped on it. There were the usual young palm-fronds around it. But Julius saw it differently as a house where the terrible artist was at work. He wiped the sole of his foot on the sandy path and hurried away, carrying another vague worry in his mind. But hurrying was no use now; the fleet-footed mask was already abroad. Perhaps it was impelled to hurry by the threatening imminence of the moon. Its voice rose high and clear in the still night air like a flaming sword. It was yet a long way away, but Julius knew that distances vanished before it. So he made straight for the cocoyam farm beside the road and threw himself on his belly, in the shelter of the broad leaves. He had hardly done this when he heard the rattling staff of the spirit and a thundering stream of esoteric speech. He shook all over. The sounds came bearing down on him, almost pressing his face into the moist earth. And now he could hear the footsteps. It was as if twenty evil men were running together. Panic sweat broke all over him and he was nearly impelled to get up and run. Fortunately he kept a firm hold on himself ... In no time at all the commotion in the air and on the earth—the thunder and torrential rain, the earthquake and flood—passed and disappeared in the distance on the other side of the road.

The next morning at the office, the Chief Clerk, a son of the soil spoke bitterly about last night's provocation of Kitikpa by the headstrong youngsters who had launched the noisy fleet-footed mask in defiance of their elders, who knew that Kitikpa would be enraged, and then ...

The trouble was that the disobedient youths had never yet experienced the power of Kitikpa themselves; they had only heard of it. But soon they would learn.

As Julius stood at the window looking out on the emptied market he lived through the terror of that night again. It was barely a week ago but already it seemed like another life, separated from the present by a vast emptiness. This emptiness deepened with every passing day. On this side of it stood Julius, and on the other Ma and Janet whom the dread artist decorated.

—1959, 1972

## from *An Image of Africa: Racism in Conrad's* Heart of Darkness

In the fall of 1974 I was walking one day from the English Department at the University of Massachusetts to a parking lot. It was a fine autumn morning such as encouraged friendliness to passing strangers. Brisk youngsters were hurrying in all directions, many of them obviously freshmen in their first flush of enthusiasm. An older man going the same way as I turned and remarked to me how very young they came these days. I agreed. Then he asked me if I was a student too. I said no, I was a teacher. What did I teach? African literature. Now that was funny, he said, because he knew a fellow who taught the same thing, or perhaps it was African history, in a certain community college not far from here. It always surprised him, he went on to say, because he never had thought of Africa as having that kind of stuff, you know. By this time I was walking much faster. "Oh well," I heard him say finally, behind me: "I guess I have to take your course to find out."

A few weeks later, I received two very touching letters from high school children in Yonkers, New York, who—bless their teacher—had just read *Things Fall Apart*. One of them was particularly happy to learn about the customs and superstitions of an African tribe.

I propose to draw from these rather trivial encounters rather heavy conclusions which at first sight might seem somewhat out of proportion to them. But only, I hope, at first sight.

The young fellow from Yonkers, perhaps partly on account of his age, but I believe also for much deeper and more serious reasons, is obviously unaware that the life of his own tribesmen in Yonkers, New York, is full of odd customs and superstitions and, like everybody else in his culture, imagines that he needs a trip to Africa to encounter those things.

The other person being fully my own age could not be excused on the grounds of his years. Ignorance might be a more likely reason; but here again I believe that something more willful than a mere lack of information was at work. For did not that erudite British historian

and Regius Professor at Oxford, Hugh Trevor-Roper,[1] also pronounce that African history did not exist?

If there is something in these utterances more than youthful inexperience, more than a lack of factual knowledge, what is it? Quite simply it is the desire—one might indeed say the need—in Western psychology to set Africa up as a foil to Europe, as a place of negations at once remote and vaguely familiar, in comparison with which Europe's own state of spiritual grace will be manifest.

This need is not new; which should relieve us all of considerable responsibility and perhaps make us even willing to look at this phenomenon dispassionately. I have neither the wish nor the competence to embark on the exercise with the tools of the social and biological sciences but do so more simply in the manner of a novelist responding to one famous book of European fiction: Joseph Conrad's *Heart of Darkness*, which better than any other work that I know displays that Western desire and need which I have just referred to. Of course there are whole libraries of books devoted to the same purpose, but most of them are so obvious and so crude that few people worry about them today. Conrad, on the other hand, is undoubtedly one of the great stylists of modern fiction and a good storyteller into the bargain. His contribution therefore falls automatically into a different class—permanent literature—read and taught and constantly evaluated by serious academics. *Heart of Darkness* is indeed so secure today that a leading Conrad scholar has numbered it "among the half-dozen greatest short novels in the English language."[2] I will return to this critical opinion in due course, because it may seriously modify my earlier suppositions about who may or may not be guilty in some of the matters I will now raise.

*Heart of Darkness* projects the image of Africa as "the other world," the antithesis of Europe and therefore of civilization, a place where man's vaunted intelligence

[1] *British ... Trevor-Roper* In 1963, Trevor-Roper made the comment, "Perhaps in the future there will be some African history to teach. But at the present there is none; there is only the history of Europeans in Africa. The rest is darkness, and darkness is not the subject of history."

[2] *among the ... language* From Albert J. Guerard's introduction to *Heart of Darkness*, 1950.

and refinement are finally mocked by triumphant bestiality. The book opens on the River Thames, tranquil, resting peacefully "at the decline of day after ages of good service done to the race that peopled its banks." But the actual story will take place on the River Congo, the very antithesis of the Thames. The River Congo is quite decidedly not a River Emeritus. It has rendered no service and enjoys no old-age pension. We are told that "going up that river was like travelling back to the earliest beginning of the world."

Is Conrad saying then that these two rivers are very different, one good, the other bad? Yes, but that is not the real point. It is not the differentness that worries Conrad but the lurking hint of kinship, of common ancestry. For the Thames too "has been one of the dark places of the earth." It conquered its darkness, of course, and is now in daylight and at peace. But if it were to visit its primordial relative, the Congo, it would run the terrible risk of hearing grotesque echoes of its own forgotten darkness, and falling victim to an avenging recrudescence of the mindless frenzy of the first beginnings. These suggestive echoes comprise Conrad's famed evocation of the African atmosphere in *Heart of Darkness*. In the final consideration his method amounts to no more than a steady, ponderous, fake-ritualistic repetition of two antithetical sentences, one about silence and the other about frenzy. We can inspect samples of this on pages 103 and 105 of the New American Library edition:[1] (a) "It was the stillness of an implacable force brooding over an inscrutable intention" and (b) "The steamer toiled along slowly on the edge of a black and incomprehensible frenzy." Of course there is a judicious change of adjective from time to time, so that instead of "inscrutable," for example, you might have "unspeakable," even plain "mysterious," etc., etc.

The eagle-eyed English critic F.R. Leavis drew attention long ago to Conrad's "adjectival insistence upon inexpressible and incomprehensible mystery."[2] That insistence must not be dismissed lightly, as many

Conrad critics have tended to do, as a mere stylistic flaw; for it raises serious questions of artistic good faith. When a writer while pretending to record scenes, incidents, and their impact is in reality engaged in inducing hypnotic stupor in his readers through a bombardment of emotive words and other forms of trickery, much more has to be at stake than stylistic felicity. Generally normal readers are well armed to detect and resist such underhand activity. But Conrad chose his subject well—one which was guaranteed not to put him in conflict with the psychological predisposition of his readers or raise the need for him to contend with their resistance. He chose the role of purveyor of comforting myths.

The most interesting and revealing passages in *Heart of Darkness* are, however, about people. I must crave the indulgence of my reader to quote almost a whole page from about the middle of the story when representatives of Europe in a steamer going down the Congo encounter the denizens of Africa:

> We were wanderers on a prehistoric earth, on an earth that wore the aspect of an unknown planet. We could have fancied ourselves the first of men taking possession of an accursed inheritance, to be subdued at the cost of profound anguish and of excessive toil. But suddenly, as we struggled round a bend, there would be a glimpse of rush walls, of peaked grass-roofs, a burst of yells, a whirl of black limbs, a mass of hands clapping, of feet stamping, of bodies swaying, of eyes rolling, under the droop of heavy and motionless foliage. The steamer toiled along slowly on the edge of the black and incomprehensible frenzy. The prehistoric man was cursing us, praying to us, welcoming us—who could tell? We were cut off from the comprehension of our surroundings; we glided past like phantoms, wondering and secretly appalled, as sane men would be before an enthusiastic outbreak in a madhouse. We could not understand because we were too far and could not remember because we were travelling in the night of first ages, of those ages that are gone, leaving hardly a sign—and no memories.
>
> The earth seemed unearthly. We are accustomed to look upon the shackled form of a conquered monster, but there—there you could look at a thing monstrous and free. It was unearthly, and the men

[1] *pages ... edition* Pages 105 and 107 of the Broadview edition (D.C.R.A. Goonetilleke, ed., 2nd edition, 1999). From this point on, all page numbers, provided in square brackets, are those of the Broadview edition.

[2] *adjectival ... mystery* From F.R. Leavis, *The Great Tradition* (1950).

were—No, they were not inhuman. Well, you know, that was the worst of it—this suspicion of their not being inhuman. It would come slowly to one. They howled and leaped, and spun, and made horrid faces; but what thrilled you was just the thought of their humanity—like yours—the thought of your remote kinship with this wild and passionate uproar. Ugly. Yes, it was ugly enough; but if you were man enough you would admit to yourself that there was in you just the faintest trace of a response to the terrible frankness of that noise, a dim suspicion of there being a meaning in it which you—you so remote from the night of first ages—could comprehend. [107–08]

Herein lies the meaning of *Heart of Darkness* and the fascination it holds over the Western mind: "What thrilled you was just the thought of their humanity—like yours … Ugly."

Having shown us Africa in the mass, Conrad then zeros in, half a page later, on a specific example, giving us one of his rare descriptions of an African who is not just limbs or rolling eyes:

And between whiles I had to look after the savage who was fireman. He was an improved specimen; he could fire up a vertical boiler. He was there below me, and, upon my word, to look at him was as edifying as seeing a dog in a parody of breeches and a feather hat, walking on his hind legs. A few months of training had done for that really fine chap. He squinted at the steam gauge and at the water gauge with an evident effort of intrepidity—and he had filed his teeth, too, the poor devil, and the wool of his pate shaved into queer patterns, and three ornamental scars on each of his cheeks. He ought to have been clapping his hands and stamping his feet on the bank, instead of which he was hard at work, a thrall to strange witchcraft, full of improving knowledge. [108]

As everybody knows, Conrad is a romantic on the side. He might not exactly admire savages clapping their hands and stamping their feet but they have at least the merit of being in their place, unlike this dog in a parody of breeches. For Conrad things being in their place is of the utmost importance. "Fine fellows—cannibals—in their place," he tells us pointedly. Tragedy begins when things leave their accustomed place, like Europe leaving its safe stronghold between the policeman and the baker to take a peep into the heart of darkness.

Before the story takes us into the Congo basin proper we are given this nice little vignette as an example of things in their place:

Now and then a boat from the shore gave one a momentary contact with reality. It was paddled by black fellows. You could see from afar the white of their eyeballs glistening. They shouted, sang; their bodies streamed with perspiration; they had faces like grotesque masks—these chaps; but they had bone, muscle, a wild vitality, an intense energy of movement, that was as natural and true as the surf along their coast. They wanted no excuse for being there. They were a great comfort to look at. [80]

Towards the end of the story Conrad lavishes a whole page quite unexpectedly on an African woman who has obviously been some kind of mistress to Mr. Kurtz and now presides (if I may be permitted a little liberty) like a formidable mystery over the inexorable imminence of his departure:

She was savage and superb, wild-eyed and magnificent … She stood looking at us without a stir and like the wilderness itself, with an air of brooding over an inscrutable purpose. [137–38]

This Amazon is drawn in considerable detail, albeit of a predictable nature, for two reasons. First, she is in her place and so can win Conrad's special brand of approval; and second, she fulfils a structural requirement of the story: a savage counterpart to the refined, European woman who will step forth to end the story:

She came forward, all in black with a pale head, floating toward me in the dusk. She was in mourning … She took both my hands in hers and murmured, "I had heard you were coming" … She had a mature capacity for fidelity, for belief, for suffering. [154]

The difference in the attitude of the novelist to these two women is conveyed in too many direct and subtle ways to need elaboration. But perhaps the most significant difference is the one implied in the author's bestowal of human expression to the one and the withholding of it from the other. It is clearly not part of Conrad's purpose to confer language on the "rudimentary souls" of Africa. In place of speech they made "a violent babble of uncouth sounds." They "exchanged short grunting phrases" even among themselves. But most of the time they were too busy with their frenzy. There are two occasions in the book, however, when Conrad departs somewhat from his practice and confers speech, even English speech, on the savages. The first occurs when cannibalism gets the better of them:

> "Catch 'im," he snapped, with a bloodshot widening of his eyes and a flash of sharp white teeth—"catch 'im. Give 'im to us." "To you, eh?" I asked; "what would you do with them?" "Eat 'im!" he said curtly. [113]

The other occasion was the famous announcement:

> "Mistah Kurtz—he dead" [148].

At first sight these instances might be mistaken for unexpected acts of generosity from Conrad. In reality they constitute some of his best assaults. In the case of the cannibals the incomprehensible grunts that had thus far served them for speech suddenly proved inadequate for Conrad's purpose of letting the European glimpse the unspeakable craving in their hearts. Weighing the necessity for consistency in the portrayal of the dumb brutes against the sensational advantages of securing their conviction by clear, unambiguous evidence issuing out of their own mouths, Conrad chose the latter. As for the announcement of Mr. Kurtz's death by the "insolent black head in the doorway," what better or more appropriate *finis* could be written to the horror story of that wayward child of civilization who wilfully had given his soul to the powers of darkness and "taken a high seat amongst the devils of the land" than the proclamation of his physical death by the forces he had joined?

It might be contended, of course, that the attitude to the African in *Heart of Darkness* is not Conrad's but that of his fictional narrator, Marlow, and that far from endorsing it Conrad might indeed be holding it up to irony and criticism. Certainly, Conrad appears to go to considerable pains to set up layers of insulation between himself and the moral universe of his story. He has, for example, a narrator behind a narrator. The primary narrator is Marlow, but his account is given to us through the filter of a second, shadowy person. But if Conrad's intention is to draw a *cordon sanitaire*[1] between himself and the moral and psychological *malaise* of his narrator, his care seems to me totally wasted because he neglects to hint, clearly and adequately, at an alternative frame of reference by which we may judge the actions and opinions of his characters. It would not have been beyond Conrad's power to make that provision if he had thought it necessary. Conrad seems to me to approve of Marlow, with only minor reservations—a fact reinforced by the similarities between their two careers.

Marlow comes through to us not only as a witness of truth, but one holding those advanced and humane views appropriate to the English liberal tradition which required all Englishmen of decency to be deeply shocked by atrocities in Bulgaria or the Congo of King Leopold of the Belgians or wherever.

Thus Marlow is able to toss out such bleeding-heart sentiments as these:

> They were all dying slowly—it was very clear. They were not enemies, they were not criminals, they were nothing earthly now—nothing but black shadows of disease and starvation, lying confusedly in the greenish gloom. Brought from all the recesses of the coast in all the legality of time contracts, lost in uncongenial surroundings, fed on unfamiliar food, they sickened, became inefficient, and were then allowed to crawl away and rest. [84]

The kind of liberalism espoused here by Marlow/Conrad touched all the best minds of the age in England, Europe, and America. It took different forms in the minds of different people but almost always managed to sidestep the ultimate question of equality between white people and black people. That extraordinary missionary Albert Schweitzer,[2] who sacrificed

---

[1] *cordon sanitaire*   French: quarantine line.

[2] *Albert Schweitzer*   M.D., humanitarian, and winner of the Nobel Peace Prize (1875–1965).

brilliant careers in music and theology in Europe for a life of service to Africans in much the same area as Conrad writes about, epitomizes the ambivalence. In a comment which has often been quoted Schweitzer says: "The African is indeed my brother but my junior brother." And so he proceeded to build a hospital appropriate to the needs of junior brothers with standards of hygiene reminiscent of medical practice in the days before the germ theory of disease came into being. Naturally he became a sensation in Europe and America. Pilgrims flocked, and I believe still flock even after he has passed on, to witness the prodigious miracle in Lambéréné,[1] on the edge of the primeval forest.

Conrad's liberalism would not take him quite as far as Schweitzer's, though. He would not use the word "brother" however qualified; the farthest he would go was "kinship." When Marlow's African helmsman falls down with a spear in his heart he gives his white master one final disquieting look:

> And the intimate profundity of that look he gave me when he received his hurt remains to this day in my memory—like a claim of distant kinship affirmed in a supreme moment. [125–26]

It is important to note that Conrad, careful as ever with his words, is concerned not so much about "distant kinship" as about someone *laying a claim* on it. The black man lays a claim on the white man which is well-nigh intolerable. It is the laying of this claim which frightens and at the same time fascinates Conrad, "the thought of their humanity—like yours ... Ugly."

The point of my observations should be quite clear by now, namely that Joseph Conrad was a thoroughgoing racist. That this simple truth is glossed over in criticisms of his work is due to the fact that white racism against Africa is such a normal way of thinking that its manifestations go completely unremarked. Students of *Heart of Darkness* will often tell you that Conrad is concerned not so much with Africa as with the deterioration of one European mind caused by solitude and sickness. They will point out to you that Conrad is, if anything, less charitable to the Europeans in the story than he is to the natives, that the point of the story is to ridicule Europe's civilizing mission in Africa. A Conrad student informed me in Scotland that Africa is merely a setting for the disintegration of the mind of Mr. Kurtz.

Which is partly the point. Africa as setting and backdrop which eliminates the African as human factor. Africa as a metaphysical battlefield devoid of all recognizable humanity, into which the wandering European enters at his peril. Can nobody see the preposterous and perverse arrogance in thus reducing Africa to the role of props for the break-up of one petty European mind? But that is not even the point. The real question is the dehumanization of Africa and Africans which this age-long attitude has fostered and continues to foster in the world. And the question is whether a novel which celebrates this dehumanization, which depersonalizes a portion of the human race, can be called a great work of art. My answer is: No, it cannot.

—1977

---

[1] *miracle in Lambéréné*  Hospital built in 1913 by Schweitzer and his wife, Helene Bresslau, in what is now Gabon.

# DEREK WALCOTT

## b. 1930

Unlike many Caribbean writers who felt they had to move to the "mother country" or other metropolises in order to achieve recognition and be published, Derek Walcott has remained rooted in the Caribbean. Although he teaches part of the year at Boston University, his home has always been in either Trinidad or St. Lucia. His love of the region and his "multicultural commitment" were noted by the Nobel committee when they awarded him the prize for literature in 1992; he became the first Caribbean writer to receive this honor. Throughout his career Walcott has grappled with the central issues of twentieth-century Caribbean writing: the use of the English language versus that of Creole; the effects of a history of slavery and colonization on the region; and the deep-seated ambivalence towards English culture that had been passed down to the colonies.

Walcott was born into a Methodist, English-speaking family in the predominantly Roman Catholic, French Creole-speaking island of St. Lucia. Instead of feeling isolated, he embraced the diverse aspects of his island, learning to love both the English language and Creole culture. His mother, a schoolteacher in the local Methodist school, instilled in Walcott a love of literature and a disciplined work ethic. After his father died when he was a year old, his mother took in sewing to support Walcott, his twin brother, and their elder sister. Walcott's passion for the arts became evident early, and he knew he wanted to be either a painter or a poet. When he was a child, his mother would give him a poem to copy and imitate before going to bed each evening. This early training instilled in him a strong sense of the importance of meter, rhyme, and metaphor.

After graduating from high school, Walcott became a junior teacher at the school he had once attended. By 1948, he was starting to be known in St. Lucia as an emerging poet; in that year he self-published his first volume of poetry, *25 Poems*. Walcott also began to write plays during this period (an interest he shared with his brother), and these plays began to be produced locally. His plays often reflect his interest in local culture (*Ti-Jean and his Brothers, Dream on Monkey Mountain*) or regional history (*Henri-Christophe*).

In the late 1940s and early 1950s many of Walcott's contemporaries left to study abroad, a path seen by many as the only way to "better oneself." Walcott's high-school marks had not been high enough to allow him to take this route, but he eventually obtained a scholarship to attend the University of the West Indies in Jamaica. There Walcott was an indifferent student, more interested in painting and doing independent reading than in his courses. By this time he was writing regularly, usually rising at 5 a.m. and writing until noon. Some of his more popular poems, including "Ruins of a Great House" and "A Far Cry From Africa," date from this period, during which Walcott also married and became a father.

"Ruins of a Great House" illustrates much of the cultural ambivalence Walcott was beginning to feel. A descendant both of Europeans and of former slaves, he felt torn between the two sides of his heritage. (He refers in another one of his works to "the ancestor who sold me ... and the ancestor who bought me.") His call for compassion in dealing with the effects of history has sometimes been criticized in the Caribbean as inadequate; some have felt that stronger measures needed to be taken—an unequivocal return to the African tradition, or a turning away from the English language in favor of Creole. In response to criticism of his commitment to the English language, he has responded that the New World use of English is "Adamic," and that English has been shaped by and continues to be shaped by those who use it.

In 1959 Walcott moved to Trinidad after spending a year studying theater in New York on a Rockefeller Fellowship. His first marriage had dissolved, he felt he needed a change from St. Lucia, and he was attracted to the diversity of Trinidad. He continued to write poetry and plays, and established The Trinidad Theatre Workshop, which produced many of his early plays. Walcott's time with the Workshop was key to developing an indigenous theatre tradition in the region. He remarried and had two daughters. In 1962 he published his breakthrough volume of poetry, *In a Green Night*. He was beginning to be known internationally, and some of his poems began appearing in *The New Statesman* and *The New Yorker*. He also began writing *Another Life*, his long autobiographical poem. Completed in 1973, this volume would win several awards, including *The New Statesman* Jock Campbell Award, and garner him international acclaim. The next two decades would cement Walcott's growing international status. He toured widely and continued to publish both poems and plays, including *The Star-Apple Kingdom, The Fortunate Traveller, Midsummer*, and *The Arkansas Testament*.

Walcott published his magnum opus in 1990. *Omeros* was the culmination of his development as a writer: 325 pages written in terza rima, re-casting as a Caribbean story the legend of Achilles, Hector, and Helen, with the story of the island of St. Lucia woven into it. The long poem touched on aspects of Walcott's own history, as he grapples with the region's historical ties to the British and the Caribbean's ties to Africa. The Nobel Committee awarded the prize in 1992 "for a poetic *oeuvre* of great luminosity, sustained by a historical vision, the outcome of multicultural commitment." In his Nobel acceptance speech Walcott expressed his wish that the people of the Caribbean would move beyond the pain that history has caused in the region; in his words, "[we] make too much of that long groan which underlines the past." He proffered instead a vision of the Caribbean as the synthesis of the past and beginning of a new history: "Antillean art is this restoration of our shattered histories."

Walcott has continued to write, publishing *The Bounty* in 1997, and *Tiepolo's Hound* in 2000, and *The Prodigal* in 2004. He divides his time between the United States and his home in St. Lucia.

⌘ ⌘ ⌘

## A Far Cry from Africa

A wind is ruffling the tawny pelt
Of Africa. Kikuyu,[1] quick as flies,
Batten upon the bloodstreams of the veldt.[2]
Corpses are scattered through a paradise.
5  Only the worm, colonel of carrion, cries:
"Waste no compassion on these separate dead!"

Statistics justify and scholars seize
The salients of colonial policy.
What is that to the white child hacked in bed?
10  To savages, expendable as Jews?

Threshed out by beaters, the long rushes break
In a white dust of ibises[3] whose cries
Have wheeled since civilization's dawn
From the parched river or beast-teeming plain.

---

[1] *Kikuyu* Bantu-speaking people of Kenya who fought against British colonial settlers as part of the eight-year Mau Mau uprising.

[2] *Batten upon* Thrive on; revel in; *veldt* Open country.

[3] *ibises* Long-legged, stork-like birds that inhabit lakes and swamps.

15 The violence of beast on beast is read
As natural law, but upright man
Seeks his divinity by inflicting pain.
Delirious as these worried beasts, his wars
Dance to the tightened carcass of a drum,
20 While he calls courage still that native dread
Of the white peace contracted by the dead.

Again brutish necessity wipes its hands
Upon the napkin of a dirty cause, again
A waste of our compassion, as with Spain,[1]
25 The gorilla wrestles with the superman.
I who am poisoned with the blood of both,
Where shall I turn, divided to the vein?
I who have cursed
The drunken officer of British rule, how choose
30 Between this Africa and the English tongue I love?
Betray them both, or give back what they give?
How can I face such slaughter and be cool?
How can I turn from Africa and live?
—1962

### Ruins of a Great House

*though our longest sun sets at right declensions*
*and makes but winter arches, it cannot be long before we*
*lie down in darkness, and have our light in ashes …*
                              —BROWNE, *Urn Burial*

Stones only, the disjecta membra[2] of this Great House,
Whose moth-like girls are mixed with candledust,
Remain to file the lizard's dragonish claws.
The mouths of those gate cherubs shriek with stain;
5 Axle and coach wheel silted under the muck
Of cattle droppings.
                    Three crows flap for the trees
And settle, creaking the eucalyptus boughs.
A smell of dead limes quickens in the nose
10 The leprosy of empire.
                    "Farewell, green fields,
                    Farewell, ye happy groves!"

---

[1] *Spain*   I.e., the Spanish Civil War (1936–39).

[2] *disjecta membra*   Latin: scattered remains.

Marble like Greece, like Faulkner's South[3] in stone,
Deciduous beauty prospered and is gone,
15 But where the lawn breaks in a rash of trees
A spade below dead leaves will ring the bone
Of some dead animal or human thing
Fallen from evil days, from evil times.

It seems that the original crops were limes
20 Grown in the silt that clogs the river's skirt;
The imperious rakes[4] are gone, their bright girls gone,
The river flows, obliterating hurt.
I climbed a wall with the grille ironwork
Of exiled craftsmen protecting that great house
25 From guilt, perhaps, but not from the worm's rent
Nor from the padded cavalry of the mouse.
And when a wind shook in the limes I heard
What Kipling[5] heard, the death of a great empire, the
     abuse
Of ignorance by Bible and by sword.

30 A green lawn, broken by low walls of stone,
Dipped to the rivulet, and pacing, I thought next
Of men like Hawkins, Walter Raleigh, Drake,[6]
Ancestral murderers and poets, more perplexed
In memory now by every ulcerous crime.
35 The world's green age then was a rotting lime
Whose stench became the charnel° galleon's text.    *mortuary*
The rot remains with us, the men are gone.
But, as dead ash is lifted in a wind
That fans the blackening ember of the mind,
40 My eyes burned from the ashen prose of Donne.[7]

Ablaze with rage I thought,
Some slave is rotting in this manorial lake,

---

[3] *Faulkner's South*   The American South as depicted in the novels of William Faulkner (1897–1962).

[4] *rakes*   Wild young noblemen.

[5] *Kipling*   Rudyard Kipling (1865–1936), English novelist and short-story writer whose works often interrogated British imperialism.

[6] *Hawkins*   John Hawkins, sixteenth-century British slave trader who brought slaves from Africa to West Indian plantations; *Walter Raleigh*   English explorer and poet (1552–1618); *Drake*   Sir Francis Drake (1543–96), British explorer and military commander who became the first Englishman to sail around the world.

[7] *Donne*   English poet John Donne (1572–1631).

But still the coal of my compassion fought
That Albion[1] too was once
45 A colony like ours, "part of the continent, piece of the
        main,"[2]
Nook-shotten, rook o'erblown, deranged
By foaming channels and the vain expense
Of bitter faction.
                    All in compassion ends
50 So differently from what the heart arranged:
"as well as if a manor of thy friend's … "
—1962


## A Letter from Brooklyn

An old lady writes me in a spidery style,
   Each character trembling, and I see a veined hand
Pellucid as paper, travelling on a skein
Of such frail thoughts its thread is often broken;
5 Or else the filament from which a phrase is hung
Dims to my sense, but caught, it shines like steel,
As touch a line and the whole web will feel.
She describes my father, yet I forget her face
More easily than my father's yearly dying;
10 Of her I remember small, buttoned boots and the place
She kept in our wooden church on those Sundays
Whenever her strength allowed;
Grey-haired, thin-voiced, perpetually bowed.

"I am Mable Rawlins," she writes, "and know both
        your parents";
15 He is dead, Miss Rawlins, but God bless your tense:
"Your father was a dutiful, honest,
Faithful, and useful person."
For such plain praise what fame is recompense?
"A horn-painter, he painted delicately on horn,
20 He used to sit around the table and paint pictures."

The peace of God needs nothing to adorn
It, nor glory nor ambition.
"He is twenty-eight years buried," she writes, "he was
        called home,
And is, I am sure, doing greater work."

25 The strength of one frail hand in a dim room
Somewhere in Brooklyn, patient and assured,
Restores my sacred duty to the Word.
"Home, home," she can write, with such short time to
        live,
Alone as she spins the blessings of her years;
30 Not withered of beauty if she can bring such tears,
Nor withdrawn from the world that breaks its lovers so;
Heaven is to her the place where painters go,
All who bring beauty on frail shell or horn,
There was all made, thence their *lux-mundi*[3] drawn,
35 Drawn, drawn, till the thread is resilient steel,
Lost though it seems in darkening periods,
And there they return to do work that is God's.

So this old lady writes, and again I believe.
I believe it all, and for no man's death I grieve.
—1962


## from *Midsummer*

### 52

I heard them marching the leaf-wet roads of my head,
   the sucked vowels of a syntax trampled to mud,
a division of dictions, one troop black, barefooted,
the other in redcoats bright as their sovereign's blood;
5 their feet scuffled like rain, the bare soles with the shod.
One fought for a queen, the other was chained in her
        service,
but both, in bitterness, travelled the same road.
Our occupation and the Army of Occupation
are born enemies, but what mortar can size
10 the broken stones of the barracks of Brimstone Hill[4]

---

[1] *Albion* England.

[2] *part of … main* From John Donne's *Devotions upon Emergent Occasions*, Meditation 17 (1624): "No man is an island, entire of itself; every man is a piece of the continent, a part of the main. If a clod be washed away by the sea, Europe is the less, as well as if a promontory were, as well as if a manor of thy friend's or of thine own were: any man's death diminishes me, because I am involved in mankind, and therefore never send to know for whom the bells tolls; it tolls for thee."

[3] *lux-mundi* Latin: light of the world.

[4] *Brimstone Hill* Fortress of St. Kitts.

to the gaping brick of Belfast? Have we changed sides
to the mustached sergeants and the horsy gentry
because we serve English, like a two-headed sentry
guarding its borders? No language is neutral;
15    the green oak of English is a murmurous cathedral
where some took umbrage, some peace, but every
     shade, all,
helped widen its shadow. I used to haunt the arches
of the British barracks of Vigie.[1] There were leaves
     there,
bright, rotting like revers or epaulettes,[2] and the stenches
20    of history and piss. Leaves piled like the dropped aitches
of soldiers from rival shires, from the brimstone
     trenches
of Agincourt to the gas of the Somme.[3] On Poppy Day[4]

our schools bought red paper flowers. They were for
     Flanders.
I saw Hotspur[5] cursing the smoke through which a
     popinjay
25    minced from the battle. Those raging commanders from
Thersites[6] to Percy, their rant is our model.
I pinned the poppy to my blazer. It bled like a vowel.
—1984

---

[1]  *barracks of Vigie*   On the island of St. Lucia.

[2]  *revers*   Reversed edge of a coat, vest, etc.; *epaulettes*   Ornamental shoulder pieces on military uniforms.

[3]  *Agincourt*   Site of Henry V's famous victory over the French in 1415; *Somme*   Site of World War I battle in France, which began on 1 July 1916 and lasted five months.

[4]  *Poppy Day*   Remembrance Day (in Britain and the Commonwealth) or Veteran's Day (in the U.S.), when poppies are worn to commemorate those killed in World Wars I and II. (See John McCrae's sonnet "In Flanders Fields.")

[5]  *Hotspur*   Nickname of Sir Henry Percy (1366–1403), an English nobleman who led an uprising against King Henry IV. He figures as the hot-headed rival to Prince Hal in Shakespeare's *I Henry IV*.

[6]  *Thersites*   Greek soldier who, according to Homer's *Iliad*, insulted Achilles during the Trojan War, provoking Achilles to kill him in a fit of rage.

# SEAMUS HEANEY
## b. 1939

The American poet Robert Lowell once referred to Seamus Heaney as "the best Irish poet since Yeats." Since winning the Nobel Prize for literature in 1995, Heaney has been one of the most popular poets writing in English. Often praised for its lyricism, Heaney's work reflects his rural upbringing, with a focus on the soil, the past, and lost friends. Many of his poems also deal with the troubles in his native Northern Ireland, and some have criticized him for an alleged ambivalence about the political conflict.

Heaney grew up in a Roman Catholic household in the predominantly Protestant north. The eldest of nine children, he was not marked in childhood by the strife that would later affect the region. Instead, he experienced a community that lived in harmony, regardless of religious affiliation. Heaney's parents were farmers in County Derry, just outside Belfast. He grew up with an appreciation for country life, for those who work the land, and for the importance of close-knit community. It was the radio that taught him the "thrill of story" and introduced him to a wider world beyond his county. His poetry is often filled with images from this period of his life.

Heaney's career as a published poet began while he was completing a teacher's certificate at St. Joseph's College in Belfast. Writing under the pseudonym "Incertus," he had just finished his Bachelor of Arts in English Language and Literature at Queen's University when he joined a poetry workshop. Known as "The Belfast Group," this forum allowed new poets to showcase their work and have it critiqued by their peers. The Group introduced him to other young poets, including his future wife, and was also a forum for the discussion of the political issues of the day. Many of Heaney's early poems were first read and discussed at Group meetings.

The publication in 1966 of Heaney's first book of poems, *Death of a Naturalist*, began what would be a career filled with awards and accolades. This volume won the Somerset Maugham Award, among others. While establishing his career as a poet, Heaney was working as a lecturer in English at various colleges in Ireland and the United States to support his growing family, which would eventually include two sons and a daughter. His move south to the Republic of Ireland in 1972 was in many respects a positive one, but moving away from the political controversies of Northern Ireland to the relative stability of the south was seen by some as a betrayal. Establishing a home just outside Dublin did not, however, lead Heaney to forget the political turmoil of his birthplace. It was during this time that he wrote some of his most political works: *North* (1975) and *Field Work* (1979). He did not want to be seen solely as a political poet, though, and felt he needed distance from the conflicts of the north to provide scope for objectivity.

Heaney's rising international fame led to his appointment as Boylston Professor of Rhetoric and Oratory at Harvard in 1984. This position allowed him to teach one semester at Harvard in the spring and spend the remaining eight months of the year at his home in Dublin. The death of Heaney's mother, also in 1984, was the occasion for some of his most touching poetry, published in *Haw Lantern* (1987). When questioned about his memorializing of lost friends and family, Heaney responded: "The elegiac Heaney? There's nothing else." Heaney uses this fascination with the past to comment indirectly on the present. In one of his "bog poems," "Punishment," Heaney compares a first-century girl who was drowned as punishment for adultery to women in Northern Ireland today. In other poems he uses the details of rural life, such as digging potatoes, churning milk, and eating wild fruit, to comment on universal issues.

In 1995 Heaney was awarded the Nobel Prize for literature. In making the award, the committee cited his "works of lyrical beauty and ethical depth, which exalt everyday miracles and the living past." In his Nobel acceptance speech he wrote that the "form of the poem … is crucial to poetry's power to do the thing which always is and always will be to poetry's credit: the power to persuade that vulnerable part of our consciousness of its rightness in spite of the evidence of wrongness all around it."

In 1999, Heaney published a translation of *Beowulf*, which won the Whitbread Book of the Year Award in 2000. When asked why he writes poetry, he responded that the "excitement of something coming out right … that is indeed its own reward."

⌘ ⌘ ⌘

## Digging

Between my finger and my thumb
The squat pen rests; snug as a gun.

Under my window, a clean rasping sound
When the spade sinks into gravelly ground:
5   My father, digging. I look down

Till his straining rump among the flowerbeds
Bends low, comes up twenty years away
Stooping in rhythm through potato drills[1]
Where he was digging.

10   The coarse boot nestled on the lug, the shaft
Against the inside knee was levered firmly.
He rooted out tall tops, buried the bright edge deep
To scatter new potatoes that we picked
Loving their cool hardness in our hands.

15   By God, the old man could handle a spade.
Just like his old man.

My grandfather cut more turf[2] in a day
Than any other man on Toner's bog.
Once I carried him milk in a bottle

20   Corked sloppily with paper. He straightened up
To drink it, then fell to right away
Nicking and slicing neatly, heaving sods
Over his shoulder, going down and down
For the good turf. Digging.

25   The cold smell of potato mould, the squelch and slap
Of soggy peat, the curt cuts of an edge
Through living roots awaken in my head.
But I've no spade to follow men like them.

Between my finger and my thumb
30   The squat pen rests.
I'll dig with it.
—1966

## Thatcher

Bespoke for weeks, he turned up some morning
Unexpectedly, his bicycle slung
With a light ladder and a bag of knives.
He eyed the old rigging, poked at the eaves,

5   Opened and handled sheaves of lashed wheat-straw.
Next, the bundled rods: hazel and willow
Were flicked for weight, twisted in case they'd snap.
It seemed he spent the morning warming up:

---

1   *potato drills*   Row of sown potatoes.

2   *turf*   Slabs of peat.

Then fixed the ladder, laid out well-honed blades
10  And snipped at straw and sharpened ends of rods
That, bent in two, made a white-pronged staple
For pinning down his world, handful by handful.

Couchant° for days on sods above the rafters,          *lying*
He shaved and flushed the butts,[1] stitched all together
15  Into a sloped honeycomb, a stubble patch,
And left them gaping at his Midas touch.[2]
—1969

## The Wife's Tale

When I had spread it all on linen cloth
Under the hedge, I called them over.
The hum and gulp of the thresher ran down
And the big belt slewed to a standstill, straw
5  Hanging undelivered in the jaws.
There was such quiet that I heard their boots
Crunching the stubble twenty yards away.

He lay down and said, "Give these fellows theirs,
I'm in no hurry," plucking grass in handfuls
10  And tossing it in the air. "That looks well."
(He nodded at my white cloth on the grass.)
"I declare a woman could lay out a field
Though boys like us have little call for cloths."
He winked, then watched me as I poured a cup
15  And buttered the thick slices that he likes.
"It's threshing better than I thought, and mind
It's good clean seed. Away over there and look."
Always this inspection has to be made
Even when I don't know what to look for.

20  But I ran my hand in the half-filled bags
Hooked to the slots. It was hard as shot,
Innumerable and cool. The bags gaped
Where the chutes ran back to the stilled drum
And forks were stuck at angles in the ground
25  As javelins might mark lost battlefields.
I moved between them back across the stubble.

They lay in the ring of their own crusts and dregs,
Smoking and saying nothing. "There's good yield,
Isn't there?"—as proud as if he were the land itself—
30  "Enough for crushing and for sowing both."
And that was it. I'd come and he had shown me,
So I belonged no further to the work.
I gathered cups and folded up the cloth
And went. But they still kept their ease,
35  Spread out, unbuttoned, grateful, under the trees.
—1969

## The Grauballe Man[3]

As if he had been poured
in tar, he lies
on a pillow of turf
and seems to weep

5  the black river of himself
The grain of his wrists
is like bog oak,[4]
the ball of his heel

like a basalt egg.
10  His instep has shrunk
cold as a swan's foot
or a wet swamp root.

His hips are the ridge
and purse of a mussel,
15  his spine an eel arrested
under a glisten of mud.

The head lifts,
the chin is a visor
raised above the vent
20  of his slashed throat

was buoyant with hindsight—

---

[1] *butts*  Branch tips.

[2] *Midas touch*  Reference to the Greek myth of King Midas, whose touch turned everything to gold.

[3] *Grauballe Man*  Man from the first century BCE whose preserved remains were found in 1952, in a peat bog near the village of Grauballe, Denmark.

[4] *bog oak*  Wood of an oak tree preserved in peat-bog.

it said Thor's[1] hammer swung
to geography and trade,
thick-witted couplings and revenges,

25  the hatreds and behindbacks
of the althing,[2] lies and women,
exhaustions nominated peace,
memory incubating the spilled blood.

It said, "Lie down
30  in the word-hoard, burrow
the coil and gleam
of your furrowed brain.

Compose in darkness.
Expect aurora borealis°            *northern lights*
35  in the long foray
but no cascade of light.

Keep your eye clear
as the bleb° of the icicle,          *air bubble*
trust the feel of what nubbed treasure
40  your hands have known."
—1975

## Punishment [3]

I can feel the tug
of the halter at the nape
of her neck, the wind
on her naked front.

5  It blows her nipples
to amber beads,

---

it shakes the frail rigging
of her ribs.

I can see her drowned
10  body in the bog,
the weighing stone,
the floating rods and boughs.

Under which at first
she was a barked sapling
15  that is dug up
oak-bone, brain-firkin:[4]

her shaved head
like a stubble of black corn,
her blindfold a soiled bandage,
20  her noose a ring

to store
the memories of love.
Little adulteress,
before they punished you

25  you were flaxen-haired,
undernourished, and your
tar-black face was beautiful.
My poor scapegoat,

I almost love you
30  but would have cast, I know,
the stones of silence.
I am the artful voyeur

of your brain's exposed
and darkened combs,
35  your muscles' webbing
and all your numbered bones:

I who have stood dumb
when your betraying sisters,
cauled° in tar,               *capped*

---

[1] *Thor*  Norse god of thunder, often pictured wielding a hammer (representing the thunderbolt).

[2] *althing*  General assembly of the islanders.

[3] *Punishment*  In 1951 the body of a fourteen-year-old girl from the first century BCE was discovered in a German bog. The left side of her head had been shaved, her eyes bandaged shut, and a collar tied around her neck. Her body had been weighed down with tree branches and a stone. Germanic people often punished adulterous women by shaving their hair and either killing them or expelling them from the village. After the girl's body was found, the brain was removed and examined.

[4] *firkin*  Small cask or barrel.

40 wept by the railings,[1]

who would connive
in civilized outrage
yet understand the exact
and tribal, intimate revenge.
—1975

## Casualty

### 1

He would drink by himself
And raise a weathered thumb
Towards the high shelf,
Calling another rum
5 And blackcurrant, without
Having to raise his voice,
Or order a quick stout
By a lifting of the eyes
And a discreet dumb-show
10 Of pulling off the top;
At closing time would go
In waders and peaked cap
Into the showery dark,
A dole-kept breadwinner
15 But a natural for work.
I loved his whole manner,
Sure-footed but too sly,
His deadpan sidling tact,
His fisherman's quick eye
20 And turned observant back.

Incomprehensible
To him, my other life.
Sometimes, on his high stool,
Too busy with his knife
25 At a tobacco plug
And not meeting my eye,
In the pause after a slug
He mentioned poetry.
We would be on our own

30 And, always politic
And shy of condescension,
I would manage by some trick
To switch the talk to eels
Or lore of the horse and cart
35 Or the Provisionals.[2]

But my tentative art
His turned back watches too:
He was blown to bits
Out drinking in a curfew
40 Others obeyed, three nights
After they shot dead
The thirteen men in Derry.
PARAS THIRTEEN, the walls said,
BOGSIDE NIL.[3] That Wednesday
45 Everybody held
His breath and trembled.

### 2

It was a day of cold
Raw silence, wind-blown
Surplice and soutane:[4]
50 Rained-on, flower-laden
Coffin after coffin
Seemed to float from the door
Of the packed cathedral
Like blossoms on slow water.
55 The common funeral
Unrolled its swaddling band,
Lapping, tightening
Till we were braced and bound
Like brothers in a ring.

60 But he would not be held
At home by his own crowd
Whatever threats were phoned,
Whatever black flags waved.
I see him as he turned
65 In that bombed offending place,

---

[1] *your betraying ... railings*  In Belfast, women who kept company with British soldiers were sometimes shaved, stripped, tarred, and handcuffed to railings by the IRA as punishment.

[2] *Provisionals*  Members of the Provisional Branch of the IRA.

[3] *PARAS ... NIL*  I.e., the British Army's Parachute Regiment had killed thirteen people, while the Roman Catholic people of the Bogside district, in Londonderry, had killed none.

[4] *Surplice and soutane*  Vestments worn by the Roman Catholic clergy.

Remorse fused with terror
In his still knowable face,
His cornered outfaced stare
Blinding in the flash.

70  He had gone miles away
For he drank like a fish
Nightly, naturally
Swimming towards the lure
Of warm lit-up places,
75  The blurred mesh and murmur
Drifting among glasses
In the gregarious smoke.
How culpable was he
That last night when he broke
80  Our tribe's complicity?
"Now you're supposed to be
An educated man,"
I hear him say. "Puzzle me
The right answer to that one."

                3

85  I missed his funeral,
Those quiet walkers
And sideways talkers
Shoaling out of his lane
To the respectable
90  Purring of the hearse ...
They move in equal pace
With the habitual
Slow consolation
Of a dawdling engine,
95  The line lifted, hand
Over fist, cold sunshine
On the water, the land
Banked under fog: that morning
I was taken in his boat,
100  The screw° purling, turning                *propeller*
Indolent fathoms white,
I tasted freedom with him.
To get out early, haul
Steadily off the bottom,
105  Dispraise the catch, and smile
As you find a rhythm
Working you, slow mile by mile,
Into your proper haunt

Somewhere, well out, beyond ...

110  Dawn-sniffing revenant,[1]
Plodder through midnight rain,
Question me again.
—1979

## Seeing Things

                1

Inishbofin[2] on a Sunday morning.
Sunlight, turfsmoke,[3] seagulls, boatslip,° diesel.    *deck*
One by one we were being handed down
Into a boat that dipped and shilly-shallied
5  Scaresomely every time. We sat tight
On short cross-benches, in nervous twos and threes,
Obedient, newly close, nobody speaking
Except the boatmen, as the gunwales sank
And seemed they might ship water any minute.
10  The sea was very calm but even so,
When the engine kicked and our ferryman
Swayed for balance, reaching for the tiller,
I panicked at the shiftiness and heft
Of the craft itself. What guaranteed us—
15  That quick response and buoyancy and swim—
Kept me in agony. All the time
As we went sailing evenly across
The deep, still, seeable-down-into water,
It was as if I looked from another boat
20  Sailing through air, far up, and could see
How riskily we fared into the morning,
And loved in vain our bare, bowed, numbered heads.

                2

*Claritas*.[4] The dry-eyed Latin word
Is perfect for the carved stone of the water
25  Where Jesus stands up to his unwet knees
And John the Baptist pours out more water
Over his head: all this in bright sunlight

---

[1]  *revenant*   One who returns to life from the dead.

[2]  *Inishbofin*   Small island west of Ireland.

[3]  *turfsmoke*   Smoke from burning slabs of peat ("turf"), which was used as fuel.

[4]  *Claritas*   Latin: clarity.

On the façade of a cathedral. Lines
Hard and thin and sinuous represent
30 The flowing river. Down between the lines
Little antic fish are all go. Nothing else.
And yet in that utter visibility
The stone's alive with what's invisible:
Waterweed, stirred sand-grains hurrying off,
35 The shadowy, unshadowed stream itself.
All afternoon, heat wavered on the steps
And the air we stood up to our eyes in wavered
Like the zigzag hieroglyph for life itself.

3

Once upon a time my undrowned father
40 Walked into our yard. He had gone to spray
Potatoes in a field on the riverbank
And wouldn't bring me with him. The horse-sprayer
Was too big and newfangled, bluestone°        *copper sulphate*
   might
Burn me in the eyes, the horse was fresh, I
45 Might scare the horse, and so on. I threw stones
At a bird on the shed roof, as much for
The clatter of the stones as anything,
But when he came back, I was inside the house
And saw him out the window, scatter-eyed
50 And daunted, strange without his hat,
His step unguided, his ghosthood immanent.
When he was turning on the riverbank,
The horse had rusted and reared up and pitched
Cart and sprayer and everything off balance,
55 So the whole rig went over into a deep
Whirlpool, hoofs, chains, shafts, cartwheels, barrel
And tackle, all tumbling off the world,
And the hat already merrily swept along
The quieter reaches. That afternoon
60 I saw him face to face, he came to me
With his damp footprints out of the river,
And there was nothing between us there
That might not still be happily ever after.

—1991

## Englands of the Mind[1]

One of the most precise and suggestive of T.S. Eliot's critical formulations was his notion of what he called "the auditory imagination," "the feeling for syllable and rhythm, penetrating far below the conscious levels of thought and feeling, invigorating every word; sinking to the most primitive and forgotten, returning to the origin and bringing something back," fusing "the most ancient and the most civilized mentality."[2] I presume Eliot was thinking here about the cultural depth-charges latent in certain words and rhythms, that binding secret between words in poetry that delights not just the ear but the whole backward and abysm of mind and body; thinking of the energies beating in and between words that the poet brings into half-deliberate play; thinking of the relationship between the word as pure vocable, as articulate noise, and the word as etymological occurrence, as symptom of human history, memory and attachments.

It is in the context of this auditory imagination that I wish to discuss the language of Ted Hughes, Geoffrey Hill, and Philip Larkin.[3] All of them return to an origin and bring something back, all three live off the hump of the English poetic achievement, all three, here and now, in England, imply a continuity with another England, there and then. All three are hoarders and shorers of what they take to be the real England. All three treat England as a region—or rather treat their region as England—in different and complementary ways. I believe they are afflicted with a sense of history that was once the peculiar affliction of the poets of other nations who were not themselves natives of England but who spoke the English language. The poets of the mother culture, I feel, are now possessed of that defensive love of their territory which was once shared only by those poets whom we might call colonial—Yeats, Mac-Diarmid, Carlos Williams.[4] They are aware of their

[1] *Englands of the Mind*   Beckman Lecture given by Heaney at the University of California, Berkeley, May 1976.

[2] *the auditory ... mentality*   From T.S. Eliot, *The Use of Poetry and the Use of Criticism* (1933).

[3] *Ted Hughes ... Larkin*   Three British poets of the twentieth century.

[4] *Yeats*   Irish poet William Butler Yeats (1865–1939);   *Mac-Diarmid*   Hugh MacDiarmid, pen name of Scottish poet Christopher Murray Grieve (1892–1978);   *Carlos Williams*   American poet

Englishness as deposits in the descending storeys of the literary and historical past. Their very terrain is becoming consciously precious. A desire to preserve indigenous traditions, to keep open the imagination's supply lines to the past, to receive from the stations of Anglo-Saxon confirmations of ancestry, to perceive in the rituals of show Saturdays and race-meetings and seaside outings, of church-going and marriages at Whitsun,[1] and in the necessities that crave expression after the ritual of church-going has passed away, to perceive in these a continuity of communal ways, and a confirmation of an identity which is threatened—all this is signified by their language.

When we examine that language, we find that their three separate voices are guaranteed by three separate foundations which, when combined, represent almost the total resources of the English language itself. Hughes relies on the northern deposits, the pagan Anglo-Saxon and Norse elements, and he draws energy also from a related constellation of primitive myths and world views. The life of his language is a persistence of the stark outline and vitality of Anglo-Saxon that became the Middle English alliterative tradition and then went underground to sustain the folk poetry, the ballads, and the ebullience of Shakespeare and the Elizabethans. Hill is also sustained by the Anglo-Saxon base, but his proper guarantor is that language as modified and amplified by the vocabularies and values of the Mediterranean, by the early medieval Latin influence; his is to a certain extent a scholastic imagination founded on an England that we might describe as Anglo-Romanesque, touched by the polysyllabic light of Christianity but possessed by darker energies which might be acknowledged as barbaric. Larkin then completes the picture, because his proper hinterland is the English language Frenchified and turned humanist by the Norman conquest and the Renaissance, made nimble, melodious, and plangent by Chaucer and Spenser, and besomed[2] clean of its inkhornisms[3] and its irrational magics by the eighteenth century.

And their Englands of the mind might be correspondingly characterized. Hughes's is a primeval landscape where stones cry out and horizons endure, where the elements inhabit the mind with a religious force, where the pebble dreams "it is the foetus of God," "where the staring angels go through," "where all the stars bow down," where, with appropriately pre-Socratic[4] force, water lies "at the bottom of all things / utterly worn out utterly clear." It is England as King Lear's heath which now becomes a Yorkshire moor where sheep and foxes and hawks persuade "unaccommodated man" that he is a poor bare forked thing, kinned not in a chain but on a plane of being with the animals themselves. There monoliths and lintels.[5] The air is menaced by God's voice in the wind, by demonic protean crow-shapes; and the poet is a wanderer among the ruins, cut off by catastrophe from consolation and philosophy. Hill's England, on the other hand, is more hospitable to the human presence. The monoliths make way for the keeps[6] and chantries[7] if also for the beheading block. The heath's loneliness is kept at bay by the natural magic of the grove and the intellectual force of the scholar's cell. The poet is not a wanderer but a clerk or perhaps an illuminator or one of a guild of masters: he is in possession of a history rather than a mythology; he has a learned rather than an oral tradition. There are wars, but there are also dynasties, ideas of inheritance and order, possibilities for the "true governaunce of England." His elegies are not laments for the irrevocable dispersal of the *comitatus*[8] and the ring-giver in the hall, but solemn requiems for Plantagenet kings[9] whose murderous wars are set in a great pattern, to be understood only when "the sea / Across daubed rocks evacuates its dead." And Larkin's England similarly reflects features from the period that his language is hived off. His trees and flowers and grasses are neither animistic, nor hallowed by half-remembered druidic lore; they are emblems of mutabilitie. Behind

William Carlos Williams (1883–1963).

[1] *whitsun*   I.e., at Whit Sunday or Whitsuntide, the Pentecost.

[2] *besomed*   Swept.

[3] *inkhornisms*   Pedantic words or expressions.

[4] *pre-Socratic*   Characteristic of the period before the philosopher Socrates (i.e., before the sixth century BCE) and his system of inquiry into the causes of things.

[5] *lintels*   Horizontal support beams over doors and windows.

[6] *keeps*   Medieval strongholds, towers.

[7] *chantries*   Chapels in which priests sing daily mass for the founders.

[8] *comitatus*   Latin: escort; imperial retinue.

[9] *Plantagenet kings*   English dynasty that ruled 1154–1485 (Henry II to Richard III).

them lies the sensibility of troubadour and courtier. "Cut grass lies frail; / Brief is the breath / Mown stalks exhale"; his landscape is dominated neither by the untamed heath nor the totemistic architectures of spire and battlement but by the civic prospects, by roofs and gardens and prospects where urban and pastoral visions interact as "postal districts packed like squares of wheat." The poet is no longer a bardic remnant nor an initiate in curious learning nor a jealous master of the secrets of a craft; he is a humane and civilized member of the customs service or the civil service or, indeed, the library service. The moon is no longer his white goddess but his poetic property, to be image rather than icon: "high and preposterous and separate," she watches over unfenced existence, over fulfilment's desolate attic, over an England of department stores, canals and floatings of industrial froth, explosions in mines, effigies in churches, secretaries in offices; and she hauls tides of life where only one ship is worth celebration, not a Golden Hind or a Victory,[1] but "black- / Sailed unfamiliar, towing at her back / A huge and birdless silence."

Hughes's sensibility is pagan in the original sense: he is a haunter of the *pagus*,[2] a heath-dweller, a heathen; he moves by instinct in the thickets beyond the *urbs*;[3] he is neither urban nor urbane. His poetry is as redolent of the lair as it is of the library. The very titles of his books are casts made into the outback of our animal recognitions. *Lupercal*, a word infested with wolfish stinks yet returning to an origin in Shakespeare's *Julius Caesar*: "You all did see that on the Lupercal / I thrice presented him a kingly crown." Yet the word passes back through Shakespeare into the Lupercal, a cave below the western corner of the Palatine Hill in Rome; and the Lupercal was also the festival held on 15 February when, after the sacrifice of goats and a dog, youths dressed only in girdles made from the skins of these victims ran about the bounds of the Palatine city, striking those whom they met, especially women, with strips of goatskin. It was a fertility rite, and it was also a ritual beating of the bounds of the city, and in a way Hughes's language is just this also. Its sensuous fetch, its redolence of blood and gland and grass and water, recalled English poetry in the fifties from a too suburban aversion of the attention from the elemental; and the poems beat the bounds of a hidden England in streams and trees, on moors and in byres.[4] Hughes appeared like Poor Tom on the heath, a civilized man tasting and testing the primitive facts; he appeared as *Wodwo*, a nosing wild man of the woods. The volume *Wodwo* appeared in 1967 and carried as its epigraph a quotation from *Gawain and the Green Knight*, and that deliberate affiliation is instructive. Like the art of Gawain, Hughes's art is one of clear outline and inner richness. His diction is consonantal, and it snicks through the air like an efficient blade, marking and carving out fast definite shapes; but within those shapes, mysteries and rituals are hinted at. They are circles within which he conjures up presences.

Hughes's vigour has much to do with this matter of consonants that take the measure of his vowels like calipers, or stud the line like rivets. "Everything is inheriting everything," as he says in one of his poems, and what he has inherited through Shakespeare and John Webster and Hopkins and Lawrence[5] is something of that primary life of stress which is the quick of the English poetic matter. His consonants are the Norsemen, the Normans, the Roundheads[6] in the world of his vocables, hacking and hedging and hammering down the abundance and luxury and possible lasciviousness of the vowels. "I imagine this midnight moment's forest"—the first line of the well-known "The Thought Fox"—is hushed, but it is a hush achieved by the quelling, battening-down action of the m's and d's and t's: I iMagine this MiDnighT MoMenT's foresT. Hughes's aspiration in these early poems is to command all the elements, to bring them within the jurisdiction of his authoritarian voice. And in "The Thought Fox" the thing at the beginning of the poem which lives beyond his jurisdiction is characteristically fluid and vowelling and sibilant: "Something else is alive" whispers of a

[1] *Golden Hind* Ship captained by Sir Francis Drake that circumnavigated the globe (1577–80); *Victory* Flagship of Admiral Lord Nelson in the Battle of Trafalgar (1805).

[2] *pagus* Latin: countryside.

[3] *urbs* Latin: city.

[4] *byres* Cow-houses.

[5] *John Webster* Jacobean dramatist John Webster (1580–1625); *Hopkins* Poet Gerard Manley Hopkins (1844–89); *Lawrence* Novelist D.H. Lawrence (1885–1930).

[6] *Roundheads* Members or supporters of the seventeenth-century Parliamentary Party before and during the Civil War; i.e., Puritans.

presence not yet accounted for, a presence that is granted its full vowel music as its epiphany—"Something more near / Though deeper within darkness / Is entering the loneliness." It is granted this dilation of its mystery before it is conjured into the possession of the poet-warden, the vowel-keeper; and its final emergence in the fully sounded i's and e's of "an eye, / A widening deepening greenness," is gradually mastered by the braking action of "brilliantly, concentratedly," and by the shooting of the monosyllabic consonantal bolts in the last stanza:

> Till, with a sudden sharp hot stink of fox
> It enters the dark hole of the head.
> The window is starless still; the clock ticks,
> The page is printed.

Next a poem whose subject might be expected to woo the tender pious vowels from a poet rather than the disciplining consonants. About a "Fern":

> Here is the fern's frond, unfurling a gesture,

The first line is an Anglo-Saxon line, four stresses, three of them picked out by alliteration; and although the frosty grip of those f's thaws out, the fern is still subsumed into images of control and discipline and regal authority:

> And, among them, the fern
> Dances gravely, like the plume
> Of a warrior returning, under the low hills,
>
> Into his own kingdom.

But of course we recognize that Hughes's "Thistles" are vegetation more kindred to his spirit than the pliant fern. And when he turns his attention to them, they become reincarnations of the Norsemen in a poem entitled "The Warriors of the North":

> Bringing their frozen swords, their salt-bleached eyes, their salt-bleached hair,
> The snow's stupefied anvils in rows,
> Bringing their envy,
> The slow ships feelered Southward, snails over the steep

sheen of the water-globe

and he imagines them resurrected in all their arctic mail "into the iron arteries of Calvin," and into "Thistles." The thistles are emblems of the Hughes voice as I see it, born of an original vigour, fighting back over the same ground; and it is not insignificant that in this poem Hughes himself imagines the thistles as images of a fundamental speech, uttering itself in gutturals from behind the sloped arms of consonants:

> Every one a revengeful burst
> Of resurrection, a grasped fistful
> Of splintered weapons and Icelandic frost thrust up
>
> From the underground stain of a decayed Viking.
> They are like pale hair and the gutturals of dialects.
> Every one manages a plume of blood.
>
> Then they grow grey, like men.
> Mown down, it is a feud. Their sons appear,
> Stiff with weapons, fighting back over the same ground.

The gutturals of dialects, which Hughes here connects with the Nordic stratum of English speech, he pronounces in another place to be the germinal secret of his own voice. In an interview published in the *London Magazine* in January 1971 he said:

> I grew up in West Yorkshire. They have a very distinctive dialect there. Whatever other speech you grow into, presumably your dialect stays alive in a sort of inner freedom ... it's your childhood self there inside the dialect and that is possibly your real self or the core of it. ... Without it, I doubt if I would ever have written verse. And in the case of the West Yorkshire dialect, of course, it connects you directly and in your most intimate self to Middle English poetry.

In other words he finds that the original grain of his speech is a chip off the old block and that his work need not be a new planting but a new bud on an old bough. What other poet would have the boldness to entitle a collection *Wodwo*? Yet *Gawain and the Green Knight*, with its beautiful alliterating and illuminated form, its interlacing and trellising of natural life and mythic life, is probably closer in spirit to Hughes's poetry than Hughes's poetry is to that of his English contemporaries. Everything inherits everything—and Hughes is the rightful heir to this alliterative tradition, and to the cleaving simplicity of the Border ballad, which he elevates to the status of touchstone later in that same interview. He says that he started writing again in 1955:

> The poems that set me off were odd pieces by Shapiro, Lowell, Merwin, Wilbur and Crowe Ransom.[1] Crowe Ransom was the one who gave me a model I felt I could use. He helped me get my words into focus. ... But this whole business of influences is mysterious. ... And after all the campaigns to make it new you're stuck with the fact that some of the Scots Border ballads still cut a deeper groove than anything written in the last forty years. Influences just seem to make it more and more unlikely that a poet will write what he alone could write.

What Hughes alone could write depended for its release on the discovery of a way to undam the energies of the dialect, to get a stomping ground for that inner freedom, to get that childhood self a disguise to roam at large in. Freedom and naturalness and homeliness are positives in Hughes's critical vocabulary, and they are linked with both the authenticity of individual poets and the genius of the language itself. Speaking of Keith Douglas[2] in 1964, Hughes could have been speaking of himself; of the way his language and his imagination alerted themselves when the hunt for the poem in the adult world became synonymous with the hunt for the animal in the world of childhood, the world of dialect:

> The impression is of a sudden mobilizing of the poet's will, a clearing of his vision, as if from sitting considering possibilities and impossibilities he stood up to act. Pictures of things no longer interest him much: he wants their substance, their nature and their consequences in life. At once, and quite suddenly, his mind is whole. ... He is a renovator of

language. It is not that he uses words in jolting combinations, or with titanic extravagance, or curious precision. His triumph is in the way he renews the simplicity of ordinary talk. ... The music that goes along with this ... is the natural path of such confident, candid thinking. ... A utility general purpose style that combines a colloquial prose readiness with poetic breadth, a ritual intensity of music with clear direct feeling, and yet in the end is nothing but casual speech.

This combination of ritual intensity, prose readiness, direct feeling, and casual speech can be discovered likewise in the best poems of *Lupercal*, because in *Hawk in the Rain* and indeed in much of *Wodwo* and *Crow*, we are often in the presence of that titanic extravagance Hughes mentions, speech not so much mobilizing and standing up to act as flexing and straining until it verges on the grotesque. But in poems like "Pike," "Hawk Roosting," "The Bull Moses," and "An Otter" we get this confident, speedy, hammer-and-tongs proficiency. And in this poem from *Wodwo*, called "Pibroch," a poem uniquely Hughesian in its very title, fetching energy and ancestry from what is beyond the Pale[3] and beneath the surface, we have the elements of the Scottish piper's *ceol mor*,[4] the high style, implicit in words like "dead," "heaven," "universe," "aeon," "angels," and in phrases like "the foetus of God," "the stars bow down"—a phrase which cunningly makes its cast and raises Blake in the pool of the ear. We have elements of this high style, ritual intensity, whatever you want to call it; and we have also the "prose readiness," the "casual speech" of "bored," "hangs on," "lets up," "tryout," and the workaday cadences of "Over the stone rushes the wind," and "her mind's gone completely." The landscape of the poem is one that the Anglo-Saxon wanderer or seafarer would be completely at home in:

> The sea cries with its meaningless voice
> Treating alike its dead and its living,
> Probably bored with the appearance of heaven
> After so many millions of nights without sleep,
> Without purpose, without self-deception.

---

[1] *Shapiro ... Ransom*  Karl Shapiro, Robert Lowell, W.S. Merwin, Richard Wilbur, and John Crowe Ransom—all twentieth-century American poets.

[2] *Keith Douglas*  British poet (1920–44).

[3] *beyond the Pale*  I.e., outside the bounds of acceptable behavior.

[4] *ceol mor*  Gaelic: the great music. Classical Scottish music played exclusively on the great highland bagpipe.

Stone likewise. A pebble is imprisoned
Like nothing in the Universe.
Created for black sleep. Or growing
Conscious of the sun's red spot occasionally,
Then dreaming it is the foetus of God.

Over the stone rushes the wind
Able to mingle with nothing,
Like the hearing of the blind stone itself.
Or turns, as if the stone's mind came feeling
A fantasy of directions.

Drinking the sea and eating the rock
A tree struggles to make leaves—
An old woman fallen from space
Unprepared for these conditions.
She hangs on, because her mind's gone completely.

Minute after minute, aeon after aeon,
Nothing lets up or develops.
And this is neither a bad variant nor a tryout.
This is where the staring angels go through.
This is where all the stars bow down.

Hughes attempts to make vocal the inner life, the simple being-thereness, "the substance, nature and consequences in life" of sea, stone, wind and tree. Blake's pebble and tiger[1] are shadowy presences in the background, as are the landscapes of Anglo-Saxon poetry. And the whole thing is founded on rock, that rock which Hughes presented in his autobiographical essay as his birthstone, holding his emergence in place just as his headstone will hold his decease:

This was the *memento mundi*[2] over my birth: my spiritual midwife at the time and my godfather ever since—or one of my godfathers. From my first day it watched. If it couldn't see me direct, a towering gloom over my pram, it watched me through a species of periscope: that is, by infiltrating the very light of my room with its particular shadow. From my home near the bottom of the south-facing slope of the valley, the cliff was both the curtain and

backdrop to existence.

I quote this piece because it links the childhood core with the adult opus, because that rock is the equivalent in his poetic landscape of dialect in his poetic speech. The rock persists, survives, sustains, endures and informs his imagination, just as it is the bedrock of the language upon which Hughes founds his version of survival and endurance. …

Finally, to come to Larkin, where what accrues in the language is not "a golden and stinking blaze," not the rank and fermenting composts of philology and history, but the bright senses of words worn clean in literate conversation. In Larkin's language as in his vision of water, "any angled light … congregate[s] endlessly." There is a gap in Larkin between the perceiver and the thing perceived, a refusal to melt through long perspectives, an obstinate insistence that the poet is neither a race memory nor a myth-kitty nor a mason, but a real man in a real place. The cadences and vocabulary of his poems are tuned to a rational music. It would seem that he has deliberately curtailed his gift for evocation, for resonance, for symbolist *frissons*. He turned from Yeats to Hardy as his master. He never followed the Laurentian success of his early poem "Wedding Wind" which ends with a kind of biblical swoon, an image of fulfilled lovers "kneeling like cattle by all generous waters." He rebukes romantic aspiration and afflatus with a scrupulous meanness. If he sees the moon, he sees it while groping back to bed after a piss. If he is forced to cry out "O wolves of memory, immensements," he is also forced to recognize that he is past all that swaddling of sentiment, even if it is "for others, undiminished, somewhere." "Undiminished"—the word, with its hovering balance between attenuated possibilities and the possibility of amplitude, is typical. And Christopher Ricks[3] has pointed out how often negatives operate in Larkin's best lines. Lovers talking in bed, for example, discover it ever more difficult

> to find
> Words at once true and kind,
> Or not untrue and not unkind.

His tongue moves hesitantly, precisely, honestly, among ironies and negatives. He is the poet of rational light, a light that has its own luminous beauty but which has also the effect of exposing clearly the truths which it

---

[1]  *Blake's … tiger*  See William Blake's "The Clod & the Pebble" and "The Tyger," from *Songs of Innocence and Experience* (1789).

[2]  *memento mundi*  Latin: reminder of the world.

[3]  *Christopher Ricks*  Renowned British scholar and literary critic (b. 1933).

touches. Larkin speaks neither a dialect nor a pulpit language; there are no "hectoring large scale verses" in his three books, nor is there the stubbly intimacy of "oath-edged talk and pipe-smoke" which he nostalgically annotates among the miners. His language would have pleased those Tudor and Augustan guardians who wanted to polish and beautify their speech, to smooth it for art. What we hear is a stripped standard English voice, a voice indeed with a unique break and remorseful tone, but a voice that leads back neither to the thumping beat of Anglo-Saxon nor to the Gregorian chant of the Middle Ages. Its ancestry begins, in fact, when the Middle Ages are turning secular, and plays begin to take their place beside the Mass as a form of communal telling and knowing. In the first few lines of Larkin's poem "Money," for example, I think I hear the cadences of *Everyman*,[1] the querulous tones of Riches reproaching the hero:

> Quarterly, is it, money reproaches me:
>     "Why do you let me lie here wastefully?
> I am all you never had of goods and sex.
>     You could get them still just by writing a few cheques."

Those endstopped lines, sliding down to rhymed conclusions, suggest the beginning of that period out of which Larkin's style arises. After *Everyman*, there is Skelton,[2] a common-sensical wobble of rhyme, a humorous wisdom, a practical lyricism:

> Oh, no one can deny
> That Arnold is less selfish than I.
> He married a wife to stop her getting away
> Now she's there all day, ...

There is as well the Cavalier[3] Larkin, the maker of songs, where the conversational note and the dainty disciplines of a metrical form are in beautiful equilibrium:

Yet still the unresting castles thresh
In fullgrown thickness every May.
Last year is dead, they seem to say.
Begin afresh, afresh, afresh.

Even in that short space, by the way, one can see the peculiar Larkin fusion of parsimony and abundance—the gorgeousness of "unresting castles," the poignant sweetness of "afresh, afresh" are held in check by the quotidian "last year is dead." Yet it is by refusing to pull out the full stops, or by almost refusing, that Larkin gains his own brand of negative capability.

As well as the Cavalier Larkin, there is a late Augustan[4] Larkin, the poet of decorous melancholy moods, of twilit propriety and shadowy melody. His poem about superannuated racehorses, for example, entitled "At Grass," could well be subtitled, "An Elegy in a Country Paddock." Behind the trees where the horses shelter there could well rise the spire of Stoke Poges church;[5] and behind the smooth numbers of wind distressing the tails and manes, there is the donnish exactitude of tresses being *dis*tressed:

> The eye can hardly pick them out
> From the cold shade they shelter in
> Till wind distresses tail and mane ...

And when, at the conclusion of the poem, "the groom and the groom's boy / With bridles in the evening come," their footsteps surely echo the ploughman homeward plodding his weary way. There is, moreover, a Tennysonian Larkin and a Hardy-esque Larkin. There is even, powerfully, an Imagist Larkin:

> There is an evening coming in
> Across the fields, one never seen before,
> That lights no lamps.
>
> Silken it seems at a distance, yet
> When it is drawn up over the knees and breast
> It brings no comfort.

---

[1] *Everyman*   Fifteenth-century morality play.

[2] *Skelton*   I.e., Skeltonesque; resembling the work of John Skelton (c. 1460–1529).

[3] *Cavalier*   Cavaliers were supporters of the Stuart monarchy during the political unrest of the mid-seventeenth century; i.e., a courtly poet.

[4] *Augustan*   I.e., characteristic of an eighteenth-century poet.

[5] *Stoke Poges church*   Church of Stoke Poges, Buckinghamshire, the churchyard of which is believed to be the setting of Thomas Gray's famous poem "Elegy Written in a Country Churchyard" (1751).

Where has the tree gone, that locked
Earth to the sky? What is under my hands,
That I cannot feel?

What loads my hands down?

Then there is Larkin, the coiner of compounds—which
we may choose to call Hopkinsian or even perhaps,
briefly, Shakespearean—who writes of "some lonely
rain-ceased midsummer evening," of "light unanswerable and tall and wide," of "the million-petalled flower
of being here," of "thin continuous dreaming," and
"wasteful, weak, propitiatory flowers."

    And to go from the sublime to the ridiculous, there
is the seaside-postcard Larkin, as true to the streak of
vulgarity in the civilization as he is sensitive to its most
delicious refinements: "Get stewed: / Books are a load of
crap." Or get this disfigurement of a poster of a bathing
beauty:

    Huge tits and a fissured crotch
    Were scored well in, and the space
    Between her legs held scrawls
    That set her fairly astride
    A tuberous cock and balls.

And then, elsewhere,

    They fuck you up, your mum and dad.
    They may not mean to but they do.
    They fill you with the faults they had
    And add some extra, just for you.

And again, in "Sad Steps":

    Groping back to bed after a piss
    I part thick curtains, and am startled by
    The rapid clouds, the moon's cleanliness.

But despite the piss, and the snigger of the demotic in
all of these places, that title, "Sad Steps," reminds us
that Larkin is solicitous for his Sidney[1] also. He too
returns to origins and brings something back, although
he does not return to "roots." He puts inverted commas
round his "roots," in fact. His childhood, he says, was a

forgotten boredom. He sees England from train windows, fleeting past and away. He is urban modern man,
the insular Englishman, responding to the tones of his
own clan, ill at ease when out of his environment. He is
a poet, indeed, of composed and tempered English
nationalism, and his voice is the not untrue, not unkind
voice of post-war England, where the cloth cap and the
royal crown have both lost some of their potent symbolism, and the categorical, socially defining functions of
the working-class accent and the aristocratic drawl have
almost been eroded. Larkin's tones are mannerly but not
exquisite, well-bred but not mealy-mouthed. If his
England and his English are not as deep as Hughes's or
as solemn as Hill's, they are nevertheless dearly beloved,
and during his sojourn in Belfast in the late fifties, he
gave thanks, by implication, for the nurture that he
receives by living among his own. The speech, the
customs, the institutions of England are, in the words of
another English poet, domiciled in Ireland, "wife to his
creating thought." That was Hopkins in Dublin in the
1880s, sensing that his individual talent was being
divorced from his tradition. Here is Larkin remembering the domicile in Belfast in the 1950s:

    Lonely in Ireland, since it was not home,
    Strangeness made sense. The salt rebuff of speech,
    Insisting so on difference, made me welcome:
    Once that was recognised, we were in touch.

    Their draughty streets, end-on to hills, the faint
    Archaic smell of dockland, like a stable,
    The herring-hawker's cry, dwindling, went
    To prove me separate, not unworkable.

    Living in England has no such excuse:
    These are my customs and establishments
    It would be much more serious to refuse.
    Here no elsewhere underwrites my existence.

Larkin's England of the mind is in many ways continuous with the England of Rupert Brooke's "Grantchester"
and Edward Thomas's "Adlestrop," an England of
customs and institutions, industrial and domestic, but
also an England whose pastoral hinterland is threatened
by the very success of those institutions. Houses and

---

[1] *Sidney*   Poet Sir Philip Sidney (1154–86).

roads and factories mean that a certain England is "Going, Going":

It seems, just now,
To be happening so very fast;
Despite all the land left free
For the first time I feel somehow
That it isn't going to last,

That before I snuff it, the whole
Boiling will be bricked in
Except for the tourist parts—
First slum of Europe: a role
It won't be so hard to win,
With a cast of crooks and tarts.

And that will be England gone,
The shadows, the meadows, the lanes,
The guildhalls, the carved choirs.
There'll be books; it will linger on
In galleries; but all that remains
For us will be concrete and tyres.

I think that sense of an ending has driven all three of these writers into a kind of piety towards their local origins, has made them look in, rather than up, to England. The loss of imperial power, the failure of economic nerve, the diminished influence of Britain inside Europe, all this has led to a new sense of the shires, a new valuing of the native English experience. Donald Davie, for example, has published a book of poems, with that very title, *The Shires*, which attempts to annex to his imagination by personal memory or historical meditation or literary connections, each shire of England. It is a book at once intimate and exclusive, a topography of love and impatience, and it is yet another symptom that English poets are being forced to explore not just the matter of England, but what is the matter with England. I have simply presumed to share in that exploration through the medium which England has, for better or worse, impressed upon us all, the English language itself.

—1980

# ALICE MUNRO
## b. 1931

Alice Munro's reputation as a writer of short fiction has grown steadily since the publication of her first volume of stories in 1968; upon the publication of her most recent collection Jonathan Franzen suggested in *The New York Review of Books* that Munro "has a strong claim to being the best fiction writer now working in North America," and the *Atlantic Monthly*'s reviewer described her as "the living writer most likely to be read in a hundred years."

Alice Munro was born into a farming community in Wingham, Huron County, Ontario. The landscape of south-western Ontario would later appear as the setting in many of her short stories. Her father's fox fur business was unsuccessful and the family found itself in an awkward position: they were not rich enough to belong to the elite of the town, but because of their education, they did not quite fit elsewhere. Munro has described the characters with whom she came into social contact as "a community of outcasts," saying that she "was always an outsider, and you just couldn't ask for a better beginning for a writer."

After graduating from high school, Munro won a partial scholarship to attend the University of Western Ontario where she completed two years towards a degree in English. It was while she was there that she had her first story published in the university magazine. Due to strained finances, she was not able to complete her degree. She married and moved with her husband to Vancouver, British Columbia in 1951, where the couple would eventually have three daughters. Munro has often commented that the genre of the short story was well-suited to a working mother who could only snatch moments of time in which to write while taking care of her family. During the 1950s and 1960s she published stories at the rate of one or two a year, in publications such as *Chatelaine* and *The Tamarack Review*. Munro lived for some time during these years in Victoria—of all Canadian cities the most English in character—where, in addition to raising a family, she and her husband also operated a bookstore, Munro's Books. These years in British Columbia have continued to provide raw material for some of Munro's best fiction, perhaps most notably in the linked stories "Chance," "Soon," and "Silence" (2004).

In 1968, Munro's growing reputation as a short story writer led Ryerson Press to request that she gather some of her stories for a collection; this was the genesis of *Dance of the Happy Shades*, for which she would win her first Governor General's Award. In 1971, she published *The Lives of Girls and Women*, a collection of interlinked stories. The collection charts the development of the young Del Jordan as she grows up in the constricting atmosphere of the small town of Jubilee; Munro later commented that the novel "is autobiographical in form but not in fact."

Munro moved back to southwestern Ontario in 1973 after the dissolution of her marriage. She taught at York University, and later at the University of Western Ontario. She continued to write and publish, and began a longstanding connection with the *The New Yorker*, which would eventually publish many of her stories. The publication of the collection *Who Do You Think You Are?* would result in Munro's second Governor General's Award; the book was also shortlisted for the Booker Prize in 1978. Munro won her third Governor General's Award in 1986 for *The Progress of Love*. Her more recent works include *Friend of My Youth* (1990), *The Love of a Good Woman* (1998), and *Hateship, Friendship, Courtship, Loveship, Marriage* (2001), and *Runaway* (2005). Munro's later stories are often longer and more complex than her earlier works—her 2005 story "The View from Castle Rock," which explores the immigrant experience, is a case in point—but she has retained a keen eye for detail and a fine sense of emotional nuance. Among her many awards are the W.H. Smith Literary Award in Britain, the National Book Critics Circle Award in the United States, and two Giller Prizes in Canada.

⌘ ⌘ ⌘

## The View from Castle Rock

On a visit to Edinburgh with his father when he is nine or ten years old, Andrew finds himself climbing the damp, uneven stone steps of the Castle. His father is in front of him, some other men behind—it's a wonder how many friends his father has found, standing in cubbyholes where there are bottles set on planks, in the High Street—until at last they crawl out on a shelf of rock, from which the land falls steeply away. It has just stopped raining, the sun is shining on a silvery stretch of water far ahead of them, and beyond that is a pale green and grayish-blue land, a land as light as mist, sucked into the sky.

"America," his father tells them, and one of the men says that you would never have known it was so near.

"It is the effect of the height we are on," another says.

"There is where every man is sitting in the midst of his own properties and even the beggars is riding around in carriages," Andrew's father says, paying no attention to them. "So there you are, my lad"—he turns to Andrew—"and God grant that one day you will see it closer, and I will myself, if I live."

Andrew has an idea that there is something wrong with what his father is saying, but he is not well enough acquainted with geography to know that they are looking at Fife. He does not know if the men are mocking his father or if his father is playing a trick on them. Or if it is a trick at all.

Some years later, in the harbor of Leith,[1] on the fourth of June, 1818, Andrew and his father—whom I must call Old James, because there is a James in every generation—and Andrew's pregnant wife, Agnes, his brother Walter, his sister Mary, and also his son James, who is not yet two years old, set foot on board a ship for the first time in their lives.

Old James makes this fact known to the ship's officer who is checking off the names.

"The first time, serra, in all my long life. We are men of the Ettrick.[2] It is a landlocked part of the world."

The officer says a word which is unintelligible to them but plain in meaning. *Move along.* He has run a line through their names. They move along or are pushed along, Young James riding on Mary's hip.

"What is this?" Old James says, regarding the crowd of people on deck. "Where are we to sleep? Where have all these rabble come from? Look at the faces on them—are they the blackamoors?"[3]

"Black Highlanders, more like," Walter says. This is a joke, muttered so that his father cannot hear, Highlanders being one of the sorts the old man despises.

"There are too many people," his father continues. "The ship will sink."

"No," Walter says, speaking up now. "Ships do not often sink because of too many people. That's what the fellow was there for, to count the people."

Barely on board the vessel and this seventeen-year-old whelp has taken on knowing airs; he has taken to contradicting his father. Fatigue, astonishment, and the weight of the greatcoat he is wearing prevent Old James from cuffing him.

The business of life aboard ship has already been

---

[1] *Leith*  Harbor town adjoining Edinburgh.

[2] *Ettrick*  Located in the Scottish borderlands.

[3] *blackamoors*  Appellation formerly used to describe any black African person.

explained to the family. In fact, it has been explained by the old man himself. He was the one who knew all about provisions, accommodations, and the kinds of people you would find on board. All Scotsmen and all decent folk. No Highlanders, no Irish.

But now he cries out that it is like the swarm of bees in the carcass of the lion.

"An evil lot, an evil lot. Oh, that ever we left our native land."

"We have not left yet," Andrew says. "We are still looking at Leith. We would do best to go below and find ourselves a place."

More lamentation. The bunks are narrow planks with horsehair pallets that are both hard and prickly.

"Better than nothing," Andrew says.

"Oh, that ever I was enticed to bring us here, onto this floating sepulchre."

Will nobody shut him up? Agnes thinks. This is the way he will go on and on, like a preacher or a lunatic, when the fit takes him. She cannot abide it. She is in more agony herself than he is ever likely to know.

"Well, are we going to settle here or are we not?" she says.

Some people have hung up their plaids[1] or shawls to make a half-private space for their families. She goes ahead and takes off her outer wrappings to do the same.

The child is turning somersaults in her belly. Her face is hot as a coal, her legs throb, and the swollen flesh in between them—the lips the child must soon part to get out—is a scalding sack of pain.

Her mother would have known what to do about that. She would have known which leaves to mash to make a soothing poultice. At the thought of her mother such misery overcomes her that she wants to kick somebody.

Why does Andrew not speak plainly to his father, reminding him of whose idea it was, who harangued and borrowed and begged to get them just where they are now? Andrew will not do it, Walter will only joke, and as for Mary she can hardly get her voice out of her throat in her father's presence.

Agnes comes from a large Hawick family of weavers, who work in the mills now but worked for generations at home. Working there they learned the art of cutting

one another down to size, of squabbling and surviving in close quarters. She is still surprised by the rigid manners, the deference and silences in her husband's family. She thought from the beginning that they were a queer sort and she thinks so still. They are as poor as her own folk but they have such a great notion of themselves. And what have they got to back it up?

Mary has taken Young James back up to the deck. She could tell that he was frightened down there in the half-dark. He does not have to whimper or complain—she knows his feelings by the way he digs his little knees into her.

The sails are furled tight. "Look up there, look up there," Mary says, and points to a sailor who is busy high up in the rigging. The boy on her hip makes his sound for bird—"peep." "Sailor-peep, sailor-peep," she says. She and he communicate in a half-and-half language—half her teaching and half his invention. She believes that he is one of the cleverest children ever born into the world. Being the eldest of her family, and the only girl, she has tended to all her brothers, and been proud of them all at one time, but she has never known a child like this. Nobody else has any idea how original and independent he is. Men have no interest in children so young, and Agnes, his mother, has no patience with him.

"Talk like folk," Agnes tells him, and if he doesn't she gives him a clout. "What are you?" she says. "Are you a folk or an elfit?"

Mary fears Agnes's temper, but in a way she doesn't blame her. She thinks that women like Agnes—men's women, mother women—lead an appalling life. First with what the men do to them—even as good a man as Andrew—and then with what the children do, coming out. She will never forget the way her own mother lay in bed, out of her mind with a fever, not knowing anyone, till she died, three days after Walter was born. She screamed at the black pot hanging over the fire, thinking it was full of devils.

Mary—her brothers call her "poor Mary"—is under five feet tall and has a tight little face with a lump of protruding chin, and skin that is subject to fiery eruptions that take a long time to fade. When she is spoken to, her mouth twitches as if the words were all mixed up

---

[1]    *plaids*    Woolen scarves used as cloaks.

with her spittle and her crooked teeth, and the response she manages is a dribble of speech so faint and scrambled that it is hard for people not to think her dim-witted. She has great difficulty looking anybody in the eyes—even the members of her own family. It is only when she gets the boy hitched onto the narrow shelf of her hip that she is capable of some coherent and decisive speech—and then it is mostly to him.

She hears the cow bawling before she can see it. Then she looks up and sees the brown beast dangling in the air, all caged in ropes and kicking and roaring frantically. It is held by a hook on a crane, which now hauls it out of sight. People around her are hooting and clapping their hands. A child cries out, wanting to know if the cow will be dropped into the sea. A man tells him no—she will go along with them on the ship.

"Will they milk her, then?"

"Aye. Keep still. They'll milk her," the man says reprovingly. And another man's voice climbs boisterously over his.

"They'll milk her till they take the hammer to her, and then ye'll have the blood pudding for yer dinner."

Now follow the hens, swung through the air in crates, all squawking and fluttering in their confinement and pecking one another when they can, so that some feathers escape and float down through the air. And after them a pig trussed up like the cow, squealing with a human note in its distress and shifting wildly in midair, so that howls of both delight and outrage rise below, depending on whether they come from those who are hit or those who see others hit.

James is laughing, too. He recognizes shite, and cries out his own word for it, which is "gruggin."

Someday he may remember this, Mary thinks. *I saw a cow and a pig fly through the air.* Then he may wonder if it was a dream. And nobody will be there—she certainly won't—to tell him that it was not, that it happened on this ship. It's possible that he will never see a ship like this again in all his waking life. She has no idea where they will go when they reach the other shore, but she imagines that it will be someplace inland, among the hills, someplace like the Ettrick.

She does not think that she will live long, wherever they go. She coughs in the summer as well as the winter,

and when she coughs her chest aches. She suffers from sties, and cramps in the stomach, and her bleeding comes rarely but may last a month when it does. She hopes, though, that she will not die while James is still in need of her, which he will be for a while yet. She knows that the time will come when he will turn away, as her brothers did, when he will become ashamed of the connection with her. At least, that is what she tells herself will happen, but like anybody in love she cannot believe it.

On a trip to Peebles, Walter bought himself a notebook to write in, but for several days he has found too much to pay attention to and too little space or quiet on the deck even to open it. Finally, after some investigating, he has discovered a favorable spot, near the cabins on the upper deck.

> We came on board on the 4th day of June and lay the 5th, 6th, 7th, and 8th in the Leith roads getting the ship to a place where we could set sail, which was on the 9th. We passed the corner of Fifeshire all well nothing occurring worth mentioning till this day the 13th in the morning when we were awakened by a cry, John o'Groat's House. We could see it plain and had a fine sail across the Pentland Firth having both wind and tide in our favour and it was in no way dangerous as we had heard tell. There was a child had died, the name of Ormiston and its body was thrown overboard sewed up in a piece of canvas with a large lump of coal at its feet.

He pauses in his writing to think of the weighted sack falling down through the water. Would the piece of coal do its job, would the sack fall straight down to the very bottom of the sea? Or would the current of the sea be strong enough to keep lifting it up and letting it fall, pushing it sideways, taking it as far as Greenland or south to the tropical waters full of rank weeds, the Sargasso Sea? Or might some ferocious fish come along and rip the sack and make a meal of the body before it had even left the upper waters and the region of light?

He pictures it now—the child being eaten. Not swallowed whole as in the case of Jonah but chewed into bits as he himself would chew a tasty chunk from a boiled sheep. But there is the matter of a soul. The soul leaves the body at the moment of death. But from which part of the body does it leave? The best guess seems to be that it emerges with the last breath, having been hidden somewhere in the chest, around the place of the heart and the lungs. Though Walter has heard a joke they used to tell about an old fellow in the Ettrick, to the effect that he was so dirty that when he died his soul came out his arsehole, and was heard to do so with a mighty explosion.

This is the sort of information that preachers might be expected to give you—not mentioning anything like an arsehole, of course, but explaining something of the proper location and exit. Yet they shy away from it. Also they cannot explain—at least, he has never heard one explain—how the souls maintain themselves outside of bodies until the Day of Judgment and how on that day each one finds and recognizes the body that is its own and reunites with it, though it be not so much as a skeleton at that time. *Though it be dust.* There must be some who have studied enough to know how all this is accomplished. But there are also some—he has learned this recently—who have studied and read and thought till they have come to the conclusion that there are no souls at all. No one cares to speak about these people, either, and indeed the thought of them is terrible. How can they live with the fear—indeed, the certainty—of Hell before them?

On the third day aboard ship Old James gets up and starts to walk around. After that, he stops and speaks to anybody who seems ready to listen. He tells his name, and says that he comes from Ettrick, from the Valley and Forest of Ettrick, where the old kings of Scotland used to hunt.

"And on the field at Flodden," he says, "after the battle of Flodden, they said you could walk up and down among the corpses and pick out the men from the Ettrick, because they were the tallest and the strongest and the finest-looking men on the ground. I have five sons and they are all good strong lads, but only two of them are with me. One of my sons is in Nova Scotia. The last I heard of him he was in a place called Economy, but we have not had any word of him since and I do not know whether he is alive or dead. My eldest son went off to work in the Highlands, and the son that is next to the youngest took it into his head to go off there, too, and I will never see either of them again. Five sons and, by the mercy of God, all grew to be men, but it was not the Lord's will that I should keep them with me. A man's life is full of sorrow. I have a daughter as well, the oldest of them all, but she is nearly a dwarf. Her mother was chased by a ram when she was carrying her."

On the afternoon of the 14th a wind from the North and the ship began to shake as if every board that was in it would fly loose from every other. The buckets overflowed from the people that were sick and vomiting and there was the contents of them slipping all over the deck. All people were ordered below but many of them crumpled up against the rail and did not care if they were washed over. None of our family was sick however and now the wind has dropped and the sun has come out and those who did not care if they died in the filth a little while ago have got up and dragged themselves to be washed where the sailors are splashing buckets of water over the decks. The women are busy too washing and rinsing and wringing out all the foul clothing. It is the worst misery and the suddenest recovery I have seen ever in my life.

A young girl ten or twelve years old stands watching Walter write. She is wearing a fancy dress and bonnet and has light-brown curly hair. Not so much a pretty face as a pert one.

"Are you from one of the cabins?" she says.

Walter says, "No. I am not."

"I knew you were not. There are only four of them, and one is for my father and me and one is for the captain and one is for his mother, and she never comes out, and one is for the two ladies. You are not supposed to be on this part of the deck unless you are from one of the cabins."

"Well, I did not know that," Walter says, but does not bestir himself to move away.

"I have seen you before writing in your book."

"I haven't seen you."

"No. You were writing, so you didn't notice. I haven't told anybody about you," she adds carelessly, as if that were a matter of choice and she might well change her mind.

When she leaves, Walter adds a sentence.

> And this night in the year 1818 we lost sight of Scotland.

The words seem majestic to him. He is filled with a sense of grandeur, solemnity, and personal importance.

> 16th was a very windy day with the wind coming out of the SW the sea was running very high and the ship got her gib-boom broken on account of the violence of the wind. And our sister Agnes was taken into the cabin.

"Sister," he has written, as if she were all the same to him as poor Mary, but that is not the case. Agnes is a tall well-built girl with thick dark hair and dark eyes. The flush on one of her cheeks slides into a splotch of pale brown as big as a handprint. It is a birthmark, which people say is a pity, because without it she would be handsome. Walter can hardly bear looking at it, but this is not because it is ugly. It is because he longs to touch it, to stroke it with the tips of his fingers. It looks not like ordinary skin but like the velvet on a deer. His feelings about her are so troubling that he can speak to her only unpleasantly, if he speaks at all. And she pays him back with a good seasoning of contempt.

Agnes thinks that she is in the water and the waves are heaving her up and slamming her down. Every time they slap her down it is worse than the time before, and she sinks farther and deeper, the moment of relief passing before she can grab it, for the next wave is already gathering its power to hit her.

Then sometimes she knows that she is in a bed, a strange bed and strangely soft, but it is all the worse for that because when she sinks down there is no resistance, no hard place where the pain has to stop. People keep rushing back and forth in front of her. They are all seen sideways and all transparent, talking very fast so she can't make them out, and maliciously taking no heed of her. She sees Andrew in the midst of them, and two or three of his brothers. Some of the girls she knows are there, too—the friends she used to lark around with in

Hawick. And they do not give a poor penny for the plight she is in now.

She never knew before that she had so many enemies. They are grinding her down and pretending they don't even know it. Their movement is grinding her to death.

Her mother bends over her and says in a drawling, cold, lackadaisical voice, "You are not trying, my girl. You must try harder." Her mother is all dressed up and talking fine, like some Edinburgh lady.

Evil stuff is poured into her mouth. She tries to spit it out, knowing it is poison.

I will just get up and get out of this, she thinks. She starts trying to pull herself loose from her body, as if it were a heap of rags on fire.

She hears a man's voice, giving some order. "Hold her," he says, and she is split and stretched wide open to the world and the fire.

"Ah—ah—anh," the man says, panting as if he had been running in a race.

Then a cow that is so heavy, bawling heavy with milk, rears up and sits down on Agnes's stomach.

"Now. Now," the man says, and he groans at the end of his strength as he tries to heave it off.

The fools. The fools, ever to have let it in.

> She was not better till the 18th when she was delivered of a daughter. We having a surgeon on board nothing happened. Nothing occurred till the 22nd this was the roughest day we had till then experienced. Agnes was mending in an ordinary way till the 29th we saw a great shoal of porpoises and the 30th (yesterday) was a very rough sea with the wind blowing from the west we went rather backwards than forwards.

"In the Ettrick there is what they call the highest house in Scotland," Old James says, "and the house that my grandfather lived in was a higher one than that. The name of the place is Phauhope—they call it Phaup. My grandfather was Will O'Phaup, and fifty years ago you would have heard of him if you came from any place south of the Forth and north of the Debatable Lands."

There are people who curse to see him coming, but others who are glad of any distraction. His sons hear his voice from far away, amid all the other commotion on the deck, and make tracks in the opposite direction.

For the first two or three days, Young James refused to be unfastened from Mary's hip. He was bold enough, but only if he could stay there. At night he slept in her cloak, curled up beside her, and she wakened aching along her left side, because she had lain stiffly all night so as not to disturb him. Then in the space of one morning he was down and running about and kicking at her if she tried to hoist him up.

Everything on the ship calls out for his attention. Even at night he tries to climb over her and run away in the dark. So she gets up aching not only from her position but from lack of sleep altogether. One night she drops off and the child gets loose, but most fortunately stumbles against his father's body in his bid for escape. Henceforth, Andrew insists that he be tied down every night. He howls, of course, and Andrew shakes him and cuffs him and then he sobs himself to sleep. Mary lies by him softly explaining that this is necessary so that he cannot fall off the ship into the ocean, but he regards her at these times as his enemy, and if she puts out a hand to stroke his face he tries to bite it with his baby teeth. Every night he goes to sleep in a rage, but in the morning when she unties him, still half asleep and full of his infant sweetness, he clings to her drowsily and she is suffused with love.

Then one day he is gone. She is in the line for wash water and she turns around and he is not beside her. She was just speaking a few words to the woman ahead of her, answering a question about Agnes and the infant, she had just told the woman its name—Isabel—and in that moment he got away.

Everything in an instant is overturned. The nature of the world is altered. She runs back and forth, crying out James's name. She runs up to strangers, to sailors who laugh at her as she begs them, "Have you seen a little boy? Have you seen a little boy this high, he has blue eyes?"

"I seen fifty or sixty of them like that in the last five minutes," a man says to her. A woman trying to be kind says that he will turn up, Mary should not worry herself, he will be playing with some of the other children. Some women even look about, as if they would help her search, but of course they cannot, they have their own responsibilities.

This is what Mary sees plainly in those moments of anguish: that the world which has turned into a horror for her is still the same ordinary world for all these other people and will remain so even if James has truly vanished, even if he has crawled through the ship's railings—she has noticed everywhere the places where this would be possible—and been swallowed by the ocean.

The most brutal and unthinkable of all events, to her, would seem to most others like a sad but not extraordinary misadventure. It would not be unthinkable to them.

Or to God. For in fact when God makes some rare and remarkable, beautiful human child is He not particularly tempted to take His creature back, as if the world did not deserve it?

Still, she is praying to Him all the time. At first she only called on the Lord's name. But as her search grows more specific and in some ways more bizarre—she is ducking under clotheslines that people have contrived for privacy, she thinks nothing of interrupting folk at any business, she flings up the lids of their boxes and roots in their bedclothes, not even hearing them when they curse her—her prayers also become more complicated and audacious. She tries to think of something to offer, something that could equal the value of James's being restored to her. But what does she have? Nothing of her own—not health or prospects or anybody's regard. There is no piece of luck or even a hope that she can offer to give up. What she has is James.

And how can she offer James for James?

This is what is knocking around in her head.

But what about her love of James? Her extreme and perhaps idolatrous, perhaps wicked love of another creature. She will give up that, she will give it up gladly, if only he isn't gone.

If only he can be found. If only he isn't dead.

She recalls all this an hour or two after somebody has noticed the boy peeping out from under a large empty bucket, listening to the hubbub. And she retracts her vow at once. Her understanding of God is shallow and unstable, and the truth is that, except in a time of terror such as she has just experienced, she does not really care. She has always felt that God or even the idea of Him was more distant from her than from other people. There is a stubborn indifference in her that nobody knows about. In fact, everybody may imagine that she clings secretly to religion because there is so little else available to her. They are quite wrong, and now that she has James back she gives no thanks but thinks what a fool she was and how she could not give up her love of him any more than stop her heart beating.

After that, Andrew insists that James be tied down not only by night but also by day, to the post of the bunk or to their clothesline on the deck. Andrew has trounced his son for the trick he played, but the look in James's eyes says that his tricks are not finished.

Agnes keeps asking for salt, till they begin to fear that she will fuss herself into a fever. The two women looking after her are cabin passengers, Edinburgh ladies, who took on the job out of charity.

"You be still now," they tell her. "You have no idea what a fortunate lassie you are that we had Mr. Suter on board."

They tell her that the baby was turned the wrong way inside her, and they were all afraid that Mr. Suter would have to cut her, and that might be the end of her. But he had managed to get it turned so that he could wrestle it out.

"I need salt for my milk," says Agnes, who is not going to let them put her in her place with their reproaches and their Edinburgh speech. They are idiots, anyway. She has to explain to them how you must put a little salt in the baby's first milk, just place a few grains on your finger and squeeze a drop or two of milk onto it and let the child swallow that before you put it to the breast. Without this precaution there is a good chance that it will grow up half-witted.

"Is she even a Christian?" one of them says to the other.

"I am as much as you," Agnes says. But to her own surprise and shame she starts to weep aloud, and the baby howls along with her, out of sympathy or hunger. And still she refuses to feed it.

Mr. Suter comes in to see how she is. He asks what all the grief is about, and they tell him the trouble.

"A newborn baby to get salt in its stomach—where did she get the idea?"

He says, "Give her the salt." And he stays to see her squeeze the milk on her salty finger, lay the finger to the infant's lips, and follow it with her nipple.

He asks her what the reason is and she tells him.

"And does it work every time?"

She tells him—a little surprised that he is as stupid as they are, though gentler—that it works without fail.

"So where you come from they all have their wits about them? And are all the girls strong and good-looking like you?"

She says that she would not know about that.

Sometimes visiting young men, educated men from the town, used to hang around her and her friends, complimenting them and trying to work up a conversation, and she always thought that any girl who allowed it was a fool, even if the man was handsome. Mr. Suter is far from handsome—he is too thin, and his face is badly pocked, so that at first she took him for an old fellow. But he has a kind voice, and if he is teasing her a little there is no harm in it. No man would have the nature left to deal with a woman after looking at her spread wide, her raw parts open to the air.

"Are you sore?" he asks, and she believes there is a shadow on his damaged cheeks, a slight blush rising. She says that she is no worse than she has to be, and he nods, picks up her wrist, and bows over it, strongly pressing her pulse.

"Lively as a racehorse," he says, with his hands still above her, as if he did not know where to put them next. Then he decides to push back her hair and press his fingers to her temples, as well as behind her ears.

She will recall this touch, this curious, gentle, tingling pressure, with an addled mixture of scorn and longing, for many years to come.

"Good," he says. "No sign of a fever."

He watches, for a moment, the child sucking.

"All's well with you now," he says, with a sigh. "You have a fine daughter, and she can say all her life that she was born at sea."

Andrew arrives later and stands at the foot of the bed. He has never looked on her in such a bed as this (a regular bed, even though bolted to the wall). He is red with shame in front of the ladies, who have brought in the basin to wash her.

"That's it, is it?" he says, with a nod—not a glance—at the bundle beside her.

She laughs in a vexed way and asks what did he think it was. That is all it takes to knock him off his unsteady perch, to puncture his pretense of being at ease. Now he stiffens up, even redder, doused with fire. It isn't just what she said. It is the whole scene—the smell of the infant and the milk and the blood, and most of all the basin, the cloths, the women standing by, with their proper looks that might seem to a man both admonishing and full of derision.

He looks as if he can't think of another word to say, so she has to tell him, with rough mercy, to get on his way, there's work to be done here.

Some of the girls used to say that when you finally gave in and lay down with a man—even granting he was not the man of your first choice—it gave you a helpless but calm and even sweet feeling. Agnes does not recall that she felt that with Andrew. All she felt was that he was an honest lad and the right one for her in her circumstances, and that it would never occur to him to run off and leave her.

Walter has continued to go to the same private place to write in his book and nobody has caught him there. Except the girl, of course. One day he arrives at the place and she is there before him, skipping with a red-tasselled rope. When she sees him she stops, out of breath. And no sooner does she catch her breath than she begins to cough, so that it is several minutes before she can speak. She sinks down against the pile of canvas that conceals the spot, flushed, her eyes full of bright tears from the coughing. He simply stands and watches her, alarmed at this fit but not knowing what to do.

"Do you want me to fetch one of the ladies?"

He is on speaking terms with the Edinburgh women now, on account of Agnes. They take a kind interest in the mother and baby and Mary and Young James, and think that the old father is comical. They are also amused by Andrew and Walter, who seem to them so bashful.

The coughing girl is shaking her curly head violently.

"I don't want them," she says, when she can gasp the words out. "I have never told anybody that you come

here. So you mustn't tell anybody about me."

"Well, you are here by rights."

She shakes her head again and gestures for him to wait till she can speak more easily.

"I mean that you saw me skipping. My father hid my skipping rope but I found where he hid it."

"It isn't the Sabbath," Walter says reasonably. "So what is wrong with you skipping?"

"How do I know?" she says, regaining her saucy tone. "Perhaps he thinks I am too old for it. Will you swear not to tell anyone?"

What a queer, self-important little thing she is, Walter thinks. She speaks only of her father, so he thinks it likely that she has no brothers or sisters and—like himself—no mother. That condition has probably made her both spoiled and lonely.

The girl—her name is Nettie—becomes a frequent visitor when Walter tries to write in his book. She always says that she does not want to disturb him, but after keeping ostentatiously quiet for about five minutes she interrupts him with some question about his life or a bit of information about hers. It is true that she is motherless and an only child. She has never even been to school. She talks most about her pets—those dead and those living at her house in Edinburgh—and a woman named Miss Anderson, who used to travel with her and teach her. It seems that she was glad to see the back of this woman, and surely Miss Anderson, too, was glad to depart, after all the tricks that were played on her—the live frog in her boot and the woollen but lifelike mouse in her bed.

Nettie has been back and forth to America three times. Her father is a wine merchant whose business takes him to Montreal.

She wants to know all about how Walter and his people live. Her questions are, by country standards, quite impertinent. But Walter does not really mind. In his own family he has never been in a position that allowed him to instruct or teach or tease anybody younger than himself, and it gives him pleasure.

What does Walter's family have for supper when they are at home? How do they sleep? Are animals kept in the house? Do the sheep have names, and what are the sheepdogs' names, and can you make pets of them? What is the arrangement of the scholars in the schoolroom? Are the teachers cruel? What do some of his words mean that she does not understand, and do all the people where he is from talk like him?

"Oh, aye," Walter says. "Even His Majesty the Duke does. The Duke of Buccleuch."

She laughs and freely pounds her little fist on his shoulder.

"Now you are teasing me. I know it. I know that Dukes are not called Your Majesty. They are not."

One day she arrives with paper and drawing pencils. She says that she has brought them to keep herself busy, so she will not be a nuisance to him. She offers to teach him to draw, if he wants to learn. But his attempts make her laugh, and he deliberately does worse and worse, till she laughs so hard she has one of her coughing fits. Then she says that she will do some drawings in the back of his notebook, so that he will have them to remember the voyage by. She draws the sails up above and a hen that has somehow escaped its cage and is trying to travel like a seabird over the water. She sketches from memory her dog that died. And she makes a picture of the icebergs she saw, higher than houses, on one of her past voyages with her father. The setting sun shone through these icebergs and made them look—she says—like castles of gold. Rose-colored and gold.

Everything that she has drawn, including the icebergs, has a look that is both guileless and mocking, peculiarly expressive of herself.

"The other day I was telling you about that Will O'Phaup that was my grandfather, but there was more to him than I told you. I did not tell you that he was the last man in Scotland to speak to the fairies. It is certain that I have never heard of any other, in his time or later."

Walter is sitting around a corner, near some sailors who are mending the torn sails, but by the sounds that are made throughout the story he can guess that the out-of-sight audience is mostly women.

There is one tall well-dressed man—a cabin passenger, certainly—who has paused to listen within Walter's view. There is a figure close to this man's other side, and at one moment in the tale this figure peeps around to look at Walter and he sees that it is Nettie. She seems about to laugh, but she puts a finger to her lips as if warning herself—and Walter—to keep silent.

The man must, of course, be her father. The two of them stand there listening quietly till the tale is over. Then the man turns and speaks directly, in a familiar yet courteous way, to Walter. "Are you writing down what you can make of this?" the man asks, nodding at Walter's notebook.

Walter is alarmed, not knowing what to say. But Nettie looks at him with calming reassurance, then drops her eyes and waits beside her father as a demure little miss should.

"I am writing a journal of the voyage," Walter says stiffly.

"Now, that is interesting. That is an interesting fact, because I, too, am keeping a journal of this voyage. I wonder if we find the same things worth writing of."

"I only write what happens," Walter says, wanting to make clear that this is a job for him and not an idle pleasure. Still, he feels that some further justification is called for. "I am writing to keep track of every day so that at the end of the voyage I can send a letter home."

The man's voice is smoother and his manner gentler than any address Walter is used to. He wonders if he is being made sport of in some way. Or if Nettie's father is the sort of person who strikes up an acquaintance in the hope of getting hold of your money for some worthless investment.

Not that Walter's looks or dress would mark him out as a likely prospect.

"So you do not describe what you see? Only what, as you say, is happening?"

Walter is about to say no, and then yes. For he has just thought, if he writes that there is a rough wind, is that not describing? You do not know where you are with this kind of person.

"You are not writing about what we have just heard?"

"No."

"It might be worth it. There are people who go around now prying into every part of Scotland and writing down whatever these old country folk have to say. They think that the old songs and stories are disappearing and that they are worth recording. I don't know about that—it isn't my business. But I would not be surprised if the people who have written it all down will find that it was worth their trouble—I mean to say, there will be money in it."

Nettie speaks up unexpectedly.

"Oh, hush, Father. The old fellow is starting again."

This is not what any daughter would say to her father in Walter's experience, but the man seems ready to laugh, looking down at her fondly.

And indeed Old James's voice has been going this little while, breaking in determinedly and reproachfully on those of his audience who might have thought it was time for their own conversations.

"And still another time, but in the long days in the summer, out on the hills late in the day but before it was well dark…"

Walter has heard the stories his father is spouting, and others like them, all his life, but the odd thing is that until they came on board this ship he had never heard them from his father. The father he knew until a short while ago would, he is certain, have had no use for them.

"This is a terrible place we live in," his father used to say. "The people is all full of nonsense and bad habits, and even our sheep's wool is so coarse you cannot sell it. The roads are so bad a horse cannot go more than four miles an hour. And for plowing here they use the spade or the old Scotch plow, though there has been a better plow in other places for fifty years. 'Oh, aye, aye,' they say when you ask them. 'Oh, aye, but it's too steep hereabouts, the land is too heavy.'

"To be born in the Ettrick is to be born in a backward place," he would say, "where the people is all believing in old stories and seeing ghosts, and I tell you it is a curse to be born in the Ettrick."

And very likely that would lead him on to the subject of America, where all the blessings of modern invention were put to eager use and the people could never stop improving the world around them.

But hearken at him now.

"You must come up and talk to us on the deck above," Nettie's father says to Walter when Old James has finished his story. "I have business to think about and I am not much company for my daughter. She is forbidden to run around, because she is not quite recovered from the cold she had in the winter, but she

is fond of sitting and talking."

"I don't believe it is the rule for me to go there," Walter says, in some confusion.

"No, no, that is no matter. My girl is lonely. She likes to read and draw, but she likes company, too. She could show you how to draw, if you like. That would add to your journal."

So they sit out in the open and draw and write. Or she reads aloud to him from her favorite book, which is "The Scottish Chiefs."[1] He already knows the story—who does not know about William Wallace?[2]—but she reads smoothly and at just the proper speed and makes some things solemn and others terrifying and others comical, so that soon he is as much in thrall to the book as she is. Even though, as she says, she has read it twelve times already.

He understands a little better now why she has so many questions to ask him. He and his folk remind her of the people in her book, such people as there were out on the hills and in the valleys in the olden times. What would she think if she knew that the old fellow, the old tale-spinner spouting all over the boat and penning people up to listen as if they were sheep—what would she think if she knew that he was Walter's father?

She would be delighted, probably, more curious about Walter's family than ever. She would not look down on them, except in a way that she could not help or recognize.

We came on the fishing bank of Newfoundland on the 12th of July and on the 19th we saw land and it was a joyful sight to us. It was a part of Newfoundland. We sailed between Newfoundland and St. Paul's Island and having a fair wind both the 18th and the 19th we found ourselves in the river on the morning of the 20th and within sight of the mainland of North America. We were awakened at about 1 o'clock in the morning and I think every passenger was out of bed at 4 o'clock gazing at the land, it being wholly covered with wood and quite a new sight to us. It was a part of Nova Scotia and

---

[1]  *The Scottish Chiefs*  An historical novel by Jane Porter (1809).

[2]  *William Wallace*  Great Scottish hero (c. 1270–1305).

a beautiful hilly country.

This is the day of wonders. The land is covered with trees like a head with hair and behind the ship the sun rises, tipping the top trees with light. The sky is clear and shining as a china plate and the water playfully ruffled with wind. Every wisp of fog has gone and the air is full of the resinous smell of the trees. Seabirds are flashing above the sails all golden like creatures of Heaven, but the sailors fire a few shots to keep them from the rigging.

Mary holds Young James up so that he may always remember this first sight of the continent that will be his home. She tells him the name of this land—Nova Scotia.

"It means New Scotland," she says.

Agnes hears her. "Then why doesn't it say so?"

Mary says, "It's Latin, I think."

Agnes snorts with impatience. The baby was woken early by all the hubbub and celebration, and now she is miserable, wanting to be on the breast all the time, wailing whenever Agnes tries to take her off. Young James, observing all this closely, makes an attempt to get on the other breast, and Agnes bats him off so hard that he staggers.

"Suckie-laddie," Agnes calls him. He yelps a bit, then crawls around behind her and pinches the baby's toes.

Another whack.

"You're a rotten egg, you are," his mother says. "Somebody's been spoiling you till you think you're the Laird's arse."

Agnes's roused voice always makes Mary feel as if she were about to catch a blow herself.

Old James is sitting with them on the deck, but pays no attention to this domestic unrest.

"Will you come and look at the country, Father?" Mary says uncertainly. "You can have a better view from the rail."

"I can see it well enough," Old James says. Nothing in his voice suggests that the revelations around them are pleasing to him.

"Ettrick was covered with trees in the old days," he says. "The monks had it first and after that it was the Royal Forest. It was the King's forest. Beech trees, oak trees, rowan trees."

"As many trees as this?" Mary says, made bolder than usual by the novel splendors of the day.

"Better trees. Older. It was famous all over Scotland. The Royal Forest of Ettrick."

"And Nova Scotia is where our brother James is," Mary continues.

"He may be or he may not. It would be easy to die here and nobody know you were dead. Wild animals could have eaten him."

Mary wonders how her father can talk in this way, about how wild animals could have eaten his own son. Is that how the sorrows of the years take hold of you—turning your heart of flesh to a heart of stone, as it says in the old song? And if it is so, how carelessly and disdainfully might he talk about her, who never meant to him a fraction of what the boys did?

Somebody has brought a fiddle onto the deck and is tuning up to play. The people who have been hanging on to the rail and pointing out to one another what they can all see on their own—likewise repeating the name that by now everyone knows, Nova Scotia—are distracted by these sounds and begin to call for dancing. Dancing, at seven o'clock in the morning.

Andrew comes up from below, bearing their supply of water. He stands and watches for a little, then surprises Mary by asking her to dance.

"Who will look after the boy?" Agnes says immediately. "I am not going to get up and chase him." She is fond of dancing, but is prevented now not only by the nursing baby but by the soreness of the parts of her body that were so battered in the birth.

Mary is already refusing, saying she cannot go, but Andrew says, "We will put him on the tether."

"No. No," Mary says. "I've no need to dance." She believes that Andrew has taken pity on her, remembering how she used to be left on the sidelines in school games and at the dancing, though she can actually run and dance perfectly well. Andrew is the only one of her brothers capable of such consideration, but she would almost rather he behaved like the others and left her ignored as she has always been. Pity galls her.

Young James begins to complain loudly, having recognized the word "tether."

"You be still," his father says. "Be still or I'll clout you."

Then Old James surprises them all by turning his attention to his grandson.

"You. Young lad. You sit by me."

"Oh, he will not sit," Mary says. "He will run off and then you cannot chase him, Father. I will stay."

"He will sit," Old James says.

"Well, settle it," Agnes says to Mary. "Go or stay."

Young James looks from one to the other, cautiously snuffling.

"Does he not know even the simplest word?" his grandfather says. "Sit. Lad. Here."

Young James lowers himself, reluctantly, to the spot indicated.

"Now go," Old James says to Mary. And all in confusion, on the verge of tears, she is led away.

People are dancing not just in the figure of the reel but quite outside of it, all over the deck. They are grabbing anyone at all and twirling around. They are even grabbing some of the sailors, if they can get hold of them. Men dance with women, men dance with men, women dance with women, children dance with one another or all alone and without any idea of the steps, getting in the way—but everybody is in everybody's way already and it is no matter.

Mary has caught hands with Andrew and is swung around by him, then passed on to others, who bend to her and fling her undersized body about. She dances down at the level of the children, though she is less bold and carefree. In the thick of so many bodies she is helpless, she cannot pause—she has to stamp and wheel to the music or be knocked down.

"Now, you listen and I will tell you," Old James says. "This old man, Will O'Phaup, my grandfather—he was my grandfather as I am yours—Will O'Phaup was sitting outside his house in the evening, resting himself. It was mild summer weather. All alone, he was. And there was three little lads hardly bigger than you are yourself, they came around the corner of Will's house. They told him good evening. 'Good evening to you, Will O'Phaup,' they says. 'Well, good evening to you, lads. What can I do for you?' 'Can you give us a bed for the night or a place to lie down?' they says. And 'Aye,' he says. 'Aye, I'm thinking three bits of lads like yourselves should not be so hard to find room for.' And he

goes into the house with them following and they says, 'And by the bye, could you give us the key, too, the big silver key that you had of us?' Well, Will looks around, and he looks for the key, till he thinks to himself, What key was that? For he knew he never had such a thing in his life. Big key or silver key, he never had it. 'What key are you talking about?' And turns himself around and they are not there. Goes out of the house, all around the house, looks to the road. No trace of them. Looks to the hills. No trace. Then Will knew it. They was no lads at all. Ah, no. They was no lads at all."

James has not made any sound. At his back is the thick and noisy wall of dancers, to the side his mother, with the small clawing beast that bites into her body. And in front of him is the old man with his rumbling voice, insistent but remote, and his blast of bitter breath.

It is the child's first conscious encounter with someone as perfectly self-centered as he is.

He is barely able to focus his intelligence, to show himself not quite defeated. "Key," he says. "Key?"

Agnes, watching the dancing, catches sight of Andrew, red in the face and heavy on his feet, linked arm to arm with various jovial women. There is not one girl whose looks or dancing gives Agnes any worries. Andrew never gives her any worries, anyway. She sees Mary tossed around, with even a flush of color in her cheeks— though she is too shy, and too short, to look anybody in the face. She sees the nearly toothless witch of a woman who birthed a child a week after her own, dancing with her hollow-cheeked man. No sore parts for her. She must have dropped the child as slick as if it were a rat, then given it to one or the other of her weedy-looking daughters to mind.

She sees Mr. Suter, the surgeon, out of breath, pulling away from a woman who would grab him, ducking through the dance and coming to greet her.

She wishes he would not. Now he will see who her father-in-law is; he may have to listen to the old fool's gabble. He will get a look at their drab, and now not even clean, country clothes. He will see her for what she is.

"So here you are," he says. "Here you are with your treasure."

It is not a word that Agnes has ever heard used to

refer to a child. It seems as if he is talking to her in the way he might talk to a person of his own acquaintance, some sort of a lady, not as a doctor talks to a patient. Such behavior embarrasses her and she does not know how to answer.

"Your baby is well?" he says, taking a more down-to-earth tack. He is still catching his breath from the dancing, and his face is covered with a fine sweat.

"Aye."

"And you yourself? You have your strength again?" She shrugs very slightly, so as not to shake the child off the nipple.

"You have a fine color, anyway. That is a good sign."

He asks then if she will permit him to sit and talk to her for a few moments, and once more she is confused by his formality but tells him that he may do as he likes.

Her father-in-law gives the surgeon—and her as well—a despising glance, but Mr. Suter does not notice it, perhaps does not even realize that the old man and the fair-haired boy who sits straight-backed facing the old man have anything to do with her.

"What will you do in Canada West?" he asks.

It seems to her the silliest question. She shakes her head—what can she say? She will wash and sew and cook and almost certainly suckle more children. Where that will be does not much matter. It will be in a house, and not a fine one.

She knows now that this man likes her, and in what way. She remembers his fingers on her skin. What harm can happen, though, to a woman with a baby at her breast? She feels stirred to show him a bit of friendliness.

"What will you do?" she says.

He smiles and says that he supposes he will go on doing what he has been trained to do, and that the people in America—so he has heard—are in need of doctors and surgeons, just like other people in the world.

"But I do not intend to get walled up in some city. I'd like to get as far as the Mississippi River, at least. Everything beyond the Mississippi used to belong to France, you know, but now it belongs to America and it is wide open—anybody can go there, except that you may run into the Indians. I would not mind that, either. Where there is fighting with the Indians, there'll be all the more need for a surgeon."

She does not know anything about this Mississippi River but she knows that Mr. Suter does not look like a fighting man himself—he does not look as if he could stand up in a quarrel with the brawling lads of Hawick, let alone red Indians.

Two dancers swing so close to them as to put a wind into their faces. It is a young girl, a child, really, whose skirts fly out—and who should she be dancing with but Agnes's brother-in-law Walter. Walter makes some sort of silly bow to Agnes and the surgeon and his father, and the girl pushes him and turns him around and he laughs at her. She is dressed like a young lady, with bows in her hair. Her face is lit up with enjoyment, her cheeks are glowing like lanterns, and she treats Walter with great familiarity, as if she had got hold of a large toy.

"That lad is your friend?" Mr. Suter says.

"No. He is my husband's brother."

The girl is laughing quite helplessly, as she and Walter—through her heedlessness—have almost knocked down another couple in the dance. She is not able to stand up for laughing, and Walter has to support her. Then it appears that she is not laughing but coughing. Walter is holding her against himself, half carrying her to the rail.

"There is one lass that will never have a child to her breast," Mr. Suter says, his eyes flitting to the sucking child before resting again on the girl. "I doubt if she will live long enough to see much of America. Does she not have anyone to look after her? She should not have been allowed to dance."

He stands up so that he can keep the girl in view as Walter holds her by the rail.

"There, she has stopped," he says.

"No hemorrhaging. At least not this time."

Agnes can see that he takes a satisfaction in the verdict he has passed on this girl. And it occurs to her that this must be because of some condition of his own—that he must be thinking that he is not so bad off by comparison.

There is a cry at the rail, nothing to do with the girl and Walter. Another cry, and many people break off dancing and rush to look at the water. Mr. Suter rises and goes a few steps in that direction, following the crowd, then turns back.

"A whale," he says. "They are saying there is a whale

to be seen off the side."

"You stay here!" Agnes shouts in an angry voice, and he turns to her in surprise. But he sees that her words are meant for Young James, who is on his feet.

"This is your lad, then?" Mr. Suter exclaims, as if he had made a remarkable discovery. "May I carry him over to have a look?"

And that is how Mary—happening to raise her face in the crush of passengers—beholds Young James, much amazed, being carried across the deck in the arms of a hurrying stranger, a pale and determined dark-haired man who is surely a foreigner. A child stealer, or child murderer, heading for the rail.

She gives so wild a shriek that anybody would think she was in the Devil's clutches herself, and people make way for her as they would for a mad dog.

"Stop, thief! Stop, thief!" she is crying. "Take the boy from him. Catch him. James! James! Jump down!"

She flings herself forward and grabs the child's ankles, yanking him so that he howls in fear and outrage. The man bearing him nearly topples over but doesn't give him up. He holds on and pushes at Mary with his foot.

"Take her arms," he shouts to those around them. He is short of breath. "She is in a fit."

Andrew has pushed his way in, through people who are still dancing and people who have stopped to watch the drama. He manages somehow to get hold of Mary and Young James and to make clear that one is his son and the other his sister and that it is not a question of fits.

All is shortly explained with courtesies and apologies from Mr. Suter.

"I had just stopped for a few minutes' talk with your wife, to ask her if she was well," the surgeon says. "I did not take time to bid her goodbye, so you must do it for me."

Mary remains unconvinced by the surgeon's story. Of course he would have to say to Agnes that he was taking the child to look at the whale. But that does not make it the truth. Whenever the picture of that devilish man carrying Young James flashes through her mind, and she feels in her chest the power of her own cry, she is astonished and happy. It is still her belief that she has saved him.

We were becalmed the 21st and 22nd but we had rather more wind the 23rd but in the afternoon were all alarmed by a squall of wind accompanied by thunder and lightning which was very terrible and we had one of our mainsails that had just been mended torn to rags again with the wind. The squall lasted about 8 or 10 minutes and the 24th we had a fair wind which sent us a good way up the River, where it became more strait so that we saw land on both sides of the River. But we becalmed again till the 31st when we had a breeze only two hours.

Nettie's father's name is Mr. Carbert. Sometimes he sits and listens to Nettie read or talks to Walter. The day after the dancing, when many people are in a bad humor from exhaustion and some from drinking whiskey, and hardly anybody bothers to look at the shore, he seeks Walter out to talk to him.

"Nettie is so taken with you," he says, "that she has got the idea that you must come along with us to Montreal."

He gives an apologetic laugh, and Walter laughs, too.

"Then she must think that Montreal is in Canada West," Walter says.

"No. No. I am not making a joke. I looked out for you on purpose when she was not with me. You are a fine companion for her and it makes her happy to be with you. And I can see that you are an intelligent lad and a prudent one and one who would do well in my office."

"I am with my father and my brother," Walter says, so startled that his voice has a youthful yelp in it. "We are going to get land."

"Well, then. You are not the only son your father has. There may not be enough good land for all of you. And you may not always want to be a farmer."

Walter tells himself that this is true.

"My daughter, now, how old do you think she is?"

Walter cannot think. He shakes his head.

"She is fourteen, nearly fifteen," Nettie's father says. "You would not think so, would you? But it does not matter—that is not what I am talking about. Not about you and Nettie, anything in years to come. You understand that? There is no question of years to come. But I would like for you to come with us and let her be the child that she is and make her happy now with your company. Then I would naturally want to repay you, and there would also be work for you in the office, and if all went well you could count on advancement."

Both of them at this point notice that Nettie is coming toward them. She sticks out her tongue at Walter, so quickly that her father apparently does not notice.

"No more now. Think about it and pick your time to tell me," her father says. "But sooner rather than later would be best."

Walter does not take long to make up his mind. He knows enough to thank Mr. Carbert, but says that he has not thought of working in an office, or at any indoor job. He means to work with his family until they are set up with land to farm and then when they do not need his help so much he thinks of being a trader to the Indians, a sort of explorer. Or a miner for gold.

"As you will," Mr. Carbert says. They walk several steps together, side by side. "I must say I had thought you were rather more serious than that. Fortunately, I said nothing to Nettie."

But Nettie has not been fooled as to the subject of their talks together. She pesters her father until he has to let her know how things have gone and then she seeks out Walter.

"I will not talk to you anymore from now on," she says, in a more grownup voice than he has ever heard from her. "It is not because I am angry but just because if I go on talking to you I will have to think all the time about how soon I'll be saying goodbye to you. But if I stop now I will have already said goodbye, so it will all be over sooner."

She spends the time that is left walking sedately with her father, in her finest clothes.

Walter feels sorry to see her—in these fine cloaks and bonnets she looks more of a child than ever, and her show of haughtiness is touching—but there is so much for him to pay attention to that he seldom thinks of her when she is out of sight.

Years will pass before she will reappear in his mind. But when she does he will find that she is a source of happiness, available to him till the day he dies. Sometimes he will even entertain himself with thoughts of what might have happened had he taken up the offer. He will imagine a radiant recovery, Nettie's acquiring a tall and maidenly body, their life together. Such foolish thoughts as a man may have in secret.

> Several boats from the land came alongside of us with fish, rum, live sheep, tobacco, etc. which they sold very high to the passengers. The 1st of August we had a slight breeze and on the morning of the 2nd we passed by the Isle of Orleans and about six in the morning we were in sight of Quebec in as good health I think as when we left Scotland. We are to sail for Montreal tomorrow in a steamboat.

> My brother Walter in the former part of this letter has written a large journal which I intend to sum up in a small ledger. We have had a very prosperous voyage being wonderfully preserved in health. We can say nothing yet about the state of the country. There is a great number of people landing here but wages is good. I can neither advise nor discourage people from coming. The land is very extensive and very thin-peopled. I think we have seen as much land as might serve all the people in Britain uncultivated and covered with wood. We will write you again as soon as settled.

When Andrew has added this paragraph, Old James is persuaded to add his signature to those of his two sons before the letter is sealed and posted to Scotland from Quebec. He will write nothing else, saying, "What does it matter to me? It cannot be my home, it can be nothing to me but the land where I will die."

"It will be that for all of us," Andrew says. "But when the time comes we will think of it more as a home."

"Time will not be given to me to do that."

"Are you not well, Father?"

"I am well and I am not."

Young James is now paying occasional attention to the old man, sometimes stopping in front of him and looking straight into his face, with a sturdy insistence.

"He bothers me," Old James says. "I don't like the boldness of him. He will go on and on and not remember a thing of Scotland, where he was born, or the ship he travelled on. He will get to talking another language the way they do when they go to England, only it will be worse than theirs. He looks at me with the kind of look that says he knows that me and my times is all over with."

"He will remember plenty of things," Mary says. Since the dancing and the incident of Mr. Suter she has grown more forthright within the family. "And he doesn't mean his look to be bold," she says. "It is just that he is interested in everything. He understands what you say, far more than you think. He takes everything in and he thinks about it."

Her eyes fill with tears of enthusiasm, but the others look down at the child with sensible reservations.

Young James stands in the midst of them—bright-eyed, fair, and straight. Slightly preening, somewhat wary, unnaturally solemn, as if he had indeed felt descend upon him the burden of the future.

The adults, too, feel the astonishment of the moment. It is as if they had been borne for these past six weeks not on a ship but on one great wave, which has landed them with a mighty thump on this bewildering shore. Thoughts invade their heads, wheeling in with the gulls' cries, their infidel commotion.

Mary thinks that she could snatch up Young James and run away into some part of the strange city of Quebec and find work as a sewing woman (talk on the boat has made her aware that such work is in demand). Then she could bring him up all by herself, as if she were his mother.

Andrew thinks of what it would be like to be here as a free man, without wife or father or sister or children, without a single burden on his back. What could he do then? He tells himself that it is no harm, surely, it is no harm to think about it.

Agnes has heard women on the boat say that the officers you see in the street here are surely the best-looking men anywhere in the world, and that they are ten or twenty times more numerous than the women. Which must mean that you can get what you want out of them—that is, marriage. Marriage to a man with enough money that you could ride in a carriage and send presents to your mother. If you were not married already and dragged down with two children.

Walter thinks that his brother is strong and Agnes is strong—she can help him on the land while Mary cares for the children. Who ever said that he should be a farmer? When they get to Montreal he will go and attach himself to the Hudson's Bay Company and they will send him to the frontier, where he will find riches as well as adventure.

Old James has sensed defection and begins to lament openly, "How shall we sing the Lord's song in a strange land?"

These travellers lie buried—all but one of them—in the graveyard of Boston Church, in Esquesing, in Halton County, Ontario, almost within sight, and well within sound, of Highway 401, which at that spot, just a few miles from Toronto, may be the busiest road in Canada.

Old James is here. And Andrew and Agnes. Nearby is the grave of Mary, married after all and buried beside Robert Murray, her husband. Women were scarce and so were prized in the new country. She and Robert did not have any children together, but after Mary's early death he married another woman and with her he had four sons who lie here, dead at the ages of two, and three, and four, and thirteen. The second wife is here, too. Her stone says "Mother." Mary's says "Wife."

Agnes is here, having survived the births of many children. In a letter to Scotland, telling of the death of Old James in 1829 (a cancer, not much pain until near the end, though "it eat away a great part of his cheek and jaw"), Andrew mentions that his wife has been feeling poorly for the past three years. This may be a roundabout way of saying that during those years she bore her sixth, seventh, and eighth children. She must have recovered her health, for she lived into her eighties.

Andrew seems to have prospered, though he spread himself less than Walter, who married an American girl from Montgomery County, in New York State. Eighteen when she married him, thirty-three when she died after the birth of her ninth child. Walter did not marry again, but farmed successfully, educated his sons, speculated in land, and wrote letters to the government complaining about his taxes. He was able, before he died, to take a trip back to Scotland, where he had himself photographed wearing a plaid and holding a bouquet of thistles.

On the stone commemorating Andrew and Agnes there appears also the name of their daughter Isabel, who, like her mother, died an old woman.

*Born at Sea.*

Here, too, is the name of Andrew and Agnes's firstborn child, Isabel's elder brother.

Young James was dead within a month of the family's landing at Quebec. His name is here, but surely he cannot be. They had not yet taken up their land when he died; they had not even seen this place. He may have been buried somewhere along the way from Montreal to York or in that hectic new town itself. Perhaps in a raw temporary burying ground now paved over, perhaps without a stone in a churchyard, where other bodies would someday be laid on top of his. Dead of some mishap in the busy streets, or of a fever, or dysentery, or any of the ailments, the accidents, that were the common destroyers of little children in his time.

—2005

# NGŨGĨ WA THIONG'O
## b. 1938

Novelist, playwright, essayist, and lecturer, Kenyan author Ngũgĩ (pronounced "Nn-goog-y") wa Thiong'o is one of East Africa's most important voices. Most of Ngũgĩ's fiction and non-fiction deals with African history and human rights issues; two acclaimed early novels, *Weep Not, Child* (1964) and *A Grain of Wheat* (1967), are sympathetic accounts of the Mau Mau uprisings of the 1950s that determined Kenya's future. These works have been followed by numerous novels, stories, essays, and plays that deal with colonialism and neo-colonialism—that state of oppression, according to Ngũgĩ, which is "nurtured in the womb of colonialism," leaving economic and spiritual control in the hands of the colonists long after they have departed. Passionate about the state of the African people's identity, Ngũgĩ has written extensively about the need to preserve African cultures and languages. He dedicated *Decolonising the Mind* (1986) "to all those who write in African languages, and to all those who over the years have maintained the dignity of the literature, culture, philosophy, and other treasures carried by African languages." For the past three decades has written all of his creative work in Gikuyu, his native tongue.

Ngũgĩ was born to Thiong'o wa Nducu and and Wanjika wa Ngũgĩ, in Kamiriithu, Kenya, in 1938. His was a large peasant family composed of his father, his mother, who was one of his father's four wives, and their twenty-eight children. His childhood was

scarred by violent struggles between the Mau Mau rebels, who were primarily from the Gikuyu tribe, and the British colonial forces; Ngũgĩ's brother was killed, his mother tortured, and his entire village obliterated. He attended Christian schools as a youth and for a time became a devout Christian himself, but he renounced the religion in 1976 and ceased using his Christian name, James Ngugi. After acquiring a BA from Makerere University in Uganda, Ngũgĩ worked as a journalist for the Nairobi *Daily Nation* and was editor of the literary journal *Zuka*—"Emerge" in Swahili—from 1967 to 1970. He eventually did graduate work at Leeds University in England, obtaining his MA and PhD. He married Nyambura, a Kenyan woman, in 1961, and they had six children.

Ngũgĩ's own literary career began in 1963 (coincidentally, the year in which Kenya achieved independence from Britain) with the successful production of his first play, *The Black Hermit*. His first novel, *The River Between* (1965), is still widely regarded as a classic of African and English literature. It is a finely observed and deeply compassionate novel of the tension between the traditional ways of rural Kenya and those of Christianity and of the modern world (including such highly charged issues as those surrounding the practice of female circumcision). *The River Between* was written in English, as were *A Grain of Wheat* (1967) and *Weep Not, Child* (1976). The popularity of Ngũgĩ's 1977 play *Ngaahika Ndeenda* (*I Will Marry When I Want*), co-written with Ngũgĩ wa Mirii, led to his exile from Kenya. Working class people and farmers were so enamored of the play and its themes of empowerment and land rights that the government feared an uprising and banned the production. Soon afterward Ngũgĩ was imprisoned for political dissent, an experience he recounts in 1981's *Detained: A Writer's Prison Diary*. He was not reinstated in his post at the University of Nairobi after his detainment, and he left the country in 1982. In 1987 he wrote

*Matigari Ma Njiruungi*, based on a Gikuyu fable about a freedom fighter; again the Kenyan government reacted in fear and anger, issuing another warrant for his arrest.

The 1977 novel *Petals of Blood* marked Ngũgĩ's "farewell to the English language as a vehicle of my writing of plays, novels and short stories," and *Decolonising the Mind* was his farewell to non-fiction writing in English. "From now on," he said, "it is Gikuyu and Kiswahili all the way." By going back to his original language, especially after having succeeded in eliminating the University of Nairobi's English Department while he was Chair, he worked to end "the domination of the mental universe of the colonised." *Petals of Blood* also marked a change in the focus of his work, from themes of colonialism to those of neo-colonialism. For Ngũgĩ, the problems in Africa did not begin, nor did they end, with the slave trade. According to him, in order to control the native people of Africa, colonizers set out to obliterate African independence both by destroying African culture and by superimposing their own culture and languages. Ngũgĩ has said that neo-colonialism continues long after the colonizers have departed, with first-world countries exploiting African goods and services, keeping the economy "still in the hands of the imperialist bourgeoisie." *Caitaani Mutharabaini*, or *Devil on the Cross* (1982), was written soon after *Petals of Blood* (while he was in a Nairobi prison) and, according to the author, is one of his most important novels.

In a 2004 interview Ngũgĩ said: "In a spiritual sense I have never left Kenya. Kenya and Africa are always in my mind. But I look forward to a physical reunion with Kenya, my beloved country," and soon afterward he made his long-awaited return. Crowds of people celebrated his homecoming, but tragedy followed in the form of an assault upon Ngũgĩ and Njeeri, his second wife (whom he married after Nyambura's death). The couple and their two children fled the country the following day.

Ngũgĩ has taught at universities in New Zealand and Germany, as well as at New York University, Yale, and Smith in the U.S.A. Most of his writing in the past fifteen years has focused on cultural theory, such as the 1993 volume *Moving the Centre: The Struggle for Cultural Freedom*. He currently works at the University of California, Irvine, as Director of the International Center for Writing and Translation, and Distinguished Professor.

⌘ ⌘ ⌘

## from *Decolonising the Mind*

### CHAPTER 3

I was born into a large peasant family: father, four wives and about twenty-eight children. I also belonged, as we all did in those days, to a wider extended family and to the community as a whole.

We spoke Gĩkũyũ as we worked in the fields. We spoke Gĩkũyũ in and outside the home. I can vividly recall those evenings of storytelling around the fireside. It was mostly the grown-ups telling the children but everybody was interested and involved. We children would re-tell the stories the following day to other children who worked in the fields picking the pyre-

thrum flowers, tea-leaves or coffee beans of our European and African landlords.

The stories, with mostly animals as the main characters, were all told in Gĩkũyũ. Hare, being small, weak but full of innovative wit and cunning, was our hero. We identified with him as he struggled against the brutes of prey like lion, leopard, hyena. His victories were our victories and we learnt that the apparently weak can outwit the strong. We followed the animals in their struggle against hostile nature—drought, rain, sun, wind—a confrontation often forcing them to search for forms of co-operation. But we were also interested in their struggles amongst themselves, and particularly between the beasts and the victims of prey. These twin struggles, against nature and other animals, reflected real-life struggles in the human world.

Not that we neglected stories with human beings as the main characters. There were two types of characters in such human-centred narratives: the species of truly human beings with qualities of courage, kindness, mercy, hatred of evil, concern for others; and a man-eat-man two-mouthed species with qualities of greed, selfishness, individualism and hatred of what was good for the larger co-operative community. Co-operation as the ultimate good in a community was a constant theme. It could unite human beings with animals against ogres and beasts of prey, as in the story of how dove, after being fed with castor-oil seeds, was sent to fetch a smith working far away from home and whose pregnant wife was being threatened by these man-eating two-mouthed ogres.

There were good and bad story-tellers. A good one could tell the same story over and over again, and it would always be fresh to us, the listeners. He or she could tell a story told by someone else and make it more alive and dramatic. The differences really were in the use of words and images and the inflexion of voices to effect different tones.

We therefore learnt to value words for their meaning and nuances. Language was not a mere string of words. It had a suggestive power well beyond the immediate and lexical meaning. Our appreciation of the suggestive magical power of language was reinforced by the games we played with words through riddles, proverbs, trans-positions of syllables, or through nonsensical but musically arranged words. So we learnt the music of our language on top of the content. The language, through images and symbols, gave us a view of the world, but it had a beauty of its own. The home and the field were then our pre-primary school but what is important, for this discussion, is that the language of our evening teach-ins, and the language of our immediate and wider community, and the language of our work in the fields were one.

And then I went to school, a colonial school, and this harmony was broken. The language of my educa-tion was no longer the language of my culture. I first went to Kamaandura, missionary run, and then to another called Maanguuu run by nationalists grouped around the Gĩkũyũ Independent and Karinga Schools[1] Association. Our language of education was still Gĩkũyũ. The very first time I was ever given an ovation for my writing was over a composition in Gĩkũyũ. So for my first four years there was still harmony between the language of my formal education and that of the Limuru[2] peasant community.

It was after the declaration of a state of emergency over Kenya in 1952 that all the schools run by patriotic nationalists were taken over by the colonial regime and were placed under District Education Boards chaired by Englishmen. English became the language of my formal education. In Kenya, English became more than a language: it was *the* language, and all the others had to bow before it in deference.

Thus one of the most humiliating experiences was to be caught speaking Gĩkũyũ in the vicinity of the school. The culprit was given corporal punishment—three to five strokes of the cane on bare buttocks—or was made to carry a metal plate around the neck with inscriptions such as I AM STUPID or I AM A DONKEY. Sometimes the culprits were fined money they could hardly afford. And how did the teachers catch the culprits? A button was initially given to one pupil who was supposed to hand it over to whoever was caught speaking his mother tongue. Whoever had the button at the end of the day would sing who had given it to him and the ensuing process would bring out all the culprits of the day. Thus children were turned into witch-hunters and in the process were being taught the lucrative value of being a traitor to one's immediate community.

The attitude to English was the exact opposite: any achievement in spoken or written English was highly rewarded; prizes, prestige, applause; the ticket to higher realms. English became the measure of intelligence and ability in the arts, the sciences, and all the other branch-es of learning. English became *the* main determinant of a child's progress up the ladder of formal education.

As you may know, the colonial system of education in addition to its apartheid racial demarcation had the structure of a pyramid: a broad primary base, a narrow-ing secondary middle, and an even narrower university apex. Selections from primary into secondary were

---

[1]  *Karinga Schools*   Run by the Orthodox and Pentecostal churches.

[2]  *Limuru*   Located in the Nairobi region.

through an examination, in my time called Kenya African Preliminary Examination, in which one had to pass six subjects ranging from Maths to Nature Study and Kiswahili.[1] All the papers were written in English. Nobody could pass the exam who failed the English language paper no matter how brilliantly he had done in the other subjects. I remember one boy in my class of 1954 who had distinctions in all subjects except English, which he had failed. He was made to fail the entire exam. He went on to become a turn boy in a bus company. I who had only passes but a credit in English got a place at the Alliance High School, one of the most elitist institutions for Africans in colonial Kenya. The requirements for a place at the University, Makerere University College, were broadly the same: nobody could go on to wear the undergraduate red gown, no matter how brilliantly they had performed in all the other subjects unless they had a credit—not even a simple pass!—in English. Thus the most coveted place in the pyramid and in the system was only available to the holder of an English language credit card. English was the official vehicle and the magic formula to colonial elitedom.

Literary education was now determined by the dominant language while also reinforcing that dominance. Orature (oral literature) in Kenyan languages stopped. In primary school I now read simplified Dickens and Stevenson alongside Rider Haggard. Jim Hawkins, Oliver Twist, Tom Brown[2]—not Hare, Leopard and Lion—were now my daily companions in the world of imagination. In secondary school, Scott and G.B. Shaw vied with more Rider Haggard, John Buchan, Alan Paton, Captain W.E. Johns. At Makerere I read English: from Chaucer to T.S. Eliot with a touch of Grahame Greene.

Thus language and literature were taking us further and further from ourselves to other selves, from our world to other worlds.

What was the colonial system doing to us Kenyan children? What were the consequences of, on the one hand, this systematic suppression of our languages and the literature they carried, and on the other the elevation of English and the literature it carried? To answer those questions, let me first examine the relationship of language to human experience, human culture, and the human perception of reality.

## Chapter 4

Language, any language, has a dual character: it is both a means of communication and a carrier of culture. Take English. It is spoken in Britain and in Sweden and Denmark. But for Swedish and Danish people English is only a means of communication with non-Scandinavians. It is not a carrier of their culture. For the British, and particularly the English, it is additionally, and inseparably from its use as a tool of communication, a carrier of their culture and history. Or take Swahili in East and Central Africa. It is widely used as a means of communication across many nationalities. But it is not the carrier of a culture and history of many of those nationalities. However in parts of Kenya and Tanzania, and particularly in Zanzibar, Swahili is inseparably both a means of communication and a carrier of the culture of those people to whom it is a mother-tongue.

Language as communication has three aspects or elements. There is first what Karl Marx once called the language of real life, the element basic to the whole notion of language, its origins and development: that is, the relations people enter into with one another in the labour process, the links they necessarily establish among themselves in the act of a people, a community of human beings, producing wealth or means of life like food, clothing, houses. A human community really starts its historical being as a community of co-operation in production through the division of labour; the simplest is between man, woman and child within a household; the more complex divisions are between branches of production such as those who are sole hunters, sole gatherers of fruits or sole workers in metal. Then there are the most complex divisions such as those in modern factories where a single product, say a shirt or a shoe, is the result of many hands and minds. Production is co-operation, is communication, is language, is expression of a relation between human beings and it is specifically human.

---

[1]   *Kiswahili*  Swahili language.

[2]   *Jim Hawkins … Tom Brown*  Characters in Robert Louis Stevenson's *Treasure Island*, Charles Dickens's *Oliver Twist*, and Thomas Hughes's *Tom Brown's Schooldays* respectively.

The second aspect of language as communication is speech and it imitates the language of real life, that is communication in production. The verbal signposts both reflect and aid communication or the relation established between human beings in the production of their means of life. Language as a system of verbal signposts makes that production possible. The spoken word is to relations between human beings what the hand is to the relations between human beings and nature. The hand through tools mediates between human beings and nature and forms the language of real life: spoken words mediate between human beings and form the language of speech.

The third aspect is the written signs. The written word imitates the spoken. Where the first two aspects of language as communication through the hand and the spoken word historically evolved more or less simultaneously, the written aspect is a much later historical development. Writing is representation of sounds with visual symbols, from the simplest knot among shepherds to tell the number in a herd or the hieroglyphics among the Agĩkuyu gicaandi singers and poets of Kenya, to the most complicated and different letter and picture writing systems of the world today.

In most societies the written and the spoken languages are the same, in that they represent each other: what is on paper can be read to another person and be received as that language, which the recipient has grown up speaking. In such a society there is broad harmony for a child between the three aspects of language as communication. His interaction with nature and with other men is expressed in written and spoken symbols or signs which are both a result of that double interaction and a reflection of it. The association of the child's sensibility is with the language of his experience of life.

But there is more to it: communication between human beings is also the basis and process of evolving culture. In doing similar kinds of things and actions over and over again under similar circumstances, similar even in their mutability, certain patterns, moves, rhythms, habits, attitudes, experiences and knowledge emerge. Those experiences are handed over to the next generation and become the inherited basis for their further actions on nature and on themselves. There is a gradual accumulation of values which in time become

almost self-evident truths governing their conception of what is right and wrong, good and bad, beautiful and ugly, courageous and cowardly, generous and mean in their internal and external relations. Over a time this becomes a way of life distinguishable from other ways of life. They develop a distinctive culture and history. Culture embodies those moral, ethical and aesthetic values, the set of spiritual eyeglasses, through which they come to view themselves and their place in the universe. Values are the basis of a people's identity, their sense of particularity as members of the human race. All this is carried by language. Language as culture is the collective memory bank of a people's experience in history. Culture is almost indistinguishable from the language that makes possible its genesis, growth, banking, articulation and indeed its transmission from one generation to the next.

Language as culture also has three important aspects. Culture is a product of the history which it in turn reflects. Culture in other words is a product and a reflection of human beings communicating with one another in the very struggle to create wealth and to control it. But culture does not merely reflect that history, or rather it does so by actually forming images or pictures of the world of nature and nurture. Thus the second aspect of language as culture is as an image-forming agent in the mind of a child. Our whole conception of ourselves as a people, individually and collectively, is based on those pictures and images which may or may not correctly correspond to the actual reality of the struggles with nature and nurture which produced them in the first place. But our capacity to confront the world creatively is dependent on how those images correspond or not to that reality, how they distort or clarify the reality of our struggles. Language as culture is thus mediating between me and my own self; between my own self and other selves; between me and nature. Language is mediating in my very being. And this brings us to the third aspect of language as culture. Culture transmits or imparts those images of the world and reality through the spoken and the written language, that is through a specific language. In other words, the capacity to speak, the capacity to order sounds in a manner that makes for mutual comprehension between human beings is universal. This is the universality of language, a quality specific to human beings. It corresponds to the universality of the struggle against nature and that between human beings. But the particularity of the sounds, the words, the word order into phrases and sentences, and the specific manner, or laws, of their ordering is what distinguishes one language from another. Thus a specific culture is not transmitted through language in its universality but in its particularity as the language of a specific community with a specific history. Written literature and orature are the main means by which a particular language transmits the images of the world contained in the culture it carries.

Language as communication and as culture are then products of each other. Communication creates culture: culture is a means of communication. Language carries culture, and culture carries, particularly through orature and literature, the entire body of values by which we come to perceive ourselves and our place in the world. How people perceive themselves affects how they look at their culture, at their politics and at the social production of wealth, at their entire relationship to nature and to other beings. Language is thus inseparable from ourselves as a community of human beings with a specific form and character, a specific history, a specific relationship to the world.

## CHAPTER 5

So what was the colonialist imposition of a foreign language doing to us children?

The real aim of colonialism was to control the people's wealth: what they produced, how they produced it, and how it was distributed; to control, in other words, the entire realm of the language of real life. Colonialism imposed its control of the social production of wealth through military conquest and subsequent political dictatorship. But its most important area of domination was the mental universe of the colonised, the control, through culture, of how people perceived themselves and their relationship to the world. Economic and political control can never be complete or effective without mental control. To control a people's culture is to control their tools of self-definition in relationship to others.

For colonialism this involved two aspects of the same process: the destruction or the deliberate undervaluing of a people's culture, their art, dances, religions, history, geography, education, orature and literature, and the conscious elevation of the language of the coloniser. The domination of a people's language by the languages of the colonising nations was crucial to the domination of the mental universe of the colonised.

Take language as communication. Imposing a foreign language, and suppressing the native languages as spoken and written, were already breaking the harmony previously existing between the African child and the three aspects of language. Since the new language as a means of communication was a product of and was reflecting the "real language of life" elsewhere, it could never as spoken or written properly reflect or imitate the real life of that community. This may in part explain why technology always appears to us as slightly external, *their* product and not *ours*. The word "missile" used to hold an alien far-away sound until I recently learnt its equivalent in Gĩkũyũ, *ngurukuhĩ* and it made me apprehend it differently. Learning, for a colonial child, became a cerebral activity and not an emotionally felt experience.

But since the new, imposed languages could never completely break the native languages as spoken, their most effective area of domination was the third aspect of language as communication, the written. The language of an African child's formal education was foreign. The language of the books he read was foreign. The language of his conceptualisation was foreign. Thought, in him, took the visible form of a foreign language. So the written language of a child's upbringing in the school (even his spoken language within the school compound) became divorced from his spoken language at home. There was often not the slightest relationship between the child's written world, which was also the language of his schooling, and the world of his immediate environment in the family and the community. For a colonial child, the harmony existing between the three aspects of language as communication was irrevocably broken. This resulted in the disassociation of the sensibility of that child from his natural and social environment, what we might call colonial alienation. The alienation became reinforced in the teaching of history, geography, music, where bourgeois Europe was always the centre of the universe.

This disassociation, divorce, or alienation from the immediate environment becomes clearer when you look at colonial language as a carrier of culture.

Since culture is a product of the history of a people which it in turn reflects, the child was now being exposed exclusively to a culture that was a product of a world external to himself. He was being made to stand outside himself to look at himself. *Catching Them Young* is the title of a book on racism, class, sex, and politics in children's literature by Bob Dixon. "Catching them young" as an aim was even more true of a colonial child. The images of his world and his place in it implanted in a child take years to eradicate, if they ever can be.

Since culture does not just reflect the world in images but actually, through those images, conditions a child to see that world a certain way, the colonial child was made to see the world and where he stands in it as seen and defined by or reflected in the culture of the language of imposition.

And since those images are mostly passed on through orature and literature it meant the child would now only see the world as seen in the literature of his language of adoption. From the point of view of alienation, that is of seeing oneself from outside oneself as if one was another self, it does not matter that the imported literature carried the great humanist tradition of the best Shakespeare, Goethe, Balzac, Tolstoy, Gorky,

Brecht, Sholokhov, Dickens. The location of this great mirror of imagination was necessarily Europe and its history and culture and the rest of the universe was seen from that centre.

But obviously it was worse when the colonial child was exposed to images of his world as mirrored in the written languages of his coloniser. Where his own native languages were associated in his impressionable mind with low status, humiliation, corporal punishment, slow-footed intelligence and ability or downright stupidity, non-intelligibility and barbarism, this was reinforced by the world he met in the works of such geniuses of racism as a Rider Haggard or a Nicholas Monsarrat; not to mention the pronouncement of some of the giants of western intellectual and political establishment, such as Hume ("… The negro is naturally inferior to the whites …"), Thomas Jefferson ("… The blacks … are inferior to the whites on the endowments of both body and mind …"), or Hegel with his Africa comparable to a land of childhood still enveloped in the dark mantle of the night as far as the development of self-conscious history was concerned. Hegel's statement that there was nothing harmonious with humanity to be found in the African character is representative of the racist images of Africans and Africa such a colonial child was bound to encounter in the literature of the colonial languages. The results could be disastrous.

—1986

# LES MURRAY
## b. 1938

Australia's most celebrated poet, Les Murray has published over twenty-five books of poetry and prose, and has edited three major anthologies of Australian poetry. In bringing Australian rural themes to an international audience, Murray relies on precise, vivid imagery and on bravura displays of wordplay, as in his poem "Bent Water in the Tasmanian Highlands." Murray is also an influential literary critic whose work has helped shape Australian cultural identity. A nationalist and a republican, he argues for the necessity of a distinctive Australian voice, which for him emanates from the bush (the remote areas of the country). His 1976 collection of poems, *The Vernacular Republic*, is a landmark in Australian literature and embodies his commitment to Australian cultural sovereignty.

Murray was born in 1938 in Nabiac, a rural village in New South Wales, Australia. His parents,

Cecil Murray and Miriam Arnall, ran a dairy farm in the nearby countryside where Murray spent his childhood and youth. An only child, he was self-educated until he started school at age 10, by which time he had memorized much of *Cassell's Encyclopedia*. His studies were interrupted at the age of 12 by the sudden death of his mother. This event, as well as his father's subsequent depression, defined his early life. During his later high school years, Murray was relentlessly bullied and teased about his large body, his unkempt appearance, and his eccentric behavior. From then on, he would always identify with society's outcasts. Both politically and in his poetry, Murray tends to side with "the genuine, not the advertised, underdog."

In 1957, Murray entered the University of Sydney on a Commonwealth Scholarship, and his skill as a writer and editor brought him notice from many accomplished writers, including the poet Geoffrey Lehmann, who encouraged Murray's focus on rural themes. The wooded landscape of the family's farm became the background for many of his poems; it also fostered

Murray's connection to bush traditions and to the language of the common folk. The harsh poverty that he endured in his early years continued through his university years and is a frequent subject of his work. Murray dropped out of university in 1961, depressed and destitute, and began to hitchhike around Australia. Shortly after his return, he married Valerie Morelli, a fellow German student, and the first of five children was born the following year. Murray converted to Catholicism, his wife's religion, and began a spiritual and emotional ascent out of his depression. (He is now a devout Catholic, and his poetry has become increasing informed by his spirituality.)

Initially, Murray supported his family by working as a translator of Western European languages (he is proficient in more than a dozen languages) at a university in Canberra. In 1961, Murray achieved literary prominence when his poetry began appearing in prestigious Australian news magazines and journals, such as *The Bulletin* and *Southerly*. His first book of poetry, *The Ilex Tree* (1965), co-written with Lehmann, won the Grace Leven Prize. In 1971 he began writing full time, and from that point on he published steadily. While his farming roots remained prominent in the themes of his poems, those roots may have hindered his acceptance in Australia. Murray says, "It's a deep dirty secret, in Australia, that I'm the wrong class to be a poet. That is never spelled out in reviews or articles, but it is signaled in the codes. Bias against rural folk does have an unspoken racial component, as well as the redneck stereotypes. Class is always at bottom racial." Murray has, however, won international acclaim, winning numerous international awards, such as the prestigious T.S. Eliot Award, the European Petrarch Prize for life's work, and the Queen's Gold Medal for poetry for his verse-novel *Fredy Neptune* (1998). Like his poetry in general, this novel displays the dexterity, perception, creativity, wit, and imaginative wordplay that has become his signature. He has also become a cultural icon, writing essays and lecturing about diverse aspects of Australian culture. Although his work remains rooted in an Australian ethos, Murray has become recognized throughout the English-speaking world as a poet, as Joseph Brodsky has put it, "by whom the language lives."

⌘ ⌘ ⌘

## An Absolutely Ordinary Rainbow

The word goes round Repins, the murmur goes round Lorenzinis,[1]
At Tattersalls,[2] men look up from sheets of numbers,
The Stock Exchange scribblers forget the chalk in their hands
And men with bread in their pockets leave the Greek Club:
5    There's a fellow crying in Martin Place.[3] They can't stop him.

The traffic in George Street is banked up for half a mile
And drained of motion. The crowds are edgy with talk
And more crowds come hurrying. Many run in the back streets
Which minutes ago were busy main streets, pointing:
10    There's a fellow weeping down there. No one can stop him.

The man we surround, the man no one approaches
Simply weeps, and does not cover it, weeps
Not like a child, not like the wind, like a man
And does not declaim it, nor beat his breast, nor even
15    Sob very loudly—yet the dignity of his weeping

Holds us back from his space, the hollow he makes about him
In the midday light, in his pentagram of sorrow,
And uniforms back in the crowd who tried to seize him
Stare out at him, and feel, with amazement, their minds
20    Longing for tears as children for a rainbow.

Some will say, in the years to come, a halo
Or force stood around him. There is no such thing.
Some will say they were shocked and would have stopped him

---

[1] *Repins ... Lorenzinis*   Once a well-known café and a well-known restaurant, respectively, in Sydney, Australia.

[2] *Tattersalls*   Exclusive Sydney sports club associated with horse racing.

[3] *Martin Place*   Busy plaza in downtown Sydney.

But they will not have been there. The fiercest manhood,
The toughest reserve, the slickest wit amongst us

Trembles with silence, and burns with unexpected
Judgements of peace. Some in the concourse scream
Who thought themselves happy. Only the smallest children
And such as look out of Paradise come near him
And sit at his feet, with dogs and dusty pigeons.

Ridiculous, says a man near me, and stops
His mouth with his hands, as if it uttered vomit—
And I see a woman, shining, stretch her hand
And shake as she receives the gift of weeping;
As many as follow her also receive it

And many weep for sheer acceptance, and more
Refuse to weep for fear of all acceptance,
But the weeping man, like the earth, requires nothing,
The man who weeps ignores us, and cries out
Of his writhen face and ordinary body

Not words, but grief, not messages, but sorrow
Hard as the earth, sheer, present as the sea—
And when he stops, he simply walks between us
Mopping his face with the dignity of one
Man who has wept, and now has finished weeping.

Evading believers, he hurries off down Pitt Street.
—1969

## Bent Water in the Tasmanian Highlands

Flashy wrists out of buttoned grass cuffs, feral whisky burning gravels,
jazzy knuckles ajitter on soakages, peaty cupfulls, soft pots overflowing,
setting out along the great curve, migrating mouse-quivering water,
mountain-driven winter water, in the high tweed, stripping off its mountains
to run faster in its skin, it swallows the above, it feeds where it is fed on,
it forms at many points and creases outwards, pleated water
shaking out its bedding soil, increasing its scale, beginning the headlong
—Bent Water, you could call this level
between droplet and planetary, not as steered by twisting beds laterally
but as upped and swayed on its swelling and outstanding own curvatures,
its floating top that sweeps impacts sidelong, its event-horizon,
a harelip round a pebble, mouthless cheeks globed over a boulder, a

finger's far-stretched holograph, skinned flow athwart a snag
—these flexures are all reflections, motion-glyphs, pitches of impediment,

15    say a log commemorated in a log-long hump of wave,
a buried rock continually noted, a squeeze-play
through a cracked basalt bar, maintaining a foam-roofed two-sided
overhang of breakneck riesling; uplifted hoseless hosings, fully circular water,
flattened water off rock sills, sandwiched between an upper

20    and a lower whizzing surface, trapped in there with airy scatter
and mingled high-speed mirrorings; water groined, produced and spiralled
—Crowded scrollwork from events, at steepening white velocities
as if the whole outline of the high country were being pulled out
along these joining channels, and proving infinite, anchored deeply as it is

25    in the groundwater scale, in the silence around racy breccia,[1]
yet it is spooling out; the great curve, drawing and driving,
of which these are the animal-sized swells and embodiments,
won't always describe this upland; and after the jut falls, the inverse
towering on gorges, these peaks will be hidden beneath

30    rivers and tree-bark, in electricity, in cattle, on the ocean
—Meditation is a standing wave, though, on the black-green inclines
of pouring and cascading, slate-dark rush and timberworker's tea
bullying the pebble-fans; if we were sketched first at this speed,
sheaths, buttocks, wings, it is mother and history and swank here

35    till our wave is drained of water. And as such it includes the writhing
down in a trench, knees, bellies, the struggling, the slack bleeding
remote enough perhaps, within its close clean film
to make the observer a god; do we come here to be gods?
or to watch an alien pouring down the slants of our anomaly

40    and be hypnotised to rest by it? So much detail's unlikely, for hypnosis;
it looks like brotherhood sought at a dreamer's remove
and, in either view, laws of falling and persistence:
the continuous ocean round a planetary stone, braiding uptilts
after swoops, echo-forms, arches built from above and standing

45    on flourish, clear storeys, translucent honey-glazed clerestories—[2]
—1983

---

[1]  *breccia*  Rock composed of pieces of stone.

[2]  *clerestories*  Upper windows in a cathedral's vault.

## The Quality of Sprawl

Sprawl is the quality
of the man who cut down his Rolls-Royce
into a farm utility truck, and sprawl
is what the company lacked when it made repeated efforts
to buy the vehicle back and repair its image.          5

Sprawl is doing your farming by aeroplane, roughly,
or driving a hitchhiker that extra hundred miles home.
It is the rococo[1] of being your own still centre.
It is never lighting cigars with ten-dollar notes:
that's idiot ostentation and murder of starving people.          10
Nor can it be bought with the ash of million-dollar deeds.

Sprawl lengthens the legs; it trains greyhounds on liver and beer.
Sprawl almost never says Why not? with palms comically raised
nor can it be dressed for, not even in running shoes worn
with mink and a nose ring. That is Society. That's Style.          15
Sprawl is more like the thirteenth banana in a dozen
or anyway the fourteenth.

Sprawl is Hank Stamper in Never Give an Inch[2]
bisecting an obstructive official's desk with a chain saw.
Not harming the official. Sprawl is never brutal          20
though it's often intransigent. Sprawl is never Simon de Montfort[3]
at a town-storming: Kill them all! God will know his own.
Knowing the man's name this was said to might be sprawl.

Sprawl occurs in art. The fifteenth to twenty-first
lines in a sonnet, for example. And in certain paintings;          25
I have sprawl enough to have forgotten which paintings.
Turner's glorious Burning of the Houses of Parliament[4]
comes to mind, a doubling bannered triumph of sprawl—
except, he didn't fire them.

Sprawl gets up the nose of many kinds of people          30
(every kind that comes in kinds) whose futures don't include it.
Some decry it as criminal presumption, silken-robed Pope Alexander

---

[1] *rococo*  Antiquated; also ornate, fanciful.

[2] *Hank Stamper in Never Give an Inch*  Character in a 1971 Paul Newman movie, entitled *Sometimes a Great Notion*, in North America.

[3] *Simon de Montfort*  King Henry III's brother-in-law and one-time advisor, who led a successful revolt against the king in 1264.

[4] *Burning of the Houses of Parliament*  An 1834 painting by British artist J.M.W. Turner (1775–1851).

dividing the new world between Spain and Portugal.[1]
If he smiled *in petto*[2] afterwards, perhaps the thing did have sprawl.

35   Sprawl is really classless, though. It's John Christopher Frederick Murray
asleep in his neighbours' best bed in spurs and oilskins
but not having thrown up:
sprawl is never Calum who, in the loud hallway of our house,
reinvented the Festoon.[3] Rather
40   it's Beatrice Miles going twelve hundred ditto in a taxi,
No Lewd Advances, No Hitting Animals, No Speeding,
on the proceeds of her two-bob-a-sonnet Shakespeare readings.
An image of my country. And would that it were more so.

No, sprawl is full-gloss murals on a council-house wall.
45   Sprawl leans on things. It is loose-limbed in its mind.
Reprimanded and dismissed
it listens with a grin and one boot up on the rail
of possibility. It may have to leave the Earth.
Being roughly Christian, it scratches the other cheek
50   and thinks it unlikely. Though people have been shot for sprawl.
—1983

## Pigs

Us all on sore cement was we.
Not warmed then with glares. Not glutting mush
under that pole the lightning's tied to.
No farrow°-shit in milk to make us randy.                    *young pig*
5   Us back in cool god-shit. We ate crisp.
We nosed up good rank in the tunnelled bush.
Us all fuckers then. And Big, huh? Tusked
the balls-biting dog and gutsed him wet.
Us shoved down the soft cement of rivers.
10   Us snored the earth hollow, filled farrow, grunted.
Never stopped growing. We sloughed, we
     soughed°                                                *sighed*
and balked no weird till the high ridgebacks was us

with weight-buried hooves. Or bristly, with milk.
Us never knowed like slitting nor hose-biff[4] then.
15   Not the terrible sheet-cutting screams up ahead.
The burnt water kicking. This gone already feeling
here in no place with our heads on upside down.
—1992

## The Mare out on the Road

Sliding round the corner on gravel
and there was a mare across the road
and a steep embankment down to the paddock.
The moment was crammed with just two choices.

5   Sliding fast, with the brakes shoaling gravel.
Five metres down, and would the car capsize?
The moment was crammed with just two choices.
One of two accidents would have to happen.

---

[1] *Pope ... Portugal*  In 1493, Spanish Pope Alexander VI divided
the area newly discovered by Europeans between Spain and Portugal.
This was later ratified in the Treaty of Tordesillas (1494).

[2] *in petto*  Italian: secretly.

[3] *Festoon*  Flower garland hung in a semi-circle; by extension, the
ornamental architectural feature that resembles this garland.

[4] *biff*  Blow or punch.

The poor horse was a beautiful innocent
10    but her owner never let a grudge go by.
No court case, just family slurs for life.
Sliding fast with the brakes shoaling gravel.

Now the mare was expanding. Would she run?
leave a gap before or behind to drive through?
15    No chance. She grew in moist astonishment.
Five metres down, and would the car capsize?

Blood hoof collision would be NOW, without a swerve.
Would the car explode in flames, below? It hung
aslant, away down. The door groaned up like a hatch.
20    No court case, just family slurs for life

because the old man didn't believe in accidents,
nor in gestures. The mare trots off
ahead of boots hobbling to find the old man's son.
The poor horse was a beautiful innocent.

25    The breeder's son on their tractor
was full of apologies and shame, winching
the mouth-full, glass-weeping car back up in secret
because the old man didn't believe in accidents.
—2005

# MARGARET ATWOOD
## *b. 1939*

When she was coming of age in the 1960s and 1970s, Margaret Atwood's work helped define and bring attention to Canadian literature; more recently she has been an international figure quite as much as a Canadian one. Always prolific, she has written over 35 books that have been translated into more than 30 languages. Her creative work—poetry, fiction, and children's literature—often uses a fantastic or speculative framework to address contentious issues. She has also been a leader in highlighting feminist concerns such as the power relations between men and women. Atwood has received numerous awards over the years, including the Booker Prize in 2000 and the Governor General's Award, Canada's national literary award, in 1966 and 1985.

The "bush," or wilderness, is important to Atwood and often appears as a thematic element in her fiction. As a child, Atwood would regularly spend the spring, summer, and fall months in isolated areas of northern Ontario with her entomologist father and her mother, a former teacher. Living for long periods surrounded by the bush left Atwood with a powerful appreciation of the natural world. She also developed a love of reading as a response to the many hours of solitude provided by living in a log cabin with no other source of entertainment.

Born in Ottawa, Atwood moved with her family to Toronto in 1946 so that her father could take up a teaching position at the University of Toronto. Her advanced reading level allowed her to move ahead a grade in high school, where she decided that she wanted to be a writer. She was, however, forced to contend with 1950s gender stereotypes; according to the social code of the time, women who wished to work should be educated as nurses, teachers or secretaries—and be prepared to resign their careers when they married and moved to the suburbs. Atwood also had to contend with the many obstacles facing aspiring writers, whether male or female, in Canada's still largely undeveloped literary culture. The graduation message printed in her yearbook turned out to be quite prophetic: "Peggy's not-so-secret ambition is to write THE Canadian novel—and with those English marks, who doubts that she will?"

Atwood moved on to Victoria College at the University of Toronto in 1957, where she studied under the scholar and critic Northrop Frye. It was while she was at university that she first started publishing her poems in university magazines and small journals. At the time, she was publishing under the non-gendered name M.E. Atwood so that she would not be discriminated against as a woman.

When Atwood completed her B.A., Frye encouraged her to go to graduate school. She arrived in Boston in 1961 to pursue a Master's degree at Harvard University. Being at Harvard allowed her the distance to consider what it meant to be Canadian. Atwood came to believe that the physical and cultural landscape was central to any conception of Canadian literature; the writer must consider what it is to write in or of the Canadian space. Atwood explored these ideas as she continued writing poetry. She completed her Master's degree in 1962 and started a doctorate the following year, but financial constraints eventually forced her to put her studies on hold. She also felt that she needed more time to devote to her creative work.

Atwood accepted a lecturer's position at the University of British Columbia in Vancouver in 1964. Vancouver turned out to be a place where she could do both creative and critical work; while there she wrote her first published book and first professionally published volume of poetry, as well as making a significant start on several other books. *The Circle Game* (poetry) was published in 1966, and resulted in her first Governor General's Award. At the time she was, at 27, the youngest writer ever to have won the award. While at UBC, Atwood also wrote *The Edible Woman*, which would eventually be published in 1969. The book depicts a woman with an eating disorder and examines the role of consumerism in our culture; in both its feminist and anti-consumerist themes the book captured the mood of the times, and became a considerable international success. Atwood had returned to Boston at this point to try to complete her doctorate. She continued to produce poetry and publish while working on her studies. Although she wrote more than two-thirds of it, she never would complete her doctoral dissertation.

In 1970 Atwood published a collection of poems, *The Journals of Susanna Moodie*, in which she adopted the point of view of a nineteenth-century immigrant newly arrived in Canada. Atwood felt that Moodie's doubleness, as British and Canadian, exemplified a characteristically Canadian ambivalence.

Atwood also continued her interest in the relationships between men and women in her influential collection *Power Politics* (1971). The following year, Atwood published a critical text on Canadian literature, *Survival: A Thematic Guide to Canadian Literature*, in which she argued that Canadian literature must confront and survive Canadian nature in order to thrive. The book was a huge success and prompted reassessments of Canadian literature in many quarters.

While working on *Survival* Atwood began a relationship with another writer, Graeme Gibson; the two remain together, and have one child. Atwood has continued to be prolific as a writer. Her major works include *Surfacing* (1973); *Lady Oracle* (1977); *Bodily Harm* (1982); *The Handmaid's Tale* (1986), for which she won her second Governor General's Award; *Cat's Eye* (1988); *The Robber Bride* (1993); *Alias Grace* (1996); *The Blind Assassin* (2000), for which she won the Booker Prize; and *Oryx and Crake* (2003). Over the years Atwood has continued to expand the range of her work. Her major novels have ventured into the genres of fantastical satire (*The Robber Bride*), historical fiction and murder mystery (*Alias Grace*), layered fiction (*Alias Grace*, which includes a novel-within-the novel), and futuristic "fantasy" with powerful political implications for the present-day world (*The Handmaid's Tale, Oryx and Crake*). She has also continued her critical work, publishing *Negotiating with the Dead: A Writer on Writing* in 2002.

Atwood has long been involved in various human rights organizations, including Amnesty International and PEN Canada. She was also a founding member of the Writers' Union of Canada. Her work continues to draw attention to a variety of issues, including the place of women in society, and the place of nature in our lives. To Atwood, nature and myth are not to be separated from our everyday lives; instead, they are a "valued and necessary part of the human mentality."

⌘ ⌘ ⌘

## Further Arrivals[1]

After we had crossed the long illness
that was the ocean, we sailed up-river

On the first island
the immigrants threw off their clothes
5   and danced like sandflies

We left behind one by one
the cities rotting with cholera,
one by one our civilized
distinctions

10   and entered a large darkness.

It was our own
ignorance we entered.

I have not come out yet

My brain gropes nervous
15   tentacles in the night, sends out
fears hairy as bears,
demands lamps; or waiting

for my shadowy husband, hears
malice in the trees' whispers.

20   I need wolf's eyes to see
the truth.

I refuse to look in a mirror.

Whether the wilderness is
real or not
25   depends on who lives there.
—1970

---

[1]   The seven poems that follow, from "Further Arrivals" through "A
Bus along St. Clair: December," are from *The Journals of Susanna
Moodie*. In this volume of poetry Atwood imagines the inner
thoughts and feelings of the author of the 1852 work *Roughing It in
the Bush or Life in Canada*, in which Moodie wrote of her pioneering
life in Upper Canada.

## Death of a Young Son by Drowning

He, who navigated with success
the dangerous river of his own birth
once more set forth

on a voyage of discovery
5   into the land I floated on
but could not touch to claim.

His feet slid on the bank,
the currents took him;
he swirled with ice and trees in the swollen water

10   and plunged into distant regions,
his head a bathysphere;[2]
through his eyes' thin glass bubbles

he looked out, reckless adventurer
on a landscape stranger than Uranus
15   we have all been to and some remember.

There was an accident; the air locked,
he was hung in the river like a heart.
They retrieved the swamped body,

cairn° of my plans and future charts,     *stone memorial*
20   with poles and hooks
from among the nudging logs.

It was spring, the sun kept shining, the new grass
leapt to solidity;
my hands glistened with details.

25   After the long trip I was tired of waves.
My foot hit rock. The dreamed sails
collapsed, ragged.

I planted him in this country
like a flag.
—1970

---

[2]   *bathysphere*  Spherical chamber used for deep-sea observation.

## The Immigrants

They are allowed to inherit
the sidewalks involved as palmlines, bricks
exhausted and soft, the deep
lawnsmells, orchards whorled
5   to the land's contours, the inflected weather

only to be told they are too poor
to keep it up, or someone
has noticed and wants to kill them; or the towns
pass laws which declare them obsolete.

10   I see them coming
up from the hold smelling of vomit,
infested, emaciated, their skins grey
with travel; as they step on shore

the old countries recede, become
15   perfect, thumbnail castles preserved
like gallstones in a glass bottle, the
towns dwindle upon the hillsides
in a light paperweight-clear.

They carry their carpetbags and trunks
20   with clothes, dishes, the family pictures;
they think they will make an order
like the old one, sow miniature orchards,
carve children and flocks out of wood

but always they are too poor, the sky
25   is flat, the green fruit shrivels
in the prairie sun, wood is for burning;
and if they go back, the towns

in time have crumbled, their tongues
stumble among awkward teeth, their ears
30   are filled with the sound of breaking glass.
I wish I could forget them
and so forget myself:

my mind is a wide pink map
across which move year after year
35   arrows and dotted lines, further and further,
people in railway cars

their heads stuck out of the windows
at stations, drinking milk or singing,
their features hidden with beards or shawls
40   day and night riding across an ocean of unknown
land to an unknown land.
—1970

## Later in Belleville: Career

Once by a bitter candle
of oil and braided
rags, I wrote
verses about love and sleighbells

5   which I exchanged for potatoes;

in the summers I painted butterflies
on a species of white fungus
which were bought by the tourists, glass-
cased for English parlours

10   and my children (miraculous)
wore shoes.

Now every day
I sit on a stuffed sofa
in my own fringed parlour, have
15   uncracked plates (from which I eat
at intervals)
and a china teaset.

There is no use for art.
—1970

## Daguerreotype Taken in Old Age

I know I change
have changed

but whose is this vapid face
pitted and vast, rotund
5   suspended in empty paper
as though in a telescope

the granular moon

I rise from my chair
pulling against gravity
10 I turn away
and go out into the garden

I revolve among the vegetables,
my head ponderous
reflecting the sun
15 in shadows from the pocked ravines
cut in my cheeks, my eye-
sockets 2 craters

along the paths
I orbit
20 the apple trees
white white spinning
stars around me

I am being
eaten away by light
—1970

## Thoughts from Underground

When I first reached this country
I hated it
and I hated it more each year:

in summer the light a
5 violent blur, the heat
thick as a swamp,
the green things fiercely
shoving themselves upwards, the
eyelids bitten by insects

10 In winter our teeth were brittle
with cold. We fed on squirrels.
At night the house cracked.
In the mornings, we thawed
the bad bread over the stove.

15 Then we were made successful
and I felt I ought to love
this country.
        I said I loved it
and my mind saw double.

20 I began to forget myself
in the middle
of sentences.  Events
were split apart

I fought.  I constructed
25 desperate paragraphs of praise, everyone
ought to love it because

and set them up at intervals

        due to natural resources, native industry, superior
        penitentiaries
30      we will all be rich and powerful

flat as highway billboards

        who can doubt it, look how
        fast Belleville is growing

(though it is still no place for an english gentleman)
—1970

## A Bus along St. Clair: December

It would take more than that to banish
me: this is my kingdom still.

Turn, look up
through the gritty window: an unexplored
5 wilderness of wires

Though they buried me in monuments
of concrete slabs, of cables
though they mounded a pyramid
of cold light over my head
10 though they said, We will build
silver paradise with a bulldozer

it shows how little they know
about vanishing: I have
my ways of getting through.

15  Right now, the snow
is no more familiar
to you than it was to me:
this is my doing.
The grey air, the roar
20  going on behind it
are no more familiar.

I am the old woman
sitting across from you on the bus,
her shoulders drawn up like a shawl;
25  out of her eyes come secret
hatpins, destroying
the walls, the ceiling

Turn, look down:
there is no city;
30  this is the centre of a forest

your place is empty
—1970

## We are hard

### I

We are hard on each other
and call it honesty,
choosing our jagged truths
with care and aiming them across
5    the neutral table.

The things we say are
true; it is our crooked
aims, our choices
turn them criminal.

### II

10  Of course your lies
are more amusing:
you make them new each time.

Your truths, painful and boring
repeat themselves over & over
15  perhaps because you own
so few of them

### III

A truth should exist,
it should not be used
like this. If I love you

20  is that a fact or a weapon?

### IV

Does the body lie
moving like this, are these
touches, hairs, wet
soft marble my tongue runs over
25  lies you are telling me?

Your body is not a word,
it does not lie or
speak truth either.

It is only
30  here or not here.
—1971

## [you fit into me]

You fit into me
like a hook into an eye

a fish hook
an open eye
—1971

## The Handmaid's Tale and Oryx and Crake[1] in Context

I'm not a science fiction expert. Nor am I an academic, although I used to be one, sort of. Although I'm a writer, I'm not primarily a writer of science fiction. In this genre I'm a dilettante and a dabbler, an amateur—which last word, rightly translated, means "lover." I got into hot water recently on a radio talk show in Britain: the radio person said she'd just been to a sci-fi conference there, and some people were really, really mad at me. Why? said I, mystified. For being mean to science fiction, said she. In what way had I been mean? I asked. For saying you didn't write it, she replied. And I having had the nerve to win the Arthur C. Clarke Award for Science Fiction.

I said I liked to make a distinction between science fiction proper—for me, this label denotes books with things in them we can't yet do or begin to do, talking beings we can never meet, and places we can't go—and speculative fiction, which employs the means already more or less to hand, and takes place on Planet Earth.

I said I made this distinction, not out of meanness, but out of a wish to avoid false advertising: I didn't want to raise people's hopes. I did not wish to promise—for instance—the talking squid of Saturn if I couldn't deliver them. But some people use both terms interchangeably, and some employ one of them as an umbrella term, under which subgenres may cluster. Speculative fiction may be used as the tree, for which science fiction, science fiction fantasy, and fantasy are the branches. The beast has at least nine heads,[2] and the ability to eat all other fictional forms in sight, and to turn them into its own substance. (In this way it's like every other form of literature: genres may look hard and fast from a distance, but up close it's nailing jelly to a wall.)

Long ago—into the time machine we go, and we get off in the cellar of one of the houses I grew up in. That cellar had a lot of books in it, and among them were the collected works of H.G. Wells, a writer who is surely the granddaddy of us all, and who was still much in vogue when my father was a young man. My father was himself a scientist, and also a keen appreciator of farfetched yarns; furthermore, he was never known to discard a book. So in the cellar I read—when I was supposed to be doing my homework—not only all the Wells stories but also many another weird tale: *Gulliver's Travels*, one of the other granddaddies of us all, and Rider Haggard, and Ray Bradbury, and *Frankenstein*, and *Dracula*, and *Dr. Jekyll and Mr. Hyde*, and Arthur Conan Doyle's *The Lost World*, and *R.U.R.* and *The War with the Newts*, and *Penguin Island*, and George Orwell of course, and *Brave New World*, and John Wyndham, AND MORE, as they are in the habit of saying these days when trying to sell you something.

That was in the early fifties. In the late fifties—by which time I was in college—I used to play hookey by going to B movie double bills, and it was thus that I saw at the time of their first release a number of the films that now appear in video guides with little turkeys beside them. *The Creeping Eye*, for instance, which was quite scary until the eye itself made its appearance, waving tentacles but with tractor treads clearly visible beneath it; or *Love Slaves of the Amazon*—the love slaves were male, and the Amazonians were female, clad in fetching potato sacks dyed green and bent on depriving the poor love slaves of every ounce of vital bodily fluid they contained. Or—one of my favorites—*The Head That Wouldn't Die*, which had a pinheaded monster with ill-fitting pyjamas. One odd thing about movie mad scientists is that they can't ever seem to measure their monsters for proper clothing sizes. I also saw … but let's just say I developed a certain feel for the genre.

Then, in the early to middle sixties, I found myself in graduate school, studying English literature at Harvard. My field was the Victorian period, and as the time came for me to choose a thesis topic, I found myself drawn toward a dark, weedy little corner, at that time not much explored. I invented a genre—"the English metaphysical romance"—which I took to mean those prose narratives of the period that were not novels in the Jane Austen sense and that contained supernatural or quasi-supernatural beings, especially goddesslike ones.

---

[1] *The Handmaid's Tale* and *Oryx and Crake*    Novels by Atwood, published in 1985 and 2003 respectively.

[2] *beast … nine heads*    Reference to the hydra, the nine-headed mythological snake-beast that would grow two more heads as quickly as one was cut off.

The line went from George Macdonald through Rider Haggard and all the way to C.S. Lewis and J.R.R. Tolkien.

These books were not science fiction as such, since they had scant interest in science. But narrative genres of all kinds are enclosed by permeable membranes and tend to combine and recombine, like Al Capp's[1] combination anti-gravity ray and marshmallow toaster; so I found myself reading everything I could get hold of that might have some bearing on my topic. This is how I came across *A Crystal Age*, by W.H. Hudson, and M.P. Shiel's *The Purple Cloud*, and Herbert Read's peculiar *The Green Child*.

I even went on a search through American sci-fi and fantasy of the first half of the twentieth century to see if the phenomena I was observing could be found there too, or were peculiarly English. Someone has suggested that the sort of book that interested me was a result of Anglicanism: the narrative motifs and the ritual forms remain, but the Real Presence—the body and blood of Christ, manifest at the Mass through transubstantiation[2]—has gone elsewhere, leaving us with stand-ins. Certainly America did not have what I was looking for, not at that time; nonetheless I read my way through all the Conan the Barbarian books, which might be seen as a kind of gloss on Henry James.

Anyone who spends much time contemplating this kind of literature will realize pretty soon that such books do not exist within the world of the novel proper. By "the novel proper," I mean the prose-fiction form that traces its lineage from *Moll Flanders* through Joseph Addison's sketches through Fanny Burney through Jane Austen through Charles Dickens through George Eliot through Thomas Hardy through George Gissing—just to mention some English practitioners—and on into our times. The setting is Middle Earth, and the middle of Middle Earth is the middle class, and the hero and heroine are usually the desirable norms, or could have been in—for instance—Thomas Hardy, if fate and society hadn't been so contrary. Grotesque variations on

the desirable norms appear, of course, but they take the form, not of monsters or vampires or space aliens, but of people with character defects or strange noses. Ideas about new forms of social organization are introduced through conversations among the characters, or in the form of thought or reverie, rather than being dramatized, as in the utopia and the dystopia.[3] The central characters are placed in social space by being given parents and other relatives, however unsatisfactory or dead these may be at the outset of the story. These central characters don't just appear as fully grown adults but are provided with a past, a history. We, the readers, expect them to be psychologically plausible—"well rounded," we are fond of saying, as in the citations for citizenship awards at high school graduations; and we expect their surroundings to be what we think of as realistic. This is fiction about the waking state.

We have shambled into the bad habit of labeling all prose fictions as novels and of judging them accordingly—by comparing them with novels or with "realistic" fiction generally. But a book can be a prose fiction without being a novel. Nathaniel Hawthorne called his fictions "romances," to distinguish them from novels. The French have two words for the short story, *conte* and *nouvelle*—"tale" and "news"—and this is a useful distinction. The tale can be set anywhere, and can move into realms that are off-limits to the novel—into the cellars and attics of the mind, where figures that can appear in novels only as dreams and nightmares and fantasies take actual shape, and walk. The news, however, is news of us; it's the daily news, as in "daily life." There can be car crashes and shipwrecks in the news, but there are not likely to be any Frankenstein monsters; not, that is, until someone in daily life manages to create one. But there's more to the news than "the news." Speculative fiction can bring us that other kind of news; it can speak of what is past and passing, but especially of what's to come.

*The Pilgrim's Progress*, although a prose narrative and a fiction, was not intended as a novel; when it was written, such a thing did not yet exist. It's a romance, a story about the adventures of a hero, coupled with an allegory—the stages of the Christian life. (It's also one

[1] *Al Capp* Cartoonist (1909–79), creator of "Li'l Abner."

[2] *transubstantiation* According to Catholicism, the conversion of the Eucharist bread into the body of Christ and the wine into His blood.

[3] *dystopia* A place or society that is the worst possible—the opposite of a utopia.

of the precursors of science fiction, although not often recognized as such.) Here are some other prose-fiction forms that are not novels proper: the confession; the symposium; the Menippean satire,[1] or anatomy; the utopia and its evil twin, the dystopia; and more.

Before the term *science fiction* appeared, in America in the thirties, stories such as H.G. Wells's *Time Machine* were called *scientific romances*. In both terms, the science element is a qualifier. The nouns are *romance* and *fiction*, and as we have seen, the word *fiction* covers a lot of ground.

These kinds of narratives can do some things that novels, as defined above, cannot do. I'll run through them, even though I know I'm preaching to the converted:[2]

1. Explore the consequences of new and proposed technologies in graphic ways, by showing them fully up and running.
2. Explore the nature and limits of what it means to be human in graphic ways, by pushing the envelope as far as it will go—see, for instance, Ursula Le Guin.
3. Explore the relation of humanity to the universe in graphic ways, an exploration that often takes us in the direction of religion and can meld easily with mythology—again, an exploration that can take place within the conventions of realism only through conversations and soliloquies.
4. Explore proposed changes in social organization in graphic ways, by showing what they might be like for those living under them. Thus the utopia and the dystopia.
5. Explore the realms of the imagination in graphic ways, by taking us boldly and daringly where no one has gone before. Thus the spaceship, the inner space of *Fantastic Voyage*, the cyberspace trips of William Gibson, and *The Matrix*—the last, by the way, an adventure romance with strong overtones of Christian allegory, and thus more closely related to *The Pilgrim's Progress* than to *Pride and Prejudice*.

You'll notice that all my examples begin with the word *explore*, which should tip us off to the fact that a work of science fiction or speculative fiction or scientific romance is more likely to find its points of reference in the romance than in the socially realistic novel. But in all kinds of fiction, the business of the author is not so much factual truth as plausibility. Not that a thing did happen or even that it could happen but that the reader believes it while reading (within the terms set by the convention, that is, whatever that convention may be).

All of which is a somewhat too lengthy preamble to my topic, which is the writing of my two works of "science fiction" or "speculative fiction," *The Handmaid's Tale* and *Oryx and Crake*. Although lumped together by commentators who have spotted what they have in common—they are not novels in the Jane Austen sense, and both take place in the future, that never-never land equivalent to the other world visited by shamans—they are in fact dissimilar. *The Handmaid's Tale* is a classic dystopia, which takes at least part of its inspiration from George Orwell's *1984*—particularly the epilogue. In a piece I did for the BBC[3] recently on the occasion of Orwell's anniversary, I said:

> Orwell has been accused of bitterness and pessimism—of leaving us with a vision of the future in which the individual has no chance, and the brutal, totalitarian boot of the all-controlling Party will grind into the human face, forever. But this view of Orwell is contradicted by the last chapter in the book, an essay on Newspeak—the doublethink language concocted by the regime. By expurgating all words that might be troublesome—"bad" is no longer permitted, but becomes "double-plus-ungood"—and by making other words mean the opposite of what they used to mean— the place where people get tortured is the Ministry of Love, the building where the past is destroyed is the Ministry of Information—the rulers of Airstrip One wish to make it literally impossible for people to think straight. However, the essay on Newspeak is written in standard English, in the third person, and in the past tense, which can only mean that the regime has fallen, and that language and individual-

---

[1]  *Menippean satire*  Form created by Menippus of Syria, a third century BCE Cynic.

[2]  *preaching to the converted*  This essay originated as a keynote address to the Fifth Academic Conference on Canadian Science Fiction and Fantasy (Toronto, 2003).

[3]  *BBC*  British Broadcasting Corporation.

ity have survived. For whoever has written the essay on Newspeak, the world of *1984* is over. Thus it's my view that Orwell had much more faith in the resilience of the human spirit than he's usually been given credit for.

Orwell became a direct model for me much later in my life—in the real 1984, the year in which I began writing a somewhat different dystopia, *The Handmaid's Tale*....

The majority of dystopias—Orwell's included—have been written by men, and the point of view has been male. When women have appeared in them, they have been either sexless automatons or rebels who've defied the sex rules of the regime. They've acted as the temptresses of the male protagonists, however welcome this temptation may be to the men themselves. Thus Julia, thus the camiknickers-wearing, orgy-porgy seducer of the Savage in *Brave New World*, thus the subversive femme fatale of Yevgeny Zamyatin's 1924 seminal classic, *We*. I wanted to try a dystopia from the female point of view—the world according to Julia, as it were. However, this does not make *The Handmaid's Tale* a "feminist dystopia," except insofar as giving a woman a voice and an inner life will always be considered "feminist" by those who think women ought not to have these things.

In other respects, the despotism I describe is the same as all real ones and most imagined ones. It has a small powerful group at the top that controls—or tries to control—everyone else, and it gets the lion's share of available goodies. The pigs in *Animal Farm* get the milk and the apples, the elite of *The Handmaid's Tale* get the fertile women. The force that opposes the tyranny in my book is one in which Orwell himself—despite his belief in the need for political organization to combat oppression—always put great store: ordinary human decency, of the kind he praised in his essay on Charles Dickens....

At the end of *The Handmaid's Tale*, there's a section that owes much to *1984*. It's the account of a symposium held several hundred years in the future, in which the repressive government described in the novel is now merely a subject for academic analysis. The parallels with Orwell's essay on Newspeak should be evident.

*The Handmaid's Tale*, then, is a dystopia. What about *Oryx and Crake*? I would argue that it is not a classic dystopia. Though it has obvious dystopian elements, we don't really get an overview of the structure of the society in it, like the one provided in the epilogue of *The Handmaid's Tale*. We just see its central characters living their lives within small corners of that society, much as we live ours. What they can grasp of the rest of the world comes to them through television and the Internet, and is thus suspect, because edited.

I'd say instead that *Oryx and Crake* is a combination antigravity ray and marshmallow toaster. It's an adventure romance—that is, the hero goes on a quest—coupled with a Menippean satire, the literary form that deals in intellectual obsession. The Laputa or floating island portion of *Gulliver's Travels* is one of these. So are the Watson-Crick[1] Institute chapters of *Oryx and Crake*. The fact that Laputa never did and never could exist—though Jonathan Swift put his finger correctly on the advantage of air superiority, an advantage that in his day he could only imagine—and that the Watson-Crick Institute is very close to being a reality doesn't have much to do with their functions as aspects of a literary form.

None of these things were in my head when I began the book. Mary Shelley started to write *Frankenstein* because of a dream she had, and so it was with Robert Louis Stevenson and *Dr. Jekyll and Mr. Hyde*; and most works of fiction begin this way, whether the writer is asleep or awake. There's a Middle English convention called the dream vision, and I'd say most fiction writing has to have an element of dream vision twisted into its roots. I began *Oryx and Crake* when I was in Australia, land of the dreamtime; I "saw" the book as I was looking over a balcony at a rare red-headed crake, during a birding expedition—and birding is a trance-inducing activity if there ever was one. The details of the story got worked out later, but without the vision there would have been no book.

As William Blake noted long ago, the human imagination drives the world. At first it drove only the human world, which was once very small in comparison with the huge and powerful natural world around it.

---

[1] *Watson-Crick* James Watson and Francis Crick discovered the structure of DNA in 1953.

Now we have our hand upon the throttle and our eye upon the rail, and we think we're in control of everything; but it's still the human imagination, in all its diversity, that propels the train. Literature is an uttering, or outering, of the human imagination. It puts the shadowy forms of thought and feeling—heaven, hell, monsters, angels, and all—out into the light, where we can take a good look at them and perhaps come to a better understanding of who we are and what we want, and what our limits may be. Understanding the imagination is no longer a pastime or even a duty but a necessity, because increasingly, if we can imagine something, we'll be able to do it.

Therefore, not farewell, dear reader/voyager, but fare forward.

—2004

# Michael Ondaatje
## b. 1943

Philip Michael Ondaatje's intricately crafted, lyrically intense works reveal his interest in narrative form—in what he refers to as the "undercurrents of shape and tone as opposed to just the meaning." His diversity as a writer makes him strikingly difficult to label. Though he started out as a poet (and continues to publish poetry), he frequently mixes prose with verse and makes use of historical documents, photographs, interviews, mythology, and autobiography. He has also made three films and adapted three of his works for the stage. Many of his books of poetry resemble novels in their extended development of character and plot. His novels, on the other hand, are frequently described as poetic; they are often written in highly figurative language, flowing from one vivid image to the next rather than developing along any linear plot line.

Ondaatje was born in 1943 in Ceylon (now Sri Lanka). His parents separated when he was two, and in 1949 his mother moved to London, where she ran a boarding school. When Ondaatje was ten he joined his mother in England, where he was educated at Dulwich College. Before Ondaatje's first return to Sri Lanka in 1978, his childhood home rarely figured in his work. "Letters and Other Worlds" (1973), one of his best-known poems, is one notable exception; here he draws on his early experiences as he comes to terms with his father's death. This surreal recollection of his father adopts a conversational tone and of makes use of startling, occasionally violent images of a sort that have since become characteristic of Ondaatje's work.

Ondaatje followed his older brother, Christopher, to Canada in 1962. At the University of Toronto, where he completed his B.A., he began to make a name for himself as a poet. He was also introduced to Coach House Press, where he came into contact with the founder Stan Bevington, as well as with influential writers and thinkers such as bp Nichol, Roy Kiyooka, and Frank Davey. Ondaatje worked as a Coach House editor for several years, and his first book of poetry, *Dainty Monsters* (1967), was designed and printed there while he was completing an M.A. at Queen's University in Kingston. Following the success of this first book, Ondaatje quickly released his next work, the long dramatic poem *The man with seven toes* (1969).

By the time that Ondaatje's novel *The English Patient* (1992) won the Booker Prize and brought him international success, he was already a prominent Canadian literary figure. He had established himself as a literary critic, an editor of anthologies of poetry and prose, and a teacher of creative writing at Toronto's York University, where he continues to teach. He had received two Governor General's Awards for poetry (for *The Collected Works of Billy the Kid* in 1970 and *There's a Trick with a Knife I'm Learning to Do* in 1979), a Books in Canada First Novel Award for *Coming Through Slaughter* (1976), and a Trillium Book Award for *In the Skin of a Lion* (1987). Ondaatje has since won another Governor General's Award and a Giller Prize for his novel *Anil's Ghost* (2000).

In whatever genre, Ondaatje's work often explores the personal stories behind known history or myth. *The Collected Works of Billy the Kid,* for example, describes legendary American killer William Bonney as Ondaatje imagines him; *Coming Through Slaughter* reconstructs the story of Buddy Bolden, a jazz musician who is said to have lost his sanity while marching in a parade. Ondaatje mixes the realistic and the fantastic as he intertwines elements of the mythic with details of everyday life. Often he makes use of gossip, rumors, and outright lies in his examinations of real historical personages. The realism of his books, he says, has more to do with "emotional or psychological rightness" than with historical accuracy.

Aspects of Ondaatje's characters frequently seem beyond our comprehension, and a mystery surrounding a central character—such as that of the unidentified patient in *The English Patient*—often drives much of the story. Ondaatje likes to keep his readers at a distance from the characters he is exploring, particularly when the character is Ondaatje himself. Even in his more personal works—such as his family history *Running in the Family* (1982) or the poetry collection *Secular Love* (1984)—Ondaatje is merely another character whom we glimpse from a variety of (sometimes contradictory) angles. This is the deliberate choice of an author who believes readers will only limit the potential of his work if they seek to interpret it autobiographically. In this respect as in so many others, Ondaatje resists being locked into established literary traditions, preferring instead to mix modes and genres in an ongoing search for original forms of expression.

⌘ ⌘ ⌘

## Letters & Other Worlds

*"for there was no more darkness for him and, no doubt
like Adam before the fall, he could see in the dark"* [1]

My father's body was a globe of fear
His body was a town we never knew
He hid that he had been where we were going
His letters were a room he seldom lived in
5   In them the logic of his love could grow

My father's body was a town of fear
He was the only witness to its fear dance
He hid where he had been that we might lose him
His letters were a room his body scared

10  He came to death with his mind drowning.
On the last day he enclosed himself
in a room with two bottles of gin, later
fell the length of his body
so that brain blood moved

15  to new compartments
that never knew the wash of fluid
and he died in minutes of a new equilibrium.

His early life was a terrifying comedy
and my mother divorced him again and again.
20  He would rush into tunnels magnetized
by the white eye of trains
and once, gaining instant fame,
managed to stop a Perahara[2] in Ceylon
—the whole procession of elephants dancers
25  local dignitaries—by falling
dead drunk onto the street.

As a semi-official, and semi-white at that,
the act was seen as a crucial
turning point in the Home Rule Movement
30  and led to Ceylon's independence in 1948.

(My mother had done her share too—
her driving so bad

---

[1]  *"for ... dark"*  Ondaatje is quoting a translation of Alfred Jarry's *La Dragonne* (1943) that is cited in Roger Shattuck's *The Banquet Years* (1955).

[2]  *Perahara*  A procession (originally of a religious nature) of praise or thanksgiving.

she was stoned by villagers
whenever her car was recognized)

35  For 14 years of marriage
each of them claimed he or she
was the injured party.
Once on the Colombo docks
saying goodbye to a recently married couple
40  my father, jealous
at my mother's articulate emotion,
dove into the waters of the harbour
and swam after the ship waving farewell.
My mother pretending no affiliation
45  mingled with the crowd back to the hotel.

Once again he made the papers
though this time my mother
with a note to the editor
corrected the report—saying he was drunk
50  rather than broken hearted at the parting of friends.
The married couple received both editions
of *The Ceylon Times* when their ship reached Aden.

And then in his last years
he was the silent drinker,
55  the man who once a week
disappeared into his room with bottles
and stayed there until he was drunk
and until he was sober.

There speeches, head dreams, apologies,
60  the gentle letters, were composed.
With the clarity of architects
he would write of the row of blue flowers
his new wife had planted,
the plans for electricity in the house,
65  how my half-sister fell near a snake
and it had awakened and not touched her.
Letters in a clear hand of the most complete empathy
his heart widening and widening and widening
to all manner of change in his children and friends
70  while he himself edged
into the terrible acute hatred
of his own privacy
till he balanced and fell

the length of his body
75  the blood screaming in
the empty reservoir of bones
the blood searching in his head without metaphor
—1973

## from *Running in the Family*

### TRAVELS IN CEYLON

Ceylon falls on a map and its outline is the shape of a tear. After the spaces of India and Canada it is so small. A miniature. Drive ten miles and you are in a landscape so different that by rights it should belong to another country. From Galle in the south to Colombo a third of the way up the coast is only seventy miles. When houses were built along the coastal road it was said that a chicken could walk between the two cities without touching ground. The country is cross-hatched with maze-like routes whose only escape is the sea. From a ship or plane you can turn back or look down at the disorder. Villages spill onto streets, the jungle encroaches on village.

The Ceylon Road and Rail Map resembles a small garden full of darting red and black birds. In the middle of the 19th century, a 17-year-old English officer was ordered to organize the building of a road from Colombo to Kandy. Workers tore paths out of the sides of mountains and hacked through jungle, even drilled a huge hole through a rock on the hairpin bend of the Kadugannawa Pass. It was finished when the officer was thirty-six. There was a lot of this sort of casual obsession going on at that time.

My father, too, seemed fated to have an obsession with trains all his life. Rail trips became his nemesis. If one was to be blind drunk in the twenties and thirties, one somehow managed it on public transport, or on roads that would terrify a sober man with mountain passes, rock cuts, and precipices. Being an officer in the Ceylon Light Infantry, my father was allowed free train passes and became notorious on the Colombo-Trincomalee run.

He began quietly enough. In his twenties he pulled out his army pistol, terrified a fellow officer—John

Kotelawala—under his seat, walked through the swaying carriages and threatened to kill the driver unless he stopped the train. The train halted ten miles out of Colombo at seven-thirty in the morning. He explained that he expected this trip to be a pleasant one and he wanted his good friend Arthur van Langenberg who had missed the train to enjoy it with him.

The passengers emptied out to wait on the tracks while a runner was sent back to Colombo to get Arthur. After a two-hour delay Arthur arrived, John Kotelawala came out from under his seat, everyone jumped back on, my father put his pistol away, and the train continued on to Trincomalee.

I think my father believed that he owned the railway by birthright. He wore the railway as if it was a public suit of clothes. Trains in Ceylon lack privacy entirely. There are no individual compartments, and most of the passengers spend their time walking through carriages, curious to see who else is on board. So people usually knew when Mervyn Ondaatje boarded the train, with or without his army revolver. (He tended to stop trains more often when in uniform.) If the trip coincided with his days of dipsomania[1] the train could be delayed for hours. Messages would be telegraphed from one station to another to arrange for a relative to meet and remove him from the train. My uncle Noel was usually called. As he was in the Navy during the war, a naval jeep would roar towards Anuradhapura to pick up the major from the Ceylon Light Infantry.

When my father removed all his clothes and leapt from the train, rushing into the Kadugannawa tunnel, the Navy finally refused to follow and my mother was sent for. He stayed in the darkness of that three-quarter-mile-long tunnel for three hours stopping rail traffic going both ways. My mother, clutching a suit of civilian clothing (the Army would not allow her to advertise his military connections), walked into that darkness, finding him and talking with him for over an hour and a half. A moment only Conrad[2] could have interpreted. She went in there alone, his clothes in one arm—but no shoes, an oversight he later complained of—and a railway lantern that she shattered as soon as she reached him. They had been married for six years.

They survived that darkness. And my mother, the lover of Tennyson and early Yeats, began to realize that she had caught onto a different breed of dog. She was to become tough and valiant in a very different world from then on, determined, when they divorced, never to ask him for money, and to raise us all on her own earnings. They were both from gracious, genteel families, but my father went down a path unknown to his parents and wife. She followed him and coped with him for fourteen years, surrounding his behaviour like a tough and demure breeze. Talking him out of suicide in a three-quarter-mile-long tunnel, for god's sake! She walked in armed with clothes she had borrowed from another passenger, and a light, and her knowledgeable love of all the beautiful formal poetry that existed up to the 1930s, to meet her naked husband in the darkness, in the black slow breeze of the Kadugannawa tunnel, unable to find him until he rushed at her, grabbed that lantern and dashed it against the wall before he realized who it was, who had come for him.

"It's me!"

Then a pause. And, "How *dare* you follow me!"

"I followed you because no one else would follow you."

If you look at my mother's handwriting from the thirties on, it has changed a good deal from her youth. It looks wild, drunk, the letters are much larger and billow over the pages, almost as if she had changed hands. Reading her letters we thought that the blue aerograms[3] were written in ten seconds flat. But once my sister saw her writing and it was the most laboured process, her tongue twisting in her mouth. As if that scrawl was the result of great discipline, as if at the age of thirty or so she had been blasted, forgotten how to write, lost the use of a habitual style and forced herself to cope with a new dark unknown alphabet.

Resthouses are an old tradition in Ceylon. The roads are so dangerous that there is one every fifteen miles. You can drive in to relax, have a drink or lunch or get a room for the night. Between Colombo and Kandy people stop at the Kegalle resthouse; from Colombo to Hatton, they stop at the Kitulgala resthouse. This was my father's favourite.

---

[1]  *dipsomania*  Excessive craving for alcohol.

[2]  *Conrad*  Joseph Conrad, author of *The Heart of Darkness* (1899).

[3]  *aerograms*  Air letters.

It was on his travels by road that my father waged war with a certain Sammy Dias Bandaranaike, a close relative of the eventual Prime Minister of Ceylon who was assassinated by a Buddhist monk.

It is important to understand the tradition of the Visitors' Book. After a brief or long stay at a resthouse, one is expected to write one's comments. The Bandaranaike-Ondaatje feud began and was contained within the arena of such visitors' books. What happened was that Sammy Dias Bandaranaike and my father happened to visit the Kitulgala resthouse simultaneously. Sammy Dias, or so my side of the feud tells it, was a scrounger for complaints. While most people wrote two or three curt lines, he would have spent his whole visit checking every tap and shower to see what was wrong and would have plenty to say. On this occasion, Sammy left first, having written half a page in the Kitulgala resthouse visitors' book. He bitched at everything, from the service to the badly made drinks, to the poor rice, to the bad beds. Almost an epic. My father left two hours later and wrote two sentences, "No complaints. Not even about Mr. Bandaranaike." As most people read these comments, they were as public as a newspaper advertisement, and soon everyone including Sammy had heard about it. And everyone but Sammy was amused.

A few months later they both happened to hit the resthouse in Avissawella for lunch. They stayed there only an hour ignoring each other. Sammy left first, wrote a half-page attack on my father, and complimented the good food. My father wrote one and a half pages of vindictive prose about the Bandaranaike family, dropping hints of madness and incest. The next time they came together, Sammy Dias allowed my father to write first and, after he had left, put down all the gossip he knew about the Ondaatjes.

This literary war broke so many codes that for the first time in Ceylon history pages had to be ripped out of visitors' books. Eventually one would write about the other even when the other was nowhere near the resthouse. Pages continued to be torn out, ruining a good archival history of two semi-prominent Ceylon families. The war petered out when neither Sammy Dias nor my father was allowed to write their impressions of a stay or a meal. The standard comment on visitors' books today about "constructive criticism" dates from this period.

...

My father's last train ride (he was banned from the Ceylon Railways after 1943) was his most dramatic. The year I was born he was a major with the Ceylon Light Infantry and was stationed away from my mother in Trincomalee. There were fears of a Japanese attack and he became obsessed with a possible invasion. In charge of Transport he would wake up whole battalions and rush them to various points of the harbour or coastline, absolutely certain that the Japanese would not come by plane but by ship. Marble Beach, Coral Beach, Nilaveli, Elephant Point, Frenchman's Pass, all suddenly began to glow like fireflies from army jeeps sent there at three in the morning. He began to drink a lot, moved onto a plateau of constant alcohol, and had to be hospitalized. Authorities decided to send him back to a military hospital in Colombo under the care of John Kotelawala, once more the unfortunate travelling companion. (Sir John Kotelawala, for he was eventually to become Prime Minister.) Somehow my father smuggled bottles of gin onto the train and even before they left Trinco he was raging. The train sped through tunnels, scrubland, careened around sharp bends, and my father's fury imitated it, its speed and shake and loudness, he blew in and out of carriages, heaving bottles out of the windows as he finished them, getting John Kotelawala's gun.

More drama was taking place off the train as his relatives tried to intercept it before he reached Colombo. For some reason it was crucial that he be taken to hospital by a member of the family rather than under military guard. His sister, my Aunt Stephy, drove to meet the train at Anuradhapura, not quite sure what his condition was but sure that she was his favourite sister. Unfortunately she arrived at the station in a white silk dress, a white feathered hat, and a long white pair of gloves—perhaps to impress John Kotelawala who was in charge of her brother and who was attracted to her. Her looks gathered such a crowd and caused such an uproar that she was surrounded and couldn't reach the carriage when the train slowed into the station. John Kotelawala glanced at her with wonder—this slight, demure, beautiful woman in white on the urine-soaked platform—while he struggled with her brother who had begun to take off his clothes.

"Mervyn!"

"Stephy!"

Shouted as they passed each other, the train pulling out, Stephy still being mobbed, and an empty bottle crashing onto the end of the platform like a last sentence.

John Kotelawala was knocked out by my father before he reached Galgamuwa. He never pressed charges. In any case my father took over the train.

He made it shunt back and forth ten miles one way, ten miles another, so that all trains, some full of troops, were grounded in the south unable to go anywhere. He managed to get the driver of the train drunk as well and was finishing a bottle of gin every hour walking up and down the carriages almost naked, but keeping his shoes on this time and hitting the state of inebriation during which he would start rattling off wonderful limericks—thus keeping the passengers amused.

But there was another problem to contend with. One whole carriage was given over to high-ranking British officers. They had retired early and, while the train witnessed small revolutions among the local military, everyone felt that the anarchic events should be kept from the sleeping foreigners. The English thought Ceylon trains were bad enough, and if they discovered that officers in the Ceylon Light Infantry were going berserk and upsetting schedules they might just leave the country in disgust. Therefore, if anyone wished to reach the other end of the train, they would climb onto the roof of the "English carriage" and tiptoe, silhouetted by the moon above them, to the next compartment. My father, too, whenever he needed to speak with the driver, climbed out into the night and strolled over the train, clutching a bottle and revolver and greeting passengers in hushed tones who were coming the other way. Fellow officers who were trying to subdue him would never have considered waking up the English. They slept on serenely with their rage for order in the tropics, while the train shunted and reversed into the night and there was chaos and hilarity in the parentheses

around them.

Meanwhile, my Uncle Noel, fearful that my father would be charged, was waiting for the train at Kelaniya six miles out of Colombo, quite near where my father had stopped the train to wait for Arthur van Langenberg. So they knew him well there. But the train kept shunting back and forth, never reaching Kelaniya, because at this point my father was absolutely certain the Japanese had mined the train with bombs, which would explode if they reached Colombo. Therefore, anyone who was without a military connection was put off the train at Polgahawela, and he cruised up and down the carriages breaking all the lights that would heat the bombs. He was saving the train and Colombo. While my Uncle Noel waited for over six hours at Kelaniya—the train coming into sight and then retreating once more to the north—my father and two officers under his control searched every piece of luggage. He alone found over twenty-five bombs and as he collected them the others became silent and no longer argued. There were now only fifteen people, save for the sleeping English, on the Trinco-Colombo train, which eventually, as night was ending and the gin ran out, drifted into Kelaniya. My father and the driver had consumed almost seven bottles since that morning.

My Uncle Noel put the bruised John Kotelawala in the back of the Navy jeep he had borrowed. And then my father said he couldn't leave the bombs on the train, they had to take them in the jeep and drop them into the river. He rushed back time and again into the train and brought out the pots of curd that passengers had been carrying. They were carefully loaded into the jeep alongside the prone body of the future Prime Minister. Before my Uncle drove to the hospital, he stopped at the Kelani-Colombo bridge and my father dropped all twenty-five pots into the river below, witnessing huge explosions as they smashed into the water.

—1982

# TOM STOPPARD
## b. 1937

Tom Stoppard has been a leading figure in British theater since the mid-1960s. Throughout his career he has been prolific, producing plays, radio dramas, screenplays for film and television, adaptations, translations, short stories, and a novel. His literary accomplishments have earned him many awards, including an OBE (Order of the British Empire), a knighthood, and an Academy Award.

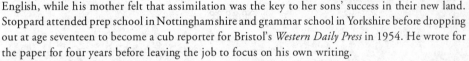

Stoppard was born Tomàš Straussler on 3 July 1937, in Zlín, Czechoslovakia. His non-observant Jewish family fled Czechoslovakia for Singapore when Nazi Germany occupied Czech lands in March 1939. When the Japanese prepared to invade Singapore in 1942, most of the family was evacuated to Darjeeling, India. His father, Eugen Straussler, a doctor, stayed in Singapore to provide medical assistance and was killed when the Japanese torpedoed his evacuation boat. While in Darjeeling, his mother re-married, to a British Army major, Kenneth Stoppard. The family moved to Bolton, England in 1946, by which time Tomàš Straussler had taken his stepfather's surname and an anglicized first name.

Stoppard's parents encouraged him and his brother to embrace English culture; his stepfather was, purportedly, chauvinistically English, while his mother felt that assimilation was the key to her sons' success in their new land. Stoppard attended prep school in Nottinghamshire and grammar school in Yorkshire before dropping out at age seventeen to become a cub reporter for Bristol's *Western Daily Press* in 1954. He wrote for the paper for four years before leaving the job to focus on his own writing.

In 1960 he finished his first script for the stage, *A Walk on the Water*, which was produced for television in 1963 and later re-adapted for the stage as *Enter a Free Man* (1968). While beginning his writing career, Stoppard worked for a year as drama critic for the now-defunct British theater magazine, *Scene*. During his short tenure at the magazine, he reportedly saw 132 plays. His first major theatrical success, and one of the most widely-produced plays of the twentieth century, was *Rosencrantz and Guildenstern Are Dead*, first staged at the Edinburgh Fringe Festival in 1966. Although this production received a tepid response from audiences and critics, the play was picked up and produced at the Old Vic Theatre in London in 1967, where it was widely acclaimed. An existentialist drama about two minor characters from Shakespeare's *Hamlet* who are controlled by narrative forces beyond their understanding, *Rosencrantz and Guildenstern Are Dead* established Stoppard as one of the rising stars of British theater.

Stoppard's plays of this era tended to be clever, absurdist dramas, in which theatricality itself is a driving force. In *The Real Inspector Hound* (1968), for instance, two theater critics become implicated in the play they are watching as it unfolds in front of them. On one level, *Jumpers* (1972) is a disquisition on moral philosophy; on another it is vibrantly theatrical, frequently enlivened by a flying striptease artist and a group of acrobats. *Travesties* (1975), ostensibly a historical play about a meeting between James Joyce, Tristan Tzara, and Vladimir Lenin, turns into a parody of Oscar Wilde's *The Importance of Being Earnest*.

In the late 1970s Stoppard began to turn his attention toward human rights issues. His Czech roots led him toward advocacy on behalf of dissident playwrights in eastern European countries then tightly and often brutally under the control of the Soviet Union. Most notable among the writers whose cause Stoppard championed was Václav Havel (later President of the Czech Republic); Stoppard has translated many of Havel's works into English.

This concern for the Czech dissident movement is evident in Stoppard's 1977 television screenplay *Professional Foul*, in which an English academic faces an ethical dilemma when one of his former students runs afoul of the Czechoslovakian authorities. The screenplay was written as a contribution to Amnesty International's 1977 Prisoner of Conscience Year. Like many of Stoppard's works, it cleverly brings together two or more disparate themes or ideas—in this case, language philosophy, Cold War politics, and professional sports—within a unified comedic structure.

Throughout Stoppard's career historical and philosophical inquiry has remained an important engine for his writing. *Arcadia* (1993), which Stoppard both wrote and directed for the Royal National Theatre, juxtaposes historical events taking place at an English country house in 1809 with their interpretation by a group of historians in the same house in 1989. The play has been added to the repertoire of the illustrious Comédie-Française of Paris, the first time that such an honor has been bestowed on a living playwright. His 2002 trilogy of plays, *The Coast of Utopia,* concerns a series of philosophical debates between literary and political characters in pre-revolutionary Russia.

Stoppard has found an even wider audience with his original screenplays and screen adaptations. He adapted and directed the screen successful film version of *Rosencrantz and Guildenstern Are Dead* in 1990. He also wrote the screenplay for Terry Gilliam's influential 1985 film *Brazil*, and adapted J.G. Ballard's novel *Empire of the Sun* for the screen in 1986. In 1998 his screenplay for *Shakespeare in Love*, co-authored with Marc Norman, won the Academy Award for best screenplay. Stoppard lives in England and has four children from two marriages.

⌘ ⌘ ⌘

## Professional Foul

CHARACTERS:

Anderson
McKendrick
Chetwyn
Hollar
Broadbent
Crisp
Stone
Captain (Man 6)
Policeman (Man 1)
Policeman (Man 2)
Policeman (Man 3)

Policeman (Man 4)
Policeman (Man 5)
Mrs. Hollar
Sacha (ten years old)
Grayson
Chamberlain
Frenchman
Chairman
Clerk, Lift Operators, Concierges, Interpreters, Customs, Police, etc.

SCENE I

(Interior. Aeroplane. In flight.

The tourist class cabin of a passenger jet. We are mainly concerned with two passengers. Anderson is an Oxbridge[1] don, a professor. He is middle-aged, or more. He is sitting in an aisle seat, on the left as we look down the gangway towards the tail. McKendrick is also in an aisle seat, but across the gangway and one row nearer the tail. McKendrick is about forty. He is also a don, but where Anderson gives a somewhat fastidious impression, McKendrick is a rougher sort of diamond. McKendrick is sitting in the first row of smokers' seats, and Anderson in the last row of the non-smokers' seats, looking aft. The plane is by no means full. The three seats across the aisle from Anderson are vacant. The seat next to Anderson on his right is also vacant but the seat beyond that, by the window, accommodates a sleeping man.

On the vacant seat between Anderson and the sleeping man is lying a sex magazine of the Penthouse type. The magazine, however, is as yet face down.

The passengers are coming to the end of a meal. They have trays of aeroplane food in front of them. McKendrick puts down his fork and lights a cigarette. Anderson dabs at his mouth with his napkin and puts it down. He glances around casually and notes the magazine next to him. He notes the sleeping man.

McKendrick has a briefcase on the seat next to him, and from this he takes a glossy brochure. In fact, this is quite an elaborate publication associated with a philosophical congress. The cover of this programme is seen to read: "Colloquium Philosophicum Prague 77."

Anderson slides out from under his lunch tray a brochure identical to McKendrick's. He glances at it for a mere moment and loses interest. He turns his attention back to the magazine on the seat. He turns the magazine over and notes the naked woman on its cover. He picks the magazine up, with a further glance at the sleeping man, and opens it to a spread of colour photographs. Consciously or unconsciously, he is holding the brochure in such a way as to provide a shield for the magazine.

McKendrick, casually glancing round, sees the twin to his own brochure.)

MCKENDRICK.  Snap.

(Anderson looks up guiltily.)

ANDERSON.  Ah …

(Anderson closes the magazine and slides it face-up under his lunch tray. McKendrick's manner is extrovert. Almost breezy. Anderson's manner is a little vague.)

MCKENDRICK.  I wasn't sure it was you. Not a very good likeness.
5 ANDERSON.  I assure you this is how I look.
MCKENDRICK.  I mean your photograph. (He flips his brochure open. It contains small photographs and pen portraits of various men and women who are in fact to be speakers at the colloquium.) The photograph is younger.
10 ANDERSON.  It must be an old photograph.

(McKendrick gets up and comes to sit in the empty seat across the aisle from Anderson.)

MCKENDRICK.  (Changing seats.) Bill McKendrick.
ANDERSON.  How odd.
MCKENDRICK.  Is it?
ANDERSON.  Young therefore old. Old therefore young.
15 Only odd at first glance.
MCKENDRICK.  Oh yes.

(Anderson takes a notebook, with pencil attached, from his pocket and writes in it as he speaks.)

ANDERSON.  The second glance is known as linguistic analysis. A lot of chaps pointing out that we don't always mean what we say, even when we manage to say
20 what we mean. Personally I'm quite prepared to believe it.[2] (He finishes writing and closes the notebook. He glances

---

[1] Oxbridge  Term used with reference to the many shared characteristics of Britain's two oldest and most prestigious universities, Oxford and Cambridge.

[2] linguistic analysis … believe it  For much of the twentieth century Western analytic philosophy endeavored to deal with philosophical questions largely through the analysis of language. Beginning with Gottlob Frege and Bertrand Russell very early in the twentieth century, language began to be looked at by philosophers as a system

*uneasily out of the window.*) Have you noticed the way the wings keep *wagging*? I try to look away and think of something else but I am drawn back irresistibly … I

25 wouldn't be nervous about flying if the wings didn't wag. Solid steel. Thick as a bank safe. Flexing like tree branches. It's not natural. There is a coldness around my heart as though I'd seen your cigarette smoke knock against the ceiling and break in two like a bread stick.

30 By the way, that is a non-smoking seat.
MCKENDRICK.   Sorry.

(*McKendrick stubs out his cigarette. Anderson puts his notebook back into his pocket.*)

ANDERSON.   Yes, I like to collect little curiosities for the language chaps. It's like handing round a bag of liquorice allsorts. They're terribly grateful. (*A thought*

35 *strikes him.*) Oh, you're not a language chap yourself?

(*The question seems to surprise McKendrick, and amuse him.*)

MCKENDRICK.   No. I'm McKendrick.
ANDERSON.   You'll be giving a paper?
MCKENDRICK.   Yes. Nothing new, actually. More of a summing up of my corner. My usual thing, you

40 know …

(*McKendrick is fishing but Anderson doesn't seem to notice.*)

ANDERSON.   Jolly good.

of logical symbols. Ludwig Wittgenstein's philosophical work shortly thereafter led to "ordinary language" philosophy—a school of thought that held that philosophical problems could be addressed by paying attention to the language that we use to discuss them; through such analysis the problems could often be solved–or made to dissolve. In its extreme form twentieth-century language philosophy came to be seen as fostering the reductionist view that all serious philosophical differences could be dealt with as verbal quibbles. In reaction, philosophers in the last two decades of the twentieth century began again to discuss philosophical problems under the assumption that when they used words to name concepts they could indeed express something meaningful. But in 1977, when *Professional Foul* was written, language philosophy still largely dominated academic philosophy in Britain and other Western countries.

MCKENDRICK.   Perhaps you've come across some of my stuff …?

(*Anderson now wakes up to the situation and is contrite.*)

ANDERSON.   Clearly that is a reasonable expectation. I

45 *am* sorry. I'm sure I know your name. I don't read the philosophical journals as much as I should, and hardly ever go to these international bunfights. No time nowadays. They shouldn't call us professors. It's more like being the faculty almoner.[1]

50 MCKENDRICK.   At least my paper will be new to you. We are the only English, actually singing for our supper, I mean. I expect there'll be a few others going for the free trip and the social life. In fact, I see we've got one on board. At the back.

(*McKendrick jerks his head towards the back of the plane. Anderson turns round to look. The object of attention is Chetwyn, asleep in the back row, on the aisle. Chetwyn is younger than McKendrick and altogether frailer and neater. Anderson squints down the plane at Chetwyn.*)

55 Do you know Prague?
ANDERSON.   (*Warily.*) Not personally. I know the name. (*Then he wakes up to that.*) Oh, *Prague*. Sorry. No, I've never been there. (*Small pause.*) Or have I? I got an honorary degree at Bratislava once. We changed planes

60 in Prague. (*Pause.*) It might have been Vienna actually. (*Pause. He looks at the window.*) Wag, wag.
MCKENDRICK.   It's Andrew Chetwyn. Do you know him?
ANDERSON.   (*Warily.*) Not personally.

65 MCKENDRICK.   I don't know him *personally*. Do you know his line at all?
ANDERSON.   Not as such.
MCKENDRICK.   (*Suspiciously.*) Have you *heard* of him?
ANDERSON.   No. In a word.

70 MCKENDRICK.   Oh. He's been quite public recently.
ANDERSON.   He's an ethics chap, is he?
MCKENDRICK.   His line is that Aristotle got it more or less right, and St. Augustine brought it up to date.

---

[1]  *almoner*  Official with a variety of duties in connection with the provision of social assistance.

ANDERSON. I can see that that might make him
75 conspicuous.

MCKENDRICK. Oh, it's not *that*. I mean politics. Letters
to *The Times* about persecuted professors with
unpronounceable names. I'm surprised the Czechs gave
him a visa.

80 ANDERSON. There are some rather dubious things
happening in Czechoslovakia.[1] Ethically.

MCKENDRICK. Oh yes. No doubt.

ANDERSON. We must not try to pretend otherwise.

MCKENDRICK. Oh quite. I mean I don't. My work is
85 pretty political. I mean by implication, of course. As
yours is. I'm looking forward to hearing you.

ANDERSON. Thank you. I'm sure your paper will be very
interesting too.

MCKENDRICK. As a matter of fact I think there's a lot of
90 juice left in the fictions problem.

ANDERSON. Is that what you're speaking on?

MCKENDRICK. No—you are.

ANDERSON. Oh, am I? (*He looks in his brochure briefly.*)
So I am.

95 MCKENDRICK. "Ethical Fictions as Ethical Foundations."

ANDERSON. Yes. To tell you the truth I have an ulterior
motive for coming to Czechoslovakia at this time. I'm
being a tiny bit naughty.

100 MCKENDRICK. Naughty?

ANDERSON. Unethical. Well, I am being paid for by the
Czech government, after all.

---

[1] *politics ... Czechoslovakia* At the end of World War II in 1945,
the countries of Western Europe (which had been liberated from the
control of Nazi Germany by Allied forces) again became independent nations, but the nations of eastern Europe (which had been
liberated by Soviet troops) were turned into satellite Communist
states under the control of Moscow. As Winston Churchill put it in
a famous 1946 speech, an "iron curtain" descended across Europe,
with both travel and the free flow of ideas into and out of eastern
Europe severely restricted. Prague was the capital of Czechoslovakia
(now divided into the Czech Republic and Slovakia), one of the
countries under Soviet control; in the late 1970s, when *Professional
Foul* was written, this control was particularly tight. (In 1968 a
widespread reaction against domination by the USSR, known as the
"Prague spring," had been crushed by Soviet tanks.) It was not until
1989–90, when the Soviet Union itself began to break apart, that
eastern European nations such as Czechoslovakia became independent of Soviet control.

MCKENDRICK. And what ...?

ANDERSON. I don't think I'm going to tell you. You see,
105 if I tell you I make you a co-conspirator whether or not
you would have wished to be one. Ethically I should
give you the opportunity of choosing to be one or not.

MCKENDRICK. Then why don't you give me the
opportunity?

110 ANDERSON. I can't without telling you. An impasse.

(*McKendrick is already putting two and two together and
cannot hide his curiosity.*)

MCKENDRICK. Look ... Professor Anderson ... if it's
political in any way I'd really be very interested.

ANDERSON. Why, are you a politics chap?

MCKENDRICK. One is naturally interested in what is
115 happening in these places. And I have an academic
interest—my field is the philosophical assumptions of
social science.

ANDERSON. How fascinating. What is that exactly?

MCKENDRICK. (*Slightly hurt.*) Perhaps my paper
120 tomorrow afternoon will give you a fair idea.

ANDERSON. (*Mortified.*) Tomorrow afternoon? I say,
what rotten luck. That's exactly when I have to play
truant. I *am* sorry.

MCKENDRICK. (*Coldly.*) That's all right.

125 ANDERSON. I expect they'll have copies.

MCKENDRICK. I expect so.

ANDERSON. The science of social philosophy, eh?

MCKENDRICK. (*Brusquely.*) More or less.

ANDERSON. (*With polite interest.*) McCarthy.

130 MCKENDRICK. McKendrick.

ANDERSON. And how are things at ... er ...

MCKENDRICK. Stoke.[2]

ANDERSON. (*Enthusiastically.*) *Stoke*! An excellent
university, I believe.

135 MCKENDRICK. You know perfectly well you wouldn't
be seen dead in it.

---

[2] *Stoke* Fictionalized "redbrick" university. Before the war, the
British government created many new universities (many of them
located in industrial cities such as Stoke). These were known
colloquially as "redbricks" for the building material used most
commonly in their construction. Social and academic snobs often
expressed disdain for the redbricks, contrasting them unfavorably
with the old traditions and old stone buildings of Oxford and
Cambridge Universities.

(*Anderson considers this.*)

ANDERSON. Even if that were true, my being seen dead in a place has never so far as I know been thought a condition of its excellence.

(*McKendrick despite himself laughs, though somewhat bitterly.*)

140 MCKENDRICK. Very good.

(*An air hostess is walking down the aisle, removing people's lunch trays. She removes Anderson's tray, revealing the cover of the sexy magazine, in the middle of McKendrick's next speech, and passes down the aisle.*)

Wit and paradox. Verbal felicity. An occupation for gentlemen. A higher civilization alive and well in the older universities. I see you like tits and bums, by the way.

145 ANDERSON. (*Embarrassed.*) Ah …

(*The turning of tables cheers McKendrick up considerably.*)

MCKENDRICK. They won't let you in with that, you know. You'll have to hide it.

ANDERSON. As a matter of fact it doesn't belong to me.

MCKENDRICK. Western decadence, you see. Marxists

150 are a terrible lot of prudes. I can say that because I'm a bit that way myself.

ANDERSON. You surprise me.

MCKENDRICK. Mind you, when I say I'm a Marxist…

ANDERSON. Oh, I see.

155 MCKENDRICK. … I don't mean I'm an apologist for everything done in the name of Marxism.

ANDERSON. No, no quite. There's nothing anti-socialist about it. Quite the reverse. The rich have always had it to themselves.

160 MCKENDRICK. On the contrary. That's why I'd be really very interested in any extra-curricular activities which might be going. I have an open mind about it.

ANDERSON. (*His wires crossed.*) Oh, yes, indeed, so have I.

165 MCKENDRICK. I sail pretty close to the wind, Marx-wise.

ANDERSON. Mind you, it's an odd thing but travel broadens the mind in a way that the proverbialist didn't quite intend. It's only at airports and railway stations

170 that one finds in oneself a curiosity about er—er—erotica, um, girlie magazines.

(*McKendrick realizes that they've had their wires crossed.*)

MCKENDRICK. Perhaps you've come across some of my articles.

ANDERSON. (*Amazed and fascinated.*) You mean you

175 write for—? (*He pulls himself up and together.*) Oh—your—er articles—I'm afraid as I explained I'm not very good at keeping up with the philosophical …. (*McKendrick has gone back to his former seat to fish about in his briefcase. He emerges with another girlie magazine*

180 *and hands it along the aisle to Anderson.*)

MCKENDRICK. I've got one here. Page sixty-one. The science fiction short story. Not a bad life. Science fiction and sex. And, of course, the philosophical assumptions of social science.

185 ANDERSON. (*Faintly.*) Thank you very much.

MCKENDRICK. Keep it by all means.

(*Anderson cautiously thumbs through pages of naked women.*)

I wonder if there'll be any decent women?

SCENE 2

(*Interior. Hotel Lobby. Prague.*

*We are near the reception desk. Anderson, McKendrick and Chetwyn have just arrived together. Perhaps with other people. Their luggage consists only of small overnight suitcases and briefcases. McKendrick is at the desk, half-way through his negotiations. The lobby ought to be rather large, with lifts,*[1] *etc. It should be large enough to make inconspicuous a man who is carefully watching the three Englishmen. This man is aged thirty-five or younger. He is poorly dressed, but not tramp-like. His name is Pavel Hollar. The lobby contains other people and a poorly equipped news-stand. We catch up with Anderson talking*

---

[1] *lifts* Elevators.

to Chetwyn.)

ANDERSON. (*Enthusiastically.*) Birmingham! Excellent university. Some very good people.

(*The Desk Clerk comes to the counter, where McKendrick is first in the queue. The Clerk and other Czech people in this script obviously speak with an accent, but there is no attempt here to reproduce it.*)

CLERK. Third floor. Dr. McKendrick.
MCKENDRICK. Only of philosophy.
5 CLERK. Your baggage is there?
MCKENDRICK. (*Hastily.*) Oh, I'll see to that. Can I have the key, please?
CLERK. Third floor. Dr. Anderson. Ninth floor. A letter for you.

(*The Clerk gives Anderson a sealed envelope and also a key. Anderson seems to have been expecting the letter. He thanks the Clerk and takes it.*)

10 Dr. Chetwyn. Ninth floor.

(*The three philosophers walk towards the lifts. Pavel watches them go. When they reach the lift Anderson glances round and sees two men some way off across the lobby, perhaps at the news-stand. These men are called Crisp and Broadbent. Crisp looks very young; he is twenty-two. He wears a very smart, slightly flashy suit and tie. Broadbent, balding but young, is in his thirties. He wears flannels and a blazer. Crisp is quite small. Broadbent is big and heavy. But both look fit.*)

ANDERSON. I say, look who's over there ... Broadbent and Crisp.

(*The lift now opens before them. Anderson goes in showing his key to the middle-aged woman in charge of the lift. McKendrick and Chetwyn do likewise. Over this:*)

CHETWYN. Who? (*He sees them and recognizes them.*) Oh yes.
15 MCKENDRICK. (*Sees them.*) Who?
CHETWYN. Crisp and Broadbent. They must be staying here too.
MCKENDRICK. Crisp? Broadbent? That kid over by the news-stand?
20 ANDERSON. That's Crisp.
MCKENDRICK. My God, they get younger all the time.

(*The lift doors close. Inside the lift.*)

ANDERSON. Crisp is twenty-two. Broadbent is past his peak but Crisp is the next genius in my opinion.
MCKENDRICK. Do you know him?
25 ANDERSON. Not personally. I've been watching him for a couple of years.
CHETWYN. He's Newcastle, isn't he?
ANDERSON. Yes.
MCKENDRICK. I've never heard of him. What's his role there?
30 ANDERSON. He's what used to be called left wing. Broadbent's in the centre. He's an opportunist more than anything. (*The lift has stopped at the third floor.*) (*To McKendrick*) This is you—see you later.

(*McKendrick steps out of the lift and looks round.*)

35 MCKENDRICK. Do you think the rooms are bugged?

(*The lift doors shut him off. Inside the lift. Anderson and Chetwyn ride up in silence for a few moments.*)

ANDERSON. What was it Aristotle said about the higher you go the further you fall ...?
CHETWYN. He was talking about tragic heroes.

(*The lift stops at the ninth floor. Anderson and Chetwyn leave the lift.*)

I'm this way. There's a restaurant downstairs. The menu
40 is very limited but it's all right.
ANDERSON. You've been here before?
CHETWYN. Yes. Perhaps see you later then, sir.

(*Chetwyn goes down a corridor, away from Anderson's corridor.*)

ANDERSON. (*To himself.*) Sir?

(*Anderson follows the arrow towards his own room number.*)

SCENE 3

(*Interior. Anderson's hotel room.*

    *The room contains a bed, a wardrobe, a chest. A telephone. A bathroom containing a bath leads off through a door. Anderson is unpacking. He puts some clothes into a drawer and closes it. His suitcase is open on the bed. Anderson turns his attention to his briefcase and brings out McKendrick's magazine. He looks round, wondering what to do with it. There is a knock on the door. Anderson tosses the girlie magazine into his suitcase and closes the case. He goes to open the door. The caller is Pavel Hollar.*)

ANDERSON. Yes?
HOLLAR. I am Pavel Hollar.
ANDERSON. Yes?
HOLLAR. Professor Anderson.

(*Hollar is Czech and speaks with an accent.*)

5 ANDERSON. Hollar? Oh, heavens, yes. How extraordinary. Come in.
HOLLAR. Thank you. I'm sorry to—
ANDERSON. No, no—what a pleasant surprise. I've only just arrived, as you can see. Sit where you can. How are
10 you? What are you doing? You live in Prague?
HOLLAR. Oh yes.

(*Anderson closes the door.*)

ANDERSON. Well, well. Well, well, well, well. How are you? Must be ten years.
HOLLAR. Yes. It is ten. I took my degree in sixty-seven.
15 ANDERSON. You got a decent degree, too, didn't you?
HOLLAR. Yes, I got a first.[1]
ANDERSON. Of course you did. Well done, well done. Are you still in philosophy?
HOLLAR. No, unfortunately.
20 ANDERSON. Ah. What are you doing now?
HOLLAR. I am a, what do you say—a cleaner.

---
[1] *a first* First-class degree.

ANDERSON. (*With intelligent interest.*) A cleaner? What is that?
HOLLAR. (*Surprised.*) Cleaning. Washing. With a brush
25 and a bucket. I am a cleaner at the bus station.
ANDERSON. You wash buses?
HOLLAR. No, not buses—the lavatories, the floors where people walk and so on.
ANDERSON. Oh. I see. You're a *cleaner*.
30 HOLLAR. Yes.

(*Pause.*)

ANDERSON. Are you married now, or anything?
HOLLAR. Yes. I married. She was almost my fiancée when I went to England. Irma. She is a country girl. No English. No philosophy. We have a son who is Sacha.
35 That is Alexander.
ANDERSON. I see.
HOLLAR. And Mrs. Anderson?
ANDERSON. She died. Did you meet her ever?
HOLLAR. No.
40 ANDERSON. (*Pause.*) I don't know what to say.
HOLLAR. Did she die recently?
ANDERSON. No, I mean—a cleaner.
HOLLAR. I had one year graduate research. My doctorate studies were on certain connections with Thomas Paine
45 and Locke. But then, since sixty-nine …
ANDERSON. Cleaning lavatories.
HOLLAR. First I was in a bakery. Later on construction, building houses. Many other things. It is the way it is for many people.
50 ANDERSON. Is it all right for you to be here talking to me?
HOLLAR. Of course. Why not? You are my old professor.

(*Hollar is carrying a bag or briefcase. He puts this down and opens it.*)

I have something here.

(*From the bag he takes out of the sort of envelope which would contain about thirty type-written foolscap pages. He also takes out a child's "magic eraser" pad, the sort of pad on which one scratches a message and then slides it out to erase it.)*

55  You understand these things of course?
ANDERSON.  (*Nonplussed.*) Er …
HOLLAR.  (*Smiling.*) Of course.

*(Hollar demonstrates the pad briefly, then writes on the pad while Anderson watches.)*

ANDERSON.  (*Stares at him.*) To England?

*(Hollar abandons the use of the pad, and whispers in Anderson's ear.)*

HOLLAR.  Excuse me.

*(Hollar goes to the door and opens it for Anderson. Hollar carries his envelope but leaves his bag in the room. Anderson goes out of the door baffled. Hollar follows him. They walk a few paces down the corridor.)*

60  Thank you. It is better to be careful.
ANDERSON.  Why? You don't seriously suggest that my room is bugged?
HOLLAR.  It is better to assume it.
ANDERSON.  Why?

*(Just then the door of the room next to Anderson's opens and a man comes out. He is about forty and wears a dark rather shapeless suit. He glances at Anderson and Hollar. And then walks off in the opposite direction towards the lift and passes out of sight. Hollar and Anderson instinctively pause until the man has gone.)*

65  I hope you're not getting me into trouble.
HOLLAR.  I hope not. I don't think so. I have friends in trouble.
ANDERSON.  I know, it's dreadful—but … well, what is it?

*(Hollar indicates his envelope.)*

70  HOLLAR.  My doctoral thesis. It is mainly theoretical. Only ten thousand words, but very formally arranged.

ANDERSON.  My goodness … ten years in the writing.
HOLLAR.  No. I wrote it this month—when I heard of this congress here and you coming. I decided. Every day
75  in the night.
ANDERSON.  Of course. I'd be very happy to read it.
HOLLAR.  It is in Czech.
ANDERSON.  Oh … well …?
HOLLAR.  I'm afraid so. But Peter Volkansky—he was
80  with me, you remember—we came together in sixty-three—
ANDERSON.  Oh yes—Volkansky—yes, I do remember him. He never came back here.
HOLLAR.  No. He didn't come back. He was a realist.
85  ANDERSON.  He's at Reading[1] or somewhere like that.
HOLLAR.  Lyster.
ANDERSON.  Leicester.[2] Exactly. Are you in touch with him?
HOLLAR.  A little. He will translate it and try to have it
90  published in English. If it's good. I think it is good.
ANDERSON.  But can't you publish it in Czech?… (*This catches up on him and he shakes his head.*) Oh, Hollar … now, you know, really, I'm a guest of the government here.
95  HOLLAR.  They would not search you.
ANDERSON.  That's not the point. I'm sorry … I mean it would be bad manners, wouldn't it?
HOLLAR.  Bad manners?
ANDERSON.  I know it sounds rather lame. But ethics
100  and manners are interestingly related. The history of human calumny is largely a series of breaches of good manners … (*Pause.*) Perhaps if I said correct behaviour it wouldn't sound so ridiculous. You do see what I mean. I am sorry. … Look, can we go back … I ought
105  to unpack.
HOLLAR.  My thesis is about correct behaviour.
ANDERSON.  Oh yes?
HOLLAR.  Here, you know, individual correctness is defined by what is correct for the state.
110 ANDERSON.  Yes, I know.
HOLLAR.  I ask how collective right can have meaning by itself. I ask where it comes from, the idea of a collective ethic.
ANDERSON.  Yes.

---

[1]  *Reading*  University of Reading.

[2]  *Leicester*  University of Leicester.

HOLLAR. I reply, it comes from the individual. One man's dealings with another man.

ANDERSON. Yes.

HOLLAR. The collective ethic can only be the individual ethic writ big.

ANDERSON. Writ large.

HOLLAR. Writ large, precisely. The ethics of the state must be judged against the fundamental ethic of the individual. The human being, not the citizen. I conclude there is an obligation, a human responsibility, to fight against the state correctness. Unfortunately that is not a safe conclusion.

ANDERSON. Quite. The difficulty arises when one asks oneself how the *individual* ethic can have any meaning by itself. Where does *that* come from? In what sense is it intelligible, for example, to say that a man has certain inherent, individual rights? It is much easier to understand how a community of individuals can decide to give each other certain rights. These rights may or may not include, for example, the right to publish something. In that situation, the individual ethic would flow from the collective ethic, just as the state says it does. (*Pause.*) I only mean it is a question you would have to deal with.

HOLLAR. I mean, it is not safe for me.

ANDERSON. (*Still misunderstanding.*) Well yes, but for example, you could say that such an arrangement between a man and the state is a sort of contract, and it is the essence of a contract that both parties enter into it freely. And you have not entered into it freely. I mean, that would be one line of attack.

HOLLAR. It is not the main line. You see, to me the idea of an inherent right is intelligible. I believe that we have such rights, and they are paramount.

ANDERSON. Yes, I see you do, but how do you justify the assertion?

HOLLAR. I observe. I observe my son for example.

ANDERSON. Your son?

HOLLAR. For example.

(*Pause.*)

ANDERSON. Look, there's no need to stand out here. There's … no point. I was going to have a bath and change … meeting some of my colleagues later …

(*Anderson moves to go but Hollar stops him with a touch on the arm.*)

HOLLAR. I am not a famous dissident. A writer, a scientist …

ANDERSON. No.

HOLLAR. If I am picked up—on the way home, let us say—there is no fuss. A cleaner. I will be one of hundreds. It's all right. In the end it must change. But I have something to say—that is all. If I leave my statement behind, then it's OK. You understand?

ANDERSON. Perhaps the correct thing for me to have done is not to have accepted their invitation to speak here. But I did accept it. It is a contract, as it were, freely entered into. And having accepted their hospitality I cannot in all conscience start smuggling … It's just not ethical.

HOLLAR. But if you didn't know you were smuggling it—

ANDERSON. Smuggling entails knowledge.

HOLLAR. If I hid my thesis in your luggage, for instance.

ANDERSON. That's childish. Also, you could be getting me into trouble, and your quarrel is not with me. Your action would be unethical on your own terms—one man's dealings with another man. I am sorry.

(*Anderson goes back towards his door, which Hollar had left ajar. Hollar follows him.*)

HOLLAR. No, it is I who must apologize. The man next door, is he one of your group?

ANDERSON. No. I don't know him.

(*Anderson opens his bedroom door. He turns as if to say goodbye.*)

HOLLAR. My bag.

ANDERSON. Oh yes.

(*Hollar follows Anderson into the room.*)

HOLLAR. You will have a bath…?

ANDERSON. I thought I would.

(*Hollar turns into the bathroom. Anderson stays in the bedroom, surprised. He hears the bath water being turned on. The bath water makes a rush of sound. Anderson enters the bathroom and sees Hollar sitting on the edge of the bath. Interior bathroom.*)

HOLLAR.   (*Quietly.*) I have not yet made a copy.
ANDERSON.   (*Loudly.*) What?

(*Hollar goes up to Anderson and speaks close to Anderson's ear. The bath taps make a loud background noise.*)

HOLLAR.   I have not yet made a copy. I have a bad feeling about carrying this home. (*He indicates his*
190 *envelope.*) I did not expect to take it away. I ask a favour. (*Smiles.*) Ethical.
ANDERSON.   (*Quietly now.*) What is it?
HOLLAR.   Let me leave this here and you can bring it to my apartment tomorrow—I have a safe place for it
195 there.

(*Hollar takes a piece of paper and a pencil from his pocket and starts writing his address in capital letters.*)

ANDERSON.  But you know my time here is very crowded—(*Then he gives in.*) Do you live nearby?
HOLLAR.   It is not far. I have written my address.

(*Hollar gives Anderson the paper.*)

ANDERSON.   (*Forgetting to be quiet.*) Do you
200 seriously—(*Hollar quietens Anderson.*) Do you seriously expect to be searched on the way home?
HOLLAR.   I don't know, but it is better to be careful. I wrote a letter to Mr. Husak.[1] Also some other things. So sometimes they follow me.
205 ANDERSON.   But you weren't worried about bringing the thesis with you.
HOLLAR.   No. If anybody watches me they want to know what books *you* give *me.*
ANDERSON.   I see. Yes, all right, Hollar. I'll bring it
210 tomorrow.

---

[1] *Mr. Husak*  Gustav Husak (1913–91), leader of Czechoslovakia between 1969 and 1987.

HOLLAR.   Please don't leave it in your room when you go to eat. Take your briefcase.

(*They go back into the bedroom. Anderson puts Hollar's envelope into his briefcase.*)

(*Normal voice.*) So perhaps you will come and meet my wife.
215 ANDERSON.   Yes. Should I telephone?
HOLLAR.   Unfortunately my telephone is removed. I am home all day. Saturday.
ANDERSON.   Oh yes.
HOLLAR.   Goodbye.
220 ANDERSON.   Goodbye.

(*Hollar goes to the door, carrying his bag.*)

HOLLAR.   I forgot—welcome to Prague. (*Hollar leaves, closing the door. Anderson stands still for a few moments. Then he hears footsteps approaching down the corridor. The footsteps appear to stop outside his room. But then the door*
225 *to the next room is opened and the unseen man enters the room next door and loudly closes the door behind him.*)

## SCENE 4

(*Interior. Anderson's room. Morning.*
*Close-up of the colloquium brochure. It is lying on Anderson's table. Then Anderson picks it up. His dress and appearance, and the light outside the window, tell us that it is morning. Dressed to go out, Anderson picks up his briefcase and leaves the room. In the corridor he walks towards the lifts. At the lifts he finds Crisp waiting. Anderson stands next to Crisp silently for a few moments.*)

ANDERSON.   Good morning. (*Pause.*) Mr. Crisp … my name is Anderson. I'm a very great admirer of yours.
CRISP.   (*Chewing gum.*) Oh … ta.
ANDERSON.   Good luck this afternoon.
5 CRISP.   Thanks. Bloody useless, the lifts in this place.
ANDERSON.   Are you all staying in this hotel?

(*Crisp doesn't seem to hear this. Crisp sees Broadbent emerging from a room. Broadbent carries a zipped bag.*

*Crisp has a similar bag.)*

CRISP.   (*Shouts.*) Here you are, Roy—it's waiting for you.

(*Broadbent arrives.*)

ANDERSON.   Good morning. Good luck this afternoon.
BROADBENT.   Right. Thanks. Are you over for the
10 match?
ANDERSON.   Yes. Well, partly. I've got my ticket.

(*Anderson takes out of his pocket the envelope he received
from the hotel Clerk and shows it.*)

CRISP.   (*Quietly.*) You didn't pull her, then?
BROADBENT.   No chance.
CRISP.   They don't trust you, do they?
15 BROADBENT.   Well, they're right, aren't they? Remember
Milan.
CRISP.   (*Laughing.*) Yeah—(*The bell sounds to indicate
that the lift is arriving.*) About bloody time.
ANDERSON.   I see from yesterday's paper that they've
20 brought in Jirasek for Vladislav.
BROADBENT.   Yes, that's right. Six foot eight, they say.
ANDERSON.   He's not very good in the air unless he's got
lots of space.

(*Broadbent looks at him curiously. The lift doors open and
the three of them get in. There is no one else in the lift
except the female Operator. Interior lift.*)

BROADBENT.   You've seen him, have you?
25 ANDERSON.   I've seen him twice. In the UEFA Cup a
few seasons ago.... I happened to be in Berlin for the
Hegel[1] Colloquium, er, bunfight. And then last season
I was in Bratislava to receive an honorary degree.
CRISP.   Tap his ankles for him. Teach him to be six foot
30 eight.
BROADBENT.   Leave off—(*He nods at the Lift Operator.*)
You never know, do you?
CRISP.   Yeah, maybe the lift's bugged.
ANDERSON.   He scored both times from the same move,
35 and came close twice more—

BROADBENT.   Oh yes?

(*Pause.*)

ANDERSON.   (*In a rush.*) I realize it's none of my
business—I mean you may think I'm an absolute ass,
but—(*Pause.*) Look, if Halas takes a corner he's going to
40 make it short—almost certainly—push it back to Deml
or Kautsky, who pulls the defence out. Jirasek hangs
about for the chip to the far post. They'll do the same
thing from a set piece. Three or four times in the same
match. *Really.* Short corners and free kicks. (*The lift stops
45 at the third floor. Broadbent and Crisp are staring at
Anderson.*) (*Lamely.*) Anyway, that's why they've
brought Jirasek back, in my opinion.

(*The lift doors open and McKendrick gets in. McKendrick's
manner is breezy and bright.*)

MCKENDRICK.   Good morning! You've got together
then?
50 ANDERSON.   A colleague. Mr. McKendrick ...
MCKENDRICK.   You're Crisp. (*He takes Crisp's hand and
shakes it.*) Bill McKendrick. I hear you're doing some
very interesting work in Newcastle.[2] Great stuff. I still
like to think of myself as a bit of a left-winger at Stoke.[3]
55 Of course, my stuff is largely empirical—I leave
epistemological questions to the scholastics—eh,
Anderson? (*He pokes Anderson in the ribs.*)
ANDERSON.   McKendrick ...
BROADBENT.   Did you say *Stoke?*

(*The lift arrives at the ground floor.*)

60 MCKENDRICK.   (*To Broadbent.*) We've met, haven't we?
Your face is familiar ...

(*Broadbent, Crisp and McKendrick in close attendance
leave the lift. Anderson is slow on the uptake but follows.*)

ANDERSON.   McKendrick—?

---

[1] *Hegel*   Georg Wilhelm Friedrich Hegel *(*1770–1831*),* German
philosopher.

[2] *Newcastle*   Northern English town, home of both Newcastle
University and the Newcastle United football club.

[3] *Stoke*   Stoke City football club traditionally plays at a much lower
level than does Newcastle United.

MCKENDRICK. (*Prattling*) There's a choice of open forums tonight—neo-Hegelians or Quinian neo-Positivists. Which do you fancy? Pity Quine[1] couldn't be here. And Hegel for that matter.

(*McKendrick laughs brazenly in the lobby. Broadbent and Crisp eye him warily. Anderson winces.*)

## SCENE 5

(*Interior. The colloquium.*

*The general idea is that a lot of philosophers sit in a sort of theatre while on stage one of their number reads a paper from behind a lectern, with a Chairman in attendance behind him. The set-up, however, is quite complicated. To one side are three glassed-in-booths, each one containing "simultaneous interpreters." These interpreters have earphones and microphones. They also have a copy of the lecture being given. One of these interpreters is translating into Czech, another into French, another into German. The audience is furnished with earphones or with those hand-held phones which are issued in theatres sometimes. Each of these phones can tune into any of the three interpreters, depending upon the language of the listener. For our purposes it is better to have the hand-held phones. It is important to the play, specifically to a later scene when Anderson is talking, that the hall and the audience should be substantial. At the moment Anderson is in the audience, sitting next to McKendrick. McKendrick is still discomfited. Chetwyn is elsewhere in the audience.*

*We begin, however, with a large close-up of the speaker, who is an American called Stone. After the first sentence or two of Stone's speech, the camera will acquaint us with the situation. At different points during Stone's speech, there is conversation between Anderson and McKendrick. In this script, these conversations are placed immediately after that part of Stone's speech which they will cover. This applies also to any other interpolations. Obviously, Stone does not pause to let these other things in.*)

STONE. The confusion which often arises from the ambiguity of ordinary language raises special problems for a logical language. This is especially so when the ambiguity is not casual and inadvertent—but when it's contrived. In fact, the limitations of a logical language are likely to appear when we ask ourselves whether it can accommodate a literature, or whether poetry can be reduced to a logical language. It is here that deliberate ambiguity for effect makes problems.

ANDERSON. Perfectly understandable mistake.

STONE. Nor must we confuse ambiguity, furthermore, with mere synonymity. When we say that a politician ran for office, that is not an ambiguous statement, it is merely an instance of a word having different applications, literal, idiomatic and so on.

MCKENDRICK. I said I knew his face.

ANDERSON. "Match of the Day."[2]

STONE. The intent is clear in each application. The show ran well on Broadway. Native Dancer ran well at Kentucky,[3] and so on. (*In the audience a Frenchman expresses dismay and bewilderment as his earphones give out a literal translation of "a native dancer" running well at Kentucky. Likewise a German listener has the same problem.*)

And what about this word "Well"? Again, it is applied as a qualifier with various intent—the show ran for a long time, the horse ran fast, and so on.

MCKENDRICK. So this pressing engagement of yours is a football match.

ANDERSON. A World Cup qualifier is not just a football match.

STONE. Again, there is no problem here so long as these variations are what I propose to call reliable. "You eat well," says Mary to John. "You cook well," says John to Mary. We know that when Mary says, "You *eat* well," she does not mean that John eats *skilfully*. Just as we know that when John says, "You cook well," he does not mean that Mary cooks *abundantly*.

ANDERSON. But I'm sorry about missing your paper, I really am.

STONE. I say that we know this, but I mean only that our general experience indicates it. The qualifier takes its meaning from the contextual force of the verb it

---

[1] *Quine* Willard Van Orman Quine (1908–2000), American analytical philosopher and logician.

[2] *Match of the Day* The pun here involves matching faces with names and the long-running British television program featuring a selected football match.

[3] *Native … Kentucky* I.e., a horse named "Native Dancer" ran well at the Kentucky Derby, the American horse-race.

qualifies. But it is the mark of a sound theory that it
should take account not merely of our general
experience but also of the particular experience, and not
merely of the particular experience but also of the
unique experience, and not merely of the unique
experience but also of the hypothetical experience. It is
when we consider the world of *possibilities,* hypothetical
experience, that we get closer to ambiguity. "You cook
well," says John to Mary. "You eat well," says Mary to
John.

MCKENDRICK.   Do you ever wonder whether all this is
worthwhile?

ANDERSON.   No.

MCKENDRICK.   I know what you mean.

(*Chetwyn is twisting the knob on his translation phone, to
try all this out in different languages. He is clearly bored.
He looks at his watch.*)

STONE.   No problems there. But I ask you to imagine a
competition when what is being judged is table
manners. (*Insert French interpreter's box—interior.*)

INTERPRETER.   … *bonne tenue à table* …[1]

STONE.   John enters this competition and afterwards
Mary says, "Well, you certainly ate well!" Now Mary
seems to be saying that John ate skilfully—*with
refinement.* And again, I ask you to imagine a
competition where the amount of food eaten is taken
into account along with refinement of table manners.
*Now* Mary says to John, "Well, you didn't eat very well,
but at least you ate well."

INTERPRETER.   *Alors, vous n'avez pas bien mangé … mais
…*[2] (*All Interpreters baffled by this.*)

STONE.   Now clearly there is no way to tell whether
Mary means that John ate abundantly but clumsily, or
that John ate frugally but elegantly. Here we have a
genuine ambiguity. To restate Mary's sentence in a
logical language we would have to ask her what she
meant.

MCKENDRICK.   By the way, I've got you a copy of my
paper.

ANDERSON.   Oh, many thanks.

---

[1] *bonne tenue à table*   French: good table manners.

[2] *Alors … mais*   A word-for-word translation into French: Well,
you did not eat well … but ….

MCKENDRICK.   It's not a long paper. You could read it
comfortably during half-time.

(*McKendrick gives Anderson his paper.*)

STONE.   But this is to assume that Mary exists. Let us say
she is a fictitious character in a story I have written. Very
well, you say to me, the author, "What did Mary
mean?" Well, I might reply—"I don't know what she
meant. Her ambiguity makes the necessary point of my
story." And here I think the idea of a logical language
which can *only* be unambiguous breaks down.

(*Anderson opens his briefcase and puts McKendrick's paper
into it. He fingers Hollar's envelope and broods over it.
Stone has concluded. He sits down to applause. The
Chairman, who has been sitting behind him, has stood up.*)

ANDERSON.   I'm going to make a discreet exit—I've got
a call to make before the match.

(*Anderson stands up.*)

CHAIRMAN.   Yes—Professor Anderson I think …?

(*Anderson is caught like a rabbit in the headlights.
McKendrick enjoys his predicament and becomes interested
in how Anderson will deal with it.*)

ANDERSON.   Ah … I would only like to offer Professor
Stone the observation that language is not the only level
of human communication, and perhaps not the most
important level. Whereof we cannot speak, thereof we
are by no means silent. (*McKendrick smiles "Bravo."*)
Verbal language is a technical refinement of our capacity
for communication, rather than the *fons et origo*[3] of that
capacity. The likelihood is that language develops in an
*ad hoc*[4] way, so there is no reason to expect its development to be logical. (*A thought strikes him.*) The
importance of language is overrated. It allows me and
Professor Stone to show off a bit, and it is very useful for
communicating detail—but the important truths are

---

[3] *fons et origo*   Latin: source and origin.

[4] *ad hoc*   Latin: literally, "to this," meaning here for a particular
purpose.

simple and monolithic. The essentials of a given situation speak for themselves, and language is as capable of obscuring the truth as of revealing it. Thank you. (*Anderson edges his way out towards the door.*)

110 CHAIRMAN.  (*Uncertainly.*) Professor Stone …

STONE.  Well, what was the question?

### SCENE 6

(*Interior. Front door of the Hollar apartment.*

*The apartment is one of two half-way up a large old building. The stairwell is dirty and uncared for. The Hollar front door is on a landing, and the front door of another flat is across the landing. Stairs go up and down. Anderson comes up the stairs and finds the right number on the door and rings the bell. He is carrying his briefcase. All the men in this scene are Czech plain-clothes Policemen. They will be identified in this text merely by number. Man 3 is the one in charge. Man 1 comes to the door.*)

ANDERSON.  I'm looking for Mr. Hollar.

(*Man 1 shakes his head. He looks behind him. Man 2 comes to the door.*)

MAN 2.  (*In Czech.*) Yes? Who are you?

ANDERSON.  English? Um. *Parlez-vous français?* Er. Spreckanzydoitch?

5 MAN 2.  (*In German.*) *Deutsch? Ein Bisschen.*[1]

ANDERSON.   Actually I don't. Does Mr. Hollar live here? Apartment Hollar?

(*Man 2 speaks to somebody behind him.*)

MAN 2.  (*In Czech.*) An Englishman. Do you know him?

(*Mrs. Hollar comes to the door. She is about the same age as Hollar.*)

---

[1] *Parlez-vous … Bisschen   Parlez-vous français* French: do you speak French? *Spreckanzydoitch?* I.e., German: *Sprechen Sie Deuetsch*, do you speak German? *Deutsch? Ein Bisschen* German: German? A bit.

ANDERSON.  Mrs. Hollar? (*Mrs. Hollar nods.*) Is your

10 husband here? Pavel …

MRS. HOLLAR.   (*In Czech.*) Pavel is arrested.

(*Inside, behind the door, Man 3 is heard shouting, in Czech.*)

MAN 3.  (*Not seen.*) What's going on there?

(*Man 3 comes to the door.*)

ANDERSON.   I am looking for Mr. Hollar. I am a friend from England. His Professor. My name is Anderson.

15 MAN 3.  (*In English.*) Not here. (*In Czech to Mrs. Hollar.*) He says he is a friend of your husband. Anderson.

ANDERSON.  He was my student.

(*Mrs. Hollar calls out.*)

MAN 3. (*In Czech.*) Shut up.

20 ANDERSON.  Student. Philosophy.

(*Mrs. Hollar calls out.*)

MAN 3.  Shut up.

(*Man 3 and Man 2 come out of the flat on to the landing, closing the door behind them.*)

ANDERSON.   I just came to see him. Just to say hello. For a minute. I have a taxi waiting. Taxi.

MAN 3.  Taxi.

25 ANDERSON.  Yes. I can't stay.

MAN 3.  (*In English.*) Moment. OK.

ANDERSON.  I can't stay.

(*Man 3 rings the bell of the adjacent flat. A rather scared woman opens the door. Man 3 asks, in Czech, to use the phone. Man 3 goes inside the other flat. Anderson begins to realize the situation.*)

Well, look, if you don't mind—I'm on my way to—an engagement …

30 MAN 2.  (*In Czech.*) Stay here.

(*Pause. Anderson looks at his watch. Then from inside the flat Mrs. Hollar is shouting in Czech.*)

MRS. HOLLAR.    (*Unseen.*) I'm entitled to a witness of my choice.

(*The door is opened violently and immediately slammed. Anderson becomes agitated.*)

ANDERSON.    What's going on in there?
MAN 2.    (*In Czech.*) Stay here, he won't be a minute.

(*Anderson can hear Mrs. Hollar shouting.*)

35    ANDERSON.  Now  look  here—(*Anderson  rings  the doorbell. The door is opened by Man 4.*) I demand to speak to Mrs. Hollar.

(*Upstairs and downstairs doors are opening and people are shouting, in Czech, "What's going on?" And so on. There is also shouting from inside the flat. Man 2 shouts up and down the staircase, in Czech.*)

MAN 2.    (*In Czech.*) Go inside!
ANDERSON.   Now look here, I am the J. S. Mill Professor
40    of Ethics at the University of Cambridge and I demand that I be allowed to leave or to telephone the British Ambassador!
MAN 4.    (*In Czech.*) Bring him inside.
MAN 2.    (*In Czech.*) In.

(*He pushes Anderson into the flat. Interior flat. The hallway. Inside it is apparent that the front door leads to more than one flat. Off the very small dirty hall there is a kitchen, a lavatory and two other doors, not counting the door to the Hollar rooms.*)

45    MAN 4.    (*In Czech.*) Stay with him. (*The Hollar interior door is opened from inside by Mrs. Hollar.*)
MRS. HOLLAR.    (*In Czech.*) If he's my witness he's allowed in here.
MAN 4.    (*In Czech.*) Go inside—he's not your witness.

(*Man 4 pushes Mrs. Hollar inside and closes the door from within. This leaves Anderson and Man 2 in the little hall.*

*Another door now opens, and a small girl, poorly dressed, looks round it. She is jerked back out of sight by someone and the door is pulled closed. The Hollar door is flung open again, by Mrs. Hollar.*)

50    MRS. HOLLAR.    (*In Czech.*) I want this door open.
MAN 2.    (*In Czech.*) Leave it open, then. He'll be back in a minute.

(*Man 4 disappears back inside the flat. Mrs. Hollar is heard.*)

MRS. HOLLAR.    (*Unseen. In Czech.*) Bastards.

(*Anderson stands in the hallway. He can hear Mrs. Hollar starting to cry. Anderson looks completely out of his depth.*)

ANDERSON.   My God …

(*Then the doorbell rings. Man 2 opens it to let in Man 3.*)

55    MAN 2.    (*In Czech.*) We had to come in to shut her up.
MAN 3.    (*In Czech.*) Well, he's coming over. (*In English to Anderson.*) Captain coming. Speak English.
ANDERSON.   I would like to telephone the British Ambassador.
60    MAN 3.    (*In English.*) OK. Captain coming.
ANDERSON.   How long will he be? I have an appointment. (*He looks at his watch.*) Yes, by God! I do have an engagement and it starts in half an hour—
MAN 3.    (*In English.*) Please.

(*A lavatory flushes. From the other interior door an Old Man comes out. Man 3 nods curtly at the Old Man. The Old Man shuffles by looking at Anderson. Man 3 becomes uneasy at being in the traffic. He decides to bring Anderson inside the flat. He does so.*

*Interior Hollar's room. There are two connecting rooms. Beyond this room is a door leading to a bedroom. This door is open. The rooms seem full of people. The rooms are small and shabby. They are being thoroughly searched, and obviously have been in this process for hours. The searchers do not spoil or destroy anything. There are no torn cushions or anything like that. However, the floor of the first room is almost covered in books. The bookcases which line perhaps two of the walls are empty. The rug could be rolled up, and there could be one or two floorboards up.*

*Man 1 is going through the books, leafing through each one and looking along the spine. He is starting to put books back on the shelves one by one. Man 5 has emptied drawers of their contents and is going through a pile of papers. Mrs. Hollar stands in the doorway between the two rooms. Beyond her Man 2 can be seen searching. [Man 4 is out of sight in the bedroom.] Man 3 indicates a chair on which Anderson should sit. Anderson sits, putting his briefcase on the floor by his feet. He looks around.*

*He sees a clock showing 2:35.*

*Mix to clock showing 2:55.*

*Anderson is where he was. Man 1 is still on the books. Man 5 is still looking through papers. Man 3 is examining the inside of a radio set.*

*Voices are heard faintly on the stairs. There is a man remonstrating. A woman's voice, too.*

*The doorbell rings.*

*Man 3 leaves the room, closing the door. Anderson hears him go to the front door. There is some conversation. The front door closes again and Man 3 re-enters the room.)*

65 MAN 3. *(In English to Anderson.)* Taxi.

ANDERSON. Oh—I forgot him. Dear me.

MAN 3. OK.

ANDERSON. I must pay him.

*(Anderson takes out his wallet. Man 3 takes it from him without snatching.)*

MAN 3. OK.

*(Man 3 looks through the wallet.)*

70 ANDERSON. Give that back—*(Furious.)* Now, you listen to me—this has gone on quite long enough—I demand—to be allowed to leave …

*(Anderson has stood up. Man 3 gently pushes him back into the chair. In Anderson's wallet Man 3 finds his envelope and discovers the football ticket. He puts it back. He looks sympathetically at Anderson.)*

MAN 3. *(In Czech.)* The old boy's got a ticket for the

England match. No wonder he's furious. *(He gives the wallet back to Anderson. In English.)* Taxi OK. No money. He go. Football no good.

ANDERSON. Serve me right.

MAN 5. *(In Czech.)* It's on the radio. Let him have it on.

*(Man 3 returns to the radio and turns it on. Mrs. Hollar enters quickly from the bedroom and turns it off.)*

MRS. HOLLAR. *(In Czech.)* That's my radio.

80 MAN 3. *(In Czech.)* Your friend wants to listen to the match.

*(Mrs. Hollar looks at Anderson. She turns the radio on. The radio is talking about the match, which is just about to begin.)*

MAN 3. *(In English.)* Is good. OK?

*(Anderson, listening, realizes that the radio is listing the names of the English team.*

*Then the match begins.*

*Mix to: The same situation about half an hour later. The radio is still on. Man 1 is still on the books. He has put aside three or four English books. Man 5 has disappeared. Man 2 is sorting out the fluff from a carpet sweeper. Man 4 is standing on a chair, examining the inside of a ventilation grating.*

*Anderson gets up off his chair and starts to walk towards the bedroom.*

*The three Men in the room look up but don't stop him. Anderson enters the bedroom. Interior bedroom.*

*Man 3 is going through pockets in a wardrobe. Man 5 is looking under floorboards. Mrs. Hollar is sitting on the bed, watching them.)*

ANDERSON. It's half-past three. I demand to be allowed to leave or to telephone the British—

85 MAN 3. Please—too slow.

ANDERSON. I demand to leave—

MAN 3. OK. Who wins football?

ANDERSON. *(Pause.)* No score.

*(The doorbell goes. Man 3 goes into the other room and to the door. Anderson follows him as far as the other room.*

*On the way through Man 3 signals to turn off the radio. Man 2 turns off the radio. Mrs. Hollar comes in and turns the radio on.)*

MRS. HOLLAR.    (*In Czech.*) Show me where it says I can't listen to my own radio.

(*Man 3 returns from the front door with Man 6. Man 6 enters the room, saying:*)

MAN 6.    (*In Czech.*) I said don't let him leave—I didn't say bring him inside. (*To Anderson in English.*) Professor Anderson? I'm sorry your friend Mr. Hollar has got himself into trouble.

ANDERSON.    Thank Christ—now listen to me—I am a professor of philosophy. I am a guest of the Czechoslovakian government. I might almost say an honoured guest. I have been invited to speak at the Colloquium in Prague. My connections in England reach up to the highest in the land

MAN 6.    Do you know the Queen?

ANDERSON.    Certainly. (*But he has rushed into that.*) No, I do not know the Queen—but I speak the truth when I say that I am personally acquainted with two members of the government, one of whom has been to my house, and I assure you that unless I am allowed to leave this building immediately there is going to be a major incident about the way my liberty has been impeded by your men. I do not know what they are doing here, I do not care what they are doing here—

MAN 6.    Excuse me, Professor. There is some mistake. I thought you were here as a friend of the Hollar family.

ANDERSON.    I know Pavel Hollar, certainly.

MAN 6.    Absolutely. You are here as a friend, at Mrs. Hollar's request.

ANDERSON.    I just dropped in to—what do you mean?

MAN 6.    Mr. Hollar unfortunately has been arrested for a serious crime against the state. It is usual for the home of an accused person to be searched for evidence, and so on. I am sure the same thing happens in your country. Well, under our law Mrs. Hollar is entitled to have a friendly witness present during the search. To be frank, she is entitled to two witnesses. So if, for example, an expensive vase is broken by mistake, and the police claim it was broken before, it will not just be her word

against theirs. And so on. I think you will agree that's fair.

ANDERSON.    Well?

MAN 6.    Well, my understanding is that she asked you to be her witness. (*In Czech to Mrs. Hollar.*) Did you ask him to be your witness?

MRS. HOLLAR.    (*In Czech.*) Yes, I did.

MAN 6.    (*In English to Anderson.*) Yes. Exactly so. (*Pause.*) You are Mr. Hollar's friend, aren't you?

ANDERSON.    I taught him in Cambridge after he left Czechoslovakia.

MAN 6.    A brave man.

ANDERSON.    Yes … a change of language … and … culture …

MAN 6.    He walked across a minefield. In 1962.[1] Brave.

ANDERSON.    Perhaps he was simply desperate.

MAN 6.    Perhaps a little ungrateful. The state, you know, educated him, fed him, for eighteen years. "Thank you very much—goodbye."

ANDERSON.    Well he came back, in the spring of sixty-eight.

MAN 6.    Oh yes.

ANDERSON.    A miscalculation.

MAN 6.    How do you mean?

ANDERSON.    Well, really … there are a lot of things wrong in England but it is still not "a serious crime against the state" to put forward a philosophical view which does not find favour with the government.

MAN 6.    Professor … Hollar is charged with currency offences. There is a black market in hard currency. It is illegal. We do not have laws about philosophy. He is an ordinary criminal.

(*Pause. The radio commentary has continued softly. But in this pause it changes pitch. It is clear to Anderson, and to us, that something particular has occurred in the match. Man 6 is listening.*)

(*In English.*) Penalty. (*He listens for a moment.*) For us, I'm afraid.

ANDERSON.    Yes, I can hear.

---

[1] *after he left Czechoslovakia … 1962*  For a citizen to move to Britain from Soviet-controlled Czechoslovakia would have been considered a defection to an enemy state.

(*This is because it is clear from the crowd noise that it's a penalty for the home side. Man 6 listens again.*)

MAN 6.  (*In English.*) Broadbent—a bad tackle when Deml had a certain goal ... a what you call it?—a necessary foul.

ANDERSON.  A professional foul.

165 MAN 6.  Yes. (*On the radio the goal is scored. This is perfectly clear from the crowd reaction.*) Not good for you. (*Man 6 turns off the radio. Pause. Man 6 considers Anderson.*) So you have had a philosophical discussion with Hollar.

170 ANDERSON.  I believe you implied that I was free to go. (*He stands up.*) I am quite sure you know that Hollar visited me at my hotel last night. It was a social call, which I was returning when I walked into this. And, furthermore, I understood nothing about being a 175 witness—I was prevented from leaving. I only came to say hello, and meet Pavel's wife, on my way to the football—

MAN 6.  (*With surprise.*) So you came to Czechoslovakia to go to the football match, Professor? (*This rattles 180 Anderson.*)

ANDERSON.  Certainly not. Well, the afternoon of the Colloquium was devoted to—well, it was not a condition of my invitation that I should attend all the sessions. (*Pause.*) I was invited to *speak,* not to listen. I 185 am speaking tomorrow morning.

MAN 6.  Why should I know Hollar visited you at the hotel?

ANDERSON.  He told me he was often followed.

MAN 6.  Well, when a man is known to be engaged in 190 meeting foreigners to buy currency—

ANDERSON.  I don't believe any of that—he was being harassed because of his letter to Husak—

MAN 6.  A letter to President Husak? What sort of letter?

ANDERSON.  (*Flustered.*) Your people knew about it—

195 MAN 6.  It is not a crime to write to the President—

ANDERSON.  No doubt that depends on what is written.

MAN 6.  You mean he wrote some kind of slander?

ANDERSON.  (*Heatedly.*) I insist on leaving now.

MAN 6.  Of course. You know, your taxi driver has made 200 a complaint against you.

ANDERSON.  What are you talking about?

MAN 6.  He never got paid.

ANDERSON.  Yes, I'm sorry but—

MAN 6.  You are not to blame. My officer told him to go.

205 ANDERSON.  Yes, that's right.

MAN 6.  Still, he is very unhappy. You told him you would be five minutes, you were delivering something—

ANDERSON.  How could I have told him that? I don't 210 speak Czech.

MAN 6.  You showed him five on your watch, and you did all the things people do when they talk to each other without a language. He was quite certain you were delivering something in your briefcase.

(*Pause.*)

215 ANDERSON.  Yes. All right. But it was not money.

MAN 6.  Of course not. You are not a criminal.

ANDERSON.  Quite so. I promised to bring Pavel one or two of the Colloquium papers. He naturally has an interest in philosophy and I assume it is not illegal.

220 MAN 6.  Naturally not. Then you won't mind showing me.

(*Anderson hesitates then opens the briefcase and takes out McKendrick's paper and his own and passes them over. Man 6 takes them and reads their English titles.*)

"Ethical Fictions as Ethical Foundations" ...
"Philosophy and the Catastrophe Theory."

(*Man 6 gives the papers back to Anderson.*)

MAN 6.  You wish to go to the football match? You will 225 see twenty minutes, perhaps more.

ANDERSON.  No. I'm going back to the university, to the Colloquium.

MRS. HOLLAR.  (*In Czech.*) Is he leaving?

MAN 6.  Mrs. Hollar would like you to remain.

230 ANDERSON.  (*To Mrs. Hollar.*) No, I'm sorry. (*A thought strikes him.*) If you spoke to the taxi driver you would have known perfectly well I was going to the England match.

(*Man 6 doesn't reply to this either in word or expression. Anderson closes his briefcase. The doorbell rings and Man*)

*3 goes to open the door. From the bedroom Man 5 enters with a small parcel wrapped in old newspaper.)*

MAN 5.   (*In Czech.*) I found this, Chief, under the
235   floorboards.

(*Man 5 gives the parcel to Man 6, who unwraps it to reveal a bundle of American dollars. Mrs. Hollar watches this with disbelief and there is an outburst.*)

MRS. HOLLAR.   (*In Czech.*) He's lying! (*To Anderson.*) It's a lie—

(*The door reopens for Man 3. Sacha Hollar, aged ten, comes in with him. He is rather a tough little boy. He runs across to his mother, who is crying and shouting, and embraces her. It is rather as though he were a small adult comforting her.*)

ANDERSON.   Oh my God … Mrs. Hollar …

(*Anderson, out of his depth and afraid, decides abruptly to leave and does so. Man 3 isn't sure whether to let him go but Man 6 nods at him and Anderson leaves.*)

### SCENE 7

(*Interior. Hotel Corridor. Evening.*
*Anderson approaches his room. He is worn out. When he gets to his door and fumbles with his key he realizes that he can hear a voice in the room next door to his. He puts his ear to this other door.*)

GRAYSON.   (*Inside.*) Yes, a new top for the running piece—OK—Prague, Saturday.

(*Grayson speaks not particularly slowly but with great deliberation, enunciating every consonant and splitting syllables up where necessary for clarity. He is, of course, dictating to a fast typist.*)

There'll be Czechs bouncing in the streets of Prague tonight as bankruptcy stares English football in the face,
5   stop, new par.

(*Anderson knocks on the door.*)

(*Inside.*) It's open!

(*Anderson opens the door and looks into the room. Interior room. It is of course a room very like Anderson's own room, if not identical. Its occupant, the man we had seen leave the room earlier, is Grayson, a sports reporter from England. He is on the telephone as Anderson cautiously enters the room.*)

Make no mistake, comma, the four-goal credit which these slick Slovaks netted here this afternoon will keep them in the black through the second leg of the World
10   Cup Eliminator at Wembley next month, stop. New par—(*To Anderson.*) Yes? (*Into phone.*) You can bank on it.
ANDERSON.   I'm next door.
GRAYSON.   (*Into phone.*)—bank on it. New par—(*To
15   Anderson.*) Look, can you come back? (*Into phone.*) But for some determined saving by third-choice Jim Bart in the injury hyphen jinxed England goal, we would have been overdrawn by four more when the books were closed, stop. Maybe Napoleon was wrong when he said
20   we were a nation of shopkeepers, stop. Today England looked like a nation of goalkeepers, stop. Davey, Petherbridge and Shell all made saves on the line. New par.
ANDERSON.   Do you mind if I listen—I missed the
25   match.

(*Grayson waves him to a chair. Anderson sits on a chair next to a door which is in fact a connecting door into the next room. Not Anderson's own room but the room on the other side of Grayson's room.*)

GRAYSON.   (*Into phone.*) Dickenson and Pratt were mostly left standing by Wolker, with a W, and Deml, D dog, E Edward, M mother, L London—who could go round the halls as a telepathy act, stop. Only Crisp
30   looked as if he had a future outside Madame Tussaud's[1]—a.u.d.s.—stop. He laid on the two best chances, comma, both wasted by Pratt, comma, who ski'ed one and stubbed his toe on the other, stop. Crisp's, apostrophe s. comment from where I was sitting

---

[1]  *Madame Tussaud's*  Famous wax museum in London.

35  looked salt and vinegar flavoured[1] …

*(Anderson has become aware that another voice is cutting in from the next room. The door between the two rooms is not quite closed. During Grayson's last speech Anderson gently pushes open the door and looks behind him and realizes that a colleague of Grayson's is also dictating in the next room. Anderson stands up and looks into the next room and is drawn into it by the rival report. This room belongs to Chamberlain.*
    *Interior Chamberlain's room. Chamberlain on phone.)*

CHAMBERLAIN.  Wilson, who would like to be thought the big bad man of the English defence, merely looked slow-footed and slow-witted stop. Deml—D.E.M. mother L.—Deml got round him five times on the trot,
40  bracket, literally, close bracket, using the same swerve, comma, making Wilson look elephantine in everything but memory, stop. On the fifth occasion there was nothing to prevent Deml scoring except what Broadbent took it on himself to do, which was to scythe Deml
45  down from behind, stop. Halas scored from the penalty, stop. *(Anderson sighs and sits down on the equivalent chair in Chamberlain's room. Chamberlain sees him.)* Can I help you—?
ANDERSON.  Sorry—I'm from next door.
50  CHAMBERLAIN.  *(Into phone.)* New paragraph—*(To Anderson.)* I won't be long—*(Into phone.)* This goal emboldened the Czechs to move Bartok, like the composer, forward and risk the consequences, stop. Ten minutes later, just before half-time, comma, he was the
55  man left over to collect a short corner from Halas and it was his chip which Jirasek rose to meet for a simple goal at the far post—
ANDERSON.  I knew it!

*(Chamberlain turns to look at him.)*

CHAMBERLAIN.  *(Into phone.)* New paragraph. As with
60  tragic opera, things got worse after the interval[2] …

---

[1]  *Crisp's … flavoured*  Pun on the word "crisp," which is the term used in England for potato chips.

[2]  *interval*  Intermission.

*(Anderson has stood up to leave. He leaves through Grayson's room. Grayson is on the phone, saying:)*

GRAYSON.  *(Into the phone.)* … Jirasek, unmarked at the far post, flapped into the air like a great stork and, rising a yard higher than Bart's outstretched hands, he put Czechoslovakia on the road to victory.

*(Anderson leaves the room without looking at Grayson or being noticed.)*

## SCENE 8

*(Interior. Hotel dining room.*
    *The cut is to gay Czech music.*
    *The dining room has a stage. A small group of Czech musicians and singers in the tourist version of peasant costume is performing. It is evening. At one of the tables Stone, the American, and a Frenchman are sitting next to each other, and sharing the table are Anderson, McKendrick and Chetwyn. The three of them are, for different reasons, subdued. Stone is unsubdued. They are reaching the end of the meal.)*

STONE.  Hell's bells. Don't you understand English? When I say to you, "Tell me what you mean," you can only reply, "I would wish to say so and so." "Never mind what you would wish to say," I reply. "Tell me
5  what you *mean*."
FRENCHMAN.  *Mais oui,* but if you ask me in French, you must say, *"Qu'est-ce que vous voulez dire?"*—"What is that which you wish to say?" *Naturellement,* it is in order for me to reply, *"Je veux dire etcetera."*[3]
10  STONE.  *(Excitedly.)* But you are making *my* point—don't you see?
MCKENDRICK.  What do you think the chances are of meeting a free and easy woman in a place like this?
STONE.  I *can't* ask you in French.
15  MCKENDRICK.  I don't mean free, necessarily.
FRENCHMAN.  *Pourquoi non? Qu'est-ce que vous voulez dire? Voilà!*[4]—now I have asked you.

---

[3]  *Mais oui*  French: But yes; *Naturellement*  French: naturally; *Je veux dire etcetera*  French: I wish to say, etc.

[4]  *Pourquoi … Voilà*  French: Why not? What is it that you want to say? There!

CHETWYN. You don't often see goose on an English menu.

(*Chetwyn is the last to finish his main course. They have all eaten the main course. There are drinks and cups of coffee on the table.*)

20 STONE. The French have no verb meaning "I mean."
CHETWYN. Why's that I wonder.
STONE. They just don't.
CHETWYN. People are always eating goose in Dickens.[1]
MCKENDRICK. Do you think it will be safe?
25 FRENCHMAN. *Par exemple. Je vous dis, "Qu'est-ce que vous voulez dire?"*[2]
MCKENDRICK. I mean, one wouldn't want to be photographed through a two-way mirror.
Stone. I don't want to ask you what you would wish to
30 say. I want to ask you what you *mean*. Let's assume there is a difference.
ANDERSON. We do have goose liver. What do they do with the rest of the goose?
STONE. Now assume that you say one but mean the
35 other.
FRENCHMAN. *Je dis quelque chose, mais je veux dire*[3]—
STONE. Right.
MCKENDRICK. (*To Stone.*) Excuse me, Brad.
STONE. Yes?
40 MCKENDRICK. You eat well but you're a lousy eater.

(*This is a fair comment. Stone has spoken with his mouth full of bread, cake, coffee, etc. and he is generally messy about it. Stone smiles forgivingly but hardly pauses.*)

STONE. Excuse us.
FRENCHMAN. *À bientôt.*[4]

(*Stone and the Frenchman get up to leave.*)

STONE. (*Leaving.*) You see, what you've got is an

incorrect statement which when corrected looks like
45 itself.

(*There is a pause.*)

MCKENDRICK. Did you have a chance to read my paper?
ANDERSON. I only had time to glance at it. I look forward to reading it carefully.
50 CHETWYN. I read it.
ANDERSON. Weren't you there for it?
MCKENDRICK. No, he sloped off for the afternoon.
ANDERSON. Well, you sly devil, Chetwyn. I bet you had a depressing afternoon. It makes the heart sick, doesn't
55 it.
CHETWYN. Yes, it does rather. We don't know we've been born.
MCKENDRICK. He wasn't at the football match.
CHETWYN. Oh—is that where you were?
60 ANDERSON. No, I got distracted.
MCKENDRICK. He's being mysterious. I think it's a woman.
ANDERSON. (*To Chetwyn.*) What were you doing?
CHETWYN. I was meeting some friends.
65 MCKENDRICK. He's being mysterious. I don't think it's a woman.
CHETWYN. I have friends here, that's all.
ANDERSON. (*To McKendrick.*) Was your paper well received?
70 MCKENDRICK. No. They didn't get it. I could tell from the questions that there'd been some kind of communications failure.
ANDERSON. The translation phones?
MCKENDRICK. No, no—they simply didn't understand
75 the line of argument. Most of them had never heard of catastrophe theory,[5] so they weren't ready for what is admittedly an audacious application of it.
ANDERSON. I must admit I'm not absolutely clear about it.
80 MCKENDRICK. It's like a reverse gear—no—it's like a breaking point. The mistake that people make is, they think a moral principle is indefinitely extendible, that it holds good for any situation, a straight line cutting

[1] *Dickens* I.e., in the novels of Charles Dickens (1812–70).

[2] *Par … dire* French: For example. I say to you, "What is it that you want to say?"

[3] *Je … dire* French: I say something, but I want to say.

[4] *À bientôt* French: see you later.

[5] *catastrophe theory* Branch of mathematics originated in the 1960s by French mathematician René Thom.

across the graph of our actual situation—here you are,
you see—(*he uses a knife to score a line in front of him
straight across the table-cloth, left to right in front of him.*)
"Morality" down there, running parallel to "Immorality" up here (*he scores a parallel line.*)—and never the
twain shall meet. They think that is what a principle
means.

ANDERSON.  And isn't it?

McKENDRICK.  No. The two lines are on the same
plane. (*He holds out his flat hand, palm down, above the
scored lines.*) They're the edges of the same plane—it's in
three dimensions, you see—and if you twist the plane in
a certain way, into what we call the catastrophe curve,
you get a model of the sort of behaviour we find in the
real world. There's a point—the catastrophe point—
where your progress along one line of behaviour jumps
you into the opposite line; the principle reverses itself at
the point where a rational man would abandon it.

CHETWYN.  Then it's not a principle.

McKENDRICK.  There aren't any principles in your
sense. There are only a lot of principled people trying to
behave as if there were.

ANDERSON.  That's the same thing, surely.

McKENDRICK.  You're a worse case than Chetwyn and
his primitive Greeks. At least he has the excuse of
*believing* in goodness and beauty. You know they're
fictions but you're so hung up on them you want to
treat them as if they were God-given absolutes.

ANDERSON.  I don't see how else they would have any
practical value—

McKENDRICK.  So you end up using a moral principle as
your excuse for acting against a moral interest. It's a sort
of funk—

(*Anderson, under pressure, slams his cup back on to its
saucer in a very uncharacteristic and surprising way. His
anger is all the more alarming for that.*)

ANDERSON.  You make your points altogether too easily,
McKendrick. What need have you of moral courage
when your principles reverse themselves so
conveniently?

McKENDRICK.  All right! I've gone too far. As usual.
Sorry. Let's talk about something else. There's quite an
attractive woman hanging about outside, loitering in the
vestibule. (*The dining-room door offers a view of the
lobby.*) Do you think it is a trap? My wife said to
me—now, Bill, don't do anything daft, you know what
you're like, if a blonde knocked on your door with the
top three buttons of her police uniform undone and
asked for a cup of sugar you'd convince yourself she was
a bus conductress brewing up in the next room.

ANDERSON.  (*Chastened.*) I'm sorry ... you're right up to
a point. There would be no moral dilemmas if moral
principles worked in straight lines and never crossed
each other. One meets test situations which have
troubled much cleverer men than us.

CHETWYN.  A good rule, I find, is to try them out on
men much *less* clever than us. I often ask my son what
*he* thinks.

ANDERSON.  Your son?

CHETWYN.  Yes. He's eight.

McKENDRICK.  She's definitely glancing this
way—seriously, do you think one could chat her up?

(*Stone turns round to look through the door and we see now
that the woman is Mrs. Hollar.*)

ANDERSON. Excuse me.

(*He gets up and starts to leave, but then comes back
immediately and takes his briefcase from under the table
and then leaves. We stay with the table. McKendrick
watches Anderson meet Mrs. Hollar and shake her hand
and they disappear.*)

McKENDRICK.  Bloody hell, it *was* a woman. Crafty old
beggar.

SCENE 9

(*Exterior. Street. Night.
Anderson and Mrs. Hollar walking.
A park. A park bench. Sacha Hollar sitting on the
bench.
Anderson and Mrs. Hollar arrive.*)

MRS. HOLLAR.  (*In Czech.*) Here he is. (*To Anderson.*)
Sacha. (*In Czech.*) Thank him for coming.

SACHA.   She is saying thank you that you come.

MRS. HOLLAR.   (*In Czech.*) We're sorry to bother him.

5  SACHA.   She is saying sorry for the trouble.

ANDERSON.   No, no I am sorry about … everything. Do you learn English at school?

SACHA.   Yes. I am learning English two years. With my father also.

10  ANDERSON.   You are very good.

SACHA.   Not good. You are a friend of my father. Thank you.

ANDERSON.   I'm afraid I've done nothing.

SACHA.   You have his writing?

15  ANDERSON.   His thesis? Yes. It's in here. (*He indicates his briefcase.*)

SACHA.   (*In Czech.*) It's all right, he's still got it.

(*Mrs. Hollar nods.*)

MRS. HOLLAR.   (*In Czech.*) Tell him I didn't know who he was today.

20  SACHA.   My mother is not knowing who you are, tomorrow at the apartment.

ANDERSON.   Today.

SACHA.   Today. Pardon. So she is saying, "Come here! Come here! Come inside the apartment!" Because she is

25  not knowing. My father is not telling her. He is telling me only.

ANDERSON.   I see. What did he tell you?

SACHA.   He will go see his friend the English professor. He is taking the writing.

30  ANDERSON.   I see. Did he return home last night?

SACHA.   No. He is arrested outside hotel. Then in the night they come to make search.

ANDERSON.   Had they been there all night?

SACHA.   At eleven o'clock they are coming. They search

35  twenty hours.

ANDERSON.   My God.

SACHA.   In morning I go to Bartolomesskaya to be seeing him.

MRS. HOLLAR.   (*Explains.*) Police.

40  SACHA.   But I am not seeing him. They say go home. I am waiting. Then I am going home. Then I am seeing you.

ANDERSON.   What were they looking for?

SACHA.   (*Shrugs.*) Western books. Also my father is

45  writing things. Letters, politics, philosophy. They find nothing. Some English books they don't like but really nothing. But the dollars, of course, they pretend to find.

(*Mrs. Hollar hears the word dollars.*)

MRS. HOLLAR.   (*In Czech.*) Tell him the dollars were put there by the police.

50  SACHA.   Not my father's dollars. He is having no moneys.

ANDERSON.   Yes. I know.

SACHA.   They must arrest him for dollars because he does nothing. No bad things. He is signing something. So

55  they are making trouble.

ANDERSON.   Yes.

MRS. HOLLAR.   (*In Czech.*) Tell him about Jan.

SACHA.   You must give back my father's thesis. Not now. The next days. My mother cannot take it.

60  ANDERSON.   He asked me to take it to England.

SACHA.   Not possible now. But thank you.

ANDERSON.   He asked me to take it.

SACHA.   Not possible. Now they search you, I think. At the aeroport. Because they are seeing you coming to the

65  apartment and you have too much contact. Maybe they are seeing us now.

(*Anderson looks around him.*)

Is possible.

ANDERSON.   (*Uncomfortably.*) I ought to tell you … (*quickly.*) I came to the apartment to give the thesis

70  back. I refused him. But he was afraid he might be stopped—I thought he just meant searched, not arrested—

SACHA.   Too quick—too quick—

(*Pause.*)

ANDERSON.   What do you want me to do?

75  SACHA.   My father's friend—he is coming to Philosophy Congress today.

ANDERSON.   Tomorrow.

SACHA.   Yes tomorrow. You give him the writing. Is called Jan. Is OK. Good friend.

(*Anderson nods.*)

80 ANDERSON.  Jan.
SACHA.  (*In Czech.*) He'll bring it to the university hall for Jan tomorrow. (*Sacha stands up.*) We go home now.

(*Mrs. Hollar gets up and shakes hands with Anderson.*)

ANDERSON.  I'm sorry … What will happen to him?
MRS. HOLLAR.  (*In Czech.* )What was that?
85 SACHA.  (*In Czech.*) He wants to know what will happen to Daddy.
MRS. HOLLAR.  Ruzyne.
SACHA.  That is the prison. Ruzyne.

(*Pause.*)

ANDERSON.  I will, of course, try to help in England. I'll
90 write letters. The Czech Ambassador … I have friends, too, in our government—

(*Anderson realizes that the boy has started to cry. He is 'specially taken aback because he has been talking to him like an adult.*)

Now listen—I am personally friendly with important people—the Minister of Education—people like that.
MRS. HOLLAR.  (*In Czech but to Anderson.*) Please help
95 Pavel—
ANDERSON.  Mrs. Hollar—I will do everything I can for him.

(*He watches Mrs. Hollar and Sacha walk away into the dark.*)

## SCENE 10

(*Interior. Anderson's room. Night.*
    *Anderson is lying fully dressed on the bed. His eyes open. Only light from the window. There are faint voices from Grayson's room. After a while Anderson gets up and leaves his room and knocks on Grayson's door.*
    *Exterior Grayson's room.*
    *Grayson opens his door.*)

GRAYSON.  Oh hello. Sorry, are we making too much noise?
ANDERSON.  No, it's all right, but I heard you were still up and I wondered if I could ask a favour of you. I
5 wonder if I could borrow your typewriter.
GRAYSON.  My typewriter?
ANDERSON.  Yes.
GRAYSON.  Well, I'm leaving in the morning.
ANDERSON.  I'll let you have it back first thing. I'm
10 leaving on the afternoon plane myself.
GRAYSON.  Oh—all right then.
ANDERSON.  That's most kind.

(*During the above the voices from the room have been semi-audible. McKendrick's voice, rather drunk, but articulate, is heard.*)

MCKENDRICK.  (*His voice only, heard underneath the above dialogue.*) Now, listen to me, I'm a professional
15 philosopher. You'll do well to listen to what I have to say.
ANDERSON.  That sounds as if you've got McKendrick in there.
GRAYSON.  Oh—is he one of yours?
20 ANDERSON.  I wouldn't put it like that.
GRAYSON.  He's getting as tight as a tick.
ANDERSON.  Yes.
GRAYSON.  You couldn't collect him, could you? He's going to get clouted in a minute.
25 ANDERSON.  Go ahead and clout him, if you like.
GRAYSON.  It's not me. It's Broadbent and a couple of the lads. Your pal sort of latched on to us in the bar. He really ought to be getting home.
ANDERSON.  I'll see what I can do.

(*Anderson follows Grayson into the room.*)

30 MCKENDRICK.  How can you expect the kids to be little gentlemen when their heroes behave like yobs[1]—answer me that—no—you haven't answered my question—if you've got yobs on the fields you're going to have yobs on the terraces.

---

[1] *yobs* Hooligans.

(*Interior Grayson's room. McKendrick is the only person standing up. He is holding court, with a bottle of whisky in one hand and his glass in the other. Around this small room are Broadbent, Crisp, Chamberlain and perhaps one or two members of the England squad. Signs of a bottle party.*)

35 GRAYSON.  (*Closing his door.*) I thought philosophers were quiet, studious sort of people.

ANDERSON.  Well, some of us are.

MCKENDRICK.  (*Shouts.*) Anderson! You're the very man I want to see! We're having a philosophical discussion
40 about the yob ethics of professional footballers—

BROADBENT.  You want to watch it, mate.

MCKENDRICK.  Roy here is sensitive because he gave away a penalty today, by a deliberate foul. To stop a certain goal he hacked a chap down. After all, a penalty
45 might be saved and broken legs are quite rare—(*Broadbent stands up but McKendrick pacifies him with a gesture.*) It's perfectly all right—you were adopting the utilitarian values of the game, for the good of the team, for England! But I'm not talking about
50 particular acts of expediency. No, I'm talking about the whole *ethos*.

ANDERSON.  McKendrick, don't you think it's about time we retired?

MCKENDRICK.  (*Ignoring him.*) Now, I've played soccer
55 for years. Years and *years*. I played soccer from the age of *eight* until I was *thirteen*. At which point I went to a rugger[1] school. Even so, Tommy here will tell you that I still consider myself something of a left-winger. (*This is to Crisp.*) Sorry about that business in the lift, by the
60 way, Tommy. Well, one thing I remember clearly from my years and *years* of soccer is that if two players go for a ball which then goes into touch, there's never any doubt *among those players* which of them touched the ball last. I can't remember one occasion in all those years
65 and *years* when the player who touched the ball last didn't realize it. So, what I want to know *is*—why is it that on "Match of the Day," every time the bloody ball goes into touch, *both* players claim the throw-in for their own side? I merely ask for information. Is it because
70 they are very, very stupid or is it because a dishonest advantage is as welcome as an honest one?

CHAMBERLAIN.  Well, look, it's been a long evening, old

---

[1] *rugger* Rugby.

chap—

ANDERSON.  Tomorrow is another day, McKendrick.

75 MCKENDRICK.  Tomorrow, in my experience, is usually the same day. Have a drink—

ANDERSON.  No thank you.

MCKENDRICK.  Here's a question for anthropologists. Name me a tribe which organizes itself into teams for
80 sporting encounters and greets every score against their opponents with paroxysms of childish glee, whooping, dancing and embracing in an ecstasy of crowing self-congratulation in the very midst of their disconsolate fellows?—Who are these primitives who pile all their
85 responses into the immediate sensation, unaware or uncaring of the long undulations of life's fortunes? Yes, you've got it! (*He chants the "Match of the Day" signature tune.*) It's the yob-of-the-month competition, entries on a postcard please. But the question is—is it because
90 they're working class, or is it because financial greed has corrupted them? Or is it both?

ANDERSON.  McKendrick, you are being offensive.

MCKENDRICK.  Anderson is one of life's cricketers. Clap, clap. (*He claps in a well-bred sort of way and puts on a
95 well-bred voice.*) Well played, sir. Bad luck, old chap. The comparison with cricket may suggest to you that yob ethics are working class.

(*Broadbent comes up to McKendrick and pushes him against the wall. McKendrick is completely unconcerned, escapes and continues without pause.*)

But you would be quite wrong. Let me refer you to a typical rugby team of Welsh miners. A score is
100 acknowledged with pride but with restraint, the scorer himself composing his features into an expressionless mask lest he might be suspected of exulting in his opponents' misfortune—my God, it does the heart good, doesn't it? I conclude that yob ethics are caused by
105 financial greed.

ANDERSON.  Don't be such an ass.

(*McKendrick takes this as an intellectual objection.*)

MCKENDRICK.  You think it's the adulation, perhaps? (*To Crisp.*) Is it the adulation, Tommy, which has corrupted you?

CRISP.  What's he flaming on about?

CHAMBERLAIN.  Well, I think it's time for my shut-eye.

CRISP.  No, I want to know what he's saying about me. He's giving me the needle.

ANDERSON.  (*To McKendrick.*) May I remind you that you profess to be something of a pragmatist yourself in matters of ethics—

McKENDRICK.  Ah yes—I—see—you think that because I don't believe in reliable signposts on the yellow brick road to rainbowland, you think I'm a bit of a yob myself—the swift kick in the kneecap on the way up the academic ladder—the Roy Broadbent of Stoke— (*To Broadbent.*) Stoke's my team, you know.

BROADBENT.  Will you tell this stupid bugger his philosophy is getting up my nostrils.

GRAYSON.  You're not making much sense, old boy.

McKENDRICK.  Ah! Grayson here has a fine logical mind. He has put his finger on the flaw in my argument, namely that the reason footballers are yobs may be nothing to do with being working class, or with financial greed, or with adulation, or even with being footballers. It may be simply that football attracts a certain kind of person, namely yobs—

(*This is as far as he gets when Broadbent smashes him in the face. McKendrick drops.*)

CRISP.  Good on you, Roy.

(*Anderson goes to McKendrick, who is flat on the floor.*)

ANDERSON.  McKendrick …

CHAMBERLAIN.  Well, I'm going to bed.

(*Chamberlain goes through the connecting door into his own room and closes the door.*)

BROADBENT.  He can't say that sort of thing and get away with it.

GRAYSON.  Where's his room?

ANDERSON.  On the third floor.

GRAYSON.  Bloody hell.

CRISP.  He's waking up.

BROADBENT.  He's all right.

ANDERSON.  Come on, McKendrick.

(*They all lift McKendrick to his feet. McKendrick makes no protest. He's just about able to walk.*)

I'll take him down in the lift. (*He sees the typewriter in its case and says to Grayson*) I'll come back for the typewriter. (*He leads McKendrick towards the door.*)

McKENDRICK.  (*Mutters.*) All right. I went too far. Let's talk about something else.

(*But McKendrick keeps walking or staggering. Anderson opens Grayson's door.*)

BROADBENT.  Here. That bloody Jirasek. Just like you said.

ANDERSON.  Yes.

BROADBENT.  They don't teach you nothing at that place, then?

ANDERSON.  No.

(*Anderson helps McKendrick out and closes the door.*)

## SCENE 11

(*Interior. The Colloquium.*

*Anderson comes to the lectern. There is a Czech Chairman behind him.*

*Chetwyn is in the audience but McKendrick is not. We arrive as Anderson approaches the microphone. Anderson lays a sheaf of typewritten paper on the lectern.*)

ANDERSON.  I propose in this paper to take up a problem which many have taken up before me, namely the conflict between the rights of individuals and the rights of the community. I will be making a distinction between rights and rules.

(*We note that the Chairman, listening politely and intently, is suddenly puzzled. He himself has some papers and from these he extracts one, which is in fact the official copy of Anderson's official paper. He starts looking at it. It doesn't take him long to satisfy himself that Anderson is giving a different paper. These things happen while Anderson speaks. At the same time the three Interpreters in their booths, while speaking into their microphones as Anderson speaks, are also in some difficulty because they have copies of Anderson's official paper.)*

I will seek to show that rules, in so far as they are related to rights, are a secondary and consequential elaboration of primary rights, and I will be associating rules generally with communities and rights generally with individuals. I will seek to show that a conflict between the two is generally a pseudo-conflict arising out of one side or the other pressing a pseudo-right. Although claiming priority for rights over rules—where they are in conflict—I will be defining rights as fictions acting as incentives to the adoption of practical values; and I will further propose that although these rights are fictions, there is an obligation to treat them as if they were truths; and further, that although this obligation can be shown to be based on values which are based on fictions, there is an obligation to treat *that* obligation as though it were based on truth; and so on *ad infinitum*.[1]

*(At this point the Chairman interrupts him.)*

CHAIRMAN. Pardon me—Professor—this is not your paper—

ANDERSON. In what sense? I am indisputably giving it.

CHAIRMAN. But it is not the paper you were invited to give.

ANDERSON. I wasn't invited to give a particular paper.

CHAIRMAN. You offered one.

ANDERSON. That's true.

CHAIRMAN. But this is not it.

ANDERSON. No. I changed my mind.

CHAIRMAN. But it is irregular.

ANDERSON. I didn't realize it mattered.

CHAIRMAN. It is a discourtesy.

ANDERSON. *(Taken aback.)* Bad manners? I am sorry.

CHAIRMAN. You cannot give this paper. We do not have copies.

ANDERSON. Do you mean that philosophical papers require some sort of clearance?

CHAIRMAN. The interpreters cannot work without copies.

ANDERSON. Don't worry. It is not a technical paper. I will speak a little slower if you like. *(Anderson turns back to the microphone.)* If we decline to define rights as fictions, albeit with the force of truths, there are only two senses in which humans could be said to have rights. Firstly, humans might be said to have certain rights if they had collectively and mutually agreed to give each other these rights. This would merely mean that humanity is a rather large club with club rules, but it is not what is generally meant by human rights. It is not what Locke[2] meant, and it is not what the American Founding Fathers meant when, taking the hint from Locke, they held certain rights to be inalienable— among them, life, liberty and the pursuit of happiness. The early Americans claimed these as the endowment of God—which is the *second* sense in which humans might be said to have rights. This is a view more encouraged in some communities than in others. I do not wish to dwell on it here except to say that it *is* a view and not a deduction, and that I do not hold it myself. What strikes us is the consensus about an individual's right put forward both by those who invoke God's authority and by those who invoke no authority at all other than their own idea of what is fair and sensible. The first Article of the American Constitution, guaranteeing freedom of religious observance, of expression, of the press, and of assembly, is closely echoed by Articles 28 and 32 of the no less admirable Constitution of Czechoslovakia, our generous hosts on this occasion. Likewise, protection from invasion of privacy, from unreasonable search and from interference with letters and correspondence guaranteed to the American people by Article 4 is likewise guaranteed to the Czech people by Article 31.

*(The Chairman, who has been more and more uncomfortable, leaves the stage at this point. He goes into the "wings." At some distance from Anderson, but still just in earshot of Anderson, i.e. one can hear Anderson's words clearly if faintly, is a telephone. Perhaps in a stage manager's office. We go with the Chairman but we can still hear Anderson.)*

---

[1] *ad infinitum* Latin: to infinity.

[2] *Locke* John Locke (1632–1704), English philosopher, whose ideas on the natural rights of human beings greatly influenced the founders of the United States.

Is such a consensus remarkable? Not at all. If there is a God, we his creations would doubtless subscribe to his values. And if there is not a God, he, our creation, would undoubtedly be credited with values which we think to be fair and sensible. But what is fairness? What is sense? What are these values which we take to be self-evident? And why are they values?

## SCENE 12

(*Interior. McKendrick's room.*

*McKendrick is fully dressed and coming round from a severe hangover. His room is untidier than Anderson's. Clothes are strewn about. His suitcase, half full, is open. His briefcase is also in evidence. McKendrick looks at his watch, but it has stopped. He goes to the telephone and dials.*)

## SCENE 13

(*Interior. Anderson's room.*

*The phone starts to ring. The camera pulls back from the phone and we see that there are two men in the room, plain-clothes Policemen, searching the room. They look at the phone but only for a moment, and while it rings they continue quietly. They search the room very discreetly. We see one carefully slide open a drawer and we cut away.*)

## SCENE 14

(*The Colloquium.*

*We have returned to Anderson's paper. There is no Chairman on stage.*)

ANDERSON. Ethics were once regarded as a sort of monument, a ghostly Eiffel Tower constructed of Platonic entities like honesty, loyalty, fairness, and so on, all bolted together and consistent with each other, harmoniously stressed so as to keep the edifice standing up: an ideal against which we measured our behaviour. The tower has long been demolished. In our own time linguistic philosophy proposes that the notion of, say,

justice has no existence outside the ways in which we choose to employ the word, and indeed *consists* only of the way in which we employ it. In other words, that ethics are not the inspiration of our behaviour but merely the creation of our utterances.

(*Over the latter part of this we have gone back to the Chairman who is on the telephone. The Chairman is doing little talking and some listening.*)

And yet common observation shows us that this view demands qualification. A small child who cries "that's not fair" when punished for something done by his brother or sister is apparently appealing to an idea of justice which is, for want of a better word, natural. And we must see that natural justice, however illusory, does inspire many people's behaviour much of the time. As an ethical utterance it seems to be an attempt to define a sense of rightness which is not simply derived from some other utterance elsewhere.

(*We cut now to a backstage area, but Anderson's voice is continuous, heard through the sort of PA system which one finds backstage at theatres.*

*The Chairman hurries along the corridor, seeking and now finding a uniformed "Fireman," a backstage official. During this Anderson speaks.*)

Now a philosopher exploring the difficult terrain of right and wrong should not be over-impressed by the argument "a child would know the difference." But when, let us say, we are being persuaded that it is ethical to put someone in prison for reading or writing the wrong books, it is well to be reminded that you can persuade a man to believe almost anything provided he is clever enough, but it is much more difficult to persuade someone less clever. There is a sense of right and wrong which precedes utterance. It is individually experienced and it concerns one person's dealings with another person. From this experience we have built a system of ethics which is the sum of individual acts of recognition of individual right.

(*During this we have returned to Anderson in person. And at this point the Chairman re-enters the stage and goes and*) *sits in his chair. Anderson continues, ignoring him.*)

If this is so, the implications are serious for a collective
or state ethic which finds itself in conflict with
40    individual rights, and seeks, in the name of the people,
to impose its values on the very individuals who
comprise the state. The illogic of this manoeuvre is an
embarrassment to totalitarian systems. An attempt is
sometimes made to answer it by consigning the whole
45    argument to "bourgeois logic," which is a concept no
easier to grasp than bourgeois physics or bourgeois
astronomy. No, the fallacy must lie elsewhere—

(*At this point loud bells, electric bells, ring. The fire alarm.
The Chairman leaps up and shouts.*)

CHAIRMAN.   (*In Czech.*) Don't panic! There appears to
be a fire. Please leave the hall in an orderly manner. (*In*
50    *English.*) Fire! Please leave quietly!

(*The philosophers get to their feet and start heading for the
exit. Anderson calmly gathers his papers up and leaves the
stage.*)

SCENE 15

(*Interior. Airport.*
*People leaving the country have to go through a baggage
check. There are at least three separate but adjacent benches
at which Customs Men and Women search the baggage of
travellers. The situation here is as follows:*
*At the first bench Chetwyn is in mid-search.*
*At the second bench Anderson is in mid-search.*
*At the third bench a traveller is in mid-search.*
*There is a short queue of people waiting for each bench.*
*The leading man in the queue waiting for the third
bench is McKendrick. The search at this third bench is
cursory. However, Anderson is being searched very
thoroughly. We begin on Anderson. We have not yet noted
Chetwyn.*
*At Anderson's bench a uniformed Customs Woman is
examining the contents of his suitcase, helped by a
uniformed Customs Man. At the same time a plain-clothes
Policeman is very carefully searching everything in*

*Anderson's briefcase.*
*We see the Customs Man take a cellophane-wrapped
box of chocolates from Anderson's case. He strips off the
cellophane and looks at the chocolates and then he digs
down to look at the second layer of chocolates. Anderson
watches this with amazement. The chocolate box is closed
and put back in the case. Meanwhile, a nest of wooden
dolls, the kind in which one doll fits inside another, is
reduced to its components.*
*The camera moves to find McKendrick arriving at the
third desk. There is no plain-clothes Policeman there. The
Customs Officer there opens his briefcase and flips, in a
rather cursory way, through McKendrick's papers. He asks
McKendrick to open his case. He digs about for a moment
in McKendrick's case. Back at Anderson's bench the plain-
clothes Policeman is taking Anderson's wallet from
Anderson's hand. He goes through every piece of paper in
the wallet.*
*We go back to McKendrick's bench to find McKendrick
closing his case and being moved on. McKendrick turns
round to Anderson to speak.*)

MCKENDRICK.   You picked the wrong queue, old man.
Russian roulette. And Chetwyn.

(*We now discover Chetwyn, who is going through a similar
search to Anderson's. He has a plain-clothes Policeman too.
This Policeman is looking down the spine of a book from
Chetwyn's suitcase. We now return to Anderson's bench.
We find that the Customs Man has discovered a suspicious
bulge in the zipped compartment on the underside of the lid
of Anderson's suitcase. Anderson's face tells us that he has a
spasm of anxiety. The bulge suggests something about the
size of Hollar's envelope. The Customs Man zips open the
compartment and extracts the copy of McKendrick's girlie
magazine. Anderson is embarrassed.*
*We return to Chetwyn, whose briefcase is being searched
paper by paper. The Customs Official searching his suitcase
finds a laundered shirt, nicely ironed and folded. He opens
the shirt up and discovers about half a dozen sheets of
writing-paper. Thin paper with typewriting on it. Also a
photograph of a man. The plain-clothes Policeman joins the
Customs Official and he starts looking at these pieces of
paper. He looks up at Chetwyn, whose face has gone white.*)

SCENE 16

(*Interior. Aeroplane.*
*The plane is taxiing.*
*McKendrick and Anderson are sitting together.*
*McKendrick looks shocked.*)

MCKENDRICK.   Silly bugger. Honestly.

ANDERSON.   It's all right—they'll put him on the next plane.

MCKENDRICK.   To Siberia.

5 ANDERSON.   No, no, don't be ridiculous. It wouldn't look well for them, would it? All the publicity. I don't think there's anything in Czech law about being in possession of letters to Amnesty International and the UN and that sort of thing. They couldn't treat Chetwyn

10 as though he were a Czech national anyway.

MCKENDRICK.   Very unpleasant for him though.

ANDERSON.   Yes.

MCKENDRICK.   He took a big risk.

ANDERSON.   Yes.

15 MCKENDRICK.   I wouldn't do it. Would you?

ANDERSON.   No. He should have known he'd be searched.

MCKENDRICK.   Why did they search you?

ANDERSON.   They thought I might have something.

20 MCKENDRICK.   Did you have anything?

ANDERSON.   I did in a way.

MCKENDRICK.   What was it?

ANDERSON.   A thesis. Apparently rather slanderous from the state's point of view.

25 MCKENDRICK.   Where did you hide it?

ANDERSON.   In your briefcase.

(*Pause.*)

MCKENDRICK.   You what?

ANDERSON.   Last night. I'm afraid I reversed a principle.

(*McKendrick opens his briefcase and finds Hollar's envelope. Anderson takes it from him. McKendrick is furious.*)

MCKENDRICK.   You utter bastard.

30 ANDERSON.   I thought you would approve.

MCKENDRICK.   Don't get clever with me. (*He relapses, shaking.*) Jesus. It's not quite playing the game is it?

ANDERSON.   No, I suppose not. But they were very unlikely to search *you*.

35 MCKENDRICK.   That's not the bloody point.

ANDERSON.   I thought it was. But you could be right. Ethics is a very complicated business. That's why they have these congresses.

(*The plane picks up speed on the runway towards take-off.*)

—1977

# CARYL CHURCHILL
## b. 1938

Caryl Churchill has been widely recognized as one of the most influential English-language playwrights of the twentieth century. Characterized by bold feminist and socialist themes, her work looks beyond the politics of personal liberation, connecting issues of gender inequality to larger systemic injustices. Her willingness to challenge the status quo has also extended to the ways in which her plays are created and structured—and in that respect she has had considerable impact on the theater world.

Churchill was born in London on 3 September 1938. Her father was a political cartoonist, and

her mother was a model and occasional movie actor. During World War II, the family moved to Montreal, but Churchill returned to England for university, studying English Literature at Oxford. It was here that she began her playwriting career, creating works for student theatrical groups. She received a Bachelor's degree in English Literature in 1960.

Her first professional works were BBC radio plays. Churchill found that writing short works was more compatible with her domestic situation; she had married in 1961 and was raising three sons. These radio works, including *The Ants* (1962), *Not, Not, Not, Not Enough Oxygen* (1971), and *Schreber's Nervous Illness* (1972), are generally set in domestic environments, and exhibit a keen sense of the effects of economic policy on day-to-day life.

Churchill's first professional stage play, *Owners*, a critique of capitalist values, was produced by London's Royal Court Theatre in 1972. As the Royal Court's first female playwright in residence in 1974–75, she began a series of associations with professional theater companies that was to mark her work indelibly. In 1976 she began working with the socialist-feminist theater company Monstrous Regiment on *Vinegar Tom* (1976). Blending a story about witch trials in England during the seventeenth century with contemporary songs and text, the play was developed over an extended period of time through a workshop with the members of the company.

Churchill took a similar approach with *Cloud Nine* (1979), developed with Joint Stock Theatre. In *Cloud Nine*, Churchill began to explore how the structure of her plays could itself address a topic. The first act of the play takes place in colonial Africa during the Victorian era. The second act takes place in contemporary England, but with the same characters, who have aged only 25 years. Through this technique of time-displacement and through unusual cross-gendered casting, Churchill addresses the power politics of colonialism and gender, providing not just a historical perspective on but also a critique of contemporary society. With *Cloud Nine* Churchill began to be recognized by critics and audiences as a major force in British theater.

Churchill's historical "double vision" also animates her 1982 work, *Top Girls*. Although not as unconventional in its dramaturgy as *Cloud Nine*, *Top Girls* integrates the experiences of historical women with those of women living in the early 1980s, during the period of the first female British Prime Minister, Margaret Thatcher. In its investigation of female identity and notions of "success" in a male-dominated business world, *Top Girls* also explicitly links the concept of women's liberation with that of economic liberation.

Churchill's plays throughout the 1980s continued to explore socialist themes. *Serious Money* (1987), a critical and commercial hit on Broadway, investigated the politics of the London Stock Exchange, and Churchill was one of the first English-language playwrights to write about the fall of communism in Eastern Europe. Within weeks of the fall of the Romanian communist dictator Nicolae Ceausescu in late 1989, Churchill went to Romania to do a workshop with a group of London theater students. The result, *Mad Forest: a Play from Romania* (1990), is a theatrical treatment of the fall of a political system and the chaos that ensued.

More recent works have probed the ethical complexities of contemporary society. *Far Away* (2000) is a nightmarish play about a future world at war with itself. In *A Number* (2002), the protagonist of Churchill's play is confronted both by clones that he has created thirty-five years earlier and by his son, from whom the clones were engendered.

Churchill has received many awards during her career, including four Obie awards for best new play (awarded for Off-Broadway plays); the 1987 Society of West End Theatre Award, for best new play; and the BBC Award for best new play.

⌘⌘⌘

## *Top Girls*

### CHARACTERS:

Marlene
Isabella Bird
Lady Nijo
Dull Gret
Pope Joan
Patient Griselda
Waitress
Jeanine
Joyce
Angie
Kit
Nell
Win
Louise
Mrs. Kidd
Shona

Note on layout
A speech usually follows the one immediately before it
BUT:
1: when one character starts speaking before the other has finished, the point of interruption is marked / .
eg. ISABELLA.  This is the Emperor of Japan? / I once
met the Emperor of Morocco.

NIJO.   In fact he was the ex-Emperor.
2: a character sometimes continues speaking right through another's speech:
eg. ISABELLA.  When I was forty I thought my life was over. / Oh I
NIJO.  I didn't say I felt it for twenty years. Not every minute.
ISABELLA.  was pitiful. I was sent on a cruise for my health and I felt even worse. Pains in my bones, pins and needles…
3: sometimes a speech follows on from a speech earlier than the one immediately before it, and continuity is marked * .
eg. GRISELDA.  I'd seen him riding by, we all had. And he'd seen me in the fields with the sheep.*
ISABELLA.  I would have been well suited to minding sheep.
NIJO.  And Mr. Nugent riding by.
ISABELLA.  Of course not, Nijo, I mean a healthy life in the open air.
JOAN.  *He just rode up while you were minding the sheep and asked you to marry him?
where "in the fields with the sheep" is the cue to both "I would have been" and "He just rode up."

## ACT 1, SCENE 1

(*Restaurant. Table set for dinner with white tablecloth. Six places. Marlene and Waitress.*)

MARLENE.    Excellent, yes, table for six. One of them's going to be late but we won't wait. I'd like a bottle of Frascati[1] straight away if you've got one really cold.

(*The Waitress goes.*)
(*Isabella Bird[2] arrives.*)

Here we are. Isabella.
5   ISABELLA.    Congratulations, my dear.
MARLENE.    Well, it's a step. It makes for a party. I haven't time for a holiday. I'd like to go somewhere exotic like you but I can't get away. I don't know how you could bear to leave Hawaii. / I'd like to lie in the
10   sun forever, except of course I
ISABELLA.    I did think of settling.
MARLENE.    can't bear sitting still.
ISABELLA.    I sent for my sister Hennie to come and join me. I said, Hennie we'll live here forever and help the
15   natives. You can buy two sirloins of beef for what a pound of chops costs in Edinburgh. And Hennie wrote back, the dear, that yes, she would come to Hawaii if I wished, but I said she had far better stay where she was. Hennie was suited to life in Tobermory.[3]
20   MARLENE.    Poor Hennie.
ISABELLA.    Do you have a sister?
MARLENE.    Yes in fact.
ISABELLA.    Hennie was happy. She was good. I did miss its face, my own pet. But I couldn't stay in Scotland. I
25   loathed the constant murk.
MARLENE.    Ah! Nijo!

(*She sees Lady Nijo[4] arrive.*)

---

[1]   *bottle of Frascati*   White wine named for a district southeast of Rome.

[2]   [Churchill's note]   Isabella Bird (1831–1904) lived in Edinburgh, travelled extensively between the ages of 40 and 70.

[3]   *Tobermory*   Town on the Isle of Mull, Scotland.

[4]   [Churchill's note]   Lady Nijo (b. 1258), Japanese, was an Emperor's courtesan and later a Buddhist nun who travelled on foot through Japan.

(*The Waitress enters with wine.*)

NIJO.    Marlene!
MARLENE.    I think a drink while we wait for the others. I think a drink anyway. What a week.

(*The Waitress pours wine.*)

30   NIJO.    It was always the men who used to get so drunk. I'd be one of the maidens, passing the sake.
ISABELLA.    I've had sake. Small hot drink. Quite fortifying after a day in the wet.
NIJO.    One night my father proposed three rounds of
35   three cups, which was normal, and then the Emperor should have said three rounds of three cups, but he said three rounds of nine cups, so you can imagine. Then the Emperor passed his sake cup to my father and said, "Let the wild goose come to me this spring."
40   MARLENE.    Let the what?
NIJO.    It's a literary allusion to a tenth-century epic, / His Majesty was very cultured.
ISABELLA.    This is the Emperor of Japan? / I once met the Emperor of Morocco.
45   NIJO.    In fact he was the ex-Emperor.
MARLENE.    But he wasn't old? / Did you, Isabella?
NIJO.    Twenty-nine.
ISABELLA.    Oh it's a long story.
MARLENE.    Twenty-nine's an excellent age.
50   NIJO.    Well I was only fourteen and I knew he meant something but I didn't know what. He sent me an eight-layered gown and I sent it back. So when the time came I did nothing but cry. My thin gowns were badly ripped. But even that morning when he left / —he'd a
55   green robe with a scarlet lining and
MARLENE.    Are you saying he raped you?
NIJO.    very heavily embroidered trousers, I already felt different about him. It made me uneasy. No, of course not, Marlene, I belonged to him, it was what I was
60   brought up for from a baby. I soon found I was sad if he stayed away. It was depressing day after day not knowing when he would come. I never enjoyed taking other women to him.
ISABELLA.    I certainly never saw my father drunk. He was
65   a clergyman. / And I didn't get married till I was fifty.

(*The Waitress brings menus.*)

NIJO.   Oh, my father was a very religious man. Just before he died he said to me, "Serve His Majesty, be respectful, if you lose his favour enter holy orders."
MARLENE.   But he meant stay in a convent, not go
70  wandering round the country.
NIJO.   Priests were often vagrants, so why not a nun? You think I shouldn't? / I still did what my father wanted.
MARLENE.   No no, I think you should. / I think it was
75  wonderful.

(*Dull Gret*[1] *arrives.*)

ISABELLA.   I tried to do what my father wanted.
MARLENE.   Gret, good. Nijo.
GRET.   I know Griselda's going to be late, but should we wait for Joan? / Let's get you a drink.
80  ISABELLA.   Hello Gret! (*Continues to Nijo.*) I tried to be a clergyman's daughter. Needlework, music, charitable schemes. I had a tumour removed from my spine and spent a great deal of time on the sofa. I studied the metaphysical poets and hymnology. / I thought I
85  enjoyed intellectual pursuits.
NIJO.   Ah, you like poetry. I come of a line of eight generations of poets. Father had a poem / in the anthology.
ISABELLA.   My father taught me Latin although I was a
90  girl. / But
MARLENE.   They didn't have Latin at my school.
ISABELLA.   really I was more suited to manual work. Cooking, washing, mending, riding horses. / Better than reading books,
95  NIJO.   Oh but I'm sure you're very clever.
ISABELLA.   eh Gret? A rough life in the open air.
NIJO.   I can't say I enjoyed my rough life. What I enjoyed most was being the Emperor's favourite / and wearing thin silk.
100  ISABELLA.   Did you have any horses, Gret?
GRET.   Pig.

(*Pope Joan*[2] *arrives.*)

MARLENE.   Oh Joan, thank God, we can order. Do you know everyone? We were just talking about learning Latin and being clever girls. Joan was by way of an
105  infant prodigy. Of course you were. What excited you when you were ten?
JOAN.   Because angels are without matter they are not individuals. Every angel is a species.
MARLENE.   There you are.

(*They laugh. They look at menus.*)

110  ISABELLA.   Yes, I forgot all my Latin. But my father was the mainspring of my life and when he died I was so grieved. I'll have the chicken, please, / and the soup.
NIJO.   Of course you were grieved. My father was saying his prayers and he dozed off in the sun. So I touched his
115  knee to rouse him. "I wonder what will happen," he said, and then he was dead before he finished the sentence. / If he'd died saying
MARLENE.   What a shock.
NIJO.   his prayers he would have gone straight to heaven.
120  / Waldorf salad.
JOAN.   Death is the return of all creatures to God.
NIJO.   I shouldn't have woken him.
JOAN.   Damnation only means ignorance of the truth. I was always attracted by the teachings of John the Scot,[3]
125  though he was inclined to confuse / God and the world.
ISABELLA.   Grief always overwhelmed me at the time.
MARLENE.   What I fancy is a rare steak. Gret?
ISABELLA.   I am of course a member of the / Church of England.
130  GRET.   Potatoes.
MARLENE.   I haven't been to church for years. / I like Christmas carols.
ISABELLA.   Good works matter more than church attendance.
135  MARLENE.   Make that two steaks and a lot of potatoes. Rare. But I don't do good works either.
JOAN.   Cannelloni, please, / and a salad.

---

[1]  [Churchill's note]  Dull Gret is the subject of the Brueghel painting, *Dulle Griet*, in which a woman in an apron and armor leads a crowd of women charging through hell and fighting the devils.

[2]  [Churchill's note]  Pope Joan, disguised as a man, is thought to have been Pope between 854–856.

[3]  *John the Scot*  Johannes Scotus Eriugena (c. 815–87), theologian, philosopher, and poet, whose ideas were greatly influenced by Plato.

ISABELLA.  Well, I tried, but oh dear. Hennie did good works.

140 NIJO.  The first half of my life was all sin and the second / all repentance.*

MARLENE.  Oh what about starters?

GRET.  Soup.

JOAN.  *And which did you like best?

145 MARLENE.  Were your travels just a penance? Avocado vinaigrette. Didn't you / enjoy yourself?

JOAN.  Nothing to start with for me, thank you.

NIJO.  Yes, but I was very unhappy. / It hurt to remember

150 MARLENE.  And the wine list.

NIJO.  the past. I think that was repentance.

MARLENE.  Well I wonder.

NIJO.  I might have just been homesick.

MARLENE.  Or angry.

155 NIJO.  Not angry, no, / why angry?

GRET.  Can we have some more bread?

MARLENE.  Don't you get angry? I get angry.

NIJO.  But what about?

MARLENE.  Yes let's have two more Frascati. And some
160 more bread, please.

(*The Waitress exits.*)

ISABELLA.  I tried to understand Buddhism when I was in Japan but all this birth and death succeeding each other through eternities just filled me with the most profound melancholy. I do like something more active.

165 NIJO.  You couldn't say I was inactive. I walked every day for twenty years.

ISABELLA.  I don't mean walking. / I mean in the head.

NIJO.  I vowed to copy five Mahayana sutras.[1] / Do you know how

170 MARLENE.  I don't think religious beliefs are something we have in common. Activity yes.

NIJO.  long they are? My head was active. / My head ached.

JOAN.  It's no good being active in heresy.

175 ISABELLA.  What heresy? She's calling the Church of England / a heresy.

JOAN.  There are some very attractive / heresies.

---

[1]  *Mahayana sutras*  Buddhist scriptures, thought by some to have been written by the Buddha, dating from the first century BCE.

NIJO.  I had never heard of Christianity. Never / heard of it. Barbarians.

180 MARLENE.  Well I'm not a Christian. / And I'm not a Buddhist.

ISABELLA.  You have heard of it?

MARLENE.  We don't all have to believe the same.

ISABELLA.  I knew coming to dinner with a pope we
185 should keep off religion.

JOAN.  I always enjoy a theological argument. But I won't try to convert you, I'm not a missionary. Anyway I'm a heresy myself.

ISABELLA.  There are some barbaric practices in the east.

190 NIJO.  Barbaric?

ISABELLA.  Among the lower classes.

NIJO.  I wouldn't know.

ISABELLA.  Well theology always made my head ache.

MARLENE.  Oh good, some food.

(*Waitress is bringing the first course.*)

195 NIJO.  How else could I have left the court if I wasn't a nun? When father died I had only His Majesty. So when I fell out of favour I had nothing. Religion is a kind of nothing / and I dedicated what was left of me to nothing.

200 ISABELLA.  That's what I mean about Buddhism. It doesn't brace.

MARLENE.  Come on, Nijo, have some wine.

NIJO.  Haven't you ever felt like that? Nothing will ever happen again. I am dead already. You've all felt / like
205 that.

ISABELLA.  You thought your life was over but it wasn't.

JOAN.  You wish it was over.

GRET.  Sad.

MARLENE.  Yes, when I first came to London I
210 sometimes … and when I got back from America I did. But only for a few hours. Not twenty years.

ISABELLA.  When I was forty I thought my life was over. / Oh I

NIJO.  I didn't say I felt it for twenty years. Not every
215 minute.

ISABELLA.  was pitiful. I was sent on a cruise for my health and I felt even worse. Pains in my bones, pins and needles in my hands, swelling behind the ears, and—oh, stupidity. I shook all over, indefinable terror.

220 And Australia seemed to me a hideous country, the
acacias stank like drains. / I had a

NIJO.  You were homesick.

ISABELLA.  photograph for Hennie but I told her I
wouldn't send it, my hair had fallen out and my clothes

225 were crooked, I looked completely insane and suicidal.

NIJO.  So did I, exactly, dressed as a nun. I was wearing
walking shoes for the first time.

ISABELLA.  I longed to go home, / but home to what?
Houses

230 NIJO.  I longed to go back ten years.

ISABELLA.  are so perfectly dismal.

MARLENE.  I thought travelling cheered you both up.

ISABELLA.  Oh it did / of course. It was on the trip from

NIJO.  I'm not a cheerful person, Marlene. I just laugh a

235 lot.

ISABELLA.  Australia to the Sandwich Isles, I fell in love
with the sea. There were rats in the cabin and ants in the
food but suddenly it was like a new world. I woke up
every morning happy, knowing there would be nothing

240 to annoy me. No nervousness. No dressing.

NIJO.  Don't you like getting dressed? I adored my
clothes. / When I was chosen to give sake to His
Majesty's brother,

MARLENE.  You had prettier colours than Isabella.

245 NIJO.  the Emperor Kameyana, on his formal visit, I
wore raw silk pleated trousers and a seven-layered gown
in shades of red, and two outer garments, / yellow lined
with green and a light

MARLENE.  Yes, all that silk must have been very …

*(The Waitress starts to clear the first course.)*

250 JOAN.  I dressed as a boy when I left home.*

NIJO.  green jacket. Lady Betto had a five-layered gown
in shades of green and purple.

ISABELLA.  *You dressed as a boy?

MARLENE.  Of course, / for safety.

255 JOAN.  It was easy, I was only twelve. / Also women
weren't allowed in the library. We wanted to study in
Athens.

MARLENE.  You ran away alone?

JOAN.  No, not alone, I went with my friend. / He was

260 sixteen

NIJO.  Ah, an elopement.

JOAN.  but I thought I knew more science than he did
and almost as much philosophy.

ISABELLA.  Well I always travelled as a lady and I

265 repudiated strongly any suggestion in the press that I
was other than feminine.

MARLENE.  I don't wear trousers in the office. / I could
but I don't.

ISABELLA.  There was no great danger to a woman of my

270 age and appearance.

MARLENE.  And you got away with it, Joan?

JOAN.  I did then.

*(The Waitress starts to bring the main course.)*

MARLENE.  And nobody noticed anything?

JOAN.  They noticed I was a very clever boy. / And when

275 I

MARLENE.  I couldn't have kept pretending for so long.

JOAN.  shared a bed with my friend, that was
ordinary—two poor students in a lodging house. I think
I forgot I was pretending.

280 ISABELLA.  Rocky Mountain Jim, Mr. Nugent,[1] showed
me no disrespect. He found it interesting, I think, that
I could make scones and also lasso cattle. Indeed he
declared his love for me, which was most distressing.

NIJO.  What did he say? / We always sent poems first.

285 MARLENE.  What did you say?

ISABELLA.  I urged him to give up whisky, / but he said
it was too late.

MARLENE.  Oh Isabella.

ISABELLA.  He had lived alone in the mountains for

290 many years.

MARLENE.  But did you—?

*(The Waitress goes.)*

ISABELLA.  Mr. Nugent was a man that any woman might
love but none could marry. I came back to England.

NIJO.  Did you write him a poem when you left? / Snow

295 on the

MARLENE.  Did you never see him again?

ISABELLA.  No, never.

---

[1] *Mr. Nugent*  Mountain man with whom Bird had a romantic
relationship, as documented in her 1879 book *A Lady's Life in the
Rocky Mountains.*

NIJO. mountains. My sleeves are wet with tears. In England no tears, no snow.

300 ISABELLA. Well, I say never. One morning very early in Switzerland, it was a year later, I had a vision of him as I last saw him / in his trapper's clothes with his hair round his face,

NIJO. A ghost!

305 ISABELLA. and that was the day, / I learnt later, he died with a

NIJO. Ah!

ISABELLA. bullet in his brain. / He just bowed to me and vanished.

310 MARLENE. Oh Isabella.

NIJO. When your lover dies—One of my lovers died. / The priest Ariake.

JOAN. My friend died. Have we all got dead lovers?

MARLENE. Not me, sorry.

315 NIJO. (To Isabella.) I wasn't a nun, I was still at court, but he was a priest, and when he came to me he dedicated his whole life to hell. / He knew that when he died he would fall into one of the three lower realms. And he died, he did die.

320 JOAN. (To Marlene.) I'd quarrelled with him over the teachings of John the Scot, who held that our ignorance of God is the same as his ignorance of himself. He only knows what he creates because he creates everything he knows but he himself is above being—do you follow?

325 MARLENE. No, but go on.

NIJO. I couldn't bear to think / in what shape would he be reborn.*

JOAN. St. Augustine maintained that the Neo-Platonic Ideas are indivisible from God, but I agreed with John 330 that the created

ISABELLA. *Buddhism is really most uncomfortable.

JOAN. world is essences derived from Ideas which derived from God. As Denys the Areopagite[1] said—the pseudo-Denys—first we give God a name, then deny it 335 / then reconcile the

NIJO. In what shape would he return?

JOAN. contradiction by looking beyond / those terms—

MARLENE. Sorry, what? Denys said what?

JOAN. Well we disagreed about it, we quarrelled. And 340 next day he was ill, / I was so annoyed with him, all the time I was

NIJO. Misery in this life and worse in the next, all because of me.

JOAN. nursing him I kept going over the arguments in 345 my mind. Matter is not a means of knowing the essence. The source of the species is the Idea. But then I realised he'd never understand my arguments again, and that night he died. John the Scot held that the individual disintegrates / and there is no personal immortality.

350 ISABELLA. I wouldn't have you think I was in love with Jim Nugent. It was yearning to save him that I felt.

MARLENE. (To Joan.) So what did you do?

JOAN. First I decided to stay a man. I was used to it. And I wanted to devote my life to learning. Do you 355 know why I went to Rome? Italian men didn't have beards.

ISABELLA. The loves of my life were Hennie, my own pet, and my dear husband the doctor, who nursed Hennie in her last illness. I knew it would be terrible 360 when Hennie died but I didn't know how terrible. I felt half of myself had gone. How could I go on my travels without that sweet soul waiting at home for my letters? It was Doctor Bishop's devotion to her in her last illness that made me decide to marry him. He and Hennie had 365 the same sweet character. I had not.

NIJO. I thought His Majesty had sweet character because when he found out about Ariake he was so kind. But really it was because he no longer cared for me. One night he even sent me out to a man who had 370 been pursuing me. / He lay awake on the other side of the screens and listened.

ISABELLA. I did wish marriage had seemed more of a step. I tried very hard to cope with the ordinary drudgery of life. I was ill again with carbuncles on the 375 spine and nervous prostration. I ordered a tricycle, that was my idea of adventure then. And John himself fell ill, with erysipelas[2] and anaemia. I began to love him with my whole heart but it was too late. He was a skeleton with transparent white hands. I wheeled him on various

[1] *Denys the Areopagite* Pseudo-Dionysius the Areopagite, an anonymous fifth-century theologian and philosopher, author of a collection of books incorrectly attributed to the Dionysius mentioned in Acts 17.34.

[2] *erysipelas* Infection of the skin caused by streptococcal bacteria.

380　seafronts in a bathchair.[1] And he faded and left me. There was nothing in my life. The doctors said I had gout / and my heart was much affected.

NIJO.　There was nothing in my life, nothing, without the Emperor's favour. The Empress had always been my
385　enemy, Marlene, she said I had no right to wear three-layered gowns. / But I was the adopted daughter of my grandfather the Prime Minister. I had been publicly granted permission to wear thin silk.

JOAN.　There was nothing in my life except my studies.
390　I was obsessed with pursuit of the truth. I taught at the Greek School in Rome, which St. Augustine had made famous. I was poor, I worked hard. I spoke apparently brilliantly, I was still very young, I was a stranger; suddenly I was quite famous, I was everyone's favourite.
395　Huge crowds came to hear me. The day after they made me cardinal I fell ill and lay two weeks without speaking, full of terror and regret. / But then I got up

MARLENE.　Yes, success is very…

JOAN.　determined to go on. I was seized again / with a
400　desperate longing for the absolute.

ISABELLA.　Yes, yes, to go on. I sat in Tobermory among Hennie's flowers and sewed a complete outfit in Jaeger flannel.[2] / I was fifty-six years old.

NIJO.　Out of favour but I didn't die. I left on foot,
405　nobody saw me go. For the next twenty years I walked through Japan.

GRET.　Walking is good.

(The Waitress enters.)

JOAN.　Pope Leo died and I was chosen. All right then. I would be Pope. I would know God. I would know
410　everything.

ISABELLA.　I determined to leave my grief behind and set off for Tibet.

MARLENE.　Magnificent all of you. We need some more wine, please, two bottles I think, Griselda isn't even here
415　yet, and I want to drink a toast to you all.

---

[1]　*bathchair*　Large chair on wheels, from Bath, a famous spa for invalids.

[2]　*Jaeger flannel*　Cloth invented by Dr. Gustav Jaeger, who developed a theory that wearing pure animal fibers against the body would help disperse noxious exhalations from the body.

ISABELLA.　To yourself surely, / we're here to celebrate your success.

NIJO.　Yes, Marlene,

JOAN.　Yes, what is it exactly, Marlene?

420　MARLENE.　Well it's not Pope but it is managing director.*

JOAN.　And you find work for people.

MARLENE.　Yes, an employment agency.

NIJO.　*Over all the women you work with. And the
425　men.

ISABELLA.　And very well deserved too. I'm sure it's just the beginning of something extraordinary.

MARLENE.　Well it's worth a party.

ISABELLA.　To Marlene.*

430　MARLENE.　And all of us.

JOAN.　*Marlene.

NIJO.　Marlene.

GRET.　Marlene.

MARLENE.　We've all come a long way. To our courage
435　and the way we changed our lives and our extraordinary achievements.

(They laugh and drink a toast.)

ISABELLA.　Such adventures. We were crossing a mountain pass at seven thousand feet, the cook was all to pieces, the muleteers suffered fever and snow
440　blindness. But even though my spine was agony I managed very well.

MARLENE.　Wonderful.

NIJO.　Once I was ill for four months lying alone at an inn. Nobody to offer a horse to Buddha. I had to live for
445　myself, and I did live.

ISABELLA.　Of course you did. It was far worse returning to Tobermory. I always felt dull when I was stationary. / That's why I could never stay anywhere.

NIJO.　Yes, that's it exactly. New sights. The shrine by the
450　beach, the moon shining on the sea. The goddess had vowed to save all living things. / She would even save the fishes. I was full of hope.

JOAN.　I had thought the Pope would know everything. I thought God would speak to me directly. But of
455　course he knew I was a woman.

MARLENE.　But nobody else even suspected?

(The Waitress brings more wine.)

JOAN.  In the end I did take a lover again.*
ISABELLA.  In the Vatican?
GRET.  *Keep you warm.
460 NIJO.  *Ah, lover.
MARLENE.  *Good for you.
JOAN.  He was one of my chamberlains. There are such
    a lot of servants when you're a Pope. The food's very
    good. And I realised I did know the truth. Because
465 whatever the Pope says, that's true.
NIJO.  What was he like, the chamberlain?*
GRET.  Big cock.
ISABELLA.  Oh Gret.
MARLENE.  *Did he fancy you when he thought you
470 were a fella?
NIJO.  What was he like?
JOAN.  He could keep a secret.
MARLENE.  So you did know everything.
JOAN.  Yes, I enjoyed being Pope. I consecrated bishops
475 and let people kiss my feet. I received the King of
    England when he came to submit to the church.
    Unfortunately there were earthquakes, and some village
    reported it had rained blood, and in France there was a
    plague of giant grasshoppers, but I don't think that can
480 have been my fault, do you?*

(*Laughter.*)

The grasshoppers fell on the English Channel / and
were
NIJO.  I once went to sea. It was very lonely. I realised it
    made very little difference where I went.
485 JOAN.  washed up on shore and their bodies rotted and
    poisoned the air and everyone in those parts died.

(*Laughter.*)

ISABELLA.  *Such superstition! I was nearly murdered in
    China by a howling mob. They thought the barbarians
    ate babies and put them under railway sleepers to make
490 the tracks steady, and ground up their eyes to make the
    lenses of cameras. / So
MARLENE.  And you had a camera!
ISABELLA.  they were shouting, "child-eater, child-eater."
    Some people tried to sell girl babies to Europeans for
495 cameras or stew!

(*Laughter.*)

MARLENE.  So apart from the grasshoppers it was a great
    success.
JOAN.  Yes, if it hadn't been for the baby I expect I'd
    have lived to an old age like Theodora of Alexandria,[1]
500 who lived as a monk. She was accused by a girl / who
    fell in love with her of being the father of her child
    and—
NIJO.  But tell us what happened to your baby. I had
    some babies.
505 MARLENE.  Didn't you think of getting rid of it?
JOAN.  Wouldn't that be a worse sin than having it? /
    But a Pope with a child was about as bad as possible.
MARLENE.  I don't know, you're the Pope.
JOAN.  But I wouldn't have known how to get rid of it.
510 MARLENE.  Other Popes had children, surely.
JOAN.  They didn't give birth to them.
NIJO.  Well you were a woman.
JOAN.  Exactly and I shouldn't have been a woman.
    Women, children and lunatics can't be Pope.
515 MARLENE.  So the only thing to do / was to get rid of it
    somehow.
NIJO.  You had to have it adopted secretly.
JOAN.  But I didn't know what was happening. I thought
    I was getting fatter, but then I was eating more and
520 sitting about, the life of a Pope is quite luxurious. I
    don't think I'd spoken to a woman since I was twelve.
    The chamberlain was the one who realised.
MARLENE.  And by then it was too late.
JOAN.  Oh I didn't want to pay attention. It was easier to
525 do nothing.
NIJO.  But you had to plan for having it. You had to say
    you were ill and go away.
JOAN.  That's what I should have done I suppose.
MARLENE.  Did you want them to find out?
530 NIJO.  I too was often in embarrassing situations, there's
    no need for a scandal. My first child was His Majesty's,
    which unfortunately died, but my second was
    Akebono's. I was seventeen. He was in love with me
    when I was thirteen, he was very upset when I had to go

---

[1] *Theodora of Alexandria*  Wealthy fifth- or sixth-century noble-
woman who entered a monastery as penance for committing
adultery, and lived as a man. She was expelled from the monastery
when she was accused of fathering a child.

535 to the Emperor, it was very romantic, a lot of poems.
Now His Majesty hadn't been near me for two months
so he thought I was four months pregnant when I was
really six, so when I reached the ninth month / I

JOAN. I never knew what month it was.

540 NIJO. announced I was seriously ill, and Akebono
announced he had gone on a religious retreat. He held
me round the waist and lifted me up as the baby was
born. He cut the cord with a short sword, wrapped the
baby in white and took it away. It was only a girl but I

545 was sorry to lose it. Then I told the Emperor that the
baby had miscarried because of my illness, and there you
are. The danger was past.

JOAN. But Nijo, I wasn't used to having a woman's
body.

550 ISABELLA. So what happened?

JOAN. I didn't know of course that it was near the time.
It was Rogation Day,[1] there was always a procession. I
was on the horse dressed in my robes and a cross was
carried in front of me, and all the cardinals were

555 following, and all the clergy of Rome, and a huge crowd
of people. / We set off from

MARLENE. Total Pope.

JOAN. St. Peter's to go to St. John's. I had felt a slight
pain earlier, I thought it was something I'd eaten, and

560 then it came back, and came back more often. I thought
when this is over I'll go to bed. There were still long
gaps when I felt perfectly all right and I didn't want to
attract attention to myself and spoil the ceremony. Then
I suddenly realised what it must be. I had to last out till

565 I could get home and hide. Then something changed,
my breath started to catch, I couldn't plan things
properly any more. We were in a little street that goes
between St. Clement's and the Colosseum, and I just
had to get off the horse and sit down for a minute.

570 Great waves of pressure were going through my body, I
heard sounds like a cow lowing, they came out of my
mouth. Far away I heard people screaming, "The Pope
is ill, the Pope is dying." And the baby just slid out onto
the road.*

575 MARLENE. The cardinals / won't have known where to
put themselves.

NIJO. Oh dear, Joan, what a thing to do! In the street!

---

[1] *Rogation Day* One of three days immediately before Ascension
Thursday in the Christian liturgical calendar.

ISABELLA. *How embarrassing.
GRET. In a field, yah.

(*They are laughing.*)

580 JOAN. One of the cardinals said, "The Antichrist!" and
fell over in a faint.

(*They all laugh.*)

MARLENE. So what did they do? They weren't best
pleased.

JOAN. They took me by the feet and dragged me out of
585 town and stoned me to death.

(*They stop laughing.*)

MARLENE. Joan, how horrible.
JOAN. I don't really remember.
NIJO. And the child died too?
JOAN. Oh yes, I think so, yes.

(*Pause.*)
(*The Waitress enters to clear the plates. They start talking quietly.*)

590 ISABELLA. (*To Joan.*) I never had any children. I was
very fond of horses.

NIJO. (*To Marlene.*) I saw my daughter once. She was
three years old. She wore a plum-red / small-sleeved
gown. Akebono's

595 ISABELLA. Birdie was my favourite. A little Indian bay
mare I rode in the Rocky Mountains.

NIJO. wife had taken the child because her own died.
Everyone thought I was just a visitor. She was being
brought up carefully so she could be sent to the palace
600 like I was.

ISABELLA. Legs of iron and always cheerful, and such a
pretty face. If a stranger led her she reared up like a
bronco.

NIJO. I never saw my third child after he was born, the
605 son of Ariake the priest. Ariake held him on his lap the
day he was born and talked to him as if he could
understand, and cried. My fourth child was Ariake's too.
Ariake died before he was born. I didn't want to see

anyone, I stayed alone in the hills. It was a boy again,
610    my third son. But oddly enough I felt nothing for him.
MARLENE.   How many children did you have, Gret?
GRET.   Ten.
ISABELLA.   Whenever I came back to England I felt I had
so much to atone for. Hennie and John were so good. I
615    did no good in my life. I spent years in self-gratification.
So I hurled myself into committees, I nursed the people
of Tobermory in the epidemic of influenza, I lectured
the Young Women's Christian Association on Thrift. I
talked and talked explaining how the East was corrupt
620    and vicious. My travels must do good to someone beside
myself. I wore myself out with good causes.
MARLENE.   Oh God, why are we all so miserable?
JOAN.   The procession never went down that street
again.
625    MARLENE.   They rerouted it specially?
JOAN.   Yes they had to go all round to avoid it. And they
introduced a pierced chair.
MARLENE.   A pierced chair?
JOAN.   Yes, a chair made out of solid marble with a hole
630    in the seat / and it was in the Chapel of the Saviour, and
after he was
MARLENE.   You're not serious.
JOAN.   elected the Pope had to sit in it.
MARLENE.   And someone looked up his skirts? / Not
635    really?
ISABELLA.   What an extraordinary thing.
JOAN.   Two of the clergy / made sure he was a man.
NIJO.   On their hands and knees!
MARLENE.   A pierced chair!
640    GRET.   Balls!

(*Griselda*[1] *arrives unnoticed.*)

NIJO.   Why couldn't he just pull up his robe?
JOAN.   He had to sit there and look dignified.
MARLENE.   You could have made all your chamberlains
sit in it.*
645    GRET.   Big one, small one.
NIJO.   Very useful chair at court.
ISABELLA.   *Or the laird of Tobermory in his kilt.

(*They are quite drunk. They get the giggles.*)
(*Marlene notices Griselda.*)

MARLENE.   Griselda! / There you are. Do you want to
eat?
650    GRISELDA.   I'm sorry I'm so late. No, no, don't bother.
MARLENE.   Of course it's no bother. / Have you eaten?
GRISELDA.   No really, I'm not hungry.
MARLENE.   Well have some pudding.[2]
GRISELDA.   I never eat pudding.
655    MARLENE.   Griselda, I hope you're not anorexic. We're
having pudding, I am, and getting nice and fat.
GRISELDA.   Oh if everyone is. I don't mind.
MARLENE.   Now who do you know? This is Joan who
was Pope in the ninth century, and Isabella Bird, the
660    Victorian traveller, and Lady Nijo from Japan,
Emperor's concubine and Buddhist nun, thirteenth
century, nearer your own time, and Gret who was
painted by Brueghel. Griselda's in Boccaccio and
Petrarch and Chaucer because of her extraordinary
665    marriage. I'd like profiteroles because they're disgusting.
JOAN.   Zabaglione, please.
ISABELLA.   Apple pie / and cream.
NIJO.   What's this?
MARLENE.   Zabaglione, it's Italian, it's what Joan's
670    having, / it's delicious.
NIJO.   A Roman Catholic / dessert? Yes please.
MARLENE.   Gret?
GRET.   Cake.
GRISELDA.   Just cheese and biscuits, thank you.
675    MARLENE.   Yes, Griselda's life is like a fairy-story, except
it starts with marrying the prince.
GRISELDA.   He's only a marquis, Marlene.
MARLENE.   Well everyone for miles around is his liege
and he's absolute lord of life and death and you were the
680    poor but beautiful peasant girl and he whisked you off.
/ Near enough a prince.
NIJO.   How old were you?
GRISELDA.   Fifteen.
NIJO.   I was brought up in court circles and it was still a
685    shock. Had you ever seen him before?
GRISELDA.   I'd seen him riding by, we all had. And he'd
seen me in the fields with the sheep.*

---

[1]   [Churchill's note]  Patient Griselda is the obedient wife whose
story is told by Chaucer in The Clerk's Tale of *The Canterbury Tales.*

---

[2]   *pudding*  Dessert.

ISABELLA. I would have been well suited to minding sheep.

690 NIJO. And Mr. Nugent riding by.

ISABELLA. Of course not, Nijo, I mean a healthy life in the open air.

JOAN. *He just rode up while you were minding the sheep and asked you to marry him?

695 GRISELDA. No, no, it was on the wedding day. I was waiting outside the door to see the procession. Everyone wanted him to get married so there'd be an heir to look after us when he died, / and at last he announced a day for the wedding but

700 MARLENE. I don't think Walter wanted to get married. It is Walter? Yes.

GRISELDA. nobody knew who the bride was, we thought it must be a foreign princess, we were longing to see her. Then the carriage stopped outside our cottage and we 705 couldn't see the bride anywhere. And he came and spoke to my father.

NIJO. And your father told you to serve the Prince.

GRISELDA. My father could hardly speak. The Marquis said it wasn't an order, I could say no, but if I said yes I 710 must always obey him in everything.

MARLENE. That's when you should have suspected.

GRISELDA. But of course a wife must obey her husband. / And of course I must obey the Marquis.*

ISABELLA. I swore to obey dear John, of course, but it 715 didn't seem to arise. Naturally I wouldn't have wanted to go abroad while I was married.

MARLENE. *Then why bother to mention it at all? He'd got a thing about it, that's why.

GRISELDA. I'd rather obey the Marquis than a boy from 720 the village.

MARLENE. Yes, that's a point.

JOAN. I never obeyed anyone. They all obeyed me.

NIJO. And what did you wear? He didn't make you get married in your own clothes? That would be perverse.*

725 MARLENE. Oh, you wait.

GRISELDA. *He had ladies with him who undressed me and they had a white silk dress and jewels for my hair.

MARLENE. And at first he seemed perfectly normal?

GRISELDA. Marlene, you're always so critical of him. / 730 Of course he was normal, he was very kind.

MARLENE. But Griselda, come on, he took your baby.

GRISELDA. Walter found it hard to believe I loved him. He couldn't believe I would always obey him. He had to prove it.

735 MARLENE. I don't think Walter likes women.

GRISELDA. I'm sure he loved me, Marlene, all the time.

MARLENE. He just had a funny way / of showing it.

GRISELDA. It was hard for him too.

JOAN. How do you mean he took away your baby?

740 NIJO. Was it a boy?

GRISELDA. No, the first one was a girl.

NIJO. Even so it's hard when they take it away. Did you see it at all?

GRISELDA. Oh yes, she was six weeks old.

745 NIJO. Much better to do it straight away.

ISABELLA. But why did your husband take the child?

GRISELDA. He said all the people hated me because I was just one of them. And now I had a child they were restless. So he had to get rid of the child to keep them 750 quiet. But he said he wouldn't snatch her, I had to agree and obey and give her up. So when I was feeding her a man came in and took her away. I thought he was going to kill her even before he was out of the room.

MARLENE. But you let him take her? You didn't 755 struggle?

GRISELDA. I asked him to give her back so I could kiss her. And I asked him to bury her where no animals could dig her up. / It

ISABELLA. Oh my dear.

760 GRISELDA. was Walter's child to do what he liked with.*

MARLENE. Walter was bonkers.

GRET. Bastard.

ISABELLA. *But surely, murder.

GRISELDA. I had promised.

765 MARLENE. I can't stand this. I'm going for a pee …

(*Marlene goes out. The Waitress brings dessert.*)

NIJO. No, I understand. Of course you had to, he was your life. And were you in favour after that?

GRISELDA. Oh yes, we were very happy together. We never spoke about what had happened.

770 ISABELLA. I can see you were doing what you thought was your duty. But didn't it make you ill?

GRISELDA. No, I was very well, thank you.

NIJO. And you had another child?

GRISELDA. Not for four years, but then I did, yes, a boy.

NIJO. Ah a boy. / So it all ended happily.

GRISELDA. Yes he was pleased. I kept my son till he was two years old. A peasant's grandson. It made the people angry. Walter explained.

ISABELLA. But surely he wouldn't kill his children / just because—

GRISELDA. Oh it wasn't true. Walter would never give in to the people. He wanted to see if I loved him enough.

JOAN. He killed his children / to see if you loved him enough?

NIJO. Was it easier the second time or harder?

GRISELDA. It was always easy because I always knew I would do what he said.

(Pause. They start to eat.)

ISABELLA. I hope you didn't have any more children.

GRISELDA. Oh no, no more. It was twelve years till he tested me again.

ISABELLA. So whatever did he do this time? / My poor John, I never loved him enough, and he would never have dreamt …

GRISELDA. He sent me away. He said the people wanted him to marry someone else who'd give him an heir and he'd got special permission from the Pope. So I said I'd go home to my father. I came with nothing / so I went with nothing. I

NIJO. Better to leave if your master doesn't want you.

GRISELDA. took off my clothes. He let me keep a slip so he wouldn't be shamed. And I walked home barefoot. My father came out in tears. Everyone was crying except me.

NIJO. At least your father wasn't dead. / I had nobody.

ISABELLA. Well it can be a relief to come home. I loved to see Hennie's sweet face again.

GRISELDA. Oh yes, I was perfectly content. And quite soon he sent for me again.

JOAN. I don't think I would have gone.

GRISELDA. But he told me to come. I had to obey him. He wanted me to help prepare his wedding. He was getting married to a young girl from France / and nobody except me knew how to arrange things the way

he liked them.

NIJO. It's always hard taking him another woman.

(Marlene comes back.)

JOAN. I didn't live a woman's life. I don't understand it.

GRISELDA. The girl was sixteen and far more beautiful than me. I could see why he loved her. / She had her younger brother with her as a page.

(The Waitress enters.)

MARLENE. Oh God, I can't bear it. I want some coffee. Six coffees. Six brandies. / Double brandies. Straightaway.

GRISELDA. They all went in to the feast I'd prepared. And he stayed behind and put his arms round me and kissed me. / I felt half asleep with the shock.

NIJO. Oh, like a dream.

MARLENE. And he said, "This is your daughter and your son."

GRISELDA. Yes.

JOAN. What?

NIJO. Oh. Oh I see. You got them back.

ISABELLA. I did think it was remarkably barbaric to kill them but you learn not to say anything. / So he had them brought up secretly I suppose.

MARLENE. Walter's a monster. Weren't you angry? What did you do?

GRISELDA. Well I fainted. Then I cried and kissed the children. / Everyone was making a fuss of me.

NIJO. But did you feel anything for them?

GRISELDA. What?

NIJO. Did you feel anything for the children?

GRISELDA. Of course, I loved them.

JOAN. So you forgave him and lived with him?

GRISELDA. He suffered so much all those years.

ISABELLA. Hennie had the same sweet nature.

NIJO. So they dressed you again?

GRISELDA. Cloth of gold.

JOAN. I can't forgive anything.

MARLENE. You really are exceptional, Griselda.

NIJO. Nobody gave me back my children.

(Nijo cries. The Waitress brings brandies.)

ISABELLA.  I can never be like Hennie. I was always so
busy in England, a kind of business I detested. The very
presence of people exhausted my emotional reserves. I
855 could not be like Hennie however I tried. I tried and
was as ill as could be. The doctor suggested a steel net to
support my head, the weight of my own head was too
much for my diseased spine. / It is dangerous to put
oneself in depressing circumstances. Why should I do it?
860 JOAN.  Don't cry.
NIJO.  My father and the Emperor both died in the
autumn. So much pain.
JOAN.  Yes, but don't cry.
NIJO.  They wouldn't let me into the palace when he was
865 dying. I hid in the room with his coffin, then I couldn't
find where I'd left my shoes, I ran after the funeral
procession in bare feet, I couldn't keep up. When I got
there it was over, a few wisps of smoke in the sky, that's
all that was left of him. What I want to know is, if I'd
870 still been at court, would I have been allowed to wear
full mourning?
MARLENE.  I'm sure you would.
NIJO.  Why do you say that? You don't know anything
about it. Would I have been allowed to wear full
875 mourning?
ISABELLA.  How can people live in this dim pale island
and wear our hideous clothes? I cannot and will not live
the life of a lady.
NIJO.  I'll tell you something that made me angry. I was
880 eighteen, at the Full Moon Ceremony. They make a
special rice gruel and stir it with their sticks, and then
they beat their women across the loins so they'll have
sons and not daughters. So the Emperor beat us all /
very hard as usual—that's not it,
885 MARLENE.  What a sod.
NIJO.  Marlene, that's normal, what made us angry, he
told his attendants they could beat us too. Well they had
a wonderful time. / So Lady Genki and I made a plan,
and the ladies all hid

(*The Waitress has entered with coffees.*)

890 MARLENE.  I'd like another brandy please. Better make
it six.
NIJO.  in his rooms, and Lady Mashimizu stood guard
with a stick at the door, and when His Majesty came in

Genki seized him and I beat him till he cried out and
895 promised he would never order anyone to hit us again.
Afterwards there was a terrible fuss. The nobles were
horrified. "We wouldn't even dream of stepping on your
Majesty's shadow." And I had hit him with a stick. Yes,
I hit him with a stick.
900 JOAN.  Suave, mari magno turbantibus aequora ventis,
e terra magnum alterius spectare laborem;
non quia vexari quemquamst iucunda voluptas,
sed quibus ipse malis careas quia cernere suave est.
Suave etiam belli certamina magna tueri
905 per campos instructa tua sine parte pericli.
Sed nil dulcius est, bene quam munita tenere
edita doctrina sapientum templa serena, /
despicere unde queas alios passimque videre
errare atque viam palantis quaerere vitae,
910 GRISELDA.  I do think—I do wonder—it would have
been nicer if Walter hadn't had to.
ISABELLA.  Why should I? Why should I?
MARLENE.  Of course not.
NIJO.  I hit him with a stick.
915 JOAN.  certare ingenio, contendere nobilitate,
noctes atque dies niti praestante labore
ad summas emergere opes retumque potiri.
O miseras / hominum mentis, o pectora caeca!*
ISABELLA.  Oh miseras!
920 NIJO.  *Pectora caeca.
JOAN.  qualibus in tenebris vitae quantisque periclis
degitur hoc aevi quodcumquest! / nonne videre
nil aliud sibi naturam latrare, nisi utqui
corpore seiunctus dolor absit, mente fruatur[1]

---

[1]  *Suave ... fruatur* Latin:
'Tis sweet, when, down the mighty main, the winds
Roll up its waste of waters, from the land
To watch another's labouring anguish far,
Not that we joyously delight that man
Should thus be smitten, but because 'tis sweet
To mark what evils we ourselves be spared;
'Tis sweet, again, to view the mighty strife
Of armies embattled yonder o'er the plains,
Ourselves no sharers in the peril; but naught
There is more goodly than to hold the high
Serene plateaus, well fortressed by the wise,
Whence thou may'st look below on other men
And see them ev'rywhere wand'ring, all dispersed
In their lone seeking for the road of life;
Rivals in genius, or emulous in rank,
Pressing through days and nights with hugest toil

(*Joan subsides.*)

925   GRET.   We come into hell through a big mouth. Hell's
black and red. / It's like the village where I come from.
There's a river and

MARLENE.   (*To Joan.*) Shut up, pet.

ISABELLA.   Listen, she's been to hell.

930   GRET.   a bridge and houses. There's places on fire like
when the soldiers come. There's a big devil sat on a roof
with a big hole in his arse and he's scooping stuff out of
it with a big ladle and it's falling down on us, and it's
money, so a lot of the women stop and get some. But

935   most of us is fighting the devils. There's lots of little
devils, our size, and we get them down all right and give
them a beating. There's lots of funny creatures round
your feet, you don't like to look, like rats and lizards,
and nasty things, a bum with a face, and fish with legs,

940   and faces on things that don't have faces on. But they
don't hurt, you just keep going. Well we'd had worse,
you see, we'd had the Spanish.[1] We'd all had family
killed. My big son die on a wheel. Birds eat him. My
baby, a soldier run her through with a sword. I'd had

945   enough, I was mad, I hate the bastards. I come out my
front door that morning and shout till my neighbours
come out and I said, "Come on, we're going where the
evil come from and pay the bastards out." And they all
come out just as they was / from baking or washing in

950   their

NIJO.   All the ladies come.

GRET.   aprons, and we push down the street and the
ground opens up and we go through a big mouth into
a street just like ours but in hell. I've got a sword in my

955   hand from somewhere and I fill a basket with gold cups
they drink out of down there. You just keep running on
and fighting / you didn't stop for nothing. Oh we give
them devils such a beating.

NIJO.   Take that, take that.

---

For summits of power and mastery of the world.
O wretched minds of men! O blinded hearts!

Joan recites from Book 2 of *De Rerum Natura* (*Of the Nature of
Things*), written by Roman poet Titus Lucretius Carus (c. 99–c. 55
BCE).

[1] *Spanish* Brueghel, who was Flemish, painted *Dulle Griet* in
1562, four years before the Netherlands revolted against Spanish
rule.

960   JOAN.   Something something something mortisque
timores turn vacuum pectus—damn. Quod si
ridicula—something something on and on and on and
something splendorem purpureai.[2]

ISABELLA.   I thought I would have a last jaunt up the

965   west river in China. Why not? But the doctors were so
very grave. I just went to Morocco. The sea was so wild
I had to be landed by ship's crane in a coal bucket. / My
horse was a terror to me a

GRET.   Coal bucket, good.

970   JOAN.   nos in luce timemus something terrorem.

ISABELLA.   powerful black charger.

(*Nijo is laughing and crying.*)
(*Joan gets up and is sick in a corner.*)
(*Marlene is drinking Isabella's brandy.*)

So off I went to visit the Berber sheikhs in full blue
trousers and great brass spurs. I was the only European
woman ever to have seen the Emperor of Morocco. I

975   was seventy years old. What lengths to go to for a last
chance of joy. I knew my return of vigour was only
temporary, but how marvelous while it lasted.

## ACT 1, SCENE 2

(*Employment Agency. Marlene and Jeanine.*)

MARLENE.   Right Jeanine, you are Jeanine aren't you?
Let's have a look. O's and A's.[3] / No A's, all those O's
you probably

JEANINE.   Six O's.

---

[2] *Something … purpureai* Here and following, Joan stumbles her
way through more lines from *De Rerum Natura*, which (correctly
spoken) are translated as:

In how great perils, in what darks of life
Are spent the human years, however brief!
O not to see that nature for herself
Barks after nothing, save that pain keep off,
Disjoined from the body, and that mind enjoy
Delightsome feeling, far from care and fear!

[3] *O's and A's* Credits earned through the British schooling system.
O levels were attained by passing tests at the Ordinary level at age
sixteen. Those interested in going on to a university were required to
study for two more years and earn A levels, granted to those passing
tests at the Advanced level.

5  MARLENE.  could have got an A. / Speeds, not brilliant, not too bad.

JEANINE.  I wanted to go to work.

MARLENE.  Well, Jeanine, what's your present job like?

JEANINE.  I'm a secretary.

10  MARLENE.  Secretary or typist?

JEANINE.  I did start as a typist but the last six months I've been a secretary.

MARLENE.  To?

JEANINE.  To three of them, really, they share me.
15  There's Mr. Ashford, he's the office manager, and Mr. Philby / is sales, and—

MARLENE.  Quite a small place?

JEANINE.  A bit small.

MARLENE.  Friendly?

20  JEANINE.  Oh it's friendly enough.

MARLENE.  Prospects?

JEANINE.  I don't think so, that's the trouble. Miss Lewis is secretary to the managing director and she's been there forever, and Mrs. Bradford / is—

25  MARLENE.  So you want a job with better prospects?

JEANINE.  I want a change.

MARLENE.  So you'll take anything comparable?

JEANINE.  No, I do want prospects. I want more money.

MARLENE.  You're getting—?

30  JEANINE.  Hundred.

MARLENE.  It's not bad you know. You're what? Twenty?

JEANINE.  I'm saving to get married.

MARLENE.  Does that mean you don't want a long-term
35  job, Jeanine?

JEANINE.  I might do.

MARLENE.  Because where do the prospects come in? No kids for a bit?

JEANINE.  Oh no, not kids, not yet.

40  MARLENE.  So you won't tell them you're getting married?

JEANINE.  Had I better not?

MARLENE.  It would probably help.

JEANINE.  I'm not wearing a ring. We thought we
45  wouldn't spend on a ring.

MARLENE.  Saves taking it off.

JEANINE.  I wouldn't take it off.

MARLENE.  There's no need to mention it when you go for an interview. / Now Jeanine do you have a feel for

50  any particular

JEANINE.  But what if they ask?

MARLENE.  kind of company?

JEANINE.  I thought advertising.

MARLENE.  People often do think advertising. I have got
55  a few vacancies but I think they're looking for something glossier.

JEANINE.  You mean how I dress? / I can dress different. I

MARLENE.  I mean experience.

60  JEANINE.  dress like this on purpose for where I am now.

MARLENE.  I have a marketing department here of a knitwear manufacturer. / Marketing is near enough advertising. Secretary

JEANINE.  Knitwear?

65  MARLENE.  to the marketing manager, he's thirty-five, married, I've sent him a girl before and she was happy, left to have a baby, you won't want to mention marriage there. He's very fair I think, good at his job, you won't have to nurse him along. Hundred and ten, so that's
70  better than you're doing now.

JEANINE.  I don't know.

MARLENE.  I've a fairly small concern here, father and two sons, you'd have more say potentially, secretarial and reception duties, only a hundred but the job's going
75  to grow with the concern and then you'll be in at the top with new girls coming in underneath you.

JEANINE.  What is it they do?

MARLENE.  Lampshades. / This would be my first choice for you.

80  JEANINE.  Just lampshades?

MARLENE.  There's plenty of different kinds of lampshade. So we'll send you there, shall we, and the knitwear second choice. Are you free to go for an interview any day they call you?

85  JEANINE.  I'd like to travel.

MARLENE.  We don't have any foreign clients. You'd have to go elsewhere.

JEANINE.  Yes I know. I don't really … I just mean …

MARLENE.  Does your fiancé want to travel?

90  JEANINE.  I'd like a job where I was here in London and with him and everything but now and then—I expect it's silly. Are there jobs like that?

MARLENE.  There's personal assistant to a top executive in a multinational. If that's the idea you need to be planning ahead. Is that where you want to be in ten years?

JEANINE.   I might not be alive in ten years.

MARLENE.   Yes but you will be. You'll have children.

JEANINE.   I can't think about ten years.

MARLENE.   You haven't got the speeds anyway. So I'll send you to these two shall I? You haven't been to any other agency? Just so we don't get crossed wires. Now Jeanine I want you to get one of these jobs, all right? If I send you that means I'm putting myself on the line for you. Your presentation's OK, you look fine, just be confident and go in there convinced that this is the best job for you and you're the best person for the job. If you don't believe it they won't believe it.

JEANINE.   Do you believe it?

MARLENE.   I think you could make me believe it if you put your mind to it.

JEANINE.   Yes, all right.

ACT 1, SCENE 3

(*Joyce's back yard. The house with back door is upstage. Downstage a shelter made of junk, made by children. Two girls, Angie and Kit, are in it, squashed together. Angie is 16, Kit is 12. They cannot be seen from the house. Joyce calls from the house.*)

JOYCE.   Angie. Angie are you out there?

(*Silence. They keep still and wait. When nothing else happens they relax.*)

ANGIE.   Wish she was dead.

KIT.   Wanna watch *The Exterminator?*

ANGIE.   You're sitting on my leg.

KIT.   There's nothing on telly. We can have an ice cream. Angie?

ANGIE.   Shall I tell you something?

KIT.   Do you wanna watch *The Exterminator?*

ANGIE.   It's X,[1] innit.[2]

KIT.   I can get into Xs.

ANGIE.   Shall I tell you something?

---

[1] *X*  Rated for adults only.

[2] *innit*  Isn't it.

KIT.   We'll go to something else. We'll go to Ipswich. What's on the Odeon?

ANGIE.   She won't let me, will she?

KIT.   Don't tell her.

ANGIE.   I've no money.

KIT.   I'll pay.

ANGIE.   She'll moan though, won't she?

KIT.   I'll ask her for you if you like.

ANGIE.   I've no money, I don't want you to pay.

KIT.   I'll ask her.

ANGIE.   She don't like you.

KIT.   I still got three pounds birthday money. Did she say she don't like me? I'll go by myself then.

ANGIE.   Your mum don't let you. I got to take you.

KIT.   She won't know.

ANGIE.   You'd be scared who'd sit next to you.

KIT.   No I wouldn't.
She does like me anyway.

ANGIE.   Tell me then.

KIT.   Tell you what?

ANGIE.   It's you she doesn't like.

KIT.   Well I don't like her so tough shit.

JOYCE.   (*Off.*) Angie. Angie. Angie. I know you're out there. I'm not coming out after you. You come in here.

(*Silence. Nothing happens.*)

ANGIE.   Last night when I was in bed. I been thinking yesterday could I make things move. You know, make things move by thinking about them without touching them. Last night I was in bed and suddenly a picture fell down off the wall.

KIT.   What picture?

ANGIE.   My gran,[3] that picture. Not the poster. The photograph in the frame.

KIT.   Had you done something to make it fall down?

ANGIE.   I must have done.

KIT.   But were you thinking about it?

ANGIE.   Not about it, but about something.

KIT.   I don't think that's very good.

ANGIE.   You know the kitten?

KIT.   Which one?

ANGIE.   There only is one. The dead one.

KIT.   What about it?

---

[3] *gran*  Grandmother.

ANGIE.  I heard it last night.

KIT.  Where?

55  ANGIE.  Out here. In the dark. What if I left you here in the dark all night?

KIT.  You couldn't. I'd go home.

ANGIE.  You couldn't.

KIT.  I'd / go home.

60  ANGIE.  No you couldn't, not if I said.

KIT.  I could.

ANGIE.  Then you wouldn't see anything. You'd just be ignorant.

KIT.  I can see in the daytime.

65  ANGIE.  No you can't. You can't hear it in the daytime.

KIT.  I don't want to hear it.

ANGIE.  You're scared that's all.

KIT.  I'm not scared of anything.

ANGIE.  You're scared of blood.

70  KIT.  It's not the same kitten anyway. You just heard an old cat, / you just heard some old cat.

ANGIE.  You don't know what I heard. Or what I saw. You don't know nothing because you're a baby.

KIT.  You're sitting on me.

75  ANGIE.  Mind my hair / you silly cunt.

KIT.  Stupid fucking cow, I hate you.

ANGIE.  I don't care if you do.

KIT.  You're horrible.

ANGIE.  I'm going to kill my mother and you're going to

80  watch.

KIT.  I'm not playing.

ANGIE.  You're scared of blood.

(*Kit puts her hand under her dress, brings it out with blood on her finger.*)

KIT.  There, see, I got my own blood, so.

(*Angie takes Kit's hand and licks her finger.*)

ANGIE.  Now I'm a cannibal. I might turn into a

85  vampire now.

KIT.  That picture wasn't nailed up right.

ANGIE.  You'll have to do that when I get mine.

KIT.  I don't have to.

ANGIE.  You're scared.

90  KIT.  I'll do it, I might do it. I don't have to just because you say. I'll be sick on you.

ANGIE.  I don't care if you are sick on me, I don't mind sick. I don't mind blood. If I don't get away from here I'm going to die.

95  KIT.  I'm going home.

ANGIE.  You can't go through the house. She'll see you.

KIT.  I won't tell her.

ANGIE.  Oh great, fine.

KIT.  I'll say I was by myself. I'll tell her you're at my

100  house and I'm going there to get you.

ANGIE.  She knows I'm here, stupid.

KIT.  Then why can't I go through the house?

ANGIE.  Because I said not.

KIT.  My mum don't like you anyway.

105  ANGIE.  I don't want her to like me. She's a slag.[1]

KIT.  She is not.

ANGIE.  She does it with everyone.

KIT.  She does not.

ANGIE.  You don't even know what it is.

110  KIT.  Yes I do.

ANGIE.  Tell me then.

KIT.  We get it all at school, cleverclogs. It's on television. You haven't done it.

ANGIE.  How do you know?

115  KIT.  Because I know you haven't.

ANGIE.  You know wrong then because I have.

KIT.  Who with?

ANGIE.  I'm not telling you / who with.

KIT.  You haven't anyway.

120  ANGIE.  How do you know?

KIT.  Who with?

ANGIE.  I'm not telling you.

KIT.  You said you told me everything.

ANGIE.  I was lying wasn't I?

125  KIT.  Who with? You can't tell me who with because / you never—

ANGIE.  Sh.

(*Joyce has come out of the house. She stops half way across the yard and listens. They listen.*)

---

1  *slag*  Derogatory term for a woman who engages sexually with numerous partners.

JOYCE.   You there Angie? Kit? You there Kitty? Want a
cup of tea? I've got some chocolate biscuits. Come on
130 now I'll put the kettle on. Want a choccy biccy, Angie?

(*They all listen and wait.*)

Fucking rotten little cunt. You can stay there and die.
I'll lock the back door.

(*They all wait.*)
(*Joyce goes back to the house.*)
(*Angie and Kit sit in silence for a while.*)

KIT.   When there's a war, where's the safest place?
ANGIE.   Nowhere.
135 KIT.   New Zealand is, my mum said. Your skin's burned
right off. Shall we go to New Zealand?
ANGIE.   I'm not staying here.
KIT.   Shall we go to New Zealand?
ANGIE.   You're not old enough.
140 KIT.   You're not old enough.
ANGIE.   I'm old enough to get married.
KIT.   You don't want to get married.
ANGIE.   No but I'm old enough.
KIT.   I'd find out where they were going to drop it and
145 stand right in the place.
ANGIE.   You couldn't find out.
KIT.   Better than walking round with your skin dragging
on the ground. Eugh. / Would you like walking round
with your skin dragging on the ground?
150 ANGIE.   You couldn't find out, stupid, it's a secret,
KIT.   Where are you going?
ANGIE.   I'm not telling you.
KIT.   Why?
ANGIE.   It's a secret.
155 KIT.   But you tell me all your secrets.
ANGIE.   Not the true secrets.
KIT.   Yes you do.
ANGIE.   No I don't.
KIT.   I want to go somewhere away from the war.
160 ANGIE.   Just forget the war.
KIT.   I can't.
ANGIE.   You have to. It's so boring.
KIT.   I'll remember it at night.
ANGIE.   I'm going to do something else anyway.

165 KIT.   What? Angie come on. Angie.
ANGIE.   It's a true secret.
KIT.   It can't be worse than the kitten. And killing your
mother. And the war.
ANGIE.   Well I'm not telling you so you can die for all I
170 care.
KIT.   My mother says there's something wrong with you
playing with someone my age. She says why haven't you
got friends your own age. People your own age know
there's something funny about you. She says you're a
175 bad influence. She says she's going to speak to your
mother.

(*Angie twists Kit's arm till she cries out.*)

ANGIE.   Say you're a liar.
KIT.   She said it not me.
ANGIE.   Say you eat shit.
180 KIT.   You can't make me.

(*Angie lets go.*)

ANGIE.   I don't care anyway. I'm leaving.
KIT.   Go on then.
ANGIE.   You'll all wake up one morning and find I've
gone.
185 KIT.   Good.
ANGIE.   I'm not telling you when.
KIT.   Go on then.
ANGIE.   I'm sorry I hurt you.
KIT.   I'm tired.
190 ANGIE.   Do you like me?
KIT.   I don't know.
ANGIE.   You do like me.
KIT.   I'm going home.

(*Kit gets up.*)

ANGIE.   No you're not.
195 KIT.   I'm tired.
ANGIE.   She'll see you.
KIT.   She'll give me a chocolate biscuit.
ANGIE.   Kitty.
KIT.   Tell me where you're going.
200 ANGIE.   Sit down.

*(Kit sits in the hut again.)*

KIT.  Go on then.

ANGIE.  Swear?

KIT.  Swear.

ANGIE.  I'm going to London. To see my aunt.

205 KIT.  And what?

ANGIE.  That's it.

KIT.  I see my aunt all the time.

ANGIE.  I don't see my aunt.

KIT.  What's so special?

210 ANGIE.  It is special. She's special.

KIT.  Why?

ANGIE.  She is.

KIT.  Why?

ANGIE.  She is.

215 KIT.  Why?

ANGIE.  My mother hates her.

KIT.  Why?

ANGIE.  Because she does.

KIT.  Perhaps she's not very nice.

220 ANGIE.  She is nice.

KIT.  How do you know?

ANGIE.  Because I know her.

KIT.  You said you never see her.

ANGIE.  I saw her last year. You saw her.

225 KIT.  Did I?

ANGIE.  Never mind.

KIT.  I remember her. That aunt. What's so special?

ANGIE.  She gets people jobs.

KIT.  What's so special?

230 ANGIE.  I think I'm my aunt's child. I think my mother's
     really my aunt.

KIT.  Why?

ANGIE.  Because she goes to America, now shut up.

KIT.  I've been to London.

235 ANGIE.  Now give us a cuddle and shut up because I'm
     sick.

KIT.  You're sitting on my arm.

*(Silence.)*

*(Joyce comes out and comes up to them quietly.)*

JOYCE.  Come on.

KIT.  Oh hello.

240 JOYCE.  Time you went home.

KIT.  We want to go to the Odeon.

JOYCE.  What time?

KIT.  Don't know.

JOYCE.  What's on?

245 KIT.  Don't know.

JOYCE.  Don't know much do you?

KIT.  That all right then?

JOYCE.  Angie's got to clean her room first.

ANGIE.  No I don't.

250 JOYCE.  Yes you do, it's a pigsty.

ANGIE.  Well I'm not.

JOYCE.  Then you're not going. I don't care.

ANGIE.  Well I am going.

JOYCE.  You've no money, have you?

255 ANGIE.  Kit's paying anyway.

JOYCE.  No she's not.

KIT.  I'll help you with your room.

JOYCE.  That's nice.

ANGIE.  No you won't. You wait here.

260 KIT.  Hurry then.

ANGIE.  I'm not hurrying. You just wait.

*(Angie goes into the house. Silence.)*

JOYCE.  I don't know.

*(Silence.)*

How's school then?

KIT.  All right.

265 JOYCE.  What are you now? Third year?

KIT.  Second year.

JOYCE.  Your mum says you're good at English.

*(Silence.)*

Maybe Angie should've stayed on.

KIT.  She didn't like it.

270 JOYCE.  I didn't like it. And look at me. If your face fits
     at school it's going to fit other places too. It wouldn't
     make no difference to Angie. She's not going to get a
     job when jobs are hard to get. I'd be sorry for anyone in
     charge of her. She'd better get married. I don't know
275 who'd have her, mind. She's one of those girls might

never leave home. What do you want to be when you
grow up, Kit?

KIT.   Physicist.

JOYCE.   What?

280   KIT.   Nuclear physicist.

JOYCE.   Whatever for?

KIT.   I could, I'm clever.

JOYCE.   I know you're clever, pet. (*Silence.*)
I'll make a cup of tea. (*Silence.*)

285   Looks like it's going to rain. (*Silence.*) Don't you have
friends your own age?

KIT.   Yes.

JOYCE.   Well then.

KIT.   I'm old for my age.

290   JOYCE.   And Angie's simple is she? She's not simple.

KIT.   I love Angie.

JOYCE.   She's clever in her own way.

KIT.   You can't stop me.

JOYCE.   I don't want to.

295   KIT.   You can't, so.

JOYCE.   Don't be cheeky, Kitty. She's always kind to
little children.

KIT.   She's coming so you better leave me alone.

(*Angie comes out. She has changed into an old best dress,
slightly small for her.*)

JOYCE.   What you put that on for? Have you done your
300   room? You can't clean your room in that.

ANGIE.   I looked in the cupboard and it was there.

JOYCE.   Of course it was there, it's meant to be there. Is
that why it was a surprise, finding something in the
right place? I should think she's surprised, wouldn't you
305   Kit, to find something in her room in the right place.

ANGIE.   I decided to wear it.

JOYCE.   Not today, why? To clean your room? You're
not going to the pictures till you've done your room.
You can put your dress on after if you like.

(*Angie picks up a brick.*)

310   Have you done your room? You're not getting out of it,
you know.

KIT.   Angie, let's go.

JOYCE.   She's not going till she's done her room.

KIT.   It's starting to rain.

315   JOYCE.   Come on, come on then. Hurry and do your
room, Angie, and then you can go to the cinema with
Kit. Oh it's wet, come on. We'll look up the time in the
paper. Does your mother know, Kit, it's going to be a
late night for you, isn't it? Hurry up, Angie. You'll spoil
320   your dress. You make me sick.

(*Joyce and Kit run in.*)
(*Angie stays where she is. Sound of rain.*)
(*Kit comes out of the house and shouts.*)

KIT.   Angie. Angie, come on, you'll get wet.

(*Kit comes back to Angie.*)

ANGIE.   I put on this dress to kill my mother.

KIT.   I suppose you thought you'd do it with a brick.

ANGIE.   You can kill people with a brick.

325   KIT.   Well you didn't, so.

## ACT 2, SCENE 1

(*Office of "Top Girls" Employment Agency. Three desks
and a small interviewing area. Monday morning. Win and
Nell have just arrived for work.*)

NELL.   Coffee coffee coffee coffee / coffee.

WIN.   The roses were smashing. / Mermaid.

NELL.   Ohhh.

WIN.   Iceberg. He taught me all their names.

(*Nell has some coffee now.*)

5   NELL.   Ah. Now then.

WIN.   He has one of the finest rose gardens in West
Sussex. He exhibits.

NELL.   He what?

WIN.   His wife was visiting her mother. It was like living
10   together.

NELL.   Crafty, you never said.

WIN.   He rang on Saturday morning.

NELL.   Lucky you were free.

WIN.   That's what I told him.

15   NELL.  Did you hell.

WIN.  Have you ever seen a really beautiful rose garden?

NELL.  I don't like flowers. / I like swimming pools.

WIN.  Marilyn. Esther's Baby. They're all called after birds.[1]

20   NELL.  Our friend's late. Celebrating all weekend I bet you.

WIN.  I'd call a rose Elvis. Or John Conteh.[2]

NELL.  Is Howard in yet?

WIN.  If he is he'll be bleeping us with a problem.

25   NELL.  Howard can just hang on to himself.

WIN.  Howard's really cut up.

NELL.  Howard thinks because he's a fella the job was his as of right. Our Marlene's got far more balls than Howard and that's that.

30   WIN.  Poor little bugger.

NELL.  He'll live.

WIN.  He'll move on.

NELL.  I wouldn't mind a change of air myself.

WIN.  Serious?

35   NELL.  I've never been a staying put lady. Pastures new.

WIN.  So who's the pirate?

NELL.  There's nothing definite.

WIN.  Inquiries?

NELL.  There's always inquiries. I'd think I'd got bad breath if there stopped being inquiries. Most of them can't afford me. Or you.

WIN.  I'm all right for the time being. Unless I go to Australia.

NELL.  There's not a lot of room upward.

45   WIN.  Marlene's filled it up.

NELL.  Good luck to her. Unless there's some prospects money wise.

WIN.  You can but ask.

NELL.  Can always but ask.

50   WIN.  So what have we got? I've got a Mr. Holden I saw last week.

NELL.  Any use?

WIN.  Pushy. Bit of a cowboy.

NELL.  Good looker?

55   WIN.  Good dresser.

NELL.  High flyer?

WIN.  That's his general idea certainly but I'm not sure he's got it up there.

NELL.  Prestel[3] wants six high flyers and I've only seen

60   two and a half.

WIN.  He's making a bomb on the road but he thinks it's time for an office. I sent him to IBM but he didn't get it.

NELL.  Prestel's on the road.

65   WIN.  He's not overbright.

NELL.  Can he handle an office?

WIN.  Provided his secretary can punctuate he should go far.

NELL.  Bear Prestel in mind then, I might put my head

70   round the door. I've got that poor little nerd I should never have said I could help. Tender heart me.

WIN.  Tender like old boots. How old?

NELL.  Yes well forty-five.

WIN.  Say no more.

75   NELL.  He knows his place, he's not after calling himself a manager, he's just a poor little bod[4] wants a better commission and a bit of sunshine.

WIN.  Don't we all.

NELL.  He's just got to relocate. He's got a bungalow in

80   Dymchurch.[5]

WIN.  And his wife says.

NELL.  The lady wife wouldn't care to relocate. She's going through the change.[6]

WIN.  It's his funeral, don't waste your time.

85   NELL.  I don't waste a lot.

WIN.  Good weekend you?

NELL.  You could say.

WIN.  Which one?

NELL.  One Friday, one Saturday.

90   WIN.  Aye-aye.

NELL.  Sunday night I watched telly.

WIN.  Which of them do you like best really?

NELL.  Sunday was best, I liked the Ovaltine.[7]

WIN.  Holden, Barker, Gardner, Duke.

---

[1]  *birds*  British slang for girls.

[2]  *John Conteh*  British Light-Heavyweight boxing champion.

[3]  *Prestel*  Now-defunct British company that provided information via text on screen through television cables.

[4]  *bod*  Person.

[5]  *Dymchurch*  Coastal town southeast of London.

[6]  *the change*  Change of life, i.e., menopause.

[7]  *Ovaltine*  Warm drink, often drunk in the morning, or at bedtime.

95 NELL. I've a lady here thinks she can sell.

WIN. Taking her on?

NELL. She's had some jobs.

WIN. Services?

NELL. No, quite heavy stuff, electric.

100 WIN. Tough bird like us.

NELL. We could do with a few more here.

WIN. There's nothing going here.

NELL. No but I always want the tough ones when I see them. Hang onto them.

105 WIN. I think we're plenty.

NELL. Derek asked me to marry him again.

WIN. He doesn't know when he's beaten.

NELL. I told him I'm not going to play house, not even in Ascot.

110 WIN. Mind you, you could play house.

NELL. If I chose to play house I would play house ace.

WIN. You could marry him and go on working.

NELL. I could go on working and not marry him.

*(Marlene arrives.)*

MARLENE. Morning ladies.

*(Win and Nell cheer and whistle.)*

115 Mind my head.

NELL. Coffee coffee coffee.

WIN. We're tactfully not mentioning you're late.

MARLENE. Fucking tube.[1]

WIN. We've heard that one.

120 NELL. We've used that one.

WIN. It's the top executive doesn't come in as early as the poor working girl.

MARLENE. Pass the sugar and shut your face, pet.

WIN. Well I'm delighted.

125 NELL. Howard's looking sick.

WIN. Howard is sick. He's got ulcers and heart. He told me.

NELL. He'll have to stop then won't he?

WIN. Stop what?

130 NELL. Smoking, drinking, shouting. Working.

WIN. Well, working.

NELL. We're just looking through the day.

MARLENE. I'm doing some of Pam's ladies. They've been piling up while she's away.

135 NELL. Half a dozen little girls and an arts graduate who can't type.

WIN. I spent the whole weekend at his place in Sussex.

NELL. She fancies his rose garden.

WIN. I had to lie down in the back of the car so the neighbours wouldn't see me go in.

140 
NELL. You're kidding.

WIN. It was funny.

NELL. Fuck that for a joke.

WIN. It was funny.

145 MARLENE. Anyway they'd see you in the garden.

WIN. The garden has extremely high walls.

NELL. I think I'll tell the wife.

WIN. Like hell.

NELL. She might leave him and you could have the rose garden.

150 
WIN. The minute it's not a secret I'm out on my ear.

NELL. Don't know why you bother.

WIN. Bit of fun.

NELL. I think it's time you went to Australia.

155 WIN. I think it's pushy Mr. Holden time.

NELL. If you've any really pretty bastards, Marlene, I want some for Prestel.

MARLENE. I might have one this afternoon. This morning it's all Pam's secretarial.

160 NELL. Not long now and you'll be upstairs watching over us all.

MARLENE. Do you feel bad about it?

NELL. I don't like coming second.

MARLENE. Who does?

165 WIN. We'd rather it was you than Howard. We're glad for you, aren't we Nell.

NELL. Oh yes. Aces.

*(Interview: Win and Louise.)*

WIN. Now Louise, hello, I have your details here. You've been very loyal to the one job I see.

170 LOUISE. Yes I have.

WIN. Twenty-one years is a long time in one place.

LOUISE. I feel it is. I feel it's time to move on.

WIN. And you are what age now?

LOUISE. I'm in my early forties.

---

[1] *tube* Subway system.

175 WIN.  Exactly?

LOUISE.  Forty-six.

WIN.  It's not necessarily a handicap, well it is of course we have to face that but it's not necessarily a disabling handicap, experience does count for something.

180 LOUISE.  I hope so.

WIN.  Now between ourselves is there any trouble, any reason why you're leaving that wouldn't appear on the form?

LOUISE.  Nothing like that.

185 WIN.  Like what?

LOUISE.  Nothing at all.

WIN.  No long term understandings come to a sudden end, making for an insupportable atmosphere?

LOUISE.  I've always completely avoided anything like
190 that at all.

WIN.  No personality clashes with your immediate superiors or inferiors?

LOUISE.  I've always taken care to get on very well with everyone.

195 WIN.  I only ask because it can affect the reference and it also affects your motivation, I want to be quite clear why you're moving on. So I take it the job itself no longer satisfies you. Is it the money?

LOUISE.  It's partly the money. It's not so much the
200 money.

WIN.  Nine thousand is very respectable. Have you dependants?

LOUISE.  No, no dependants. My mother died.

WIN.  So why are you making a change?

205 LOUISE.  Other people make changes.

WIN.  But why are you, now, after spending most of your life in the one place?

LOUISE.  There you are, I've lived for that company, I've given my life really you could say because I haven't had
210 a great deal of social life, I've worked in the evenings. I haven't had office entanglements for the very reason you just mentioned and if you are committed to your work you don't move in many other circles. I had management status from the age of twenty-seven and you'll
215 appreciate what that means. I've built up a department. And there it is, it works extremely well, and I feel I'm stuck there. I've spent twenty years in middle management. I've seen young men who I trained go on, in my own company or elsewhere, to higher things.

220 Nobody notices me, I don't expect it, I don't attract attention by making mistakes, everybody takes it for granted that my work is perfect. They will notice me when I go, they will be sorry I think to lose me, they will offer me more money of course, I will refuse. They
225 will see when I've gone what I was doing for them.

WIN.  If they offer you more money you won't stay?

LOUISE.  No I won't.

WIN.  Are you the only woman?

LOUISE.  Apart from the girls of course, yes. There was
230 one, she was my assistant, it was the only time I took on a young woman assistant, I always had my doubts. I don't care greatly for working with women, I think I pass as a man at work. But I did take on this young woman, her qualifications were excellent, and she did
235 well, she got a department of her own, and left the company for a competitor where she's now on the board and good luck to her. She has a different style, she's a new kind of attractive well-dressed—I don't mean I don't dress properly. But there is a kind of woman who
240 is thirty now who grew up in a different climate. They are not so careful. They take themselves for granted. I have had to justify my existence every minute, and I have done so, I have proved—well.

WIN.  Let's face it, vacancies are going to be ones where
245 you'll be in competition with younger men. And there are companies that will value your experience enough you'll be in with a chance. There are also fields that are easier for a woman, there is a cosmetic company here where your experience might be relevant. It's eight and
250 a half, I don't know if that appeals.

LOUISE.  I've proved I can earn money. It's more important to get away. I feel it's now or never. I sometimes / think—

WIN.  You shouldn't talk too much at an interview.

255 LOUISE.  I don't. I don't normally talk about myself. I know very well how to handle myself in an office situation. I only talk to you because it seems to me this is different, it's your job to understand me, surely. You asked the questions.

260 WIN.  I think I understand you sufficiently.

LOUISE.  Well good, that's good.

WIN.  Do you drink?

LOUISE.  Certainly not. I'm not a teetotaller, I think that's very suspect, it's seen as being an alcoholic if

265 you're teetotal. What do you mean? I don't drink. Why?

WIN.   I drink.

LOUISE.   I don't.

WIN.   Good for you.

(*Main office*)

(*Marlene and Angie. Angie arrives.*)

ANGIE.   Hello.

270 MARLENE.   Have you an appointment?

ANGIE.   It's me. I've come.

MARLENE.   What? It's not Angie?

ANGIE.   It was hard to find this place. I got lost.

MARLENE.   How did you get past the receptionist? The
275 girl on the desk, didn't she try to stop you?

ANGIE.   What desk?

MARLENE.   Never mind.

ANGIE.   I just walked in. I was looking for you.

MARLENE.   Well you found me.

280 ANGIE.   Yes.

MARLENE.   So where's your mum? Are you up in town
for the day?

ANGIE.   Not really.

MARLENE.   Sit down. Do you feel all right?

285 ANGIE.   Yes thank you.

MARLENE.   So where's Joyce?

ANGIE.   She's at home.

MARLENE.   Did you come up on a school trip then?

ANGIE.   I've left school.

290 MARLENE.   Did you come up with a friend?

ANGIE.   No. There's just me.

MARLENE.   You came up by yourself, that's fun. What
have you been doing? Shopping? Tower of London?

ANGIE.   No, I just come here. I come to you.

295 MARLENE.   That's very nice of you to think of paying
your aunty a visit. There's not many nieces make that
the first port of call. Would you like a cup of coffee?

ANGIE.   No thank you.

MARLENE.   Tea, orange?

300 ANGIE.   No thank you.

MARLENE.   Do you feel all right?

ANGIE.   Yes thank you.

MARLENE.   Are you tired from the journey?

ANGIE.   Yes, I'm tired from the journey.

305 MARLENE.   You sit there for a bit then. How's Joyce?

ANGIE.   She's all right.

MARLENE.   Same as ever.

ANGIE.   Oh yes.

MARLENE.   Unfortunately you've picked a day when I'm
310 rather busy, if there's ever a day when I'm not, or I'd
take you out to lunch and we'd go to Madame
Tussaud's.[1] We could go shopping. What time do you
have to be back? Have you got a day return?

ANGIE.   No.

315 MARLENE.   So what train are you going back on?

ANGIE.   I came on the bus.

MARLENE.   So what bus are you going back on? Are you
staying the night?

ANGIE.   Yes.

320 MARLENE.   Who are you staying with? Do you want me
to put you up for the night, is that it?

ANGIE.   Yes please.

MARLENE.   I haven't got a spare bed.

ANGIE.   I can sleep on the floor.

325 MARLENE.   You can sleep on the sofa.

ANGIE.   Yes please.

MARLENE.   I do think Joyce might have phoned me. It's
like her.

ANGIE.   This is where you work is it?

330 MARLENE.   It's where I have been working the last two
years but I'm going to move into another office.

ANGIE.   It's lovely.

MARLENE.   My new office is nicer than this. There's just
the one big desk in it for me.

335 ANGIE.   Can I see it?

MARLENE.   Not now, no, there's someone else in it now.
But he's leaving at the end of next week and I'm going
to do his job.

ANGIE.   Is that good?

340 MARLENE.   Yes, it's very good.

ANGIE.   Are you going to be in charge?

MARLENE.   Yes I am.

ANGIE.   I knew you would be.

MARLENE.   How did you know?

345 ANGIE.   I knew you'd be in charge of everything.

MARLENE.   Not quite everything.

ANGIE.   You will be.

MARLENE.   Well we'll see.

---

[1] *Madame Tussaud's*   Madame Tussaud's Wax Museum, a popular
tourist destination.

ANGIE.  Can I see it next week then?

350 MARLENE.  Will you still be here next week?

ANGIE.  Yes.

MARLENE.  Don't you have to go home?

ANGIE.  No.

MARLENE.  Why not?

355 ANGIE.  It's all right.

MARLENE.  Is it all right?

ANGIE.  Yes, don't worry about it.

MARLENE.  Does Joyce know where you are?

ANGIE.  Yes of course she does.

360 MARLENE.  Well does she?

ANGIE.  Don't worry about it.

MARLENE.  How long are you planning to stay with me
     then?

ANGIE.  You know when you came to see us last year?

365 MARLENE.  Yes, that was nice wasn't it?

ANGIE.  That was the best day of my whole life.

MARLENE.  So how long are you planning to stay?

ANGIE.  Don't you want me?

MARLENE.  Yes yes, I just wondered.

370 ANGIE.  I won't stay if you don't want me.

MARLENE.  No, of course you can stay.

ANGIE.  I'll sleep on the floor. I won't be any bother.

MARLENE.  Don't get upset.

ANGIE.  I'm not, I'm not. Don't worry about it.

375 (*Mrs. Kidd comes in.*)

MRS. KIDD.  Excuse me.

MARLENE.  Yes.

MRS. KIDD.  Excuse me.

MARLENE.  Can I help you?

380 MRS. KIDD.  Excuse me bursting in on you like this but
     I have to talk to you.

MARLENE.  I am engaged at the moment. / If you could
     go to reception—

MRS. KIDD.  I'm Rosemary Kidd, Howard's wife, you
385     don't recognise me but we did meet, I remember you of
     course / but you wouldn't—

MARLENE.  Yes of course, Mrs. Kidd, I'm sorry, we did
     meet. Howard's about somewhere I expect, have you
     looked in his office?

390 MRS. KIDD.  Howard's not about, no. I'm afraid it's you
     I've come to see if I could have a minute or two.

MARLENE.  I do have an appointment in five minutes.

MRS. KIDD.  This won't take five minutes. I'm very
     sorry. It is a matter of some urgency.

395 MARLENE.  Well of course. What can I do for you?

MRS. KIDD.  I just wanted a chat, an informal chat. It's
     not something I can simply—I'm sorry if I'm
     interrupting your work. I know office work isn't like
     housework / which is all interruptions.

400 MARLENE.  No no, this is my niece. Angie. Mrs. Kidd.

MRS. KIDD.  Very pleased to meet you.

ANGIE.  Very well thank you.

MRS. KIDD.  Howard's not in today.

MARLENE.  Isn't he?

405 MRS. KIDD.  He's feeling poorly.

MARLENE.  I didn't know. I'm sorry to hear that.

MRS. KIDD.  The fact is he's in a state of shock. About
     what's happened.

MARLENE.  What has happened?

410 MRS. KIDD.  You should know if anyone. I'm referring
     to you being appointed managing director instead of
     Howard. He hasn't been at all well all weekend. He
     hasn't slept for three nights. I haven't slept.

MARLENE.  I'm sorry to hear that, Mrs. Kidd. Has he
415     thought of taking sleeping pills?

MRS. KIDD.  It's very hard when someone has worked all
     these years.

MARLENE.  Business life is full of little setbacks. I'm sure
     Howard knows that. He'll bounce back in a day or two.
420     We all bounce back.

MRS. KIDD.  If you could see him you'd know what I'm
     talking about. What's it going to do to him working for
     a woman? I think if it was a man he'd get over it as
     something normal.

425 MARLENE.  I think he's going to have to get over it.

MRS. KIDD.  It's me that bears the brunt. I'm not the
     one that's been promoted. I put him first every inch of
     the way. And now what do I get? You women this, you
     women that. It's not my fault. You're going to have to
430     be very careful how you handle him. He's very hurt.

MARLENE.  Naturally I'll be tactful and pleasant to him,
     you don't start pushing someone round. I'll consult him
     over any decisions affecting his department. But that's
     no different, Mrs. Kidd, from any of my other
435     colleagues.

MRS. KIDD.  I think it is different, because he's a man.

MARLENE.   I'm not quite sure why you came to see me.

MRS. KIDD.   I had to do something.

MARLENE.   Well you've done it, you've seen me. I think
440  that's probably all we've time for. I'm sorry he's been
taking it out on you. He really is a shit, Howard.

MRS. KIDD.   But he's got a family to support. He's got
three children. It's only fair.

MARLENE.   Are you suggesting I give up the job to him
445  then?

MRS. KIDD.   It had crossed my mind if you were
unavailable after all for some reason, he would be the
natural second choice I think, don't you? I'm not
asking.

450  MARLENE.   Good.

MRS. KIDD.   You mustn't tell him I came. He's very
proud.

MARLENE.   If he doesn't like what's happening here he
can go and work somewhere else.

455  MRS. KIDD.   Is that a threat?

MARLENE.   I'm sorry but I do have some work to do.

MRS. KIDD.   It's not that easy, a man of Howard's age.
You don't care. I thought he was going too far but he's
right. You're one of these ballbreakers / that's what you
460  are. You'll end up

MARLENE.   I'm sorry but I do have some work to do.

MRS. KIDD.   miserable and lonely. You're not natural.

MARLENE.   Could you please piss off?

MRS. KIDD.   I thought if I saw you at least I'd be doing
465  something.

(*Mrs. Kidd goes.*)

MARLENE.   I've got to go and do some work now. Will
you come back later?

ANGIE.   I think you were wonderful.

MARLENE.   I've got to go and do some work now.

470  ANGIE.   You told her to piss off.

MARLENE.   Will you come back later?

ANGIE.   Can't I stay here?

MARLENE.   Don't you want to go sightseeing?

ANGIE.   I'd rather stay here.

475  MARLENE.   You can stay here I suppose, if it's not
boring.

ANGIE.   It's where I most want to be in the world.

MARLENE.   I'll see you later then.

(*Marlene goes.*)

(*Angie sits at Win's desk.*)

(*Interview: Nell and Shona.*)

NELL.   Is this right? You are Shona?

480  SHONA.   Yeh.

NELL.   It says here you're twenty-nine.

SHONA.   Yeh.

NELL.   Too many late nights, me. So you've been where
you are for four years, Shona, you're earning six basic
485  and three commission.[1] So what's the problem?

SHONA.   No problem.

NELL.   Why do you want a change?

SHONA.   Just a change.

NELL.   Change of product, change of area?

490  SHONA.   Both.

NELL.   But you're happy on the road?

SHONA.   I like driving.

NELL.   You're not after management status?

SHONA.   I would like management status.

495  NELL.   You'd be interested in titular management status
but not come off the road?

SHONA.   I want to be on the road, yeh.

NELL.   So how many calls have you been making a day?

SHONA.   Six.

500  NELL.   And what proportion of those are successful?

SHONA.   Six.

NELL.   That's hard to believe.

SHONA.   Four.

NELL.   You find it easy to get the initial interest do you?

505  SHONA.   Oh yeh, I get plenty of initial interest.

NELL.   And what about closing?

SHONA.   I close, don't I?

NELL.   Because that's what an employer is going to have
doubts about with you a lady as I needn't tell you,
510  whether she's got the guts to push through to a closing
situation. They think we're too nice. They think we
listen to the buyer's doubts. They think we consider his
needs and his feelings.

SHONA.   I never consider people's feelings.

515  NELL.   I was selling for six years, I can sell anything, I've
sold in three continents, and I'm jolly as they come but

---

[1] *six ... commission*   £600 salary per month and £300 on commission.

I'm not very nice.

SHONA.  I'm not very nice.

NELL.  What sort of time do you have on the road with
520   the other reps? Get on all right? Handle the chat?

SHONA.  I get on. Keep myself to myself.

NELL.  Fairly much of a loner are you?

SHONA.  Sometimes.

NELL.  So what field are you interested in?

525 SHONA.  Computers.

NELL.  That's a top field as you know and you'll be up
  against some very slick fellas there, there's some very
  pretty boys in computers, it's an American-style field.

SHONA.  That's why I want to do it.

530 NELL.  Video systems appeal? That's a high-flying
  situation.

SHONA.  Video systems appeal OK.

NELL.  Because Prestel have half a dozen vacancies I'm
  looking to fill at the moment. We're talking in the area
535   of ten to fifteen thousand here and upwards.

SHONA.  Sounds OK.

NELL.  I've half a mind to go for it myself. But it's good
  money here if you've got the top clients. Could you
  fancy it do you think?

540 SHONA.  Work here?

NELL.  I'm not in a position to offer, there's nothing
  officially going just now, but we're always on the
  lookout. There's not that many of us. We could keep in
  touch.

545 SHONA.  I like driving.

NELL.  So the Prestel appeals?

SHONA.  Yeh.

NELL.  What about ties?

SHONA.  No ties.

550 NELL.  So relocation wouldn't be a problem.

SHONA.  No problem.

NELL.  So just fill me in a bit more could you about
  what you've been doing.

SHONA.  What I've been doing. It's all down there.

555 NELL.  The bare facts are down here but I've got to
  present you to an employer.

SHONA.  I'm twenty-nine years old.

NELL.  So it says here.

SHONA.  We look young. Youngness runs in the family
560   in our family.

NELL.  So just describe your present job for me.

SHONA.  My present job at present. I have a car. I have
  a Porsche. I go up the M1[1] a lot. Burn up the M1 a lot.
  Straight up the M1 in the fast lane to where the clients
565   are, Staffordshire, Yorkshire, I do a lot in Yorkshire. I'm
  selling electric things. Like dishwashers, washing
  machines, stainless steel tubs are a feature and the
  reliability of the programme. After sales service, we offer
  a very good after sales service, spare parts, plenty of spare
570   parts. And fridges, I sell a lot of fridges specially in the
  summer. People want to buy fridges in the summer
  because of the heat melting the butter and you get fed
  up standing the milk in a basin of cold water with a
  cloth over, stands to reason people don't want to do that
575   in this day and age. So I sell a lot of them. Big ones with
  big freezers. Big freezers. And I stay in hotels at night
  when I'm away from home. On my expense account. I
  stay in various hotels. They know me, the ones I go to.
  I check in, have a bath, have a shower. Then I go down
580   to the bar, have a gin and tonic, have a chat. Then I go
  into the dining room and have dinner. I usually have
  fillet steak and mushrooms, I like mushrooms. I like
  smoked salmon very much. I like having a salad on the
  side. Green salad. I don't like tomatoes.

585 NELL.  Christ what a waste of time.

SHONA.  Beg your pardon?

NELL.  Not a word of this is true is it?

SHONA.  How do you mean?

NELL.  You just filled in the form with a pack of lies.

590 SHONA.  Not exactly.

NELL.  How old are you?

SHONA.  Twenty-nine.

NELL.  Nineteen?

SHONA.  Twenty-one.

595 NELL.  And what jobs have you done? Have you done
  any?

SHONA.  I could though, I bet you.

(*Main office. Angie sitting as before. Win comes in.*)

WIN.  Who's sitting in my chair?

ANGIE.  What? Sorry.

600 WIN.  Who's been eating my porridge?

ANGIE.  What?

---

[1]  *M1*  British highway running north from western London and
passing through the Midlands.

WIN. It's all right, I saw Marlene. Angie isn't it? I'm Win. And I'm not going out for lunch because I'm knackered.[1] I'm going to set me down here and have a
605    yoghurt. Do you like yoghurt?

ANGIE. No.

WIN. That's good because I've only got one. Are you hungry?

ANGIE. No.

610    WIN. There's a cafe on the corner.

ANGIE. No thank you. Do you work here?

WIN. How did you guess?

ANGIE. Because you look as if you might work here and you're sitting at the desk. Have you always worked here?

615    WIN. No I was headhunted. That means I was working for another outfit like this and this lot came and offered me more money. I broke my contract, there was a hell of a stink. There's not many top ladies about. Your aunty's a smashing bird.

620    ANGIE. Yes I know.

MARLENE. Fan are you? Fan of your aunty's?

ANGIE. Do you think I could work here?

WIN. Not at the moment.

ANGIE. How do I start?

625    WIN. What can you do?

ANGIE. I don't know. Nothing.

WIN. Type?

ANGIE. Not very well. The letters jump up when I do capitals. I was going to do a CSE[2] in commerce but I
630    didn't.

WIN. What have you got?

ANGIE. What?

WIN. CSE's, O's.

ANGIE. Nothing, none of that. Did you do all that?

635    WIN. Oh yes, all that, and a science degree funnily enough. I started out doing medical research but there's no money in it. I thought I'd go abroad. Did you know they sell Coca-Cola in Russia and Pepsi-Cola in China? You don't have to be qualified as much as you might
640    think. Men are awful bullshitters, they like to make out jobs are harder than they are. Any job I ever did I started doing it better than the rest of the crowd and they didn't like it. So I'd get unpopular and I'd have a drink

---

[1]  *knackered*  Exhausted.

[2]  *CSE*  Certificate of Secondary Education, a level of academic achievement for those not planning to attend university.

to cheer myself up. I lived with a fella and supported
645    him for four years, he couldn't get work. After that I went to California. I like the sunshine. Americans know how to live. This country's too slow. Then I went to Mexico, still in sales, but it's no country for a single lady. I came home, went bonkers for a bit, thought I
650    was five different people, got over that all right, the psychiatrist said I was perfectly sane and highly intelligent. Got married in a moment of weakness and he's inside[3] now, he's been inside four years, and I've not been to see him too much this last year. I like this
655    better than sales, I'm not really that aggressive. I started thinking sales was a good job if you want to meet people, but you're meeting people that don't want to meet you. It's no good if you like being liked. Here your clients want to meet you because you're the one doing
660    them some good. They hope.

(*Angie has fallen asleep. Nell comes in.*)

NELL. You're talking to yourself, sunshine.

WIN. So what's new?

NELL. Who is this?

WIN. Marlene's little niece.

665    NELL. What's she got, brother, sister? She never talks about her family.

WIN. I was telling her my life story.

NELL. Violins?

WIN. No, success story.

670    NELL. You've heard Howard's had a heart attack?

WIN. No, when?

NELL. I heard just now. He hadn't come in, he was at home, he's gone to hospital. He's not dead. His wife was here, she rushed off in a cab.

675    WIN. Too much butter, too much smoke. We must send him some flowers.

(*Marlene comes in.*)

You've heard about Howard?

MARLENE. Poor sod.

NELL. Lucky he didn't get the job if that's what his
680    health's like.

MARLENE. Is she asleep?

---

[3]  *inside*  In prison.

WIN.   She wants to work here.
MARLENE.   Packer in Tesco[1] more like.
WIN.   She's a nice kid. Isn't she?
685 MARLENE.   She's a bit thick. She's a bit funny.
WIN.   She thinks you're wonderful.
MARLENE.   She's not going to make it.


ACT 2, SCENE 2

(*A year earlier. Sunday evening. Joyce's kitchen. Joyce, Angie, Marlene. Marlene is taking presents out of a bright carrier bag. Angie has already opened a box of chocolates.*)


MARLENE.   Just a few little things. / I've no memory for
JOYCE.   There's no need.
MARLENE.   birthdays have I, and Christmas seems to slip by. So I think I owe Angie a few presents.
5 JOYCE.   What do you say?
ANGIE.   Thank you very much. Thank you very much, Aunty Marlene.

(*She opens a present. It is the dress from Act One, new.*)

ANGIE.   Oh look, Mum, isn't it lovely?
MARLENE.   I don't know if it's the right size. She's
10  grown up since I saw her. / I knew she was always tall for her age.
ANGIE.   Isn't it lovely?
JOYCE.   She's a big lump.
MARLENE.   Hold it up, Angie, let's see.
15 ANGIE.   I'll put it on, shall I?
MARLENE.   Yes, try it on.
JOYCE.   Go on to your room then, we don't want / a strip show thank you.
ANGIE.   Of course I'm going to my room, what do you
20  think? Look Mum, here's something for you. Open it, go on. What is it? Can I open it for you?
JOYCE.   Yes, you open it, pet.
ANGIE.   Don't you want to open it yourself? / Go on.
JOYCE.   I don't mind, you can do it.
25 ANGIE.   It's something hard. It's—what is it? A bottle. Drink is it? No, it's what? Perfume, look. What a lot. Open it, look, let's smell it. Oh it's strong. It's lovely.

Put it on me. How do you do it? Put it on me.
JOYCE.   You're too young.
30 ANGIE.   I can play wearing it like dressing up.
JOYCE.   And you're too old for that. Here give it here, I'll do it, you'll tip the whole bottle over yourself / and we'll have you smelling all summer.
ANGIE.   Put it on you. Do I smell? Put it on Aunty too.
35  Put it on Aunty too. Let's smell.
MARLENE.   I didn't know what you'd like.
JOYCE.   There's no danger I'd have it already, / that's one thing.
ANGIE.   Now we all smell the same.
40 MARLENE.   It's a bit of nonsense.
JOYCE.   It's very kind of you Marlene, you shouldn't.
ANGIE.   Now I'll put on the dress and then we'll see.

(*Angie goes.*)

JOYCE.   You've caught me on the hop[2] with the place in a mess. / If you'd let me know you was coming I'd have
45  got
MARLENE.   That doesn't matter.
JOYCE.   Something to eat. We had our dinner dinnertime. We're just going to have a cup of tea. You could have an egg.
50 MARLENE.   No, I'm not hungry. Tea's fine.
JOYCE.   I don't expect you take sugar.
MARLENE.   Why not?
JOYCE.   You take care of yourself.
MARLENE.   How do you mean you didn't know I was
55  coming?
JOYCE.   You could have written. I know we're not on the phone but we're not completely in the dark ages, / we do have a postman.
MARLENE.   But you asked me to come.
60 JOYCE.   How did I ask you to come?
MARLENE.   Angie said when she phoned up.
JOYCE.   Angie phoned up, did she?
MARLENE.   Was it just Angie's idea?
JOYCE.   What did she say?
65 MARLENE.   She said you wanted me to come and see you. / It was a couple of weeks ago. How was I to know that's a
JOYCE.   Ha.

---

[1]  *Tesco*  British grocery store chain.

[2]  *on the hop*  By surprise.

MARLENE.  ridiculous idea? My diary's always full a
couple of weeks ahead so we fixed it for this weekend. I
was meant to get here earlier but I was held up. She gave
me messages from you.

JOYCE.  Didn't you wonder why I didn't phone you
myself?

MARLENE.  She said you didn't like using the phone.
You're shy on the phone and can't use it. I don't know
what you're like, do I.

JOYCE.  Are there people who can't use the phone?

MARLENE.  I expect so.

JOYCE.  I haven't met any.

MARLENE.  Why should I think she was lying?

JOYCE.  Because she's like what she's like.

MARLENE.  How do I know / what she's like?

JOYCE.  It's not my fault you don't know what she's like.
You never come and see her.

MARLENE.  Well I have now / and you don't seem over
the moon.*

JOYCE.  Good.

*Well I'd have got a cake if she'd told me.

(Pause.)

MARLENE.  I did wonder why you wanted to see me.

JOYCE.  I didn't want to see you.

MARLENE.  Yes, I know. Shall I go?

JOYCE.  I don't mind seeing you.

MARLENE.  Great, I feel really welcome.

JOYCE.  You can come and see Angie any time you
like, I'm not stopping you. / You know where we are.
You're the

MARLENE.  Ta[1] ever so.

JOYCE.  one went away, not me. I'm right here where I
was.
And will be a few years yet I shouldn't wonder.

MARLENE.  All right. All right.

(Joyce gives Marlene a cup of tea.)

JOYCE.  Tea.

MARLENE.  Sugar?

(Joyce passes Marlene the sugar.)

---

[1]  Ta  Thank you.

It's very quiet down here.

JOYCE.  I expect you'd notice it.

MARLENE.  The air smells different too.

JOYCE.  That's the scent.

MARLENE.  No, I mean walking down the lane.

JOYCE.  What sort of air you get in London then?

(Angie comes in, wearing the dress. It fits.)

MARLENE.  Oh, very pretty. / You do look pretty,
Angie.

JOYCE.  That fits all right.

MARLENE.  Do you like the colour?

ANGIE.  Beautiful. Beautiful.

JOYCE.  You better take it off, / you'll get it dirty.

ANGIE.  I want to wear it. I want to wear it.

MARLENE.  It is for wearing after all. You can't just
hang it up and look at it.

ANGIE.  I love it.

JOYCE.  Well if you must you must.

ANGIE.  If someone asks me what's my favourite
colour I'll tell them it's this. Thank you very much,
Aunty Marlene.

MARLENE.  You didn't tell your mum you asked me
down.

ANGIE.  I wanted it to be a surprise.

JOYCE.  I'll give you a surprise / one of these days.

ANGIE.  I thought you'd like to see her. She hasn't
been here since I was nine. People do see their aunts.

MARLENE.  Is it that long? Doesn't time fly?

ANGIE.  I wanted to.

JOYCE.  I'm not cross.

ANGIE.  Are you glad?

JOYCE.  I smell nicer anyhow, don't I?

(Kit comes in without saying anything, as if she lived
there.)

MARLENE.  I think it was a good idea, Angie, about
time. We are sisters after all. It's a pity to let that go.

JOYCE.  This is Kitty, / who lives up the road. This is
Angie's Aunty Marlene.

KIT.  What's that?

ANGIE.  It's a present. Do you like it?

KIT.  It's all right. / Are you coming out?*

MARLENE.  Hello, Kitty.
ANGIE.  *No.
145 KIT.  What's that smell?
ANGIE.  It's a present.
KIT.  It's horrible. Come on.*
MARLENE.  Have a chocolate.
ANGIE.  *No, I'm busy.
150 KIT.  Coming out later?
ANGIE.  No.
KIT.  (To Marlene.) Hello.

(Kit goes without a chocolate.)

JOYCE.  She's a little girl Angie sometimes plays with
   because she's the only child lives really close. She's like
155  a little sister to her really. Angie's good with little
   children.
MARLENE.  Do you want to work with children,
   Angie? / Be a teacher or a nursery nurse?
JOYCE.  I don't think she's ever thought of it.
160 MARLENE.  What do you want to do?
JOYCE.  She hasn't an idea in her head what she wants
   to do. / Lucky to get anything.
MARLENE.  Angie?
JOYCE.  She's not clever like you.

(Pause.)

165 MARLENE.  I'm not clever, just pushy.
JOYCE.  True enough.

(Marlene takes a bottle of whisky out of the bag.)

   I don't drink spirits.
ANGIE.  You do at Christmas.
JOYCE.  It's not Christmas, is it?
170 ANGIE.  It's better than Christmas.
MARLENE.  Glasses?
JOYCE.  Just a small one then.
MARLENE.  Do you want some, Angie?
ANGIE.  I can't, can I?
175 JOYCE.  Taste it if you want. You won't like it.
MARLENE.  We got drunk together the night your
   grandfather died.
JOYCE.  We did not get drunk.

MARLENE.  I got drunk. You were just overcome with
180  grief.
JOYCE.  I still keep up the grave with flowers.
MARLENE.  Do you really?
JOYCE.  Why wouldn't I?
MARLENE.  Have you seen Mother?
185 JOYCE.  Of course I've seen Mother.
MARLENE.  I mean lately.
JOYCE.  Of course I've seen her lately, I go every
   Thursday.
MARLENE.  (To Angie.) Do you remember your
190  grandfather?
ANGIE.  He got me out of the bath one night in a
   towel.
MARLENE.  Did he? I don't think he ever gave me a
   bath. Did he give you a bath, Joyce? He probably got
195  soft in his old age. Did you like him?
ANGIE.  Yes of course.
MARLENE.  Why?
ANGIE.  What?
MARLENE.  So what's the news? How's Mrs. Paisley?
200  Still going crazily? / And Dorothy. What happened to
   Dorothy?*
ANGIE.  Who's Mrs. Paisley?
JOYCE.  *She went to Canada.
MARLENE.  Did she? What to do?
205 JOYCE.  I don't know. She just went to Canada.
MARLENE.  Well / good for her.
ANGIE.  Mr. Connolly killed his wife.
MARLENE.  What, Connolly at Whitegates?
ANGIE.  They found her body in the garden. / Under
210  the cabbages.
MARLENE.  He was always so proper.
JOYCE.  Stuck up git. Connolly. Best lawyer money
   could buy but he couldn't get out of it. She was
   carrying on with Matthew.
215 MARLENE.  How old's Matthew then?
JOYCE.  Twenty-one. / He's got a motorbike.
MARLENE.  I think he's about six.
ANGIE.  How can he be six? He's six years older than
   me. / If he was six I'd be nothing, I'd be just born this
220  minute.
JOYCE.  Your aunty knows that, she's just being silly.
   She means it's so long since she's been here she's
   forgotten about Matthew.

ANGIE.   You were here for my birthday when I was
nine. I had a pink cake. Kit was only five then, she
was four, she hadn't started school yet. She could read
already when she went to school. You remember my
birthday? / You remember me?

MARLENE.   Yes, I remember the cake.

ANGIE.   You remember me?

MARLENE.   Yes, I remember you.

ANGIE.   And Mum and Dad was there, and Kit was.

MARLENE.   Yes, how is your dad? Where is he tonight?
Up the pub?

JOYCE.   No, he's not here.

MARLENE.   I can see he's not here.

JOYCE.   He moved out.

MARLENE.   What? When did he? / Just recently?*

ANGIE.   Didn't you know that? You don't know
much.

JOYCE.*No, it must be three years ago. Don't be rude,
Angie.

ANGIE.   I'm not, am I Aunty? What else don't you
know?

JOYCE.   You was in America or somewhere. You sent a
postcard.

ANGIE.   I've got that in my room. It's the Grand
Canyon. Do you want to see it? Shall I get it? I can get
it for you.

MARLENE.   Yes, all right.

(*Angie goes.*)

JOYCE.   You could be married with twins for all I
know. You must have affairs and break up and I don't
need to know about any of that so I don't see what
the fuss is about.

MARLENE.   What fuss?

(*Angie comes back with the postcard.*)

ANGIE.   "Driving across the states for a new job in L.A.
It's a long way but the car goes very fast. It's very hot.
Wish you were here. Love from Aunty Marlene."

JOYCE.   Did you make a lot of money?

MARLENE.   I spent a lot.

ANGIE.   I want to go to America. Will you take me?

JOYCE.   She's not going to America, she's been to
America, stupid.

ANGIE.   She might go again, stupid. It's not something
you do once. People who go keep going all the time,
back and forth on jets. They go on Concorde[1] and
Laker[2] and get jet lag. Will you take me?

MARLENE.   I'm not planning a trip.

ANGIE.   Will you let me know?

JOYCE.   Angie, / you're getting silly.

ANGIE.   I want to be American.

JOYCE.   It's time you were in bed.

ANGIE.   No it's not. / I don't have to go to bed at all
tonight.

JOYCE.   School in the morning.

ANGIE.   I'll wake up.

JOYCE.   Come on now, you know how you get.

ANGIE.   How do I get? / I don't get anyhow.

JOYCE.   Angie. Are you staying the night?

MARLENE.   Yes, if that's all right. / I'll see you in the
morning.

ANGIE.   You can have my bed. I'll sleep on the sofa.

JOYCE.   You will not, you'll sleep in your bed. / Think
I can't

ANGIE.   Mum.

JOYCE.   see through that? I can just see you going to
sleep / with us talking.

ANGIE.   I would, I would go to sleep, I'd love that.

JOYCE.   I'm going to get cross, Angie.

ANGIE.   I want to show her something.

JOYCE.   Then bed.

ANGIE.   It's a secret.

JOYCE.   Then I expect it's in your room so off you go.
Give us a shout when you're ready for bed and your
aunty'll be up and see you.

ANGIE.   Will you?

MARLENE.   Yes of course.

(*Angie goes. Silence.*)

It's cold tonight.

JOYCE.   Will you be all right on the sofa? You can /
have my bed.

MARLENE.   The sofa's fine.

[1] *Concorde*  Supersonic commercial passenger jet.

[2] *Laker*  British discount airline.

JOYCE.   Yes the forecast said rain tonight but it's held off.

MARLENE.   I was going to walk down to the estuary but I've left it a bit late. Is it just the same?

JOYCE.   They cut down the hedges a few years back. Is that since you were here?

MARLENE.   But it's not changed down the end, all the mud? And the reeds? We used to pick them when they were bigger than us. Are there still lapwings?[1]

JOYCE.   You get strangers walking there on a Sunday. I expect they're looking at the mud and the lapwings, yes.

MARLENE.   You could have left.

JOYCE.   Who says I wanted to leave?

MARLENE.   Stop getting at me then, you're really boring.

JOYCE.   How could I have left?

MARLENE.   Did you want to?

JOYCE.   I said how, / how could I?

MARLENE.   If you'd wanted to you'd have done it.

JOYCE.   Christ.

MARLENE.   Are we getting drunk?

JOYCE.   Do you want something to eat?

MARLENE.   No, I'm getting drunk.

JOYCE.   Funny time to visit, Sunday evening.

MARLENE.   I came this morning. I spent the day.

ANGIE.   (Off.) Aunty! Aunty Marlene!

MARLENE.   I'd better go.

JOYCE.   Go on then.

MARLENE.   All right.

ANGIE.   (Off.) Aunty! Can you hear me? I'm ready.

(*Marlene goes. Joyce goes on sitting. Marlene comes back.*)

JOYCE.   So what's the secret?

MARLENE.   It's a secret.

JOYCE.   I know what it is anyway.

MARLENE.   I bet you don't. You always said that.

JOYCE.   It's her exercise book.

MARLENE.   Yes, but you don't know what's in it.

JOYCE.   It's some game, some secret society she has with Kit.

MARLENE.   You don't know the password. You don't know the code.

JOYCE.   You're really in it, aren't you. Can you do the handshake?

MARLENE.   She didn't mention a handshake.

JOYCE.   I thought they'd have a special handshake. She spends hours writing that but she's useless at school. She copies things out of books about black magic, and politicians out of the paper. It's a bit childish.

MARLENE.   I think it's a plot to take over the world.

JOYCE.   She's been in the remedial class the last two years.

MARLENE.   I came up this morning and spent the day in Ipswich.[2] I went to see mother.

JOYCE.   Did she recognise you?

MARLENE.   Are you trying to be funny?

JOYCE.   No, she does wander.

MARLENE.   She wasn't wandering at all, she was very lucid thank you.

JOYCE.   You were very lucky then.

MARLENE.   Fucking awful life she's had.

JOYCE.   Don't tell me.

MARLENE.   Fucking waste.

JOYCE.   Don't talk to me.

MARLENE.   Why shouldn't I talk? Why shouldn't I talk to you? / Isn't she my mother too?

JOYCE.   Look, you've left, you've gone away, / we can do without you.

MARLENE.   I left home, so what, I left home. People do leave home / it is normal.

JOYCE.   We understand that, we can do without you.

MARLENE.   We weren't happy. Were you happy?

JOYCE.   Don't come back.

MARLENE.   So it's just your mother is it, your child, you never wanted me round, / you were jealous of me because I was the

JOYCE.   Here we go.

MARLENE.   little one and I was clever.

JOYCE.   I'm not clever enough for all this psychology / if that's what it is.

MARLENE.   Why can't I visit my own family / without all this?*

---

[1]   *lapwings*   Wading birds that inhabit shorelines.

[2]   *Ipswich*   Town in Suffolk, northeast of London.

JOYCE. Aah.

385 *Just don't go on about Mum's life when you haven't been to see her for how many years. / I go and see her every week.*

MARLENE. It's up to me.

*Then don't go and see her every week.*

390 JOYCE. Somebody has to.

MARLENE. No they don't. / Why do they?

JOYCE. How would I feel if I didn't go?

MARLENE. A lot better.

JOYCE. I hope you feel better.

395 MARLENE. It's up to me.

JOYCE. You couldn't get out of here fast enough.

MARLENE. Of course I couldn't get out of here fast enough. What was I going to do? Marry a dairyman who'd come home pissed? / Don't you fucking this

400 fucking that fucking bitch

JOYCE. Christ.

MARLENE. fucking tell me what to fucking do fucking.

JOYCE. I don't know how you could leave your own child.

405 MARLENE. You were quick enough to take her.

JOYCE. What does that mean?

MARLENE. You were quick enough to take her.

JOYCE. Or what? Have her put in a home? Have some stranger / take her would you rather?

410 MARLENE. You couldn't have one so you took mine.

JOYCE. I didn't know that then.

MARLENE. Like hell, / married three years.

JOYCE. I didn't know that. Plenty of people / take that long.

415 MARLENE. Well it turned out lucky for you, didn't it?

JOYCE. Turned out all right for you by the look of you. You'd be getting a few less thousand a year.

MARLENE. Not necessarily.

JOYCE. You'd be stuck here / like you said.

420 MARLENE. I could have taken her with me.

JOYCE. You didn't want to take her with you. It's no good coming back now, Marlene, / and saying—

MARLENE. I know a managing director who's got two children, she breast feeds in the board room, she pays a

425 hundred pounds a week on domestic help alone and she can afford that because she's an extremely high-powered lady earning a great deal of money.

JOYCE. So what's that got to do with you at the age of seventeen?

430 MARLENE. Just because you were married and had somewhere to live—

JOYCE. You could have lived at home. / Or live with me

MARLENE. Don't be stupid.

JOYCE. and Frank. / You said you weren't keeping it.

435 You

MARLENE. You never suggested.

JOYCE. shouldn't have had it / if you wasn't going to keep it.

MARLENE. Here we go.

440 JOYCE. You was the most stupid, / for someone so clever you was the most stupid, get yourself pregnant, not go to the doctor, not tell.

MARLENE. You wanted it, you said you were glad, I remember the day, you said I'm glad you never got rid

445 of it, I'll look after it, you said that down by the river. So what are you saying, sunshine, you don't want her?

JOYCE. Course I'm not saying that.

MARLENE. Because I'll take her, / wake her up and pack now.

450 JOYCE. You wouldn't know how to begin to look after her.

MARLENE. Don't you want her?

JOYCE. Course I do, she's my child.

MARLENE. Then what are you going on about / why did

455 I have her?

JOYCE. You said I got her off you / when you didn't—

MARLENE. I said you were lucky / the way it—

JOYCE. Have a child now if you want one. You're not old.

460 MARLENE. I might do.

JOYCE. Good.

(*Pause.*)

MARLENE. I've been on the pill so long / I'm probably sterile.

JOYCE. Listen when Angie was six months I did get

465 pregnant and I lost it because I was so tired looking after your fucking baby / because she cried so much—yes I did tell

MARLENE. You never told me.

JOYCE. you— / and the doctor said if I'd sat down all

470 day with

MARLENE.   Well I forgot.

JOYCE.   my feet up I'd've kept it / and that's the only chance I ever had because after that—

MARLENE.   I've had two abortions, are you interested?
475   Shall I tell you about them? Well I won't, it's boring, it wasn't a problem. I don't like messy talk about blood / and what a bad

JOYCE.   If I hadn't had your baby. The doctor said.

MARLENE.   time we all had. I don't want a baby. I don't
480   want to talk about gynaecology.

JOYCE.   Then stop trying to get Angie off of me.

MARLENE.   I come down here after six years. All night you've been saying I don't come often enough. If I don't come for another six years she'll be twenty-one, will that
485   be OK?

JOYCE.   That'll be fine, yes, six years would suit me fine.

(*Pause.*)

MARLENE.   I was afraid of this.
I only came because I thought you wanted … I just want …

(*Marlene cries.*)

490   JOYCE.   Don't grizzle, Marlene, for God's sake. Marly? Come on, pet. Love you really. Fucking stop it, will you?

MARLENE.   No, let me cry. I like it.

(*They laugh, Marlene begins to stop crying.*)

I knew I'd cry if I wasn't careful.

495   JOYCE.   Everyone's always crying in this house. Nobody takes any notice.

MARLENE.   You've been wonderful looking after Angie.

JOYCE.   Don't get carried away.

MARLENE.   I can't write letters but I do think of you.

500   JOYCE.   You're getting drunk. I'm going to make some tea.

MARLENE.   Love you.   .

(*Joyce gets up to make tea.*)

JOYCE.   I can see why you'd want to leave. It's a dump here.

505   MARLENE.   So what's this about you and Frank?

JOYCE.   He was always carrying on, wasn't he? And if I wanted to go out in the evening he'd go mad, even if it was nothing, a class, I was going to go to an evening class. So he had this girlfriend, only twenty-two poor
510   cow, and I said go on, off you go, hoppit.[1] I don't think he even likes her.

MARLENE.   So what about money?

JOYCE.   I've always said I don't want your money.

MARLENE.   No, does he send you money?

515   JOYCE.   I've got four different cleaning jobs. Adds up. There's not a lot round here.

MARLENE.   Does Angie miss him?

JOYCE.   She doesn't say.

MARLENE.   Does she see him?

520   JOYCE.   He was never that fond of her to be honest.

MARLENE.   He tried to kiss me once. When you were engaged.

JOYCE.   Did you fancy him?

MARLENE.   No, he looked like a fish.

525   JOYCE.   He was lovely then.

MARLENE.   Ugh.

JOYCE.   Well I fancied him. For about three years.

MARLENE.   Have you got someone else?

JOYCE.   There's not a lot round here. Mind you, the
530   minute you're on your own, you'd be amazed how your friends' husbands drop by. I'd sooner do without.

MARLENE.   I don't see why you couldn't take my money.

JOYCE.   I do, so don't bother about it.

535   MARLENE.   Only got to ask.

JOYCE.   So what about you? Good job?

MARLENE.   Good for a laugh. / Got back from the US of A a bit

JOYCE.   Good for more than a laugh I should think.

540   MARLENE.   wiped out and slotted into this speedy employment agency and still there.

JOYCE.   You can always find yourself work then.

MARLENE.   That's right.

JOYCE.   And men?

545   MARLENE.   Oh there's always men.

JOYCE.   No one special?

---

[1]   *hoppit*   Get lost.

MARLENE. There's fellas who like to be seen with a high-flying lady. Shows they've got something really good in their pants. But they can't take the day to day.
550 They're waiting for me to turn into the little woman. Or maybe I'm just horrible of course.

JOYCE. Who needs them?

MARLENE. Who needs them? Well I do. But I need adventures more. So on on into the sunset. I think the
555 eighties are going to be stupendous.

JOYCE. Who for?

MARLENE. For me. / I think I'm going up up up.

JOYCE. Oh for you. Yes, I'm sure they will.

MARLENE. And for the country, come to that. Get the
560 economy back on its feet and whoosh. She's a tough lady, Maggie.[1] I'd give her a job. / She just needs to hang in there. This country

JOYCE. You voted for them, did you?

MARLENE. needs to stop whining. / Monetarism is not
565 stupid.

JOYCE. Drink your tea and shut up, pet.

MARLENE. It takes time, determination. No more slop. / And

JOYCE. Well I think they're filthy bastards.

570 MARLENE. who's got to drive it on? First woman prime minister. Terrifico. Aces. Right on. / You must admit. Certainly gets my vote.

JOYCE. What good's first woman if it's her? I suppose you'd have liked Hitler if he was a woman. Ms. Hitler.
575 Got a lot done, Hitlerina. / Great adventures.

MARLENE. Bosses still walking on the workers' faces? Still Dadda's little parrot? Haven't you learned to think for yourself? I believe in the individual. Look at me.

JOYCE. I am looking at you.

580 MARLENE. Come on, Joyce, we're not going to quarrel over politics.

JOYCE. We are though.

MARLENE. Forget I mentioned it. Not a word about the slimy unions will cross my lips.

(Pause.)

---

[1] *Maggie* Margaret Thatcher, Conservative Prime Minister of the United Kingdom between 1979 and 1990. In the early 1980s her controversial policies of reducing government spending, limiting union powers, and privatizing government-owned industries were widely blamed for high unemployment rates.

585 JOYCE. You say Mother had a wasted life.

MARLENE. Yes I do. Married to that bastard.

JOYCE. What sort of life did he have? / Working in the fields like

MARLENE. Violent life?

590 JOYCE. an animal. / Why wouldn't he want a drink?

MARLENE. Come off it.

JOYCE. You want a drink. He couldn't afford whisky.

MARLENE. I don't want to talk about him.

JOYCE. You started, I was talking about her. She had a
595 rotten life because she had nothing. She went hungry.

MARLENE. She was hungry because he drank the money. / He used to hit her.

JOYCE. It's not all down to him. / Their lives were rubbish. They

600 MARLENE. She didn't hit him.

JOYCE. were treated like rubbish. He's dead and she'll die soon and what sort of life / did they have?

MARLENE. I saw him one night. I came down.

JOYCE. Do you think I didn't? / They didn't get to
605 America and

MARLENE. I still have dreams.

JOYCE. drive across it in a fast car. / Bad nights, they had bad days.

MARLENE. America, America, you're jealous. / I had to
610 get out

JOYCE. Jealous?

MARLENE. I knew when I was thirteen, out of their house, out of them, never let that happen to me, / never let him, make my own way, out.

615 JOYCE. Jealous of what you've done, you're ashamed of me if I came to your office, your smart friends, wouldn't you, I'm ashamed of you, think of nothing but yourself, you've got on, nothing's changed for most people / has it?

620 MARLENE. I hate the working class / which is what you're going

JOYCE. Yes you do.

MARLENE. to go on about now, it doesn't exist any more, it means lazy and stupid. / I don't like the way
625 they talk. I don't

JOYCE. Come on, now we're getting it.

MARLENE. like beer guts and football vomit and saucy tits / and brothers and sisters—

JOYCE.   I spit when I see a Rolls Royce, scratch it with
630  my ring / Mercedes it was.

MARLENE.   Oh very mature—

JOYCE.   I hate the cows I work for / and their dirty dishes
with blanquette of fucking veau.[1]

MARLENE.   and I will not be pulled down to their level
635  by a flying picket[2] and I won't be sent to Siberia / or a
loony bin

JOYCE.   No, you'll be on a yacht, you'll be head of Coca-
Cola and you wait, the eighties is going to be
stupendous all right because we'll get you lot off our
640  backs—

MARLENE.   just because I'm original. And I support
Reagan[3] even if he is a lousy movie star because the reds
are swarming up his map and I want to be free in a free
world—

645  JOYCE.   What? / What?

MARLENE.   I know what I mean / by that—not shut up
here.

JOYCE.   So don't be round here when it happens because
if someone's kicking you I'll just laugh.

(Silence.)

650  MARLENE.   I don't mean anything personal. I don't
believe in class. Anyone can do anything if they've got
what it takes.

JOYCE.   And if they haven't?

MARLENE.   If they're stupid or lazy or frightened, I'm
655  not going to help them get a job, why should I?

JOYCE.   What about Angie?

MARLENE.   What about Angie?

JOYCE.   She's stupid, lazy and frightened, so what about
her?

660  MARLENE.   You run her down too much. She'll be all
right.

JOYCE.   I don't expect so, no. I expect her children will
say what a wasted life she had. If she has children.
Because nothing's changed and it won't with them in.

665  MARLENE.   Them, them. / Us and them?

JOYCE.   And you're one of them.

MARLENE.   And you're us, wonderful us, and Angie's us
/ and Mum and Dad's us.

JOYCE.   Yes, that's right, and you're them.

670  MARLENE.   Come on, Joyce, what a night. You've got
what it takes.

JOYCE.   I know I have.

MARLENE.   I didn't really mean all that.

JOYCE.   I did.

675  MARLENE.   But we're friends anyway.

JOYCE.   I don't think so, no.

MARLENE.   Well it's lovely to be out in the country. I
really must make the effort to come more often.
I want to go to sleep.
680  I want to go to sleep.

(Joyce gets blankets for the sofa.)

JOYCE.   Goodnight then. I hope you'll be warm enough.

MARLENE.   Goodnight. Joyce—

JOYCE.   No, pet. Sorry.

(Joyce goes. Marlene sits wrapped in a blanket and has
another drink. Angie comes in.)

ANGIE.   Mum?

685  MARLENE.   Angie? What's the matter?

ANGIE.   Mum?

MARLENE.   No, she's gone to bed. It's Aunty Marlene.

ANGIE.   Frightening.

MARLENE.   Did you have a bad dream? What happened
690  in it? Well you're awake now, aren't you pet?

ANGIE.   Frightening.

—1982

---

[1]  *blanquette ... veau*  Veal and vegetables in a cream sauce.

[2]  *flying picket*  Group of labor activists who support strike actions,
regardless of whether or not they are personally involved in the labor
dispute.

[3]  *Reagan*  Ronald Reagan, who began his career as a Hollywood
actor, became Governor of California, and eventually 40th President
of the United States. Reagan was a lifelong conservative.

# Angela Carter
## 1940 – 1992

Fiction writer Angela Carter spent much of her life out of step with dominant literary trends, creating works that both fascinated and baffled her readers. Carter (whom Margaret Atwood described as "born subversive") liked to disrupt conventions and deny expectations. Her writing inhabits a gray area between the fantastic and the real, and makes innovative use of numerous familiar genres—most of which (Gothic, fantasy, science fiction, magic realism) are somewhat outside the literary mainstream. Her unusually dense, allusive texts revel in linguistic play as they combine material from a myriad of sources, including folklore, tabloid headlines, French surrealism, Hollywood movies, and eighteenth-century allegorical fiction. Since her death, appreciation for her inventiveness and for the originality of her artistic vision has continued to grow; she is one of the most widely taught British writers of fiction.

Carter was born Angela Olive Stalker in Sussex in 1940. Much of her early childhood was spent with her grandmother in industrial Yorkshire, to which she and her brother had been evacuated to

escape war-time bombings. After she finished high school, Carter's father, a journalist, got her a job as a reporter for a south London paper. Direct, factual reporting of events was not her forte, however, and in 1960 she left that job to follow her new husband, Paul Carter, to Bristol. There she entered Bristol University, where she studied medieval literature.

Her first published novel, *Shadow Dance* (1966), marked the beginning of a fertile creative period; two more novels, *The Magic Toyshop* (1967) and *Several Perceptions* (1968) quickly followed. Though many of her early works are set in the Bristol of her youth, they are permeated with elements of the Gothic fairy tale and an underlying threat of violence, while distinctions between reality and daydream are often blurred.

*Several Perceptions* won the prestigious Somerset Maugham award; the £500 prize enabled Carter to depart for Japan, where she lived for two years, leaving her husband behind. In Japan, Carter began what she referred to as an apprenticeship in signs. She had gone seeking a culture that had never been Judeo-Christian, and in attempting to interpret such an utterly foreign culture—with no knowledge of the language—she was forced to rely on a heightened awareness of visual social cues, observing how roles (particularly those of gender) and customs were created and maintained. After her return to Britain in 1972, the new, radical self-awareness that resulted from her life in Japan led her to examine her own social and cultural heritage aggressively from her newly gained viewpoint of an outsider.

*The Sadeian Woman* (1979), her first book of nonfiction and one of her most controversial works, attacks the prestige she sees as often being accorded to the suffering of women, and criticizes portrayals of women as blameless victims. These strategies, she believes, only valorize the role of the powerless outsider. *The Sadeian Woman* also stated Carter's particular aims for her narratives, which she believed should provide means of exploring ideas and serve as arguments, presented in fictional terms, for the ways in which we should interpret and respond to the world around us. As she says, "Fine art, that exists for itself alone, is art in a final state of impotence. If nobody, including the artist, acknowledges art as a means of *knowing* the world, then art is relegated to a kind of rumpus room of the mind."

Published in the same year as the *Sadeian Woman*, Carter's collection of short fiction *The Bloody Chamber* (1979) takes characters from stories such as "Red Riding Hood" (Carter's version of which, "The Company of Wolves," was made into a successful film), "Sleeping Beauty," "Beauty and the Beast," and "Bluebeard," and brings them to life in a contemporary setting. Carter claimed she was interested in myths "because they are extraordinary lies designed to make people unfree," and by opening up the timeless realms of these myths to historical consciousness, she demonstrated how she believed they can—and should—end differently.

Carter's fiction from this period relies heavily on allegory, and also makes use of many elements of science fiction and magic realism. *The Infernal Desire Machine of Doctor Hoffman* (1972), in particular, is often classified as science fiction, though it also draws heavily on the picaresque. This novel has remained one of her most controversial, frequently criticized for an alleged male chauvinistic viewpoint that seems to celebrate the pornographic. With Carter's use of multiple voices and ever-shifting narrative positions, however, it is sometimes difficult to tell whether she is embracing or parodying the gender roles she sets out.

In the late 1970s and early 1980s, Carter's work began to be more favorably reviewed, and she took on a demanding lecturing and teaching schedule that saw her traveling around the world. In 1983 she also began a family, giving birth to a son, Alexander, with Mark Pearce, whom she married in 1991. Despite her busy schedule, Carter produced her longest novel, *Nights at the Circus*, in 1984. This story about a Cockney trapeze artist with wings has often been compared to Gabriel Garcia Marquez's *One Hundred Years of Solitude* (1967)—a comparison that brought Carter more into the mainstream than she had perhaps ever been. This and her final novel, *Wise Children* (1991), were both very well received, and when Carter died of lung cancer in 1992, she was mourned as a central literary figure of her day.

Many lamented that her obituary notices spoke of her work more generously than most of her reviews had. But critical acceptance had never been a goal of Carter's; she was always suspicious of critical consensus of any kind. Indeed, her writing seeks to provoke those whose opinions are widely accepted, and, in doing so, to produce fruitful critical debate. As one of her critics said, "I'll please no one, least of all her, by trying to say she's not offensive."

⌘ ⌘ ⌘

## The Bloody Chamber[1]

I remember how, that night, I lay awake in the wagon-lit[2] in a tender, delicious ecstasy of excitement, my burning cheek pressed against the impeccable linen of the pillow and the pounding of my heart mimicking that of the great pistons ceaselessly thrusting the train that bore me through the night, away from Paris, away from girlhood, away from the white, enclosed quietude of my mother's apartment, into the unguessable country of marriage.

And I remember I tenderly imagined how, at this very moment, my mother would be moving slowly about the narrow bedroom I had left behind for ever, folding up and putting away all my little relics, the tumbled garments I would not need any more, the scores for which there had been no room in my trunks, the concert programmes I'd abandoned; she would linger over this torn ribbon and that faded photograph with all the half-joyous, half-sorrowful emotions of a woman on her daughter's wedding day. And, in the midst of my bridal triumph, I felt a pang of loss as if,

---

[1]  *The Bloody Chamber*   Cf. Charles Perrault's "La Barbe Bleue" ("Bluebeard"), 1697.

[2]  *wagon-lit*   French: sleeping coach (on a train).

when he put the gold band on my finger, I had, in some way, ceased to be her child in becoming his wife.

Are you sure, she'd said when they delivered the gigantic box that held the wedding dress he'd bought me, wrapped up in tissue paper and red ribbon like a Christmas gift of crystallized fruit. Are you sure you love him? There was a dress for her, too; black silk, with the dull, prismatic sheen of oil on water, finer than anything she'd worn since that adventurous girlhood in Indo-China, daughter of a rich tea planter. My eagle-featured, indomitable mother; what other student at the Conservatoire could boast that her mother had outfaced a junkful[1] of Chinese pirates, nursed a village through a visitation of the plague, shot a man-eating tiger with her own hand and all before she was as old as I?

"Are you sure you love him?"

"I'm sure I want to marry him," I said.

And would say no more. She sighed, as if it was the reluctance that she might at last banish the spectre of poverty from its habitual place at our meager table. For my mother herself had gladly, scandalously, defiantly beggared herself for love; and, one fine day, her gallant soldier never returned from the wars, leaving his wife and child a legacy of tears that never quite dried, a cigar box full of medals and the antique service revolver that my mother, grown magnificently eccentric in hardship, kept always in her reticule,[2] in case—how I teased her—she was surprised by footpads[3] on her way home from the grocer's shop.

Now and then a starburst of lights spattered the drawn blinds as if the railway company had lit up all the stations through which we passed in celebration of the bride. My satin nightdress had just been shaken from its wrappings; it had slipped over my young girl's pointed breasts and shoulders, supple as a garment of heavy water, and now teasingly caressed me, egregious, insinuating, nudging between my thighs as I shifted restlessly in my narrow berth. His kiss, his kiss with tongue and teeth in it and a rasp of beard, had hinted to me, though with the same exquisite tact as this nightdress he'd given me, of the wedding night, which would be voluptuously deferred until we lay in his great ancestral bed in the sea-

girt, pinnacled domain that lay, still, beyond the grasp of my imagination ... that magic place, the fairy castle whose walls were made of foam, that legendary habitation in which he had been born. To which, one day, I might bear an heir. Our destination, my destiny.

Above the syncopated roar of the train, I could hear his even, steady breathing. Only the communicating door kept me from my husband and it stood open. If I rose up on my elbow, I could see the dark, leonine shape of his head and my nostrils caught a whiff of the opulent male scent of leather and spices that always accompanied him and sometimes, during his courtship, had been the only hint he gave me that he had come into my mother's sitting room, for, though he was a big man, he moved as softly as if all his shoes had soles of velvet, as if his footfall turned the carpet into snow.

He had loved to surprise me in my abstracted solitude at the piano. He would tell them not to announce him, then soundlessly open the door and softly creep up behind me with his bouquet of hot-house flowers or his box of marrons glacés,[4] lay his offering upon the keys and clasp his hands over my eyes as I was lost in a Debussy[5] prelude. But that perfume of spiced leather always betrayed him; after my first shock, I was forced always to mimic surprise, so that he would not be disappointed.

He was older than I. He was much older than I; there were streaks of pure silver in his dark mane. But his strange, heavy, almost waxen face was not lined by experience. Rather, experience seemed to have washed it perfectly smooth, like a stone on a beach whose fissures have been eroded by successive tides. And sometimes that face, in stillness when he listened to me playing, with the heavy eyelids folded over eyes that always disturbed me by their absolute absence of light, seemed to me like a mask, as if his real face, the face that truly reflected all the life he had led in the world before he met me, before, even, I was born, as though that face lay underneath this mask. Or else, elsewhere. As though he had laid by the face in which he had lived for so long in order to offer my youth a face unsigned by the years.

And, elsewhere, I might see him plain. Elsewhere. But, where?

[1] *junk*   Common Chinese boat with a flat bottom and square prow.

[2] *reticule*   Handbag.

[3] *footpads*   Thieves.

[4] *marrons glacés*   Chestnuts glazed with icing sugar.

[5] *Debussy*   French composer Claude Achille Debussy (1862–1918).

In, perhaps, that castle to which the train now took us, that marvellous castle in which he had been born.

Even when he asked me to marry him, and I said: "Yes," still he did not lose that heavy, fleshy composure of his. I know it must seem a curious analogy, a man with a flower, but sometimes he seemed to me like a lily. Yes. A lily. Possessed of that strange, ominous calm of a sentient vegetable, like one of those cobra-headed, funereal lilies whose white sheaths are curled out of a flesh as thick and tensely yielding to the touch as vellum. When I said that I would marry him, not one muscle in his face stirred, but he let out a long, extinguished sigh. I thought: Oh! how he must want me! And it was as though the imponderable weight of his desire was a force I might not withstand, not by virtue of its violence but because of its very gravity.

He had the ring ready in a leather box lined with crimson velvet, a fire opal the size of a pigeon's egg set in a complicated circle of dark antique gold. My old nurse, who still lived with my mother and me, squinted at the ring askance: opals are bad luck, she said. But this opal had been his own mother's ring, and his grandmother's, and her mother's before that, given to an ancestor by Catherine de Medici[1] ... every bride that came to the castle wore it, time out of mind. And did he give it to his other wives and have it back from them? asked the old woman rudely; yet she was a snob. She hid her incredulous joy at my marital coup—her little Marquise—behind a façade of fault-finding. But, here, she touched me. I shrugged and turned my back pettishly on her. I did not want to remember how he had loved other women before me, but the knowledge often teased me in the threadbare self-confidence of the small hours.

I was seventeen and knew nothing of the world; my Marquis had been married before, more than once, and I remained a little bemused that, after those others, he should now have chosen me. Indeed, was he not still in mourning for his last wife? Tsk, tsk, went my old nurse. And even my mother had been reluctant to see her girl whisked off by a man so recently bereaved. A Romanian countess, a lady of high fashion. Dead just three short months before I met him, a boating accident, at his home, in Brittany. They never found her body but I rummaged through the back copies of the society magazines my old nanny kept in a trunk under her bed and tracked down her photograph. The sharp muzzle of a pretty, witty, naughty monkey; such potent and bizarre charm, of a dark, bright, wild yet worldly thing whose natural habitat must have been some luxurious interior decorator's jungle filled with potted palms and tame, squawking parakeets.

Before that? *Her* face is common property; everyone painted her but the Redon[2] engraving I liked best, *The Evening Star Walking on the Rim of Night*. To see her skeletal, enigmatic grace, you would never think she had been a barmaid in a café in Montmartre until Puvis de Chavannes[3] saw her and had her expose her flat breasts and elongated thighs to his brush. And yet it was the absinthe doomed her, or so they said.

The first of all his ladies? That sumptuous diva; I had heard her sing Isolde,[4] precociously musical child that I was, taken to the opera for a birthday treat. My first opera; I had heard her sing Isolde. With what white-hot passion had she burned from the stage! So that you could tell she would die young. We sat high up, halfway to heaven in the gods, yet she half-blinded me. And my father, still alive (oh, so long ago), took hold of my sticky little hand, to comfort me, in the last act, yet all I heard was the glory of her voice.

Married three times within my own brief lifetime to three different graces, now, as if to demonstrate the eclecticism of his taste, he had invited me to join this gallery of beautiful women, I, the poor widow's child with my mouse-coloured hair that still bore the kinks of the plaits from which it had so recently been freed, my bony hips, my nervous, pianist's fingers.

He was rich as Croesus.[5] The night before our wedding—a simple affair, at the Mairie,[6] because his countess was so recently gone—he took my mother and me, curious coincidence, to see *Tristan*. And, do you

---

[1] *Catherine de Medici* Queen of France; wife of King Henry II (1519–89).

[2] *Redon* French painter and lithographer Odilon Redon (1840–1916).

[3] *Puvis de Chavannes* French painter (1824–98).

[4] *Isolde* I.e., in composer Richard Wagner's opera *Tristan und Isolde* (first performed 1865).

[5] *Croesus* Sixth-century BCE king of Lydia, famous for his wealth.

[6] *Mairie* French: town hall, mayor's residence.

know, my heart swelled and ached so during the Liebestod[1] that I thought I must truly love him. Yes. I did. On his arm, all eyes were upon me. The whispering crowd in the foyer parted like the Red Sea to let us through. My skin crisped at his touch.

How my circumstances had changed since the first time I heard those voluptuous chords that carry such a charge of deathly passion in them! Now, we sat in a loge,[2] in red velvet armchairs, and a braided, bewigged flunkey brought us a silver bucket of iced champagne in the interval. The froth spilled over the rim of my glass and drenched my hands, I thought: My cup runneth over. And I had on a Poiret[3] dress. He had prevailed upon my reluctant mother to let him buy my trousseau;[4] what would I have gone to him in, otherwise? Twice-darned underwear, faded gingham, serge skirts, hand-me-downs. So, for the opera, I wore a sinuous shift of white muslin tied with a silk string under the breasts. And everyone stared at me. And at his wedding gift.

His wedding gift, clasped round my throat. A choker of rubies, two inches wide, like an extraordinarily precious slit throat.

After the Terror, in the early days of the Directory,[5] the aristos who'd escaped the guillotine had an ironic fad of tying a red ribbon round their necks at just the point where the blade would have sliced it through, a red ribbon like the memory of a wound. And his grandmother, taken with the notion, had her ribbon made up in rubies; such a gesture of luxurious defiance! That night at the opera comes back to me even now … the white dress; the frail child within it; and the flashing crimson jewels round her throat, bright as arterial blood.

I saw him watching me in the gilded mirrors with the assessing eye of a connoisseur inspecting horseflesh, or even of a housewife in the market, inspecting cuts on the slab. I'd never seen, or else had never acknowledged, that regard of his before, the sheer carnal avarice of it; and it was strangely magnified by the monocle lodged in his left eye. When I saw him look at me with lust, I dropped my eyes but, in glancing away from him, I caught sight of myself in the mirror. And I saw myself, suddenly, as he saw me, my pale face, the way the muscles in my neck stuck out like thin wire. I saw how much that cruel necklace became me. And, for the first time in my innocent and confined life, I sensed in myself a potentiality for corruption that took my breath away.

The next day, we were married.

The train slowed, shuddered to a halt. Lights; clank of metal; a voice declaring the name of an unknown, never-to-be visited station; silence of the night; the rhythm of his breathing, that I should sleep with, now, for the rest of my life. And I could not sleep. I stealthily sat up, raised the blind a little and huddled against the cold window that misted over with the warmth of my breathing, gazing out at the dark platform towards those rectangles of domestic lamplight that promised warmth, company, a supper of sausages hissing in a pan on the stove for the station master, his children tucked up in bed asleep in the brick house with the painted shutters … all the paraphernalia of the everyday world from which I, with my stunning marriage, had exiled myself.

Into marriage, into exile; I sensed it, I knew it—that, henceforth, I would always be lonely. Yet that was part of the already familiar weight of the fire opal that glimmered like a gypsy's magic ball, so that I could not take my eyes off it when I played the piano. This ring, the bloody bandage of rubies, the wardrobe of clothes from Poiret and Worth,[6] his scent of Russian leather—all had conspired to seduce me so utterly that I could not say I felt one single twinge of regret for the world of tartines[7] and maman that now receded from me as if drawn away on a string, like a child's toy, as the train began to throb again as if in delighted anticipation of the distance it would take me.

---

[1] *Liebestod*  Aria describing the suicide of lovers.

[2] *loge*  Opera-house box.

[3] *Poiret*  Dressmaker Paul Poiret (1879–1944).

[4] *trousseau*  Bride's collection of clothing and linens.

[5] *Terror … Directory*  Reign of Terror, during the French Revolution (1793–94), during which thousands of people, considered by the political regime to be enemies of the state, were executed; *Directory* I.e., the *Directoire*, the period at the end of the French Revolution during which five Directors shared executive power over the state.

[6] *Worth*  Charles Frederick Worth (1825–95), British and French fashion designer and founder of Maison Worth.

[7] *tartines*  Slices of bread with butter or jam; a child's meal.

The first grey streamers of the dawn now flew in the sky and an eldritch half-light seeped into the railway carriage. I heard no change in his breathing but my heightened, excited senses told me he was awake and gazing at me. A huge man, an enormous man, and his eyes, dark and motionless as those eyes the ancient Egyptians painted upon their sarcophagi, fixed upon me. I felt a certain tension in the pit of my stomach, to be so watched, in such silence. A match struck. He was igniting a Romeo y Julieta[1] fat as a baby's arm.

"Soon," he said in his resonant voice that was like the tolling of a bell and I felt, all at once, a sharp premonition of dread that lasted only as long as the match flared and I could see his white, broad face as if it were hovering, disembodied, above the sheets, illuminated from below like a grotesque carnival head. Then the flame died, the cigar glowed and filled the compartment with a remembered fragrance that made me think of my father, how he would hug me in a warm fug[2] of Havana, when I was a little girl, before he kissed me and left me and died.

As soon as my husband handed me down from the high step of the train, I smelled the amniotic salinity of the ocean. It was November; the trees, stunted by the Atlantic gales, were bare and the lonely halt was deserted but for his leather-gaitered chauffeur waiting meekly beside the sleek black motor car. It was cold; I drew my furs about me, a wrap of white and black, broad stripes of ermine and sable, with a collar from which my head rose like the calyx of a wildflower. (I swear to you, I had never been vain until I met him.) The bell clanged; the straining train leapt its leash and left us at that lonely wayside halt where only he and I had descended. Oh, the wonder of it; how all that might of iron and steam had paused only to suit his convenience. The richest man in France.

"Madame."

The chauffeur eyed me; was he comparing me, invidiously, to the countess, the artist's model, the opera singer? I hid behind my furs as if they were a system of soft shields. My husband liked me to wear my opal over my kid glove, a showy, theatrical trick—but the moment the ironic chauffeur glimpsed its simmering flash

he smiled, as though it was proof positive I was his master's wife. And we drove towards the widening dawn, that now streaked half the sky with a wintry bouquet of pink of roses, orange of tiger-lilies, as if my husband had ordered me a sky from a florist. The day broke around me like a cool dream.

Sea; sand; a sky that melts into the sea—a landscape of misty pastels with a look about it of being continuously on the point of melting. A landscape with all the deliquescent harmonies of Debussy, of the études[3] I played for him, the reverie I'd been playing that afternoon in the salon of the princess where I'd first met him, among the teacups and the little cakes, I, the orphan, hired out of charity to give them their digestive of music.

And, ah! his castle. The faery solitude of the place; with its turrets of misty blue, its courtyard, its spiked gate, his castle that lay on the very bosom of the sea with seabirds mewing about its attics, the casements opening on to the green and purple, evanescent departures of the ocean, cut off by the tide from land for half a day … that castle, at home neither on the land nor on the water, a mysterious, amphibious place, contravening the materiality of both earth and the waves, with the melancholy of a mermaiden who perches on her rock and waits, endlessly, for a lover who had drowned far away, long ago. That lovely, sad, sea-siren of a place!

The tide was low; at this hour, so early in the morning, the causeway rose up out of the sea. As the car turned on to the wet cobbles between the slow margins of water, he reached out for my hand that had his sultry, witchy ring on it, pressed my fingers, kissed my palm with extraordinary tenderness. His face was as still as ever I'd seen it, still as a pond iced thickly over, yet his lips, that always looked so strangely red and naked between the black fringes of his beard, now curved a little. He smiled; he welcomed his bride home.

No room, no corridor that did not rustle with the sound of the sea and all the ceilings, the walls on which his ancestors in the stern regalia of rank lined up with their dark eyes and white faces, were stippled with refracted light from the waves which were always in motion; that luminous, murmurous castle of which I

---

[1] *Romeo y Julieta*   Brand of Havana cigar.

[2] *fug*   Thick, close atmosphere.

[3] *études*   Class of musical compositions.

was the chatelaine,[1] I, the little music student whose mother had sold all her jewellery, even her wedding ring, to pay the fees at the Conservatoire.

First of all, there was the small ordeal of my initial interview with the housekeeper, who kept this extraordinary machine, this anchored, castellated ocean liner, in smooth running order no matter who stood on the bridge; how tenuous, I thought, might be my authority here! She had a bland, pale, impassive, dislikeable face beneath the impeccably starched white linen head-dress of the region. Her greeting, correct but lifeless, chilled me; daydreaming, I dared presume too much on my status ... briefly wondered how I might install my old nurse, so much loved, however cosily incompetent, in her place. Ill-considered schemings! He told me this one had been his foster mother; was bound to his family in the utmost feudal complicity, "as much part of the house as I am, my dear." Now her thin lips offered me a proud little smile. She would be my ally as long as I was his. And with that, I must be content.

But, here, it would be easy to be content. In the turret suite he had given me for my very own, I could gaze out over the tumultuous Atlantic and imagine myself the Queen of the Sea. There was a Bechstein[2] for me in the music room and, on the wall, another wedding present—an early Flemish primitive of Saint Cecilia[3] at her celestial organ. In the prim charm of this saint, with her plump, sallow cheeks and crinkled brown hair, I saw myself as I could have wished to be. I warmed to a loving sensitivity I had not hitherto suspected in him. Then he led me up a delicate spiral staircase to my bedroom; before she discreetly vanished, the housekeeper set him chuckling with some, I dare say, lewd blessing for newlyweds in her native Breton. That I did not understand. That he, smiling, refused to interpret.

And there lay the grand, hereditary matrimonial bed, itself the size, almost, of my little room at home, with the gargoyles carved on its surfaces of ebony, vermilion lacquer, gold leaf; and its white gauze curtains, billowing in the sea breeze. Our bed. And surrounded by so many mirrors! Mirrors on all the walls, in stately frames of

contorted gold, that reflected more white lilies than I'd ever seen in my life before. He'd filled the room with them, to greet the bride, the young bride. The young bride, who had become that multitude of girls I saw in the mirrors, identical in their chic navy blue tailor-mades, for travelling, madame, or walking. A maid had dealt with the furs. Henceforth, a maid would deal with everything.

"See," he said, gesturing towards those elegant girls. "I have acquired a whole harem for myself!"

I found that I was trembling. My breath came thickly. I could not meet his eye and turned my head away, out of pride, out of shyness, and watched a dozen husbands approach me in a dozen mirrors and slowly, methodically, teasingly, unfasten the buttons of my jacket and slip it from my shoulders. Enough! No; more! Off comes the skirt; and, next, the blouse of apricot linen that cost more than the dress I had for First Communion. The play of the waves outside in the cold sun glittered on his monocle; his movements seemed to me deliberately coarse, vulgar. The blood rushed to my face again, and stayed there.

And yet, you see, I guessed it might be so—that we should have a formal disrobing of the bride, a ritual from the brothel. Sheltered as my life had been, how could I have failed, even in the world of prim bohemia in which I lived, to have heard hints of *his* world?

He stripped me, gourmand that he was, as if he were stripping the leaves off an artichoke—but do not imagine much finesse about it; this artichoke was no particular treat for the diner nor was he yet in any greedy haste. He approached his familiar treat with a weary appetite. And when nothing but my scarlet, palpitating core remained, I saw, in the mirror, the living image of an etching by Rops[4] from the collection he had shown me when our engagement permitted us to be alone together ... the child with her sticklike limbs, naked but for her button boots, her gloves, shielding her face with her hand as though her face were the last repository of her modesty; and the old, monocled lecher who examined her, limb by limb. He in his London tailoring; she, bare as a lamb chop. Most pornographic of all confrontations. And so my purchaser unwrapped his bargain. And, as at the opera, when I had first seen

---

[1]  *chatelaine*  Mistress.

[2]  *Bechstein*  Type of piano created by Carl Bechstein in 1853.

[3]  *Saint Cecilia*  Patron saint of music and musicians.

[4]  *Rops*  Belgian artist Félicien Rops (1833–98).

my flesh in his eyes, I was aghast to feel myself stirring.

At once he closed my legs like a book and I saw again the rare movement of his lips that meant he smiled.

Not yet. Later. Anticipation is the greater part of pleasure, my little love.

And I began to shudder, like a racehorse before a race, yet also with a kind of fear, for I felt both a strange, impersonal arousal at the thought of love and at the same time a repugnance I could not stifle for his white, heavy flesh that had too much in common with the armfuls of arum lilies that filled my bedroom in great glass jars, those undertakers' lilies with the heavy pollen that powders your fingers as if you had dipped them in turmeric. The lilies I always associate with him; that are white. And stain you.

This scene from a voluptuary's life was now abruptly terminated. It turns out he has business to attend to; his estates, his companies—even on your honeymoon? Even then, said the red lips that kissed me before he left me alone with my bewildered senses—a wet, silken brush from his beard; a hint of the pointed tip of the tongue. Disgruntled, I wrapped a négligé of antique lace around me to sip the little breakfast of hot chocolate the maid brought me; after that, since it was second nature to me, there was nowhere to go but the music room and soon I settled down at my piano.

Yet only a series of subtle discords flowed from beneath my fingers: out of tune … only a little out of tune; but I'd been blessed with perfect pitch and could not bear to play any more. Sea breezes are bad for pianos; we shall need a resident piano-tuner on the premises if I'm to continue with my studies! I flung down the lid in a little fury of disappointment; what should I do now, how shall I pass the long, sea-lit hours until my husband beds me?

I shivered to think of *that*.

His library seemed the source of his habitual odour of Russian leather. Row upon row of calf-bound volumes, brown and olive, with gilt lettering on their spines, the octavo[1] in brilliant scarlet morocco. A deep-buttoned leather sofa to recline on. A lectern, carved like a spread eagle, that held open upon it an edition of Huysmans's *Là-bas*,[2] from some over-exquisite private press; it had been bound like a missal,[3] in brass, with gems of coloured glass. The rugs on the floor, deep, pulsing blues of heaven and red of the heart's dearest blood, came from Isfahan and Bokhara;[4] the dark panelling gleamed; there was the lulling music of the sea and a fire of apple logs. The flames flickered along the spines inside a glass-fronted case that held books still crisp and new. Eliphas Levy;[5] the name meant nothing to me. I squinted at a title or two: *The Initiation*, *The Key of Mysteries*, *The Secret of Pandora's Box*, and yawned. Nothing, here, to detain a seventeen-year-old girl waiting for her first embrace. I should have liked, best of all, a novel in yellow paper;[6] I wanted to curl up on the rug before the blazing fire, lose myself in a cheap novel, munch sticky liqueur chocolates. If I rang for them, a maid would bring me chocolates.

Nevertheless, I opened the doors of that bookcase idly to browse. And I think I knew, I knew by some tingling of the fingertips, even before I opened that slim volume with no title at all on the spine, what I should find inside it. When he showed me the Rops, newly bought, dearly prized, had he not hinted that he was a connoisseur of such things? Yet I had not bargained for this, the girl with tears hanging on her cheeks like stuck pearls, her cunt a split fig below the great globes of her buttocks on which the knotted tails of the cat were about to descend, while a man in a black mask fingered with his free hand his prick, that curved upwards like the scimitar he held. The picture had a caption: "Reproof of curiosity." My mother, with all the precision of her eccentricity, had told me what it was that lovers did; I was innocent but not naive. *The Adventures of Eulalie at the Harem of the Grand Turk* had been printed, according to the flyleaf, in Amsterdam in 1748, a rare collector's piece. Had some ancestor brought it back himself from that northern city? Or had my husband

---

[1] *octavo* Book size. The pages of an octavo are produced by folding a standard-sized printing sheet three times to form eight leaves.

[2] *Huysmans's Là-bas* 1891 novel by French novelist Joris Karl Huysmans.

[3] *missal* Prayer book; contains the service of the Mass for the liturgical year.

[4] *Isfahan and Bokhara* Cities in Iran and Uzbekistan.

[5] *Eliphas Levy* Pseudonym of French magician Alphonse Louis Constant (1810–75).

[6] *novel in yellow paper* I.e., a popular novel.

bought it for himself, from one of those dusty little bookshops on the Left Bank where an old man peers at you through spectacles an inch thick, daring you to inspect his wares … I turned the pages in the anticipation of fear; the print was rusty. Here was another steel engraving: "Immolation of the wives of the Sultan." I knew enough for what I saw in that book to make me gasp.

There was a pungent intensification of the odour of leather that suffused his library; his shadow fell across the massacre.

"My little nun has found the prayerbooks, has she?" he demanded, with a curious mixture of mockery and relish; then, seeing my painful, furious bewilderment, he laughed at me aloud, snatched the book from my hands and put it down on the sofa.

"Have the nasty pictures scared Baby? Baby mustn't play with grownups' toys until she's learned how to handle them, must she?"

Then he kissed me. And with, this time, no reticence. He kissed me and laid his hand imperatively upon my breast, beneath the sheath of ancient lace. I stumbled on the winding stair that led to the bedroom, to the carved, gilded bed on which he had been conceived. I stammered foolishly: We've not taken luncheon yet; and, besides, it is broad daylight …

All the better to see you.

He made me put on my choker, the family heirloom of one woman who had escaped the blade. With trembling fingers, I fastened the thing about my neck. It was cold as ice and chilled me. He twined my hair into a rope and lifted it off my shoulders so that he could the better kiss the downy furrows below my ears; that made me shudder. And he kissed those blazing rubies, too. He kissed them before he kissed my mouth. Rapt, he intoned: "Of her apparel she retains/Only her sonorous jewellery."

A dozen husbands impaled a dozen brides while the mewing gulls swung on invisible trapezes in the empty air outside.

I was brought to my senses by the insistent shrilling of the telephone. He lay beside me, felled like an oak, breathing stertorously, as if he had been fighting with me. In the course of that one-sided struggle, I had seen his deathly composure shatter like a porcelain vase flung against a wall; I had heard him shriek and blaspheme at the orgasm; I had bled. And perhaps I had seen his face without its mask; and perhaps I had not. Yet I had been infinitely dishevelled by the loss of my virginity.

I gathered myself together, reached into the cloisonné[1] cupboard beside the bed that concealed the telephone and addressed the mouthpiece. His agent in New York. Urgent.

I shook him awake and rolled over on my side, cradling my spent body in my arms. His voice buzzed like a hive of distant bees. My husband. My husband, who, with so much love, filled my bedroom with lilies until it looked like an embalming parlour. Those somnolent lilies, that wave their heavy heads, distributing their lush, insolent incense reminiscent of pampered flesh.

When he'd finished with the agent, he turned to me and stroked the ruby necklace that bit into my neck, but with such tenderness now, that I ceased flinching and he caressed my breasts. My dear one, my little love, my child, did it hurt her? He's so sorry for it, such impetuousness, he could not help himself; you see, he loves her so … and this lover's recitative of his brought my tears in a flood. I clung to him as though only the one who had inflicted the pain could comfort me for suffering it. For a while, he murmured to me in a voice I'd never heard before, a voice like the soft consolations of the sea. But then he unwound the tendrils of my hair from the buttons of his smoking jacket, kissed my cheek briskly and told me the agent from New York had called with such urgent business that he must leave as soon as the tide was low enough. Leave the castle? Leave France! And would be away for at least six weeks.

"But it is our honeymoon!"

A deal, an enterprise of hazard and chance involving several millions, lay in the balance, he said. He drew away from me into that waxworks stillness of his; I was only a little girl, I did not understand. And, he said unspoken to my wounded vanity, I have had too many honeymoons to find them in the least pressing commitments. I know quite well that this child I've bought with a handful of coloured stones and the pelts of dead beasts won't run away. But, after he'd called his Paris agent to

---

[1] *cloisonné* Enamel.

book a passage for the States next day—just one tiny call, my little one—we should have time for dinner together.

And I had to be content with that.

A Mexican dish of pheasant with hazelnuts and chocolate; salad; white, voluptuous cheese; a sorbet of muscat grapes and Asti spumante. A celebration of Krug exploded festively. And then acrid black coffee in precious little cups so fine it shadowed the birds with which they were painted. I had Cointreau, he had cognac in the library, with the purple velvet curtains drawn against the night, where he took me to perch on his knee in a leather armchair beside the flickering log fire. He had made me change into that chaste little Poiret shift of white muslin; he seemed especially fond of it, my breasts showed through the flimsy stuff, he said, like little soft white doves that sleep, each one, with a pink eye open. But he would not let me take off my ruby choker, although it was growing very uncomfortable, nor fasten up my descending hair, the sign of a virginity so recently ruptured that still remained a wounded presence between us. He twined his fingers in my hair until I winced; I said, I remember, very little.

"The maid will have changed our sheets already," he said. "We do not hang the bloody sheets out of the window to prove to the whole of Brittany you are a virgin, not in these civilized times. But I should tell you it would have been the first time in all my married lives I could have shown my interested tenants such a flag."

Then I realized, with a shock of surprise, how it must have been my innocence that captivated him—the silent music, he said, of my unknowingness, like *La Terrasse des audiences au clair de lune*[1] played upon a piano with keys of ether. You must remember how ill at ease I was in that luxurious place, how unease had been my constant companion during the whole length of my courtship by this grave satyr who now gently martyrized my hair. To know that my naivety gave him some pleasure made me take heart. Courage! I shall act the fine lady to the manner born one day, if only by virtue of default.

Then, slowly yet teasingly, as if he were giving a child a great, mysterious treat, he took out a bunch of keys from some interior hidey-hole in his jacket—key after key, a key, he said, for every lock in the house. Keys of all kinds—huge, ancient things of black iron; others slender, delicate, almost baroque; wafer-thin Yale keys for safes and boxes. And, during his absence, it was I who must take care of them all.

I eyed the heavy bunch with circumspection. Until that moment, I had not given a single thought to the practical aspects of marriage with a great house, great wealth, a great man, whose key ring was as crowded as that of a prison warder. Here were the clumsy and archaic keys for the dungeons, for dungeons we had in plenty although they had been converted to cellars for his wines; the dusty bottles inhabited in racks all those deep holes of pain in the rock on which the castle was built. These are the keys to the kitchens, this is the key to the picture gallery, a treasure house filled by five centuries of avid collectors—ah! he foresaw I would spend hours there.

He had amply indulged his taste for the Symbolists, he told me with a glint of greed. There was Moreau's great portrait of his first wife, the famous *Sacrificial Victim* with the imprint of the lacelike chains on her pellucid skin. Did I know the story of the painting of that picture? How, when she took off her clothes for him for the first time, she fresh from her bar in Montmartre, she had robed herself involuntarily in a blush that reddened her breasts, her shoulders, her arms, her whole body? He had thought of that story, of that dear girl, when first he had undressed me ... Ensor, the great Ensor, his monolithic canvas: *The Foolish Virgins*. Two or three late Gauguins, his special favourite the one of the tranced brown girl in the deserted house which was called: *Out of the Night We Come, Into the Night We Go*. And, besides the additions he had made himself, his marvellous inheritance of Watteaus, Poussins and a pair of very special Fragonards, commissioned for a licentious ancestor who, it was said, had posed for the master's brush himself with his own two daughters ... He broke off his catalogue of treasures abruptly.

Your thin white face, chérie; he said, as if he saw it for the first time. Your thin white face, with its promise of debauchery only a connoisseur could detect.

A log fell in the fire, instigating a shower of sparks; the opal on my finger spurted green flame. I felt as

---

[1] *La Terrasse des audiences au clair de lune* Piano solo by Claude Debussy (1912–13).

giddy as if I were on the edge of a precipice; I was afraid, not so much of him, of his monstrous presence, heavy as if he had been gifted at birth with more specific *gravity* than the rest of us, the presence that, even when I thought myself most in love with him, always subtly oppressed me … No. I was not afraid of him; but of myself. I seemed reborn in his unreflective eyes, reborn in unfamiliar shapes. I hardly recognized myself from his descriptions of me and yet, and yet—might there not be a grain of beastly truth in them? And, in the red firelight, I blushed again, unnoticed, to think he might have chosen me because, in my innocence, he sensed a rare talent for corruption.

Here is the key to the china cabinet—don't laugh, my darling; there's a king's ransom in Sèvres in that closet, and a queen's ransom in Limoges.[1] And a key to the locked, barred room where five generations of plate[2] were kept.

Keys, keys, keys. He would trust me with the keys to his office, although I was only a baby; and the keys to his safes, where he kept the jewels I should wear, he promised me, when we returned to Paris. Such jewels! Why, I would be able to change my earrings and necklaces three times a day, just as the Empress Josephine used to change her underwear. He doubted, he said, with that hollow, knocking sound that served him for a chuckle, I would be quite so interested in his share certificates although they, of course, were worth infinitely more.

Outside our firelit privacy, I could hear the sound of the tide drawing back from the pebbles of the foreshore; it was nearly time for him to leave me. One single key remained unaccounted for on the ring and he hesitated over it; for a moment, I thought he was going to unfasten it from its brothers, slip it back into his pocket and take it away with him.

"What is *that* key?" I demanded, for his chaffing had made me bold. "The key to your heart? Give it me!"

He dangled the key tantalizingly above my head, out of reach of my straining fingers; those bare red lips of his cracked sidelong in a smile.

"Ah, no," he said. "Not the key to my heart. Rather, the key to my enfer."[3]

He left it on the ring, fastened the ring together, shook it musically, like a carillon. Then threw the keys in a jingling heap in my lap. I could feel the cold metal chilling my thighs through my thin muslin frock. He bent over me to drop a beard-masked kiss on my forehead.

"Every man must have one secret, even if only one, from his wife," he said. "Promise me this, my whey-faced piano-player; promise me you'll use all the keys on the ring except that last little one I showed you. Play with anything you find, jewels, silver plate; make toy boats of my share certificates, if it pleases you, and send them sailing off to America after me. All is yours, everywhere is open to you—except the lock that this single key fits. Yet all it is is the key to a little room at the foot of the west tower, behind the still-room, at the end of a dark little corridor full of horrid cobwebs that would get into your hair and frighten you if you ventured there. Oh, and you'd find it such a dull little room! But you must promise me, if you love me, to leave it well alone. It is only a private study, a hideaway, a 'den,' as the English say, where I can go, sometimes, on those infrequent yet inevitable occasions when the yoke of marriage seems to weigh too heavily on my shoulders. There I can go, you understand, to savour the rare pleasure of imagining myself wifeless."

There was a little thin starlight in the courtyard as, wrapped in my furs, I saw him to his car. His last words were, that he had telephoned the mainland and taken a piano-tuner on to the staff; this man would arrive to take up his duties the next day. He pressed me to his vicuna[4] breast, once, and then drove away.

I had drowsed away that afternoon and now I could not sleep. I lay tossing and turning in his ancestral bed until another daybreak discoloured the dozen mirrors that were iridescent with the reflections of the sea. The perfume of the lilies weighed on my senses; when I thought that, henceforth, I would always share these sheets with a man whose skin, as theirs did, contained

---

[1] *Sèvres … Limoges*  Fine china.

[2] *plate*  I.e., silver dishes and utensils.

[3] *enfer*  French: Hell.

[4] *vicuna*  Fine, silky wool made from the coat of a South American animal of the same name.

that toad-like, clammy hint of moisture, I felt a vague desolation that within me, now my female wound had healed, there had awoken a certain queasy craving like the cravings of pregnant women for the taste of coal or chalk or tainted food, for the renewal of his caresses. Had he not hinted to me, in his flesh as in his speech and looks, of the thousand, thousand baroque intersections of flesh upon flesh? I lay in our wide bed accompanied by a sleepless companion, my dark newborn curiosity.

I lay in bed alone. And I longed for him. And he disgusted me.

Were there jewels enough in all his safes to recompense me for this predicament? Did all that castle hold enough riches to recompense me for the company of the libertine[1] with whom I must share it? And what, precisely, was the nature of my desirous dread for this mysterious being who, to show his mastery over me, had abandoned me on my wedding night?

Then I sat straight up in bed, under the sardonic masks of the gargoyles carved above me, riven by a wild surmise. Might he have left me, not for Wall Street but for an importunate mistress tucked away God knows where who knew how to pleasure him far better than a girl whose fingers had been exercised, hitherto, only by the practice of scales and arpeggios? And, slowly, soothed, I sank back on to the heaping pillows; I acknowledged that the jealous scare I'd just given myself was not unmixed with a little tincture of relief.

At last I drifted into slumber, as daylight filled the room and chased bad dreams away. But the last thing I remembered, before I slept, was the tall jar of lilies beside the bed, how the thick glass distorted their fat stems so they looked like arms, dismembered arms, drifting drowned in greenish water.

Coffee and croissants to console this bridal, solitary waking. Delicious. Honey, too, in a section of comb on a glass saucer. The maid squeezed the aromatic juice from an orange into a chilled goblet while I watched her as I lay in the lazy, midday bed of the rich. Yet nothing, this morning, gave me more than a fleeting pleasure except to hear that the piano-tuner had been at work already. When the maid told me that, I sprang out of bed and pulled on my old serge skirt and flannel blouse,

costume of a student, in which I felt far more at ease with myself than in any of my fine new clothes.

After my three hours of practice, I called the piano-tuner in, to thank him. He was blind, of course; but young, with a gentle mouth and grey eyes that fixed upon me although they could not see me. He was a blacksmith's son from the village across the causeway; a chorister in the church whom the good priest had taught a trade so that he could make a living. All most satisfactory. Yes. He thought he would be happy here. And if, he added shyly, he might sometimes be allowed to hear me play ... for, you see, he loved music. Yes. Of course, I said. Certainly. He seemed to know that I had smiled.

After I dismissed him, even though I'd woken so late, it was still barely time for my "five o'clock."[2] The housekeeper, who, thoughtfully forewarned by my husband, had restrained herself from interrupting my music, now made me a solemn visitation with a lengthy menu for a late luncheon. When I told her I did not need it, she looked at me obliquely, along her nose. I understood at once that one of my principal functions as chatelaine was to provide work for the staff. But, all the same, I asserted myself and said I would wait until dinner-time, although I looked forward nervously to the solitary meal. Then I found I had to tell her what I would like to have prepared for me; my imagination, still that of a schoolgirl, ran riot. A fowl in cream—or should I anticipate Christmas with a varnished turkey? No; I have decided. Avocado and shrimp, lots of it, followed by no entree at all. But surprise me for dessert with every ice-cream in the ice box. She noted all down but sniffed; I'd shocked her. Such tastes! Child that I was, I giggled when she left me.

But, now ... what shall I do, now?

I could have spent a happy hour unpacking the trunks that contained my trousseau but the maid had done that already, the dresses, the tailor-mades hung in the wardrobe in my dressing room, the hats on wooden heads to keep their shape, the shoes on wooden feet as if all these inanimate objects were imitating the appearance of life, to mock me. I did not like to linger in my overcrowded dressing room, nor in my lugubriously lily-scented bedroom. How shall I pass the time?

1 *libertine* Immoral, dissolute man.

2 *"five o'clock"* Late afternoon tea.

I shall take a bath in my own bathroom! And found the taps were little dolphins made of gold, with chips of turquoise for eyes. And there was a tank of goldfish, who swam in and out of moving fronds of weeds, as bored, I thought, as I was. How I wished he had not left me. How I wished it were possible to chat with, say, a maid; or, the piano-tuner ... but I knew already my new rank forbade overtures of friendship to the staff.

I had been hoping to defer the call as long as I could, so that I should have something to look forward to in the dead waste of time I foresaw before me, after my dinner was done with, but, at a quarter before seven, when darkness already surrounded the castle, I could contain myself no longer. I telephoned my mother. And astonished myself by bursting into tears when I heard her voice.

No, nothing was the matter. Mother, I have gold bath taps.

I said, gold bath taps!

No; I suppose that's nothing to cry about, Mother.

The line was bad, I could hardly make out her congratulations, her questions, her concern, but I was a little comforted when I put the receiver down.

Yet there still remained one whole hour to dinner and the whole, unimaginable desert of the rest of the evening.

The bunch of keys lay, where he had left them, on the rug before the library fire which had warmed their metal so that they no longer felt cold to the touch but warm, almost, as my own skin. How careless I was; a maid, tending the logs, eyed me reproachfully as if I'd set a trap for her as I picked up the clinking bundle of keys, the keys to the interior doors of this lovely prison of which I was both the inmate and the mistress and had scarcely seen. When I remembered that, I felt the exhilaration of the explorer.

Lights! More lights!

At the touch of a switch, the dreaming library was brilliantly illuminated. I ran crazily about the castle, switching on every light I could find—I ordered the servants to light up all their quarters, too, so the castle would shine like a seaborne birthday cake lit with a thousand candles, one for every year of its life, and everybody on shore would wonder at it. When everything was lit as brightly as the café in the Gare du Nord,

the significance of the possessions implied by that bunch of keys no longer intimidated me, for I was determined, now, to search through them all for evidence of my husband's true nature.

His office first, evidently.

A mahogany desk half a mile wide, with an impeccable blotter and a bank of telephones. I allowed myself the luxury of opening the safe that contained the jewellery and delved sufficiently among the leather boxes to find out how my marriage had given me access to a jinn's[1] treasury—parures,[2] bracelets, rings ... While I was thus surrounded by diamonds, a maid knocked on the door and entered before I spoke; a subtle discourtesy. I would speak to my husband about it. She eyed my serge skirt superciliously; did madame plan to dress for dinner?

She made a moue[3] of disdain when I laughed to hear that, she was far more the lady than I. But, imagine—to dress up in one of my Poiret extravaganzas, with the jewelled turban and aigrette[4] on my head, roped with pearl to the navel, to sit down all alone in the baronial dining hall at the head of that massive board at which King Mark[5] was reputed to have fed his knights ... I grew calmer under the cold eye of her disapproval. I adopted the crisp inflections of an officer's daughter. No, I would not dress for dinner. Furthermore, I was not hungry enough for dinner itself. She must tell the housekeeper to cancel the dormitory feast I'd ordered. Could they leave me sandwiches and a flask of coffee in my music room? And would they all dismiss for the night?

Mais oui, madame.

I knew by her bereft intonation I had let them down again but I did not care; I was armed against them by the brilliance of his hoard. But I would not find his heart amongst the glittering stones; as soon as she had gone, I began a systematic search of the drawers of his desk.

---

[1]  *jinn*  Shape-changing demon of Islamic folklore; a genie.

[2]  *parures*  Sets of several pieces of jewelry.

[3]  *moue*  Pout.

[4]  *aigrette*  Spray of jewels.

[5]  *King Mark*  Of Arthurian legend.

All was in order, so I found nothing. Not a random doodle on an old envelope, nor the faded photograph of a woman. Only the files of business correspondence, the bills from the home farms, the invoices from tailors, the billets-doux from international financiers. Nothing. And this absence of the evidence of his real life began to impress me strangely; there must, I thought, be a great deal to conceal if he takes such pains to hide it.

His office was a singularly impersonal room, facing inwards, on to the courtyard, as though he wanted to turn his back on the siren sea in order to keep a clear head while he bankrupted a small businessman in Amsterdam or—I noticed with a thrill of distaste —engaged in some business in Laos that must, from certain cryptic references to his amateur botanist's enthusiasm for rare poppies, be to do with opium. Was he not rich enough to do without crime? Or was the crime itself his profit? And yet I saw enough to appreciate his zeal for secrecy.

Now I had ransacked his desk, I must spend a cool-headed quarter of an hour putting every last letter back where I had found it, and, as I covered the traces of my visit, by some chance, as I reached inside a little drawer that had stuck fast, I must have touched a hidden spring, for a secret drawer flew open within that drawer itself; and this secret drawer contained—at last!—a file marked: *Personal*.

I was alone, but for my reflection in the uncurtained window.

I had the brief notion that his heart, pressed flat as a flower, crimson and thin as tissue paper, lay in this file. It was a very thin one.

I could have wished, perhaps, I had not found that touching, ill-spelt note, on a paper napkin marked *La Coupole*, that began: "My darling, I cannot wait for the moment when you may make me yours completely." The diva had sent him a page of the score of *Tristan*, the Liebestod, with the single, cryptic word: "Until ..." scrawled across it. But the strangest of all these love letters was a postcard with a view of a village graveyard, among mountains, where some black-coated ghoul enthusiastically dug at a grave; this little scene, executed with the lurid exuberance of Grand Guignol,[1] was captioned: "Typical Transylvanian Scene—Midnight, All Hallows." And, on the other side, the message: "On the occasion of this marriage to the descendant of Dracula—always remember, 'the supreme and unique pleasure of love is the certainty that one is doing evil.' Toutes amitiés,[2] C."

A joke. A joke in the worst possible taste; for had he not been married to a Romanian countess? And then I remembered her pretty, witty face, and her name—Carmilla. My most recent predecessor in this castle had been, it would seem, the most sophisticated.

I put away the file, sobered. Nothing in my life of family love and music had prepared me for these grown-up games and yet these were clues to his self that showed me, at least, how much he had been loved, even if they did not reveal any good reason for it. But I wanted to know still more; and, as I closed the office door and locked it, the means to discover more fell in my way.

Fell, indeed; and with the clatter of a dropped canteen of cutlery, for, as I turned the slick Yale lock, I contrived, somehow, to open up the key ring itself, so that all the keys tumbled loose on the floor. And the very first key I picked out of that pile was, as luck or ill fortune had it, the key to the room he had forbidden me, the room he would keep for his own so that he could go there when he wished to feel himself once more a bachelor.

I made my decision to explore it before I felt a faint resurgence of my ill-defined fear of his waxen stillness. Perhaps I half-imagined, then, that I might find his real self in his den, waiting there to see if indeed I had obeyed him; that he had sent a moving figure of himself to New York, the enigmatic, self-sustaining carapace[3] of his public person, while the real man, whose face I had glimpsed in the storm of orgasm, occupied himself with pressing private business in the study at the foot of the west tower, behind the still-room. Yet, if that were so, it was imperative that I should find him, should know

---

[1] *Grand Guignol* Drama dealing with macabre subject matter and containing graphic violence. Originally, the name of a Paris theater that shocked its audience members in the early twentieth century with the graphic nature of its performances.

[2] *Toutes amitiés* French: all the best.

[3] *carapace* Shell.

him; and I was too deluded by his apparent taste for me to think my disobedience might truly offend him.

I took the forbidden key from the heap and left the others lying there.

It was now very late and the castle was adrift, as far as it could go from the land, in the middle of the silent ocean where, at my orders, it floated, like a garland of light. And all silent, all still, but for the murmuring of the waves.

I felt no fear, no intimation of dread. Now I walked as firmly as I had done in my mother's house.

Not a narrow, dusty little passage at all; why had he lied to me? But an ill-lit one, certainly; the electricity, for some reason, did not extend here, so I retreated to the still-room and found a bundle of waxed tapers in a cupboard, stored there with matches to light the oak board at grand dinners. I put a match to my little taper and advanced with it in my hand, like a penitent, along the corridor hung with heavy, I think Venetian, tapestries. The flame picked out, here, the head of a man, there, the rich breast of a woman spilling through a rent in her dress—the Rape of the Sabines,[1] perhaps? The naked swords and immolated horses suggested some grisly mythological subject. The corridor wound downwards; there was an almost imperceptible ramp to the thickly carpeted floor. The heavy hangings on the wall muffled my footsteps, even my breathing. For some reason, it grew very warm; the sweat sprang out in beads on my brow. I could no longer hear the sound of the sea.

A long, a winding corridor, as if I were in the viscera of the castle; and this corridor led to a door of worm-eaten oak, low, round-topped, barred with black iron. And still I felt no fear, no raising of the hairs on the back of the neck, no prickling of the thumbs.

The key slid into the new lock as easily as a hot knife into butter.

No fear; but a hesitation, a holding of the spiritual breath.

If I had found some traces of his heart in a file marked: *Personal*, perhaps, here, in his subterranean privacy, I might find a little of his soul. It was the consciousness of the possibility of such a discovery, of its possible strangeness, that kept me for a moment motionless, before, in the foolhardiness of my already subtly tainted innocence, I turned the key and the door creaked slowly back.

"There is a striking resemblance between the act of love and the ministrations of a torturer," opined my husband's favourite poet;[2] I had learned something of the nature of that similarity on my marriage bed. And now my taper showed me the outlines of a rack. There was also a great wheel, like the ones I had seen in woodcuts of the martyrdoms of the saints, in my old nurse's little store of holy books. And—just one glimpse of it before my little flame caved in and I was left in absolute darkness—a metal figure, hinged at the side, which I knew to be spiked on the inside and to have the name: the Iron Maiden.

Absolute darkness. And, about me, the instruments of mutilation.

Until that moment, this spoiled child did not know she had inherited nerves and a will from the mother who had defied the yellow outlaws of Indo-China. My mother's spirit drove me on, into that dreadful place, in a cold ecstasy to know the very worst. I fumbled for the matches in my pocket; what a dim, lugubrious light they gave! And yet, enough, oh, more than enough, to see a room designed for desecration and some dark night of unimaginable lovers whose embraces were annihilation.

The walls of this stark torture chamber were the naked rock; they gleamed as if they were sweating with fright. At the four corners of the room were funerary urns, of great antiquity, Etruscan, perhaps, and, on three-legged ebony stands, the bowls of incense he had left burning which filled the room with a sacerdotal[3] reek. Wheel, rack, and Iron Maiden were, I saw, displayed as grandly as if they were items of statuary and I was almost consoled, then, and almost persuaded myself that I might have stumbled only upon a little museum of his perversity, that he had installed these monstrous

---

[1] *Rape ... Sabines*  Legendary event in early Roman history, in which young Roman men abducted and raped large numbers of women from neighboring Sabine in order to try to quicken the growth of the population of early Rome. The scene has been widely depicted in works of art, including paintings by Rubens, Poussin, and David.

[2] *There is ... poet*  Unidentified.

[3] *sacerdotal*  Belonging to the priesthood.

items here only for contemplation.

Yet at the centre of the room lay a catafalque,[1] a doomed, ominous bier of Renaissance workmanship, surrounded by long white candles and, at its foot, an armful of the same lilies with which he had filled my bedroom, stowed in a four-foot-high jar glazed with a sombre Chinese red. I scarcely dared examine this catafalque and its occupant more closely; yet I knew I must.

Each time I struck a match to light those candles round her bed, it seemed a garment of that innocence of mine for which he had lusted fell away from me.

The opera singer lay, quite naked, under a thin sheet of very rare and precious linen, such as the princes of Italy used to shroud those whom they had poisoned. I touched her, very gently, on the white breast; she was cool, he had embalmed her. On her throat I could see the blue imprint of his strangler's fingers. The cool, sad flame of the candles flickered on her white, closed eyelids. The worst thing was, the dead lips smiled.

Beyond the catafalque, in the middle of the shadows, a white, nacreous glimmer; as my eyes accustomed themselves to the gathering darkness, I at last—oh, horrors!—made out a skull; yes, a skull, so utterly denuded, now, of flesh, that it scarcely seemed possible the stark bone had once been richly upholstered with life. And this skull was strung up by a system of unseen cords, so that it appeared to hang, disembodied, in the still, heavy air, and it had been crowned with a wreath of white roses, and a veil of lace, the final image of his bride.

Yet the skull was still so beautiful, had shaped with its sheer planes so imperiously the face that had once existed above it, that I recognized her the moment I saw her; face of the evening star walking on the rim of night. One false step, oh, my poor, dear girl, next in the fated sisterhood of his wives; one false step and into the abyss of the dark you stumbled.

And where was she, the latest dead, the Romanian countess who might have thought her blood would survive his depredations? I knew she must be here, in the place that had wound me through the castle towards it on a spool of inexorability. But, at first, I could see no sign of her. Then, for some reason—perhaps some change of atmosphere wrought by my presence—the metal shell of the Iron Maiden emitted a ghostly twang; my feverish imagination might have guessed its occupant was trying to clamber out, though, even in the midst of my rising hysteria, I knew she must be dead to find a home there.

With trembling fingers, I prised open the front of the upright coffin, with its sculpted face caught in a rictus[2] of pain. Then, overcome, I dropped the key I still held in my other hand. It dropped into the forming pool of her blood.

She was pierced, not by one but by a hundred spikes, this child of the land of the vampires who seemed so newly dead, so full of blood … oh God! how recently had he become a widower? How long had he kept her in this obscene cell? Had it been all the time he had courted me, in the clear light of Paris?

I closed the lid of her coffin very gently and burst into a tumult of sobbing that contained both pity for his other victims and also a dreadful anguish to know I, too, was one of them.

The candles flared, as if in a draught from a door to elsewhere. The light caught the fire opal on my hand so that it flashed, once, with a baleful light, as if to tell me the eye of God—his eye—was upon me. My first thought, when I saw the ring for which I had sold myself to this fate, was, how to escape it.

I retained sufficient presence of mind to snuff out the candles round the bier with my fingers, to gather up my taper, to look around, although shuddering, to ensure I had left behind me no traces of my visit.

I retrieved the key from the pool of blood, wrapped it in my handkerchief to keep my hands clean, and fled the room, slamming the door behind me. It crashed to with a juddering reverberation, like the door of hell.

I could not take refuge in my bedroom, for that retained the memory of his presence trapped in the fathomless silvering of his mirrors. My music room seemed the safest place, although I looked at the picture of Saint Cecilia with a faint dread; what had been the nature of her martyrdom? My mind was in a tumult; schemes for flight jostled with one another … as soon as the tide receded from the causeway, I would make for the

---

1   *catafalque*   Decorative platform for a coffin.

2   *rictus*   Gape.

mainland—on foot, running, stumbling; I did not trust that leather-clad chauffeur, nor the well-behaved housekeeper, and I dared not take any of the pale, ghostly maids into my confidence, either, since they were his creatures, all. Once at the village, I would fling myself directly on the mercy of the gendarmerie.[1]

But—could I trust them, either? His forefathers had ruled this coast for eight centuries, from this castle whose moat was the Atlantic. Might not the police, the advocates, even the judge, all be in his service, turning a common blind eye to his vices since he was milord whose word must be obeyed? Who, on this distant coast, would believe the white-faced girl from Paris who came running to them with a shuddering tale of blood, of fear, of the ogre murmuring in the shadows? Or, rather, they would immediately know it to be true. But were all honour-bound to let me carry it no further.

Assistance. My mother. I ran to the telephone; and the line, of course, was dead.

Dead as his wives.

A thick darkness, unlit by any star, still glazed the windows. Every lamp in my room burned, to keep the dark outside, yet it seemed still to encroach on me, to be present beside me but as if masked by my lights, the night like a permeable substance that could seep into my skin. I looked at the precious little clock made from hypocritically innocent flowers long ago, in Dresden; the hands had scarcely moved one single hour forward from when I first descended to that private slaughter-house of his. Time was his servant, too; it would trap me, here, in a night that would last until he came back to me, like a black sun on a hopeless morning.

And yet the time might still be my friend; at that hour, that very hour, he set sail for New York.

To know that, in a few moments, my husband would have left France calmed my agitation a little. My reason told me I had nothing to fear; the tide that would take him away to the New World would let me out of the imprisonment of the castle. Surely I could easily evade the servants. Anybody can buy a ticket at a railway station. Yet I was still filled with unease. I opened the lid of the piano; perhaps I thought my own particular magic might help me, now, that I could create a penta-

cle[2] out of music that would keep me from harm for, if my music had first ensnared him, then might it not also give me the power to free myself from him?

Mechanically, I began to play but my fingers were stiff and shaking. At first, I could manage nothing better than the exercises of Czerny but simply the act of playing soothed me and, for solace, for the sake of the harmonious rationality of its sublime mathematics, I searched among his scores until I found *The Well-Tempered Clavier*. I set myself the therapeutic task of playing all Bach's equations, every one, and, I told myself, if I played them all through without a single mistake—then the morning would find me once more a virgin.

Crash of a dropped stick.

His silver-headed cane! What else? Sly, cunning, he had returned; he was waiting for me outside the door!

I rose to my feet; fear gave me strength. I flung back my head defiantly.

"Come in!" My voice astonished me by its firmness, its clarity.

The door slowly, nervously opened and I saw, not the massive, irredeemable bulk of my husband but the slight, stooping figure of the piano-tuner, and he looked far more terrified of me than my mother's daughter would have been of the Devil himself. In the torture chamber, it seemed to me that I would never laugh again; now, helplessly, laugh I did, with relief, and, after a moment's hesitation, the boy's face softened and he smiled a little, almost in shame. Though they were blind, his eyes were singularly sweet.

"Forgive me," said Jean-Yves. "I know I've given you grounds for dismissing me, that I should be crouching outside your door at midnight ... but I heard you walking about, up and down—I sleep in a room at the foot of the west tower—and some intuition told me you could not sleep and might, perhaps, pass the insomniac hours at your piano. And I could not resist that. Besides, I stumbled over these—"

And he displayed the ring of keys I'd dropped outside my husband's office door, the ring from which one key was missing. I took them from him, looked round for a place to stow them, fixed on the piano stool as if to hide them would protect me. Still he stood

[1] *gendarmerie*  French: police force.

[2] *pentacle*  Magic symbol enclosed in a circle.

smiling at me. How hard it was to make everyday conversation.

"It's perfect," I said. "The piano. Perfectly in tune."

But he was full of the loquacity of embarrassment, as though I would only forgive him for his impudence if he explained the cause of it thoroughly.

"When I heard you play this afternoon, I thought I'd never heard such a touch. Such technique. A treat for me, to hear a virtuoso! So I crept up to your door now, humbly as a little dog might, madame, and put my ear to the keyhole and listened, and listened—until my stick fell to the floor through a momentary clumsiness of mine, and I was discovered."

He had the most touchingly ingenuous smile.

"Perfectly in tune," I repeated. To my surprise, now I had said it, I found I could not say anything else. I could only repeat: "In tune … perfect … in tune," over and over again. I saw a dawning surprise in his face. My head throbbed. To see him, in his lovely, blind human-ity, seemed to hurt me very piercingly, somewhere inside my breast; his figure blurred, the room swayed about me. After the dreadful revelation of that bloody chamber, it was his tender look that made me faint.

When I recovered consciousness, I found I was lying in the piano-tuner's arms and he was tucking the satin cushion from the piano-stool under my head.

"You are in some great distress," he said. "No bride should suffer so much, so early in her marriage."

His speech had the rhythms of the countryside, the rhythms of the tides.

"Any bride brought to this castle should come ready dressed in mourning, should bring a priest and a coffin with her," I said.

"What's this?"

It was too late to keep silent; and if he, too, were one of my husband's creatures, then at least he had been kind to me. So I told him everything, the keys, the interdiction, my disobedience, the room, the rack, the skull, the corpses, the blood.

"I can scarcely believe it," he said, wondering. "That man … so rich; so well-born."

"Here's proof," I said and tumbled the fatal key out of my handkerchief on to the silken rug.

"Oh God," he said. "I can smell the blood."

He took my hand; he pressed his arms about me. Although he was scarcely more than a boy, I felt a great strength flow into me from his touch.

"We whisper all manner of strange tales up and down the coast," he said. "There was a Marquis, once, who used to hunt young girls on the mainland; he hunted them with dogs, as though they were foxes. My grandfather had it from his grandfather, how the Marquis pulled a head out of his saddle bag and showed it to the blacksmith while the man was shoeing his horse. 'A fine specimen of the genus, brunette, eh, Guillaume?' And it was the head of the blacksmith's wife."

But, in these more democratic times, my husband must travel as far as Paris to do his hunting in the salons. Jean-Yves knew the moment I shuddered.

"Oh, madame! I thought all these were old wives' tales, chattering of fools, spooks to scare bad children into good behaviour! Yet how could you know, a stranger, that the old name for this place is the Castle of Murder?"

How could I know, indeed? Except that, in my heart, I'd always known its lord would be the death of me.

"Hark!" said my friend suddenly. "The sea has changed key; it must be near morning, the tide is going down."

He helped me up. I looked from the window, towards the mainland, along the causeway where the stones gleamed wetly in the thin light of the end of the night and, with an almost unimaginable horror, a horror the intensity of which I cannot transmit to you, I saw, in the distance, still far away yet drawing moment by moment inexorably nearer, the twin headlamps of his great black car, gouging tunnels through the shifting mist.

My husband had indeed returned; this time, it was no fancy.

"The key!" said Jean-Yves. "It must go back on the ring, with the others. As though nothing had hap-pened."

But the key was still caked with wet blood and I ran to my bathroom and held it under the hot tap. Crimson water swirled down the basin but, as if the key itself were hurt, the bloody token stuck. The turquoise eyes of the dolphin taps winked at me derisively; they knew my husband had been too clever for me! I scrubbed the stain with my nail brush but still it would not budge. I thought how the car would be rolling silently towards the closed courtyard gate; the more I scrubbed the key, the more vivid grew the stain.

The bell in the gatehouse would jangle. The porter's drowsy son would push back the patchwork quilt, yawning, pull the shirt over his head, thrust his feet into his sabots … slowly, slowly; open the door for your master as slowly as you can …

And still the bloodstain mocked the fresh water that spilled from the mouth of the leering dolphin.

"You have no more time," said Jean-Yves. "He is here. I know it. I must stay with you."

"You shall not!" I said. "Go back to your room, now. Please."

He hesitated. I put an edge of steel in my voice, for I knew I must meet my lord alone.

"Leave me!"

As soon as he had gone, I dealt with the keys and went to my bedroom. The causeway was empty; Jean-Yves was correct, my husband had already entered the castle. I pulled the curtains close, stripped off my clothes and pulled the bedcurtains round me as a pungent aroma of Russian leather assured me my husband was once again beside me.

"Dearest!"

With the most treacherous, lascivious tenderness, he kissed my eyes, and, mimicking the new bride newly wakened, I flung my arms around him, for on my seeming acquiescence depended my salvation.

"Da Silva of Rio outwitted me," he said wryly. "My New York agent telegraphed Le Havre and saved me a wasted journey. So we may resume our interrupted pleasures, my love."

I did not believe one word of it. I knew I had behaved exactly according to his desires; had he not bought me so that I should do so? I had been tricked into my own betrayal to that illimitable darkness whose source I had been compelled to seek in his absence and, now that I had met that shadowed reality of his that came to life only in the presence of its own atrocities, I must pay the price of my new knowledge. The secret of Pandora's box;[1] but he had given me the box, himself, knowing I must learn the secret. I had played a game in which every move was governed by a destiny as oppressive and omnipotent as himself, since that destiny was himself; and I had lost. Lost at that charade of innocence and vice in which he had engaged me. Lost, as the victim loses to the executioner.

His hand brushed my breast, beneath the sheet. I strained my nerves yet could not help but flinch from the intimate touch, for it made me think of the piercing embrace of the Iron Maiden and of his lost lovers in the vault. When he saw my reluctance, his eyes veiled over and yet his appetite did not diminish. His tongue ran over red lips already wet. Silent, mysterious, he moved away from me to draw off his jacket. He took the gold watch from his waistcoat and laid it on the dressing table, like a good bourgeois; scooped out his rattling loose change and now—oh God!—makes a great play of patting his pockets officiously, puzzled lips pursed, searching for something that has been mislaid. Then turns to me with a ghastly, a triumphant smile.

"But of course! I gave the keys to you!"

"Your keys? Why, of course. Here, they're under the pillow; wait a moment—what—Ah! No … now, where can I have left them? I was whiling away the evening without you at the piano, I remember. Of course! The music room!"

Brusquely he flung my négligé of antique lace on the bed.

"Go and get them."

"Now? This moment? Can't it wait until morning, my darling?"

I forced myself to be seductive. I saw myself, pale, pliant as a plant that begs to be trampled underfoot, a dozen vulnerable, appealing girls reflected in as many mirrors, and I saw how he almost failed to resist me. If he had come to me in bed, I would have strangled him, then.

But he half-snarled: "No. It won't wait. Now."

The unearthly light of dawn filled the room; had only one previous dawn broken upon me in that vile place? And there was nothing for it but to go and fetch the keys from the music stool and pray he would not

---

[1] *Pandora's box*  In Greek myth, a box that contained all human evils, said to have been opened by a girl named Pandora.

examine them too closely, pray to God his eyes would fail him, that he might be struck blind.

When I came back into the bedroom carrying the bunch of keys that jangled at every step like a curious musical instrument, he was sitting on the bed in his immaculate shirtsleeves, his head sunk in his hands.

And it seemed to me he was in despair.

Strange. In spite of my fear of him, that made me whiter than my wrap, I felt there emanate from him, at that moment, a stench of absolute despair, rank and ghastly, as if the lilies that surrounded him had all at once begun to fester, or the Russian leather of his scent were reverting to the elements of flayed hide and excrement of which it was composed. The chthonic[1] gravity of his presence exerted a tremendous pressure on the room, so that the blood pounded in my ears as if we had been precipitated to the bottom of the sea, beneath the waves that pounded against the shore.

I held my life in my hands amongst those keys and, in a moment, would place it between his well-manicured fingers. The evidence of that bloody chamber had showed me I could expect no mercy. Yet, when he raised his head and stared at me with his blind, shuttered eyes as though he did not recognize me, I felt a terrified pity for him, for this man who lived in such strange, secret places that, if I loved him enough to follow him, I should have to die.

The atrocious loneliness of that monster!

The monocle had fallen from his face. His curling mane was disordered, as if he had run his hands through it in his distraction. I saw how he had lost his impassivity and was now filled with suppressed excitement. The hand he stretched out for those counters in his game of love and death shook a little; the face that turned towards me contained a sombre delirium that seemed to me compounded of a ghastly, yes, shame but also of a terrible, guilty joy as he slowly ascertained how I had sinned.

That tell-tale stain had resolved itself into a mark the shape and brilliance of the heart on a playing card. He disengaged the key from the ring and looked at it for a while, solitary, brooding.

"It is the key that leads to the kingdom of the unimaginable," he said. His voice was low and had in it

the timbre of certain great cathedral organs that seem, when they are played, to be conversing with God.

I could not restrain a sob.

"Oh, my love, my little love who brought me a white gift of music," he said, almost as if grieving. "My little love, you'll never know how much I hate daylight!" Then he sharply ordered: "Kneel!"

I knelt before him and he pressed the key lightly to my forehead, held it there for a moment. I felt a faint tingling of the skin and, when I involuntarily glanced at myself in the mirror, I saw the heart-shaped stain had transferred itself to my forehead, to the space between the eyebrows, like the caste mark of a brahmin woman. Or the mark of Cain. And now the key gleamed as freshly as if it had just been cut. He clipped it back on the ring, emitting that same, heavy sigh as he had done when I said that I would marry him.

"My virgin of the arpeggios, prepare yourself for martyrdom."

"What form shall it take?" I said.

"Decapitation," he whispered, almost voluptuously. "Go and bathe yourself; put on that white dress you wore to hear *Tristan* and the necklace that prefigures your end. And I shall take myself off to the armoury, my dear, to sharpen my great-grandfather's ceremonial sword."

"The servants?"

"We shall have absolute privacy for our last rites; I have already dismissed them. If you look out of the window you can see them going to the mainland."

It was now the full, pale light of morning; the weather was grey, indeterminate, the sea had an oily, sinister look, a gloomy day on which to die. Along the causeway I could see trouping every maid and scullion, every pot-boy and pan-scourer, valet, laundress and vassal who worked in that great house, most on foot, a few on bicycles. The faceless housekeeper trudged along with a great basket in which, I guessed, she'd stowed as much as she could ransack from the larder. The Marquis must have given the chauffeur leave to borrow the motor for the day, for it went last of all, at a stately pace, as though the procession were a cortège and the car already bore my coffin to the mainland for burial.

But I knew no good Breton earth would cover me, like a last, faithful lover; I had another fate.

---

[1]    *chthonic*  Dwelling below the earth's surface.

"I have given them all a day's holiday, to celebrate our wedding," he said. And smiled.

However hard I stared at the receding company, I could see no sign of Jean-Yves, our latest servant, hired but the preceding morning.

"Go, now. Bathe yourself; dress yourself. The lustratory ritual and the ceremonial robing; after that, the sacrifice. Wait in the music room until I telephone for you. No, my dear!" And he smiled, as I started, recalling the line was dead. "One may call inside the castle just as much as one pleases; but, outside—never."

I scrubbed my forehead with the nail brush as I had scrubbed the key but this red mark would not go away, either, no matter what I did, and I knew I should wear it until I died, though that would not be long. Then I went to my dressing room and put on that white muslin shift, costume of a victim of an auto-da-fe,[1] he had bought me to listen to the Liebestod in. Twelve young women combed out twelve listless sheaves of brown hair in the mirrors; soon, there would be none. The mass of lilies that surrounded me exhaled, now, the odour of their withering. They looked like the trumpets of the angels of death.

On the dressing table, coiled like a snake about to strike, lay the ruby choker.

Already almost lifeless, cold at heart, I descended the spiral staircase to the music room but there I found I had not been abandoned.

"I can be of some comfort to you," the boy said. "Though not much use."

We pushed the piano stool in front of the open window so that, for as long as I could, I would be able to smell the ancient, reconciling smell of the sea that, in time, will cleanse everything, scour the old bones white, wash away all the stains. The last little chambermaid had trotted along the causeway long ago and now the tide, fated as I, came tumbling in, the crisp wavelets splashing on the old stones.

"You do not deserve this," he said.

"Who can say what I deserve or no?" I said. "I've done nothing; but that may be sufficient reason for condemning me."

"You disobeyed him," he said. "That is sufficient reason for him to punish you."

"I only did what he knew I would."

"Like Eve," he said.

The telephone rang a shrill imperative. Let it ring. But my lover lifted me up and set me on my feet; I knew I must answer it. The receiver felt heavy as earth.

"The courtyard. Immediately."

My lover kissed me, he took my hand. He would come with me if I would lead him. Courage. When I thought of courage, I thought of my mother. Then I saw a muscle in my lover's face quiver.

"Hoofbeats!" he said.

I cast one last, desperate glance from the window and, like a miracle, I saw a horse and rider galloping at a vertiginous speed along the causeway, though the waves crashed, now, high as the horse's fetlocks. A rider, her black skirts tucked up around her waist so she could ride hard and fast, a crazy, magnificent horsewoman in widow's weeds.

As the telephone rang again.

"Am I to wait all morning?"

Every moment, my mother drew nearer.

"She will be too late," Jean-Yves said and yet he could not restrain a note of hope that, though it must be so, yet it might not be so.

The third, intransigent call.

"Shall I come up to heaven to fetch you down, Saint Cecilia? You wicked woman, do you wish me to compound my crimes by desecrating the marriage bed?"

So I must go to the courtyard where my husband waited in his London-tailored trousers and the shirt from Turnbull and Asser,[2] beside the mounting block, with, in his hand, the sword which his great-grandfather had presented to the little corporal, in token of surrender to the Republic, before he shot himself. The heavy sword, unsheathed, grey as that November morning, sharp as childbirth, mortal.

When my husband saw my companion, he observed: "Let the blind lead the blind, eh? But does even a youth as besotted as you are think she was truly blind to her own desires when she took my ring? Give it me back, whore."

The fires in the opal had all died down. I gladly slipped it from my finger and, even in that dolorous place, my heart was lighter for the lack of it. My hus-

---

[1] *auto-da-fe* Public burning of heretics by the Spanish Inquisition.

[2] *Turnbull and Asser* Exclusive British tailor.

band took it lovingly and lodged it on the tip of his little finger; it would go no further.

"It will serve me for a dozen more fiancées," he said. "To the block, woman. No—leave the boy; I shall deal with him later, utilizing a less exalted instrument than the one with which I do my wife the honour of her immolation, for do not fear that in death you will be divided."

Slowly, slowly, one foot before the other, I crossed the cobbles. The longer I dawdled over my execution, the more time it gave the avenging angel to descend …

"Don't loiter, girl! Do you think I shall lose appetite for the meal if you are so long about serving it? No; I shall grow hungrier, more ravenous with each moment, more cruel … Run to me, run! I have a place prepared for your exquisite corpse in my display of flesh!"

He raised the sword and cut bright segments from the air with it, but still I lingered although my hopes, so recently raised, now began to flag. If she is not here by now, her horse must have stumbled on the causeway, have plunged into the sea … One thing only made me glad; that my lover would not see me die.

My husband laid my branded forehead on the stone and, as he had done once before, twisted my hair into a rope and drew it away from my neck.

"Such a pretty neck," he said with what seemed to be a genuine, retrospective tenderness. "A neck like the stem of a young plant."

I felt the silken bristle of his beard and the wet touch of his lips as he kissed my nape. And, once again, of my apparel I must retain only my gems; the sharp blade ripped my dress in two and it fell from me. A little green moss, growing in the crevices of the mounting block, would be the last thing I should see in all the world.

The whizz of that heavy sword.

And—a great battering and pounding at the gate, the jangling of the bell, the frenzied neighing of a horse! The unholy silence of the place shattered in an instant. The blade did *not* descend, the necklace did *not* sever, my head did *not* roll. For, for an instant, the beast wavered in his stroke, a sufficient split second of astonished indecision to let me spring upright and dart to the assistance of my lover as he struggled sightlessly with the great bolts that kept her out.

The Marquis stood transfixed, utterly dazed, at a loss. It must have been as if he had been watching his beloved *Tristan* for the twelfth, the thirteenth time and Tristan stirred, then leapt from his bier in the last act, announced in a jaunty aria interposed from Verdi[1] that bygones were bygones, crying over spilt milk did nobody any good and, as for himself, he proposed to live happily ever after. The puppet master, open-mouthed, wide-eyed, impotent at the last, saw his dolls break free of their strings, abandon the rituals he had ordained for them since time began and start to live for themselves; the king, aghast, witnesses the revolt of his pawns.

You never saw such a wild thing as my mother, her hat seized by the winds and blown out to sea so that her hair was her white mane, her black lisle legs exposed to the thigh, her skirts tucked round her waist, one hand on the reins of the rearing horse while the other clasped my father's service revolver and, behind her, the breakers of the savage, indifferent sea, like the witnesses of a furious justice. And my husband stood stock-still, as if she had been Medusa,[2] the sword still raised over his head as in those clockwork tableaux of Bluebeard that you see in glass cases at fairs.

And then it was as though a curious child pushed his centime into the slot and set all in motion. The heavy, bearded figure roared out aloud, braying with fury, and, wielding the honourable sword as if it were a matter of death or glory, charged us, all three.

On her eighteenth birthday, my mother had disposed of a man-eating tiger that had ravaged the villages in the hills north of Hanoi. Now, without a moment's hesitation, she raised my father's gun, took aim and put a single, irreproachable bullet through my husband's head.

We lead a quiet life, the three of us. I inherited, of course, enormous wealth but we have given most of it away to various charities. The castle is now a school for the blind, though I pray that the children who live there are not haunted by any sad ghosts looking for, crying for, the husband who will never return to the bloody chamber, the contents of which are buried or burned,

[1]  *Verdi*  Italian opera composer Guiseppe Verdi (1813–1901).

[2]  *Medusa*  Powerful female from Greek myth, a look at whose face would turn one to stone.

the door sealed.

I felt I had a right to retain sufficient funds to start a little music school here, on the outskirts of Paris, and we do well enough. Sometimes we can even afford to go to the Opera, though never to sit in a box, of course. We know we are the source of many whisperings and much gossip but the three of us know the truth of it and mere chatter can never harm us. I can only bless the—what shall I call it?—the *maternal telepathy* that sent my mother running headlong from the telephone to the station after I had called her, that night. I never heard you cry before, she said, by way of explanation. Not when you were happy. And who ever cried because of gold bath taps?

The night train, the one I had taken; she lay in her berth, sleepless as I had been. When she could not find a taxi at that lonely halt, she borrowed old Dobbin from a bemused farmer, for some internal urgency told her

that she must reach me before the incoming tide sealed me away from her for ever. My poor old nurse, left scandalized at home—what? interrupt milord on his honeymoon?—she died soon after. She had taken so much secret pleasure in the fact that her little girl had become a marquise; and now here I was, scarcely a penny the richer, widowed at seventeen in the most dubious circumstances and busily engaged in setting up house with a piano-tuner. Poor thing, she passed away in a sorry state of disillusion! But I do believe my mother loves him as much as I do.

No paint nor powder, no matter how thick or white, can mask that red mark on my forehead; I am glad he cannot see it—not for fear of his revulsion, since I know he sees me clearly with his heart—but, because it spares my shame.

—1979

# JOHN CLEESE AND GRAHAM CHAPMAN
## 1939 – , and 1941 – 1989

Graham Chapman and John Cleese were the founders of the influential British comedy troupe Monty Python's Flying Circus. Their work with fellow Pythons Michael Palin (1943–), Eric Idle (1943–), Terry Jones (1942–), and Terry Gilliam (1940–) attracted huge followings not just in Britain but also throughout the English-speaking world. In 2000, the British Film Institute named their television series, *Monty Python's Flying Circus*, number five in their listing of the top 100 greatest British television programs.

John Cleese was born on 27 October 1939 in Weston-Super-Mare, Somerset, England. He studied at Clifton College, Bristol, and then at Cambridge University's Downing College, where he completed a degree in law. He began working in comedy as part of the Cambridge Footlights Revue, an amateur theatrical club run by students. It was here that he met Graham Chapman.

Chapman was born in Leicester on 8 January 1941. As a schoolboy, he participated in school productions, including plays by Shakespeare and Gilbert and Sullivan, and revue shows. In 1959, he was admitted to Emmanuel College at Cambridge University, where he studied medicine. He eventually qualified as a doctor at St. Bartholomew's Hospital Medical College, London.

Like Cleese, Chapman joined the Cambridge Footlights Revue and toured to New Zealand and New York. Upon returning in 1965, Cleese and Chapman wrote and performed in various British radio and television comedy series, including *The Dick Emery Show* (1965–84), *Doctor in the House* (1969–70), *At Last the 1948 Show* (1967), and *I'm Sorry, I'll Read That Again* (1964–72). When the two were hired to write for *The Frost Report* (1966–67), a BBC comedy/variety series, they were introduced to Eric Idle, Terry Jones, and Michael Palin. It was here that the future colleagues developed their trademark comedy style.

In 1969, Chapman and Cleese were offered their own television series. Their partnership was not an easy one; Chapman had developed a drinking problem, and Cleese found himself bearing most of the burden of the show. As a result, Cleese invited Palin, Idle, Jones, and Terry Gilliam (an American animator he had met while in New York) to work on the show, and the Monty Python troupe was born. Their television show, *Monty Python's Flying Circus,* ran between 1969 and 1974. The show's humor was quirky and irreverent, featuring cartoonish authority figures, strange satirical takes on the idiosyncrasies of British life, and frequent references to philosophers, literary figures, and famous works of art.

The troupe produced 45 episodes of *Monty Python's Flying Circus*, in four series. They also made five films: *And Now for Something Completely Different* (1971), a collection of re-filmed sketches from the television show; *Monty Python and the Holy Grail* (1974), a spoof of the Arthurian legends; *Monty Python's Life of Brian* (1979), a controversial send-up of organized religion and epic Bible movies; *Monty Python Live at the Hollywood Bowl* (1982), a live film of a public performance; and *Monty Python's The Meaning of Life* (1983), a darkly comic philosophical meditation.

Cleese left the show after its third series, unhappy with the strain of working with the alcoholic Chapman. He went on to co-write and star as Basil Fawlty in the very popular television series *Fawlty Towers* and to continue making films, most notably *A Fish Called Wanda* (1988), one of the most financially successful British films in history. Graham Chapman's career faltered after Monty Python. He gave up drinking in 1977, but his only solo film project, *Yellowbeard* (1983), suffered both critically and commercially. In late 1988, Chapman was diagnosed with throat cancer, which quickly spread to his spine. He died on 4 October 1989.

⌘⌘⌘

## from *Monty Python's Flying Circus*

### DEAD PARROT SKETCH[1]

#### THE CAST:

PRALINE: John Cleese
SHOPKEEPER: Michael Palin
PORTER: Terry Jones

PRALINE.   Hello, I wish to register a complaint. ... Hello? Miss?

SHOPKEEPER.   What do you mean, miss?

PRALINE.   Oh, I'm sorry, I have a cold. I wish to make a
5    complaint.

SHOPKEEPER.   Sorry, we're closing for lunch.

PRALINE.   Never mind that my lad, I wish to complain about a parrot what I purchased not half an hour ago from this very boutique.

10  SHOPKEEPER.  Oh yes, the Norwegian Blue. What's wrong with it?

PRALINE.   I'll tell you what's wrong with it. It's dead, that's what's wrong with it.

SHOPKEEPER.   No, no it's resting look!

15  PRALINE.   Look my lad, I know a dead parrot when I see one and I'm looking at one right now.

SHOPKEEPER.   No, no sir, it's not dead. It's resting.

PRALINE.   Resting?

SHOPKEEPER.   Yeah, remarkable bird the Norwegian
20    Blue, beautiful plumage, innit?[2]

PRALINE.   The plumage don't enter into it—it's stone dead.

SHOPKEEPER.   No, no—it's just resting.

PRALINE.   All right then, if it's resting I'll wake it up.
25    (*Shouts in into cage.*) Hello Polly! I've got a nice cuttlefish for you when you wake up, Polly Parrot!

SHOPKEEPER.   (*Jogging cage.*) There it moved.

PRALINE.   No he didn't. That was you pushing the cage.

SHOPKEEPER.   I did not.

30  PRALINE.   Yes, you did. (*Takes parrot out of cage, shouts.*) Hello Polly, Polly. (*Bangs it against the counter.*) Polly

Parrot, wake up. Polly. (*Throws it in the air and it lands on the floor.*) Now that's what I call a dead parrot.

SHOPKEEPER.   No, no it's stunned.

35  PRALINE.   Look my lad, I've had just about enough of this. That parrot is definitely deceased. And when I bought it not half an hour ago, you assured me that its lack of movement was due to it being tired and shagged out after a long squawk.

40  SHOPKEEPER.   It's probably pining for the fjords.

PRALINE.   Pining for the fjords, what kind of talk is that? Look, why did it fall flat on its back the moment I got it home?

SHOPKEEPER.   The Norwegian Blue prefers kipping[3] on
45    its back. Beautiful bird, lovely plumage.

PRALINE.   Look, I took the liberty of examining the parrot, and I discovered that the only reason that it had been sitting on its perch in the first place was that it had been nailed there.

50  SHOPKEEPER.   Well of course it was nailed there. Otherwise it would muscle up to those bars and voom.

PRALINE.   Look matey (*Picks up parrot.*) this parrot wouldn't go voom if I put four thousand volts through it. It's bleeding demised.

55  SHOPKEEPER.   It's not. It's pining.

PRALINE.   It's not pining, it's passed on. This parrot is no more. It has ceased to be. It's expired and gone to meet its maker. This is a late parrot. It's a stiff. Bereft of life, it rests in peace. If you hadn't nailed it to the perch, it
60    would be pushing up the daisies. It's rung down the curtain and joined the choir invisible. This is an ex-parrot.

SHOPKEEPER.   Well I'd better replace it then.

PRALINE.   (*To camera.*) If you want to get anything done
65    in this country you've got to complain till you're blue in the mouth.

SHOPKEEPER.   Sorry guv, we're right outa parrots.

PRALINE.   I see. I see. I get the picture.

SHOPKEEPER.   I've got a slug.

70  PRALINE.   Does it talk?

SHOPKEEPER.   Not really, no.

PRALINE.   Well, it's scarcely a replacement, then is it?

---

[1]  *Dead Parrot Sketch*   From *Monty Python's Flying Circus*, Episode 9.

[2]  *innit*   I.e., Isn't it.

[3]  *kipping*   Sleeping.

SHOPKEEPER.   Listen, I'll tell you what, (*Handing over a card.*) tell you what, if you go to my brother's pet shop in Bolton[1] he'll replace your parrot for you.

PRALINE.   Bolton eh?

SHOPKEEPER.   Yeah.

PRALINE.   All right.

(*He leaves, holding the parrot.*
*Caption: "A similar pet shop in Bolton, Lancs"*[2]
*Close-up of sign on door reading: "Similar Pet Shops Ltd."*
*Pull back from sign to see same pet shop. Shopkeeper now has a moustache. Praline walks into the shop. He looks around with interest, noticing the empty parrot cage on the floor.*)

PRALINE.   Er, excuse me. This is Bolton, is it?

SHOPKEEPER.   No, no it's, er, Ipswich.[3]

PRALINE.   (*To camera,*) That's Inter-City Rail for you.

(*Leaves.*)
(*Man in porter's outfit standing at complaints desk for railways. Praline approaches.*)

PRALINE.   I wish to make a complaint.

PORTER.   I don't have to do this, you know.

PRALINE.   I beg your pardon?

PORTER.   I'm a qualified brain surgeon. I only do this because I like being my own boss.

PRALINE.   Er, excuse me, this is irrelevant, isn't it?

PORTER.   Oh yeah, it's not easy to pad these out in thirty minutes.

PRALINE.   Well I wish to make a complaint. I got on to the Bolton train and found myself deposited here in Ipswich.

PORTER.   No, this is Bolton.

PRALINE.   (*To camera.*) The pet shop owner's brother was lying.

PORTER.   Well you can't blame British Rail for that.

PRALINE.   If this is Bolton, I shall return to the pet shop.

(*Caption: "A Little Later Ltd"*
*Praline walks into the shop again.*)

PRALINE.   I understand this *is* Bolton.

SHOPKEEPER.   Yes.

PRALINE.   Well, you told me it was Ipswich.

SHOPKEEPER.   It was a pun.

PRALINE.   A pun?

SHOPKEEPER.   No, no, not a pun, no. What's the other thing which reads the same backwards as forwards?

PRALINE.   A palindrome?

SHOPKEEPER.   Yes, yes.

PRALINE.   It's not a palindrome. The palindrome of Bolton would be Notlob. It don't work.

SHOPKEEPER.   Look, what do you want?

PRALINE.   No, I'm sorry, I'm not prepared to pursue my line of enquiry any further as I think this is getting too silly.

—1969

## PET CONVERSION[4]

### THE CAST:

MAN: John Cleese
SHOPKEEPER: Michael Palin
HARRY: Graham Chapman

(*Superimposed caption: A Pet Shop Somewhere Near Melton Mowbray.*[5])

MAN.   Good morning, I'd like to buy a cat.

SHOPKEEPER.   Certainly sir. I've got a lovely terrier. (*Indicates a box on the counter.*)

MAN.   (*Glancing in box.*) No, I want a cat really.

SHOPKEEPER.   (*Taking box off counter and then putting it back on counter as if it is a different box.*) Oh yeah, how about that?

MAN.   (*Looking in box.*) No, that's the terrier.

SHOPKEEPER.   Well, it's as near as dammit.

MAN.   Well what do you mean? I want a cat.

SHOPKEEPER.   Listen, tell you what. I'll file its legs down a bit, take its snout out, stick a few wires through its cheeks. There you are, a lovely pussy cat.

MAN.   It's not a proper cat.

SHOPKEEPER.   What do you mean?

---

[1] *Bolton*   Town near Manchester in northern England.

[2] *Lancs*   Lancashire, a county in the north of England.

[3] *Ipswich*   County town in East Anglia, in the east of England, 390 kilometers (243 miles) from Bolton.

[4] *Pet Conversion*   Featured in *Monty Python's Flying Circus*, Episode 10.

[5] *Melton Mowbray*   Town in county Leicestershire.

MAN. Well it wouldn't miaow.

SHOPKEEPER. Well it would howl a bit.

MAN. No, no, no, no. Er, have you got a parrot?

20 SHOPKEEPER. No, It's afraid not actually guv, we're fresh out of parrots. I'll tell you what though … I'll lop its back legs off, make good, strip the fur, stick a couple of wings on and staple on a beak of your own choice. (*Taking small box and rattling it.*) No problem. Lovely parrot.

25 MAN. And how long would that take?

SHOPKEEPER. Oh, let me see … er, stripping the fur off, no legs … (*Calling.*) Harry … can you do a parrot job on this terrier straight away?

HARRY. (*Off screen.*) No, I'm still putting a tuck in the
30 Airedale, and then I got the frogs to let out.

SHOPKEEPER. Friday?

MAN. No I need it for tomorrow. It's a present.

SHOPKEEPER. Oh dear, it's a long job. You see parrot conversion … Tell you what though, for free, terriers
35 make lovely fish. I mean I could do that for you straight away. Legs off, fins on, stick a little pipe through the back of its neck so it can breathe, bit of gold paint, make good …

MAN. You'd need a very big tank.

40 SHOPKEEPER. It's a great conversation piece.

MAN. Yes, all right, all right … but, er, only if I can watch.

—1969

DIRTY HUNGARIAN PHRASEBOOK[1]

THE CAST:

HUNGARIAN: John Cleese
TOBACCONIST: Terry Jones
POLICEMAN: Graham Chapman

(*Set: A tobacconist's shop.*)
(*Roller caption: In 1970, the British Empire lay in ruins, and foreign nationalists frequented the streets—many of them Hungarians [not the streets—the foreign nationals]. Anyway, many of these Hungarians went into tobacconists' shops to buy cigarettes … *)

(*Enter Hungarian gentleman with phrase book. He is looking for the right phrase.*)

HUNGARIAN. I will not buy this record. It is scratched.

TOBACCONIST. Sorry?

HUNGARIAN. I will not buy this record. It is scratched.

TOBACCONIST. No, no, no. This … tobacconist's.

5 HUNGARIAN. Ah! I will not buy this tobacconist's. It is scratched.

TOBACCONIST. No, no, no … tobacco … er, cigarettes?

HUNGARIAN. Yes, cigarettes. My hovercraft is full of eels.

10 TOBACCONIST. What?

HUNGARIAN. (*Miming matches.*) My hovercraft is full of eels.

TOBACCONIST. Matches, matches?

HUNGARIAN. Yah, yah. (*He takes cigarettes and matches
15 and pulls out loose change; he consults his book.*) Er, do you want … do you want to come back to my place, bouncy bouncy?

TOBACCONIST. I don't think you're using that thing right.

20 HUNGARIAN. You great pouf.[2]

TOBACCONIST. That'll be six and six,[3] please.

HUNGARIAN. If I said you had a beautiful body, would you hold it against me? I am no longer infected.

TOBACCONIST. (*Miming that he wants to see the book; he
25 takes the book.*) It costs six and six … (*Mumbling as he searches*) Costs six and six … Here we are … Yandelvayasna grldenwi stravenka.

(*Hungarian hits him between the eyes. Policeman walking along street suddenly stops and puts his hand to his ear. He starts running down the street, round corner and down another street, round yet another corner and down another street into the shop.*)

POLICEMAN. What's going on here then?

HUNGARIAN. (*Opening book and pointing at
30 Tobacconist.*) You have beautiful thighs.

POLICEMAN. What?

TOBACCONIST. He hit me.

HUNGARIAN. Drop your panties, Sir William, I cannot wait till lunchtime.

---

[1] *Dirty Hungarian Phrasebook* Featured in *Monty Python's Flying Circus*, Episode 25.

[2] *pouf* Derogatory British slang for gay man.

[3] *six and six* Six shillings and sixpence.

35 POLICEMAN.   Right! (*Grabs him and drags him out.*)
HUNGARIAN.   My nipples explode with delight.

(*Cut to a courtroom.*)

CAST:
    JUDGE: Terry Jones
    CLERK: Eric Idle
    LAWYER: John Cleese
    POLICEMAN: Graham Chapman (still)
    YAHLT: Michael Palin

CLERK.   Call Alexander Yahlt!
VOICES.   Call Alexander Yahlt. Call Alexander Yahlt. Call Alexander Yahlt.

(*They do this three times, finishing with harmony.*)

40 MAGISTRATE.   Oh, shut up.

(*Alexander Yahlt enters.  He is not Hungarian but an ordinary man in a mac.*)[1]

CLERK.   (*To publisher.*) You are Alexander Yahlt?
YAHLT.   (*Derek Nimmo's[2] voice dubbed on.*) Oh, I am.
CLERK.   Skip the impersonations. You are Alexander Yahlt?
45 YAHLT.   (*Normal voice.*) I am.
CLERK.   You are hereby charged that on the 28th day of May 1970 you did wilfully, unlawfully, and with malice aforethought publish an alleged English-Hungarian phrase book with intent to cause a breach of the peace.
50 How do you plead?
YAHLT.   Not guilty.
CLERK.   You live at 46, Horton Terrace?
YAHLT.   I do live at 46 Horton Terrace.
CLERK.   You are the director of a publishing company?
55 YAHLT.   I am the director of a publishing company.
CLERK.   Your company publishes phrasebooks?
YAHLT.   My company does publish phrasebooks.
CLERK.   You did say 46, Horton Terrace did you?
YAHLT.   Yes.

(*He claps his hand to his mouth; gong sounds—general applause.*)

60 CLERK.   Ha, ha, ha, I got him.
MAGISTRATE.   Get on with it! Get on with it!
CLERK.   Yes, m'lud,[3] on the 28th of May you published this phrasebook.
YAHLT.   I did.
65 CLERK.   I quote one example. The Hungarian phrase meaning "Can you direct me to the station?" is translated by the English phrase, "please fondle my bum."
YAHLT.   I wish to plead incompetence.

(*The Policeman stands up.*)

POLICEMAN.   Please may I ask for an adjournment,
70 m'lud?
MAGISTRATE.   An adjournment? Certainly not.

(*The Policeman sits down; there is a loud raspberry;[4] the policeman goes bright red.*)

Why on earth didn't you say *why* you wanted an adjournment?
POLICEMAN.   I didn't know an acceptable legal phrase,
75 m'lud.

(*Cut to stock film of Women's Institute[5] applauding.  Cut back to the magistrate.*)

MAGISTRATE.   If there's any more stock film of women applauding I shall clear the court.
—1970

SPAM [6]

THE CAST:
    MR. BUN: Eric Idle
    MRS. BUN: Graham Chapman
    WAITRESS: Terry Jones
    HUNGARIAN: John Cleese

---

[1]   *mac*  I.e., mackintosh, a raincoat.

[2]   *Derek Nimmo*  British comedic actor and BBC Radio game show panelist who had a distinctive, aristocratic voice.

[3]   *m'lud*  I.e., my lord.

[4]   *raspberry*  Rude sound, generally made with the lips and tongue. Here, denotes flatulence.

[5]   *Women's Institute*  Organization for women in England and Wales.

[6]   *Spam*  Featured in *Monty Python's Flying Circus*, Episode 25.

HISTORIAN: Michael Palin

(*Scene: A cafe. All the customers are Vikings. Mr. and Mrs. Bun enter—downwards, on wires.*)

MR. BUN.  Morning.

WAITRESS.  Morning.

MR. BUN.  What have you got, then?

WAITRESS.  Well there's egg and bacon; egg sausage and
5  bacon; egg and spam; egg, bacon and spam; egg, bacon,
sausage and spam; spam, bacon, sausage and spam;
spam, egg, spam, spam, bacon and spam; spam, spam,
spam, egg and spam; spam, spam, spam, spam, spam,
spam, baked beans, spam, spam, spam, and spam; or
10  lobster thermidor aux crevettes with a mornay sauce
garnished with truffle pâté, brandy and a fried egg on
top and spam.

MRS. BUN.  Have you got anything without spam in it?

WAITRESS.  Well, there's spam, egg, sausage and spam.
15  That's not got *much* spam in it.

MRS. BUN.  I don't want *any* spam.

MR. BUN.  Why can't she have egg, bacon, spam and
sausage?

MRS. BUN.  That's got spam in it!
20  MR. BUN.  Not as much as spam, egg, sausage and spam.

MRS. BUN.  Look, could I have egg, bacon, spam and
sausage without the spam.

WAITRESS.  Uuuuuugggggh!

MRS. BUN.  What do you mean uuugggh! I don't like
25  spam.

VIKINGS.  (*Singing.*) Spam, spam, spam, spam, spam …
spam, spam, spam, spam … lovely spam, wonderful
spam …

(*Brief stock shot of a Viking ship.*)

WAITRESS.  Shut up! Shut up! Shut up! You can't have
30  egg, bacon, spam and sausage without the spam.

MRS. BUN.  (*Shrieks.*) I don't like spam!

MR. BUN.  Don't make a fuss, dear. I'll have your spam.
I love it. I'm having spam, spam, spam, spam, spam …

VIKINGS.  (*Singing.*) Spam, spam, spam, spam …
35  MR. BUN.  … baked beans, spam, spam and spam.

WAITRESS.  Baked beans are off.

MR. BUN.  Well can I have spam instead?

WAITRESS.  You mean spam, spam, spam, spam, spam,
spam, spam, spam, spam, spam?
40  VIKINGS.  (*Still singing.*) Spam, spam, spam, spam …
(*etc.*)

MR. BUN.  Yes.

WAITRESS.  Arrggh!

VIKINGS.  … lovely spam, wonderful, spam.
45  WAITRESS.  Shut up! Shut up!

(*The Vikings shut up momentarily. Enter the Hungarian.*)

HUNGARIAN.  Great boobies, honeybun, my lower
intestine is full of spam, egg, spam, bacon, spam,
tomato, spam …

VIKINGS.  (*Starting up again.*) Spam, spam, spam, spam …
50  WAITRESS.  Shut up.

(*A policeman rushes in and bundles the Hungarian out.*)

HUNGARIAN.  My nipples explode …

(*Cut to a historian. Superimposed caption: "A HISTORIAN."*)

HISTORIAN.  Another great Viking victory was at the
Green Midget café at Bromley. Once again the Viking
strategy was the same. They sailed from these fiords here
55  (*indicating map with arrows on it*), assembled at
Trondheim and waited for the strong north-easterly
winds to blow their oaken galleys to England whence
they sailed on May 23rd. Once in Bromley they
assembled at the Green Midget café and spam selecting
60  a spam particular spam item from the spam menu
would spam, spam, spam, spam, spam …

(*The backdrop behind him rises to reveal the café again. The Vikings start singing again and the historian conducts them.*)

VIKINGS.  (*Singing.*) Spam, spam, spam, spam, spam,
lovely spam, wonderful spam. Lovely spam, wonderful
spam …

(*Mr. and Mrs. Bun rise slowly in the air.*)
—1970

# SALMAN RUSHDIE
## b. 1947

Salman Rushdie has become recognized as one of the key figures of postmodernist fiction, and of postcolonial writing of all sorts. He has been honored with many prestigious awards and has helped to shape an entire generation of Indian writing in English. But his achievements were for many years overshadowed by a furor created by the violent opposition of Islamic fundamentalists to his novel, *The Satanic Verses* (1988); this became one of the major artistic and religious controversies of the twentieth century.

Born Ahmed Salman Rushdie to devout Muslim parents in Bombay (now Mumbai), India, he was educated at the Cathedral School in Bombay, and then moved to England at age 14, where he

attended Rugby School, one of England's most prestigious boarding schools. It was far from an entirely pleasant experience; Rushdie has recounted how he was the object of racially motivated attacks by white students. He moved back to Bombay after graduating, but returned to England to attend Cambridge University's King's College, where he studied history and joined a student theater group. After earning his BA in 1968, Rushdie worked in television in Pakistan for several years, and then returned to England to become a copywriter for an advertising agency.

In his first novel, *Grimus* (1975), Rushdie concocted a literary mixture of fantasy and realism of a sort that would become characteristic of his work. An adaptation of an old Sufi poem, *Grimus* is a fantastical work that borders on science fiction. It met with little success. But his next novel, *Midnight's Children* (1981), catapulted Rushdie to the top of the English-language literary world. *Midnight's Children* presents the life of its protagonist, a pickle-factory worker named Saleem Sinai who was born (like Rushdie) at the time of India's independence from Britain, as an allegory for the history of post-colonial India. The tone of the novel again partakes both of realism and of fantasy—as its famous first sentence signals: "I was born in the city of Bombay ... once upon a time. No, that won't do, there's no getting away from the date: I was born in Doctor Narlikar's Nursing Home on August 15th, 1947." The novel was very much in tune with its age. In the literary world, this was the dawn of literary postmodernism, and writers of fiction were increasingly interested in self-conscious or ironic explorations of the play of illusion and reality. And in the world of literary theory and criticism, works on post-colonial themes were coming more and more to be considered central to the literature of the English-speaking world; from this angle too, *Midnight's Children* was of intense interest. In 1981 the novel won the prestigious Booker Prize for Fiction, and in 1993 it won the Booker of Bookers' Prize for the novel deemed to have been the best of all those awarded the Booker in the award's first twenty-five years.

His next work was a short novel, *Shame* (1983), in which Rushdie shifted his focus to neighboring Pakistan. His treatment of the rulers of Pakistan, particularly former Prime Minister Zulfikar Ali Bhutto and General Muhammad Zia-ul-Haq, explored the connection between shame and violence. This novel was also shortlisted for the Booker Prize.

In 1988 Rushdie published a novel that was to change the course of his life. Like *Midnight's Children* and *Shame*, *The Satanic Verses* was critically acclaimed (it won the Whitbread Novel Award in 1988), and like them it featured elements that hover between fantasy and reality. But to some it was altogether too real; the novel was condemned by a number of prominent Muslim leaders on the grounds that the book's unflattering portrayal of the prophet Mohammed was blasphemous; it was banned in eleven countries, and was the subject of violent protests. The controversy over the book escalated on 14 February 1989, when Iran's spiritual and political leader, the Ayatollah Ruhollah Khomeini, issued a *fatwa* (or legal pronouncement) calling for Rushdie's death. Ten days later Khomeini placed a $3 million (U.S.) bounty on Rushdie's head (the amount was doubled in 1997). Rushdie went into hiding, under the protection of British authorities. The Japanese translator of the book was murdered in Toyko in 1991. Other translators were attacked and harassed. In 1998 the Iranian government made a public pledge not to carry out the death sentence against Rushdie. Nevertheless, the *fatwa* still stands.

While in hiding, Rushdie published a children's book, *Haroun and the Sea of Stories* (1990), an allegory for India and Pakistan's dispute over the State of Kashmir. The book also contains harsh criticisms of literary censorship. He followed up with a book of essays, entitled *Imaginary Homelands: Essays and Criticism 1981–1991* (1991), from which the essay below is taken.

Rushdie's later work expands his artistic vision to treat the intersection of Indian culture with western cultures. In *The Moor's Last Sigh* (1995) Rushdie explores the connection between descendants of Portuguese settlers and their Indian neighbors. The novel won the Whitbread Novel Award in 1995. *The Ground Beneath Her Feet* (1999), a variation on the Greek Orpheus myth, deals with the influence of American rock and roll music on Indian culture. His 2001 novel, *Fury*, is set in New York, and features a transplanted Bombay-born intellectual as its protagonist. *Shalimar the Clown* (2005) returns to the Indian subcontinent for its subject matter, telling the story of two Kashmiri villages whose inhabitants get caught up in a cycle of escalating violence.

Rushdie is Honorary Professor in the Humanities at the Massachusetts Institute of Technology (MIT), and a Fellow of Britain's Royal Society of Literature. He continues to live in hiding in New York City.

⌘ ⌘ ⌘

### Is Nothing Sacred?[1]

I grew up kissing books and bread. In our house, whenever anyone dropped a book or let fall a chapati or a "slice," which was our word for a triangle of buttered leavened bread, the fallen object was required not only to be picked up but also kissed, by way of apology for the act of clumsy disrespect. I was as careless and butter-fingered as any child and, accordingly, during my childhood years, I kissed a large number of "slices" and also my fair share of books.

Devout households in India often contained, and still contain, persons in the habit of kissing holy books. But we kissed everything. We kissed dictionaries and atlases. We kissed Enid Blyton novels and Superman comics. If I'd ever dropped the telephone directory I'd probably have kissed that, too.

All this happened before I had ever kissed a girl. In fact it would almost be true, true enough for a fiction writer, anyhow, to say that once I started kissing girls, my activities with regard to bread and books lost some of their special excitement. But one never forgets one's first loves.

[1] *Is Nothing Sacred?*   This essay was the Herbert Read Memorial Lecture for 1990, delivered at the Institute of Contemporary Arts in London on 6 February 1990. It was read by playwright Harold Pinter. Rushdie himself was for many years prevented from making public appearances by the widely publicized call for his death issued by Iran's Ayatollah Khomeini.

Bread and books: food for the body and food for the soul—what could be more worthy of our respect, and even love?

It has always been a shock to me to meet people for whom books simply do not matter, and people who are scornful of the act of reading, let alone writing. It is perhaps always astonishing to learn that your beloved is not as attractive to others as she is to you. My most beloved books have been fictions, and in the last twelve months I have been obliged to accept that for many millions of human beings, these books are entirely without attraction or value. We have been witnessing an attack upon a particular work of fiction that is also an attack upon the very ideas of the novel form, an attack of such bewildering ferocity that it has become necessary to restate what is most precious about the art of literature—to answer the attack, not by an attack, but by a declaration of love.

Love can lead to devotion, but the devotion of the lover is unlike that of the True Believer in that it is not militant. I may be surprised—even shocked—to find that you do not feel as I do about a given book or work of art or even person; I may very well attempt to change your mind; but I will finally accept that your tastes, your loves, are your business and not mine. The True Believer knows no such restraints. The True Believer knows that he is simply right, and you are wrong. He will seek to convert you, even by force, and if he cannot he will, at the very least, despise you for your unbelief.

Love need not be blind. Faith must, ultimately, be a leap in the dark.

The title of this lecture is a question usually asked, in tones of horror, when some personage or idea or value or place held dear by the questioner is treated to a dose of iconoclasm. White cricket balls for night cricket? Female priests? A Japanese takeover of Rolls-Royce cars? *Is nothing sacred?*

Until recently, however, it was a question to which I thought I knew the answer. The answer was No.

No, nothing is sacred in and of itself, I would have said. Ideas, texts, even people can be made sacred—the word is from the Latin *sacrare,* "to set apart as holy"— but even though such entities, once their sacredness is established, seek to proclaim and to preserve their own

absoluteness, their inviolability, the act of making sacred is in truth an event in history. It is the product of the many and complex pressures of the time in which the act occurs. And events in history must always be subject to questioning, deconstruction, even to declarations of their obsolescence. To respect the sacred is to be paralysed by it. The idea of the sacred is quite simply one of the most conservative notions in any culture, because it seeks to turn other ideas—Uncertainty, Progress, Change—into crimes.

To take only one such declaration of obsolescence: I would have described myself as living in the aftermath of the death of God. On the subject of the death of God, the American novelist and critic William H. Gass had this to say, as recently as 1984:

> The death of god represents not only the realization that gods have never existed, but the contention that such a belief is no longer even irrationally possible: that neither reason nor the taste and temper of the times condone it. The belief lingers on, of course, but it does so like astrology or a faith in a flat earth.

I have some difficulty with the uncompromising bluntness of this obituary notice. It has always been clear to me that God is unlike human beings in that it can die, so to speak, in parts. In other parts, for example India, God continues to flourish, in literally thousands of forms. So that if I speak of living after this death, I am speaking in a limited, personal sense—my sense of God ceased to exist long ago, and as a result I was drawn towards the great creative possibilities offered by surrealism, modernism and their successors, those philosophies and aesthetics born of the realization that, as Karl Marx said, "all that is solid melts into air."

It did not seem to me, however, that my ungodliness, or rather my post-godliness, need necessarily bring me into conflict with belief. Indeed, one reason for my attempt to develop a form of fiction in which the miraculous might coexist with the mundane was precisely my acceptance that notions of the sacred and the profane both needed to be explored, as far as possible without pre-judgement, in any honest literary portrait of the way we are.

That is to say: the most secular of authors ought to be capable of presenting a sympathetic portrait of a devout believer. Or, to put it another way: I had never felt the need to totemize my lack of belief, and so make it something to go to war about.

Now, however, I find my entire world-picture under fire. And as I find myself obliged to defend the assumptions and processes of literature, which I had believed that all free men and women could take for granted, and for which all unfree men and women continue every day to struggle, so I am obliged to ask myself questions I admit to finding somewhat unnerving.

Do I, perhaps, find something sacred after all? Am I prepared to set aside as holy the idea of the absolute freedom of the imagination and alongside it my own notions of the World, the Text and the Good? Does this add up to what the apologists of religion have started calling "secular fundamentalism"? And if so, must I accept that this "secular fundamentalism" is as likely to lead to excesses, abuses and oppressions as the canons of religious faith?

A lecture in memory of Herbert Read is a highly appropriate occasion for such an exploration, and I am honoured to have been asked to deliver it. Herbert Read, one of the leading British advocates of the modernist and surrealist movements, was a distinguished representative of the cultural values closest to my heart. "Art is never transfixed," Read wrote. "Change is the condition of art remaining art." This principle is also mine. Art, too, is an event in history, subject to the historical process. But it is also *about* that process, and must constantly strive to find new forms to mirror an endlessly renewed world. No aesthetic can be a constant, except an aesthetic based on the idea of inconstancy, metamorphosis, or, to borrow a term from politics, "perpetual revolution."

The struggle between such ideas and the eternal, revealed truths of religion is dramatized this evening, as I hope I may be excused for pointing out, by my absence. I must apologize for this. I did, in fact, ask my admirable protectors how they would feel if I were to deliver my text in person. The answer was, more or less, "What have we done to deserve this?" With regret, I took the point.

It is an agony and a frustration not be able to re-enter my old life, not even for such a moment. However, I should like to thank Harold Pinter, through his own mouth, for standing in my place. Perhaps this event could be thought of as a form of secular revelation: a man receives a text by mysterious processes from Elsewhere—above? below? New Scotland Yard?[1]—and brings it out before the people, and recites …

More than twenty years ago, I stood packed in at the back of this theatre, listening to a lecture by Arthur Koestler.[2] He propounded the thesis that language, not territory, was the prime cause of aggression, because once language reached the level of sophistication at which it could express abstract concepts, it acquired the power of totemization; and once peoples had erected totems, they would go to war to defend them. (I ask pardon of Koestler's ghost. I am relying on an old memory, and that's an untrustworthy shoulder to lean on.)

In support of his theory, he told us about two tribes of monkeys living on, I think, one of the northern islands of Japan. The two tribes lived in close proximity in the woods near a certain stream, and subsisted, not unusually, on a diet of bananas. One of the tribes, however, had developed the curious habit of washing its bananas in the stream before eating them, while the other tribe continued to be non-banana-washers. And yet, said Koestler, the two tribes continued to live contentedly as neighbours, without quarrelling. And why was this? It was because their language was too primitive to permit them to totemize either the act of banana-washing or that of eating bananas unwashed. With a more sophisticated language at their disposal, both wet and dry bananas could have become the sacred objects at the heart of a religion, and then, look out!—Holy war.

A young man rose from the audience to ask Koestler a question. Perhaps the real reason why the two tribes did not fight, he suggested, was that there were enough bananas to go round. Koestler became extremely angry.

---

[1] *New Scotland Yard*  Headquarters for the metropolitan police force of Greater London.

[2] *Arthur Koestler*  Hungarian-born novelist (1905–83), political activist, and social philosopher, whose most famous work, *Darkness at Noon* (1940), depicts extremes of censorship and oppression under a Soviet-style Marxist dictatorship.

He refused to answer such a piece of Marxist claptrap. And, in a way, he was right. Koestler and his questioner were speaking different languages, and their languages were in conflict. Their disagreement could even be seen as the proof of Koestler's point. If he, Koestler, were to be considered the banana-washer and his questioner the dry-banana man, then their command of a language more complex than the Japanese monkeys' had indeed resulted in totemizations. Now each of them had a totem to defend: the primacy of language versus the primacy of economics: and dialogue therefore became impossible. They were at war.

Between religion and literature, as between politics and literature, there is a linguistically based dispute. But it is not a dispute of simple opposites. Because whereas religion seeks to privilege one language above all others, one set of values above all others, one text above all others, the novel has always been *about* the way in which different languages, values and narratives quarrel, and about the shifting relations between them, which are relations of power. The novel does not seek to establish a privileged language, but it insists upon the freedom to portray and analyse the struggle between the different contestants for such privileges.

Carlos Fuentes has called the novel "a privileged *arena.*" By this he does not mean that it is the kind of holy space which one must put off one's shoes to enter; it is not an arena to revere; it claims no special rights *except the right to be the stage upon which the great debates of society can be conducted.* "The novel," Fuentes writes, "is born from the very fact that we do not understand one another, because unitary, orthodox language has broken down. Quixote and Sancho, the Shandy brothers, Mr. and Mrs. Karenin:[1] their novels are the comedy (or the drama) of their misunderstandings. Impose a unitary language: you kill the novel, but you also kill the society."

He then poses the question I have been asking myself throughout my life as a writer: *Can the religious mentality survive outside of religious dogma and hierarchy?* Which is to say: Can art be the third principle that mediates between the material and spiritual worlds;

might it, by "swallowing" both worlds, offer us something new—something that might even be called a secular definition of transcendence?

I believe it can. I believe it must. And I believe that, at its best, it does.

What I mean by transcendence is that flight of the human spirit outside the confines of its material, physical existence which all of us, secular or religious, experience on at least a few occasions. Birth is a moment of transcendence which we spend our lives trying to understand. The exaltation of the act of love, the experience of joy and very possibly the moment of death are other such moments. The soaring quality of transcendence, the sense of being more than oneself, of being in some way joined to the whole of life, is by its nature short-lived. Not even the visionary or mystical experience ever lasts very long. It is for art to capture that experience, to offer it to, in the case of literature, its readers; to be, for a secular, materialist culture, some sort of replacement for what the love of god offers in the world of faith.

It is important that we understand how profoundly we all feel the needs that religion, down the ages, has satisfied. I would suggest that these needs are of three types: firstly, the need to be given an articulation of our half-glimpsed knowledge of exaltation, of awe, of wonder; life is an awesome experience, and religion helps us understand why life so often makes us feel small, by telling us what we are *smaller than;* and, contrariwise, because we also have a sense of being special, of being *chosen,* religion helps us by telling us what we have been chosen by, and what for. Secondly, we need answers to the unanswerable: How did we get here? How did "here" get here in the first place? Is this, this brief life, all there is? How can it be? What would be the point of that? And, thirdly, we need codes to live by, "rules for every damn thing." The idea of god is at once a repository for our awestruck wonderment at life and an answer to the great questions of existence, and a rule book, too. The soul needs all these explanations—not simply rational explanations, but explanations of the heart.

It is also important to understand how often the language of secular, rationalist materialism has failed to

---

[1]  *Quixote ... Karenin*  Characters from Cervantes's *Don Quixote,* Laurence Sterne's *Tristam Shandy,* and Tolstoy's *Anna Karenina,* respectively.

answer these needs. As we witness the death of communism in Central Europe, we cannot fail to observe the deep religious spirit with which so many of the makers of these revolutions are imbued, and we must concede that it is not only a particular political ideology that has failed, but the idea that men and women could ever define themselves in terms that exclude their spiritual needs.

It seems obvious, but relevant, to point out that in all the countries now moving towards freedom, art was repressed as viciously as was religion. That the Czech revolution began in the theatres and is led by a writer is proof that people's spiritual needs, more than their material needs, have driven the commissars from power. What appears plain is that it will be a very long time before the peoples of Europe will accept any ideology that claims to have a complete, totalized explanation of the world. Religious faith, profound as it is, must surely remain a private matter. This rejection of totalized explanations is the modern condition. And this is where the novel, the form created to discuss the fragmentation of truth, comes in. The film director Luis Buñuel used to say: "I would give my life for a man who is looking for the truth. But I would gladly kill a man who thinks he has found the truth." (This is what we used to call a joke, before killing people for their ideas returned to the agenda.) The elevation of the quest for the Grail over the Grail itself, the acceptance that all that is solid has melted into air, that reality and morality are not givens but imperfect human constructs, is the point from which fiction begins. This is what J.-F. Lyotard called, in 1979, *La Condition Postmoderne*. The challenge of literature is to start from this point, and still find a way of fulfilling our unaltered spiritual requirements.

*Moby Dick* meets that challenge by offering us a dark, almost Manichean vision[1] of a universe (the *Pequod*)[2] in the grip of one demon, Ahab, and heading inexorably towards another; namely the Whale. The ocean always was our Other, manifesting itself to us in the form of beasts—the worm Ouroboros, Kraken, Leviathan.[3] Herman Melville delves into these dark waters in order to offer us a very modern parable: Ahab, gripped by his possession, perishes; Ishmael, a man without strong feeling or powerful affiliations, survives. The self-interested modern man is the sole survivor; those who worship the Whale—for pursuit is a form of worship—perish by the Whale.

Joyce's wanderers, Beckett's tramps, Gogol's tricksters, Bulgakov's devils, Bellow's[4] high-energy meditations on the stifling of the soul by the triumphs of materialism; these, and many more, are what we have instead of prophets and suffering saints. But while the novel answers our need for wonderment and understanding, it brings us harsh and unpalatable news as well.

It tells us there are no rules. It hands down no commandments. We have to make up our own rules as best we can, make them up as we go along.

And it tells us there are no answers; or, rather, it tells us that answers are easier to come by, and less reliable, than questions. If religion is an answer, if political ideology is an answer, then literature is an inquiry; great literature, by asking extraordinary questions, opens new doors in our minds.

Richard Rorty, in *Philosophy and the Mirror of Nature,* insists on the importance of historicity, of giving up the illusions of being in contact with Eternity. For him, the great error is what he calls "foundationalism," which the theologian Don Cupitt, commenting on Rorty, calls "the attempt, as old as (and even much older than) Plato, to give permanence and authority to our knowledge and values by purporting to found them in some unchanging cosmic realm, natural or noumenal, outside the flux of our human conversation." It is better, Cupitt concludes, "to be an adaptable pragmatist, a nomad."

---

[1] *Manichean vision*  Form of dualism, in which the world is seen to be determined by the tension between the forces of good and evil.

[2] *the Pequod*  Captain Ahab's ship (in Herman Melville's novel *Moby Dick* [1851]).

[3] *Ouroboros ... Leviathan*  Ouroboros is an ancient symbol from many cultures that depict a snake or a dragon devouring itself. The Kraken is an enormous sea monster said to be living in the ocean between Norway and Iceland. Leviathan is a sea monster referred to in various places in the Bible.

[4] *Joyce ... Bellow*  Authors James Joyce (1882–1941), Samuel Beckett (1906–89), Nikolai Gogol (1809–52), Mikhail Bulgakov (1891–1940), and Saul Bellow (b. 1915).

Michel Foucault, also a confirmed historicist, discusses the role of the author in challenging sacralized absolutes in his essay, "What is an Author?" This essay argues, in part, that "texts, books and discourses really began to have authors ... to the extent that authors became subject to punishment, that is, to the extent that discourses could be transgressive." This is an extraordinary, provocative idea, even if it is stated with Foucault's characteristic airiness and a complete absence of supporting evidence: *that authors were named only when it was necessary to find somebody to blame.* Foucault continues:

> In our culture (and doubtless in many others), discourse was not originally a product, a thing, a kind of goods; it was essentially an act—an act placed in the bipolar field of the sacred and the profane, the licit and the illicit, the religious and the blasphemous. Historically it was a gesture fraught with risks ...

In our beginnings we find our essences. To understand a religion, look at its earliest moments. (It is regrettable that Islam, of all religions the easiest to study in this way, because of its birth during the age of recorded history, has set its face so resolutely against the idea that it, like all ideas, is an event inside history.) And to understand an artistic form, too, Foucault suggests, look at its origins. If he is right about the novel, then literature is, of all the arts, the one best suited to challenging absolutes of all kinds; and, because it is in its origin the schismatic Other of the sacred (and authorless) text, so it is also the art mostly likely to fill our god-shaped holes.

There are other reasons, too, for proposing the novel as the crucial art form of what I can no longer avoid calling the post-modern age. For one thing, literature is the art least subject to external control, because it is made in private. The act of making it requires only one person, one pen, one room, some paper. (Even the room is not absolutely essential.) Literature is the most low-technology of the art forms. It requires neither a stage nor a screen. It calls for no interpreters, no actors, producers, camera crews, costumers, musicians. It does not even require the traditional apparatus of publishing,

as the long-running success of samizdat literature[1] demonstrates. The Foucault essay suggests that literature is as much at risk from the enveloping, smothering forces of the market economy, which reduces books to mere products. This danger is real, and I do not want to seem to be minimizing it. But the truth is that of all the forms, literature can still be the most free. The more money a piece of work costs, the easier it is to control it. Film, the most expensive of art forms, is also the least subversive. This is why, although Carlos Fuentes cites the work of film-makers like Buñuel, Bergman and Fellini as instances of successful secular revolts into the territory of the sacred, I continue to believe in the greater possibilities of the novel. Its singularity is its best protection.

Among the childhood books I devoured and kissed were large numbers of cheap comics of a most unliterary nature. The heroes of these comic books were, or so it seemed, almost always mutants or hybrids or freaks: as well as the Batman and the Spiderman there was Aquaman, who was half-fish, and of course Superman, who could easily be mistaken for a bird or a plane. In those days, the middle 1950s, the super-heroes were all, in their various ways, hawkish law-and-order conservatives, leaping to work in response to the Police Commissioner's Bat-Signal, banding together to form the Justice League of America, defending what Superman called "truth, justice and the American way." But in spite of this extreme emphasis on crime-busting, the lesson they taught children—or this child, at any rate—was the perhaps unintentionally radical truth that exceptionality was the greatest and most heroic of values; that those who were unlike the crowd were to be treasured the most lovingly; and that this exceptionality was a treasure so great and so easily misunderstood that it had to be concealed, in ordinary life, beneath what the comic books called a "secret identity." Superman could not have survived without "mild-mannered" Clark Kent; "millionaire socialite" Bruce Wayne made possible the nocturnal activities of the Batman.

Now it is obviously true that those other freakish, hybrid, mutant, exceptional beings—novelists—those

---

[1] *samizdat literature* Underground, self-published literature, originally created in the Soviet Union to undermine the system of state censorship.

creators of the most freakish, hybrid and metamorphic of forms, the novel, have frequently been obliged to hide behind secret identities, whether for reasons of gender or terror. But the most wonderful of the many wonderful truths about the novel form is that the greater the writer, the greater his or her exceptionality. The geniuses of the novel are those whose voices are fully and undisguisably their own, who, to borrow William Gass's[1] image, *sign every word they write*. What draws us to an author is his or her "unlikeness," even if the apparatus of literary criticism then sets to work to demonstrate that he or she is really no more than an accumulation of influences. Unlikeness, the thing that makes it impossible for a writer to stand in any regimented line, is a quality novelists share with the Caped Crusaders of the comics, though they are only rarely capable of leaping tall buildings in a single stride.

What is more, the writer is there, in his work, in the reader's hands, utterly exposed, utterly defenceless, entirely without the benefit of an alter ego to hide behind. What is forged, in the secret act of reading, is a different kind of identity, as the reader and writer merge, through the medium of the text, to become a collective being that both writes as it reads and reads as it writes, and creates, jointly, that unique work, "their" novel. This "secret identity" of writer and reader is the novel form's greatest and most subversive gift.

And this, finally, is why I elevate the novel above other forms, why it has always been, and remains, my first love: not only is it the art involving least compromises, but it is also the only one that takes the "privileged arena" of conflicting discourses *right inside our heads*. The interior space of our imagination is a theatre that can never be closed down; the images created there make up a movie that can never be destroyed.

In this last decade of the millennium, as the forces of religion are renewed in strength and as the all-pervasive power of materialism wraps its own weighty chains around the human spirit, where should the novel be looking? It seems clear that the renewal of the old, bipolar field of discourse, between the sacred and the profane, which Michel Foucault proposes, will be of central importance. It seems probable, too, that we may be heading towards a world in which there will be no

real alternative to the liberal-capitalist social model (except, perhaps, the theocratic, foundationalist model of Islam). In this situation, liberal capitalism or democracy or the free world will require novelists' most rigorous attention, will require reimagining and questioning and doubting as never before. "Our antagonist is our helper," said Edmund Burke, and if democracy no longer has communism to help it clarify, by opposition, its own ideas, then perhaps it will have to have literature as an adversary instead.

I have made a large number of sweeping claims for literature during the course of this piece, and I am aware of a slightly messianic tone in much of what I've written. The reverencing of books and writers, by writers, is nothing particularly new, of course. "Since the early 19th century," writes Cupitt, "imaginative writers have claimed—have indeed enjoyed—a guiding and representative role in our culture. Our preachers are novelists, poets, dramatists, film-makers and the like, purveyors of fiction, ambiguous people, deceivers. Yet we continue to think of ourselves as rational."

But now I find myself backing away from the idea of sacralizing literature with which I flirted at the beginning of this text; I cannot bear the idea of the writer as secular prophet; I am remembering that one of the very greatest writers of the century, Samuel Beckett, believed that all art must inevitably end in failure. This is, clearly, no reason for surrender. "Ever tried. Ever failed. Never mind. Try again. Fail better."

Literature is an interim report from the consciousness of the artist, and so it can never be "finished" or "perfect." Literature is made at the frontier between the self and the world, and in the act of creation that frontier softens, becomes permeable, allows the world to flow into the artist and the artist to flow into the world. Nothing so inexact, so easily and frequently misconceived, deserves the protection of being declared sacrosanct. We shall just have to get along without the shield of sacralization, and a good thing, too. We must not become what we oppose.

The only privilege literature deserves—and this privilege it requires in order to exist—is the privilege of being the arena of discourse, the place where the struggle of languages can be acted out.

---

[1] *William Gass*  American novelist, essayist and critic.

Imagine this. You wake up one morning and find yourself in a large, rambling house. As you wander through it you realize it is so enormous that you will never know it all. In the house are people you know, family members, friends, lovers, colleagues; also many strangers. The house is full of activity: conflicts and seductions, celebrations and wakes. At some point you understand that there is no way out. You find that you can accept this. The house is not what you'd have chosen, it's in fairly bad condition, the corridors are often full of bullies, but it will have to do. Then one day you enter an unimportant-looking little room. The room is empty, but there are voices in it, voices that seem to be whispering just to you. You recognize some of the voices, others are completely unknown to you. The voices are talking about the house, about everyone in it, about everything that is happening and has happened and should happen. Some of them speak exclusively in obscenities. Some are bitchy. Some are loving. Some are funny. Some are sad. The most interesting voices are all these things at once. You begin to go to the room more and more often. Slowly you learn that most of the people in the house use such rooms sometimes. Yet the rooms are all discreetly positioned and unimportant-looking.

Now imagine that you wake up one morning and you are still in the large house, but all the voice-rooms have disappeared. It is as if they have been wiped out. Now there is nowhere in the whole house where you can go to hear voices talking about everything in every possible way. There is nowhere to go for the voices that can be funny one minute and sad the next, that can sound raucous and melodic in the course of the same sentence. Now you remember: there is no way out of this house. Now this fact begins to seem unbearable. You look into the eyes of the people in the corridors—family, lovers, friends, colleagues, strangers, bullies, priests. You see the same thing in everybody's eyes. *How do we get out of here?* It becomes clear that the house is a prison. People begin to scream, and pound the walls. Men arrive with guns. The house begins to shake. You do not wake up. You are already awake.

Literature is the one place in any society where, within the secrecy of our own heads, we can hear *voices talking about everything in every possible way.* The reason for ensuring that that privileged arena is preserved is not that writers want the absolute freedom to say and do whatever they please. It is that we, all of us, readers and writers and citizens and generals and godmen, need that little, unimportant-looking room. We do not need to call it sacred, but we do need to remember that it is necessary.

"Everybody knows," wrote Saul Bellow in *The Adventures of Augie March,* "there is no fineness or accuracy of suppression. If you hold down one thing, you hold down the adjoining."

Wherever in the world the little room of literature has been closed, sooner or later the walls have come tumbling down.

—1990

# Ian McEwan
## b. 1948

Ian McEwan is known as a contemporary master of unease. From the 1970s, his writing has been well respected, though his reputation has changed through his career. Early in his career he was a vaunted *enfant terrible* with a black sense of humor and an extraordinary sense of the bleakness of many childhoods. As time has passed he has come to be regarded as more of a wise, wry curmudgeon, full of insight, who entertains and instructs through unflinching, clear prose, and who is unafraid to portray the darker side of life.

Born in 1948 in Aldershot, England, a self-named "army brat," McEwan spent most of his childhood abroad in Africa, Asia, and Europe. He was educated at the University of Sussex and then at the University of East Anglia, studying with the novelists Malcolm Bradbury and Angus Wilson. In 1972, he returned from a trip overseas that was financed by the proceeds from his first published short story ("Homemade") and began to teach English as a second language in addition to writing.

*First Love, Last Rites* (1975), a volume of short stories, won the prestigious Somerset Maugham Award and was widely credited with helping to revitalize the short story as a literary genre in 1970s Britain. McEwan's subsequent works include his second collection of short stories, *In Between the Sheets* (1978) and his novels: *The Cement Garden* (1978); *The Comfort of Strangers* (1981); *The Child in Time* (1987), which won the Whitbread Prize for literature; *The Innocent* (1989); *Enduring Love* (1997); *Amsterdam* (1998), which won the Booker Prize; *Atonement* (2001); and *Saturday* (2005). McEwan has also written frequently in the popular press and he has published two children's books, *Rose Blanche* (1985) and *The Daydreamer* (1994).

Critically, the works of Ian McEwan have been well received, though there is a consistent and subtle factionalism among those who comment on his work. Some praise it as edgy, stark, and unflinching in dealing with the seedy and uncomfortable underbelly of difficult topics such as adolescent and deviant sexuality, murder, and the horrors that may emerge in everyday life. Others see his work as verging on the salacious, as being too much oriented towards the pursuit of shock value. But even this latter camp lauds McEwan for his clean, unadorned prose and his ability to place the reader in proximity to the narrative. It is telling that even his staunchest critics find little fault in the technique and execution of his writing.

There are clear lines to the evolution of McEwan's fiction. In his early works, the primary focus is on some of the most dark and uncomfortable aspects of sexuality and of death, and on lives that are lived largely in isolation from the world. His later works are less frequently focused on human grotesques, and often take place very much in the world (*Atonement* is set against the backdrop of World War Two, for example, and *Saturday* in the context of early twenty-first century terrorism). But the differences are of degree rather than of kind; precise imagery, elliptical social commentary, and deft handling of human emotion are constants in his writing, from early stories such as "Last Day of Summer," with its child's-eye view of life in a hippie commune, to the very adult perspectives of his recent novels.

⌘⌘⌘

## Last Day of Summer

I am twelve and lying near-naked on my belly out on the back lawn in the sun when for the first time I hear her laugh. I don't know, I don't move, I just close my eyes. It's a girl's laugh, a young woman's, short and nervous like laughing at nothing funny. I got half my face in the grass I cut an hour before and I can smell the cold soil beneath it. There's a faint breeze coming off the river, the late afternoon sun stinging my back and that laugh jabbing at me like it's all one thing, one taste in my head. The laughing stops and all I can hear is the breeze flapping the pages of my comic, Alice crying somewhere upstairs and a kind of summer heaviness all over the garden. Then I hear them walking across the lawn towards me and I sit up so quickly it makes me dizzy, and the colours have gone out of everything. And there's this fat woman, or girl, walking towards me with my brother. She's so fat her arms can't hang right from her shoulders. She's got rubber tyres round her neck. They're both looking at me and talking about me, and when they get really close I stand up and she shakes my hand and still looking right at me she makes a kind of yelping noise like a polite horse. It's the noise I heard just now, her laugh. Her hand is hot and wet and pink like a sponge, with dimples at the base of each finger. My brother introduces her as Jenny. She's going to take the attic bedroom. She's got a very large face, round like a red moon, and thick glasses which make her eyes as big as golf balls. When she lets go of my hand I can't think of one thing to say. But my brother Peter talks on and on, he tells her what vegetables we are growing and what flowers, he makes her stand where she can get a view of the river between the trees and then he leads her back to the house. My brother is exactly twice my age and he's good at that sort of thing, just talking.

Jenny takes the attic. I've been up there a few times looking for things in the old boxes, or watching the river out of the small window. There's nothing much in the boxes really, just cloth scraps and dressmaking patterns. Perhaps some of them actually belonged to my mother. In one corner there's a pile of picture frames without pictures. Once I was up there because it was raining outside, and downstairs there was a row going on between Peter and some of the others. I helped José clear out the place ready for a bedroom. José used to be Kate's boyfriend and then last spring he moved his things out of Kate's bedroom and moved into the spare room next to mine. We carried the boxes and frames to the garage, we stained the wooden floor black and put down rugs. We took apart the extra bed in my room and carried it up. With that, a table and a chair, a small cupboard and the sloping ceiling, there is just room for two people standing up. All Jenny has for luggage is a small suitcase and a carrier bag. I take them up to her room for her and she follows, breathing harder and harder and stopping halfway up the third set of stairs to get a rest. My brother Peter comes up behind and we squeeze in as if we are all going to be living there and we're seeing it for the first time. I point out the window for her so she can see the river. Jenny sits with her big elbows on the table. Sometimes she dabs at her damp red face with a large white handkerchief while she's listening to some story of Peter's. I'm sitting on the bed behind her looking at how immense her back is, and under her chair I can see her thick pink legs, how they taper away and squeeze into tiny shoes at the bottom. Everywhere she's pink. The smell of her sweat fills the room. It smells like the new cut grass outside, and I get this idea that I mustn't breathe it in too deeply or I'll get fat too. We stand up to go so she can get on with her unpacking and she's saying thank you for everything, and as I go through the door she makes her little yelp, her nervous laugh. Without meaning to I glance back at her through the doorway and she's looking right at me with her magnified golf-balls eyes.

"You don't say much, do you?" she says. Which sort of makes it even harder to think of something to say. So I just smile at her and carry on down the stairs.

Downstairs it's my turn to help Kate cook the supper. Kate is tall and slim and sad. Really the opposite of Jenny. When I have girl friends I'm going to have them like Kate. She's very pale, though, even at this time in the summer. She has strange-coloured hair.

Once I heard Sam say it was the colour of a brown envelope. Sam is one of Peter's friends who also lives here and who wanted to move his things into Kate's bedroom when José moved his out. But Kate is sort of haughty and she doesn't like Sam because he's too noisy. If Sam moved into Kate's room he'd always be waking up Alice, Kate's little girl. When Kate and José are in the same room I always watch them to see if they ever look at each other, and they never do. Last April I went into Kate's room one afternoon to borrow something and she and José were in bed asleep. José's parents come from Spain and his skin is very dark. Kate was lying on her back with one arm stretched out, and José was lying on her arm, snuggling up to her side. They didn't have pyjamas on, and the sheet came up to their waists. They were so black and so white. I stood at the foot of the bed a long time, watching them. It was like some secret I'd found out. Then Kate opened her eyes and saw me there and told me very softly to get out. It seems pretty strange to me that they were lying there like that and now they don't even look at each other. That wouldn't happen with me if I was lying on some girl's arm. Kate doesn't like cooking. She has to spend a lot of time making sure Alice doesn't put knives in her mouth or pull boiling pots off the stove. Kate prefers dressing-up and going out, or talking for hours on the telephone, which is what I would rather do if I was a girl. Once she stayed out late and my brother Peter had to put Alice to bed. Kate always looks sad when she speaks to Alice, when she's telling her what to do she speaks very softly as if she doesn't really want to be speaking to Alice at all. And it's the same when she talks to me, as if it's not really talking at all. When she sees my back in the kitchen she takes me through to the downstairs bath-room and dabs calamine lotion over me with a piece of cotton wool. I can see her in the mirror, she doesn't seem to have any particular expression on her face. She makes a sound between her teeth, half a whistle and half a sigh, and when she wants a different part of my back towards the light she pushes or pulls me about by my arm. She asks me quickly and quietly what the girl upstairs is like, and when I tell her, "She's very fat and she's got a funny laugh," she doesn't make any reply. I cut up vegetables for Kate and lay the table. Then I walk down to the river to look at my boat. I bought it with

some money I got when my parents died. By the time I get to the jetty it's past sunset and the river is black with scraps of red like the cloth scraps that used to be in the attic. Tonight the river is slow and the air is warm and smooth. I don't untie the boat, my back is too sore from the sun to row. Instead I climb in and sit with the quiet rise and fall of the river, watching the red cloth sink in the black water and wondering if I breathed in too much of Jenny's smell.

When I get back they are about to start eating. Jenny is sitting next to Peter and when I come in she doesn't look up from her plate, even when I sit down on the other side of her. She's so big beside me, and yet so bowed down over her plate, looking as if she doesn't really want to exist, that I feel sorry for her in a way and I want to speak to her. But I can't think of anything to say. In fact no one has anything to say this meal, they're all just pushing their knives and forks backwards and forwards over their plates, and now and then someone murmurs for something to be passed. It doesn't usually happen like this when we're eating, there's usually something going on. But Jenny's here, more silent than any of us, and bigger, too, and not looking up from her plate. Sam clears his throat and looks down our end of the table at Jenny, and everyone else looks up too, except for her, waiting for something. Sam clears his throat again and says,

"Where were you living before, Jenny?" Because no one's been speaking it comes out flat, as if Sam's in an office filling in a form for her. And Jenny, still looking down at her plate, says,

"Manchester." Then she looks at Sam. "In a flat." And she gives a little yelp of a laugh, probably because we're all listening and looking at her, and then she sinks back into her plate while Sam's saying something like, "Ah, I see," and thinking of the next thing to say. Upstairs, Alice starts crying so Kate goes and brings her down and lets her sit on her lap. When she stops crying she points at each one of us in turn and shouts, "UH, UH, UH," and so on right round the table while we all sit there eating and not speaking. It's like she's telling us off for not thinking of things to say. Kate tells her to be quiet in the sad way she always has when she's with Alice. Sometimes I think she's like that because Alice doesn't have a father. She doesn't look at all like Kate, she has very fair hair and ears that are too large for her head. A year or two ago when Alice was very little I used to think that José was her father. But his hair is black, and he never pays much attention to Alice. When everybody's finished the first course and I'm helping Kate collect the dishes, Jenny offers to have Alice on her lap. Alice is still shouting and pointing at different things in the room, but once she's on Jenny's lap she goes very quiet. Probably because it's the biggest lap she's ever seen. Kate and I bring in fruit and tea, and when we are peeling oranges and bananas, eating the apples from our tree in the garden, pouring tea and passing cups with milk and sugar round, everyone starts talking and laughing like they usually do, like there never was anything holding them back. And Jenny is giving Alice a really good time on her lap, making her knees gallop like a horse, making her hand swoop down like a bird on to Alice's belly, showing her tricks with her fingers, so that all the time Alice is shouting for more. It's the first time I've heard her laugh like that. And then Jenny glances down the table at Kate who's been watching them play with the same kind of look she might have on her face if she was watching the telly. Jenny carries Alice to her mother like she's suddenly feeling guilty about having Alice on her lap for such a long time and having so much fun. Alice is shouting, "More, more, more," when she's back at the other end of the table, and she's still shouting it five minutes later when her mother carries her up to bed.

Because my brother asks me to, I take coffee up to Jenny's room early next morning. When I go in she's already up, sitting at her table putting stamps on letters. She looks smaller than she did last night. She has her window wide open and her room is full of morning air, it feels like she's been up for a long time. Out of her window I can see the river stretching between the trees, light and quiet in the sun. I want to get outside, I want to see my boat before breakfast. But Jenny wants to talk. She makes me sit on her bed and tell her about myself. She doesn't ask me any questions and since I'm not sure how to start off telling someone about myself I sit there and watch while she writes addresses on her letters and sips her coffee. But I don't mind, it's all right in Jenny's room. She's put two pictures on the wall. One is a framed photograph taken in a zoo of a monkey walking

upside down along a branch with its baby hanging on to its stomach. You can tell it is a zoo because in the bottom corner there's a zookeeper's cap and part of his face. The other is a colour picture taken out of a magazine of two children running along the seashore holding hands. The sun is setting and everything in the picture is deep red, even the children. It's a very good picture. She finishes with her letters and asks me where I go to school. I tell her about the new school I'm going to when the holidays are over, the big comprehensive[1] in Reading. But I haven't been there yet, so there isn't much I can tell her about it. She sees me looking out the window again.

"Are you going down to the river?"

"Yes, I have to see my boat."

"Can I come with you? Will you show me the river?" I wait for her by the door, watching her squeeze her round, pink feet into small, flat shoes and brush her very short hair with a brush which has a mirror on the back. We walk across the lawn to the kissing gate[2] at the bottom of the garden and along the path through the high ferns. Half way down I stop to listen to a yellow-hammer, and she tells me that she doesn't know the song of one bird. Most grown-up people will never tell you that they don't know things. So farther on down the path just before it opens out on to the jetty we stop under an old oak tree so she can hear a blackbird. I know there's one up there, it's always up there singing this time in the morning. Just as we get there it stops and we have to wait quietly for it to begin again. Standing by that half-dead old trunk I can hear other birds in other trees and the river just round the corner washing under the jetty. But our bird is taking a rest. Something about waiting in silence makes Jenny nervous and she pinches her nose tight to stop her yelp of a laugh getting out. I want her to hear the blackbird so much I put my hand on her arm, and when I do that she takes her hand away from her nose and smiles. Just a few seconds after that the blackbird sets out on its long complicated song. It was waiting all the time for us to get settled. We walk

---

[1]  *comprehensive* Secondary school for children of all levels of ability, stereotypically seen as working class.

[2]  *kissing gate* From "kisting gate," a small swinging gate set in a cupped enclosure to allow one person to pass at a time and keep livestock out.

out on to the jetty and I show her my boat tied up at the end. It's a rowing boat, green on the outside and red on the inside like a fruit. I've been down here every day all this summer to row it, paint it, wipe it down, and sometimes just to look at it. Once I rowed it seven miles upstream and spent the rest of the day drifting back down. We sit on the edge of the jetty looking at my boat, the river and the trees on the other side. Then Jenny looks downstream and says,

"London's down there." London is a terrible secret I try to keep from the river. It doesn't know about it yet while it's flowing past our house. So I just nod and say nothing. Jenny asks me if she can sit in the boat. It worries me at first that she's going to be too heavy. But of course I cannot tell her that. I lean over the jetty and hold the painter rope for her to climb in. She does it with a lot of grunting and rocking around. And since the boat doesn't look any lower now than it usually does, I get in too and we watch the river from this new level where you can see how strong and old it really is. We sit talking for a long time. First I tell her about how my parents died two years ago in a car crash and how my brother had ideas for turning the house into a kind of commune. At first he was going to have over twenty people living here. But now I think he wants to keep it down to about eight. Then Jenny tells me about the time she was a teacher in a big school in Manchester where all the children were always laughing at her because she was fat. She doesn't seem to mind talking about it, though. She has some funny stories of her time there. When she's telling me of the time when the children locked her in a book cupboard we both laugh so much the boat rocks from side to side and pushes small waves out into the river. This time Jenny's laugh is easy and kind of rhythmic, not hard and yelping like before. On the way back she recognizes two blackbirds by their songs, and when we're crossing the lawn she points out another. I just nod. It's a song-thrush really, but I'm too hungry to tell her the difference.

Three days later I hear Jenny singing. I'm in the back yard trying to put together a bicycle out of bits and pieces and I hear her through the open kitchen window. She's in there cooking lunch and looking after Alice while Kate visits friends. It's a song she doesn't know the words for, halfway between happy and sad, and she's singing like an old croaky Negress to Alice. New morning man la-la, la-la-la-, l'la, new morning man la-la-la, la-la, l'la, new morning man take me 'way from here. That afternoon I row her out on the river and she has another song with the same kind of tune, but this time with no words at all. Ya-la-la, ya-laaa, ya-eeeee. She spreads her hands out and rolls her big magnified eyes around like it's a serenade especially for me. A week later Jenny's songs are all over the house, sometimes with a line or two if she can remember it, most often with no words at all. She spends a lot of her time in the kitchen and that's where she does most of her singing. Somehow she makes more space in there. She scrapes paint off the north window to let in more light. No one can think why it was painted over in the first place. She carries out an old table, and when it's out everyone realizes that it was always in the way. One afternoon she paints the whole of one wall white to make the kitchen look bigger, and she arranges the pots and plates so that you always know where they are and even I can reach them. She makes it into the kind of kitchen you can sit around in when you've got nothing else to do. Jenny makes her own bread and bakes cakes, things we usually go to the shop for. On the third day she's here I find clean sheets on my bed. She takes the sheets I've been using all summer and most of my clothes away for washing. She spends all of one afternoon making a curry, and that night I eat the best meal in two years. When the others tell her how good they think it is Jenny gets nervous and does her yelping laugh. I can see the others are still bothered when she does it, they sort of look away as if it is something disgusting that would be rude to look at. But it doesn't worry me at all when she does that laugh, I don't even hear it except when the others are there at the table looking away. Most afternoons we go out on the river together and I try to teach her to row, and listen to her stories of when she was teaching, and when she was working in a supermarket, how she used to watch old people come in each day to shoplift bacon and butter, I teach her some more birdsongs, but the only one she can really remember is the first one, the blackbird. In her room she shows me pictures of her parents and her brother and she says,

"I'm the only fat one." I show her some pictures of my parents, too. One of them was taken a month before they died, and in it they are walking down some steps holding hands and laughing at something outside the picture. They were laughing at my brother who was fooling around to make them laugh for the picture I was taking. I had just got the camera for my tenth birthday and that was one of the first pictures I took with it. Jenny looks at it for a long time and says something about her looking like a very nice woman, and suddenly I see my mother as just a woman in a picture, it could be any woman, and for the first time she's far off, not in my head looking out, but outside my head being looked at by me, Jenny or anyone who picks up the photo. Jenny takes it out of my hand and puts it away with the others in the shoebox. As we go downstairs she starts off on a long story about a friend of hers who was producing a play which ended strangely and quietly. The friend wanted Jenny to start off the clapping at the end but Jenny got it all wrong somehow and started everyone clapping fifteen minutes before the end during a quiet bit so that the last part of the play was lost and the clapping was all the louder because no one knew what the play was about. All this, I suppose, is to make me stop thinking about my mother, which it does.

Kate spends more time with her friends in Reading. One morning I'm in the kitchen when she comes in very smartly dressed in a kind of leather suit and high leather boots. She sits down opposite me to wait for Jenny to come down so she can tell her what food to give Alice that day, and what time she'll be back. It reminds me of another morning almost two years ago when Kate came into the kitchen in the same kind of suit. She sat down at the table, undid her blouse and started to knead with her fingers blueish-white milk into a bottle from one tit and then the other. She didn't seem to notice me sitting there.

"What are you doing that for?" I asked her.

She said, "It's for Janet to give to Alice later on today. I've got to go out." Janet was a black girl who used to be living here. It was strange watching Kate milk herself into a bottle. It made me think how we're just animals with clothes on doing very peculiar things, like monkeys at a tea party. But we get so used to each other most of the time. I wonder if Kate is thinking of that time now, sitting with me in the kitchen first thing in the morning. She's got orange lipstick on and her hair

tied back and that makes her look even thinner than usual. Her lipstick is sort of fluorescent, like a road sign. Every minute she looks at her watch and her leather creaks. She looks like some beautiful woman from outer space. Then Jenny comes down, wearing a huge old dressing-gown made out of patches and yawning because she's just got out of bed, and Kate speaks to her very quickly and quietly about Alice's food for the day. It's as if it makes her sad, talking about that sort of thing. She picks up her bag and runs out the kitchen and calls, "Bye," over her shoulder. Jenny sits down at the table and drinks tea and it's like she really is the big mama left behind at home to look after the rich lady's daughter. Yo' daddy's rich and yo' mama's goodlookin', lah la-la-la la-la don' yo' cry. And there's something in the way the others treat Jenny. Like she's outside things, and not really a person like they are. They've got used to her cooking big meals and making cakes. No one says anything about it now. Sometimes in the evenings Peter, Kate, José and Sam sit around and smoke hashish in Peter's homemade water-pipe and listen to the stereo turned up loud. When they do that Jenny usually goes up to her room, she doesn't like to be with them when they're doing that, and I can see they sort of resent it. And though she's a girl she's not beautiful like Kate or Sharon, my brother's girlfriend. She doesn't wear jeans and Indian shirts like they do, either, probably because she can't find any to fit her. She wears dresses with flowers on and ordinary things like my mother or the lady in the post office wear. And when she gets nervous about something and does her laugh I can tell they think of her like some sort of mental patient, I know that by the way they turn their eyes away. And they still think about how fat she is. Sometimes when she's not there Sam calls her Slim Jim, and it always makes the others laugh. It's not that they're unfriendly to her or anything like that, it's just that in some way that's hard to describe they keep her apart from themselves. One time we're out on the river she asks me about hashish.

"What do you think about it all?" she says, and I tell her my brother won't let me try it till I'm fifteen. I know she's dead against it, but she doesn't mention it again. It's that same afternoon I take a photograph of her leaning by the kitchen door holding Alice and squinting a little into the sun. She takes mine too, riding no-hands round the back yard on the bicycle I put together out of bits and pieces.

It's hard to say exactly when Jenny becomes Alice's mother. At first she's just looking after her while Kate visits friends. Then the visits get more often till they are almost every day. So the three of us, Jenny, Alice and me, spend a lot of time together by the river. By the jetty there's a grass bank which slopes down on to a tiny sand beach about six feet across. Jenny sits on the bank playing with Alice while I do things to my boat. When we first put Alice in the boat she squeals like a baby pig. She doesn't trust the water. It's a long time before she'll stand on the small beach, and when she does at last she never takes her eyes off the water's edge to make sure it doesn't creep up on her. But when she sees Jenny waving to her from the boat, and quite safe, she changes her mind and we make a trip to the other side of the river. Alice doesn't mind about Kate being away because she likes Jenny, who sings her the bits of songs she knows and talks to her all the time when they are sitting on the grass bank by the river. Alice does not understand a word of it but she likes the sound of Jenny's voice going on and on. Sometimes Alice points up to Jenny's mouth and says, "More, more." Kate is always so quiet and sad with her she doesn't hear many voices speaking right at her. One night Kate stays away and doesn't come back till the next morning. Alice is sitting on Jenny's knee spreading her breakfast across the kitchen table when Kate comes running in, scoops her up, hugs her and asks over and over again without giving anyone time to reply,

"Has she been all right? Has she been all right? Has she been all right?" The same afternoon Alice is back with Jenny because Kate has to go off somewhere again. I'm in the hall outside the kitchen when I hear her tell Jenny she'll be back in the early evening, and a few minutes later I see her walking down the drive carrying a small suitcase. When she gets back two days later she just puts her head round the door to see if Alice is still there, and then she goes up to her room. It's not always such a good thing having Alice with us all the time. We can't go very far in the boat. After twenty minutes Alice gets suspicious of the water again and wants to be back on the shore. And if we want to walk somewhere Alice has to be carried most of the way. It means I can't show

Jenny some of my special places along the river. By the end of the day Alice gets pretty miserable, moaning and crying about nothing because she's tired. I get fed up spending so much time with Alice. Kate stays up in her room most of the day. One afternoon I take her up some tea and she's sitting in a chair asleep. With Alice there so much of the time Jenny and I don't talk together as much as we did when she first came. Not because Alice is listening, but because all Jenny's time is taken up with her. She doesn't think of anything else, really, it seems like she doesn't want to talk with anyone but Alice. One evening we are all sitting around in the front room after supper. Kate is in the hall having a long argument with someone on the telephone. She finishes, comes in, sits down in a noisy kind of way and carries on reading. But I can see she's angry and not really reading at all. No one speaks for a while, then Alice starts crying upstairs and shouting for Jenny. Jenny and Kate both look up at once and stare at each other for a moment. Then Kate gets up and leaves the room. We all pretend to go on reading but really we are listening to Kate's footsteps on the stairs. We hear her walk into Alice's room, which is right over this one, and we hear Alice shout louder and louder for Jenny to come up. Kate comes back down the stairs, this time quickly. When she comes in the room Jenny looks up and they stare at each other again. And all the time Alice goes on shouting for Jenny. Jenny gets up and squeezes past Kate at the door. They don't speak. The rest of us, Peter, Sam, José and me, we carry on with our pretend reading and listen to Jenny's footsteps upstairs. The crying stops and she stays up there a long time. When she comes down Kate is back in her chair with her magazine. Jenny sits down and no one looks up, no one speaks.

Suddenly the summer is over. Jenny comes into my room early one morning to drag the sheets off my bed and all the clothes she can find in the room. Everything has to be washed before I go to school. Then she gets me to clean out my room, all the old comics and plates and cups which have been collecting under my bed all summer, all the dust and the pots of paint I've been using on my boat. She finds a small table in the garage and I help her carry it to my room. It's going to be my desk for doing homework on. She takes me into the village for a treat, and she won't tell me what it is. When we get there it turns out to be a haircut. I'm about to walk away when she puts her hand on my shoulder.

"Don't be silly," she says. "You can't go to school looking like that, you won't last a day." So I sit still for the barber and let him cut away my whole summer while Jenny sits behind me, laughing at me scowling at her in the mirror. She gets some money from my brother Peter and takes me on the bus into town to buy a school uniform. It's strange having her tell me what to do all of a sudden after our times out on the river. But I don't mind, really, I can't think of any good reasons for not doing the things she says. She steers me through the main shopping streets, into shoe shops and outfitters, she buys me a red blazer and a cap, two pairs of black leather shoes, six pairs of grey socks, two pairs of grey trousers and five grey shirts, and all the time she's saying, "Do you like these ones? Do you like this?" and since I don't have any special feeling for one particular shade of grey, I agree with whatever she thinks is the best. It's all over in an hour. That evening she empties my drawers of my rock collection to make room for the new clothes, and she gets me to put on the whole uniform. They all laugh downstairs, especially when I put the red cap on. Sam says I look like an inter-galactic postman. For three nights in a row she has me scrubbing my knees with a nailbrush to get the dirt out from under the skin.

Then on Sunday, the day before I start back at school, I go down to the boat with Jenny and Alice for the last time. In the evening I'm going to help Peter and Sam drag my boat up the path and across the lawn into the garage for the winter. Then we're going to build another jetty, a stronger one. It's the last boat trip of the summer. Jenny lifts Alice in and climbs in herself while I hold the boat steady from the jetty. As I'm pushing us off with an oar, Jenny starts one of her songs. Jeeesus won't you come on down, Jeeesus won't you come on down, Jeeesus won't you come on down, lah, la-la-la-lah, la-la. Alice stands between Jenny's knees watching me row. She thinks it's funny, the way I strain backwards and forwards. She thinks it's a game I'm playing with her, moving close up to her face and away again. It's strange, our last day on the river. When Jenny's finished her song no one speaks for a long time. Just

Alice laughing at me. It's so still on the river, her laugh carries across the water to nowhere. The sun is a kind of pale yellow like it's burnt out at the end of summer, there's no wind in the trees on the banks, and no birdsong. Even the oars make no sound in the water. I row upstream with the sun on my back, but it's too pale to feel it, it's too pale to make shadows, even. Up ahead there's an old man standing under an oak tree, fishing. When we are level with him he looks up and stares at us in our boat and we stare back at him on the bank. His face does not change when he's looking at us. Our faces do not change, either, no one says hello. He has a long piece of grass in his mouth and when we've passed he takes it out and spits quietly into the river. Jenny trails her hand in the thick water and watches the bank as if it's something she's only seeing in her mind. It makes me think she doesn't really want to be out there on the river with me. She only came because of all the other times we've been rowing together, and because this is the last time this summer. It sort of makes me sad, thinking that, it makes it harder to row. Then after we've been going for about half an hour she looks at me and smiles and I can tell it's all in my head about her not wanting to be on the river because she starts talking about the summer, about all the things we've been doing. She makes it sound really great, much better than it was really. About the long walks we went on, and paddling at the edge of the river with Alice, how I tried to teach her to row and remember different birdsongs, and the times we used to get up while the others were still asleep and row on the river before breakfast. She gets me going too, remembering all the things we did, like the time we thought we saw a waxwing, and another time we waited one evening behind a bush for a badger to come out of its hole. Pretty soon we get really excited about what a summer it's been and the things we're going to do next year, shouting and laughing into the dead air. And then Jenny says,

"And tomorrow you put on your red cap and go to school." There's something in the way she says it, pretending to be serious and telling me off, with one finger wagging in the air, that makes it the funniest thing I ever heard. And the idea of it too, of doing all those things in the summer and then at the end of it putting on a red cap and going to school. We start laughing and it seems like we're never going to stop. I have to put down the oars. Our hooting and cackling gets louder and louder because the still air doesn't carry it across the water and the noise of it stays with us in the boat. Each time we catch the other's eye we laugh harder and louder till it begins to hurt down my sides, and more than anything I want to stop. Alice starts to cry because she doesn't know what's happening, and that makes us laugh more. Jenny leans over the side of the boat so she can't see me. But her laugh is getting tighter and drier, little hard yelps like pieces of stone from her throat. Her big pink face and her big pink arms are shaking and straining to catch a mouthful of air, but it's all going out of her in little pieces of stone. She leans back into the boat. Her mouth is laughing but her eyes look kind of scared and dry. She drops to her knees, holding her stomach with the pain of laughing, and knocks Alice down with her. And the boat tips over. It tips over because Jenny falls against the side, because Jenny is big and my boat is small. It goes over quickly, like the click of my camera shutter, and suddenly I'm at the deep green bottom of the river touching the cold soft mud with the back of my hand and feeling the reeds on my face. I can hear laughter like sinking pieces of stone by my ear. But when I push upwards to the surface I feel no one near me. When I come up it's dark on the river. I've been down a long time. Something touches my head and I realize I'm inside the upturned boat. I go down again and up the other side. It takes me a long time to get my breath. I work my way round the boat shouting over and over for Jenny and Alice. I put my mouth in the water and shout their names. But no one answers, nothing breaks the surface. I'm the only one on the river. So I hang on to the side of the boat and wait for them to come up. I wait a long time, drifting along with the boat, with the laughter still in my head, watching the river and the yellow patches on it from the sun getting low. Sometimes great shivers run through my legs and back, but mostly I'm calm, hanging on to the green shell with nothing in my mind, nothing at all, just watching the river, waiting for the surface to break and the yellow patches to scatter. I drift past the place where the old man was fishing and it seems like a very long time ago. He's gone now, there's just a paper bag in the place where he was standing. I get so tired I close my eyes and it feels like I'm at home in bed and it's winter and my mother's coming into my room to say goodnight. She turns out the light and I slip off the boat into the river. Then I remember and I shout for Jenny and Alice and watch the river again and my eyes start to close and my mother comes into my room and says goodnight and turns out the light and I sink back into the water again. After a long time I forget to shout for Jenny and Alice, I just hang there and drift down. I'm looking at a place on the bank I used to know very well a long time ago. There's a patch of sand and a grass bank by a jetty. The yellow patches are sinking into the river when I push away from the boat. I let it drift on down to London and I swim slowly through the black water to the jetty.

—1972

# PAUL MULDOON

## b. 1951

Since first beginning to publish in the early 1970s, Irish poet Paul Muldoon has been hailed as a fresh and distinctive voice. Suffused with dark humor, startling images, and unusual language, his poetry constantly challenges the validity of our knowledge about ourselves, our methods of perception, and our conceptions of others. As he has said, his poems generally "seem to be saying one thing but in fact couldn't possibly be saying that."

Muldoon was born in County Armagh, Northern Ireland, and was raised a Roman Catholic in that largely Protestant region. In secondary school he learned Gaelic and began studying Irish

literature; he also began writing poetry in Gaelic, later switching to English. At Queen's University in Belfast, where Muldoon studied literature and philosophy, fellow poet Seamus Heaney became his tutor. The two met weekly, along with Michael Longley, James Simmons, and Derek Mahon, to discuss poetry and critique one another's work. When the members of this group each gained international recognition in the 1960s and '70s, the five began to be referred to as the Ulster Poets.

While in university, Muldoon published a small pamphlet of poems, *Knowing My Place* (1971), and Heaney included some of Muldoon's poems in a magazine he was guest editing, bringing him to the attention of the publisher Faber & Faber. Muldoon's first collection, *New Weather* (1973), was published by Faber & Faber the year he graduated. In *New Weather* Muldoon introduces the theme of the quest, which has been prominent throughout his work. The poems of this collection, like those of his later ones, mix references to Greco-Roman, British, American, and Native American cultures with frequent references to Irish history and politics. Muldoon's work tends simultaneously to reach back to Irish mythological roots and forward into a metaphysical world of his own creation.

Muldoon's subsequent collections have continued to extend the reach of his poetry. *Mules* (1977) deals with Ireland's troubled political situation; it is more experimental and more overtly ironic than *New Weather*. *Why Brownlee Left* (1980), which is at least superficially autobiographical, chronicles the end of a marriage. His 1983 volume *Quoof* (named after his family's private word for a hot water bottle) toys with issues of identity, home, and the nature of the imagination.

Muldoon says that his poetry deals with "everything and anything." Elements of pop culture, such as references to film and television, are combined with political statements and elements of mythology or autobiography. Concrete descriptions of the landscape of his native Ulster are often transformed into a moral or psychological landscape. Similarly, a public event can be suddenly transformed by private consciousness. Frequently, words and images have multiple meanings; the title of *Kerry Slides* (1996), for example, refers both to an Irish dance of that name and to the accompanying photos of County Kerry by Bill Doyle.

In addition to puns and unusual language, Muldoon frequently makes use of disparate, conflicting images and unconventional rhymes to challenge his readers. His experiments with form—which have been a source of criticism as well as of praise—have touched on nearly every poetic genre, from the sonnet to the libretto. Many collections, such as *Brownlee*, begin with a series of short poems, including ballads, sonnets, and short lyrics, which builds to a long poem.

Muldoon worked as a producer for BBC Northern Ireland from his graduation from university until 1986, when he chose to pursue an academic career. He held fellowships at Cambridge, the University of East Anglia, and at various American institutions before accepting a position at Princeton in 1990. From 1999 to 2004 he was Professor of Poetry at Oxford University.

Muldoon's poetry marks a creative break from earlier Irish poetical tradition, long dominated by the influence of Yeats, and he has been instrumental in the development of new trends in Irish poetry in recent years—through his own poetry as well as through his work as an editor (for example, of the *Faber Book of Contemporary Irish Poetry*, 1980) and a scholar. Muldoon published a collection of his lectures on Irish literature, *To Ireland, I* in 2000. Among his numerous literary awards are the Geoffrey Faber Memorial Prize (for *Brownlee*), a Guggenheim Fellowship (1990), and the T.S. Eliot Award (for his 1995 volume *The Annals of Chile*). *Moy Sand and Gravel* (2002) won both the Pulitzer Prize and the International Griffin Poetry Prize.

⌘⌘⌘

## Good Friday, 1971. Driving Westward[1]

It was good going along with the sun
Through Ballygawley, Omagh and Strabane.[2]
I started out as it was getting light
And caught sight of hares all along the road
5   That looked to have been taking a last fling,
Doves making the most of their offerings
As if all might not be right with the day

Where I moved through morning towards the sea.
I was glad that I would not be alone.
10  Those children who travel badly as wine
Waved as they passed in their uppity cars
And now the first cows were leaving the
     byres,°                                        cow-houses
The first lorry° had delivered its load.          truck
A whole country was fresh after the night

15  Though people were still fighting for the last
Dreams and changing their faces where I paused
To read the first edition of the truth.
I gave a lift to the girl out of love

And crossed the last great frontier at Lifford.[3]
20  Marooned by an iffing and butting herd
Of sheep, Letterkenny had just then laid

Open its heart and we passed as new blood
Back into the grey flesh of Donegal.
The sky went out of its way for the hills
25  And life was changing down for the sharp bends
Where the road had put its thin brown arm round
A hill and held on tight out of pure fear.
Errigal[4] stepped out suddenly in our

Path and the thin arm tightened round the waist
30  Of the mountain and for a time I lost
Control and she thought we hit something big
But I had seen nothing, perhaps a stick
Lying across the road. I glanced back once
And there was nothing but a heap of stones.
35  We had just dropped in from nowhere for lunch

In Gaoth Dobhair, I happy and she convinced
Of the death of more than lamb or herring.
She stood up there and then, face full of drink,

---

1  *Good Friday ... Westward*   Reference to John Donne's poem "Good Friday, 1613. Riding Westward" (1633).

2  *Ballygawley ... Strabane*   Three towns in County Tyrone (bordering County Donegal) in Northern Ireland.

3  *Lifford*   Town in County Donegal, in the Republic of Ireland. Letterkenny, mentioned in line 21, and Gaoth Dobhair, in line 36, are also in Donegal.

4  *Errigal*   Tallest peak in the Derryveagh Mountains.

And announced that she and I were to blame
40  For something killed along the way we came.
Children were warned that it was rude to stare,
Left with their parents for a breath of air.
—1973

## Our Lady Of Ardboe[1]

### 1

Just there, in a corner of the whin°-field,        *heather*
Just where the thistles bloom.
She stood there as in Bethlehem
One night in nineteen fifty-three or four.

5   The girl leaning over the half-door
Saw the cattle kneel, and herself knelt.

### 2

I suppose that a farmer's youngest daughter
Might, as well as the next, unravel
The winding road to Christ's navel.

10  Who's to know what's knowable?
Milk from the Virgin Mother's breast,
A feather off the Holy Ghost?
The fairy thorn? The holy well?[2]

Our simple wish for there being more to life
15  Than a job, a car, a house, a wife—
The fixity of running water.

For I like to think, as I step these acres,
That a holy well is no more shallow
Nor plummetless than the pools of Shiloh,[3]
20  The fairy thorn no less true than the Cross.

### 3

Mother of our Creator, Mother of our Saviour,
Mother most amiable, Mother most admirable.
Virgin most prudent, Virgin most venerable,
Mother inviolate, Mother undefiled.

25  And I walk waist-deep among purples and golds
With one arm as long as the other.
—1977

## The Sightseers

My father and mother, my brother and sister
and I, with uncle Pat, our dour best-loved uncle,
had set out that Sunday afternoon in July
in his broken-down Ford

5   not to visit some graveyard—one died of shingles,
one of fever, another's knees turned to jelly—
but the brand-new roundabout[4] at Ballygawley,
the first in mid-Ulster.[5]

Uncle Pat was telling us how the B-Specials[6]
10  had stopped him one night somewhere near Ballygawley
and smashed his bicycle

and made him sing the Sash[7] and curse the Pope of
    Rome.
They held a pistol so hard against his forehead
there was still the mark of an O when he got home.
—1983

---

[1] *Ardboe* Town in County Tyrone, Northern Ireland.

[2] *fairy … well* Sacred symbols in both pre-Christian and Irish-Christian religions.

[3] *Shiloh* Village in Palestine northwest of the Dead Sea that provided a sanctuary for the Israelites.

[4] *roundabout* Merry-go-round.

[5] *mid-Ulster* Region consisting of the northern, western, and eastern parts of County Tyrone, in Northern Ireland.

[6] *B-Specials* Auxiliary force of the Royal Ulster Constabulary, formed in 1920 by the government of Northern Ireland to combat IRA secessionist fighters and any potential subversion within the state. The B-Special force was exclusively Protestant, was several times larger than the normal police force, and was regarded by many as a "Protestant army." The B-Specials were disbanded in 1972, at the beginning of Direct Rule by the British.

[7] *the Sash* Irish Protestant ballad commemorating the victory of the Protestants in the Williamite war of 1690–91.

## Cherish The Ladies

In this, my last poem about my father,
there may be time enough
for him to fill their drinking-trough
and run his eye over

5    his three mooley° heifers.                    *hornless*
Such a well-worn path,
I know, from here to the galvanized[1] bath.
I know, too, you would rather

*I saw behind the hedge to where the pride*
10   *of the herd, though not an Irish*
*bull, would cherish*
*the ladies with his electric cattle-prod.*

As it is, in my last poem about my father
he opens the stand-pipe[2]
15   and the water scurries along the hose
till it's curled

in the bath. One heifer
may look up
and make a mental note, then put her nose
20   back to the salt-lick of the world.
—1983

## Milkweed And Monarch

As he knelt by the grave of his mother and father
the taste of dill, or tarragon—
he could barely tell one from the other—

filled his mouth. It seemed as if he might smother.

5    Why should he be stricken
with grief, not for his mother and father,

but a woman slinking from the fur of a sea-otter
in Portland, Maine, or, yes, Portland, Oregon—
he could barely tell one from the other—

10   and why should he now savour
the tang of her, her little pickled gherkin,
as he knelt by the grave of his mother and father?

———

He looked about. He remembered her palaver
on how both earth and sky would darken—
15   "You could barely tell one from the other"—

while the Monarch butterflies passed over
in their milkweed-hunger: "A wing-beat, some reckon,
may trigger off the mother and father

of all storms, striking your Irish Cliffs of Moher
20   with the force of a hurricane."
Then: "Milkweed and Monarch 'invented' each
       other."

———

He looked about. Cow's-parsley in a samovar.[3]
He'd mistaken his mother's name, "Regan," for
       "Anger":
as he knelt by the grave of his mother and father
25   he could barely tell one from the other.
—1994

---

[1]   *galvanized*   Coated with metal.
[2]   *stand-pipe*   Outdoor pipe connected to a water-main.
[3]   *samovar*   Russian tea urn.

## The Plot

*He said, my pretty fair maid, if it is as you say,*
*I'll do my best endeavors in cutting of your hay,*
*For in your lovely countenance I never saw a frown,*
*So, my lovely lass, I'll cut your grass, that's ne'er been*
    *trampled down.*

                    —Traditional Ballad

```
a l f a l f a l f a l f a l f a l f a
l f a l f a l f a l f a l f a l f a l
f a l f a l f a l f a l f a l f a l f
a l f a                   a l f a
l f a l                   l f a l
f a l f                   f a l f
a l f a       a l p h a       a l f a
l f a l                   l f a l
f a l f                   f a l f
a l f a                   a l f a
l f a l f a l f a l f a l f a l f a l
f a l f a l f a l f a l f a l f a l f
a l f a l f a l f a l f a l f a l f a
```
—1998


## Anonymous: Myself And Pangur

Myself and Pangur, my white cat,
have much the same calling, in that
much as Pangur goes after mice
I go hunting for the precise

5   word. He and I are much the same
in that I'm gladly "lost to fame"

when on the *Georgics*,[1] say, I'm bent
while he seems perfectly content

with his lot. Life in the cloister
10  can't possibly lose its luster
so long as there's some crucial point
with which we might by leaps and bounds

yet grapple, into which yet sink
our teeth. The bold Pangur will think
15  through mouse snagging much as I muse
on something naggingly abstruse,

then fix his clear, unflinching eye
on our lime-white cell wall, while I
focus, insofar as I can,
20  on the limits of what a man

may know. Something of his rapture
at his most recent mouse capture
I share when I, too, get to grips
with what has given me the slip.

25  And so we while away our whiles,
never cramping each other's styles
but practicing the noble arts
that so lift and lighten our hearts,

Pangur going in for the kill
30  with all his customary skill
while I, sharp-witted, swift, and sure,
shed light on what had seemed obscure.
                          —1998

---

[1]  *Georgics*  Long poem on agriculture and the role of the husband-
man by the Greek first-century BCE poet Virgil.

# Kazuo Ishiguro
## b. 1954

Kazuo Ishiguro is best known for his Booker Prize-winning novel *The Remains of the Day* (1989), but his other novels have also received extraordinary international acclaim. He has been hailed—along with writers such as Salman Rushdie, Michael Ondaatje, Vikram Seth, and Timothy Mo—as part of a new movement of "world fiction." Like these writers, he writes in English but is of non-Anglo-Saxon ancestry, and often depicts characters and settings which differ from those traditionally found in English literature. With influences that include Japanese pop culture of the 1940s and 1950s, nineteenth-century American writers, and Russian authors Dostoevski and Chekhov, Ishiguro often produces work that challenges his readers' expectations.

Ishiguro was born in Nagasaki, Japan, in 1954. When he was five his father accepted a one-year research position at the National Institute of Oceanography in Britain, and the family left for England. Ishiguro's parents educated him in the expectation that the family would return to Japan—providing him with Japanese magazines, books, and movies—but their return continued to be postponed, and eventually they became permanent British residents. Ishiguro studied English and philosophy at the University of Kent at Canterbury, where he received his B.A. He went on to a Master's degree in Creative Writing at the University of East Anglia in Norwich, where he was a member of a postgraduate class directed by Malcolm Bradbury.

Ishiguro, who for several years had attempted unsuccessfully to become a singer/songwriter, enjoyed almost immediate success as a writer of fiction. His first two novels, *A Pale View of Hills* (1982) and *An Artist of the Floating World* (1986), won prestigious literary awards in England and established him as an important new novelist. Both these early novels are set in Japan, although Ishiguro would not make his first return to Japan until 1989; Ishiguro has said that the Japan of these novels is one of his own personal imagination, constructed on a foundation of childhood memories.

Throughout his life Ishiguro has retained something of the outsider's perspective. When he began writing he realized he "wasn't a very English Englishman, and [he] wasn't a very Japanese Japanese either." This unique perspective enables him to pinpoint and dissect cultural myths, norms, and stereotypes—indeed, Ishiguro believes one of an artist's most important jobs is to "tackle and rework myths." Lurking behind the faintly comic resolution of *An Artist of the Floating World* is Ishiguro's knowledge that many Western readers—familiar only with stereotypes of Japanese society—would expect at the novel's end the cultural cliché of the protagonist's ritual suicide by *seppuku*.

*The Remains of the Day* is widely regarded as one of the most accomplished works of fiction of the twentieth century. Its story concerns Stevens, an aging butler who looks back in the summer of 1956 on the events of his life—in particular, on the great events that had transpired in his presence in the mid-1930s when his employer, Lord Darlington, had been organizing clandestine support in Britain for Germany's Nazi government; and on the unacknowledged love that had existed over the same period between himself and the housekeeper at Darlington Hall, Miss Kenton. The story is told in

Stevens's voice; from between the lines of the butler's spare and formal narrative the reader is led to piece together a tale of misplaced loyalty, lost opportunity, and almost unbearable sadness.

Ishiguro has been compared to novelist Graham Swift in his intertwining of personal and world histories. His novels often center on characters who attempt to cope with traumatic events of history, but he has little interest in investigating the historic events themselves. *The Remains of the Day* looks back from the 1950s to the impending Nazi threat of the 1930s, with barely a glance at its culmination during World War II; similarly, although *A Pale View of Hills* is set in Nagasaki in the late 1940s, no mention is ever made of the atomic bomb, the effects of which permeate every aspect of the protagonist's life. As Ishiguro says, this is because he is "more interested in what people tell themselves happened … than what actually happened." Often recounted in the first person by an unreliable narrator who is haunted by events in his or her past, Ishiguro's narratives frequently center on distortions of perception or of memory. His very writing style mimics the workings of memory, moving fluidly across time and through tangentially connected episodes.

Ishiguro's settings are often loosely defined, as is the case in "A Village After Dark" (2001) or in *The Unconsoled* (1995), which could be set in any European city. Whether they take place in Japan, England, or Shanghai—the setting of *When We Were Orphans* (2002)— there is often a somewhat unsettling universality to the experiences described; the locations are important only in that they provide backdrops for, and insights into, Ishiguro's characters. As a result, Ishiguro's fiction—which has been printed in over thirty languages—is well suited for translation.

*Never Let Me Go* (2005) has been widely praised as Ishiguro's most accomplished work since *The Remains of the Day*. Set largely in a boarding school where the atmosphere is at once warmly familiar and deeply disturbing, the novel explores against a futuristic dystopian background the roots of social exclusion, the sometimes frightening conjunction of medical science and human notions of progress, the nature of love, and the shadow cast by death on human existence.

Ishiguro lives with his wife and daughter in London.

⌘ ⌘ ⌘

## A Village After Dark

There was a time when I could travel England for weeks on end and remain at my sharpest—when, if anything, the travelling gave me an edge. But now that I am older I become disoriented more easily. So it was that on arriving at the village just after dark I failed to find my bearings at all. I could hardly believe I was in the same village in which not so long ago I had lived and come to exercise such influence.

There was nothing I recognized, and I found myself walking forever around twisting, badly lit streets hemmed in on both sides by the little stone cottages characteristic of the area. The streets often became so narrow I could make no progress without my bag or my elbow scraping one rough wall or another. I persevered nevertheless, stumbling around in the darkness in the hope of coming upon the village square— where I could at least orient myself—or else of encountering one of the villagers. When after a while I had done neither, a weariness came over me, and I decided my best course was just to choose a cottage at random, knock on the door, and hope it would be opened by someone who remembered me.

I stopped by a particularly rickety-looking door, whose upper beam was so low that I could see I would have to crouch right down to enter. A dim light was leaking out around the door's edges, and I could hear voices and laughter. I knocked loudly to insure that the occupants would hear me over their talk. But just then someone behind me said, "Hello."

I turned to find a young woman of around twenty, dressed in raggedy jeans and a torn jumper, standing in the darkness a little way away.

"You walked straight past me earlier," she said, "even though I called to you."

"Did I really? Well, I'm sorry. I didn't mean to be rude."

"You're Fletcher, aren't you?"

"Yes," I said, somewhat flattered.

"Wendy thought it was you when you went by our cottage. We all got very excited. You were one of that lot, weren't you? With David Maggis and all of them."

"Yes," I said, "but Maggis was hardly the most important one. I'm surprised you pick him out like that. There were other, far more important figures." I reeled off a series of names and was interested to see the girl nodding at each one in recognition. "But this must have all been before your time," I said. "I'm surprised you know about such things."

"It was before our time, but we're all experts on your lot. We know more about all that than most of the older ones who were here then. Wendy recognized you instantly just from your photos."

"I had no idea you young people had taken such an interest in us. I'm sorry I walked past you earlier. But you see, now that I'm older, I get a little disoriented when I travel."

I could hear some boisterous talk coming from behind the door. I banged on it again, this time rather impatiently, though I was not so eager to bring the encounter with the girl to a close.

She looked at me for a moment, then said, "All of you from those days are like that. David Maggis came here a few years ago. In '93, or maybe it was '94. He was like that. A bit vague. It must get to you after a while, travelling all the time."

"So Maggis was here. How interesting. You know, he wasn't one of the really important figures. You mustn't get carried away with such an idea. Incidentally, perhaps you could tell me who lives in this cottage." I thumped the door again.

"The Petersons," the girl said. "They're an old house. They'll probably remember you."

"The Petersons," I repeated, but the name meant nothing to me.

"Why don't you come to our cottage? Wendy was really excited. So were the rest of us. It's a real chance for us, actually talking to someone from those days."

"I'd very much like to do that. But first of all I'd better get myself settled in. The Petersons, you say."

I thumped the door again, this time quite ferociously. At last it opened, throwing warmth and light out into the street. An old man was standing in the doorway. He looked at me carefully, then asked, "It's not Fletcher, is it?"

"Yes, and I've just got into the village. I've been travelling for several days."

He thought about this for a moment, then said, "Well, you'd better come in."

I found myself in a cramped, untidy room full of rough wood and broken furniture. A log burning in the fireplace was the only source of light, by which I could make out a number of hunched figures sitting around the room. The old man led me to a chair beside the fire with a grudgingness that suggested it was the very one he had just vacated. Once I sat down, I found I could not easily turn my head to see my surroundings or the others in the room. But the warmth of the fire was very welcome, and for a moment I just stared into its flames, a pleasant grogginess drifting over me. Voices came from behind me, inquiring if I was well, if I had come far, if I was hungry, and I replied as best I could, though I was aware that my answers were barely adequate. Eventually, the questions ceased, and it occurred to me that my presence was creating a heavy awkwardness, but I was so grateful for the warmth and the chance to rest that I hardly cared.

Nonetheless, when the silence behind me had gone unbroken for several minutes, I resolved to address my hosts with a little more civility, and I turned in my chair. It was then, as I did so, that I was suddenly seized by an intense sense of recognition. I had chosen the cottage quite at random, but now I could see that it was none other than the very one in which I had spent my years in this village. My gaze moved immediately to the far corner—at this moment shrouded in darkness—to the spot that had been *my* corner, where once my mattress had been and where I had spent many tranquil hours browsing through books or conversing with whoever happened to drift in. On summer days, the windows, and often the door, were left open to allow a refreshing breeze to blow right through. Those were the days when the cottage was surrounded by open fields and there would come from outside the voices of my friends, lazing in the long grass, arguing over poetry or philosophy. These precious fragments of the past came back to me so powerfully that it was all I could do not to make straight for my old corner then and there.

Someone was speaking to me again, perhaps asking another question, but I hardly listened. Rising, I peered through the shadows into my corner, and could now make out a narrow bed, covered by an old curtain, occupying more or less the exact space where my mattress had been. The bed looked extremely inviting, and I found myself cutting into something the old man was saying.

"Look," I said, "I know this is a bit blunt. But, you see, I've come such a long way today. I really need to lie down, close my eyes, even if it's just for a few minutes. After that, I'm happy to talk all you like."

I could see the figures around the room shifting uneasily. Then a new voice said, rather sullenly, "Go ahead then. Have a nap. Don't mind us."

But I was already picking my way through the clutter toward my corner. The bed felt damp, and the springs creaked under my weight, but no sooner had I curled up with my back to the room than my many hours of travelling began to catch up with me. As I was drifting off, I heard the old man saying, "It's Fletcher, all right. God, he's aged."

A woman's voice said, "Should we let him go to sleep like that? He might wake in a few hours and then we'll have to stay up with him."

"Let him sleep for an hour or so," someone else said. "If he's still asleep after an hour, we'll wake him."

At this point, sheer exhaustion overtook me.

It was not a continuous or comfortable sleep. I drifted between sleep and waking, always conscious of voices behind me in the room. At some point, I was aware of a woman saying, "I don't know how I was ever under his spell. He looks such a ragamuffin now."

In my state of near-sleep, I debated with myself whether these words applied to me or, perhaps, to David Maggis, but before long sleep engulfed me once more.

When I next awoke, the room appeared to have grown both darker and colder. Voices were continuing behind me in lowered tones, but I could make no sense

of the conversation. I now felt embarrassed at having gone to sleep in the way I had, and for a few further moments remained motionless with my face to the wall. But something about me must have revealed that I was awake, for a woman's voice, breaking off from the general conversation, said, "Oh, look, look." Some whispers were exchanged, then I heard the sound of someone coming toward my corner. I felt a hand placed gently on my shoulder, and looked up to find a woman kneeling over me. I did not turn my body sufficiently to see the room, but I got the impression that it was lit by dying embers, and the woman's face was visible only in shadow.

"Now, Fletcher," she said. "It's time we had a talk. I've waited a long time for you to come back. I've thought about you often."

I strained to see her more clearly. She was somewhere in her forties, and even in the gloom I noticed a sleepy sadness in her eyes. But her face failed to stir in me even the faintest of memories.

"I'm sorry," I said. "I have no recollection of you. But please forgive me if we met some time ago. I do get very disoriented these days."

"Fletcher," she said, "when we used to know one another, I was young and beautiful. I idolized you, and everything you said seemed like an answer. Now here you are, back again. I've wanted to tell you for many years that you ruined my life."

"You're being unfair. All right, I was mistaken about a lot of things. But I never claimed to have any answers. All I said in those days was that it was our duty, all of us, to contribute to the debate. We knew so much more about the issues than the ordinary people here. If people like us procrastinated, claiming we didn't yet know enough, then who was there to act? But I never claimed I had the answers. No, you're being unfair."

"Fletcher," she said, and her voice was oddly gentle, "you used to make love to me, more or less every time I wandered in here to your room. In this corner, we did all kinds of beautifully dirty things. It's odd to think how I could have once been so physically excited by you. And here you're just a foul-smelling bundle of rags now. But look at me—I'm still attractive. My face has got a bit lined, but when I walk in the village streets I wear dresses I've made specially to show off my figure.

A lot of men want me still. But you, no woman would look at you now. A bundle of stinking rags and flesh."

"I don't remember you," I said. "And I've no time for sex these days. I've other things to worry about. More serious things. Very well, I was mistaken about a lot in those days. But I've done more than most to try and make amends. You see, even now I'm travelling. I've never stopped. I've travelled and travelled trying to undo what damage I may once have caused. That's more than can be said of some others from those days. I bet Maggis, for instance, hasn't worked nearly as hard to try and put things right."

The woman was stroking my hair.

"Look at you. I used to do this, run my fingers through your hair. Look at this filthy mess. I'm sure you're contaminated with all sorts of parasites." But she continued slowly to run her fingers through the dirty knots. I failed to feel anything erotic from this, as perhaps she wished me to do. Rather, her caresses felt maternal. Indeed, for a moment it was as though I had finally reached some cocoon of protectiveness, and I began once more to feel sleepy. But suddenly she stopped and slapped me hard on the forehead.

"Why don't you join the rest of us now? You've had your sleep. You've got a lot of explaining to do." With that she got up and left.

For the first time, I turned my body sufficiently to survey the room. I saw the woman making her way past the clutter on the floor, then sitting down in a rocking chair by the fireplace. I could see three other figures hunched around the dying fire. One I recognized to be the old man who had opened the door. The two others—sitting together on what looked like a wooden trunk—seemed to be women of around the same age as the one who had spoken to me.

The old man noticed that I had turned, and he indicated to the others that I was watching. The four of them proceeded to sit stiffly, not speaking. From the way they did this, it was clear that they had been discussing me thoroughly while I was asleep. In fact, as I watched them I could more or less guess the whole shape their conversation had taken. I could see, for instance, that they had spent some time expressing concern for the young girl I had met outside, and about the effect I might have on her peers.

"They're all so impressionable," the old man would have said. "And I heard her inviting him to visit them."

To which, no doubt, one of the women on the trunk would have said, "But he can't do much harm now. In our time, we were all taken in because all his kind—they were young and glamorous. But these days the odd one passing through from time to time, looking all decrepit and burned out like that—if anything, it goes to demystify all that talk about the old days. In any case, people like him have changed their position so much these days. They don't know themselves what they believe."

The old man would have shaken his head. "I saw the way that young girl was looking at him. All right, he looks a pitiful mess over there just now. But once his ego's fed a little, once he has the flattery of the young people, sees how they want to hear his ideas, then there'll be no stopping him. It'll be just like before. He'll have them all working for his causes. Young girls like that, there's so little for them to believe in now. Even a stinking tramp like this could give them a purpose."

Their conversation, all the time I slept, would have gone something very much like that. But now, as I observed them from my corner, they continued to sit in guilty silence, staring at the last of their fire. After a while, I rose to my feet. Absurdly, the four of them kept their gazes averted from me. I waited a few moments to see if any of them would say anything. Finally, I said, "All right, I was asleep earlier, but I've guessed what you were saying. Well, you'll be interested to know I'm going to do the very thing you feared. I'm going this moment to the young people's cottage. I'm going to tell them what to do with all their energy, all their dreams, their urge to achieve something of lasting good in this world. Look at you, what a pathetic bunch. Crouching in your cottage, afraid to do anything, afraid of me, of Maggis, of anyone else from those times. Afraid to do anything in the world out there, just because once we made a few mistakes. Well, those young people haven't yet sunk so low, despite all the lethargy you've been preaching at them down the years. I'll talk to them. I'll undo in half an hour all of your sorry efforts."

"You see," the old man said to the others. "I knew it would be this way. We ought to stop him, but what can we do?"

I crashed my way across the room, picked up my bag, and went out into the night.

The girl was still standing outside when I emerged. She seemed to be expecting me and with a nod began to lead the way.

The night was drizzly and dark. We twisted and turned along the narrow paths that ran between the cottages. Some of the cottages we passed looked so decayed and crumbling that I felt I could destroy one of them simply by running at it with all my weight.

The girl kept a few paces ahead, occasionally glancing back at me over her shoulder. Once she said, "Wendy's going to be so pleased. She was sure it was you when you went past earlier. By now, she'll have guessed she was right, because I've been away this long, and she'll have brought the whole crowd together. They'll all be waiting."

"Did you give David Maggis this sort of reception, too?"

"Oh, yes. We were really excited when he came."

"I'm sure he found that very gratifying. He always had an exaggerated sense of his own importance."

"Wendy says Maggis was one of the interesting ones, but that you were, well, important. She thinks you were really important."

I thought about this for a moment.

"You know," I said, "I've changed my mind on very many things. If Wendy's expecting me to say all the things I used to all those years ago, well, she's going to be in for a disappointment."

The girl did not seem to hear this, but continued to lead me purposefully through the clusters of cottages.

After a little while, I became aware of footsteps following a dozen or so paces behind us. At first, I assumed this was just some villager out walking and refrained from turning round. But then the girl halted under a street lamp and looked behind us. I was thus obliged also to stop and turn. A middle-aged man in a dark overcoat was coming toward us. As he approached, he held out his hand and shook mine, though without smiling.

"So," he said, "you're here."

I then realized I knew the man. We had not seen each other since we were ten years old. His name was Roger Button, and he had been in my class at the school I had attended for two years in Canada before my family returned to England. Roger Button and I had not been especially close, but, because he had been a timid boy, and because he, too, was from England, he had for a while followed me about. I had neither seen nor heard from him since that time. Now, as I studied his appearance under the street lamp, I saw the years had not been kind to him. He was bald, his face was pocked and lined, and there was a weary sag to his whole posture. For all that, there was no mistaking my old classmate.

"Roger," I said, "I'm just on my way to visit this young lady's friends. They've gathered together to receive me. Otherwise I'd have come and looked you up straightaway. As it was, I had it in my mind as the next thing to do, even before getting any sleep tonight. I was just thinking to myself, However late things finish at the young people's cottage, I'll go and knock on Roger's door afterward."

"Don't worry," said Roger Button as we all started to walk again. "I know how busy you are. But we ought to talk. Chew over old times. When you last saw me—at school, I mean—I suppose I was a rather feeble specimen. But, you know, that all changed when I got to fourteen, fifteen. I really toughened up. Became quite a leader type. But you'd long since left Canada. I always wondered what would have happened if we'd come across each other at fifteen. Things would have been rather different between us, I assure you."

As he said this, memories came flooding back. In those days, Roger Button had idolized me, and in return I had bullied him incessantly. However, there had existed between us a curious understanding that my bullying him was all for his own good; that when, without warning, I suddenly punched him in the stomach on the playground, or when, passing him in the corridor, I impulsively wrenched his arm up his back until he started to cry, I was doing so in order to help him toughen up. Accordingly, the principal effect such attacks had on our relationship was to keep him in awe of me. This all came back to me as I listened to the weary-looking man walking beside me.

"Of course," Roger Button went on, perhaps guessing my train of thought, "it might well be that if you hadn't treated me the way you did I'd never have become what I did at fifteen. In any case, I've often wondered how it would have been if we'd met just a few years later. I really was something to be reckoned with by then."

We were once again walking along the narrow twisted passages between cottages. The girl was still leading the way, but she was now walking much faster. Often we would only just manage to catch a glimpse of her turning some corner ahead of us, and it struck me that we would have to keep alert if we were not to lose her.

"Today, of course," Roger Button was saying, "I've let myself go a bit. But I have to say, old fellow, you seem to be in much worse shape. Compared with you, I'm an athlete. Not to put too fine a point on it, you're just a filthy old tramp now, really, aren't you? But, you know, for a long time after you left I continued to idolize you. Would Fletcher do this? What would Fletcher think if he saw me doing that? Oh, yes. It was only when I got to fifteen or so that I looked back on it all and saw through you. Then I was very angry, of course. Even now, I still think about it sometimes. I look back and think, Well, he was just a thoroughly nasty so-and-so. He had a little more weight and muscle at that age than I did, a little more confidence, and he took full advantage. Yes, it's very clear, looking back, what a nasty little person you were. Of course, I'm not implying you still are today. We all change. That much I'm willing to accept."

"Have you been living here long?" I asked, wishing to change the subject.

"Oh, seven years or so. Of course, they talk about you a lot around here. I sometimes tell them about our early association. 'But he won't remember me,' I always tell them. 'Why would he remember a skinny little boy he used to bully and have at his beck and call?' Anyway, the young people here, they talk about you more and more these days. Certainly, the ones who've never seen you tend to idealize you the most. I suppose you've come back to capitalize on all that. Still, I shouldn't blame you. You're entitled to try and salvage a little self-respect."

We suddenly found ourselves facing an open field, and we both halted. Glancing back, I saw that we had

walked our way out of the village; the last of the cottages were some distance behind us. Just as I had feared, we had lost the young woman; in fact, I realized we had not been following her for some time.

At that moment, the moon emerged, and I saw we were standing at the edge of a vast grassy field—extending, I supposed, far beyond what I could see by the moon.

Roger Button turned to me. His face in the moonlight seemed gentle, almost affectionate.

"Still," he said, "it's time to forgive. You shouldn't keep worrying so much. As you see, certain things from the past will come back to you in the end. But then we can't be held accountable for what we did when we were very young."

"No doubt you're right," I said. Then I turned and looked around in the darkness. "But now I'm not sure where to go. You see, there were some young people waiting for me in their cottage. By now they'd have a warm fire ready for me and some hot tea. And some home-baked cakes, perhaps even a good stew. And the moment I entered, ushered in by that young lady we were following just now, they'd all have burst into applause. There'd be smiling, adoring faces all around me. That's what's waiting for me somewhere. Except I'm not sure where I should go."

Roger Button shrugged. "Don't worry, you'll get there easily enough. Except, you know, that girl was being a little misleading if she implied you could walk to Wendy's cottage. It's much too far. You'd really need to catch a bus. Even then, it's quite a long journey. About two hours, I'd say. But don't worry, I'll show you where you can pick up your bus."

With that, he began to walk back toward the cottages. As I followed, I could sense that the hour had got very late and my companion was anxious to get some sleep. We spent several minutes walking around the cottages again, and then he brought us out into the village square. In fact, it was so small and shabby it hardly merited being called a square; it was little more than a patch of green beside a solitary street lamp. Just visible beyond the pool of light cast by the lamp were a few shops, all shut up for the night. There was complete silence and nothing was stirring. A light mist was hovering over the ground.

Roger Button stopped before we had reached the green and pointed.

"There," he said. "If you stand there, a bus will come along. As I say, it's not a short journey. About two hours. But don't worry, I'm sure your young people will wait. They've so little else to believe in these days, you see."

"It's very late," I said. "Are you sure a bus will come?"

"Oh, yes. Of course, you may have to wait. But eventually a bus will come." Then he touched me reassuringly on the shoulder. "I can see it might get a little lonely standing out here. But once the bus arrives your spirits will rise, believe me. Oh, yes. That bus is always a joy. It'll be brightly lit up, and it's always full of cheerful people, laughing and joking and pointing out the window. Once you board it, you'll feel warm and comfortable, and the other passengers will chat with you, perhaps offer you things to eat or drink. There may even be singing— that depends on the driver. Some drivers encourage it, others don't. Well, Fletcher, it was good to see you."

We shook hands, then he turned and walked away. I watched him disappear into the darkness between two cottages.

I walked up to the green and put my bag down at the foot of the lamppost. I listened for the sound of a vehicle in the distance, but the night was utterly still. Nevertheless, I had been cheered by Roger Button's description of the bus. Moreover, I thought of the reception awaiting me at my journey's end—of the adoring faces of the young people—and felt the stirrings of optimism somewhere deep within me.

—2001

# HANIF KUREISHI

## b. 1954

Hanif Kureishi is known as much for his work on films such as *My Beautiful Laundrette* (which won an Academy Award nomination in 1986 for best screenplay) and *Sammy and Rosie Get Laid* as he is for his novels, short stories, plays, and essays. His films and his fiction—which includes the novel *The Black Album* (1995) and the short story collection *Love in a Blue Time* (1997)—reflect the tense dynamics of inter-racial life in Thatcher-era Britain and are animated by realistic dialogue and picaresque characters.

Born in Bromley, a suburb of London, the son of a Pakistani father and English mother, Kureishi grew up feeling alienated in both groups. He recalls racial violence and taunts when he was growing up (being referred to regularly by one teacher as "Paki Pete," for instance). He speaks about having wanted to escape both his skin color and the Indian and Pakistani communities. Yet he has become a central figure in the new, multicultural, literary landscape of modern Britain, where he writes openly about the experiences of "hybridity" and alienation.

Kureishi expressed a desire to write at a young age, but his passion for learning led him to study philosophy at King's College, London, where he graduated with a B.A. He returned to writing soon afterward and saw his first play, *Soaking the Heat*, produced in 1976 at London's Royal Court Theatre. Many plays followed, including *Outskirts* (1981), first produced by the Royal Shakespeare Company. Four years later he wrote the screenplay for *My Beautiful Laundrette*, a successful film that was directed by Stephen Frears. 1990 saw the publication of Kureishi's first novel, *The Buddha of Suburbia*, which won the Whitbread First Novel Award. A semi-autobiographical novel, *The Buddha of Suburbia* focuses on a young "in-betweener" who has an Indian father and English mother, is bisexual, and moves between suburban and urban life in London. *The Black Album* (1995), Kureishi's second novel, also portrays a young "hybrid" Londoner—in this case one who is as much attracted to Western pop culture (as represented by his acid-dropping college supervisor Deedee Osgood) as he is to the culture of the campus Islamic fundamentalists (who call for the burning of Salman Rushdie's *The Satanic Verses*).

Kureishi wrote the screenplay for and directed the film *London Kills Me* (1991) and the screenplay for the film version of his short story "My Son the Fanatic" (1997). The short story touches on familiar Kureishi themes of father-and-son tensions, cultural longings, and Islamic fundamentalism. When the film version appeared, many in the Pakistani community condemned what they saw as racial stereotyping and a negative portrayal of the Asian community. Kureishi has said, however, that he is more interested in exploring the problems of immigration, hybridity, religious fundamentalism, sexual politics, and racial tensions than he is in becoming a spokesperson for the Asian community. "Does Shakespeare present Hamlet as a nice Danish prince?" he once asked. A "shrewd observer of human folly," as *Time Out* magazine has called him, Kureishi is concerned with exposing the pretense, hypocrisy, and immorality of a wide range of human beings whether Anglo-English, Asian, or "in-betweeners."

Kureishi has broadened the range of his work in recent years, writing in *Intimacy* (1998) of a man's experience with infidelity (his own and his wife's) and his abandonment of his family; of the pop culture world of rock musicians in *Gabriel's Gift* (2001); and of a Faustian, hedonistic search for youth and beauty in *The Body* (2004). But Kureishi continues to write with his signature irony, which he calls "the modern mode, a way of commenting on bleakness and cruelty without falling into dourness and didacticism."

⌘ ⌘ ⌘

## My Son the Fanatic

Surreptitiously the father began going into his son's bedroom. He would sit there for hours, rousing himself only to seek clues. What bewildered him was that Ali was getting tidier. Instead of the usual tangle of clothes, books, cricket bats, video games, the room was becoming neat and ordered; spaces began appearing where before there had been only mess.

Initially Parvez had been pleased; his son was outgrowing his teenage attitudes. But one day, beside the dustbin, Parvez found a torn bag which contained not only old toys, but computer discs, video tapes, new books and fashionable clothes the boy had bought just a few months before. Also without explanation, Ali had parted from the English girlfriend who used to come often to the house. His old friends had stopped ringing.

For reasons he didn't himself understand, Parvez wasn't able to bring up the subject of Ali's unusual behaviour. He was aware that he had become slightly afraid of his son, who, alongside his silences, was developing a sharp tongue. One remark Parvez did make, "You don't play your guitar any more," elicited the mysterious but conclusive reply, "There are more important things to be done."

Yet Parvez felt his son's eccentricity as an injustice. He had always been aware of the pitfalls which other men's sons had fallen into in England. And so, for Ali, he had worked long hours and spent a lot of money paying for his education as an accountant. He had bought him good suits, all the books he required and a computer. And now the boy was throwing his possessions out!

The TV, video and sound system followed the guitar. Soon the room was practically bare. Even the unhappy walls bore marks where Ali's pictures had been removed.

Parvez couldn't sleep; he went more to the whisky bottle, even when he was at work. He realised it was imperative to discuss the matter with someone sympathetic.

Parvez had been a taxi driver for twenty years. Half that time he'd worked for the same firm. Like him, most of the other drivers were Punjabis. They preferred to work at night, the roads were clearer and the money better. They slept during the day, avoiding their wives. Together they led almost a boy's life in the cabbies' office, playing cards and practical jokes, exchanging lewd stories, eating together and discussing politics and their problems.

But Parvez had been unable to bring this subject up with his friends. He was too ashamed. And he was afraid, too, that they would blame him for the wrong turning his boy had taken, just as he had blamed other fathers whose sons had taken to running around with bad girls, truanting from school and joining gangs.

For years Parvez had boasted to the other men about how Ali excelled at cricket, swimming and football, and how attentive a scholar he was, getting straight "A"s in most subjects. Was it asking too much for Ali to get a good job now, marry the right girl and start a family? Once this happened, Parvez would be happy. His dreams of doing well in England would have come true. Where had he gone wrong?

But one night, sitting in the taxi office on busted chairs with his two closest friends watching a Sylvester Stallone film, he broke his silence.

"I can't understand it!" he burst out. "Everything is going from his room. And I can't talk to him any more. We were not father and son—we were brothers! Where has he gone? Why is he torturing me!"

And Parvez put his head in his hands.

Even as he poured out his account the men shook their heads and gave one another knowing glances. From their grave looks Parvez realised they understood the situation.

"Tell me what is happening!" he demanded.

The reply was almost triumphant. They had guessed something was going wrong. Now it was clear. Ali was taking drugs and selling his possessions to pay for them. That was why his bedroom was emptying.

"What must I do then?"

Parvez's friends instructed him to watch Ali scrupulously and then be severe with him, before the boy went mad, overdosed or murdered someone.

Parvez staggered out into the early morning air, terrified they were right. His boy—the drug addict killer!

To his relief he found Bettina sitting in his car.

Usually the last customers of the night were local "brasses" or prostitutes. The taxi drivers knew them well, often driving them to liaisons. At the end of the girls' shifts, the men would ferry them home, though sometimes the women would join them for a drinking session in the office. Occasionally the drivers would go with the girls. "A ride in exchange for a ride," it was called.

Bettina had known Parvez for three years. She lived outside the town and on the long drive home, where she sat not in the passenger seat but beside him, Parvez had talked to her about his life and hopes, just as she talked about hers. They saw each other most nights.

He could talk to her about things he'd never be able to discuss with his own wife. Bettina, in turn, always reported on her night's activities. He liked to know where she was and with whom. Once he had rescued her from a violent client, and since then they had come to care for one another.

Though Bettina had never met the boy, she heard about Ali continually. That late night, when he told Bettina that he suspected Ali was on drugs, she judged neither the boy nor his father, but became businesslike and told him what to watch for.

"It's all in the eyes," she said. They might be bloodshot; the pupils might be dilated; he might look tired.

He could be liable to sweats, or sudden mood changes. "Okay?"

Parvez began his vigil gratefully. Now he knew what the problem might be, he felt better. And surely, he figured, things couldn't have gone too far? With Bettina's help he would soon sort it out.

He watched each mouthful the boy took. He sat beside him at every opportunity and looked into his eyes. When he could he took the boy's hand, checking his temperature. If the boy wasn't at home Parvez was active, looking under the carpet, in his drawers, behind the empty wardrobe, sniffing, inspecting, probing. He knew what to look for; Bettina had drawn pictures of capsules, syringes, pills, powders, rocks.

Every night she waited to hear news of what he'd witnessed.

After a few days of constant observation, Parvez was able to report that although the boy had given up sports, he seemed healthy, with clear eyes. He didn't, as his father expected, flinch guiltily from his gaze. In fact the boy's mood was alert and steady in this sense; as well as being sullen, he was very watchful. He returned his father's long looks with more than a hint of criticism, of reproach even, so much so that Parvez began to feel that it was he who was in the wrong, and not the boy!

"And there's nothing else physically different?" Bettina asked.

"No!" Parvez thought for a moment. "But he is growing a beard."

One night, after sitting with Bettina in an all-night coffee shop, Parvez came home particularly late. Reluctantly he and Bettina had abandoned their only explanation, the drug theory, for Parvez had found nothing resembling any drug in Ali's room. Besides, Ali wasn't selling his belongings. He threw them out, gave them away or donated them to charity shops.

Standing in the hall, Parvez heard his boy's alarm clock go off. Parvez hurried into his bedroom where his wife was still awake, sewing in bed. He ordered her to sit down and keep quiet, though she had neither stood up nor said a word. From this post, and with her watching him curiously, he observed his son through the crack in the door.

The boy went into the bathroom to wash. When he returned to his room Parvez sprang across the hall and set his ear at Ali's door. A muttering sound came from within. Parvez was puzzled but relieved.

Once this clue had been established, Parvez watched him at other times. The boy was praying. Without fail, when he was at home, he prayed five times a day.

Parvez had grown up in Lahore[1] where all the boys had been taught the Koran. To stop him falling asleep when he studied, the Moulvi[2] had attached a piece of string to the ceiling and tied it to Parvez's hair, so that if his head fell forward, he would instantly awake. After this indignity Parvez had avoided all religions. Not that the other taxi drivers had more respect. In fact they made jokes about the local mullahs[3] walking around with their caps and beards, thinking they could tell people how to live, while their eyes roved over the boys and girls in their care.

Parvez described to Bettina what he had discovered. He informed the men in the taxi office. The friends, who had been so curious before, now became oddly silent. They could hardly condemn the boy for his devotions.

Parvez decided to take a night off and go out with the boy. They could talk things over. He wanted to hear how things were going at college; he wanted to tell him stories about their family in Pakistan. More than anything he yearned to understand how Ali had discovered the "spiritual dimension," as Bettina described it.

To Parvez's surprise, the boy refused to accompany him. He claimed he had an appointment. Parvez had to insist that no appointment could be more important than that of a son with his father.

The next day, Parvez went immediately to the street where Bettina stood in the rain wearing high heels, a short skirt and a long mac[4] on top, which she would open hopefully at passing cars.

"Get in, get in!" he said.

They drove out across the moors and parked at the spot where on better days, with a view unimpeded for many miles by nothing but wild deer and horses, they'd lie back, with their eyes half closed, saying "This is the

life." This time Parvez was trembling. Bettina put her arms around him.

"What's happened?"

"I've just had the worst experience of my life."

As Bettina rubbed his head Parvez told her that the previous evening he and Ali had gone to a restaurant. As they studied the menu, the waiter, whom Parvez knew, brought him his usual whisky and water. Parvez had been so nervous he had even prepared a question. He was going to ask Ali if he was worried about his imminent exams. But first, wanting to relax, he loosened his tie, crunched a popadom[5] and took a long drink.

Before Parvez could speak, Ali made a face.

"Don't you know it's wrong to drink alcohol?" he said.

"He spoke to me very harshly," Parvez told Bettina. "I was about to castigate the boy for being insolent, but managed to control myself."

He had explained patiently to Ali that for years he had worked more than ten hours a day, that he had few enjoyments or hobbies and never went on holiday. Surely it wasn't a crime to have a drink when he wanted one?

"But it is forbidden," the boy said.

Parvez shrugged, "I know."

"And so is gambling, isn't it?"

"Yes. But surely we are only human?"

Each time Parvez took a drink, the boy winced, or made a fastidious face as an accompaniment. This made Parvez drink more quickly. The waiter, wanting to please his friend, brought another glass of whisky. Parvez knew he was getting drunk, but he couldn't stop himself. Ali had a horrible look on his face, full of disgust and censure. It was as if he hated his father.

Halfway through the meal Parvez suddenly lost his temper and threw a plate on the floor. He had felt like ripping the cloth from the table, but the waiters and other customers were staring at him. Yet he wouldn't stand for his own son telling him the difference between right and wrong. He knew he wasn't a bad man. He had a conscience. There were a few things of which he was ashamed, but on the whole he had lived a decent life.

"When have I had time to be wicked?" he asked Ali.

---

[1] *Lahore*  Capital of Punjab province in Pakistan.

[2] *Moulvi*  Muslim doctor of the law; an imam or priest; a learned man.

[3] *mullahs*  Muslim clerics.

[4] *mac*  I.e., macintosh, or raincoat.

[5] *popadom*  Thin wafer made from chickpea flour.

In a low monotonous voice the boy explained that Parvez had not, in fact, lived a good life. He had broken countless rules of the Koran.

"For instance?" Parvez demanded.

Ali hadn't needed time to think. As if he had been waiting for this moment, he asked his father if he didn't relish pork pies?[1]

"Well ..."

Parvez couldn't deny that he loved crispy bacon smothered with mushrooms and mustard and sandwiched between slices of fried bread. In fact he ate this for breakfast every morning.

Ali then reminded Parvez that he had ordered his own wife to cook pork sausages, saying to her, "You're not in the village now, this is England. We have to fit in!"

Parvez was so annoyed and perplexed by this attack that he called for more drink.

"The problem is this," the boy said. He leaned across the table. For the first time that night his eyes were alive. "You are too implicated in Western civilisation."

Parvez burped; he thought he was going to choke.

"Implicated!" he said. "But we live here!"

"The Western materialists hate us," Ali said. "Papa, how can you love something which hates you?"

"What is the answer then?" Parvez said miserably. "According to you."

Ali addressed his father fluently, as if Parvez were a rowdy crowd that had to be quelled and convinced. The Law of Islam would rule the world; the skin of the infidel would burn off again and again; the Jews and Christers would be routed. The West was a sink of hypocrites, adulterers, homosexuals, drug takers and prostitutes.

As Ali talked, Parvez looked out of the window as if to check that they were still in London.

"My people have taken enough. If the persecution doesn't stop there will be *jihad*.[2] I, and millions of others, will gladly give our lives for the cause."

"But why, why?" Parvez said.

"For us the reward will be in paradise."

"Paradise!"

Finally, as Parvez's eyes filled with tears, the boy urged him to mend his ways.

"How is that possible?" Parvez asked.

"Pray," Ali said. "Pray beside me."

Parvez called for the bill and ushered his boy out of the restaurant as soon as he was able. He couldn't take any more. Ali sounded as if he'd swallowed someone else's voice.

On the way home the boy sat in the back of the taxi, as if he were a customer.

"What has made you like this?" Parvez asked him, afraid that somehow he was to blame for all this. "Is there a particular event which has influenced you?"

"Living in this country."

"But I love England," Parvez said, watching his boy in the mirror. "They let you do almost anything here."

"That is the problem," he replied.

For the first time in years Parvez couldn't see straight. He knocked the side of the car against a lorry, ripping off the wing mirror. They were lucky not to have been stopped by the police; Parvez would have lost his licence and therefore his job.

Getting out of the car back at the house, Parvez stumbled and fell in the road, scraping his hands and ripping his trousers. He managed to haul himself up. The boy didn't even offer him his hand.

Parvez told Bettina he was now willing to pray, if that was what the boy wanted, if that would dislodge the pitiless look from his eyes.

"But what I object to," he said, "is being told by my own son that I am going to hell!"

What finished Parvez off was that the boy had said he was giving up accountancy. When Parvez had asked why, Ali had said sarcastically that it was obvious.

"Western education cultivates an anti-religious attitude."

And, according to Ali, in the world of accountants it was usual to meet women, drink alcohol and practise usury.

"But it's well-paid work," Parvez argued. "For years you've been preparing!"

Ali said he was going to begin to work in prisons, with poor Muslims who were struggling to maintain

---

[1] *pork pies*  Muslims are forbidden to eat pork.

[2] *jihad*  Jihad, or "struggle" has had two meanings, historically: one suggests the struggle in which a Muslim should engage spiritually, with himself, and the other suggests the Muslim struggle against non-believers, which can be understood as a call to war.

their purity in the face of corruption. Finally, at the end of the evening, as Ali was going to bed, he had asked his father why he didn't have a beard, or at least a moustache.

"I feel as if I've lost my son," Parvez told Bettina. "I can't bear to be looked at as if I'm a criminal. I've decided what to do."

"What is it?"

"I'm going to tell him to pick up his prayer mat and get out of my house. It will be the hardest thing I've ever done, but tonight I'm going to do it."

"But you mustn't give up on him," said Bettina. "Many young people fall into cults and superstitious groups. It doesn't mean they'll always feel the same way."

She said Parvez had to stick by his boy, giving him support, until he came through.

Parvez was persuaded that she was right, even though he didn't feel like giving his son more love when he had hardly been thanked for all he had already given.

Nevertheless, Parvez tried to endure his son's looks and reproaches. He attempted to make conversation about his beliefs. But if Parvez ventured any criticism, Ali always had a brusque reply. On one occasion Ali accused Parvez of "grovelling" to the whites; in contrast, he explained, he was not "inferior"; there was more to the world than the West, though the West always thought it was best.

"How is it you know that?" Parvez said, "seeing as you've never left England?"

Ali replied with a look of contempt.

One night, having ensured there was no alcohol on his breath, Parvez sat down at the kitchen table with Ali. He hoped Ali would compliment him on the beard he was growing but Ali didn't appear to notice.

The previous day Parvez had been telling Bettina that he thought people in the West sometimes felt inwardly empty and that people needed a philosophy to live by.

"Yes," said Bettina. "That's the answer. You must tell him what your philosophy of life is. Then he will understand that there are other beliefs."

After some fatiguing consideration, Parvez was ready to begin. The boy watched him as if he expected nothing.

Haltingly Parvez said that people had to treat one another with respect, particularly children their parents. This did seem, for a moment, to affect the boy. Heartened, Parvez continued. In his view this life was all there was and when you died you rotted in the earth. "Grass and flowers will grow out of me, but something of me will live on—"

"How?"

"In other people. I will continue—in you." At this the boy appeared a little distressed. "And your grandchildren," Parvez added for good measure. "But while I am here on earth I want to make the best of it. And I want you to, as well!"

"What d'you mean by 'make the best of it'?" asked the boy.

"Well," said Parvez. "For a start … you should enjoy yourself. Yes. Enjoy yourself without hurting others."

Ali said that enjoyment was a "bottomless pit."

"But I don't mean enjoyment like that!" said Parvez. "I mean the beauty of living!"

"All over the world our people are oppressed," was the boy's reply.

"I know," Parvez replied, not entirely sure who "our people" were, "but still—life is for living!"

Ali said, "Real morality has existed for hundreds of years. Around the world millions and millions of people share my beliefs. Are you saying you are right and they are all wrong?"

Ali looked at his father with such aggressive confidence that Parvez could say no more.

One evening Bettina was sitting in Parvez's car, after visiting a client, when they passed a boy on the street.

"That's my son." Parvez said suddenly. They were on the other side of town, in a poor district, where there were two mosques.

Parvez set his face hard.

Bettina turned to watch him. "Slow down then, slow down!" She said, "He's good-looking. Reminds me of you. But with a more determined face. Please, can't we stop?"

"What for?"

"I'd like to talk to him."

Parvez turned the cab round and stopped beside the boy.

"Coming home?" Parvez asked. "It's quite a way."

The sullen boy shrugged and got into the back seat. Bettina sat in the front. Parvez became aware of Bettina's short skirt, gaudy rings and ice-blue eyeshadow. He became conscious that the smell of her perfume, which he loved, filled the cab. He opened the window.

While Parvez drove as fast as he could, Bettina said gently to Ali, "Where have you been?"

"The mosque," he said.

"And how are you getting on at college? Are you working hard?"

"Who are you to ask me these questions?" he said, looking out of the window. Then they hit bad traffic and the car came to a standstill.

By now Bettina had inadvertently laid her hand on Parvez's shoulder. She said, "Your father, who is a good man, is very worried about you. You know he loves you more than his own life."

"You say he loves me," the boy said.

"Yes!" said Bettina.

"Then why is he letting a woman like you touch him like that?"

If Bettina looked at the boy in anger, he looked back at her with twice as much cold fury.

She said, "What kind of woman am I that deserves to be spoken to like that?"

"You know," he said. "Now let me out."

"Never," Parvez replied.

"Don't worry, I'm getting out," Bettina said.

"No, don't!" said Parvez. But even as the car moved she opened the door, threw herself out and ran away across the road. Parvez shouted after her several times, but she had gone.

Parvez took Ali back to the house, saying nothing more to him. Ali went straight to his room. Parvez was unable to read the paper, watch television or even sit down. He kept pouring himself drinks.

At last he went upstairs and paced up and down outside Ali's room. When, finally, he opened the door, Ali was praying. The boy didn't even glance his way.

Parvez kicked him over. Then he dragged the boy up by his shirt and hit him. The boy fell back. Parvez hit him again. The boy's face was bloody. Parvez was panting. He knew that the boy was unreachable, but he struck him nonetheless. The boy neither covered himself nor retaliated; there was no fear in his eyes. He only said, through his split lip: "So who's the fanatic now?"

—1994

# DAVID DABYDEEN
## *b. 1955*

David Dabydeen emerged as one of the voices of postcolonial literature during the 1980s and 90s. His writing, both in the academic realm of art history and in the worlds of poetry and fiction, investigates the notion of personal identity after the violence of colonization by Britain, exploring the boundary lines between the country of his birth, Guyana, and the United Kingdom, where he now lives and works. His writing has earned him numerous literary and cultural honors, including the prestigious Commonwealth Poetry Prize and the Quiller-Couch Prize.

Dabydeen was born in Berbice, in the British colony of Guyana. His parents were of the agricultural working class, descended from East Indian indentured laborers. During Dabydeen's early years, Guyana's political climate was marked by an atmosphere of hostility stemming from racial tensions between those of African and Indian descent. Because of this, the family relocated several times to avoid race riots. At the age of ten, Dabydeen moved to Guyana's capital, Georgetown, to continue his education on a full scholarship. This move, heartily urged by his mother, allowed him to escape the backbreaking labor of the sugar cane fields. He remained in Georgetown for several years, lodging in various private homes; during this period he met several teachers who encouraged his ambition to write.

In 1969, Dabydeen moved with his family to England and continued his education there. Despite being told by one London teacher that "he would be lucky to make university," Dabydeen earned a scholarship to Cambridge, and completed a BA with honors in 1978. He went on to earn a doctorate in Eighteenth-century Art and Literature at the University of London in 1981. Since then, Dabydeen has completed post-doctoral study at Oxford and Yale, and has lectured on Caribbean Studies at both institutions, as well as heading the Centre for Caribbean Studies at Warwick University, and serving as the Guyanese ambassador to the United Nations Education, Scientific and Cultural Organization (UNESCO).

While studying at Cambridge, Dabydeen began work on the poems that would eventually earn him the Quiller-Couch Prize, a poetry award issued by Cambridge University. These poems were published along with others in his first volume of poetry, *Slave Song* (1984), a collection that is written in the voice of African slaves and Indian laborers in Guyanese Creole and that includes English translations of the poems, as well as extensive commentaries. The book was awarded the 1984 Commonwealth Poetry Prize. He followed up with another book of poetry, *Coolie Odyssey* (1988), a cautious celebration of Indo-Caribbean culture. Dabydeen's first novel, *The Intended* (1991), drew on autobiographical experience in telling the story of a young man's Guyanese childhood and his immigrant experience in London. His next novel, *Disappearance* (1993), draws on the works of Joseph Conrad and V.S. Naipaul to investigate the remnants of an Empire mentality in Britain, and the challenge this mentality undergoes in the face of a culturally diversifying population. The novel also features a Guyanese protagonist.

Dabydeen's next work, *Turner—New and Selected Poems* (1994), received much critical attention. The title work, a long narrative poem, analyzes British painter J.M.W. Turner's masterwork, "Slavers

Throwing Overboard the Dead & Dying," looking past the surface aesthetic of the painting to explore its colonial assumptions. His most recent novels, *The Counting House* (1996) and *A Harlot's Progress* (1999), continue to investigate the intersection of British, East Indian, and African cultures. *The Counting House* tells the history of the meeting of Africans and Indians in Guyana, while *A Harlot's Progress* draws again on Dabydeen's interest in the world of painting. Dabydeen's protagonist in this novel is a fictional character inspired by a figure in William Hogarth's engraving of the same name.

In addition to his works of fiction, Dabydeen has written several critical works about art and literature.

⌘ ⌘ ⌘

## Slave Song

Tie me haan up.
Juk out me eye.
Haal me teet out
So me na go bite.
5   Put chain rung me neck.
Lash me foot tight.
Set yu daag fo gyaad
Maan till nite—

Bu yu caan stap me cack floodin in de goldmine
10  Caan stap me cack splashin in de sunshine!

Whip me till me bleed
Till me beg.
Tell me how me hanimal
African orang-utan
15  Tell me how me cannibal
Fit fo slata fit fo hang.
Slice waan lip out
Waan ear an waan leg—

Bu yu caan stap me cack dippin in de honeypot
20  Drippin at de tip an happy as a Hottentot!¹

Look how e'ya leap from bush to bush like a black
    crappau
Seeking out a watahole,
Blind by de sunflare, tongue like a dussbowl—
See how e'ya sip laang an full an slow!

25  Till e swell an heavy, stubban, chupit, full o sleep
Like camoudie swalla calf an stretch out in de grass,
    content,
Full o peace …
Hibiscus bloom, a cool breeze blow
An from a hill a wataflow
30  Canary singin saaf an low …

Is so when yu dun dream she pink tit,
Totempole she puss,
Leff yu teetmark like a tattoo in she troat!

She gi me taat
35  She gi me wife
So tear out me liver
Or stake me haat
Me still gat life!²
—1984

¹ *Hottentot*  One of a nomadic tribe of southern Africa.

² [Dabydeen's note]  Tie my hands up/ Pierce my eyes/ Haul my teeth out/ So I'll not bite/ Put chains around my neck/ Lash my feet tight/ Set your dogs to guard/ Morning till night—

But you can't stop my cock flooding in the goldmine/ Can't stop my cock splashing in the sunshine!

Whip me till I bleed/ Tell me I'm an animal/ An African orang-utan/ Tell me I'm a cannibal/ Fit only to slaughter or to hang/ Slice one lip out/ One ear and one leg—

But you can't stop my cock dipping in the honeypot,/ Dripping at the tip and happy as a Hottentot!

Look how he leaps from bush to bush like a black toad/ Seeking out a waterhole/ Blind by the sunflare, tongue like a dust-bowl—/ See how he sips long and full and slow!

Till he's swollen and heavy, stubborn, dazed, full of sleep/ Like camoudie snake after swallowing a calf, stretched out in the grass,

## Coolie[1] Odyssey

### (For Ma, d. 1985)

Now that peasantry is in vogue,
Poetry bubbles from peat bogs,[2]
People strain for the old folk's fatal gobs
Coughed up in grates North or North East
5  'Tween bouts o' living dialect,
It should be time to hymn your own wreck,
Your house the source of ancient song:
Dry coconut shells cackling in the fireside
Smoking up our children's eyes and lungs,
10  Plantains[3] spitting oil from a clay pot,
Thick sugary black tea gulped down.

The calves hustle to suck,
Bawling on their rope but are beaten back
Until the cow is milked.
15  Frantic children call to be fed.
Roopram the Idiot goes to graze his father's goats
    backdam
Dreaming that the twig he chews so viciously in his
    mouth
Is not a twig.

In a winter of England's scorn
20  We huddle together memories, hoard them from
The opulence of our masters.

You were always back home, forever
As canefield and whiplash, unchanging
As the tombstones in the old Dutch plot

25  Which the boys used for wickets[4] playing ball.

Over here Harilall who regularly dodged his duties at
    the marketstall
To spin bowl for us in the style of Ramadhin[5]
And afterwards took his beatings from you heroically
In the style of England losing
30  Is now known as the local Paki[6]
Doing slow trade in his Balham cornershop.
Is it because his heart is not in business
But in the tumble of wickets long ago
To the roar of wayward boys?
35  Or is it because he spends too much time
Being chirpy with his customers, greeting
The tight-wrapped pensioners stalking the snow
With tropical smile, jolly small chat, credit?
They like Harilall, these muted claws of Empire,
40  They feel privileged by his grinning service,
They hear steelband[7] in his voice
And the freeness of the sea.
The sun beams from his teeth.

Heaped up beside you Old Dabydeen
45  Who on Albion Estate[8] clean dawn
Washed obsessively by the canal bank,
Spread flowers on the snake-infested water,
Fed the gods the food that Chandra[9] cooked,
Bathed his tongue of the creole
50  Babbled by low-caste infected coolies.[10]
His Hindi chants terrorised the watertoads
Flopping to the protection of bush.
He called upon Lord Krishna[11] to preserve
The virginity of his daughters

---

content/ Full of peace … / Hibiscus bloom, a cool breeze blows/ And from a hill a water-flow/ Canaries singing soft and low …

It's so when you've done dreamt her pink nipples/ Totempoled her cunt/ Left your teeth mark like a tattoo in her throat!

She gives me thought/ She gives me wife/ So tear out my liver/ Or stake my heart/ I'll still have life.

[1] *Coolie*  Derogatory term for an unskilled laborer, usually of Asian origin.

[2] *Poetry … bogs*  See the "Bog Poems" of Seamus Heaney, Irish poet (b. 1939).

[3] *Plantains*  Staple fruits in tropical regions, resembling bananas.

[4] *wickets*  Targets used in the game of cricket.

[5] *Ramadhin*  Sonny Ramadhin (b. 1929), professional cricket player who was the first East Indian to represent the West Indies.

[6] *Paki*  Derogatory term for a person of Pakistani origin.

[7] *steelband*  Caribbean band composed chiefly of steel drums, instruments fashioned from oil drums.

[8] *Albion Estate*  Large plantation in St. Thomas, West Indies.

[9] *Chandra*  Hindu god of the moon and fertility.

[10] *low-caste*  Low on the hereditary caste system of the Hindus.

[11] *Lord Krishna*  Aspect of Vishnu, god of order and justice. Krishna, one of the most important of the Hindu gods, is defender of humankind and symbolic of the love between the gods and humans.

55 From the Negroes,
   Prayed that the white man would honour
   The end-of-season bonus to Poonai
   The canecutter, his strong, only son:
   Chandra's womb being cursed by deities
60 Like the blasted land
   Unconquerable jungle or weed
   That dragged the might of years from a man.
   Chandra like a deaf-mute moved about the house
   To his command,
65 A fearful bride barely come-of-age
   Year upon year swelling with female child.
   Guilt clenched her mouth
   Smothered the cry of bursting apart:
   Wrapped hurriedly in a bundle of midwife's cloth
70 The burden was removed to her mother's safekeeping.
   He stamped and cursed and beat until he turned old
   With the labour of chopping tree, minding cow,
        building fence
   And the expense of his daughters' dowries.
   Dreaming of India
75 He drank rum
   Till he dropped dead
   And was buried to the singing of Scottish Presbyterian
        hymns
   And a hell-fire sermon from a pop-eyed bawling
        catechist,
   By Poonai, lately baptised, like half the village.

80 Ever so old,
   Dabydeen's wife,
   Hobbling her way to fowl-pen,
   Cussing low, chewing her cud, and lapsed in dream,
   Sprinkling rice from her shrivelled hand.
85 Ever so old and bountiful,
   Past where Dabydeen lazed in his mudgrave,
   Idle as usual in the sun,
   Who would dip his hand in a bowl of dhall[1] and rice—
   Nasty man, squelching and swallowing like a
        low-caste sow—
90 The bitch dead now!

The first boat chugged to the muddy port
Of King George's Town.° Coolies          Georgetown, Guyana
     come to rest
In El Dorado,[2]
Their faces and best saris black with soot.
95 The men smelt of saltwater mixed with rum.
The odyssey was plank between river and land,
Mere yards but months of plotting
In the packed bowel of a white man's boat
The years of promise, years of expanse.

100 At first the gleam of the green land and the white folk
        and the Negroes,
The earth streaked with colour like a toucan's beak,
Kiskidees° flame across a fortunate sky,          tropical birds
Canefields ripening in the sun
Wait to be gathered in armfuls of gold.

105 I have come back late and missed the funeral.
You will understand the connections were difficult.
Three airplanes boarded and many changes
Of machines and landscapes like reincarnations
To bring me to this library of graves,
110 This small clearing of scrubland.
There are no headstones, epitaphs, dates.
The ancestors curl and dry to scrolls of parchment.
They lie like texts
Waiting to be written by the children
115 For whom they hacked and ploughed and saved
To send to faraway schools.
*Is foolishness fill your head.*
*Me dead.*
*Dog-bone and dry-well*
120 *Got no story to tell.*
*Just how me born stupid is so me gone.*
Still we persist before the grave
Seeking fables.
We plunder for the maps of El Dorado
125 To make bountiful our minds in an England
Starved of gold.

Albion village sleeps, hacked
Out between bush and spiteful lip of river.

---

[1]  *dhall*  Spicy Indian dish made with lentils, tomatoes, onions and various seasonings.

[2]  *El Dorado*  Legendary city of wealth and beauty thought to have existed in the New World.

Folk that know bone
130  Fatten themselves on dreams
For the survival of days.
Mosquitoes sing at a nipple of blood.
A green-eyed moon watches
The rheumatic agony of houses crutched up on stilts
135  Pecked about by huge beaks of wind,
That bear the scars of ancient storms.
Crappeau° clear their throats in hideous serenade,    *frogs*
Candleflies burst into suicidal flame.
In a green night with promise of rain
140  You die.

We mark your memory in songs
Fleshed in the emptiness of folk,
Poems that scrape bowl and bone
In English basements far from home,
145  Or confess the lust of beasts
In rare conceits
To congregations of the educated
Sipping wine, attentive between courses—
See the applause fluttering from their fair hands
150  Like so many messy table napkins.
—1988


from *Turner: New and Selected Poems*

PREFACE

1

In 1840 J.M.W. Turner exhibited at the Royal Academy[1] his finest painting in the sublime style, "Slavers Throwing Overboard the Dead and Dying" (commonly known as "Slave Ship"). It was not unusual for ship captains to order the drowning of sick slaves (who would fetch a low price on landing in the Caribbean), and to claim their insurance value on the basis of goods lost at sea.

Ruskin[2] thought that "Slave Ship" represented "the noblest sea that Turner ever painted … the noblest certainly ever painted by man." He wrote a detailed account of the composition of the painting, dwelling on the genius with which Turner illuminated sea and sky in an intense and lurid splendour of colours. "If I were to rest Turner's immortality upon any single work, I should choose this." (He did, by buying the painting.) Its subject, the shackling and drowning of Africans, was relegated to a brief footnote in Ruskin's essay. The footnote reads like an afterthought, something tossed overboard.

2

My poem focuses on the submerged head of the African in the foreground of Turner's painting. It has been drowned in Turner's (and other artists') sea for centuries. When it awakens it can only partially recall the sources of its life, so it invents a body, a biography, and peoples an imagined landscape. Most of the names of birds, animals and fruit are made up. Ultimately, however, the African rejects the fabrication of an idyllic past. His real desire is to begin anew in the sea but he is too trapped by grievous memory to escape history. Although the sea has transformed him—bleached him of colour and complicated his sense of gender—he still recognises himself as "nigger." The desire for transfiguration or newness or creative amnesia is frustrated. The agent of self-recognition is a stillborn child tossed overboard from a future ship. The child floats towards him. He wants to give it life, to mother it, but the child—his unconscious and his origin—cannot bear the future and its inventions, drowned as it is in memory of ancient cruelty. Neither can escape Turner's representation of them as exotic and sublime victims. Neither can describe themselves anew but are indelibly stained by Turner's language and imagery.

The intensity of Turner's painting is such that I believe the artist in private must have savoured the sadism he publicly denounced. I make Turner the captain of the slave ship (the stillborn child is also named Turner). Turner's well-chronicled love of children is seen in another light, as is his extreme prudence with money.

[1] *J.M.W. Turner … Academy* Joseph Mallord William Turner, British artist (1775–1851); *Royal Academy* British institution dedicated to the cultivation painting, sculpture, and architecture.

[2] *Ruskin* John Ruskin (1819–1900), British artist, author, art and social critic.

J.M.W. Turner, *Slavers Throwing Overboard the Dead and Dying* (1840). Figures of the drowning are barely visible in the foreground, lower right. Turner's painting depicts a 1781 incident in which Captain Luke Collingwood of the slave ship "Zong," whose ship was running short of water and other supplies when it had been blown off-course during a severe storm, ordered that all sick and dying slaves be thrown overboard. 133 were killed as a result. Insurance was a factor in Collingwood's decision; compensation could be claimed for property lost or jettisoned in storms, but not for slaves killed by disease or other natural causes. The incident became widely publicized and spurred support for the abolitionist movement. In the ensuing legal case the court upheld the insurance company's financial liability, and no criminal charges were brought against the captain. In the twentieth century the incident became the basis for several literary works, including this long poem by David Dabydeen and a novel by Fred D'Aguiar.

## Turner

### I

Stillborn from all the signs. First a woman sobs
Above the creak of timbers and the cleaving
Of the sea, sobs from the depths of true
Hurt and grief, as you will never hear
5  But from woman giving birth, belly
Blown and flapping loose and torn like sails,
Rough sailors' hands jerking and tugging
At ropes of veins, to no avail. Blood vessels

10  Burst asunder, all below—deck are drowned.
Afterwards, stillness, but for the murmuring
Of women. The ship, anchored in compassion
And for profit's sake (what well-bred captain
Can resist the call of his helpless
15  Concubine, or the prospect of a natural
Increase in cargo?), sets sail again,
The part—born, sometimes with its mother,
Tossed overboard. Such was my bounty
Delivered so unexpectedly that at first
I could not believe this miracle of fate,

20   This longed-for gift of motherhood.
    What was deemed mere food for sharks will become
    My fable. I named it Turner
    As I have given fresh names to birds and fish
    And humankind, all things living but unknown,
25   Dimly recalled, or dead.

2

    It plopped into the water and soon swelled
    Like a brumplak seed that bursts buckshot
    From its pod, falling into the pond
    In the backdam of my mother's house, and fattening,
30   Where small boys like I was hold sticks to the water
    For fish; branches stripped and shaped from the impala
    Tree, no other, for we know—only the gods
    Can tell how—that they bend so supple,
    Almost a circle without snapping, yet strong
35   Enough to pull in a baby alligator.
    Maybe by instinct, maybe the wisdom
    Of our village elders passed down forever
    (Until Turner came) which we suck in from birth
    Like wood-smoke in my mother's kitchen,
40   Coconut shells stoking up a fire,
    And I squat with my two sisters, small we are,
    I don't know exactly how much in age—
    Though since Turner's days I have learnt to count,
    Weigh, measure, abstract, rationalise—
45   But we are small enough nearly to pass
    Upright under the belly of the cow
    Whilst our father pulls the teats and wheezes
    Milk into a pakreet shell, swoosh, swoosh
    Swoosh, the sound still haunts, survives the roar
50   And crash and endless wash and lap
    Of waves, and we stoop under the belly
    Of the cow and I can see I am just
    Taller than its haunches, and when my sisters
    Kneel their heads reach its knees. We play
55   Games as our father milks, crawling under
    The belly like warriors, then springing up
    At the other side to hurl spears at enemies
    Hiding behind the chaltee tree in the cow-pen,
    From which we pick twigs each morning, chew the ends,
60   Brush our teeth clean. The cow moves its head
    To one side, watches us with covetous eyes
    As if it wants to play, but my father

    Will forbid it, for even when the milking is done,
    He will not let us jump on the cow's back,
65   Nor decorate its heels with the blue and yellow
    Bark of hemlik, nor put a chaktee straw
    Into its nostrils until it sneezes
    And snorts with laughter, but will lead it
    Straight to pasture, and send us off to school,
70   To Manu, the magician, who will teach
    Us how to squeeze, drain, blend, boil the juices
    Of herbs for medicines, or bandage the sprained
    Foot of a chicken. So the cow stands still,
    But looks at us with a harlot's eye and winks,
75   And we can see the mischief in its face
    Which our father can't because he's so far
    Behind, concentrating on his fingers as if
    Worshipping the gods, and it flicks its tail,
    Beating off flies, but really to join in,
80   To lash and surprise us as we wait in ambush
    Under its belly for the English
    To come from another village, who will plunder
    The crops, burn the huts, stampede the goats,
    Drag girls away by ropes.

3

85   I dream to be small again, even though
    My mother caught me with my fingers
    In a panoose jar, and whilst I licked them clean
    And reached for more, she came upon me,
    Put one load of licks with a tamarind
90   Stick on my back, boxed my ears; the jar fell,
    Broke, panoose dripped thickly to the floor.
    Ants appeared cautiously, marched with tongues
    Hanging out, like a gang of slavers;
    Even though I cut myself on a sharp stone
95   Plunging headlong into the pond, feet splayed,
    Hands folded at my chest like a straplee monkey
    Diving from a branch into water, swimming
    About, climbing again for another go.
    I sit in the savannah minding cows,
100  Watching it climb and plunge all day. When I strip,
    Mount the tree and dive I hit my head
    On a stone waiting at the bottom of the pond.
    I come up dazed, I float half-dead, I bleed
    For days afterwards, for even Manu cannot
105  Stem the flow with his poultices soaked

In goat-dung mixed with the skin of abara fruit,
The smell of which makes me retch. My mother
Watches over me, eyes big like our cow's
But full of sadness. My sisters laugh at me,
110 They steal my toys and play with them, knowing
I am too weak to complain. When I awake
The house I built from barak shells, painted
With the green juice of a siddam, is in shambles,
Stilts fallen off, big holes in the roof
115 Where they poked their clumsy fingers in.
Girls are stupid, they know only how to wash
And cook, my father will marry them off
Soon, two goats each for bride-price.° That will          *dowry*
     teach
Them not to tamper with my things and thieve.

4

120 It plopped into the water from a passing ship
Like a lime-seed spat from the scurvied mouth
Of a sailor, shooting out between
A gap in his teeth, a cannonball
From the square hole at the side of the ship
125 That makes me duck below the water in fright
As it booms and breaks against another's mast.
All day they spit fire to each other
Like lovers, like Sensu courting Zain
Rolling out her long red tongue whilst he
130 Sits sternly and cross-legged, refusing
To surrender (clay statues in the hearth
In the front-room of my father's house where
Dawntime he prayed earnestly, fed them,
Washed his fingers in a sacred bowl
135 Repeatedly, his tongue, his face; smeared
His forehead with green dye. When he departed
To the savannah,° my sisters and me,          *plain*
Awakened, hungry, our mother still lighting
The fireside and peeling yams, stole
140 Some of the food, nibbling sinfully
At the sweetballs of ocho and sarabell)
For if the fire of her tongue should play
Upon his body and he should melt,
The earth would tumble uncontrollably,
145 People spew off the edges, clutching roots
Like they do now at each other, as one ship sinks.

For days afterwards the sea is strewn with companions:
The gods have taken revenge on all of us.
We float together for days before the waves
150 Divide us. I have known them all, briefly,
I have always known them, year after year
From different sunken ships. Turner are the ones
With golden hair. His blue eyes smile at children
As he gives us sweets and a ladle from a barrel
155 Of shada juice. Five of us hold his hand,
Each takes a finger, like jenti cubs
Clinging to their mother's teats, as he leads us
To the ship. Why is my mother screaming
Like a harch, and where is my father?
160 Why does Turner forbid her to touch us
Before we board? Why are all the elders in chains?
All the fair men are Turner, I can tell
Even when sea-quats have swallowed their eyes,
Dug holes in their faces to lay their eggs.
165 I can tell from the silver buckles
On the black leather boots which he lets us
Polish, till we can see our faces.
Each day boys scramble at his feet, fighting
To clean them first. He promises that the most
170 Faithful will be given them when we land.
Only the silver survives the sea and all
Its creatures, his most faithful possession.
Even the sharks crack their teeth against it.

5

The women are less familiar
175 But I name them Adra, Zentu, Danjera,
The names of my mother and my father's wives.
They are not so ample as our women
Though the sea bloats them, the salt hardens
On their skin, a crust of white that hides
180 Lines of neglect, indelicacies. The sea prepares
Their festive masks, salt crystals like a myriad
Of sequins hemmed into their flesh through golden
Threads of hair. The sea decorates, violates.
Limbs break off, crabs roost between their breasts
185 Feeding. The sea strips them clean. I am ashamed
To look upon the nakedness of my mothers.
—1995

# CAROL ANN DUFFY
## *b. 1955*

As the British newspaper *The Guardian* has put it, "in the world of British poetry, Carol Ann Duffy is a superstar." Lauded by reviewers and by academic critics, her work has also been enormously popular with the general public; perhaps not since Philip Larkin's *High Windows* became a bestseller in the mid-1970s has a British poet simultaneously enjoyed such high levels of critical esteem and such a broad readership. Duffy first made her mark in the 1980s as a writer of dramatic monologues, many of them poems of controlled edginess (such as "Stealing") that give voice to tough, working class personae. She has since become equally well known for tightly crafted lyrics of concentrated emotional force, especially on the themes of love and loss.

The eldest child of five, Duffy was born in Glasgow to an Irish mother and Scottish father, and raised largely in the north Midlands town of Stafford, where her father became a member of the local council and was a Labour Party candidate for Parliament. She attended St. Joseph's Convent School and Stafford Girls High School before studying philosophy at Liverpool University. She then worked for some years in London, where she was editor of the poetry magazine *Ambit*. In 1996 Duffy moved to Manchester, and since then she has taught at Manchester Metropolitan University, where in 2005 she was appointed Creative Director of the Writing School.

With her early collections—most notably her first book, *Standing Female Nude* (1985)—Duffy established a reputation as a powerful feminist voice, as a poet of considerable versatility, and as an entertainer, as capable of writing in a comic as in a dramatic or lyric mode. In *Mean Time* (1993), the emotional as well as technical range of her work broadened, as can be seen in poems such as "Nostalgia," "The Good Teachers," and "Crush." Her 1999 book *The World's Wife* is a striking *tour de force* in which each poem is written in the persona of a wife, sister, or lover of a famous man from history or mythology, from "Mrs. Faust" and "Anne Hathaway" to "Mrs. Lazarus." Her 2005 collection *Rapture* is also a unified work, though of a very different sort; here she presents a chronologically-ordered series of poems that trace the emotional trajectory of a relationship of love—poems, as Duffy puts it in the sonnet from which the book takes its title, of "desire and passion on the thinking air." *Rapture* is confessedly autobiographical, but in the only interview on the collection that Duffy consented to give, she declined to discuss any specifics: "I could not feel more deeply than I have in these poems," she said, "but these are not journals or diaries or letters, they are works of art. A transformation takes place—it has to, if the feeling is to be revealed to others."

Though Duffy's poetry often bristles with contemporaneity in its tone and subject matter, it also exhibits a remarkable range of formal accomplishment; many of her poems follow accentual-syllabic metrical patterns, and many use rhyme extensively. It is perhaps more a reflection on reading habits that took root in the second half of the twentieth century than it is on Duffy's work itself that as formal patterns of rhythm and rhyme began to play a larger and larger role in her work, some began to wonder, in Jeannette Winterson's words, "whether Duffy had lost her balance. Had she stopped writing poetry and slopped into verse?" Unlike many poets who are inclined toward formal complexity, Duffy eschews unusual diction: as she has put it, "I'm not interested, as a poet, in words like 'plash'—Seamus Heaney words, interesting words. I like to use simple words but in a complicated way."

Among lesbian writers, Duffy is noteworthy for her rejection of any exceptionalist status. "I'm not a lesbian poet, whatever that is. If I am a lesbian icon and a role model, that's great, but if it is a word that is used to reduce me, then you have to ask why.… I define myself as a poet and a mother—that's all." Duffy's daughter Ella was born in 1995.

Duffy has written or edited over thirty books, including several plays, collections of poetry for children, and a variety of edited volumes. Among the many awards she has received are the 2003 Forward Poetry Prize, the 2003 Whitbread Poetry Award (for *Mean Time*), and the 2005 T.S. Eliot Prize (for *Rapture*). She was appointed an Officer of the British Empire in 1993 and a Commander of the British Empire in 2001.

⌘ ⌘ ⌘

## Stealing

The most unusual thing I ever stole? A snowman.
Midnight. He looked magnificent; a tall, white
      mute
beneath the winter moon. I wanted him, a mate
with a mind as cold as the slice of ice
5   within my own brain. I started with the head.

Better off dead than giving in, not taking
what you want. He weighed a ton; his torso,
frozen stiff, hugged to my chest, a fierce chill
piercing my gut. Part of the thrill was knowing
10  that children would cry in the morning. Life's tough.

Sometimes I steal things I don't need. I joy-ride cars
to nowhere, break into houses just to have a look.
I'm a mucky ghost, leave a mess, maybe pinch a
      camera.
I watch my gloved hand twisting the doorknob.
15  A stranger's bedroom. Mirrors. I sigh like this—Aah.

It took some time. Reassembled in the yard,
he didn't look the same. I took a run
and booted him. Again. Again. My breath ripped out
in rags. It seems daft now. Then I was standing
20  alone among lumps of snow, sick of the world.

Boredom. Mostly I'm so bored I could eat myself.
One time, I stole a guitar and thought I might

learn to play. I nicked[1] a bust of Shakespeare once,
flogged[2] it, but the snowman was the strangest.
25  You don't understand a word I'm saying, do you?
—1987

## Adultery

Wear dark glasses in the rain.
      Regard what was unhurt
as though through a bruise.
Guilt. A sick, green tint.

5   New gloves, money tucked in the palms,
the handshake crackles. Hands
can do many things. Phone.
Open the wine. Wash themselves. Now

you are naked under your clothes all day,
10  slim with deceit. Only the once
brings you alone to your knees,
miming, more, more, older and sadder,

creative. Suck a lie with a hole in it
on the way home from a lethal, thrilling night
15  up against a wall, faster. Language
unpeels to a lost cry. You're a bastard.

---

[1] *nicked*  Slang for stole.
[2] *flogged*  Slang for sold.

Do it do it do it. Sweet darkness
in the afternoon; a voice in your ear
telling you how you are wanted,
20 which way, now. A telltale clock

wiping the hours from its face, your face
on a white sheet, gasping, radiant, yes.
Pay for it in cash, fiction, cab-fares back
to the life which crumbles like a wedding-cake.

25 Paranoia for lunch; too much
to drink, as a hand on your thigh
tilts the restaurant. You know all about love,
don't you. Turn on your beautiful eyes

for a stranger who's dynamite in bed, again
30 and again; a slow replay in the kitchen
where the slicing of innocent onions
scalds you to tears. Then, selfish autobiographical sleep

in a marital bed, the tarnished spoon of your body
stirring betrayal, your heart over-ripe at the core.
35 You're an expert, darling; your flowers
dumb and explicit on nobody's birthday.

So write the script—illness and debt,
a ring thrown away in a garden
no moon can heal, your own words
40 commuting to bile in your mouth, terror—

and all for the same thing twice. And all
for the same thing twice. You did it.
What. Didn't you. Fuck. Fuck. No. That was
the wrong verb. This is only an abstract noun.
—1993

## The Good Teachers

You run round the back to be in it again.
No bigger than your thumbs, those virtuous
    women
size you up from the front row. Soon now,
Miss Ross will take you for double History.

5 You breathe on the glass, making a ghost of her, say
South Sea Bubble Defenestration of Prague.[1]

You love Miss Pirie. So much, you are top
of her class. So much, you need two of you
to stare out from the year, serious, passionate.
10 The River's Tale by Rudyard Kipling[2] by heart.
Her kind intelligent green eye. Her cruel blue one.
You are making a poem up for her in your head.

But not Miss Sheridan. Comment vous appelez.[3]
But not Miss Appleby. Equal to the square
15 of the other two sides. Never Miss Webb.
Dar es Salaam. Kilimanjaro.[4] Look. The good teachers
swish down the corridor in long, brown skirts,
snobbish and proud and clean and qualified.

And they've got your number. You roll the waistband
20 of your skirt over and over, all leg, all
dumb insolence, smoke-rings. You won't pass.
You could do better. But there's the wall you climb
into dancing, lovebites, marriage, the Cheltenham
and Gloucester,[5] today. The day you'll be sorry one
    day.
—1993

## Drunk

Suddenly the rain is hilarious.
The moon wobbles in the dusk.

What a laugh. Unseen frogs
belch in the damp grass.

5 The strange perfumes of darkening trees.
Cheap red wine

[1] *South Sea ... Prague* Two unconnected historical incidents.

[2] *Rudyard Kipling* English novelist, poet and short-story writer who was born in Bombay (1865–1936).

[3] *Comment vous appelez* French: what do you call.

[4] *Dar es Salaam. Kilimanjaro* The largest city and the tallest mountain, respectively, in Tanzania.

[5] *Cheltenham and Gloucester* The name of a commercial bank in the United Kingdom.

and the whole world a mouth.
Give me a double, a kiss.
—1993

### Mean Time

The clocks slid back an hour
and stole light from my life
as I walked through the wrong part of town,
mourning our love.

5  And, of course, unmendable rain
fell to the bleak streets
where I felt my heart gnaw
at all our mistakes.

If the darkening sky could lift
10  more than one hour from this day
there are words I would never have said
nor have heard you say.

But we will be dead, as we know,
beyond all light.
15  These are the shortened days
and the endless nights.
—1993

### Mrs. Lazarus[1]

I had grieved. I had wept for a night and a day
over my loss, ripped the cloth I was married in
from my breasts, howled, shrieked, clawed
at the burial stones till my hands bled, retched
5  his name over and over again, dead, dead.

[1] *Mrs. Lazarus*  In the story recounted in John 11.41–44, "a man named Lazarus" is sick; his sisters Martha and Mary send for Jesus asking for help. Jesus sends a reply asserting that "the sickness will not end in death," but does not come at once to help. When he does arrive a few days later Lazarus is dead and has been entombed for four days, but when Jesus has the stone covering the entrance to the tomb rolled back, Lazarus emerges in his grave-cloths. There is no mention of Lazarus's wife in the Biblical account.

Gone home. Gutted the place. Slept in a single cot,
widow, one empty glove, white femur
in the dust, half. Stuffed dark suits
into black bags, shuffled in a dead man's shoes,
10  noosed the double knot of a tie round my bare neck,

gaunt nun in the mirror, touching herself. I learnt
the Stations of Bereavement, the icon of my face
in each bleak frame; but all those months
he was going away from me, dwindling
15  to the shrunk size of a snapshot, going,

going. Till his name was no longer a certain spell
for his face. The last hair on his head
floated out from a book. His scent went from the
house.
The will was read. See, he was vanishing
20  to the small zero held by the gold of my ring.

Then he was gone. Then he was legend, language;
my arm on the arm of the schoolteacher—the shock
of a man's strength under the sleeve of his coat—
along the hedgerows. But I was faithful
25  for as long as it took. Until he was memory.

So I could stand that evening in the field
in a shawl of fine air, healed, able
to watch the edge of the moon occur to the sky
and a hare thump from a hedge; then notice
30  the village men running towards me, shouting,

behind them the women and children, barking dogs,
and I knew. I knew by the sly light
on the blacksmith's face, the shrill eyes
of the barmaid, the sudden hands bearing me
35  into the hot tang of the crowd parting before me.

He lived. I saw the horror on his face.
I heard his mother's crazy song. I breathed
his stench; my bridegroom in his rotting shroud,
moist and dishevelled from the grave's slack chew,
40  croaking his cuckold name, disinherited, out of his
time.
—1999

## Wish

But what if, in the clammy soil, her limbs
grew warmer, shifted, stirred, kicked off
the covering of earth, the drowsing corms,[1]
the sly worms, what if her arms reached out
5   to grab the stone, the grooves of her dates
under her thumb, and pulled her up? I wish.
Her bare feet walk along the gravel path
between the graves, her shroud like washing
blown onto the grass, the petals of her wreath
10  kissed for a bride. Nobody died. Nobody
wept. Nobody slept who couldn't be woken
by the light. If I can only push open this heavy door
she'll be standing there in the sun, dirty, tired,
wondering why do I shout, why do I run.

—2002

## Rapture

Thought of by you all day, I think of you.
The birds sing in the shelter of a tree.
Above the prayer of rain, unacred blue,
not paradise, goes nowhere endlessly.
5   How does it happen that our lives can drift
far from our selves, while we stay trapped in time,
queuing[2] for death? It seems nothing will shift
the pattern of our days, alter the rhyme
we make with loss to assonance with bliss.
10  Then love comes, like a sudden flight of birds
from earth to heaven after rain. Your kiss,
recalled, unstrings, like pearls, this chain of words.
Huge skies connect us, joining here to there.
Desire and passion on the thinking air.

—2005

---

[1]  *corms*  Bulbs.

[2]  *queuing*  Lining up.

# DIRECTIONS IN LATE TWENTIETH- AND EARLY TWENTY-FIRST-CENTURY POETRY

Modernism, the most important movement in twentieth-century British poetry before the Second World War, has remained an important influence in the post-war period. The densely allusive style of Geoffrey Hill, for example, has often been seen as an extension of the traditions of Modernism. And the language poetry of such writers as Veronica Forrest-Thomson, Maggie O'Sullivan, and J.H. Prynne[1] (whose work we would have liked to have included here), is often said to represent a different sort of offshoot of Modernism (described by some as a form of postmodernism), one that lends itself less to the unpacking of meaning than to the free association of images—and, especially, of sounds. The poetry of Prynne or of Forrest-Thomson, indeed, may tend to frustrate any efforts to locate expressible meaning, and often calls into question assumptions about the nature and function of poetry.

At a far extreme from language poetry (and from Modernism) stands the verse of Philip Larkin,[2] whose poems for the most part employ familiar and accessible forms to convey meanings that may fairly readily be articulated. In the 1950s, 60s, and 70s, when, for the most part, the practice of poetry was moving away from accentual-syllabic forms (and from rhyme), Larkin continued to develop his extraordinary versatility in those traditional forms. The degree to which Larkin, together with W.H. Auden, was able to demonstrate poetic possibility in traditional forms may in part explain the degree to which the mainstream of British poetry over the past 30 years has returned to those paths. (Certainly British poetry in recent generations has been far less dominated by free verse than has poetry in the United States or in Canada.) A poet such as Carol Ann Duffy may, in the attitudes behind her work, be light years away from the social and political conservatism of Larkin, but poetically the two share a surprising amount of common ground. Respected by critics and academics while also appealing to a broad, popular readership, their work connects strongly with readers not only through its emotional intelligence but also through its technical virtuosity—not least of all through rhyme and other aural qualities.

The leading lights of British poetry in the 1970s were considered to be Larkin, Ted Hughes, and Seamus Heaney. Whereas Larkin's work is rooted most strongly in unvarnished observations of the human, that of Hughes and, especially, of Heaney might fairly be said to be rooted in the earth—in the elemental suggestiveness of nature imagery. They, too, have exerted considerable influence on subsequent writers; echoes may be heard, for example, in the work of poets such as Medbh McGuckian and Alice Oswald. (It should be emphasized, however, that these poets have found their own distinctive voices; they are successors to poets such as Hughes and Heaney, not their imitators.)

The prominence of writers such as Duffy, McGuckian, Oswald, and a host of other women writers in contemporary British and Irish poetry points to a striking change over the past 30 years.

---

[1] *J.H. Prynne*   Prynne informed the editors that he makes it his regular practice to decline to release his work for inclusion in anthologies.

[2] The work of several of the poets mentioned in this headnote (Auden, Larkin, Gunn, Hughes, Heaney, Walcott, Dabydeen, Muldoon, and Duffy) is represented elsewhere in this volume; it is touched on here by way of contextualizing the work of the poets whose work is included in this section.

As late as the 1980s, almost any list of acknowledged major living poets in England, Scotland, Wales, and Ireland would have been composed overwhelmingly of men. That is no longer true: the past generation is perhaps the first in the history of British poetry in which significant women poets have emerged in numbers at least as great as those of their male counterparts.

Another shift has been towards increasing identification of poets with national groups. Liz Lochhead is one often identified strongly as a Scottish poet; Gwyneth Lewis and Nuala Ní Dhomhnaill have led the way in forging fresh traditions as bilingual poets in Welsh and English (in the case of Lewis) and Irish and English (in the case of Dhomhnaill), finding immense poetic resources in the sounds as well as the meanings of the two languages. And there has been an extraordinary outpouring of work from poets born and raised in Northern Ireland; Seamus Heaney, Derek Mahon, Paul Muldoon, Tom Paulin, and McGuckian are among the most notable names. (It is essential here to note, however, that many of these poets have self-identified as Irish rather than as Northern Irish.) In their different ways all have created work that has connected with readers in its sense of place—as well as through imagery and through aural qualities.

A very different sort of aural connection with readers and listeners has been created by dub poetry, a form that constitutes another important direction in the British poetry of the past thirty years. The blending of reggae music and poetry into dub in the work of writers and performers such as Linton Kwesi Johnson and Jean Binta Breeze is one important way in which poets have created hybrid expressions of the traditions of the Caribbean and the realities of present-day Britain. More broadly, poets such as Derek Walcott, David Dabydeen, Kamau Brathwaite, and Grace Nichols have brought from their backgrounds in the Caribbean a range of styles and of concerns that have broadened the scope of "British" poetry immeasurably. In like fashion, poets such as Moniza Alvi connect with the roots of their own cultural heritage and the heritage of British colonialism.

Finally, mention should be given here to the degree to which poetry in Britain—and the public discussion of this poetry—has often been infused in recent generations with strongly political content. The politics of postcolonialism and of race are here important strands, but the politics of gender, of class, and of aesthetics have often been just as hotly contested. (Sexual orientation, on the other hand, is no longer in itself an object of controversy; with the coming into prominence over the course of the twentieth century first of openly gay poets—W.H. Auden and Thom Gunn chief among them—and then of openly lesbian poets such as Duffy and Jackie Kay, and with the overall change in societal attitudes in the late twentieth and early twenty-first centuries, a gay or lesbian sexual orientation has come to be regarded almost universally as unexceptionable.) Poets such as Tony Harrison have powerfully addressed issues relating to social class; Heaney, Muldoon, Tom Paulin, and others have spoken out provocatively on issues in British and Irish politics; poets such as Johnson and Kay have focused strongly in their work on issues of race and culture; and so on.

Poets such as James Fenton, Craig Raine, and Andrew Motion, on the other hand, have often been labeled (whether fairly or not) representatives of the "Oxbridge" establishment; the choice of Motion as Poet Laureate in 1999 was highly controversial, with many suggesting that Duffy would have been a more forward-looking choice. Through these controversies various observers have depicted British poetry as divided into politically-charged binaries of poetic style as well as of politics, positing a mainstream tradition stemming from the work of Larkin, Hughes, and Heaney, contrasted with a rival tradition of bold experimentation with roots in Modernism and post-modernism. British poets themselves, however, with only a few exceptions, have been reluctant to enlist in movements that have aimed to make a battleground of the field of British poetry—and have remained powerfully aware of the degree to which the actual work of poets alleged to be in entirely different camps often cuts across the supposed lines of demarcation. In this as in so many other respects, it is diversity that has above all characterized British poetry in the generations since World War II.

⌘ ⌘ ⌘

### GEOFFREY HILL (b. 1932)

Geoffrey Hill, often referred to as a "late modernist" poet, has been publishing important work since the 1950s. Hill grew up in a small town in Worcestershire, and the history and geography of the West Midlands have been a continuing presence in his writing, perhaps most notably in *Mercian Hymns* (1971); more broadly, his poetry often explores connections with history and poetic tradition. His books include *For the Unfallen* (1959), *Tenebrae* (1978), and *The Orchards of Syon* (2002).

### from *Mercian Hymns*

I

King[1] of the perennial holly-groves, the riven sandstone: overlord of the M5: architect of the historic rampart and ditch, the citadel at Tamworth, the summer hermitage in Holy Cross: guardian of the Welsh Bridge and the Iron Bridge:[2] contractor to the desirable new estates: saltmaster: money-changer:

commissioner for oaths: martyrologist: the friend of Charlemagne.[3]

"I liked that," said Offa, "sing it again."

4

I was invested in mother-earth,[4] the crypt of roots and endings. Child's-play. I abode there, bided my time: where the mole

shouldered the clogged wheel, his gold solidus;[5] where dry-dust badgers thronged the Roman flues, the long-unlooked-for mansions of our tribe.

7

Gasholders, russet among fields. Milldams, marlpools[6] that lay unstirring. Eel-swarms. Coagulations of frogs: once, with branches and half-bricks, he battered a ditchful; then sidled away from the stillness and silence.

Ceolred[7] was his friend and remained so, even after the day of the lost fighter: a biplane, already obsolete and irreplaceable, two inches of heavy snub silver. Ceolred let it spin through a hole in the classroom-floorboards, softly, into the rat-droppings and coins.

---

[1] [Hill's note]   The historical King Offa reigned over Mercia (and the greater part of England south of the Humber) in the years AD 757–96. During early medieval times he was already becoming a creature of legend. The Offa who figures in this sequence might perhaps most usefully be regarded as the presiding genius of the West Midlands, his dominion enduring from the middle of the eighth century until the middle of the twentieth (and possibly beyond). The indication of such a timespan will, I trust, explain and to some extent justify a number of anachronisms.

[2] *M5 … Iron Bridge*   These lines include a number of historical and geographical references to the West Midlands. The M5 is a modern superhighway running north-south near the Severn River; King Offa built a palace at Tamworth and made it the effective capital of Mercia (later the Normans built a castle there); the Welsh Bridge crosses the Severn at Shrewsbury; the Iron Bridge (a landmark in the history of the Industrial Revolution) crosses the same river near Telford.

[3] *Charlemagne*   (742–814), King of the Franks and conqueror of much of continental Europe.

[4] [Hill's note]   To the best of my recollection, the expression "to invest in mother-earth" was the felicitous (and correct) definition of "yird" given by Mr. Michael Hordern in the program *Call My Bluff* televised on BBC 2 on Thursday January 19th 1970.

[5] *solidus*   Gold coin of the Roman Empire.

[6] *marlpools*   Marl is a clay-like deposit in lakebeds, often used to make bricks.

[7] *Ceolred*   Cousin to Offa, and his successor as King of Mercia.

After school he lured Ceolred, who was sniggering with
   fright, down to the old quarries, and flayed him.
   Then, leaving Ceolred, he journeyed for hours, calm
   and alone, in his private derelict sandlorry named
10   *Albion*.[1]

8

The mad are predators. Too often lately they harbour
   against us. A novel heresy exculpates all maimed
   souls. Abjure it! I am the King of Mercia, and I
   know.

5  Threatened by phone-calls at midnight, venomous
   letters, forewarned I have thwarted their imminent
   devices.

Today I name them; tomorrow I shall express the new
   law. I dedicate my awakening to this matter.

10

He adored the desk, its brown-oak inlaid with ebony,
   assorted prize pens, the seals of gold and
   base metal into which he had sunk his name.

It was there that he drew upon grievances from the
5   people; attended to signatures and retributions;
   forgave the death-howls of his rival. And there he
   exchanged gifts with the Muse[2] of History.

What should a man make of remorse, that it might
   profit his soul? Tell me. Tell everything to Mother,
10   darling, and God bless.

He swayed in sunlight, in mild dreams. He tested the
   little pears. He smeared catmint on his palm for his
   cat Smut to lick. He wept, attempting to master
   *ancilla* and *servus*.[3]

22

We ran across the meadow scabbed with cow-dung, past
   the crab-apple trees and camouflaged nissen hut.[4] It
   was curfew-time for our war-band.

At home the curtains were drawn. The wireless[5] boomed
5   its commands. I loved the battle-anthems and the
   gregarious news.

Then, in the earthy shelter, warmed by a blue-glassed
   storm-lantern, I huddled with stories of dragon-
   tailed airships and warriors who took wing immortal
10   as phantoms.

23

In tapestries, in dreams, they gathered, as it was enacted,
   the return, the re-entry of transcendence into this
   sublunary world. *Opus Anglicanum*,[6] their stringent
   mystery riddled by needles: the silver veining, the
5   gold leaf, voluted[7] grape-vine, master-works of
   treacherous thread.

They trudged out of the dark, scraping their boots free
   from lime-splodges and phlegm. They munched
   cold bacon. The lamps grew plump with oily reliable
10   light.
—1971

## A Short History of British India (2)

Suppose they sweltered here three thousand years
  patient for our destruction. There is a greeting
beyond the act. Destiny is the great thing,
true lord of annexation and arrears.

5  Our law-books overrule the emperors.
The mango is the bride-bed of light. Spring

---

[1] *Albion*  Great Britain.

[2] *Muse*  In classical mythology, one of the nine daughters of Zeus
and Mnemosyne, each of whom presided over, and provided
inspiration for, an aspect of the arts and sciences.

[3] *ancilla and servus*  Latin: female servant and male slave.

[4] *nissen hut*  Tunnel-shaped hut with a cement floor and corrugated
iron roof.

[5] *wireless*  Radio.

[6] *Opus Anglicanum*  Latin: English work; a term used in the
thirteenth and fourteenth centuries to refer to fine embroidery
produced in England.

[7] *voluted*  Grooved.

jostles the flame-tree. But new mandates bring
new images of faith, good subahdars![1]

The flittering candles of the wayside shrines
10 melt into dawn. The sun surmounts the dust.
Krishna from Radha[2] lovingly untwines.

Lugging the earth, the oxen bow their heads.
The alien conscience of our days is lost
among the ruins and on endless roads.
—1978

### from *The Triumph of Love*[3]

#### 35

Even now, I tell myself, there is a language
to which I might speak and which
would rightly hear me;
responding with eloquence; in its turn,
5 negotiating sense without insult
given or injury taken.
Familiar to those who already know it
elsewhere as justice,
it is met also in the form of silence.

#### 39

Rancorous, narcissistic old sod—what
makes him go on? We thought, hoped rather,
he might be dead. Too bad. So how
much more does he have of injury time?[4]

#### 148

Obnoxious means, far back within itself,
easily wounded. But vulnerable, proud

anger is, I find, a related self
of covetousness. I came late
5 to seeing that. Actually, I had to be
shown it. What I saw was rough, and still
pains me. Perhaps it should pain me more.
Pride is our crux: be angry, but not proud
where that means vainglorious. Take Leopardi's
10 words or—to be accurate—BV's English
cast of them: when he found Tasso's poor
scratch of a memorial barely showing
among the cold slabs of defunct pomp.[5] It
seemed *a sad and angry consolation.*
15 So—Croker, MacSikker, O'Shem[6]—I ask you:
what are poems for? They are to console us
with their own gift, which is like perfect pitch.
Let us commit that to our dust. What
ought a poem to be? Answer, *a sad*
20 *and angry consolation.* What is
the poem? What figures? Say,
*a sad and angry consolation.* That's
beautiful. Once more? A *sad and angry*
*consolation.*

#### 149

Obstinate old man—*senex*
*sapiens,*[7] it is not. Is he still
writing? What is he writing now? He
has just written: I find it hard
5 to forgive myself. We are immortal. Where
was I?—

#### 150

Sun-blazed, over Romsley,[8] the livid rain-scarp.
—1998

---

[1] *subahdars* Nobles.

[2] *Krishna from Radha* In Hinduism the relationship between Krishna and Radha is expressive of the utmost passion and devotion, and of the harmony of souls.

[3] *The Triumph of Love* The complete poem comprises 150 sections (echoing the 150 Psalms of the Bible).

[4] *injury time* Extra time at the end of a soccer game, added to make up for earlier time lost due to injury.

[5] *Leopardi ... pomp* BV was the pseudonym used by James Thomson (1834–82), who translated work by Giacomo Leopardi (1798–1837), an Italian writer who drew on the work of the great sixteenth-century Italian poet Torquato Tasso (1544–95).

[6] *Croker ... O'Shem* Earlier in *The Triumph of Love*, Hill assigns these names to three critics.

[7] *senex sapiens* Latin: wise old man.

[8] *Romsley* Village near Bromsgrove (where Hill was born), now part of the city of Birmingham.

## TONY HARRISON (b. 1937)

The northern English writer Tony Harrison is among the most versatile and prolific of British poets. His many books of poetry include *The Loiners* (1970), the long poem *V* (1985), *The Gaze of the Gorgon* (1992), *The Shadow of Hiroshima* (1995), and *Under the Clock* (2005); he is also the author of numerous translations and adaptations of poetic drama. Much of Harrison's poetry is infused with political content, particularly on subjects such as class and modern warfare.

## Them & [uz]

*for Professors Richard Hoggart & Leon Cortez[1]*

### 1

α ιχî,  ay, ay! … stutterer Demosthenes[2]
gob full of pebbles outshouting seas—

4 words only of *mi'art*[3] aches and … "Mine's broken,
you barbarian, T.W.!" *He* was nicely spoken.
5 "Can't have our glorious heritage done to death!"

I played the Drunken Porter in *Macbeth*.[4]

"Poetry's the speech of kings. You're one of those
Shakespeare gives the comic bits to: prose!
All poetry (even Cockney Keats?)[5] you see
10 's been dubbed by [Ës]  into RP,
Received Pronunciation, please believe [Ës]
your speech is in the hands of the Receivers."

"We say [Ës]  not [uz] T.W.!" That shut my trap.
I doffed my flat a's (as in "flat cap")
15 my mouth all stuffed with glottals, great
lumps to hawk up and spit out … *E-nun-ci-ate!*

### 2

So right, yer buggers, then! We'll occupy
your lousy leasehold Poetry.

I chewed up Littererchewer and spat the bones
20 into the lap of dozing Daniel Jones,
dropped the initials I'd been harried as
and used my *name* and own voice: [uz] [uz] [uz],
ended sentences with by, with, from,[6]
and spoke the language that I spoke at home.
25 R.I.P. RP. R.I.P. T.W.
I'm *Tony* Harrison no longer you!

You can tell the Receivers where to go
(and not aspirate[7] it) once you know
Wordsworth's *matter/water* are full rhymes,
30 [uz] can be loving as well as funny.

My first mention in the *Times*
automatically made Tony Anthony!
—1981

## t'Ark[8]

S ilence and poetry have their own reserves.
The numbered creatures flourish less and less.
A language near extinction best preserves
the deepest grammar of our nothingness.

5 Not only dodo, oryx and great auk[9]
waddled on their tod[10] to t'monster ark,

---

[1] *Richard Hoggart* (b. 1918), British sociologist and cultural commentator; *Leon Cortez* (1898–1970) British film, radio, and television actor.

[2] *Demosthenes*  Greatest of all orators in ancient Greece, Demosthenes (384–322 BCE) is said to have placed rocks in his mouth in an effort to improve his enunciation.

[3] *'art*  Heart. The dropped "h" has often been regarded in Britain as a sign of "lower class" pronunciation. "My heart aches" are the first words of John Keats's "Ode to a Nightingale" (see l. 9, below).

[4] *Drunken Porter … Macbeth*  Servant with a small, comic role in Shakespeare's play.

[5] *Cockney Keats*  The Romantic poet John Keats (1795–1821) came from a Cockney (i.e., east London) background and was attacked for allegedly representing a "Cockney School of Poetry."

[6] *by, with, from*  Three examples of prepositions; strict grammarians assert that a sentence must not end with a preposition.

[7] *aspirate*  Pronounce the "h" when it appears at the beginning of a word (as opposed to dropping it).

[8] *t'Ark*  The ark. T' is a northern English dialect pronunciation of "the."

[9] *dodo … great auk*  Species that are now extinct.

[10] *on their tod*  On their own.

but "leg," "night," "origin" in crushed people's talk,
tongues of fire last witnessed mouthing: *dark!*

Now when the future couldn't be much darker,
10  there being fewer epithets for sun,
and Cornish and the Togoland *Restsprache*[1]
name both the animals and hunter's gun,
celebrate before things go too far
Papua's last reported manucode,
15  the pygmy hippo of the Cote d'Ivoire,
and Upper Guinea's oviparous toad—[2]

(or mourn in Latin their imminent death,
then translate these poems into *cynghanedd*).[3]
—1981


## from *V*

...

Next millennium you'll have to search quite hard
to find out where I'm buried but I'm near
the grave of haberdasher Appleyard,
the pile of HARPs,[4] or some new neonned beer.

5  Find Byron, Wordsworth,[5] or turn left between
one grave marked Broadbent, one marked Richardson.
Bring some solution with you that can clean
whatever new crude words have been sprayed on.

If love of art, or love, gives you affront
10  that the grave I'm in's graffitied then, maybe,
erase the more offensive FUCK and CUNT
but leave, with the worn UNITED, one small v.[6]

---

[1]  *Cornish ... Restsprache*  Two endangered languages—Cornish from Cornwall in southwest England, and Restsprache from Togo in West Africa.

[2]  *Papua's ... toad*  All examples of severely endangered species.

[3]  *cynghanedd*  Welsh: literally, "harmony," also "poetic form." The Welsh language, once classed as endangered, began to be more widely used in the late twentieth century.

[4]  *HARP*  Brand of lager beer.

[5]  *Byron, Wordsworth*  Romantic poets George Gordon, Lord Byron (1788–1824), and William Wordsworth (1770–1850).

[6]  *UNITED*  In this case, short for "Leeds United Football Club"; *v.* Short for "victory," a common piece of graffiti during World War II.

Victory? For vast, slow, coal-creating forces
that hew the body's seams to get the soul.
15  Will Earth run out of her "diurnal courses"
before repeating her creation of black coal?

But choose a day like I chose in mid-May
or earlier when apple and hawthorn tree,
no matter if boys boot their ball all day,
20  cling to their blossoms and won't shake them free.

If, having come this far, somebody reads
these verses, and he/she wants to understand,
face this grave on Beeston Hill,[7] your back to Leeds,
and read the chiselled epitaph I've planned:

25  *Beneath your feet's a poet, then a pit.*
*Poetry supporter, if you're here to find*
*how poems can grow from* (beat you to it!) SHIT
*find the beef, the beer, the bread, then look behind.*
—1985


## from *Sonnets for August 1945*[8]

### THE MORNING AFTER

#### I

The fire left to itself might smoulder weeks.
Phone cables melt. Paint peels from off back gates.
Kitchen windows crack; the whole street reeks
of horsehair blazing. Still, it celebrates.

5  Though people weep, their tears dry from the heat.
Faces flushed with flame, beer, sheer relief
and such a sense of celebration in our street
for me it still means joy though banked with grief.

And that, now clouded, sense of public joy
10  with war-worn adults wild in their loud fling
has never come again since as a boy
I saw Leeds people dance and heard them sing.

---

[7]  *Beeston Hill*  Western suburb of the city of Leeds.

[8]  *August 1945*  The United States dropped atomic bombs on the Japanese cities of Hiroshima and Nagasaki on 6 August and 9 August, respectively.

There's still that dark, scorched circle on the road.
The morning after kids like me helped spray
15  hissing upholstery spring wire that still glowed
and cobbles boiling with black gas tar for VJ.[1]
—1990

## TOM RAWORTH (b. 1942)

An artist as well as a prolific poet, Tom Raworth
roots his work strongly in both sound and image;
the connections forged through what Angela
Leighton has called his "jump-cut lyricism" tend to
be intuitive rather than intellectual. Born in
London, Raworth has lived largely in Cambridge
but has also lived and worked in the United States,
Mexico, and South Africa. Since 1966, he has
published over 40 books and pamphlets; his
*Collected Poems* appeared in 2003.

### Out of A Sudden

the alphabet wonders
what it should do
paper feels useless
colours lose hue

5  while all musical notes
perform only in blue

a lombardy poplar
shadows the ground
drifted with swansdown
10  muffling the sound

at the tip of the lake
of the road to the south

above in the night sky
scattered by chance
15  stars cease their motion
poppies don't dance

---

[1]  *VJ*  Day on which victory by the Allies over Japan was celebrated.

in the grass standing still
by the path no-one walks.
—1995

### Looking for Language

Physical pulled to a stop
acting interested reactions

a history for rejection
inherited recognisable energy

5  whacked holes in gone scenarios
chrome plated folds

dedicated to dazzle conviction
shapes suitable for previous sites
—2000

## DAVID HARSENT (b. 1942)

For many years a bookseller and a publisher, David
Harsent made writing his vocation in the late 1980s;
in addition to his numerous volumes of poetry he is
the author (under the name Jack Curtis) of several
crime novels. His books of poetry include *The
Sorrow of Sarajevo* (1996), *A Bird's Idea of Flight*
(1998), and *Marriage* (2002). The poems in *Legion*
(2005), which won the Forward Prize for the year's
best collection of poetry, largely concern the horrors
of an unnamed war.

### Art

Before this, I liked a sketchiness in art,
figures, say three or four, half-done in white on
    almost-white,
or something much like a bruise
seeping up through the wash, so you might make out,
5  if you stood side-on to the thing, eye-hollows, a nose,
or a mouth saying O-O-O: whites, but also blues
deep enough to make mauve in moonlight or snowlight
(was it?) and these few standing still, standing apart,

but more at their backs, a hidden weight in the canvas.
10  It's everywhere, now, in the city's broken stone, in the
        glint
off smashed glass, in the much-told tale
of the bombed-out house where someone peeled off the
        wall
a face stuck flat came away whole
still wearing the puckish stare of the hierophant,[1]
15  just a touch or two left on the whitewash, the art of
        hint.
—2005

## CRAIG RAINE (b. 1944)

With his first book *The Onion, Memory* (1978) and
particularly with his second, *A Martian Sends a
Postcard Home* (1979), Craig Raine created something of a sensation, and for a time it was suggested
that his ability to make the familiar fresh and
strange through striking metaphor would spawn a
new school of British poetry. That never occurred,
but Raine himself has continued to produce a body
of interesting and important work, including the
long poems *History: The Home Movie* and *A la
recherche du temps perdu* (2000). An outspoken critic
as well as a poet, Raine was from 1981 to 1991
poetry editor at the publishing house Faber &
Faber, and has taught for many years at Oxford
University.

## A Martian Sends a Postcard Home

Caxtons[2] are mechanical birds with many wings
and some are treasured for their markings—

they cause the eyes to melt
or the body to shriek without pain.

5   I have never seen one fly, but
sometimes they perch on the hand.

---

[1] *hierophant*   One who presides over sacred ceremonies or esoteric
revelations.
[2] *Caxtons*   William Caxton (1422–91) introduced the printing
press to England.

Mist is when the sky is tired of flight
and rests its soft machine on ground:

then the world is dim and bookish
10  like engravings under tissue paper.

Rain is when the earth is television.
It has the property of making colours darker.

Model T[3] is a room with the lock inside—
a key is turned to free the world

15  for movement, so quick there is a film
to watch for anything missed.

But time is tied to the wrist
or kept in a box, ticking with impatience.

In homes, a haunted apparatus sleeps,
20  that snores when you pick it up.

If the ghost cries, they carry it
to their lips and soothe it to sleep

with sounds. And yet, they wake it up
deliberately, by tickling with a finger.

25  Only the young are allowed to suffer
openly. Adults go to a punishment room

with water but nothing to eat.
They lock the door and suffer the noises

alone. No one is exempt
30  and everyone's pain has a different smell.

At night, when all the colours die,
they hide in pairs

and read about themselves—
in colour, with their eyelids shut.
—1979

---

[3] *Model T*   Early model of the automobile, produced by the Ford
Motor Company; the Model T was the first car to enjoy mass
popularity.

## Eavan Boland (b. 1944)

With a body of work extending over four decades, Eavan Boland has broken new ground as the first Irish woman to achieve widespread recognition as a poet of the first rank. Like many Irish poets, she has maintained a strong interest in history and in myth, but she has explored them with a strong awareness of the power of myth to distort as well as to shape reality. Her poetry has also cast a fresh and powerful eye on the dynamics of family life. Among her many books of poetry are *Night Feed* (1982), *In a Time of Violence* (1994), and *Against Love Poetry* (2001). Boland has for some years divided her time between Dublin and California; she is Director of the Creative Writing Program at Stanford University.

## Night Feed

This is dawn.
Believe me
This is your season, little daughter.
The moment daisies open,
5   The hour mercurial rainwater
Makes a mirror for sparrows.
It's time we drowned our sorrows.

I tiptoe in.
I lift you up
10  Wriggling
In your rosy, zipped sleeper.
Yes, this is the hour
For the early bird and me
When finder is keeper.

15  I crook the bottle.
How you suckle!
This is the best I can be,
Housewife
To this nursery
20  Where you hold on,
Dear life.

A slit of milk.
The last suck.
And now your eyes are open,

25  Birth-coloured and offended.
Earth wakes.
You go back to sleep.
The feed is ended.

Worms turn.
30  Stars go in.
Even the moon is losing face.
Poplars stilt for dawn
And we begin
The long fall from grace.
35  I tuck you in.
—1982

## Anna Liffey[1]

*L*ife, the story goes,
Was the daughter of Cannan,
And came to the plain of Kildare.
She loved the flatlands and the ditches
5   And the unreachable horizon.
She asked that it be named for her.
The river took its name from the land.
The land took its name from a woman.

\*

A woman in the doorway of a house.
10  A river in the city of her birth.

\*

There, in the hills above my house,
The river Liffey rises, is a source.
It rises in rush and ling[2] heather and
Black peat and bracken and strengthens
15  To claim the city it narrated.

---

[1] *Anna Liffey*  Before it reaches Dublin, the River Liffey in Ireland runs through flatlands in County Kildare that were at one time known as the plains of Liffe; "Abha" is the Irish word for "river," and over the centuries the Liffey has been variously known as Alyffy, Analiffy, and (more commonly) Anna Liffey.

[2] *ling*  Another name for heather, used primarily in the north of England.

Swans. Steep falls. Small towns.
The smudged air and bridges of Dublin.

\*

Dusk is coming.
Rain is moving east from the hills.

\*

20  If I could see myself
I would see
A woman in a doorway
Wearing the colours that go with red hair.
Although my hair is no longer red.

\*

25  I praise
The gifts of the river.
Its shiftless and glittering
Retelling of a city,
Its clarity as it flows,
30  In the company of runt flowers and herons,
Around a bend at Islandbridge
And under thirteen bridges to the sea.
Its patience at twilight—
Swans nesting by it,
35  Neon wincing into it.

\*

Maker of
Places, remembrances,
Narrate such fragments for me:

\*

One body. One spirit.
40  One place. One name.
The city where I was born.
The river that runs through it.
The nation which eludes me.

Fractions of a life
45  It has taken me a lifetime
To claim.

\*

I came here in a cold winter.

I had no children. No country.
I did not know the name for my own life.

50  My country took hold of me.
My children were born.

I walked out in a summer dusk
To call them in.

One name. Then the other one.
55  The beautiful vowels sounding out home.

\*

Make a nation what you will
Make of the past
What you can—

There is now
60  A woman in a doorway.

It has taken me
All my strength to do this.

Becoming a figure in a poem.

Usurping a name and a theme.

\*

65  A river is not a woman.
Although the names it finds,
The history it makes
And suffers—
The Viking blades beside it,

70   The muskets of the Redcoats,
    The flames of the Four Courts
 Blazing into it—
   Are a sign.
    Any more than
75 A woman is a river,
   Although the course it takes,
    Through swans courting and distraught willows
 Its patience
   Which is also its powerlessness,
80    From Callary to Islandbridge,
     And from source to mouth,
 Is another one.
     And in my late forties
 Past believing
85   Love will heal
    What language fails to know
 And needs to say—
   What the body means—
    I take this sign
90 And I make this mark:
   A woman in the doorway of her house.
    A river in the city of her birth.
 The truth of a suffered life.
    The mouth of it.

   *

95 The seabirds come in from the coast.
 The city wisdom is they bring rain.
 I watch them from my doorway.
 I see them as arguments of origin—
 Leaving a harsh force on the horizon,
100 Only to find it
 Slanting and falling elsewhere.

 Which water—
 The one they leave or the one they pronounce—
 Remembers the other?

105 I am sure
 The body of an ageing woman
 Is a memory
 And to find a language for it
 Is as hard

110 As weeping and requiring
 These birds to cry out as if they could
 Recognize their element
 Remembered and diminished in
 A single tear.

   *

115 An ageing woman
 Finds no shelter in language.
 She finds instead
 Single words she once loved
 Such as "summer" and "yellow"
120 And "sexual" and "ready"
 Have suddenly become dwellings
 For someone else—
 Rooms and a roof under which someone else
 Is welcome, not her. Tell me,
125 Anna Liffey,
 Spirit of water,
 Spirit of place,
 How is it on this
 Rainy Autumn night
130 As the Irish sea takes
 The names you made, the names
 You bestowed, and gives you back
 Only wordlessness?

   *

 Autumn rain is
135 Scattering and dripping
 From car-ports
 And clipped hedges.
 The gutters are full.

 When I came here
140 I had neither
 Children nor country.
 The trees were arms.
 The hills were dreams.

 I was free
145 To imagine a spirit
 In the blues and greens,

The hills and fogs
Of a small city.

My children were born.
150  My country took hold of me.
A vision in a brick house.
Is it only love
That makes a place?

I feel it change.
155  My children are
Growing up, getting older.
My country holds on
To its own pain.

I turn off
160  The harsh yellow
Porch light and
Stand in the hall.
Where is home now?

Follow the rain
165  Out to the Dublin hills.
Let it become the river.
Let the spirit of place be
A lost soul again.

        *

In the end
170  It will not matter
That I was a woman. I am sure of it.
The body is a source. Nothing more.
There is a time for it. There is a certainty
About the way it seeks its own dissolution.
175  Consider rivers.
They are always en route to
Their own nothingness. From the first moment
They are going home. And so
When language cannot do it for us,
180  Cannot make us know love will not diminish us,
There are these phrases
Of the ocean
To console us.
Particular and unafraid of their completion.

185  In the end
Everything that burdened and distinguished me
Will be lost in this:
I was a voice.
    —1994

## Listen. This is the Noise of Myth

This is the story of a man and woman
 under a willow and beside a weir
near a river in a wooded clearing.
They are fugitives. Intimates of myth.

5   Fictions of my purpose. I suppose
I shouldn't say that yet or at least
before I break their hearts or save their lives
I ought to tell their story and I will.

When they went first it was winter; cold,
10  cold through the Midlands and as far West[1]
as they could go. They knew they had to go—
through Meath, Westmeath, Longford,

their lives unravelling like the hours of light—
and then there were lambs under the snow
15  and it was January, aconite[2] and jasmine
and the hazel yellowing and puce berries on the ivy.

They could not eat where they had cooked,
nor sleep where they had eaten
nor at dawn rest where they had slept.
20  They shunned the densities

of trees with one trunk and of caves
with one dark and the dangerous embrace
of islands with a single landing place.
And all the time it was cold, cold:

25  the fields still gardened by their ice,
the trees stitched with snow overnight,

---

[1]  *West*  Historically, the West of Ireland has always been the poorest and most rural area.

[2]  *aconite*  Small flower (also known as "winter aconite").

the ditches full; frost toughening lichen,
darning lace into rock crevices.

And then the woods flooded and buds
30  blunted from the chestnut and the foxglove
put its big leaves out and chaffinches
chinked and flirted in the branches of the ash.

And here we are where we started from—
under a willow and beside a weir
35  near a river in a wooded clearing.
The woman and the man have come to rest.

Look how light is coming through the ash.
The weir sluices kingfisher blues.
The woman and the willow tree lean forward, forward.
40  Something is near; something is about to happen;

something more than Spring
and less than history. Will we see
hungers eased after months of hiding?
Is there a touch of heat in that light?

45  If they stay here soon it will be summer; things
returning, sunlight fingering minnowy deeps,
seedy greens, reeds, electing lights
and edges from the river. Consider

legend, self-deception, sin, the sum
50  of human purposes and its end; remember
how our poetry depends on distance,
aspect: gravity will bend starlight.

Forgive me if I set the truth to rights.
Bear with me if I put an end to this:
55  She never turned to him; she never leaned
under the sallow-willow[1] over to him.

They never made love; not there; not here;
not anywhere; there was no winter journey;
no aconite, no birdsong and no jasmine,
60  no woodland and no river and no weir.

Listen. This is the noise of myth. It makes
the same sound as shadow. Can you hear it?
Daylight greys in the preceptories.[2]
Her head begins to shine

65  pivoting the planets of a harsh nativity.
They were never mine. This is mine.
This sequence of evicted possibilities.
Displaced facts. Tricks of light. Reflections.

Invention. Legend. Myth. What you will.
70  The shifts and fluencies are infinite.
The moving parts are marvellous. Consider
how the bereavements of the definite

are easily lifted from our heroine.
She may or she may not. She was or wasn't
75  by the water at his side as dark
waited above the Western countryside.

O consolations of the craft.
How we put
the old poultices on the old sores,
80  the same mirrors to the old magic. Look.

The scene returns. The willow sees itself
drowning in the weir and the woman
gives the kiss of myth her human heat.
Reflections. Reflections. He becomes her lover.

85  The old romances make no bones about it.
The long and short of it. The end and the beginning.
The glories and the ornaments are muted.
And when the story ends the song is over.
—1986

## Against Love Poetry

We were married in summer, thirty years ago.
I have loved you deeply from that moment
to this. I have loved other things as well. Among
them the idea of women's freedom. Why do I put

---

[1]  *sallow-willow*  Type of low-growing willow.

[2]  *preceptories*  Estates housing subordinate communities of the Knights Templars, a medieval military and religious order of knighthood.

5   these words side by side? Because I am a woman.
Because marriage is not freedom. Therefore, every
word here is written against love poetry. Love
poetry can do no justice to this. Here, instead, is a
remembered story from a faraway history: A great
10   king lost a war and was paraded in chains through
the city of his enemy. They taunted him. They
brought his wife and children to him—he showed
no emotion. They brought his former courtiers—he
showed no emotion. They brought his old
15   servant—only then did he break down and weep. I
did not find my womanhood in the servitudes of
custom. But I saw my humanity look back at me
there. It is to mark the contradictions of a daily love
that I have written this. Against love poetry.

—2001

## VERONICA FORREST-THOMSON (1947–1975)

Influential as a theorist as well as a poet, Veronica
Forrest-Thomson published three volumes of poetry
during her lifetime. *Collected Poems and Translations*
(1990) and *Poetic Artifice: A Theory of Twentieth-
Century Poetry* (1978) were published posthumously.

## Identi-Kit

L ove is the oldest camera.
   Snap me with your eyes.
Wearied with myself I want
a picture that simplifies.

5   Likeness is not important
provided the traits cohere.
Dissolve doubts and contradictions
to leave the exposure clear.

Erase shadows and negative
10   that confused the tired sight.
Develop as conclusive definition
a pattern of black and white.

For I wish to see me reassembled
in that dark-room of your mind.

—1967

## Phrase-Book

W ords are a monstrous excrescence.
   Everything green is extended. It
is apricot, orange, lemon, olive and cherry,
and other snakes in the linguistic grass;
5   also a white touch of marble which evokes
no ghosts, the taste of squid, the ...
Go away. I shall call a policeman.
Acrocorinth[1] which evokes no
goats under the lemon blossom.

10   World is a monstrous excrescence;
he is following me everywhere, one
Nescafé and twenty Athenes, everything
green; I am not responsible for it.
I don't want to speak to you.
15   Leave me alone. I shall stay here.
I refuse a green extension. Beware.
I have paid you. I have paid you
enough, sea, sun, and octopodi.
It is raining cats and allomorphs.[2]

20   "Where" is the British Embassy.
—1967

## JAMES FENTON (b. 1949)

James Fenton has ranged extraordinarily widely both
geographically (he lived for some time in Southeast
Asia) and in his work. A political correspondent,
translator, and literary critic as well as a poet,
Fenton was Professor of Poetry at Oxford University
from 1994 to 1999. His books of poetry include *The
Memory of War* (1982) and *Out of Danger* (1993).

---

[1] *Acrocorinth* Fortress overlooking the ancient Greek city of
Corinth, on the Isthmus of Corinth. It was the site of a temple of
Aphrodite (Greek goddess of love) and was strongly fortified in the
Middle Ages.

[2] *allomorphs* Variants of a particular morpheme (a meaningful
linguistic unit that cannot be divided into smaller parts), such as the
"plural" morpheme, or the "past" morpheme. Also, distinct
crystalline forms of the same substance that have the same chemical
composition.

## A German Requiem

It is not what they built. It is what they knocked
   down.
It is not the houses. It is the spaces between the houses.
It is not the streets that exist. It is the streets that no
   longer exist.
It is not your memories which haunt you.
5  It is not what you have written down.
It is what you have forgotten, what you must forget.
What you must go on forgetting all your life.
And with any luck oblivion should discover a ritual.
You will find out that you are not alone in the enterprise.
10  Yesterday the very furniture seemed to reproach you.
Today you take your place in the Widow's Shuttle.

❡

The bus is waiting at the southern gate
To take you to the city of your ancestors
Which stands on the hill opposite, with gleaming
   pediments,
15  As vivid as this charming square, your home.
Are you shy? You should be. It is almost like a wedding,
The way you clasp your flowers and give a little tug at
   your veil. Oh,
The hideous bridesmaids, it is natural that you should
   resent them
Just a little, on this first day.
20  But that will pass, and the cemetery is not far.
Here comes the driver, flicking a toothpick into the
   gutter,
His tongue still searching between his teeth.
See, he has not noticed you. No one has noticed you.
It will pass, young lady, it will pass.

❡

25  How comforting it is, once or twice a year,
To get together and forget the old times.
As on those special days, ladies and gentlemen,
When the boiled shirts[1] gather at the graveside
And a leering waistcoat approaches the rostrum.[2]
30  It is like a solemn pact between the survivors.

The mayor has signed it on behalf of the freemasonry.[3]
The priest has sealed it on behalf of all the rest.
Nothing more need be said, and it is better that way—

❡

The better for the widow, that she should not live in
   fear of surprise,
35  The better for the young man, that he should move at
   liberty between the armchairs,
The better that these bent figures who flutter among the
   graves
Tending the nightlights and replacing the
   chrysanthemums
Are not ghosts,
That they shall go home.
40  The bus is waiting, and on the upper terraces
The workmen are dismantling the houses of the dead.

❡

But when so many had died, so many and at such speed,
There were no cities waiting for the victims.
They unscrewed the name-plates from the shattered
   doorways
45  And carried them away with the coffins.
So the squares and parks were filled with the eloquence
   of young cemeteries:
The smell of fresh earth, the improvised crosses
And all the impossible directions in brass and enamel.

❡

"Doctor Gliedschirm, skin specialist, surgeries 14–16
   hours or by appointment."
50  Professor Sargnagel was buried with four degrees, two
   associate memberships
And instructions to tradesmen to use the back entrance.
Your uncle's grave informed you that he lived on the
   third floor, left.
You were asked please to ring, and he would come down
   in the lift[4]
To which one needed a key …

---

1  *boiled shirts*  White linen shirts; dress shirts.

2  *rostrum*  Pulpit; platform for public speaking.

3  *freemasonry*  Fraternal society in which members meet as societies, or "lodges." Freemasons have often played a leading role in local public affairs in various western societies.

4  *lift*  Elevator.

¶

55  Would come down, would ever come down
With a smile like thin gruel, and never too much to say.
How he shrank through the years.
How you towered over him in the narrow cage.
How he shrinks now …

¶

60  But come. Grief must have its term? Guilt too, then.
And it seems there is no limit to the resourcefulness of
    recollection.
So that a man might say and think:
When the world was at its darkest,
When the black wings passed over the rooftops
65  (And who can divine His purposes?) even then
There was always, always a fire in this hearth.
You see this cupboard? A priest-hole![1]
And in that lumber-room[2] whole generations have been
    housed and fed.
Oh, if I were to begin, if I were to begin to tell you
70  The half, the quarter, a mere smattering of what we
    went through!

¶

His wife nods, and a secret smile,
Like a breeze with enough strength to carry one dry leaf
Over two pavingstones, passes from chair to chair.
Even the enquirer is charmed.
75  He forgets to pursue the point.
It is not what he wants to know.
It is what he wants not to know.
It is not what they say.
It is what they do not say.
—1980

## GRACE NICHOLS (b. 1950)

A native of Guyana, Grace Nichols moved to
England in 1977 and began to make a mark as a
poet in the 1980s with work of challenging and

exuberant directness, often written with a view as
much to performance as to the printed page. Her
books include *I is a long-memoried woman* (1983),
*The Fat Black Woman's Poems* (1984) and *Everybody
Got a Gift* (2005).

## Skanking[3] Englishman Between Trains

Met him at Birmingham Station[4]
small yellow hair Englishman
hi fi stereo swinging in one hand
walking in rhythm to reggae sound/Man

5   he was alive
he was full-o-jive
said he had a lovely
Jamaican wife

Said he couldn't remember
10  the taste of English food
I like mih drops[5]
me johnny cakes[6]
me peas and rice
me soup/Man

15  he was alive
he was full-o-jive
said he had a lovely
Jamaican wife

Said, showing me her photo
20  whenever we have a little quarrel
you know/to sweeten her up
I surprise her with a nice mango/Man

he was alive
he was full-o-jive
25  said he had a lovely Jamaican wife
—1984

---

[1]  *priest-hole*  Hiding place for Roman Catholic priests, built during the time of the penal laws, which imposed penalties upon those who did not practice the religion of the Church of England.

[2]  *lumber-room*  Storeroom.

[3]  *Skanking*  Walking.

[4]  *Birmingham Station*  Located in the British Midlands, the city of Birmingham's railway station is a hub where many train lines meet.

[5]  *drops*  Drop-shaped cakes; also, sugar plums or candies.

[6]  *johnny cakes*  In the West Indies, a term for dumplings or scones.

## Epilogue

I have crossed an ocean
  I have lost my tongue
from the root of the old one
a new one has sprung
—1984

## Love

Love is not a grindstone
  constantly grinding
wearing down to bone

Love is not an interlocking
5  deadlock
of inseparable flesh
or a merging of metals
to smooth alloy

Love is a sunshawl
10 that keeps the beloved warm

Even the undeserving
love floods
risking all.
—1989

## White

Never mind how or why—
  this slow delight
of waking to a room
that comes out of the
5  memory of night,
A dusky dawning—
paintings, wardrobe,
hangings …

Then walking, a sleepwalker,
10 holding on to walls of vanilla,
great solid slabs

you could sink your mouth into.
The memories of ancestors,
all that blackness
15 against whiteness.
The starched religiousness of it.

O I could hold
the globe like a face,
Januslike[1] spinning
20 from the depths of my dreaming
I could face-up
to the stark white page
already seeded
with the best invisible poem.
—1996

## MEDBH McGUCKIAN (b. 1950)

Medbh McGuckian came into prominence as a writer in the 1980s and 1990s. Her poems, at once light in tone and densely suggestive, often embed large issues of history, gender and language within focused, personal contexts. Her books include *The Flower Master* (1982), *Marconi's Cottage* (1991), *The Face of the Earth* (2002), and *The Book of the Angel* (2004).

## Slips

The studied poverty of a moon roof
  The earthenware of dairies cooled by apple trees,
The apple tree that makes the whitest wash …

But I forget names, remembering them wrongly
5  Where they touch upon another name,
A town in France like a woman's Christian name.

My childhood is preserved as a nation's history,
My favourite fairytales the shells
Leased by the hermit crab.

---

[1] *Januslike*  I.e., having two faces; referring to Janus, the Roman god of doorways and of beginnings and endings, who was depicted with two faces, one looking in either direction.

10  I see my grandmother's death as a piece of ice,
    My mother's slimness restored to her,
    My own key slotted in your door—

    Tricks you might guess from this unfastened button,
    A pen mislaid, a word misread,
15  My hair coming down in the middle of a conversation.
    —1982

### The Sofa

D o not be angry if I tell you
      Your letter stayed unopened on my table
    For several days. If you were friend enough
    To believe me, I was about to start writing
5   At any moment; my mind was savagely made up,
    Like a serious sofa moved
    Under a north window. My heart, alas,

    Is not the calmest of places.
    Still it is not my heart that needs replacing:
10  And my books seem real enough to me,
    My disasters, my surrenders, all my loss …
    Since I was child enough to forget
    That you loathe poetry, you ask for some—
    About nature, greenery, insects, and, of course,

15  The sun—surely that would be to open
    An already open window? To celebrate
    The impudence of flowers? If I could
    Interest you instead in his large, gentle stares,
    How his soft shirt is the inside of pleasure
20  To me, why I must wear white for him,
    Imagine he no longer trembles

    When I approach, no longer buys me
    Flowers for my name day[1] … But I spread
    On like a house, I begin to scatter
25  To a tiny to-and-fro at odds
    With the wear on my threshold. Somewhere

A curtain rising wonders where I am,
My books sleep, pretending to forget me.
—1982

### The Dream-Language of Fergus

                    1

Y our tongue has spent the night
      in its dim sack as the shape of your foot
in its cave. Not the rudiment
of half a vanquished sound,
5   the excommunicated shadow of a name,
has rumpled the sheets of your mouth.

                    2

So Latin sleeps, they say, in Russian speech,
so one river inserted into another
becomes a leaping, glistening, splashed
10  and scattered alphabet
jutting out from the voice,
till what began as a dog's bark
ends with bronze, what began
with honey ends with ice;
15  as if an aeroplane in full flight
launched a second plane,
the sky is stabbed by their exits
and the mistaken meaning of each.

                    3

Conversation is as necessary
20  among these familiar campus trees
as the apartness of torches;
and if I am a threader
of double-stranded words, whose
Quando[2] has grown into now,
25  no text can return the honey
in its path of light from a jar,
only a seed-fund, a pendulum,
pressing out the diasporic snow.
—1991

---

[1]  *name day*  Feast day of the saint for whom a person is named.

[2]  *Quando*  Latin: when.

## MAGGIE O'SULLIVAN (b. 1951)

A visual artist and publisher as well as a poet, Maggie O'Sullivan came to be recognized as an important voice in British experimental poetry in the 1980s and 1990s. Her work is deeply rooted in the sensations of language. O'Sullivan's books include *An Incomplete Natural History* (1984), *In the House of the Shaman* (1993), and *Palace of Reptiles* (2003).

## from *Starlings*

Lived Daily
  or Both

   Daily
the Living
5    structuring
      Bone-Seed,

   Pelage,
    Aqueous,

       YONDERLY—
10          lazybed of need—
CLOUD-SANG
     Tipsy Bobbles, Dowdy
     wander. Halt upon

     grinned jeers, gin's note
15   someone's in the leading
      of small & the pitch meander ears

tune me gold
Dulthie pods,

    Lipper
    "Ochre harled
20

   ELECTRIC

CONTORTIONS—

—1993

## LINTON KWESI JOHNSON (b. 1952)

Born in Jamaica, Linton Kwesi Johnson has lived for most of his life in south London. The first and best-known practitioner of "dub poetry" (a term coined by Johnson to describe a blend of poetry and reggae music), he has worked as a journalist and broadcaster as well as as a poet and musician. His books include *Dread, Beat, an' Blood* (1975), *Tings an' Times* (1991), and *Mi Revalueshanary Fren* (2002).

## *Inglan Is a Bitch*

w'en mi jus' come to Landan toun
mi use to work pan di andahgroun[1]
but workin' pan di andahgroun
y'u don't get fi know your way aroun'

5   Inglan is a bitch
dere's no escapin' it
Inglan is a bitch
dere's no runnin' whey fram it

mi get a lickle jab in a big 'otell
10  an' awftah a while, mi woz doin' quite well
dem staat mi aaf as a dish-washah
but w'en mi tek a stack, mi noh tun clack-watchah!

Inglan is a bitch
dere's no escapin' it
15  Inglan is a bitch
noh baddah try fi hide fram it

w'en dem gi' yu di lickle wage packit
fus dem rab it wid dem big tax racket
y'u haffi struggle fi mek en's meet
20  an' w'en y'u goh a y'u bed y'u jus' cant sleep

Inglan is a bitch
dere's no escapin' it
Inglan is a bitch fi true
a noh lie mi a tell, a true

25  mi use to work dig ditch w'en it cowl noh bitch

---

[1] *andahgroun* Underground (i.e., subway).

mi did strang like a mule, but, bwoy, mi did fool
den awftah a while mi jus' stap dhu ovahtime
den awftah a while mi jus' phu dung mi tool

Inglan is a bitch
30  dere's no escapin' it
Inglan is a bitch
y'u haffi know how fi suvvive in it

well mi dhu day wok an' mi dhu nite wok
mi dhu clean wok an' mi dhu dutty wok
35  dem seh dat black man is very lazy
but if y'u si how mi wok y'u woulda seh mi crazy

Inglan is a bitch
dere's no escapin' it
Inglan is a bitch
40  y'u bettah face up to it

dem have a lickle facktri up inna Brackly[1]
inna disya facktri all dem dhu is pack crackry
fi di laas fifteen years dem get mi laybah
now awftah fifteen years mi fall out a fayvah

45  Inglan is a bitch
dere's no escapin' it
Inglan is a bitch
dere's no runnin' whey fram it

mi know dem have work, work in abundant
50  yet still, dem mek mi redundant[2]
now, at fifty-five mi gettin' quite ol'
yet still, dem sen' mi fi goh draw dole

Inglan is a bitch
dere's no escapin' it
55  Inglan is a bitch fi true
is whey wi a goh dhu 'bout it?
    —1991

---

[1]  *Brackly*  Industrial area of London.

[2]  *mek mi redundant*  Make me redundant (i.e., lay me off).

## MONIZA ALVI (b. 1954)

An important voice in the generation of British poets who came to prominence in the 1990s, Moniza Alvi has been a school teacher and college tutor as well as a poet. Born in Pakistan, she has lived in England since infancy; much of her poetry concerns issues of identity. Alvi's books include *The Country at My Shoulder* (1993), *A Bowl of Warm Air* (1996), and *How the Stone Found its Voice* (2005).

### And If

If you could choose a country
    to belong to—
perhaps you had one
snatched away,
5  once offered to you
like a legend
in a basket covered with a cloth—

and if the sun were a simple flare,
the streets beating out
10  the streets, and your breath
lost on the road
with the Yadavs,[3] herding cattle,
then you could rest, absorb
it all in the cool of the hills,

15  but still you might peel back one face
to retrieve another
and another, down to the face that is
unbearable, so clear
so complex, hinting at nations,
20  castes and sub-castes
and you would touch it once—

and if this Eastern track were
a gusty English lane
where rain makes mirrors
25  in the holes,
a rat lies lifeless, sodden

---

[3]  *Yadavs*  One of the most ancient Aryan groups of Bharata, the Yadavs live in part of India, Nepal and Bangladesh and mostly follow the Hindu religion.

as an old floorcloth,
you'd be untouchable[1]—as one

defined by someone else—
30    one who cleans the toilets,
burns the dead.
—1996

## How the World Split in Two

Was it widthways or lengthways?
a quarrel with the equator?
Did the rawness of the inside sparkle?

Only this is true:
5    there was an arm on one side
and a hand on the other,
a thought on one side
and a hush on the other.

And a luminous tear
10   carried on the back of a beetle
went backwards and forwards
from one side to the other.
—2005

### JEAN BINTA BREEZE (b. 1957)

One of Britain's leading "dub" poets (and a female
pioneer in that male-dominated genre), Jean Binta
Breeze spent her early years in Jamaica; she has lived
primarily in London since the late 1970s. Her work
deals extensively with political themes and exhibits
a global reach, with a frequent focus on the cultural
connections between Britain and the Caribbean.

## earth cries

She doesn't cry for water
she runs rivers deep

she doesn't cry for food
she has suckled trees
5    she doesn't cry for clothing
she weaves all that she wears
she doesn't cry for shelter
she grows thatch everywhere
she doesn't cry for children
10   she's got more than she can bear
she doesn't cry for heaven
she knows it's everywhere
you don't know why she's crying
when she's got everything
15   how could you know she's crying
for just one humane being
—2000

### GWYNETH LEWIS (b. 1959)

A leading poet in both Welsh and English, Gwyneth
Lewis has expressed through her work an abiding
fascination with issues relating to culture and
language. Among her books of poetry in English are
*Parables and Faxes* (1995), *Zero Gravity* (1998), and
*Keeping Mum* (2003). In 2005 she was appointed
the first National Poet for Wales.

## Mother Tongue

"I started to translate in seventy-three
in the schoolyard. For a bit of fun
to begin with—the occasional 'fuck'
for the bite of another language's smoke
5    at the back of my throat, its bitter chemicals.
Soon I was hooked on whole sentences
behind the shed, and lessons in Welsh
seemed very boring. I started on print,
Jeeves & Wooster, Dick Francis, James Bond,[2]
10   in Welsh covers. That worked for a while
until Mam discovered Jean Plaidy[3] inside

---

[1]  *untouchable*  In the caste system of Hindu societies, the lowest
caste is that of the untouchables, who are effectively restricted from
any jobs other than menial ones (such as cleaning toilets and
cremating bodies).

[2]  *Jeeves & Wooster*  Main characters in a series of popular English
comic novels by P.G. Wodehouse (1881–1975); *Dick Francis*  A
former jockey and the author of dozens of popular thrillers set
against a backdrop of horseracing (b. 1920).

[3]  *Jean Plaidy*  Popular English author of romance novels (1910–
83).

a Welsh concordance[1] one Sunday night.
There were ructions:[2] a language, she screamed,
should be for a lifetime. Too late for me.
15  Soon I was snorting Simenon
and Flaubert.[3] Had to read much more
for any effect. One night I OD'd
after reading far too much Proust.[4]
I came to, but it scared me. For a while
20  I went Welsh-only but it was bland
and my taste was changing. Before too long
I was back on translating, found that three
languages weren't enough. The 'ch'
in German was easy, Rilke[5] a buzz ...
25  For a language fetishist like me
sex is part of the problem. Umlauts[6] make me sweat,
so I need a multilingual man
but they're rare in West Wales and tend to be
married already. If only I'd kept
30  myself much purer, with simpler tastes,
the Welsh might be living ...
Detective, you speak
Russian, I hear, and Japanese.
Could you whisper some softly?
35  I'm begging you. Please ..."
    —2004

---

[1] *concordance* Alphabetical list of the main words contained in a book, with excerpts from the passages in which they occur.

[2] *ructions* Quarrels.

[3] *Simenon* Georges Simenon (1903–89), a Belgian novelist best known for his popular detective stories; *Flaubert* Gustave Flaubert (1821–80), a French novelist perhaps most celebrated for his novel *Madame Bovary* (1856).

[4] *Proust* Marcel Proust (1871–1922), a French novelist who was one of the most celebrated literary figures of the late nineteenth and early twentieth centuries; best known for his seven-volume work *À la recherche du temps perdu*.

[5] *Rilke* Renowned German poet Rainer Maria Rilke (1875–1926).

[6] *Umlauts* Diacritical sign (¨) placed over a vowel to express a change in the sound of that vowel because of the influence of an adjacent vowel.

## JACKIE KAY (b. 1961)

Born in Scotland to a Nigerian father and Scottish mother, Jackie Kay was brought up by adoptive parents; her first book of poetry, *The Adoption Papers* (1991), focuses on issues of personal and cultural identity. Among her widely praised subsequent works are *Other Lovers* (1993), *Life Mask* (2005), and the novel *Trumpet* (1998).

## In My Country

Walking by the waters
down where an honest river
shakes hands with the sea,
a woman passed round me
5  in a slow watchful circle,
as if I were a superstition;

or the worst dregs of her imagination,
so when she finally spoke
her words spliced into bars
10  of an old wheel. A segment of air.
*"Where do you come from?"*
"Here," I said. "Here. These parts."
    —1991

## High Land

I don't remember who kissed who first,
who touched who first, who anything to whom.
All I remember in the highland night—
the sheep loose outside,
5  the full moon smoking in the sky—
was that you led me and I led you.
And all of a sudden we were in a small room
in a big house with the light coming in
and your legs open; mine too.
10  And it was this swirling, twirling thing.
It's hard to fasten it down;
it is hard to remember what was what—
who was who when the wind was coming in.
    —2005

## SIMON ARMITAGE (b. 1963)

Perhaps the most celebrated British poet of his generation, Simon Armitage is equally at home with subtle lyricism and with poetry of politics and performance. A native of northern England, Armitage has written widely in many genres; his books of poetry include *Zoom* (1989), *Kid* (1992), and *The Universal Home Doctor* (2002).

## The English

They are a gentleman farmer, living
on reduced means, a cricketer's widow
sowing a kitchen garden with sweet peas.
A lighthouse-keeper counting aeroplanes.

5  Old blackout curtains staunch the break of day.
Regard the way they dwell, the harking back:
how the women at home went soldiering on
with pillows for husbands, fingers for sons,

how man after man emerged at dawn
10  from his house, in his socks, then laced his boots
on the step, locked up, then steadied himself
to post a key back through the letterbox.

The afternoon naps, the quaint hours they keep.
But since you ask them, that is how they sleep.
—2002

## It Could Be You

We interrupt our live coverage of the War
for details of tonight's National Lottery draw:

the winning numbers are fourteen, eighteen,
thirty-nine, forty-four, eighty-two, and ninety-one.

5  The bonus ball is number two-thousand-and-some.
A record jackpot pay-out will be shared between

winning ticket holders in Belfast, Aberdeen,
Milford Haven and East Acton. Now back to the action.
—2002

## ALICE OSWALD (b. 1967)

Trained as a classicist and as a gardener, Alice Oswald has established herself as one of Britain's most distinctive poetic voices: a poet of nature, of the mysterious, and of the musical. Her books include *The Gap-Stone Stile* (1996), *Dart* (2002), and *Woods etc.* (2005).

## Wedding

From time to time our love is like a sail
and when the sail begins to alternate
from tack to tack, it's like a swallowtail
and when the swallow flies it's like a coat;
5  and if the coat is yours, it has a tear
like a wide mouth and when the mouth begins
to draw the wind, it's like a trumpeter
and when the trumpet blows, it blows like millions …
and this, my love, when millions come and go
10  beyond the need of us, is like a trick;
and when the trick begins, it's like a toe
tip-toeing on a rope, which is like luck;
and when the luck begins, it's like a wedding,
which is like love, which is like everything.
—1996

## Woods etc.

footfall, which is a means so steady
and in small sections wanders through the mind
unnoticed, because it beats constantly,
sweeping together the loose tacks of sound

5  I remember walking once into increasing
woods, my hearing like a widening wound
first your voice and then the rustling ceasing.
the last glow of rain dead in the ground

that my feet kept time with the sun's imaginary
10  changing position, hoping it would rise
suddenly from scattered parts of my body
into the upturned apses of my eyes.

no clearing in that quiet, no change at all.
in my throat the little mercury line
15   that regulates my speech began to fall
rapidly the endless length of my spine
—2005

## CAITRIONA O'REILLY (b. 1973)

A native of Dublin, Caitriona O'Reilly holds a
doctorate in American literature from Trinity
College. Her books include the award-winning *The
Nowhere Birds* (2001) and *The Sea Cabinet* (2005).

## Hide

Because it tells me most when it is most alone,
I hold myself at bay to watch the world
regain its level-headedness, as harbours do
when keels are lifted out of them in autumn.
5   This is not unconsciousness. Seen from above,
the trees are guanoed[1] sea-stacks in a greeny cove
full of gulls' primeval shrieks and waves' extinctions.
Here birds safely crawl between the bushes,
wearing their wings like macs[2] with fretted hems.
10   The air's a room they fill to bursting with their songs.
All day the common warblers wing it up
and down the scale, see-saw, hammer-and-tongs.
This is not aimlessness. It is something industrial.
A starling cocks its head at a blackbird's coppery top
      notes.
15   All I hear of them in the hide reminds me
that the body must displace itself for music,
as my body has, inside this six-inch slot of light.
What converges in a thrush's throat, burnished,
      tarnished?
Its news endures no longer than the day does.
—2001

---

[1]  *guanoed*   Coated with guano, the excrement of sea-fowl.

[2]  *macs*   Macintoshes; raincoats.

## A Brief History of Light

*And the light shineth in darkness;
and the darkness comprehended it not.*[3]

The dazzle of ocean was their first infatuation,
its starry net, and the fish that mirrored it.
They knew enough to know it was not theirs.
Over the hill a dozen furnaces glowed,
5   the gold gleamed that was smelted in secret,
and the trapped white light shone bitterly
at the heart of the hardest stone on earth.
But they knew enough to know it was not theirs.
Then their hoards of light grew minor,
10   since none could view the sun straightly,
and jealousy burned their lives to the core.
So they made a god of it, shedding glory,
shedding his light on all their arguments.
Did they know enough to know it was not theirs?
15   The god in his wisdom preceded them westwards,
and the forests, in whose pillared interiors
black shapes dwelled, were banished for good.
They promised an end to the primitive darkness:
soon there was nothing that was not known.
20   They thought: *Our light is made, not merely reflected—
even the forked lightning we have braided!*
And they banished the god from the light of their minds.
But they mistook the light for their knowledge of the
      light,
till light, and only light, was everywhere.
25   And they vanished in this, their last illumination,
Knowing barely enough to know it was not theirs.
—2001

---

[3]  *And the light … it not*   John 1.5.

# BERNARDINE EVARISTO
## b. 1959

During the 1990s, novelist Bernardine Evaristo emerged as one of Britain's most innovative and powerful writers. Evaristo's postcolonial writing is fueled by her diasporic heritage and her self-conscious sense of being both from and not from her native country. Together with other British-born writers of color, such as Hanif Kureshi and Andrea Levy, Evaristo redefines what it means to be British, opening up the history of her nation to include the often-overlooked stories of global movement and migration that have been ongoing since the Middle Ages. While challenging the familiar conception of the nation, Evaristo transgresses the boundaries of genre, preferring to write "novels" that blur the lines between drama, poetry, and prose.

Bernardine Evaristo was born in London in 1959 to an English mother and Nigerian father. She trained to be an actress at a college of speech and drama, and her first writings were dramatic poems composed for the theater. Dismayed to discover that her college library contained no plays written by, or featuring, black women, she was determined to create her own. Her play *Moving Through* was performed by the Royal Court Theater Upstairs in 1982, the same year she also became a co-founder of the Theater of Black Women (1982–89). From drama she moved to poetry, publishing *Island of Abraham* (1994), which deals with her experiences visiting Madagascar and feeling both an insider and foreigner. Evaristo continues to write poetry and drama (and poetry-drama) for radio, theater, and various print media.

Evaristo exploded on to Britain's literary scene with her first full-length work of fiction, *Lara* (1997). This long poem, frequently described as a "novel-in-verse," tells the story of a family in which the parents come from divergent cultures: Taiwo is of Yoruba ancestry and Ellen of poor Irish Catholic stock. They meet in London in the late 1940s (as described in the book's first chapter, reproduced here) and their bittersweet marriage produces numerous children—of whom Lara is the fourth. The novel's kaleidoscopic narrative carries the story of the extended English-Nigerian-Irish-Brazilian family through seven generations and across several continents, while focusing particularly on Lara, who, growing up in a white London suburb, becomes increasingly aware of her racial difference. This first novel was a huge critical success; readers were intrigued by its unique form and its subtle blending of fantasy, history, and myth. It was shortlisted for numerous prizes and awarded the EMMA Best Novel Award (1999).

*Lara*'s blending of historical and contemporary settings was a tactic Evaristo continued in her later writing, which she says is inspired by "history and its commentary on contemporary writing" and by "all those untold stories that have been sewn out of the Great British Narrative." *Emperor's Babe* (2001), her second novel-in-verse, goes further than her first in uncovering the buried history of the early black experience in Britain; it takes the reader back to Roman times, to Londinium Britannia (an outpost of the Roman Empire) in 211 CE. Through the story of Zuleika, a discontented woman of Sudanese descent who has an affair with Emperor Septimus Severus, readers glimpse a larger story of black diaspora and its effects on the face of cities and empires. Written in unrhymed couplets, the novel incorporates the mixture of British slang and Latin spoken by its characters.

The devotion to historical detail evident in *Emperor's Babe* is present too in *Soul Brothers* (2005), but here Evaristo takes a more playful turn, demonstrating the effects of the past on the present by collapsing historical periods and transporting the ghosts of historical figures into the present day. The novel's protagonists take a cross-continental tour that turns into a journey through European history as they encounter the ghosts of numerous famous black figures, including Jamaican nurse and Crimean war heroine Mary Seacole, sixteenth-century Italian prince Alessandro de Medici, and great nineteenth-century Russian author Aleksandr Pushkin. This novel is not, like her earlier work, entirely formed of verse; it combines dramatic dialogue and prose with poetry. But as in her other work, Evaristo examines the history of diaspora not only to uncover buried narratives, but also to challenge the myth that multiculturalism is solely a twentieth-century phenomenon. She shows Britain as a nation that, rather than being inhabited solely by white Anglo-Saxons, has always been at the center of a series of global migrations. She then uses the revised narratives of Britain's past to explore some of the problems associated with its contemporary urban life.

Evaristo was made a Fellow of the Royal Society of Literature in 2004, and has been on over fifty international writers' tours; her writing and teaching residencies include positions at Columbia University, the University of East Anglia, and the University of the Western Cape, Cape Town.

⌘ ⌘ ⌘

## from *Lara*

### One
### 1949
### TAIWO

Oh Mama! Your pride when I boarded The Apapa!
Your son, a man now, riding the whale to paradise!
Remember the man's voice from Broadcasting House
calling us over the air waves from England?
5 "London calling The Empire! Calling The Empire!
Come in Nigeria!" *I'm coming! I'm coming!*
I shouted at night into the warm winds on deck.
Mama, my dreams have been my fuel for years,
all those British films for sixpence at the movie house.
10 See London, then die! I was desperate to get here!
When I finally landed in Liverpool it was Heaven,
I had hoped for snow but it was just very cold.
These people run everywhere and wear mufflers.
Older cousin Sam came to greet me at the docks,
15 just as well because I thought the fast automobiles
would kill me. I asked Sam if many people are killed
by cars. He laughed, "You will get used to life here."
The Africans have European wives and sailor's children.
Sam has a house in Princess Park in Toxteth district,

20 his wife Maureen is Irish and their six year old
daughter is Beatrice. I said, "Why a white wife, Sam?"
He replied, "When in Rome do as the Romans do."
Mama, I will write a letter soon. I promise you.

Sam says this country is like fisherman's bait, Mama.
25 It attracts, you bite, then you are trapped. I told him
I'd be here five years, get my degree and leave.
Tomorrow I head for London. Centre of the Empire!
Sam drinks stout every night complaining that John Bull[1]
only gives him work on the railways, and I've met elders
30 in the Yoruba Club in Croxteth Street who came
in the last century as stowaways or seamen,
fought in two world wars for Britain, but believe
back home is paradise. I argue Nigeria is small time.
Why eat rice and stew when you can taste Yorkshire
35 pud, meat and two veg. You can buy anything here,
there are so many shops, pubs on every street corner
and houses have all the modern conveniences.
Many people are respectful but some idiots shout
"Oi! Johnny! Sambo! Darkie! Nigger!" at us.
40 The elders tell us to take no nonsense from them,
so if I am abused I say quietly, "Just call me Taiwo,"
and boof! I fight them. Even the West Indians say

---
[1] *John Bull* Personification of England.

"Do you people still live in trees in the bush?" Mama,
in this country I am coloured. Back home I was just me.

45 My nickname is Bill now, after William the Great,
I have found that an African name closes doors.
You would not believe the size of London, Mama,
but people live like mice, scurry into their houses
at night and draw the curtains, the streets are quiet
50 as cemeteries. You think they are dead, but come
morning they unlock their doors, charge back down
the pavement as if life is somewhere else. If I say
hello they are frightened or angry or cross the road.
When we coloureds laugh freely they scowl at us
55 and on the Underground everyone stares into space.
I need warm clothes because it is so cold and heating
is expensive: the sun avoids this country, Mama.
I found a room in Kilburn for one pound a week,
the family were nice, the wife gave me Sunday dinner
60 but now I rent a cheaper room in Brixton where many
immigrants live. The landlord is Polish, the wife—Irish
and strict. No phone calls—in or out! No visitors!
It is so hard to find a good place to live here because
they do not want us in their houses. Mama, I know
65 I have not written you a letter yet but you must
know that I think of you and Kehinde often.

Winter's arthritic trees lace evening's broody sky,
miniature waterfalls mid-motion frozen from
sloping
roof gutters; window frames display icicles—
70 January's modern sculptures; bushes drip ephemeral
jewellery, coughing coal fires steam quartered panes
like frost. Chimneys, ordered as sentries, discharge
bulbous smoke; buses crawl through blizzards past
snow-filled bomb craters, faceless back-to-backs,
75 timbers dangling mid-air like dismembered limbs,
winds creaking, no-man's land.
For men are needed
to replace the fallen dead. In the War like cards
stacked one by one they fell. A clarion call[1] bugled
80 the colonies and to a city burnt out from doodlebug
and Luftwaffe,[2] they doffed cap, donned great coat,

dreams of prosperity, milk and gold, they were sold.
Now the emperor's disowned sons
congregate in Commonwealth dance halls.
85 At the Catholic Overseas Club, Victoria, Taiwo,
proud of his zoot suit[3] and loafers, partners the excited,
nubile, paleskins who flock in from the snow
for the heat brought in from the tropics.

Ellen thought British boys danced like ironing boards.
90 The students from Strawberry Hill's Jesuit College
sought the pristine convent ladies of Maria Assumpta
at Kensington's balls, tantalised by copious layers
of pink sequinned tulle, boned strapless tops, stoles,
corsage, lace gloves, silk purse and score cards.
95 Fearful of being lumped with the miserable wallflowers:
Mary with the hare lip and Deidre with the hairy lip,
Ellen waltzed under the ballroom's cut crystal chandeliers,
with earnest pallid suitors to bland, suited dance bands,
but before the stroke of twelve, Assumpta's flushed
100 Cinderellas were gliding exquisitely through hushed
lamp-lit streets to curfew and their rooms in the Square.
Sunday mornings in the refectory Ellen relished tales,
along with tea and buttered toast, of the Overseas Club,
Victoria, brimming with foreign students of the darker
105 variety and before long her twitching antennae led her
to the jumping church hall where she jitterbugged
to rock n' roll, did the quick-step to swing while Taiwo,
from his discreet observation post by the door, beamed
at the homely type in polka dot dress, a shy, dimpled
smile
110 and knew she was the girl he would take for a wife.

Ellen wanted to marry the Heavenly Bridegroom,
imbued from birth in the sanctity of the Catholic
Church,
she worshipped Her Lord in daily prayer, did penance
for man's original sin and her inherent wickedness.
115 She embraced suffering for infinite Love and Happiness
awaited her at the Eternal Bridal Feast in the sky.
A life of love, duty, self-sacrifice to God and souls
would be embodied in her role as a White Sister,
a teaching missionary enlightening the dark continent.

---

[1] *clarion call* Loud, clear calls.

[2] *doodlebug* Nickname of the V-1 flying bomb, or buzz bomb;
*Luftwaffe* German air force.

[3] *zoot suit* Style of men's suit popular in the forties, characterized
by tapered pants and a long, draped jacket.

120 This Assumpta virgin bought black babies from
        photographs,
    paid for their upkeep, for they who were born in the
        southern
    wild (she read) were bereft of light, though their souls
    were white; but white as an angel was the English child.
    She adored the choir nuns of the Assumption, well-to-
        do
125 women who as postulants gave their wealth to the
        convent,
    striking medieval figures in purple habits, lush as drapes,
    topped by a cream wimple, leather belt, rosary, crucifix.
    Unlike the lay nuns, in plain black and white, content
    to stir the stewing pot with floor-scrubbed hands.
130 Ripe for the plucking—Her Purity, small wonder
    that Ellen's Divine Lover came in the guise of Taiwo
    and in His Vivacious Company her heart was elevated
    by cherubims and seraphims who trilled sweetly in her
        ears
    and she was thrilled to be in His Noble Presence.

135 The supreme test of submission to the Will of God
        was the acceptance of pain; life was not to be a joyride
    but during the spring of nineteen fifty-two, Ellen,
    hitherto shaped in the fashion of clay spun into a pot,
    lived with a passion she'd reserved for the hereafter.
140 With Taiwo umbilically attached she bubbled,
        unbearably
    excited like a five year old on Christmas Eve; to him
    she revealed the goodies of a country he'd only known
    as a stranger peering through snug windows on icy
        nights.
    His tour began with Seven Brides for Seven Brothers[1]
145 in the neon lit cinema in London's Leicester Square;
    boating on the Serpentine's[2] waveless waters filled
    Sunday afternoons along with rambles on Hampstead's
    wild city heath; trains to Epping Forest—picture
        postcard
    picnics of cheese, pickles, apples, orangeade, under fairy-
150 tale ancient trees; cycle rides over London's evening
    bridges, following the controlled curve of the Thames

from the Tower[3] to the glamorous lights of Chelsea
        Bridge;
Soho's tempting finger beckoned on busy Friday nights
to Hi-life basement dives replete with emigrés and
        sailors,
155 or quiet tea-sipping at Lyons Corner House on the
        Strand.
    Soon, betrothal to The Son was replaced by devotion
    to potential husband and dreams of a huge brood of
    children so lots of souls could be saved in Heaven.

"You will go to your husband as an uncrushed
        flower,"
160 I fondly recall Mother Superior's eloquent sermon,
    delivered to the sixth form, my last day at school.
    I am so proud to know that simile will prevail for me.
    It is a summer evening, warm as I imagine Taiwo's land.
    I write at my oak desk overlooking Kensington Square;
165 the scent of honeysuckle travels in through my open
        window
    from the flower-filled gardens where young lovers linger.
    I think I have always felt worthless, really, of no account,
    yet he makes me feel so important, I am so loved by
        him.
    He phones me in the early hours and feel cherished.
170 I cannot believe how my love for Taiwo grows daily.
    I love him with every limb, every bone, each beat of my
        heart,
    every thought of my weak brain, every living part of me.
    I love him more than life, until I die and go home to
        God.
    I wanted to help Africa but Africa was brought to me!
175 My friends Mavis, Gwennie and Amy are overjoyed for
        my
    happiness. We will graduate as teachers, marry our
        beloveds,
    go forth and multiply! My childhood has now been shed
    as a caterpillar leaves its chrysalis; it will remain as
        anecdotes
    to entertain my darling Taiwo on cosy winter married
        nights.
—1997

---

[1] Seven ... Brothers  Popular 1954 movie.

[2] Serpentine  Body of water in Hyde Park, London.

[3] Tower  Tower of London.

# JEANETTE WINTERSON
## b. 1959

Described by one literary journal as having "a reputation as a holy terror, a lesbian desperado and a literary genius," Jeanette Winterson is as complex as her often outlandish and magical characters. Blatantly and often outrageously self-promoting and outspoken, she tells numerous (sometimes conflicting) stories about her own past. More importantly, she has been able to bring her talent for invention to her art. Best known for her numerous novels, Winterson has also written numerous short stories, a collection of essays on art and culture, a television screenplay on aviation, regular columns in newspapers, a radio drama, a theatrical play, and children's books. In her fiction, Winterson continues to experiment in language, form, and subject matter, bringing surreal elements down to earth and "marginal" characters to the fore.

Winterson was born in Manchester in 1959 and raised by adoptive Evangelical parents in a small town in Lancashire, where her father, John Winterson, worked in a factory. Her mother, Constance Brownrigg Winterson, was very religious and raised her daughter to be a preacher and missionary. There were few books in the house other than religious texts; Winterson's mother was said to have read *Jane Eyre* to her, but in doing so to have changed the ending so that Jane marries St. John Rivers, a missionary, rather than the "immoral" Rochester. In her sixteenth year Winterson admitted to having an affair with a young woman whom she had converted to the Pentecostal church, and both her mother and others in the church denounced her and attempted to exorcise her "demon." This incident led to Winterson's leaving her family home that year and working at odd jobs—driving an ice-cream truck, putting makeup on cadavers at a funeral home, working as an orderly in a hospital for the mentally ill—in order to put herself through school.

Eventually Winterson studied at Oxford, earning a degree in English in 1982. A few years later during an interview with Pandora House (where she succeeded in obtaining a job as an editor), she related some aspects of her life to her interviewer. Philippa Brewster found the details fascinating, but she was also impressed with the eloquent and creative way in which Winterson told her stories. Thus encouraged to put her thoughts into print, Winterson created her first novel, *Oranges Are Not the Only Fruit* (1985), in which a fictional character named Jeanette is manipulated by a fundamentalist religious mother, Mrs. Winterson, who eventually denounces her adopted daughter for her relationship with a girl. Although Winterson does admit that she was "trying to make sense of a bizarre childhood and an unusual personal history," she insists that her story is fictional, with its embedded fairy tales and a narrator who at times speaks directly to the reader. Described as a "daring, unconventionally comic novel" by the *Chicago Tribune, Oranges* won England's Whitbread First Novel Award and earned substantial public and critical acclaim.

Winterson's second novel, *Boating for Beginners*, followed *Oranges* in the same year. Her third novel, *The Passion* (1987), solidified Winterson's reputation in the literary world. Based partly on historical events, *The Passion* uses magic realism to tell the story of Henri—an androgynous military cook who works to feed Napoleon and his army—and Villanelle, the beautiful webbed-footed daughter of a Venetian boatman who incites passion in both men and women.

*Sexing the Cherry* (1989) and *Written on the Body* (1992) also explore problems of gender and sexuality. Winterson has been outspoken about the didactic element in her novels: "I started writing before I could read because I wanted to write sermons, because I was driven by a need to preach to people and convert them, which possibly I still am, except that now I do it for art's sake, and then I did it for God's sake." Winterson has continued (in the words of a New York *Times* reviewer) to "combine the biting satire of Swift with the ethereal magic of Garcia Márquez" in her more recent work—notably her collection of short fiction *The World and Other Places* (1998) and her novels, *The PowerBook* (2000) and *Lighthousekeeping* (2004).

⌘ ⌘ ⌘

## Lives of Saints

That day we saw three Jews in full length black coats and black hats[1] standing on identical stools, looking into the funnel of a pasta machine.

One stepped down from his little stool and went round to the front of the machine where the pasta was stretching out in orange strands. He took two strands and held them up high, so that they dropped against his coat. He looked like he had been decorated with medal ribbon.

They bought the machine. The Italian boys in T-shirts carried it to the truck. The Jews had bought the machine so that they could make pasta like ringlets to sell in their shop. Their shop sold sacred food and the blinds were always half drawn. The floor was just floorboard not polished and the glass counter stood chest high. They served together in their hats and coats. They wrapped things in greaseproof paper. They did this every day except Saturday and when the machine came they made pasta too. They lined the top of the glass counter with wooden trays and they lined the trays with greaseproof paper. Then they laid out the ringlets of fusilli in colours they liked, liking orange best, in memory of the first day. The shop was dark but for the pasta that glowed and sang from the machine.

*    *    *

It is true that on bright days we are happy. This is true because the sun on the eyelids effects chemical changes in the body. The sun also diminishes the pupils to pinpricks, letting the light in less. When we can hardly see we are most likely to fall in love. Nothing is commoner in summer than love, and I hesitate to tell you of the commonplace, but I have only one story to tell and this is it.

In the shop where the Jews stood in stone relief, like Shadrach, Meshach and Abednego in the fiery furnace,[2] there was a woman who liked to do her shopping in four ounces.

Even the pasta that fell from the scales in flaming waterfalls trickled into her bag. I was always behind her, coming in from the hot streets to the cool dark that hit like a church. What did she do with her tiny parcels laid in lines on the glass top?

Before she paid for them she counted them. If there were not sixteen, she asked for something else, if there were more than sixteen, she had a thing taken away.

I began following her. To begin with I followed just a little way, then, as my obsession increased, I followed in ever greater circles, from the shop to her home, through the park past the hospital. I lost all sense of time and space and sometimes it seemed to me that I was in the desert or the jungle and still following. Sometimes we were aboriginal in our arcane pathways

---

[1]  *full length ... black hats*  The conventional dress of male Hasidic Jews (a branch of orthodox Judaism).

[2]  *Shadrach ... furnace*  Shadrach, Meshach, and Abednego obeyed God's demands and refused to worship any other god. When they refused to worship the idol built by Nebuchadnezzar, King of Babylon, he had them thrown in a fiery furnace. The three men were able to walk out unscathed, however. See Daniel 3.

and other times we walked one street.

I say we. She was oblivious of me. To begin with I kept a respectful distance. I walked on the other side of the road. Then, because she did not notice, I came closer and closer. Close enough to see that she coloured her hair; the shade was not consistent. One day her skirt had a hanging thread and I cut it off without disturbing her. At last, I started to walk beside her. We fell in step without the least difficulty. And still she gave no sign of my presence.

I rummaged through the out-of-print sections in second hand bookshops and spent all my spare time in the library. I learned astronomy and studied mathematics and pored over the drawings of Leonardo da Vinci in order to explain how a watermill worked. I was so impatient to tell her what I had discovered that I began to wait for her outside her house. Eventually I knocked on the door and knocked on the door sharp at 7 a.m. every morning after that. She was always ready. In winter she carried a torch.

After a few months we were spending the whole of the day together. I made sandwiches for our lunch. She never questioned my choice of filling though I noticed she threw away the ones with sardine.

St. Teresa of Avila:[1] "I have no defence against affection. I could be bribed with a sardine."

So it is for me for whom kindness has always been a surprise.

In the lives of saints I look for confirmation of excess. To them it is not strange to spend nights on a mountain or to forgo food. For them, the visionary and the everyday coincide. Above all, they have no domestic virtues, preferring intensity to comfort. Despite their inhospitable ways, they ferment with unexpected life, like those bleak railway cuttings that host horizontal dandelions. They know there is no passion without pain.

As I told her this, as I had told her so many things, she turned to me and said, "Sixteen years ago I lived in a hot country with my husband who was important. We had servants and three children. There was a young man who worked for us. I used to watch his body through the window. In the house we lived such clean lives, always washed and talcumed against the sweat. Not the heavy night nor the heat of the day could unsettle us. We knew how to dress.

"One evening, when the boards were creaking under the weather, he came past us, where we sat eating small biscuits and drinking tea, and he dropped two baskets of limes on the floor. He was so tired that he spilt the baskets and went down on his knees under my husband's feet. I looked down and saw my husbands black socks within his black shoes. His toe kicked at a lime. I ducked under the table collecting what I could, and I could smell the young man, smelling of the day and the sun. My husband crossed his legs and I heard him say, 'No need for that, Jane.'

"Later, when we put out the lamps, and I went to my room and Stephen went to his, my armpits were wet and my face glowed as though I'd been drinking.

"I knew he would come. I took off my nightgown four or five times, wondering how to greet him. It didn't matter. Not then or afterwards. Not any of the two months that followed. My heart swelled. I had a whale's heart. The arteries of a whale's heart are so wide that a child could crawl through. I found I was pregnant.

"On the night I told him, he told me he had to go away. He asked me to go with him and I looked at the verandah and the lamps and Stephen's door that was closed and the children's door that was ajar. I looked at his body. I said I had to stay and he put his head on my stomach and cried.

"On the day he left I lay in my room and when I heard his flight booming over the house, I wrapped my head in a towel. Stephen opened the door and asked, 'Are you staying?'

"I told him I was. He said, 'Never mention this again.'

"I never did. Not that nor anything else."

We walked on in silence. We walked through the hours of the day until we arrived at nightfall and came to a castle protected by a moat. Lions guarded the gateway.

"I'm going in now," she said.

I looked up from my thoughts and saw an ordinary

---

[1] *St. Teresa of Avila* Spanish Carmelite nun who was a leading figure in the Counter-Reformation (1515–82). She is one of the principal saints of the Roman Catholic Church.

house fronted by a pretty garden with a pair of tabby cats washing their paws. Which was the story and which was real? Could it be true that a woman who had not spoken for sixteen years, except to order her food in four ounces, was now walking into this small house full of everyday things? Was it not more likely that she would disappear into her magic kingdom and leave me on the other side of the water, my throat clogged with feelings that resist words?

I followed her across the moat and saw our reflection in the water. I wanted to reach down and scoop her in my arms, let her run over my body until both of us were wet through. I wanted to swim inside her.

We crossed the moat. She fed me on boiled cabbage. I have heard it is a cure for gout. She never spoke as we ate, and afterwards she lit a candle and led me upstairs. I was surprised to see a mosquito net[1] in England.

Time is not constant. Time in stories least of all. Anyone can fall asleep and lose generations in their dreams. The night I spent with her has taken up my whole life and now I live attached to myself like a codicil.[2] It is not because I lack interests; indeed, I have recently reworked Leonardo's drawings and built for myself a fine watermill. It is that being with her allowed me to be myself. There was no burden to live normally. Now I know so many stories and such a collection of strange things that I wonder who would like them since I cannot do them

justice on my own. The heart of a whale is the height of a man....

* * *

I left her at dawn. The street was quiet, only a cat and the electric whirr of the milk van. I kept looking back at the candle in the window until it was as far away as the faint point of a fading star. In the early sky the stars had faded by the time I reached home. There was the retreating shape of the moon and nothing more.

Every day I went into the shop where the Jews stood in stone relief and I bought things that pleased me. I took my time, time being measured in four ounces. She never came in.

I waited outside her house for some years until a FOR SALE sign appeared and a neighbour told me that the woman next door had vanished. I felt such pleasure then, to know that she was wandering the world, and that one day, one day I might find her again.

When I do, all the stories that are folded into this one can be shaken out and let loose, but until then, like the lives of saints, more is contained than can be revealed. The world itself will roll up like a scroll taking time and space away.

All stories end here.

—1989

---

[1] *mosquito net*   Net hung around a bed to protect against malaria-carrying mosquitoes.

[2] *codicil*   Additional item appended to a legal document.

# Zadie Smith
## b. 1975

By the time Zadie Smith's first novel, *White Teeth*, was published in 2000, her name had already been bandied about by so many critics that it seemed as though she had been on the writing scene for years. After seeing one of her short stories in a university anthology, a literary agent approached Smith; a feeding frenzy in the publishing world ensued, ending with a publisher offering an extraordinary advance for an unpublished novel by a previously unknown author. Smith expanded the story into a novel, which became *White Teeth*, a major literary success and one of the bestselling books of 2001. *White Teeth* garnered the Commonwealth, *Guardian*, and Whitbread First Novel Awards, as well as the James Tait Black Memorial Prize. Called "a preternaturally gifted new writer" by the *New York Times* and "a major new talent" by the *Guardian*, Zadie Smith became widely characterized as the hip new voice of a postcolonial, multicultural England.

Born Sadie Smith in a North London borough, the daughter of a black Jamaican mother and a white English father, at the age of 14 she changed her name to Zadie, thinking it sounded more exotic (Smith dreamed at that time of becoming a dancer or a singer). In 1998 she earned a BA in English Literature from King's College, Cambridge, where she began publishing her short stories in the Oxford/Cambridge *May Anthologies*. It was there that the idea for *White Teeth* was born. Although some reviewers have likened the novel to those of Charles Dickens, a more frequent comparison has been to the work of Salman Rushdie. Rushdie himself is enthusiastic about *White Teeth*, describing it as "fizzing," and saying that it is "about how we all got here—from the Caribbean, from the Indian subcontinent, from thirteenth place in a long-ago Olympic bicycle race—about what 'here' turned out to be. It's an astonishingly assured debut, funny and serious, and the voice has real writerly idiosyncrasy." Some of these idiosyncrasies come from the eccentricities of the characters, who have come to England from various postcolonial countries and are in search of their new identities. Races, religions, cultures, customs, and personalities all clash in the polyglot melting pot that is North London. As the narrator of *White Teeth* says, "This has been the century of strangers, brown, yellow, and white. This has been the century of the great immigrant experiment.... [I]t makes an immigrant laugh to hear the fears of the nationalist, scared of infection, penetration, miscegenation, when this is small fry, peanuts, compared to what the immigrant fears—dissolution, disappearance."

The BBC released a miniseries based on *White Teeth* in 2002, and the same year saw publication of Smith's second novel, *The Autograph Man*, about a Londoner of Chinese and Jewish descent, who makes his living buying and selling autographs. Her third novel, *On Beauty* (2005), has been described as a "transatlantic comic saga." In 2003 Smith was a Radcliffe Institute Fellow at Harvard and was also featured in the *Granta 81: Best of Young British Novelists 2003*, which published her short story "Martha Martha." "Hanwell in Hell" was published in *The New Yorker* in 2004.

⌘ ⌘ ⌘

## Hanwell in Hell

*I am looking to enter into correspondence with anyone who remembers my father, Mr. —— Hanwell, who was living in the central Bristol area between 1970 and 1973. Any details at all will be gratefully received by daughter trying to piece together the jigsaw. Please write back to P.O. Box 187.*

I spent just one night with your father, in Bristol, thirty-four years ago. He was down on his luck at the time, as was I. We had both suffered dramatic reversals of fortune and recognized immediately that we had failure in common—a rare example of masculine intuition. Each sniffed out the other's catastrophe. For my part, I had lost my livelihood and my house; I spent the spring of that year bewildered and outraged, almost unable to comprehend that I now lived in a gruesome basement flat in which lichen seemed to grow upon every damp surface. A crooked business partner who took cash under the counter, compounded by my own careless accounting, had separated me from my business (a small chain of Bristol off-licenses[1]) so completely that I was reduced to a salesman's existence. I hawked the new American fridge-freezers from a catalogue, door-to-door. It was a dismal job and one that required me to spend a humiliating amount of time—or so I thought then—with women. In the off-licenses, all my staff had been men, and I always appreciated the fact; emotionally men are so much simpler. My new job made me feel as if I were being returned to the domestic scenes of my childhood. I seemed always to be in kitchens having cups of tea pressed upon me, repelling the timid advances of motherly women. Hanwell's situation was of course somewhat reversed: he valued the domestic and lamented its loss; with it went all the things he cared for—women, the home, family. You ask in your letter if I know why you and your sisters were left in London—I don't know, but it must have been against his will. No one would choose the life that Hanwell had.

When I met him, he was washing dishes in Barry Franks's first restaurant, halfway up the hill on Park Street. It is easy to forget now that Barry Franks was not born on the BBC holding a glass of red in one hand and his own cookery book in the other. That came later, at a time in England when people seemed able to lasso the moon quite as easily as Hanwell and I, ten years earlier, had managed to plummet beneath acceptability. In 1970, Barry Franks was only the owner of a mediocre Continental bistro, eponymously named. The cassoulet was gray, the veal chewy. You didn't go to Franks for the food. It was that rare thing: a place with atmosphere. Franks was a legendary drunk even then, and he brought the freewheeling uncertainty of that condition to every corner of his place. Although its pretense of sophistication seems ridiculous now—the Chianti bottles hugged by raffia, the red-and-white checked tablecloths—its clientele never were; the mix of the great, the good, and the not-so-good was exhilarating. Franks was the most popular place in the city after nine in the evening, and it was natural to assume, as I did, that the owner of a place like this need only flip the "OPEN" sign and watch the money roll in, but it was not so. Franks was steadily drinking away the profits. He was in such severe debt with the local heavies that he had been compelled to give up the entire back room to them and their pleasures. You could never get a table in that room; you could only sit at the curious walnut church pews that lined two walls and look on at the scene—table after table of wardrobe-shouldered goons with girls on their knees. I never saw them pay a penny for anything. Barry Franks once admitted to me that the unpaid tab came to six thousand pounds, an astronomical sum at the time. I could have bought a good flat in town for that money. Supposedly the goons were the scions of two local Italian families in the ice-cream business, but whatever Italian blood they possessed had been thoroughly diluted in the Avon. West Country people are as sallow as any European, and these ones looked and sounded no different from the rest of us. Their suits were tighter, that was all. And they were sentimental about beauty—sometimes it seemed that all their criminal machinations were merely the quickest route at their disposal to those high roads that lead to beautiful food and beautiful music and beautiful women. It was their idea to turn Franks into a kind of jazz bar, and to this end a five-piece band of white Bristolians meticulously and earnestly imitated Louis

---

[1] *off-licenses*  Drink shops.

Armstrong's Hot Five on a little makeshift stage in the back room. I liked the band, especially their precise fingers, neither inspired nor fussy but always accurate. When you feel lost in the world, there is some joy to be gleaned from exact imitations of familiar things.

The night I met Hanwell, I came in very late with a girl I was seeing at the time. Her name is lost to me, but the outline of her chest is not—huge, carefully wrapped and cantilevered, like a present on a shelf which she had not yet decided to give away. She was thirty years my junior and also a diluted Italian, although she was still taking her Catholicism neat.[1] I had spent the better part of five hours that evening—in my flat, in my car, in the cinema, and in a park—persistently trying to get my hand to go where she would not have it go. By the time we reached Franks, we were both exhausted and bad-tempered and the maître d's familiar complacent explanation that the back room was "fully occupied" suddenly enraged me. I kicked up the kind of fuss that I, having no power, had no right to kick up, while the fellow nodded solicitously, all the time continuing to discreetly direct his waiters to this table and that.

"But it is *occupied*," he repeated in that odious way, as if the back room were a bathroom; he was waiting for me to finish making a fool of myself. I remember the girl laid her hand on my biceps as if in expectation of one of those ludicrous displays of machismo so common in the kind of Hollywood schlock we had just seen at the Odeon. But she was out with the wrong type of man for that. We were led meekly to the church pews to sit alongside other couples with drinks on their knees, but at the last minute a fat man and his friend rose to leave a table just behind me—I pushed the girl quickly into the vacated seat and took the one beside her. The maître d' shrugged as if to say the consequences would not be his responsibility. I ordered two osso bucos,[2] although it was already eleven and neither of us was remotely hungry. I was perversely determined to get the maximum of whatever enjoyment was available out of the best seats at Franks. How good could it possibly feel to sit here? The band was loud, and the two of us turned our chairs to face the stage—a welcome relief from looking at each other. The trumpeter stood up to do his

solo, and then the clarinet player did the same; the bassist leaned forward for his minute in the sun and jauntily spun his massive instrument; the pianist lifted lightly from his seat when his turn came; the drummer, not able to change his position much, liked to bend his head low and lean into his drums, raising his elbows high at the moment the rest of the band fell silent. The solos went round three or four times before I remembered our food and noticed the angry mutterings from other tables. It was not uncommon for meals to turn up late at Franks, but this was a complete meltdown; the whole room was waiting to be served.

Suddenly, a sandy-haired, balding man with a pensioner's forlorn pink bulb on the end of his nose plonked down two plates in front of us. On both plates three French crêpes, stuffed with a creamy prawn-and-mushroom mixture, sat in a pretty triangle formation. The man was dressed not like a waiter or a chef but like a dishwasher, his dirty sleeves turned up. Sweat sprung from every pink pore in his innocent face. He smiled at us hopefully. Before we had a chance to object, he had moved on to the next table, passing out more of these crêpes that nobody had ordered. For a minute the noise of consternation reached a pitch and threatened to topple over into revolution—but most of the clientele, like me, were too drunk and too weary, and then the first mouthful was sampled, and it was extremely good; we quieted down. The crêpes were not fussy like Barry Franks's food, and they had no pinchbeck[3] pretensions—if your Parisian grandmother had to rustle something up at the last minute, she might cook those crêpes. Since that evening, I have passed many nights in restaurants far better than Franks, but I can't think of a meal I've enjoyed more. Just after midnight, the man passed by our table again, and I stopped him.

"Malfunction in the kitchen?"

He looked at me warily and said nothing. I wondered then whether his innocence went all the way down; his face was so devoid of guile your first instinct was to think him a simpleton of some kind.

"What's your name?"

"Hanwell, sir."

"I'm Clive, Clive Black. I'd like to shake the hand of the chef."

---

[1] *neat* Without ice.

[2] *osso buco* Italian veal stew.

[3] *pinchbeck* Deceptive; imitative.

He looked at my hand but did not touch it. It was strange to have him call me sir—Franks wasn't restaurant enough for such civilities. And looking at him more closely I realized Hanwell was too bald too early; he was still in his very early forties, and I was only ten years older.

"Did you make these?" I tried again.

"They were *delicious*," the girl said, extravagantly. Maybe she even licked one of her stubby fingers. Hanwell bit his lip. He seemed to be preparing to lie but then thought better of it.

"Well, yes. Were they all right?"

"They were more than all right. Best food I've ever had in here."

"I'm sure that's not true, sir."

"It's completely true. What's wrong with Franks, then? Tight again, is he?"

"He's feeling a bit under the weather. High temperature," Hanwell said, loyally, looking away. I smiled.

"It's amazing how many high temperatures Franks gets. He's like a five-year-old child."

I took out a cigarillo—the one luxury I refused to give up—and offered him one. He declined. "He's very lucky to have you to cover for him last minute."

"I'm glad you enjoyed the food, sir," said Hanwell tersely, and turned to go. But I wouldn't let him. There was something so compelling to me about him; I had the sense that he came from better things than this but that his fall had not debilitated him or made him as bitter as mine had made me.

"Where did you learn to cook like that?"

Hanwell was looking about him fearfully for whoever it was who was going to give him his next instruction. I had already guessed that he had the lowest job in the place, and a quick glance at the floor confirmed this. The toes of both his shoes were soaking wet.

"What, sir?"

"Don't call me sir. I've told you, it's Clive. Cooking—where did you learn?"

"Well, you pick up a bit here, a bit there, don't you," he said, reddening. "And I was in France in '44—I suppose that helped a bit."

"Were you? So was I. You must have been barely out of short trousers."

We exchanged ranks, regiments, places, and dates. He was fluent but not overly forthcoming. He had been

a private, I a lieutenant. I asked him to sit down, but again he refused.

"Come on, now, one drink—won't kill you. I can square it with Franks, if he's still conscious. He owes me a favor. By the bye, do you know what those crêpes reminded me of? The French House—in London, in Soho. They have a starter just like that."

For the first time, Hanwell smiled at me, a coy operation that used only half of his mouth.

"Yes, I've eaten them there—I used to work in Soho. Dean Street."

"But what in God's name are you doing in this hellhole?"

Hanwell's face shut up shop for the day. His bulb nose ceased to shine, his eyelids sunk low.

"I should be getting back to work."

"Look, sit down, sit down, ten minutes—honestly, we'd like you to."

My girl smiled falsely, excused herself, and went to the bathroom. Hanwell sat. We talked of France a little, especially of Paris (I remember very clearly a funny phrase he used: "It was Paris that gave me a polish"), and discovered we were both East Anglians, he from dreary Ipswich, I from dreary Norwich—quieter, altogether less dramatic surroundings than we found ourselves in now. I realized we had both spent a training period in bleak Felixstowe before leaving for Normandy, though we had landed at the beach at different times. I am not averse to war stories and tried to push him for a little more, but Hanwell wouldn't have it.

"Different life," he said dully, and finally accepted a cigarillo from me.

In all my probing, I could not get from him what I wanted: a clear sense of his class. He could have been a butcher's son or a schoolteacher's son or even a civil servant's son—upon every topic he knew just enough to get by, veering away whenever he was in the slightest trouble. He was the kind of man who knew two things about every book you could mention, though he might never have held the book itself in his hands. Several times, one waiter or another came over to retrieve him, but I waved them off. No one could produce Franks, the real authority in the place, and there was only half an hour till closing. After a while, Hanwell relaxed and told a filthy story about a German brothel, all the time

wearing that half smile, and ingratiating himself with
my girl by answering her un-Catholic questions concerning what German whores wore and what their
bedrooms looked like and whether or not they reclined
in chaise lounges, an item of furniture she pronounced
in as strange a manner as could be imagined. That
Hanwell was more of a success with the girl than I was
irritated me, but for some reason I took it out on her,
not him. I began to tailor the conversation strictly to
"men's business"—cars and the Bristol dog tracks and
other subjects I had no real interest in. The girl fell into
a deep sulk and finally left without me.

"She's a beauty," Hanwell said as we watched her go.
"It makes me feel better, knowing there are women as
beautiful as that in the world."

"Really. It makes me feel worse."

"It's like a signal …" Hanwell began, and said no
more.

"What do you mean, a signal?"

"It's only a notion I have … stupid notion."

"No, go on—I didn't understand you."

"A signal that the world is good. Beautiful women
help you know that."

I laughed out loud at this.

"Even if you can't bloody have them?"

"*Especially* then."

The band came to a clattering stop after playing
something terribly fast in which the trumpet squealed
like a train braking. Hanwell was pushing the wet butt
of his cigarillo round and round a small china plate.

"You're an odd one, Hanwell," I said into the silence.

"I'm just an optimist," said Hanwell.

Just then, Hanwell was called away once and for all.
Franks had finally roused himself in the kitchen and
sent for him. I remember that it was only when he left
the table that I realized Hanwell's glass of Chianti had
barely been touched; the girl didn't drink; *I* must have
drunk the whole bottle that was now sitting empty
before me. I ordered a tumbler of water, drained it, and
began discreetly to refill it with whiskey from my own
flask. I dreaded going back to that awful flat. I sat and
watched the night fold itself up around me, pack itself
away. The double bass was zipped into its big black
pajamas. The clarinet player delicately removed his reed
and put it to bed in a swaddle of cotton. At some point

I must have put my head on the table.

"Mr. Black? Mr. Black?"

Hanwell's hands were on my shoulders, gently
shaking me.

"Mr. Black, we're closing now."

"Hanwell?"

"Yes, Mr. Black—Hanwell. You'll have to be going
now, sir."

"It's Clive—how many times? What time is it,
anyway?"

"It's one in the morning, Clive," said Hanwell solemnly, and I saw that his first instinct had been right—
"sir" sounded so much more natural in his mouth.

Hanwell walked me to the door. We both took our
coats and hats from the hooks in the hallway.

"You leaving, too?"

"I've got a home to go to," he said, a little defen-
sively. "Just like anyone."

"What about a nightcap, Hanwell? Finish the night
off properly. You had a great success tonight—we
should celebrate. But maybe your wife wouldn't like it."

"My wife's in London."

"And mine's in Timbuktu. How about it, then?"

We agreed to go to his flat. I had some whiskey left
and shared it with him, and for at least a minute the
plan to continue the night seemed by far the best plan
any man could have devised. We walked silently and
contentedly down Park Street, but when we reached the
bottom the rain began to come down sideways, and
three minutes later I was soaked to the skin. We took a
series of rapid rights and lefts; I remember registering
the point at which I could no longer be sure that it
would be quicker and less painful to go back to my flat
than to go to Hanwell's.

"Have we much farther to go?" I asked him, blinking away water, trying to keep up with his swift pace.

"Just a bit," he said, and in the darkness I heard the
squeak of a hinge. I followed him through the iron gate
he had opened. We were in a small park, really just a
green square, with beautiful Georgian properties looming white and expensive overhead.

"This is Cabot Square, very nice," said Hanwell. "It's
a shortcut for me through the square. Imagine living
with your family in one of these huge buggers."

I thought it very strange, that addition—"with your

family." I hadn't the heart or the will to tell him that a house very like one of these "huge buggers" had recently been mine; that I had had the run of the place all for myself; that a life like that was possible.

"Barry Franks lives here," said Hanwell chirpily—he was as indefatigable as a tour guide—"with his wife and their four children."

"The way he's going, he'll be lucky to keep it," I said, too angrily. I wanted people to have the kind of bad luck I now knew existed. I didn't want anyone to think that what had happened to me could not happen to them. I wanted to spread my black gospel whenever I had the opportunity. But here was Hanwell, whistling at the house, in admiration of its owner's good fortune.

"Do you hear that?" he said. The rain had stopped; we were about to leave the park. A child, I thought, was crying in one of the houses.

"That's a fox," said Hanwell. "They scream that strange scream. It's very close by us."

He stopped and looked around. He pulled his hat low over his eyes, as if wishing to camouflage himself. Exasperated, I took off my own hat and tipped the water out of its brim. That must have been the last year I wore a hat in England. Certainly, even by the following year there wasn't a hat check left in any restaurant or public building in the country. People like Hanwell and me were the last dinosaurs as far as hats were concerned.

"Quiet a minute," said Hanwell as I opened my mouth to complain. Some lights went on in one of the grand houses across the way. I hated that subtle sign of concern and what it was meant to signal to the man outside: *I don't know what you're doing out there, but I am awake, and should I have to I will not hesitate to call the police.* When I had a house, I had the same smug habit. I well imagined the man peeling back his half of the bedcovers, pompously reassuring his wife, treading carefully on the stairs, proudly entering that great space he had worked so hard to own—his high-ceilinged living room—and peering out at these two dark figures in the square who might try to take it all away from him. When you lived where I lived now, when you heard the violent city noises, you didn't switch any lights on. I coughed loudly and lit another cigarillo.

"It's not moving away. Listen to it!" said Hanwell, slowly approaching a big, well-maintained hedge by the

exit. It was a piteous wail, and its human shape was irresistible even after one told oneself it was a fox, even after Hanwell pushed the greenery away with a long stick to reveal the trembling fox itself, collapsed on its knees upon the ground.

"Pretty thing," I said, and I can remember now what a deliberate understatement that was. It was, in truth, extraordinary to be standing this close to something so wild, so usually elusive, so slender-legged, so orange-tailed, so yellow-eyed, so unexpected. We were face to snout with the animal.

"What's wrong with it?" I asked gruffly. "Why the bloody hell doesn't it move?"

Hanwell gently poked it with the stick; it wailed again, but it didn't stand.

"It must be maimed somehow," said Hanwell.

There wasn't a mark on it. It was as spotless as if it had been stuffed, and it was perfectly serene apart from this terrible screaming. From the lit house came the sound of a sash window being forced up. Hanwell put his wet boot on the fox's slim throat.

"What are you doing?" I said with alarm, and at the same moment Hanwell brought his boot down hard and broke its neck.

"Better to put it out of its misery," said Hanwell blandly.

Quite unexpectedly—for I am almost never sick—I turned around and threw up.

"Are you all right?" said Hanwell, although he did not make any move to help me. I thought, Men like us don't know how to comfort each other. We need women for that. I felt a little throb of despair pass through me; the absolute certainty that there would be no one waiting for me tonight, no matter what time I came home.

"Ridiculous of me," I said, straightening up. "I think maybe I should go home."

It was now that Hanwell left his fox and turned to me, his face full of distress.

"But we're almost there—"

"All the same," I said firmly, trying to clean myself up a little with a handkerchief, that other obsolete item, "I think my night is over."

"But—I'd hoped—" He bit his lip as he had in the restaurant, like a small child fearing a punishment.

"What? What had you hoped?"

I was angry with him now. It seemed as if all the failures of my evening were somehow connected to him—not getting the girl, losing the drink I had spent good money putting inside me, being wet, being cold—and if I could only get away from him my life would immediately begin to improve.

"I'd hoped you'd help me."

"If it's money you wanted, you can forget it. I'm poor as a church mouse," I said, and set off in the opposite direction. I'd barely taken a step when I slid on the wet paving stones. Hanwell broke the better part of my fall, but I still found that my will deserted me inches before the ground. I resisted Hanwell's help and instead gave myself to a shallow puddle, tinted orange in the street lights. I sat there quietly for a minute. I had the keen sense that this was the lowest moment of my decline, that there would be nothing beneath this. Time has proved that instinct correct. Two wet strangers, outdoors, without women, at night, and with death curled up nearby. Whenever I am in need of spiritual nourishment, I remember that moment and feel gratitude to God for never allowing me to fall so low again. Only a certain kind of man could find himself in such a situation. I am not that man anymore. The memory of what I was makes me shudder now, but at the time the only appropriate reaction was laughter. I laughed so loud that two more lights turned on in the square.

"I suppose it is quite funny, Clive," said Hanwell, very sadly. I stopped laughing.

I looked up at the stranger with his hand on my shoulder. He had that same hopeful look on his face with which he had delivered the marvellous crêpes.

"I don't know you, Hanwell."

I examined his face—his prosaic Suffolk profile, the pouchy, boyish jaw—and I remember thinking, I'm wrong, we've met before, a thousand times. Men in England have looked like Hanwell since the days of King Raedwald;[1] there are hundreds of Hanwells in that fearful mound in Sutton Hoo.[2] It was impossible not to

[1] *King Raedwald*   Great king of East Anglia from c. 599 to c. 625.

[2] *Sutton Hoo*   Excavations at Sutton Hoo in 1938–39 led to the discovery of the remains of a Saxon ship and a large quantity of gold and silver artifacts; the site is thought to hold the remains of King Raedwald.

be reassured by this.

"No. That's true. But it's so nearby. You could get dry and then set off again in the morning."

"I haven't any money, you know."

"Don't insult me again," Hanwell said as firmly as any gentleman. I wondered whether this was a glimmer of the polish he'd picked up in Paris. And he hadn't lied: in a minute more we were climbing the lurid iron steps to his second-floor flat, every step wet and slick and heavy with the possibility of a lethal accident. Inside, the flat was no bigger than mine, but it was a good deal cleaner. At once, one noticed evidence of a previous, family existence. Pretty blue china plates hung above the doorway. Doilies seemed to cover all the limited surfaces, and on top of them stray ornaments were lined up, all too clearly snatched from a larger gathering of better examples. My eyes were drawn immediately to a large black-and-white photo pinned above the oven (which was in a corner of the lounge): three appealing dark-haired teenage girls sitting on a bench. Of course, one of them—the prettiest, if I may say so—was you. As soon as he saw me looking at it, Hanwell plucked the photo from the wall. I had the impression he would have done this anyway, whether I'd looked or no. Hanwell offered his family to his guest in the same way most men would offer a drink. I smiled and nodded, but I was distracted by the dryness of my throat. I needed to be drunk so as to explain to myself why, in the middle of the night, I had decided to come to the flat of a man who washed dishes for the thugs at Barry Franks's place.

"That's Emily," said Hanwell, happily. "And that's Carol and that's Claire. Claire's got all her mother's beauty, you can see that."

Having never seen your mother, I was at a loss as to how to continue this line of conversation.

"Very nice." I took my cigarillos out of my breast pocket. They were sodden and smelled of compost. "Any chance of a fag, Hanwell? And maybe a drink?"

"You see, the thing is," said Hanwell, quickly, "I was hoping you could do me a favour. It's a bit embarrassing."

"I'm beyond embarrassment, Hanwell, my friend. I'm sitting here begging you for a whiskey. Let's have a whiskey and then we'll deal with all other business in turn. I'm going to take my trousers off and put them on the radiator, if that's all right."

"It'll need a shilling for the meter," Hanwell said worriedly, in the tone of a Gypsy grandmother recalling a family curse, and disappeared out of the room for a minute with my trousers. To my enormous relief, he returned with a bottle of very good Irish malt. It was improbably good, and I asked him how he had come by it.

"Oh, you meet people who help you here and there," said Hanwell, pouring me out a measure.

"Do you? I don't seem to."

"It's only that you don't realize they're helping you. The heating's on now—your trousers'll be dry in a jiffy."

Hanwell stood up and began pottering around the room like a woman, straightening the meagre curtains, tidying away little things into drawers. I drank three shots, one after the other, and sat back in my chair. A small embroidered pillow connected softly with the back of my head. It was such an unlikely luxury that I let out an involuntary whimper of pleasure.

"Laura made that."

"Laura?"

"Laura, my wife."

"Ah. The one in London."

Hanwell nodded.

"And why isn't she with you again?" I asked. I realized that I knew nothing at all about Hanwell or why he was alone and washing dishes so late in his life. The greater part of it I never found out—until you told me. At the time, he offered only a painful series of incredibly delicate euphemisms, and it was a minute or so before I understood the sad truth.

"Did you find her?" I asked, unforgivably. When one is drunk, morbid curiosity is undisguisable. But Hanwell did not seem at all offended by it.

"She was in the stairwell on the way to the cellar," he said, matter-of-factly. "She'd hung herself with the wotsit you tie a bathrobe with, the cord. It was a terrible thing."

We were both quiet for a minute, considering death in the incompetent way that people do.

"But why did you tell me she was in London?"

"She is."

"I'm sorry, Hanwell. It *is* a terrible thing. Have another drink."

We didn't know each other; there was nothing else to say.

"Excuse me," said Hanwell. He left the room again. I remember drinking my drink and then another one, and letting my eye wander around this strange amalgamation of lounge and kitchen, with its junk-store furniture and filthy net curtains. Here and there one could spot the sad, cheap family heirlooms that were all a man like Hanwell could claim of his endless English ancestry. A jug and bowl, both painted with a sentimental swan, sat incongruously in the nook of the fireplace, reminding one of the Hanwells of the past who did their ablutions in their bedrooms for lack of a bathroom. Hung over the back of one chair was a stringy fur with the little feet still attached, the kind of thing women used to wear over their shoulders before the war. His wife's? His mother's? It made me think of Hanwell's fox again. I wondered what would put Hanwell out of his misery or what would put me out of mine. The next thing I remember is smelling turpentine. I stood up and moved to the door. I had no idea what the door led onto. For all I knew, Hanwell's flat bordered the edge of the world and by passing through this door I would simply fall into whatever hole contains forever. In fact, the door led directly to another room, no bigger than the room we had been in but stripped of decoration. All the furniture was piled in the middle of the room under a white dust sheet, like an obscene heap of bodies. The rest of the room was being painted a violent, hellish deep red by Hanwell, who was on a stepladder with a brush in his hand.

"I thought you'd fallen asleep," said Hanwell, seriously.

"Why would you think that?"

"I looked in. It looked like you were sleeping."

I had no watch on and no idea if this was true or not.

"Hanwell, what are you doing, for Christ's sake? It's two in the morning or something like it."

"This is the girls' room," said Hanwell, climbing down from his ladder, looking sheepish. "I mean, I hope it will be for them. I hoped you might help me, actually."

"Paint it? I suggest you hire a bloody painter, Hanwell—I came for a drink, not to be your skivvy."[1]

"No—" said Hanwell, urgently, "not that. I wanted an opinion. Is it the right kind of yellow? I'm color-

---

[1] *skivvy* Servant.

blind—I didn't like to ask the assistant—it's called Deepest Sun. I want them to wake up and feel that the place is always full of sunshine, you see."

"Yellow?"

"Don't tell me it's not right," he said, looking at me rather desperately. "This is all the paint I can afford at the moment. But there's that small pot left there—I'm going to do the skirting with that now. And the window frames. I want it to be just like sunset wall to wall, do you see? I think they blame me," he said suddenly, and sat down on the penultimate step of his little ladder. He was a ridiculous sight: weary and pink and softly weeping in this terrifying red box.

"It's nobody's fault, Hanwell."

He looked up at me curiously, as if we had just met.

"No," he said finally. "That's true." He wiped his eyes. "It's a small room, though, for three girls that age."

"How old are they?"

"Seventeen, sixteen, and fourteen. They're with their uncle and aunt at the moment, in Bromley. I write, but they don't send back."

"Have you got another paintbrush, Hanwell?"

I went to work on the windows while Hanwell got on his knees for the skirting board. He was meticulous about it. He had a tiny brush for the corners and he went over the whole thing three times. By the time I'd done my second coat on the window frames, the real yellow sun was coming up. The red paint was so dark that it repelled the light, and though we could see the day beginning outside, inside the room it felt as though my night and Hanwell's would never end. I had passed through tiredness to the other side; I felt as if I needed no sleep at all. In my underwear I could have painted that window frame a thousand times if it meant not going back out into the world. I was happy, I think. At about 6 A.M., it was clear even to poor Hanwell's color-blind eyes that we could put no more red on the red wall. I stepped down from my ladder and brought in two more shots of whiskey. We sat on the floor and admired our handiwork. We had made a room for you and your sisters. It was a good feeling. It had been so

long since I made anything at all.

"What will you do with them when they're here?" I asked Hanwell.

He spoke for a long time; he had elaborate plans. He imagined that you would be happy to hang around Franks in the daytime and watch him wash dishes, or maybe your sister would sing with the band, and when he couldn't keep an eye on you, you could spend time with Barry Franks's two odious sluttish daughters, whom I knew to be the girlfriends of two of the worst thugs in town. This was another piece of information I kept to myself.

"Are you sure they'll come, Hanwell?" I asked him when he'd finished outlining his strange ideas. He smiled broadly. I thought it extremely unlikely that any daughter of Hanwell's would ever spend a night in this room as we just had, but again I held my counsel. More and more, I suspect that men of our generation were not to be lived with. We made people unhappy because we ourselves were made unhappy in irrevocable ways. My own daughter takes great pleasure in knowing the measure of me, of judging and convicting me, and maybe she is right, and maybe you are, too. These days, everyone passes the blame backward—but we couldn't do that. We kept blame close, we held it tight. I'm sorry your father made you so unhappy. Maybe the other replies you receive will help you put the blame in the right place and "come to terms," as people say now. But when I saw your request in the paper my first thought was of a man likable enough to remember—this is no small feat. Almost everyone I met back then I'd rather forget. Even writing this I feel happy at the thought of Hanwell's prawn-and-mushroom crêpes and the care with which he touched up the skirting board. I think you are too hard on him. And I think you were wrong to think that he knew all the time you and your sisters wouldn't come, or that he didn't want you to. Hanwell had a beautiful way of hoping. Not many men can hope red yellow.

—2004

# Reading Poetry

## WHAT IS A POEM?

Most of us know what a poem is when we see one. Still, even poets find it difficult to define a poem, or poetry. In a lecture on "The Name and Nature of Poetry" (1933), the English poet A.E. Housman stated that he could "no more define poetry than a terrier can define a rat"; however, he added, "we both recognize the object by the symptoms which it provokes in us." Housman knew he was in the presence of poetry if he experienced a shiver down the spine, or "a constriction of the throat and a precipitation of water to the eyes." Implicit in Housman's response is a recognition that we have to go beyond mere formal characteristics—stanzas, rhymes, rhythms—if we want to know what poetry is, or why it differs from prose. Poetry both represents and *creates* emotions in a highly condensed way. Therefore, any definition of the genre needs to consider, as much as possible, the impact of poetry on us as readers or listeners.

Worth consideration too is the role of the listener or reader not only as passive recipient of a poem, but also as an active participant in its performance. Poetry is among other things the locus for a communicative exchange. A section below deals with the sub-genre of performance poetry, but in a very real sense all poetry is subject to performance. Poems are to be read aloud as well as on the page, and both in sensing meaning and in expressing sound the reader plays a vital role in bringing a poem to life, no matter how long dead its author may be; as W.H. Auden wrote memorably of his fellow poet W.B. Yeats, "the words of a dead man / Are modified in the guts of the living."

For some readers, poetry is, in William Wordsworth's phrase, "the breath and finer spirit of all knowledge" ("Preface" to the *Lyrical Ballads*). They look to poetry for insights into the nature of human experience, and expect elevated thought in carefully-wrought language. In contrast, other readers distrust poetry that seems moralistic or didactic. "We hate poetry that has a palpable design upon us," wrote John Keats to his friend J.H. Reynolds; rather, poetry should be "great & unobtrusive, a thing which enters into one's soul, and does not startle it or amaze it with itself but with its subject." The American poet Archibald MacLeish took Keats's idea a step further: in his poem "Ars Poetica" he suggested that "A poem should not mean / But be." MacLeish was not suggesting that a poem should lack meaning, but rather that meaning should inhere in the poem's expressive and sensuous qualities, not in some explicit statement or versified idea.

Whatever we look for in a poem, the infinitude of forms, styles, and subjects that make up the body of literature we call "poetry" is, in the end, impossible to capture in a definition that would satisfy all readers. All we can do, perhaps, is to agree that a poem is a discourse that is characterized by a heightened attention to language, form, and rhythm, by an expressiveness that works through figurative rather than literal modes, and by a capacity to stimulate our imagination and arouse our feelings.

## THE LANGUAGE OF POETRY

To speak of "the language of poetry" implies that poets make use of a vocabulary that is somehow different from the language of everyday life. In fact, all language has the capacity to be "poetic," if by poetry we understand a use of language to which some special importance is attached. The ritualistic utterances of religious ceremonies sometimes have this force; so do the skipping rhymes of children in the schoolyard. We can distinguish such uses of language from the kind of writing we find in, say, a computer user's manual: the author of the manual can describe a given function in a variety of ways, whereas the magic of the skipping rhyme can be invoked only by getting the right words in the right order. So with the poet: he or she chooses particular words in a particular order; the *way* the poet speaks is as important to our understanding as what is said. This doesn't mean that an instruction manual couldn't have poetic qualities—indeed, modern poets have created "found" poems from even less likely materials—but it does mean that in poetry there is an intimate relation amongst language, form, and meaning, and that the writer deliberately structures and manipulates language to achieve very particular ends.

### THE BEST WORDS IN THE BEST ORDER

Wordsworth provides us with a useful example of the way that poetry can invest quite ordinary words with a high emotional charge:

> No motion has she now, no force,
> She neither hears nor sees;
> Rolled round in earth's diurnal course
> With rocks, and stones, and trees.

To paraphrase the content of this stanza from "A Slumber Did My Spirit Seal," "she" is dead and buried. But the language and structures used here give this prosaic idea great impact. For example, the regular iambic meter of the two last lines conveys something of the inexorable motion of the earth and of Lucy embedded in it; the monosyllabic last line is a grim reminder of her oneness with objects in nature; the repeated negatives in the first two lines drive home the irreparable destructiveness of death; the alliteration in the third and fourth lines gives a tangible suggestion of roundness, circularity, repetition in terms of the earth's shape and motion, suggesting a cycle in which death is perhaps followed by renewal. Even the unusual word "diurnal" (which would not have seemed so unusual to Wordsworth's readers) seems "right" in this context; it lends more weight to the notion of the earth's perpetual movement than its mundane synonym "daily" (which, besides, would not scan here). It is difficult to imagine a change of any kind to these lines; they exemplify another attempted definition of poetry, this time by Wordsworth's friend Samuel Taylor Coleridge: "the best words in the best order" (*Table Talk*, 1827).

### POETIC DICTION AND THE ELEVATED STYLE

Wordsworth's diction in the "Lucy" poem cited above is a model of clarity; he has chosen language that, in its simplicity and bluntness, conveys the strength of the speaker's feelings far more strongly than an elaborate description of grief in more conventionally "poetic" language might have done. Wordsworth, disturbed by what he felt was a deadness and artificiality in the poetry of his day, sought to "choose incidents and situations from common life" and to describe them in "a selection of language really used by men" ("Preface" to *Lyrical Ballads*). His plan might seem an implicit reproach of the "raised" style, the elevated diction of epic poetry we associate with John Milton's *Paradise Lost*:

> Anon out of the earth a fabric huge
> Rose like an exhalation, with the sound
> Of dulcet symphonies and voices sweet,

> Built like a temple, where pilasters round
> Were set, and Doric pillars overlaid
> With golden architrave; nor did there want
> Cornice or frieze, with bossy sculptures graven;
> The roof was fretted gold.
>
>                              (*Paradise Lost* I.710–17)

At first glance this passage, with its Latinate vocabulary and convoluted syntax, might seem guilty of inflated language and pretentiousness. However, Milton's description of the devils' palace in Hell deliberately seeks to distance us from its subject in order to emphasize the scale and sublimity of the spectacle, far removed from ordinary human experience. In other words, language and style in *Paradise Lost* are well adapted to suit a particular purpose, just as they are in "A Slumber Did My Spirit Seal," though on a wholly different scale. Wordsworth criticized the poetry of his day, not because of its elevation, but because the raised style was too often out of touch with its subject; in his view, the words did not bear any significant relation to the "truths" they were attempting to depict.

### "PLAIN" LANGUAGE IN POETRY

Since Wordsworth's time, writers have been conscious of a need to narrow the apparent gap between "poetic" language and the language of everyday life. In much of the poetry of the past century, especially free verse, we can observe a growing approximation to speech—even to conversation—in the diction and rhythms of poetry. This may have something to do with the changed role of the poet, who today has discarded the mantle of teacher or prophet that was assumed by poets of earlier times, and who is ready to admit all fields of experience and endeavor as appropriate for poetry. The modern poet looks squarely at life, and can often find a provoking beauty in even the meanest of objects.

We should not assume, however, that a greater concern with the "ordinary," with simplicity, naturalness, and clarity, means a reduction in complexity or suggestiveness. A piece such as Stevie Smith's "Mother, Among the Dustbins," for all the casual and playful domesticity of some of its lines, skilfully evokes a range of emotions and sense impressions defying simple paraphrase.

### IMAGERY, SYMBOLISM, AND FIGURES OF SPEECH

The language of poetry is grounded in the objects and phenomena that create sensory impressions. Sometimes the poet renders these impressions quite literally, in a series of *images* that seek to recreate a scene in the reader's mind:

> Only a man harrowing clods
> In a slow silent walk
> With an old horse that stumbles and nods
> Half asleep as they stalk.
>
> Only thin smoke without flame
> From the heaps of couch-grass;
> Yet this will go onward the same
> Though Dynasties pass.

    Yonder a maid and her wight
    Come whispering by:
    War's annals will cloud into night
    Ere their story die.
                (Thomas Hardy, "In Time of 'The Breaking of Nations'")

Here, the objects of everyday life are re-created with sensory details designed to evoke in us the sensations or responses felt by the speaker viewing the scene. At the same time, the writer invests the objects with such significance that the poem's meaning extends beyond the literal to the symbolic: that is, the images come to stand for something much larger than the objects they represent. Hardy's poem moves from the presentation of stark images of rural life to a sense of their timelessness. By the last stanza we see the ploughman, the burning grass, and the maid and her companion as symbols of recurring human actions and motives that defy the struggles and conflicts of history.

IMAGISM

The juxtaposition of clear, forceful images is associated particularly with the Imagist movement that flourished at the beginning of the twentieth century. Its chief representatives (in their early work) were the American poets H.D. and Ezra Pound, who defined an image as "that which represents an intellectual and emotional complex in an instant of time." Pound's two-line poem "In a Station of the Metro" provides a good example of the Imagists' goal of representing emotions or impressions through the use of concentrated images:

    The apparition of these faces in the crowd,
      Petals on a wet, black bough.

As in a Japanese *haiku,* a form that strongly influenced the Imagists, the poem uses sharp, clear, concrete details to evoke both a sensory impression and the emotion or the atmosphere of the scene. Though the Imagist movement itself lasted only a short time (from about 1912 to 1917), it had a far-reaching influence on modern poets such as T. S. Eliot, and William Carlos Williams.

FIGURES OF SPEECH

Imagery often works together with figurative expression to extend and deepen the meaning or impact of a poem. "Figurative" language means language that is metaphorical, not literal or referential. Through "figures of speech" such as metaphor and simile, metonymy, synecdoche, and personification, the writer may alter the ordinary, denotative meanings of words in order to convey greater force and vividness to ideas or impressions, often by showing likenesses between unlike things.

With *simile,* the poet makes an explicit comparison between the subject (called the *tenor*) and another object or idea (known as the *vehicle*), using "as" or "like":

    It is a beauteous evening, calm and free,
    The holy time is quiet as a Nun
    Breathless with adoration. ...

In this opening to a sonnet, Wordsworth uses a visual image of a nun in devout prayer to convey in concrete terms the less tangible idea of evening as a "holy time." The comparison also introduces an emotional dimension, conveying something of the feeling that the scene induces in the poet. The simile can thus illuminate and expand meaning in a compact way. The poet may also extend the simile to elaborate at length on any points of likeness.

In *metaphor*, the comparison between tenor and vehicle is implied: connectives such as "like" are omitted, and a kind of identity is created between the subject and the term with which it is being compared. Thus in John Donne's "The Good-Morrow," a lover asserts the endless joy that he and his beloved find in each other:

> My face in thine eye, thine in mine appears,
> And true plain hearts do in the faces rest;
> Where can we find two better hemispheres,
> Without sharp north, without declining west?

Here the lovers are transformed into "hemispheres," each of them a half of the world not subject to the usual natural phenomena of wintry cold ("sharp north") or the coming of night ("declining west"). Thus, they form a perfect world in balance, in which the normal processes of decay or decline have been arrested. Donne renders the abstract idea of a love that defies change in pictorial and physical terms, making it more real and accessible to us. The images here are all the more arresting for the degree of concentration involved; it is not merely the absence of "like" or "as" that gives the metaphor such direct power, but the fusion of distinct images and emotions into a new idea.

*Personification* is the figure of speech in which the writer endows abstract ideas, inanimate objects, or animals with human characteristics. In other words, it is a type of implied metaphorical comparison in which aspects of a non-human subject are compared to the feelings, appearance, or actions of a human being. In the second stanza of his ode "To Autumn," Keats personifies the concept of autumnal harvesting in the form of a woman, "sitting careless on a granary floor, / Thy hair soft-lifted by the winnowing wind." Personification may also help to create a mood, as when Thomas Gray attributes human feelings to a hooting owl in "Elegy Written in a Country Church-Yard"; using such words as "moping" and "complain," Gray invests the bird's cries with the quality of human melancholy:

> … from yonder ivy-mantled tow'r
> The moping owl does to the moon complain
> Of such, as wand'ring near her secret bow'r,
> Molest her ancient solitary reign.

In his book *Modern Painters* (1856), the English critic John Ruskin criticized such attribution of human feelings to objects in nature. Calling this device the "pathetic fallacy," he objected to what he saw as an irrational distortion of reality, producing "a falseness in all our impressions of external things." Modern criticism, with a distrust of any notions of an objective "reality," tends to use Ruskin's term as a neutral label simply to describe instances of extended personification of natural objects.

*Apostrophe*, which is closely related to personification, has the speaker directly addressing a non-human object or idea as if it were a sentient human listener. Blake's "The Sick Rose," Shelley's "Ode to the West Wind" and his ode "To a Sky-Lark" all employ apostrophe, personifying the object addressed. Keats's "Ode on a Grecian Urn" begins by apostrophizing the urn ("Thou still unravish'd bride of quietness"), then addresses it in a series of questions and reflections through which the speaker attempts to unravel the urn's mysteries.

Apostrophe also appeals to or addresses a person who is absent or dead. W. H. Auden's lament "In Memory of W. B. Yeats" apostrophizes both the earth in which Yeats is to be buried ("Earth, receive an honoured guest") and the dead poet himself ("Follow, poet, follow right / To the bottom of the night …"). Religious prayers offer an illustration of the usefulness of apostrophe, since they are direct appeals from an earth-bound supplicant to an invisible god. The suggestion of strong emotion associated with such appeals is a common feature of apostrophe in poetry also, especially poetry with a religious theme, like Donne's "Holy Sonnets" (e.g., "Batter My Heart, Three-Personed God").

*Metonymy* and *synecdoche* are two closely related figures of speech that further illustrate the power of metaphorical language to convey meaning more intensely and vividly than is possible with prosaic statement. *Metonymy* (from the Greek, meaning "change of name") involves referring to an object or concept by substituting the name of another object or concept with which it is usually associated: for example, we might speak of "the Crown" when we mean the monarch, or describe the U.S. executive branch as "the White House." When the writer uses only part of something to signify the whole, or an individual to represent a class, we have an instance of *synecdoche*. T. S. Eliot provides an example in "The Love Song of J. Alfred Prufrock" when a crab is described as "a pair of ragged claws." Similarly, synecdoche is present in Milton's contemptous term "blind mouths" to describe the "corrupted clergy" he attacks in "Lycidas."

Dylan Thomas employs both metonymy and synecdoche in his poem "The Hand That Signed the Paper":

> The hand that signed the paper felled a city;
> Five sovereign fingers taxed the breath,
> Doubled the globe of dead and halved a country;
> These five kings did a king to death.
>
> The mighty hand leads to a sloping shoulder,
> The finger joints are cramped with chalk;
> A goose's quill has put an end to murder
> That put an end to talk.
>
> The hand that signed the treaty bred a fever,
> And famine grew, and locusts came;
> Great is the hand that holds dominion over
> Man by a scribbled name.
>
> The five kings count the dead but do not soften
> The crusted wound nor stroke the brow;
> A hand rules pity as a hand rules heaven;
> Hands have no tears to flow.

The "hand" of the poem is evidently a synecdoche for a great king who enters into treaties with friends and foes to wage wars, conquer kingdoms, and extend his personal power—all at the expense of his suffering subjects. The "goose quill" of the second stanza is a metonymy, standing for the pen used to sign the treaty or the death warrant that brings the war to an end.

Thomas's poem is an excellent example of the power of figurative language, which, by its vividness and concentrated force, can add layers of meaning to a poem, make abstract ideas concrete, and intensify the poem's emotional impact.

## THE POEM AS PERFORMANCE: WRITER AND PERSON

Poetry is always dramatic. Sometimes the drama is explicit, as in Robert Browning's monologues, in which we hear the voice of a participant in a dialogue; in "My Last Duchess" we are present as the Duke reflects on the portrait of his late wife for the benefit of a visitor who has come to negotiate on behalf of the woman who is to become the Duke's next wife. Or we listen with amusement and pity as the dying Bishop addresses his venal and unsympathetic sons and tries to bargain with them for a fine burial ("The Bishop Orders His Tomb at St. Praxed's"). In such poems, the notion of a speaking voice is paramount: the speaker is a personage in a play, and the poem a means of conveying plot and character.

Sometimes the drama is less apparent, and takes the form of a plea, or a compliment, or an argument addressed to a silent listener. In Donne's "The Flea" we can infer from the poem the situation that has called it forth: a lover's advances are being rejected by his beloved, and his poem is an argument intended to overcome her reluctance by means of wit and logic. We can see a similar example in Marvell's "To His Coy Mistress": here the very shape of the poem, its three-paragraph structure, corresponds to the stages of the speaker's argument as he presents an apparently irrefutable line of reasoning. Much love poetry has this kind of background as its inspiration; the yearnings or lamentations of the lover are part of an imagined scene, not merely versified reflections about an abstraction called "love."

Meditative or reflective poetry can be dramatic too. Donne's "Holy Sonnets" are pleas from a tormented soul struggling to find its god; Tennyson's "In Memoriam" follows the agonized workings of a mind tracing a path from grief and anger to acceptance and renewed hope.

We should never assume that the speaker, the "I" of the poem, is simply a voice for the writer's own views. The speaker in W. H. Auden's "To an Unknown Citizen," presenting a summary of the dead citizen's life, appears to be an official spokesperson for the society which the citizen served ("Our report on his union"; "Our researchers ..." etc.). The speaker's words are laudatory, yet we perceive immediately that Auden's own views of this society are anything but approving. The speaker seems satisfied with the highly regimented nature of his society, one in which every aspect of the individual's life is under scrutiny and subject to correction. The only things necessary to the happiness of the "Modern Man," it seems, are "A phonograph, a radio, a car, and a frigidaire." The tone here is subtly ironic, an irony created by the gap between the imagined speaker's perception and the real feelings of the writer.

### PERFORMANCE POETRY

Poetry began as an oral art, passed on in the form of chants, myths, ballads, and legends recited to an audience of listeners rather than readers. Even today, the dramatic qualities of a poem may extend beyond written text. "Performance poets" combine poetry and stagecraft in presenting their work to live audiences. Dramatic uses of voice, rhythm, body movement, music, and sometimes other visual effects make the "text" of the poem multi-dimensional. For example, Edith Sitwell's poem-sequence *Façade* (1922) was originally set to music: Sitwell read from behind a screen, while a live orchestra played. This performance was designed to enhance the verbal and rhythmic qualities of her poetry:

Beneath the flat and paper sky
The sun, a demon's eye
Glowed through the air, that mask of glass;
All wand'ring sounds that pass

Seemed out of tune, as if the light
Were fiddle-strings pulled tight.
The market-square with spire and bell
Clanged out the hour in Hell.
    (from *Façade*)

By performing their poetry, writers can also convey cultural values and traditions. The cultural aspect of performance is central to Black poetry, which originates in a highly oral tradition of folklore and storytelling. From its roots in Africa, this oral tradition has been manifested in the songs and stories of slaves, in spirituals, in the jazz rhythms of the Twenties and the Thirties and in the rebelliousness of reggae and of rap. Even when it remains "on the page," much Black poetry written in the oral tradition has a compelling rhythmic quality. The lines below from Linton Kwesi Johnson's "Mi Revalueshanary Fren," for example, blur the line between spoken poetry and song. Johnson often performs his "dub poetry" against reggae or hip-hop musical backings.

yes, people powa jus a showa evry howa
an evrybady claim dem democratic
but some a wolf an some a sheep
an dat is problematic

The chorus of Johnson's poems, with its constant repetitions, digs deeply into the roots of African song and chant. Its performance qualities become clearer when the poem is read aloud:

Husak
e ad to go
Honnicka
e ad to go
Chowcheskhu
e ad to go
Just like apartied
will av to go

To perform a poem is one way to see and hear poetry as multi-dimensional, cultural, historical, and often also political. Performance is also another way to discover how poetic "meaning" can be constructed in the dynamic relation between speaker and listener.

TONE: THE SPEAKER'S ATTITUDE

In understanding poetry, it is helpful to imagine a poem as having a "voice." The voice may be close to the poet's own, or that of an imagined character, a *persona* adopted by the poet. The tone of the voice will reveal the speaker's attitude to the subject, thus helping to shape our understanding and response. In speech we can indicate our feelings by raising or lowering our voices, and we can accompany words with physical actions. In writing, we must try to convey the tonal inflections of the speaking voice through devices of language and rhythm, through imagery and figures of speech, and through allusions and contrasts.

## THE IRONIC TONE

Housman's poem "Terence, This Is Stupid Stuff" offers a useful example of ways in which manipulating tone can reinforce meaning. When Housman, presenting himself in the poem as "Terence," imagines himself to be criticized for writing gloomy poems, his response to his critics takes the form of an ironic alternative: perhaps they should stick to drinking ale:

> Oh, many a peer of England brews
> Livelier liquor than the Muse,
> And malt does more than Milton can
> To justify God's ways to man.

The tone here is one of heavy scorn. The speaker is impatient with those who refuse to look at the realities of life and death, and who prefer to take refuge in simple-minded pleasure. The ludicrous comparisons, first between the brewers who have been made peers of England and the classical Muse of poetry, then between malt and Milton, create a sense of disproportion and ironic tension; the explicit allusion to *Paradise Lost* ("To justify God's ways to man") helps to drive home the poet's bitter recognition that his auditors are part of that fallen world depicted by Milton, yet unable or unwilling to acknowledge their harsh condition. The three couplets that follow offer a series of contrasts: in each case, the first line sets up a pleasant expectation and the second dashes it with a blunt reminder of reality:

> Ale, man, ale's the stuff to drink
> For fellows whom it hurts to think:
> Look into the pewter pot
> To see the world as the world's not.
> And faith, 'tis pleasant till 'tis past:
> The mischief is that 'twill not last.

These are all jabs at the "sterling lads" who would prefer to lie in "lovely muck" and not think about the way the world is. Housman's sardonic advice is all the more pointed for its sharp and ironic tone.

## POETIC FORMS

In poetry, language is intimately related to form, which is the structuring of words within identifiable patterns. In prose we speak of phrases, sentences, and paragraphs; in poetry, we identify structures by lines, stanzas, or complete forms such as the sonnet or the ode (though poetry in complete or blank verse has paragraphs of variable length, not formal stanzas: see below).

Rightly handled, the form enhances expression and meaning, just as a frame can define and enhance a painting or photograph. Unlike the photo frame, however, form in poetry is an integral part of the whole work. At one end of the scale, the term "form" may describe the *epic,* the lengthy narrative governed by such conventions as division into books, a lofty style, and the interplay between human and supernatural characters. At the other end lies the *epigram*, a witty and pointed saying whose distinguishing characteristic is its brevity, as in Alexander Pope's famous couplet,

> I am his Highness' dog at Kew;
> Pray tell me sir, whose dog are you?

Between the epic and the epigram lie many other poetic forms, such as the sonnet, the ballad, or the ode. "Form" may also describe stanzaic patterns like *couplets* and *quatrains*.

### "FIXED FORM" POEMS

The best-known poetic form is probably the sonnet, the fourteen-line poem inherited from Italy (the word itself is from the Italian *sonetto*, little song or sound). Within those fourteen lines, whether the poet chooses the "Petrarchan" rhyme scheme or the "English" form (see below in the section on "Rhyme"), the challenge is to develop an idea or situation that must find its statement and its resolution within the strict confines of the sonnet frame. Typically, there is an initial idea, description, or statement of feeling, followed by a "turn" in the thought that takes the reader by surprise, or that casts the situation in an unexpected light. Thus in Sonnet 130, "My Mistress' Eyes Are Nothing Like the Sun," William Shakespeare spends the first three quatrains apparently disparaging his lover in a series of unfavorable comparisons—"If snow be white, why then her breasts are dun"—but in the closing couplet his point becomes clear:

> And yet, by heaven, I think my love as rare
> As any she belied with false compare.

In other words, the speaker's disparaging comparisons have really been parodies of sentimental clichés which falsify reality; his mistress has no need of the exaggerations or distortions of conventional love poetry.

Other foreign forms borrowed and adapted by English-language poets include the *ghazal* and the *pantoum*. The *ghazal*, strongly associated with classical Urdu literature, originated in Persia and Arabia and was brought to the Indian subcontinent in the twelfth century. It consists of a series of couplets held together by a refrain, a simple rhyme scheme (a/a, b/a, c/a, d/a…), and a common rhythm, but only loosely related in theme or subject. Some English-language practitioners of the form have captured the epigrammatic quality of the ghazal, but most do not adhere to the strict pattern of the classical form.

The *pantoum*, based on a Malaysian form, was imported into English poetry via the work of nineteenth-century French poets. Typically it presents a series of quatrains rhyming *abab*, linked by a pattern of repetition in which the second and fourth lines of a quatrain become the first and third lines of the stanza that follows. In the poem's final stanza, the pattern is reversed: the second line repeats the third line of the first stanza, and the last line repeats the poem's opening line, thus creating the effect of a loop.

Similar to the pantoum in the circularity of its structure is the *villanelle*, originally a French form, with five *tercets* and a concluding *quatrain* held together by only two rhymes (aba, aba, aba, aba, aba, abaa) and by a refrain that repeats the first line at lines 6, 12, and 18, while the third line of the first tercet reappears as lines 9, 15, and 19. With its interlocking rhymes and elaborate repetitions, the villanelle can create a variety of tonal effects, ranging from lighthearted parody to the sonorous and earnest exhortation of Dylan Thomas's "Do Not Go Gentle Into That Good Night."

STANZAIC FORMS

Recurring formal groupings of lines within a poem are usually described as "stanzas." Both the recurring and the formal aspects of stanzaic forms are important; it is a common misconception to think that any group of lines in a poem, if it is set off by line spaces, constitutes a stanza. If such a group of lines is not patterned as one of a recurring group sharing similar formal characteristics, however, then it may be more appropriate to refer to such irregular groupings in the way we do for prose—as paragraphs. A ballad is typically divided into stanzas; a prose poem or a poem written in free verse, on the other hand, will rarely be divided into stanzas.

A stanza may be identified by the number of lines and the patterns of rhyme repeated in each grouping. One of the simpler traditional forms is the *ballad stanza*, with its alternating four and three-foot lines and its *abcb* rhyme scheme. Drawing on this form's association with medieval ballads and legends, Keats produces the eerie mystery of "La Belle Dame Sans Merci":

I saw pale kings and princes too,
Pale warriors, death-pale were they all;
They cried—"La Belle Dame sans Merci
Hath thee in thrall!"

Such imitations are a form of literary allusion; Keats uses a traditional stanza form to remind us of poems like "Sir Patrick Spens" or "Barbara Allen" to dramatize the painful thralldom of love by placing it within a well-known tradition of ballad narratives with similar forms and themes.

The four-line stanza, or *quatrain*, may be used for a variety of effects: from the elegiac solemnity of Gray's "Elegy Written in a Country Churchyard" to the apparent lightness and simplicity of some of Emily Dickinson's poems. Tennyson used a rhyming quatrain to such good effect in *In Memoriam* that the form he employed (four lines of iambic tetrameter rhyming *abba*) is known as the "In Memoriam stanza."

Other commonly used forms of stanza include the *rhyming couplet, terza rima, ottava rima, rhyme royal,* and the *Spenserian stanza.* Each of these is a rhetorical unit within a longer whole, rather like a paragraph within an essay. The poet's choice among such forms is dictated, at least in part, by the effects that each may produce. Thus the *rhyming couplet* often expresses a complete statement within two lines, creating a sense of density of thought, of coherence and closure; it is particularly effective where the writer wishes to set up contrasts, or to achieve the witty compactness of epigram:

Of all mad creatures, if the learn'd are right,
It is the slaver kills, and not the bite.
A fool quite angry is quite innocent:
Alas! 'tis ten times worse when they repent.

(from Pope, "Epistle to Dr. Arbuthnot")

*Ottava rima*, as its Italian name implies, is an eight-line stanza, with the rhyme scheme *abababcc*. Like the sonnet, it is long enough to allow the development of a single thought in some detail and complexity, with a concluding couplet that may extend the central idea or cast it in a wholly unexpected light. W.B. Yeats uses this stanza form in "Sailing to Byzantium" and "Among Schoolchildren." Though much used by Renaissance poets, it is particularly associated with George Gordon, Lord Byron's *Don Juan*, in which the poet exploits to the full its potential for devastating irony and bathos. It is long enough to allow the development of a single thought in some detail and complexity; the concluding couplet can then, sonnet-like, turn that thought upon its head, or cast it in a wholly unexpected light:

Sagest of women, even of widows, she
    Resolved that Juan should be quite a paragon,
And worthy of the noblest pedigree
    (His sire was of Castile, his dam from Aragon).
Then for accomplishments of chivalry,
    In case our lord the king should go to war again,
He learned the arts of riding, fencing, gunnery,
And how to scale a fortress—or a nunnery.

                                      *(Don Juan* I.38)

## FREE VERSE

Not all writers want the order and symmetry—some might say the restraints and limitations—of traditional forms, and many have turned to *free verse* as a means of liberating their thoughts and feelings. Deriving its name from the French "vers libre" made popular by the French Symbolistes at the end of the nineteenth century, free verse is characterized by irregularity of metre, line length, and rhyme. This does not mean that it is without pattern; rather, it tends to follow more closely than other forms the unforced rhythms and accents of natural speech, making calculated use of spacing, line breaks, and "cadences," the rhythmic units that govern phrasing in speech.

    Free verse is not a modern invention. Milton was an early practitioner, as was Blake; however, it was the great modern writers of free verse—first Walt Whitman, then Pound, Eliot, and William Carlos Williams (interestingly, all Americans, at least originally)—who gave this form a fluidity and flexibility that could free the imagination to deal with any kind of feeling or experience. Perhaps because it depends so much more than traditional forms upon the individual intuitions of the poet, it is the form of poetic structure most commonly found today. The best practitioners recognize that free verse, like any other kind of poetry, demands clarity, precision, and a close connection between technique and meaning.

## PROSE POETRY

At the furthest extreme from traditional forms lies poetry written in prose. Contradictory as this label may seem, the two have much in common. Prose has at its disposal all the figurative devices available to poetry, such as metaphor, personification, or apostrophe; it may use structuring devices such as verbal repetition or parallel syntactical structures; it can draw on the same tonal range, from pathos to irony. The difference is that prose poetry accomplishes its ends in sentences and paragraphs, rather than lines or stanzas. First given prominence by the French poet Charles Baudelaire (*Petits Poèmes en prose*, 1862), the form is much used to present fragments of heightened sensation, conveyed through vivid or impressionistic description. It draws upon such prosaic forms as journal entries, lists, even footnotes. Prose poetry should be distinguished from "poetic prose," which may be found in a variety of settings (from the King James Bible to the fiction of Jeanette Winterson); the distinction—which not all critics would accept—appears to lie in the writer's intention.

    Christan Bok's *Eunoia* is an interesting example of the ways in which a writer of prose poetry may try to balance the demands of each medium. *Eunoia* is an avowedly experimental work in which each chapter is restricted to the use of a single vowel. The text is governed by a series of rules described by the author in an afterword; they include a requirement that all chapters "must allude to the art of writing. All sentences must accent internal rhyme through the use of syntactical parallelism. The text must exhaust the lexicon for each vowel, citing at least 98% of the available repertoire...." Having imposed such constraints upon the language and form of the work, Bok then sets himself the task of showing that "even under such improbable conditions of duress, language can still express an uncanny, if not sublime, thought." The result is a surrealistic narrative that blends poetic and linguistic devices to almost hypnotic effect.

### THE POEM AS A MATERIAL OBJECT

Both free verse and prose poetry pay attention in different ways to the poem as a living thing on the printed page. But the way in which poetry is presented in material form is an important part of the existence of almost any form of poetry. In the six volumes of this anthology the material form of the poem is highlighted by the inclusion of a number of facsimile reproductions of poems of other eras in their earliest extant material form.

## RHYTHM AND SCANSION

When we read poetry, we often become aware of a pattern of rhythm within a line or set of lines. The formal analysis of that rhythmic pattern, or "metre," is called *scansion*. The verb "to scan" may carry different meanings, depending upon the context: if the *critic* "scans" a line, he or she is attempting to determine the metrical pattern in which it is cast; if the *line* "scans," we are making the observation that the line conforms to particular metrical rules. Whatever the context, the process of scansion is based on the premise that a line of verse is built on a pattern of stresses, a recurring set of more or less regular beats established by the alternation of light and heavy accents in syllables and words. The rhythmic pattern so distinguished in a given poem is said to be the "metre" of that poem. If we find it impossible to identify any specific metrical pattern, the poem is probably an example of free verse.

### QUANTITATIVE, SYLLABIC, AND ACCENTUAL-SYLLABIC VERSE

Although we owe much of our terminology for analyzing or describing poetry to the Greeks and Romans, the foundation of our metrical system is quite different from theirs. They measured a line of verse by the duration of sound ("quantity") in each syllable, and by the combination of short and long syllables. Such poetry is known as *quantitative* verse.

Unlike Greek or Latin, English is a heavily accented language. Thus poetry of the Anglo-Saxon period, such as *Beowulf*, was *accentual:* that is, the lines were based on a fixed number of accents, or stresses, regardless of the number of syllables in the line:

> Oft Scyld Scefing   sceapena þreatum
>    monegum maegþum   meodosetla ofteah.

Few modern poets have written in the accentual tradition. A notable exception was Gerard Manley Hopkins, who based his line on a pattern of strong stresses that he called "sprung rhythm." Hopkins experimented with rhythms and stresses that approximate the accentual quality of natural speech; the result is a line that is emphatic, abrupt, even harsh in its forcefulness:

> I caught this morning morning's minion, kingdom of daylight's dauphin, dapple-dawn-drawn
>    Falcon, in his riding

Of the rolling level underneath him steady air ....

(from "The Windhover")

Under the influence of French poetry, following the Norman invasion of the eleventh century, English writers were introduced to *syllabic* prosody: that is, poetry in which the number of syllables is the determining factor in the length of any line, regardless of the number of stresses or their placement. A few modern writers have successfully produced syllabic poetry.

However, the accentual patterns of English, in speech as well as in poetry, were too strongly ingrained to disappear. Instead, the native accentual practice combined with the imported syllabic conventions to produce the *accentual-syllabic* line, in which the writer works with combinations of stressed and unstressed syllables in lines of equal syllabic length. Geoffrey Chaucer was the first great writer to employ the accentual-syllabic line in English poetry:

Ther was also a Nonne, a Prioresse,
That of hir smiling was ful simple and coy.
Hir gretteste ooth was but by sainté Loy,
And she was clepéd Madame Eglantine.

(from *The Canterbury Tales*)

The fundamental pattern here is the ten-syllable line (although the convention of sounding the final "e" at the end of a line in Middle English verse sometimes produces eleven syllables). Each line contains five stressed syllables, each of which alternates with one or two unstressed syllables. This was to become the predominant metre of poetry in English until the general adoption of free verse in the twentieth century.

IDENTIFYING POETIC METER

Conventionally, meter is established by dividing a line into roughly equal parts, based on the rise and fall of the rhythmic beats. Each of these divisions, conventionally marked by a bar, is known as a "foot," and within the foot there will be a combination of stressed and unstressed syllables, indicated by the prosodic symbols / (stressed) and x (unstressed).

I know | that I | shall meet | my fate
Somewhere | among | the clouds | above ...

(from *Yeats*, "An Irish Airman Foresees His Death")

To describe the meter used in a poem, we must first determine what kind of foot predominates, and then count the number of feet in each line. To describe the resultant meter we use terminology borrowed from classical prosody. In identifying the meter of English verse we commonly apply the following labels:

*iambic* (x /): a foot with one weak stress followed by one strong stress

("Look home | ward, Ang | el, now, | and melt | with ruth")

*trochaic* (/ x): strong followed by weak

("Ty | ger! Ty | ger! bur | ning bright")

*anapaestic* (x x /): two weak stresses, followed by a strong

("I have passed | with a nod | of the head")

*dactylic* (/ x x): strong stress followed by two weak

("Hickory | dickory | dock")

*spondaic* (/ /): two strong stresses

("If hate | killed men,| Brother | Lawrence,
God's blood,| would not | mine kill | you?")

We also use classical terms to describe the number of feet in a line. Thus, a line with one foot is *monometer*; with two feet, *dimeter*; three feet, *trimeter*; four feet, *tetrameter*; five feet, *pentameter*; and six feet, *hexameter*.

Scansion of the two lines from Yeats's "Irish Airman" quoted above shows that the predominant foot is iambic (x /), that there are four feet to each line, and that the poem is therefore written in *iambic tetrameters*. The first foot of the second line, however, may be read as a trochee ("Somewhere"); the variation upon the iambic norm here is an example of *substitution*, a means whereby the writer may avoid the monotony that would result from adhering too closely to a set rhythm. We very quickly build up an expectation about the dominant meter of a poem; the poet will sometimes disturb that expectation by changing the beat, and so through substitution create a pleasurable tension in our awareness.

The prevailing meter in English poetry is iambic, since the natural rhythm of spoken English is predominantly iambic. Nonetheless, poets may employ other rhythms where it suits their purpose. Thus W.H. Auden can create a solemn tone by the use of a trochaic meter(/ x):

Earth, receive an honoured guest;
William Yeats is laid to rest:
Let the Irish vessel lie
Emptied of its poetry.

The same meter may be much less funereal, as in Ben Jonson's song "*To Celia*":

Come, my Celia, let us prove,
While we may, the sports of love.
Time will not be ours forever;
He, at length, our good will sever.

The sense of greater pace in this last example derives in part from the more staccato phrasing, and also from the greater use of monosyllabic words. A more obviously lilting, dancing effect is obtained from anapaestic rhythm (x x /):

I sprang to the stirrup, and Joris, and he;
I galloped, Dirck galloped, we galloped all three.
"Good speed!" cried the watch, as the gatebolts undrew;
"Speed!" echoed the wall to us galloping through.
(from *Browning*, "How They Brought the Good News from Ghent to Aix")

Coleridge wittily captured the varying effects of different meters in "Metrical Feet: Lesson for a Boy," which the poet wrote for his sons, and in which he marked the stresses himself:

> Trochee trips from long to short;
> From long to long in solemn sort
> Slow Spondee stalks; strong foot! yet ill able
> Ever to come up with Dactyl trisyllable.
> Iambics march from short to long:—
> With a leap and a bound the swift Anapaests throng....

A meter which often deals with serious themes is unrhymed iambic pentameter, also known as *blank verse*. This is the meter of Shakespeare's plays, notably his great tragedies; it is the meter, too, of Milton's *Paradise Lost*, to which it lends a desired sonority and magnificence; and of Wordsworth's "Lines Composed a Few Miles above Tintern Abbey," where the flexibility of the meter allows the writer to move by turns from description, to narration, to philosophical reflection.

## RHYME, CONSONANCE, ASSONANCE, AND ALLITERATION

Perhaps the most obvious sign of poetic form is rhyme: that is, the repetition of syllables with the same or similar sounds. If the rhyme words are placed at the end of the line, they are known as *end-rhymes*. The opening stanza of Housman's "To an Athlete Dying Young" has two pairs of end-rhymes:

> The time you won your town the *race*
> We chaired you through the market-*place*;
> Man and boy stood cheering *by*,
> And home we brought you shoulder-*high*.

Words rhyming within a line are *internal rhymes*, as in the first and third lines of this stanza from Coleridge's "The Rime of the Ancient Mariner":

> The fair breeze *blew*, the white foam *flew*
> The furrow followed free;
> We were the *first* that ever *burst*
> Into that silent sea.

When, as is usually the case, the rhyme occurs in a stressed syllable, it is known as a *masculine rhyme*; if the rhyming word ends in an unstressed syllable, it is referred to as *feminine*. The difference is apparent in the opening stanzas of Alfred Tennyson's poem "The Lady of Shalott," where the first stanza establishes the basic iambic meter with strong stresses on the rhyming words:

> On either side the river *lie*
> Long fields of barley and of *rye*,
> That clothe the wold and meet the *sky*;
> And through the field the road runs *by*
> To many-towered Camelot ...

In the second stanza Tennyson changes to trochaic lines, ending in unstressed syllables and feminine rhymes:

> Willows whiten, aspens *quiver*,
> Little breezes dusk and *shiver*
> Through the wave that runs *forever*
> By the island in the *river*
> Flowing down to Camelot.

Not only does Tennyson avoid monotony here by his shift to feminine rhymes, he also darkens the mood by using words that imply a contrast with the bright warmth of day—"quiver," "dusk," "shiver"—in preparation for the introduction of the "silent isle" that embowers the Lady.

NEAR RHYMES

Most of the rhymes in "The Lady of Shalott" are exact, or "*perfect*" rhymes. However, in the second of the stanzas just quoted, it is evident that "forever" at the end of the third line is not a "perfect" rhyme; rather, it is an instance of "*near*" or "*slant*" rhyme. Such "*imperfect*" rhymes are quite deliberate; indeed, two stanzas later we find the rhyming sequence "early," "barley," "cheerly," and "clearly," followed by the rhymes "weary," "airy," and "fairy." As with the introduction of feminine rhymes, such divergences from one dominant pattern prevent monotony and avoid a too-mechanical sing-song effect.

More importantly, near-rhymes have an oddly unsettling effect, perhaps because they both raise and frustrate our expectation of a perfect rhyme. Their use certainly gives added emphasis to the words at the end of these chilling lines from Wilfred Owen's "*Strange Meeting*":

> For by my glee might many men have laughed,
> And of my weeping something had been left,
> Which must die now. I mean the truth untold,
> The pity of war, the pity war distilled.
> Now men will go content with what we spoiled,
> Or, discontent, boil bloody, and be spilled.

CONSONANCE AND ASSONANCE

In Owen's poem, the near-rhymes "laughed / left" and "spoiled / spilled" are good examples of *consonance*, which pairs words with similar consonants but different intervening vowels. Other examples from Owen's poem include "groined / groaned," "hall / Hell," "years / yours," and "mystery / mastery."

Related to consonance as a linking device is *assonance*, the echoing of similar vowel sounds in the stressed syllables of words with differing consonants (lane/hail, penitent/reticence). A device favored particularly by descriptive poets, it appears often in the work of the English Romantics, especially Shelley and Keats, and their great Victorian successor Tennyson, all of whom had a good ear for the musical quality of language. In the following passage, Tennyson makes effective use of repeated "o" and "ow" sounds to suggest the soft moaning of the wind as it spreads the seed of the lotos plant:

> The Lotos blooms below the barren peak,
> The Lotos blows by every winding creek;

All day the wind breathes low with mellower tone;
Through every hollow cave and alley lone
Round and round the spicy downs the yellow Lotos dust is blown.

(from "The Lotos-Eaters")

## ALLITERATION

*Alliteration* connects words which have the same initial consonant. Like consonance and rhyme, alliteration adds emphasis, throwing individual words into strong relief, and lending force to rhythm. This is especially evident in the work of Gerard Manley Hopkins, where alliteration works in conjunction with the heavy stresses of *sprung rhythm*:

Brute beauty and valour and act, oh, air, pride, plume, here
Buckle! AND the fire that breaks from thee then, a billion
Times told lovelier, more dangerous, O my chevalier!

(from "The Windhover")

Like assonance, alliteration is useful in descriptive poetry, reinforcing an impression or mood through repeated sounds:

Thou on whose stream, 'mid the steep sky's commotion,
Loose clouds like Earth's decaying leaves are shed,
Shook from the tangled boughs of Heaven and Ocean ....

(from Percy Shelley, "Ode to the West Wind")

The repetition of "s" and "sh" sounds conveys the rushing sound of a wind that drives everything before it. This effect is also an example of *onomatopoeia*, a figure of speech in which the sound of the words seems to echo the sense.

## RHYME AND POETIC STRUCTURE

Rhyme may play a central role in the structure of a poem. This is particularly apparent in the *sonnet* form, where the expression of the thought is heavily influenced by the poet's choice of rhyme-scheme. The "English" or "Shakespearean" sonnet has three quatrains rhyming *abab, cdcd, efef,* and concludes with a rhyming couplet, *gg.* This pattern lends itself well to the statement and restatement of an idea, as we find, for example, in Shakespeare's sonnet "That time of year thou mayst in me behold." Each of the quatrains presents an image of decline or decay—a tree in winter, the coming of night, a dying fire; the closing couplet then relates these images to the thought of an impending separation and attendant feelings of loss.

The organization of the "Italian" or "Petrarchan" sonnet, by contrast, hinges on a rhyme scheme that creates two parts, an eight-line section (the *octave*) typically rhyming *abbaabba,* and a concluding six-line section (the *sestet*) rhyming *cdecde* or some other variation. In the octave, the writer describes a thought or feeling; in the sestet, the writer may elaborate upon that thought, or may introduce a sudden "turn" or change of direction. A good example of the Italian form is Donne's "Batter My Heart, Three-Personed God."

The rhyming pattern established at the beginning of a poem is usually followed throughout; thus the opening sets up an expectation in the reader, which the poet may sometimes play on by means of an unexpected or surprising rhyme. This is especially evident in comic verse, where peculiar or unexpected rhymes can contribute a great deal to the comic effect:

> I shoot the Hippopotamus
> with bullets made of platinum,
> Because if I use leaden ones
> his hide is sure to flatten 'em.
>
> (*Hilaire Belloc,* "The Hippopotamus")

Finally, one of the most obvious yet important aspects of rhyme is its sound. It acts as a kind of musical punctuation, lending verse an added resonance and beauty. And as anyone who has ever had to learn poetry by heart will testify, the sound of rhyme is a powerful aid to memorization and recall, from helping a child to learn numbers—

> One, two,
> Buckle my shoe,
> Three, four,
> Knock at the door—

—to selling toothpaste through an advertising jingle in which the use of rhyme drives home the identity of a product:

> You'll wonder where the yellow went,
> When you brush your teeth with Pepsodent.

OTHER FORMS WITH INTERLOCKING RHYMES

Other forms besides the sonnet depend upon rhyme for their structural integrity. These include the *rondeau*, a poem of thirteen lines in three stanzas, with two half lines acting as a refrain, and having only two rhymes. The linking effect of rhyme is also essential to the three-line stanza called *terza rima*, the form chosen by Shelley for his "Ode to the West Wind," where the rhyme scheme (*aba, bcb, cdc* etc.) gives a strong sense of forward movement. But a poet need not be limited to particular forms to use interlocking rhyme schemes.

## THE POET'S TASK

The poet's task, in Sir Philip Sidney's view, is to move us to virtue and well-doing by coming to us with

> words set in delightful proportion, either accompanied with, or prepared for, the well-
> enchanting skill of music; and with a tale forsooth he cometh unto you, with a tale which
> holdeth children from play, and old men from the chimney corner; and pretending no more,

doth intend the winning of the mind from wickedness to virtue: even as the child is often brought to take most wholesome things by hiding them in such other as have a pleasant taste.

(*The Defence of Poesy,* 1593)

Modern poets have been less preoccupied with the didactic or moral force of poetry, its capacity to win the mind to virtue; nonetheless, like their Renaissance counterparts, they view poetry as a means to understanding, a point of light in an otherwise dark universe. To Robert Frost, a poem "begins in delight and ends in wisdom":

It begins in delight, it inclines to the impulse, it assumes direction with the first line laid down, it runs a course of lucky events, and ends in a clarification of life—not necessarily a great clarification, such as sects and cults are founded on, but in a momentary stay against confusion.

("The Figure a Poem Makes," *Collected Poems,* 1939)

Rhyme and metre are important tools at the poet's disposal, and can be valuable aids in developing thought as well as in creating rhythmic or musical effects. However, the technical skills needed to turn a good line or create metrical complexities should not be confused with the ability to write good poetry. Sidney wryly observes in his *Defence of Poesy* that "there have been many excellent poets that never versified, and now swarm many versifiers that need never answer to the name of poets.…it is not rhyming and versing that maketh a poet, no more than a long gown maketh an advocate." Technical virtuosity may arouse our admiration, but something else is needed to bring that "constriction of the throat and … precipitation of water to the eyes" that A.E. Housman speaks about. What that "something" is will always elude definition, and is perhaps best left for readers and listeners to determine for themselves through their own encounters with poetry.

# MAPS

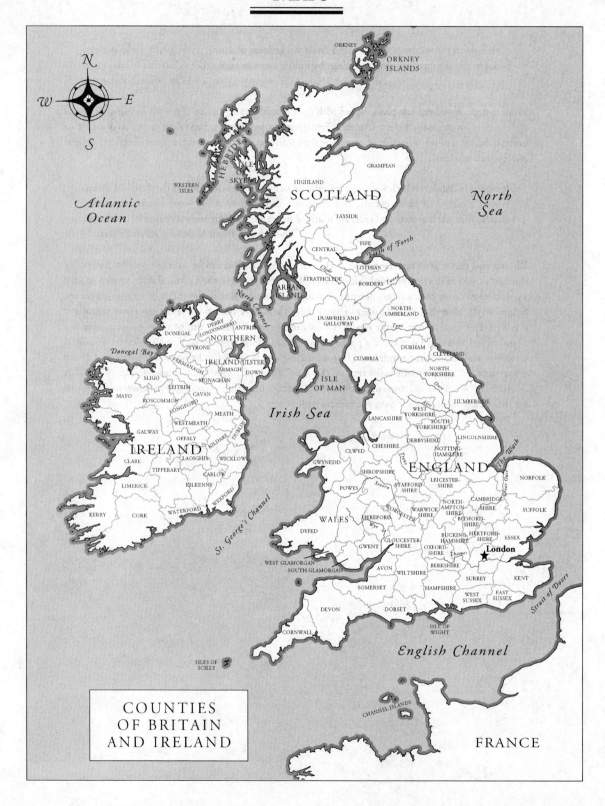

COUNTIES
OF BRITAIN
AND IRELAND

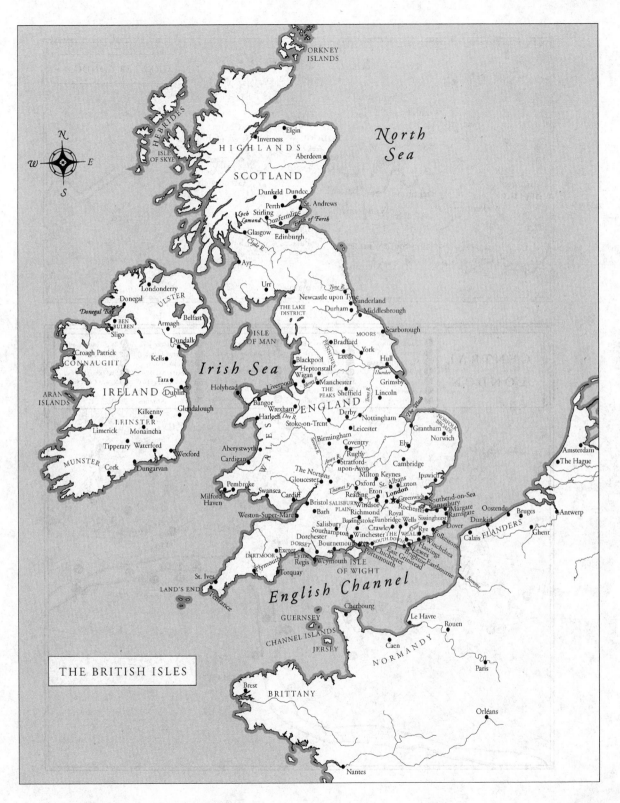

THE BRITISH ISLES

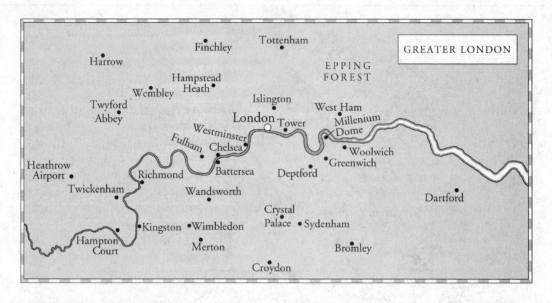

**GREATER LONDON**

Tottenham · Finchley · Harrow · Hampstead Heath · Wembley · Islington · EPPING FOREST · Twyford Abbey · London · Tower · West Ham · Millenium Dome · Westminster · Chelsea · Fulham · Woolwich · Greenwich · Heathrow Airport · Richmond · Battersea · Deptford · Twickenham · Wandsworth · Dartford · Kingston · Wimbledon · Crystal Palace · Sydenham · Hampton Court · Merton · Bromley · Croydon

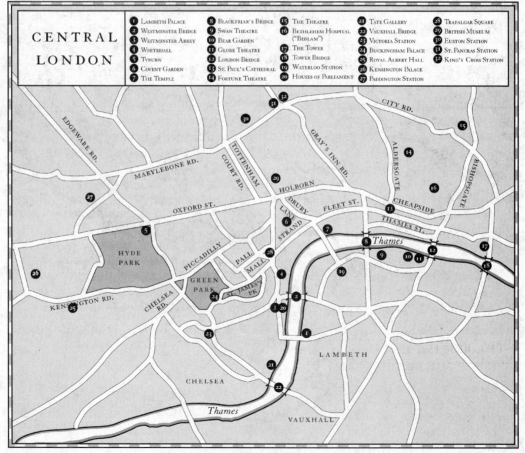

# CENTRAL LONDON

1. Lambeth Palace
2. Westminster Bridge
3. Westminster Abbey
4. Whitehall
5. Tyburn
6. Covent Garden
7. The Temple
8. Blackfriar's Bridge
9. Swan Theatre
10. Bear Garden
11. Globe Theatre
12. London Bridge
13. St. Paul's Cathedral
14. Fortune Theatre
15. The Theatre
16. Bethlehem Hospital ("Bedlam")
17. The Tower
18. Tower Bridge
19. Waterloo Station
20. Houses of Parliament
21. Tate Gallery
22. Vauxhall Bridge
23. Victoria Station
24. Buckingham Palace
25. Royal Albert Hall
26. Kensington Palace
27. Paddington Station
28. Trafalgar Square
29. British Museum
30. Euston Station
31. St. Pancras Station
32. King's Cross Station

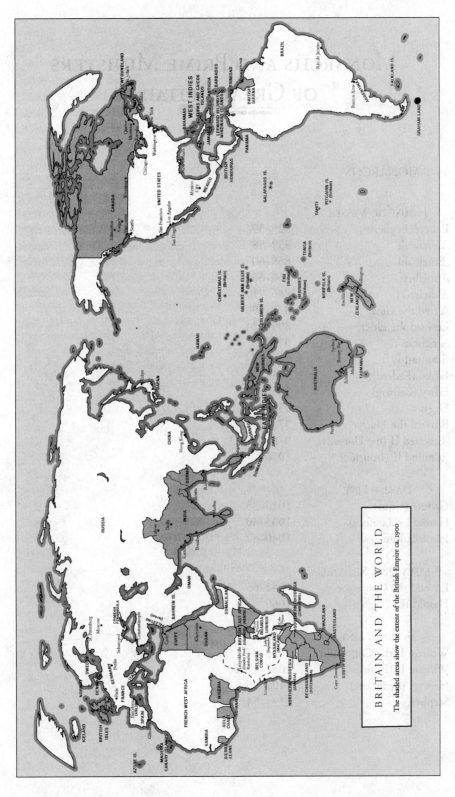

BRITAIN AND THE WORLD

The shaded areas show the extent of the British Empire ca. 1900

# Monarchs and Prime Ministers of Great Britain

## MONARCHS

### House of Wessex

| | |
|---|---|
| Egbert (Ecgberht) | 829–39 |
| Æthelwulf | 839–58 |
| Æthelbald | 858–60 |
| Æthelbert | 860–66 |
| Æthelred I | 866–71 |
| Alfred the Great | 871–99 |
| Edward the Elder | 899–924 |
| Athelstan | 924–40 |
| Edmund I | 940–46 |
| Edred (Eadred) | 946–55 |
| Edwy (Eadwig) | 955–59 |
| Edgar | 959–75 |
| Edward the Martyr | 975–78 |
| Æthelred II (the Unready) | 978–1016 |
| Edmund II (Ironside) | 1016 |

### Danish Line

| | |
|---|---|
| Canute (Cnut) | 1016–35 |
| Harold I (Harefoot) | 1035–40 |
| Hardecanute | 1040–42 |

### Wessex Line, Restored

| | |
|---|---|
| Edward the Confessor | 1042–66 |
| Harold II | 1066 |

### Norman Line

| | |
|---|---|
| William I (the Conqueror) | 1066–87 |
| William II (Rufus) | 1087–1100 |
| Henry I (Beauclerc) | 1100–35 |
| Stephen | 1135–54 |

## MONARCHS

### PLANTAGENET, ANGEVIN LINE

| | |
|---|---|
| Henry II | 1154–89 |
| Richard I (Coeur de Lion) | 1189–99 |
| John (Lackland) | 1199–1216 |
| Henry III | 1216–72 |
| Edward I (Longshanks) | 1272–1307 |
| Edward II | 1307–27 |
| Edward III | 1327–77 |
| Richard II | 1377–99 |

### PLANTAGENET, LANCASTRIAN LINE

| | |
|---|---|
| Henry IV | 1399–1413 |
| Henry V | 1413–22 |
| Henry VI | 1422–61 |

Henry VIII

### PLANTAGENET, YORKIST LINE

| | |
|---|---|
| Edward IV | 1461–83 |
| Edward V | 1483 |
| Richard III | 1483–85 |

### HOUSE OF TUDOR

| | |
|---|---|
| Henry VII | 1485–1509 |
| Henry VIII | 1509–47 |
| Edward VI | 1547–53 |
| Mary I | 1553–58 |
| Elizabeth I | 1558–1603 |

### HOUSE OF STUART

| | |
|---|---|
| James I | 1603–25 |
| Charles I | 1625–49 |

Mary I

| | |
|---|---|
| (The Commonwealth) | 1649–60 |
| Oliver Cromwell | 1649–58 |
| Richard Cromwell | 1658–59 |

## MONARCHS

### HOUSE OF STUART, RESTORED

| | |
|---|---|
| Charles II | 1660–85 |
| James II | 1685–88 |

### HOUSE OF ORANGE AND STUART

| | |
|---|---|
| William III and Mary II | 1689–94 |
| William III | 1694–1702 |

### HOUSE OF STUART

| | |
|---|---|
| Anne | 1702–14 |

### HOUSE OF BRUNSWICK, HANOVER LINE

| | |
|---|---|
| George I | 1714–27 |
| George II | 1727–60 |
| George III | 1760–1820 |

George, Prince of Wales,
Prince Regent

## PRIME MINISTERS

George III

| | |
|---|---|
| Sir Robert Walpole (Whig) | 1721–42 |
| Earl of Wilmington (Whig) | 1742–43 |
| Henry Pelham (Whig) | 1743–54 |
| Duke of Newcastle (Whig) | 1754–56 |
| Duke of Devonshire (Whig) | 1756–57 |
| Duke of Newcastle (Whig) | 1757–62 |
| Earl of Bute (Tory) | 1762–63 |
| George Grenville (Whig) | 1763–65 |
| Marquess of Rockingham (Whig) | 1765–66 |
| William Pitt the Elder (Earl of Chatham) (Whig) | 1766–68 |
| Duke of Grafton (Whig) | 1768–70 |
| Frederick North (Lord North) (Tory) | 1770–82 |
| Marquess of Rockingham (Whig) | 1782 |
| Earl of Shelburne (Whig) | 1782–83 |
| Duke of Portland | 1783 |
| William Pitt the Younger (Tory) | 1783–1801 |
| Henry Addington (Tory) | 1801–04 |
| William Pitt the Younger (Tory) | 1804–06 |
| William Wyndham Grenville (Baron Grenville) (Whig) | 1806–07 |

| MONARCHS | | PRIME MINISTERS | |
|---|---|---|---|
| | | Duke of Portland (Whig) | 1807–09 |
| George, Prince of Wales, | 1811–20 | Spencer Perceval (Tory) | 1809–12 |
| Prince Regent | | Earl of Liverpool (Tory) | 1812–27 |
| George IV | 1820–30 | | |
| | | George Canning (Tory) | 1827 |
| | | Viscount Goderich (Tory) | 1827–28 |
| | | Duke of Wellington (Tory) | 1828–30 |
| William IV | 1830–37 | | |
| | | Earl Grey (Whig) | 1830–34 |
| | | Viscount Melbourne (Whig) | 1834 |
| Victoria | 1837–1901 | | |
| | | Sir Robert Peel (Tory) | 1834–35 |
| | | Viscount Melbourne (Whig) | 1835–41 |
| | | Sir Robert Peel (Tory) | 1841–46 |
| | | Lord John Russell (later | 1846–52 |
| | | Earl) (Liberal) | |
| | | Earl of Derby (Con.) | 1852 |
| | | Earl of Aberdeen (Tory) | 1852–55 |
| | | Viscount Palmerston (Lib.) | 1855–58 |
| | | Earl of Derby (Con.) | 1858–59 |
| | | Viscount Palmerston (Lib.) | 1859–65 |
| | | Earl Russell (Liberal) | 1865–66 |
| | | Earl of Derby (Con.) | 1866–68 |
| | | Benjamin Disraeli (Con.) | 1868 |
| | | William Gladstone (Lib.) | 1868–74 |
| | | Benjamin Disraeli (Con.) | 1874–80 |
| | | William Gladstone (Lib.) | 1880–85 |
| | | Marquess of Salisbury (Con.) | 1885–86 |
| | | William Gladstone (Lib.) | 1886 |
| | | Marquess of Salisbury (Con.) | 1886–92 |
| HOUSE OF SAXE- | | William Gladstone (Lib.) | 1892–94 |
| COBURG-GOTHA | | Earl of Rosebery (Lib.) | 1894–95 |
| Edward VII | 1901–10 | Marquess of Salisbury (Con.) | 1895–1902 |
| | | Arthur Balfour (Con.) | 1902–05 |
| | | Sir Henry Campbell- | 1905–08 |
| | | Bannerman (Lib.) | |
| HOUSE OF WINDSOR | | Herbert Asquith (Lib.) | 1908–15 |
| George V | 1910–36 | | |
| | | Herbert Asquith (Lib.) | 1915–16 |

Victoria

## MONARCHS

Edward VIII      1936
George VI      1936–52

Elizabeth II      1952–

## PRIME MINISTERS

| | |
|---|---|
| Andrew Bonar Law (Con.) | 1922–23 |
| Stanley Baldwin (Con.) | 1923–24 |
| James Ramsay MacDonald (Labour) | 1924 |
| Stanley Baldwin (Con.) | 1924–29 |
| James Ramsay MacDonald (Labour) | 1929–31 |
| James Ramsay MacDonald (Labour) | 1931–35 |
| Stanley Baldwin (Con.) | 1935–37 |
| Neville Chamberlain (Con.) | 1937–40 |
| Winston Churchill (Con.) | 1940–45 |
| Winston Churchill (Con.) | 1945 |
| Clement Attlee (Labour) | 1945–51 |
| Sir Winston Churchill (Con.) | 1951–55 |
| Sir Anthony Eden (Con.) | 1955–57 |
| Harold Macmillan (Con.) | 1957–63 |
| Sir Alex Douglas-Home (Con.) | 1963–64 |
| Harold Wilson (Labour) | 1964–70 |
| Edward Heath (Con.) | 1970–74 |
| Harold Wilson (Labour) | 1974–76 |
| James Callaghan (Labour) | 1976–79 |
| Margaret Thatcher (Con.) | 1979–90 |
| John Major (Con.) | 1990–97 |
| Tony Blair (Labour) | 1997– |

# Glossary of Terms

**Accent:**  the natural emphasis (stress) speakers place on a syllable.

**Accentual Verse:**  poetry in which a line is measured only by the number of accents or stresses, not by the number of syllables.

**Accentual-Syllabic Verse:**  the most common metrical system in traditional English verse, in which a line is measured by the number of syllables and by the pattern of accented (stressed) and unaccented (unstressed) syllables.

**Aesthetes:**  members of a late nineteenth-century movement that valued "art for art's sake"—for its purely aesthetic qualities, as opposed to valuing art for the moral content it may convey, for the intellectual stimulation it may provide, or for a range of other qualities.

**Alexandrine:**  a line of verse that is 12 syllables long. In English verse, the alexandrine is always an iambic hexameter: that is, it has six iambic feet. The most-often quoted example is the second line in a couplet from Alexander Pope's "Essay on Criticism" (1711): "A needless Alexandrine ends the song / That, like a wounded snake, drags its slow length along." See also *Spenserian stanza*.

**Allegory:**  a narrative with both a literal meaning and secondary, often symbolic meaning or meanings. Allegory frequently employs personification to give concrete embodiment to abstract concepts or entities, such as feelings or personal qualities. It may also present one set of characters or events in the guise of another, using implied parallels for the purposes of satire or political comment, as in John Dryden's poem "Absalom and Achitophel."

**Alliteration:**  the grouping of words with the same initial consonant (e.g., "break, blow, burn, and make me new"). The repetition of sound acts as a connector. See also *assonance* and *consonance*.

**Alliterative Verse:**  poetry that employs alliteration of stressed syllables in each line as its chief structural principle.

**Allusion:**  a reference, often indirect or unidentified, to a person, thing, or event. A reference in one literary work to another literary work, whether to its content or its form, also constitutes an allusion.

**Ambiguity:**  an "opening" of language created by the writer to allow for multiple meanings or differing interpretations. In literature, ambiguity may be deliberately employed by the writer to enrich meaning; this differs from any unintentional, unwanted, ambiguity in non-literary prose.

**Amphibrach:**  a metrical foot with three syllables, the second of which is stressed: x / x (e.g., sensation).

**Analogy:**  a broad term that refers to our processes of noting similarities among things or events. Specific forms of analogy in poetry include *simile* and *metaphor* (see below).

**Anapaest:**  a metrical foot containing two unstressed syllables followed by one stressed syllable: xx / (e.g., underneath, intervene).

**Anglican Church / Church of England:**  formed after Henry VIII's break with Rome in the 1530s, the Church of England had acquired a permanently Protestant cast by the 1570s. There has remained considerable variation within the Church, however, with distinctions often drawn among High Church, Broad Church, and Latitudinarian. At one extreme High Church Anglicans (some of whom prefer to be known as "Anglo-Catholics") prefer relatively elaborate church rituals not dissimilar in form to those of the Roman Catholic Church and place considerable emphasis on church hierarchy, while in the other direction Latitudinarians prefer relatively informal religious services and tend far more towards egalitarianism.

**Antistrophe:**  from Greek drama, the chorus's countermovement or reply to an initial movement (strophe). See *ode* below.

**Apostrophe:**  a figure of speech (a trope; see figures of speech below) in which a writer directly addresses an object—or a dead or absent person—as if the imagined audience were actually listening.

**Archetype:**  in literature and mythology, a recurring idea, symbol, motif, character, or place. To some scholars and psychologists, an archetype represents universal human thought-patterns or experiences.

**Assonance:**  the repetition of identical or similar vowel sounds in stressed syllables in which the surrounding consonants are different: for example, "shame" and "fate"; "gale" and "cage"; or the long "i" sounds in "Beside the pumice isle..."

**Aubade:**  a lyric poem that greets or laments the arrival of dawn.

**Ballad:**  a folk song, or a poem originally recited to an audience, which tells a dramatic story based on legend or history.

**Ballad Stanza:**  a quatrain with alternating four-stress and three-stress lines, rhyming *abcb*. A variant is "common measure," in which the alternating lines are strictly iambic, and rhyme *abab*.

**Ballade:**  a fixed form most commonly characterized by only three rhymes, with an 8-line stanza rhyming *ababbcbc* and an envoy rhyming *bcbc*. Both Chaucer and Dante Gabriel Rossetti ("Ballad of the Dead Ladies") adopted this form.

**Baroque:**  powerful and heavily ornamented in style. "Baroque" is a term from the history of visual art and of music that is sometimes also used to describe certain literary styles, such as that of Richard Crashaw.

**Bathos:**  an anticlimactic effect brought about by a writer's descent from an elevated subject or tone to the ordinary or trivial.

**Benedictine Rule:**  set of instructions for monastic communities, composed by Saint Benedict of Nursia (died c. 457).

**Blank Verse:**  unrhymed lines written in iambic pentameter, a form introduced to English verse by Henry Howard, Earl of Surrey, in his translation of parts of Virgil's *Aeneid* in 1547.

**Bombast:**  inappropriately inflated or grandiose language.

**Broadside:**  individual sheet of paper printed on only one side. From the sixteenth through to the eighteenth centuries broadsides of a variety of different sorts (e.g., ballads, political tracts, short satires) were sold on the streets.

**Broken Rhyme:**  in which a multi-syllable word is split at the end of a line and continued onto the next, to allow an end-rhyme with the split syllable.

**Burlesque:**  satire of a particularly exaggerated sort, particularly that which ridicules its subject by emphasising its vulgar or ridiculous aspects.

**Caesura:**  a pause or break in a line of verse occurring where a phrase, clause, or sentence ends, and indicated in scansion by the mark II. If it occurs in the middle of the line, it is known as a "medial" caesura.

**Canon:**  in literature, those works that are commonly accepted as possessing authority or importance. In practice, "canonical" texts or authors are those that are discussed most frequently by scholars and taught most frequently in university courses.

**Canto:**  a sub-section of a long (usually epic) poem.

**Canzone:**  a short song or poem, with stanzas of equal length and an envoy.

**Carpe Diem:**  Latin (from Horace) meaning "seize the day." The idea of enjoying the moment is a common one in Renaissance love poetry. See, for example, Marvell's "To His Coy Mistress."

**Catalexis:**  the omission of unstressed syllables from a line of verse (such a line is referred to as "catalectic"). In iambic verse it is usually the first syllable of the line that is omitted; in trochaic, the last. For example, in the first stanza of Housman's "To an Athlete Dying Young" the third line is catalectic: i.e., it has dropped the first, unstressed syllable called for by the poem's iambic tetrameter form: "The time you won your town the race / We chaired you through the market-place; / Man and boy stood cheering by, / And home we brought you shoulder-high."

**Catharsis:**  the arousal through the performance of a dramatic tragedy of "emotions of pity and fear" to a point where "purgation" or "purification" occurs and the feelings are released or transformed. The concept was developed by Aristotle in his *Poetics* from an ancient Greek medical concept, and adapted by him into an aesthetic principle.

**Chiasmus:**  a figure of speech (a scheme) that reverses word order in successive parallel clauses. If the word order is A-B-C in the first clause, it becomes C-B-A in the second: for example, Donne's line "She is all states, and all princes, I" ("The Sun Rising") incorporates this reversal (though with an ellipsis).

**Classical:**   originating in or relating to ancient Greek or Roman culture. As commonly conceived, *classical* implies a strong sense of formal order. The term *neoclassical* is often used with reference to literature of the Restoration and eighteenth century that was strongly influenced by ancient Greek and Roman models.

**Closet Drama:**   a play (typically in verse) written for private performance. The term came into use in the first half of the nineteenth century.

**Colored Narrative:**   alternative term for *free indirect discourse.*

**Comedy:**   as a literary term, used originally to denote that class of ancient Greek drama in which the action ends happily. More broadly the term has been used to describe a wide variety of literary forms of a more or less light-hearted character.

*Commedia dell'arte*:   largely improvised comic performances conducted by masked performers and involving considerable physical activity. The genre of *commedia dell'arte* originated in Italy in the sixteenth century; it was influential throughout Europe for more than two centuries thereafter.

**Commonwealth:**   from the fifteenth century, a term roughly equivalent to the modern "state," but tending to emphasize the commonality of interests among all citizens. In the seventeenth century Britain was named a commonwealth under Oliver Cromwell. In the twentieth century, the term came to be applied to associations of many nations; the British Commonwealth became the successor to the British Empire.

**Conceit:**   an unusually elaborate metaphor or simile that extends beyond its original tenor and vehicle, sometimes becoming a "master" analogy for the entire poem (see, for example, Donne's "The Flea," and Robert Frost's sonnet "She is as in a field a silken tent"). Ingenious or fanciful images and comparisons were especially popular with the metaphysical poets of the seventeenth century, giving rise to the term "metaphysical conceit."

**Concrete Poetry:**   an experimental form, most popular during the 1950s and 60s, in which the printed type itself forms a visual image of the poem's key words or ideas. See also *pattern poetry, assonance.*

**Connotation:**   the implied, often unspoken meaning(s) of a given word, as distinct from its denotation, or literal meaning. Connotations may have highly emotional undertones and are usually culturally specific.

**Conservative Party:**   See *Political Parties.*

**Consonance:**   the pairing of words with similar initial and ending consonants, but with different vowel sounds (live/love, wander/wonder). See also *alliteration.*

**Convention:**   aesthetic approach, technique, or practice accepted as characteristic and appropriate for a particular form. It is a convention of certain sorts of plays, for example, that the characters speak in blank verse, of other sorts of plays that characters speak in rhymed couplets, and of still other sorts of dramatic performances that characters frequently break into song to express their feelings.

**Couplet:** a pair of rhyming lines, usually in the same meter. If they form a complete unit of thought and are grammatically complete, the lines are known as a closed couplet. See also *heroic couplet* below.

**Dactyl:** a metrical foot containing one strong stress followed by two weak stresses: / xx (e.g., muttering, helplessly). A minor form known as "double dactyls" makes use of this meter for humorous purposes, e.g., "Jiggery pokery" or "Higgledy Piggledy."

**Denotation:** See *connotation* above.

**Devolution:** process through which a degree of political power was transferred in the late twentieth and early twenty-first centuries from the British government to assemblies in Scotland and in Wales.

**Dialogue:** words spoken by characters to one another. (When a character is addressing him or her self or the audience directly, the words spoken are referred to as a *monologue*.)

**Diction:** word choice. Whether the diction of a literary work (or of a literary character) is colloquial, conversational, formal, or of some other type contributes significantly to the tone of the text as well as to characterization.

**Didacticism:** aesthetic approach emphasizing moral instruction.

**Dimeter:** a poetic line containing two metrical feet.

**Dirge:** a song or poem that mourns someone's death. See also *elegy* and *lament* below.

**Disestablishmentarianism:** movement opposing an official state-supported religion, in particular the Church of England in that role.

**Dissonance:** harsh, unmusical sounds or rhythms which poets may use deliberately to achieve certain effects.

**Dramatic Irony:** this form of irony occurs when the audience's reception of a speech by a character on the stage is affected by the possession by the audience of information not available to the character.

**Dramatic Monologue:** a lyric poem that takes the form of an utterance by a single person addressing a silent listener. The speaker may be an historical personage (as in some of Robert Browning's dramatic monologues), a figure drawn from myth or legend (as in some of Tennyson's), or an entirely imagined figure, as in Webster's "A Castaway."

**Dub Poetry:** a form of protest poetry originating in Jamaica, with its roots in dance rhythms, especially reggae, and often accompanied in performance by drums and music. See also *rap* and *hip-hop*.

**Duple Foot:** A duple foot of poetry has two syllables. The possible duple forms are iamb (in which the stress is on the second of the two syllables), trochee (in which the stress is on the first of the two syllables), spondee (in which both are stressed equally), and pyrrhic (in which both syllables are unstressed).

**Eclogue:**  now generally used simply as an alternative name for a pastoral poem. In classical times and in the early modern period, however, an *eclogue* (or *idyll*) was a specific type of pastoral poem—a dialogue or dramatic monologue involving rustic characters. (The other main sub-genre of the pastoral was the *georgic*.)

**Elegiac Stanza:**  a quatrain of iambic pentameters rhyming *abab*, often used in poems meditating on death or sorrow. The best-known example is Thomas Gray's "Elegy Written in a Country Churchyard."

**Elegy:**  a poem which formally mourns the death of a particular person (e.g., Tennyson's "In Memoriam") or in which the poet meditates on other serious subjects (e.g., Gray's "Elegy"). See also *dirge*.

**Elision:**  omitting or suppressing a letter or an unstressed syllable at the beginning or end of a word, so that a line of verse may conform to a given metrical scheme. For example, the three syllables at the beginning of Shakespeare's sonnet 129 are reduced to two by the omission of the first vowel: "Th' expense of spirit in a waste of shame." See also *syncope*.

**Ellipsis:**  the omission of a word or words necessary for the complete grammatical construction of a sentence, but not necessary for our understanding of the sentence.

**End-Rhyme:**  See *rhyme*.

**End-stopped:**  a line of poetry is said to be end-stopped when the end of the line coincides with a natural pause in the syntax, such as the conclusion of a sentence; e.g., in this couplet from Pope's "Essay on Criticism," both lines are end-stopped: "A little learning is a dangerous thing; / Drink deep, or taste not the Pierian spring." Compare this with *enjambement*.

**Enjambement:**  the "running-on" of the sense from one line of poetry to the next, with no pause created by punctuation or syntax. (The more commonly found alternative is referred to as an *end-stopped line*.)

**Envoy (Envoi):**  a stanza or half-stanza that forms the conclusion of certain French poetic forms, such as the *sestina* or the *ballade*. It often sums up or comments upon what has gone before.

**Epic:**  a lengthy narrative poem, often divided into books and sub-divided into cantos. It generally celebrates heroic deeds or events, and the style tends to be lofty and grand. Examples in English include Spenser's *The Faerie Queene* and Milton's *Paradise Lost*.

**Epic Simile:**  an elaborate simile, developed at such length that the vehicle of the comparison momentarily displaces the primary subject with which it is being compared.

**Epigram:**  a very short poem, sometimes in closed couplet form, characterized by pointed wit.

**Epigraph:**  a quotation placed at the beginning of a discourse to indicate or foreshadow the theme.

**Epiphany:** a moment at which matters of significance are suddenly illuminated for a literary character (or for the reader), typically triggered by something small and seemingly of little import. The term first came into wide currency in connection with the fiction of James Joyce.

**Episodic Plot:** plot comprising a variety of episodes that are only loosely connected by threads of story material (as opposed to plots that present one or more continually unfolding narratives where successive episodes build one on another).

**Epithalamion:** a poem celebrating a wedding. The best-known example in English is probably Edmund Spenser's "Epithalamion" (1595).

**Eulogy:** text expressing praise, especially for a distinguished person recently deceased.

**Euphemism:** mode of expression through which aspects of reality considered to be vulgar, crudely physical, or unpleasant are referred to indirectly rather than named explicitly. A variety of euphemisms exist for the processes of urination and defecation; *passed away* is often used as a euphemism for *died*. (The word *euphemism* has the same root as *Euphuism* (see below), but has taken on a different meaning.)

**Euphony:** pleasant, musical sounds or rhythms—the opposite of dissonance.

**Euphuism:** In the late sixteenth century John Lyly published a prose romance, *Euphues*, which employed a style that featured long sentences filled with balanced phrases and clauses, many of them adding little to the content. This highly mannered style was popular in the court of Elizabeth I for a few years following the publication of Lyly's famous work, and the style became known as *Euphuism*.

**European Union:** (EU) Group of nations formed in 1993 as the successor to the European Economic Community (Common Market). Britain first applied for membership in the latter in 1961; at first its efforts to join were blocked by the French government, but in 1973 Prime Minister Edward Heath successfully negotiated Britain's entry into the group. Britain has resisted some moves towards full integration with the European community, in particular retaining its own currency when other European nations adopted the Euro on 1 January 2002.

**Exchequer:** In earlier eras, the central royal financial office, responsible for receiving and keeping track of crown revenues. In later eras, part of the bureaucracy equivalent to the Ministry of Finance in Canada or the Treasury in the United States (the modern post of Chancellor of the Exchequer is equivalent to the American post of Secretary of the Treasury, the Canadian post of Minister of Finance or the Australian post of Treasurer).

**Exposition:** the setting out of material in an ordered form, either in speech or in writing. In a play those parts of the action that do not occur on stage but are rather recounted by the characters are frequently described as being presented in exposition. Similarly, when the background narrative is filled in near the beginning of a novel, such material is often described as having been presented in exposition. Somewhat confusingly, however, the term "expository prose" is usually used with reference not to fiction but to the setting forth of arguments or descriptions in the context of essays or other works of prose non-fiction.

**Eye-Rhyme:**   See *rhyme* below.

**Feminine Ending:**   the ending of a line of poetry on an "extra," and, especially, on an unstressed syllable. See, for example, the first line of Keat's "Ode on a Grecian Urn": "A thing of beauty is a joy forever," a line of iambic pentameter in which the final foot is an amphibrach rather than an iamb.

**Feminine Rhyme:**   See *rhyme* below.

**Figures of Speech:**   deliberate, highly concentrated uses of language to achieve particular purposes or effects on an audience. There are two kinds of figures: schemes and tropes. Schemes involve changes in word-sound and word-order, such as *alliteration* and *chiasmus*. Tropes play on our understandings of words to extend, alter, or transform meaning, as in *metaphor* and *personification*.

**First-Person Narrative:**   narrative recounted using *I* and *me*. See also *narrative perspective*.

**Fixed Forms:**   the term applied to a number of poetic forms and stanzaic patterns, many derived from French models, such as *ballade, rondeau, sestina, triolet,* and *villanelle*. Other "fixed forms" include the *sonnet, rhyme royal, haiku,* and *ottava rima*.

**Folio:**   largest of several sizes of book page commonly used in the first few centuries after the introduction of the printing press. A folio size results from sheets of paper of at least 14 inches by 20 inches being folded in half (a folio page size will thus be at least 7 inches by 10 inches). When the same sheet is folded twice a quarto is produced, and when it is folded 3 times an octavo.

**Foot:**   a unit of a line of verse which contains a particular combination of stressed and unstressed syllables. Dividing a line into metrical feet (*iambs, trochees,* etc.), then counting the number of feet per line, is part of *scansion*. See also *meter*.

**Franklin:**   in the late medieval period, a landholder of free status, but ranking below the gentry.

**Free Indirect Discourse:**   in prose fiction, commentary in which a seemingly objective and omniscient narrative voice assumes the point of view of one or more characters. When we hear through the third person narrative voice of Jane Austen's *Pride and Prejudice*, for example, that Mr. Darcy "was the proudest, most disagreeable man in the world, and every body hoped that he would never come there again," the narrative voice has assumed the point of view of "every body" in the community; we as readers are not meant to take it that Mr. Darcy is indeed the most disagreeable man in the world. Similarly, in the following passage from the same novel, we are likely to take it to read it as being the view of the character Charlotte that marriage is "the only honourable provision for well-educated young women of small fortune," not to take it to be an objective statement of perceived truth on the part of the novel's third person narrative voice:

> [Charlotte's] reflections were in general satisfactory. Mr. Collins to be sure was neither sensible nor agreeable; his society was irksome, and his attachment to her must be imaginary. But still he would be her husband. Without thinking highly either of men or of matrimony, marriage had always been her object; it was the only honourable provision for well-educated young women of small fortune, and however uncertain of giving happiness, must be their pleasantest preservative from want.

The term free indirect discourse may also be applied to situations in which it may not be entirely clear if the thoughts expressed emanate from the character, the narrator, or some combination of the two. (In the above-quoted passage expressing Charlotte's thoughts, indeed, some might argue that the statement concerning marriage should be taken as the expression of a belief that the narrative voice shares, at least in part.)

**Free Verse:**  poetry that does not follow any regular meter, line length, or rhyming scheme. In many respects, though, free verse follows the complex natural "rules" and rhythmic patterns (or cadences) of speech.

**Gaelic:**  Celtic language, variants of which are spoken in Ireland and Scotland.

**Genre:**  a particular literary form. The concept of genre may be used with different levels of generality. At the most general, poetry, drama, and prose fiction are distinguished as separate genres. At a lower level of generality various sub-genres are frequently distinguished, such as (within drama) comedy and tragedy, or, at a still lower level of generality, Elizabethan domestic tragedy, Edwardian drawing-room comedy, and so on.

**Georgic:**  (from Virgil's *Georgics*) a poem that celebrates the natural wealth of the countryside and advises how to cultivate and live in harmony with it. Pope's *Windsor Forest* and James Thomson's *Seasons* are classed as georgics. They were often said to make up, with eclogues, the two alliterative forms of pastoral poetry.

**Ghazal:**  derived from Persian and Indian precedents, the ghazal presents a series of thoughts in closed couplets joined by a simple rhyme-scheme: *ab bb cb eb fb*, etc.

**Gothic:**  in architecture and the visual arts, a term used to describe styles prevalent from the twelfth to the fourteenth centuries, but in literature a term used to describe work with a sinister or grotesque tone that seeks to evoke a sense of terror on the part of the reader or audience. Gothic literature originated as a genre in the eighteenth century with works such as Horace Walpole's *The Castle of Otranto*. To some extent the notion of the medieval itself then carried with it associations of the dark and the grotesque, but from the beginning an element of intentional exaggeration (sometimes verging on self-parody) attached itself to the genre. The Gothic trend of youth culture that began in the late twentieth century is less clearly associated with the medieval, but shares with the various varieties of Gothic literature (from Walpole in the eighteenth century, to Bram Stoker in the early twentieth, to Stephen King and Anne Rice in the late twentieth) a fondness for the sensational and the grotesque, as well as a propensity to self-parody.

**Guilds:**  non-clerical associations that arose in the late Anglo-Saxon period, devoted both to social purposes (such as the organization of feasts for the members) and to piety. In the later medieval period guilds developed strong associations with particular occupations.

**Haiku:**  a Japanese form, using three unrhymed lines of five, seven, and five syllables. Conventionally, it uses precise, concentrated images to suggest states of feeling.

**Heptameter:**  a line containing seven metrical feet.

**Heroic Couplet:**   a pair of rhymed iambic pentameters, so called because the form was much used in seventeenth and eighteenth-century poems and plays on heroic subjects.

**Hexameter:**   a line containing six metrical feet.

**Home Rule:**   movement dedicated to making Ireland politically independent from Britain.

**Horatian Ode:**   inspired by the work of the Roman poet Horace, an ode that is usually calm and meditative in tone, and homostrophic (i.e., having regular stanzas) in form. Keats's odes are English examples.

**House of Commons:**   elected legislative body, in Britain currently consisting of six hundred and fifty-nine members of Parliament. See also *Parliament*.

**House of Lords:**   the "Upper House" of the British Houses of Parliament. Since the nineteenth century the House of Lords has been far less powerful than the elected House of Commons. The House of Lords is currently made up of both hereditary peers (Lords whose title is passed on from generation to generation) and life peers. As a result of legislation enacted by the Labour government of Tony Blair, the role of hereditary peers in Parliament is being phased out.

**Humors:**   The four humors were believed in until the sixteenth and seventeenth centuries to be elements in the makeup of all humans; a person's temperament was thought to be determined by the way in which the humors were combined. When the *choleric* humor was dominant, the person would tend towards anger; when the *sanguine* humor was dominant, towards pleasant affability; when the *phlegmatic* humor was dominant, towards a cool and calm attitude and/or a lack of feeling or enthusiasm; and when the *melancholic* humor was dominant, towards withdrawal and melancholy.

**Hymn:**   a song whose theme is usually religious, in praise of divinity. Literary hymns may praise more secular subjects.

**Hyperbole:**   a *figure of speech* (a trope) that deliberately exaggerates or inflates meaning to achieve particular effects, such as the irony in A.E. Housman's claim (from "Terence, this is stupid stuff") that "malt does more than Milton can / To justify God's ways to man."

**Iamb:**   the most common metrical foot in English verse, containing one unstressed syllable followed by a stressed syllable: x / (e.g., between, achieve).

**Idyll:**   traditionally, a short pastoral poem that idealizes country life, conveying impressions of innocence and happiness.

**Image:**   the recreation in words of objects perceived by the senses, sometimes thought of as "pictures," although other senses besides sight are involved. Besides this literal application, the term also refers more generally to the descriptive effects of figurative language, especially in *metaphor* and *simile*.

**Imagism:**   a poetic movement that was popular mainly in the second decade of the twentieth century. The goal of Imagist poets (such as H.D. and Ezra Pound in their early work) was to represent emotions or impressions through highly concentrated imagery.

**In Memoriam Stanza:**  a four-line stanza in iambic tetrameter, rhyming *abba*: the type of stanza used by Tennyson in *In Memoriam*.

**Incantation:**  a chant or recitation of words that are believed to have magical power. A poem can achieve an "incantatory" effect through a compelling rhyme scheme and other repetitive patterns.

**Interlocking Rhyme:**  See *rhyme*.

**Internal Rhyme:**  See *rhyme*.

**Irony:**  a subtle form of humor in which a statement is understood to convey a quite different (and often entirely opposite) meaning. A writer achieves this by carefully making sure that the statement occurs in a context which undermines or twists the statement's "literal" meaning. *Hyperbole* and *litotes* are often used for ironic effect. *Sarcasm* is a particularly strong or crude form of irony (usually spoken), in which the meaning is conveyed largely by the tone of voice adopted; something said sarcastically is meant clearly to imply its opposite.

**Labour Party:**  See *Political Parties.*

**Lament:**  a poem which expresses profound regret or grief either because of a death, or because of the loss of a former, happier state.

**Language Poetry:**  a movement that defies the usual lyric and narrative conventions of poetry, and that challenges the structures and codes of everyday language. Often seen as both politically and aesthetically subversive, its roots lie in the works of modernist writers like Ezra Pound and Gertrude Stein.

**Liberal Party:**  See *Political Parties.*

**Litotes:**  a *figure of speech* (a trope) in which a writer deliberately uses understatement to highlight the importance of an argument, or to convey an ironic attitude.

**Liturgical Drama:**  drama based on and/or incorporating text from the liturgy—the text recited during religious services.

**Lollard:**  member of the group of radical Christians that took its inspiration from the ideas of John Wyclif (c. 1330–84). The Lollards, in many ways precursors of the Protestant Reformation, advocated making the Bible available to all, and dedication to the principles of evangelical poverty in imitation of Christ.

**Luddites:**  protestors against the mechanization of industry on the grounds that it was leading to the loss of employment and to an increase in poverty. In the years 1811 to 1816 there were several Luddite protests in which machines were destroyed.

**Lyric:**  a poem, usually short, expressing an individual speaker's feelings or private thoughts. Originally a song performed with accompaniment on a lyre, the lyric poem is often noted for musicality of rhyme and rhythm. The lyric genre includes a variety of forms, including the *sonnet*, the *ode*, the *elegy*, the *madrigal*, the *aubade*, the *dramatic monologue*, and the *hymn*.

**Madrigal:** a lyric poem, usually short and focusing on pastoral or romantic themes. A madrigal is often set to music.

**Masculine Ending:** a metrical line ending on a stressed syllable. *Masculine Rhyme*: see *rhyme*.

**Masque:** an entertainment typically combining music and dance, with a limited script, extravagant costumes and sets, and often incorporating spectacular special effects. Masques, which were performed before court audiences in the early seventeenth century, often focused on royal themes and frequently drew on classical mythology.

**Mass:** Within Christianity, a church service that includes the sacrament of the Eucharist (Holy Communion), in which bread and wine are consumed which are believed by those of many Christian denominations to have been transubstantiated into the body and blood of Christ. Anglicans (Episcopalians) are more likely to believe the bread and wine merely symbolizes the body and blood.

**Melodrama:** originally a term used to describe nineteenth-century-plays featuring sensational story lines and a crude separation of characters into moral categories, with the pure and virtuous pitted against evil villains. Early melodramas employed background music throughout the action of the play as a means of heightening the emotional response of the audience. By extension, certain sorts of prose fictions or poems are often described as having melodramatic elements.

**Metaphor:** a *figure of speech* (in this case, a trope) in which a comparison is made or identity is asserted between two unrelated things or actions without the use of "like" or "as." The primary subject is known as the *tenor*; to illuminate its nature, the writer links it to wholly different images, ideas, or actions referred to as the *vehicle*. Unlike a *simile*, which is a direct comparison of two things, a metaphor "fuses" the separate qualities of two things, creating a new idea. For example, Shakespeare's "Let slip the dogs of war" is a metaphorical statement. The tenor, or primary subject, is "war"; the vehicle of the metaphor is the image of hunting dogs released from their leash. The line fuses the idea of war with the qualities of ravening bloodlust associated with hunting dogs.

**Metaphysical Poets:** a group of seventeenth-century English poets, notably Donne, Cowley, Marvell, and Herbert, who employed unusual difficult imagery and *conceits* (see above) in order to develop intellectual and religious themes. The term was first applied to these writers to mark as far-fetched their use of philosophical and scientific ideas in a poetic context.

**Meter:** the pattern of stresses, syllables, and pauses that constitutes the regular rhythm of a line of verse. The meter of a poem written in the English accentual-syllabic tradition is determined by identifying the stressed and unstressed syllables in a line of verse, and grouping them into recurring units known as feet. See *accent*, *accentual-syllabic*, *caesura*, *elision*, and *scansion*. For some of the better known meters, see *iamb*, *trochee*, *dactyl*, *anapaest*, and *spondee*. See also *monometer*, *dimeter*, *trimeter*, *tetrameter*, *pentameter*, and *hexameter*.

**Methodist:** Protestant denomination formed in the eighteenth century as part of the religious movement led by John and Charles Wesley. Originally a movement within the Church of England, Methodism entailed enthusiastic evangelism, a strong emphasis on free will, and a strict regimen of Christian living.

**Metonymy:**  a *figure of speech* (a trope), meaning "change of name," in which a writer refers to an object or idea by substituting the name of another object or idea closely associated with it: for example, the substitution of "crown" for monarchy, "the press" for journalism, or "the pen" for writing. *Synecdoche* (see below) is a kind of metonymy.

**Mock-heroic:**  a style applying the elevated diction and vocabulary of epic poetry to low or ridiculous subjects. An example is Alexander Pope's "The Rape of the Lock."

**Monologue:**  words spoken by a character to him or herself or to an audience directly.

**Monometer:**  a line containing one metrical foot.

**Mood:**  This can describe the writer's attitude, implied or expressed, towards the subject (see *tone* below); or it may refer to the atmosphere that a writer creates in a passage of description or narration.

**Motif:**  an idea, image, action, or plot element that recurs throughout a literary work, creating new levels of meaning and strengthening structural coherence. The term is taken from music, where it describes recurring melodies or themes. See also *theme*.

**Narrative Perspective:**  in fiction, the point of view from which the story is narrated. A first-person narrative is recounted using *I* and *me*, whereas a third person narrative is recounted using *he, she, they*, and so on. When a narrative is written in the third person and the narrative voice evidently "knows" all that is being done and thought, the story is typically described as being recounted by an "omniscient narrator."

**Neoclassical:**  adapted from or substantially influenced by the cultures of ancient Greece and Rome. The term *neoclassical* is often used to describe the ideals of Restoration and eighteenth-century writers and artists who looked to ancient Greek and Roman civilization for models.

**Nobility:**  privileged class, the members of which are distinguished by the holding of titles. Dukes, Marquesses, Earls, Viscounts, and Barons (in that order of precedence) are all holders of hereditary titles—that is to say, in the British patrilineal tradition, titles passed on from generation to generation to the eldest son. The title of Baronet, also hereditary, was added to this list by James I. Holders of non-hereditary titles include Knights and Dames.

**Nonconformist:**  general term used to describe one who does subscribe to the Church of England.

**Nonsense Verse:**  light, humorous poetry which contradicts logic, plays with the absurd, and invents words for amusing effects. Lewis Carroll is one of the best-known practitioners of nonsense verse.

**Octave:**  also known as "octet," the first eight lines in an Italian/Petrarchan sonnet, rhyming *abbaabba*. See also *sestet* and *sonnet*.

**Octosyllabic:**  a line of poetry with eight syllables, as in iambic tetrameter.

**Ode:**  originally a classical poetic form, used by the Greeks and Romans to convey serious themes. English poetry has evolved three main forms of ode: the Pindaric (imitative of the odes of the Greek poet Pindar); the Horatian (modeled on the work of the Roman writer Horace); and the irregular ode.

The Pindaric ode was an irregular stanza in English, has a tripartite structure of "strophe," "antistrophe," and "epode" (meaning turn, counterturn, and stand), modeled on the songs and movements of the Chorus in Greek drama. The Horatian ode is more personal, reflective, and literary, and employs a pattern of repeated stanzas. The irregular ode, as its name implies, avoids a recurrent stanza pattern, and is sometimes irregular in line length also (see, for example, Wordsworth's "Ode: Intimations of Immortality").

**Onomatopoeia:** a *figure of speech* (a scheme) in which a word "imitates" a sound, or in which the sound of a word seems to reflect its meaning.

**Ottava Rima:** an 8-line stanza, usually in iambic pentameter, with the rhyme scheme *abababcc*. For an example, see Byron's *Don Juan*, or Yeats's "Sailing to Byzantium."

**Oxymoron:** a *figure of speech* (a trope) in which two words whose meanings seem contradictory are placed together, a paradox: for example, the phrase "darkness visible," from Milton's *Paradise Lost*.

**Paean:** a triumphant, celebratory song, often associated with a military victory.

**Pale:** in the medieval period, term for a protective zone around a fortress. As of the year 1500 three of these had been set up to guard frontiers of territory controlled by England—surrounding Calais in France, Berwick-upon-Tweed on the Scottish frontier, and Dublin in Ireland. The Dublin Pale was the largest of the three, and the term remained in use for a longer period there.

**Pantoum:** a poem in linked quatrains that rhyme *abab*. The second and fourth lines of one stanza are repeated as the first and third lines of the stanza that follows. In the final stanza the pattern is reversed: the second line repeats the third line of the first stanza, the fourth and final line repeats the first line of the first stanza.

**Parliament:** in Britain, the legislative body, comprising both the House of Commons and the House of Lords. Since the eighteenth century, the most powerful figure in the British government has been the Prime Minister rather than the monarch, the House of Commons has been the dominant body in Parliament, and members of the House of Commons have been organized in political parties. Since the mid-nineteenth century the effective executive in the British Parliamentary system has been the Cabinet, each member of which is typically in charge of a department of government. Unlike the American system, the British Parliamentary system (sometimes called the "Westminster system," after the location of the Houses of Parliament) brings together the executive and legislative functions of government, with the Prime Minister leading the government party in the House of Commons as well as directing the cabinet. By convention it is understood that the House of Lords will not contravene the wishes of the House of Commons in any fundamental way, though the "Upper House," as it is often referred to, may sometimes modify or reject legislation.

**Parody:** a close, usually mocking imitation of a particular literary work, or of the well-known style of a particular author, in order to expose or magnify weaknesses. Parody is a form of satire—that is, humor that may ridicule and scorn its object.

**Pastiche:** a discourse which borrows or imitates other writers' characters, forms, style, or ideas. Unlike a parody, a pastiche is usually intended as a compliment to the original writer.

**Pastoral:**   in general, pertaining to country life; in prose, drama, and poetry, a stylized type of writing that idealizes the lives and innocence of country people, particularly shepherds and shepherdesses. Also see *eclogue, georgic, idyll*, above.

**Pastoral Elegy:**   a poem in which the poet uses the pastoral style to lament the death of a friend, usually represented as a shepherd. Milton's "Lycidas" provides a good example of the form, including its use of such conventions as an invocation of the muse and a procession of mourners.

**Pathetic Fallacy:**   a form of personification in which inanimate objects are given human emotions: for example, rain clouds "weeping." The word "fallacy" in this connection is intended to suggest the distortion of reality or the false emotion that may result from an exaggerated use of personification.

**Pathos:**   the emotional quality of a discourse; or the ability of a discourse to appeal to our emotions. It is usually applied to the mood conveyed by images of pain, suffering, or loss that arouse feelings of pity or sorrow in the reader.

**Pattern Poetry:**   a predecessor of modern concrete poetry, in which the shape of the poem on the page is intended to suggest or imitate an aspect of the poem's subject. George Herbert's "Easter Wings" is an example of pattern poetry.

**Penny Dreadful:**   Victorian term for a cheap and poorly produced work of short fiction, usually of a sensational nature.

**Pentameter:**   a line of verse containing five metrical feet.

**Performance Poetry:**   poetry composed primarily for oral performance, often very theatrical in nature. See also *dub poetry* and *rap*.

**Persona:**   the assumed identity or "speaking voice" that a writer projects in a discourse. The term "persona" literally means "mask." Even when a writer speaks in the first person, we should be aware that the attitudes or opinions we hear may not necessarily be those of the writer in real life.

**Personification:**   a *figure of speech* (a trope), also known as "prosopopoeia," in which a writer refers to inanimate objects, ideas, or animals as if they were human, or creates a human figure to represent an abstract entity such as Philosophy or Peace.

**Petrarchan Sonnet:**   the earliest form of the sonnet, also known as the Italian sonnet, with an 8-line octave and a 6-line sestet. The Petrarchan sonnet traditionally focuses on love and descriptions of physical beauty.

**Phoneme:**   a linguistic term denoting the smallest unit of sound that it is possible to distinguish. The words *fun* and *phone* each have three phonemes, though one has three letters and one has five. (Each makes up a single syllable.)

**Pindaric:**   See *ode*.

**Plot:**   the organization of story materials within a literary work. The order in which story material is presented (especially causes and consequences); the inclusion of elements that allow or encourage the reader or audience to form expectations as to what is likely to happen; the decision to present some story material through exposition rather than in more extended form as part of the main action of the narrative—all these are matters of plotting.

**Political Parties:**  The party names "Whig" and "Tory" began to be used in the late seventeenth century; before that time members of the House of Commons acted individually or through shifting and very informal factions. At first the Whigs and Tories had little formal organization either, but by the mid-eighteenth century parties had acknowledged leaders, and the leader of the party with the largest number of members in the House of Commons had begun to be recognized as the Prime Minister. The Tories evolved into the modern Conservative Party, and the Whigs into the Liberal Party. In the late nineteenth century the Labour Party was formed in an effort to provide better representation in Parliament for the working class, and since the 1920s Labour and the Conservatives have alternated as the party of government, with the Liberals reduced to third-party status. (Since 1988, when the Liberals merged with a breakaway faction from Labour known as the Social Democrats, this third party has been named the Liberal Democrats.)

**Pre-Raphaelites:**  originally a group of Victorian artists and writers, formed in 1848. Their goal was to revive what they considered the simpler, fresher, more natural art that existed before Raphael (1483-1520). The poet Dante Gabriel Rossetti was one of the founders of the group.

**Presbyterian:**  term applied to a group of Protestants (primarily English and Scottish) who advocated replacing the traditional hierarchical church in which bishops and archbishops governed lower level members of the clergy with a system in which all presbyters (or ministers) would be equal. The Presbyterians, originally led by John Knox, were strongly influenced by the ideas of John Calvin.

**Prose Poem:**  a poetic discourse that uses prose formats (e.g., it may use margins and paragraphs rather than line breaks or stanzas) yet is written with the kind of attention to language, rhythm and cadence that characterizes verse.

**Prosody:**  the study and analysis of meter, rhythm, rhyme, stanzaic pattern, and other devices of versification.

**Protagonist:**  the central character in a literary work.

**Prothalamion:**  a wedding song; a term coined by the poet Edmund Spenser, adapted from "epithalamion" (see above).

**Public School:**  See *schools* below.

**Pun:**  a play on words, in which a word with two or more distinct meanings, or two words with similar sounds, may create humorous ambiguities. Also known as *paranomasia*.

**Puritan:**  term, originally applied only in a derogatory fashion but later widely accepted as descriptive, referring to those in England who favored religious reforms that went beyond those instituted as part of the Protestant Reformation, or, more generally, who were more forceful and uncompromising in pressing for religious purity both within the Church and in society as a whole.

**Pyrrhic:**  a metrical foot containing two weak stresses: xx.

**Quadrivium:** group of four academic subjects (arithmetic, astronomy, geometry, and music) that made up part of the university coursework in the Middle Ages. There were studied after the more basic subjects of the *Trivium*.

**Quantitative Meter:** a metrical system used by Greek and Roman poets, in which a line of verse was measured by the "quantity," or length of sound of each syllable. A foot was measured in terms of syllables classed as long or short.

**Quantity:** duration of syllables in poetry. The line "There is a Garden in her face" (the first line from the poem of the same name by Thomas Campion) is characterized by the short quantities of the syllables. The last line of Thomas Hardy's "During Wind and Rain" has the same number of syllables as the line by Campion, but the quantities of the syllables are much longer—in other words, the line take much longer to say: "Down their carved names the rain drop ploughs."

**Quatrain:** a four-line stanza, usually rhymed.

**Quintet:** a five-line stanza. Sometimes given as *quintain*.

**Rap:** originally coined to describe informal conversation, "rap" now usually describes a style of performance poetry in which a poet will chant rhymed verse, sometimes improvised and usually with musical accompaniment that has a heavy beat.

**Realism:** as a literary term, the presentation through literature of material closely resembling real life. As notions both of what constitutes "real life" and of how it may be most faithfully represented in literature have varied widely, "realism" has taken a variety of meanings. The term *naturalistic* has sometimes been used a synonym for *realistic*; *naturalism* originated in the nineteenth century as a term denoting a form of realism focusing in particular on grim, unpleasant, or ugly aspects of the real.

**Refrain:** one or more words or lines repeated at regular points throughout a poem, often at the end of each stanza or group of stanzas. Sometimes a whole stanza may be repeated to create a refrain, like the chorus in a song.

**Reggae:** a style of heavily-rhythmic music from the West Indies with lyrics that are colloquial in language and often anti-establishment in content and flavor. First popularized in the 1960s and 1970s, reggae has had a lasting influence on performance poetry, rap, and dub.

**Rhetoric:** in classical Greece and Rome, the art of persuasion and public speaking. From the Middle Ages onwards, the study of rhetoric gave greater attention to style, particularly figures of speech. Today in poetics, the term rhetoric may encompass not only figures of speech, but also the persuasive effects of forms, sounds and word choices.

**Rhyme:** the repetition of identical or similar sounds, usually in pairs and generally at the ends of metrical lines.

    **End-rhyme:** a rhyming word or syllable at the end of a line.

    **Eye Rhyme:** rhyming that pairs words whose spellings are alike but whose pronunciations are different: for example, though/slough.

**Feminine Rhyme:**  a two-syllable (also known as "double") rhyme. The first syllable is stressed and the second unstressed: for example, hasty/tasty. See also *triple rhyme* below.

**Interlocking Rhyme:**  the repetition of rhymes from one stanza to the next, creating links that add to the poem's continuity and coherence. Examples may be found in Shelley's use of *terza rima* in "Ode to the West Wind" and in Dylan Thomas's villanelle "Do Not Go Gentle Into That Good Night."

**Internal Rhyme:**  the placement of rhyming words within lines so that at least two words in a line rhyme with each other.

**Masculine Rhyme:**  a correspondence of sound between the final stressed syllables at the end of two or more lines, as in grieve/leave, arr-ive/sur-vive.

**Slant Rhyme:**  an imperfect or partial rhyme (also known as "near" or "half" rhyme) in which the final consonants of stressed syllables match but the vowel sounds do not. E.g., spoiled / spilled, taint / stint.

**Triple Rhyme:**  a three-syllable rhyme in which the first syllable of each rhyme-word is stressed and the other two unstressed (e.g., lottery / coterie).

**True Rhyme:**  a rhyme in which everything but the initial consonant matches perfectly in sound and spelling.

**Rhyme Royal:**  a stanza of seven iambic pentameters, with a rhyme-scheme of *ababbcc*. This is also known as the Chaucerian stanza, as Chaucer was the first English poet to use this form. See also *septet*.

**Rhythm:**  in speech, the arrangement of stressed and unstressed syllables creates units of sound. In song or verse, these units usually form a regular rhythmic pattern, a kind of beat, described in prosody as *meter*.

**Romanticism:**  a major social and cultural movement, originating in Europe, that shaped much of Western artistic thought in the late eighteenth and nineteenth centuries. Opposing the ideal of controlled, rational order of the Enlightenment, Romanticism emphasizes the importance of spontaneous self-expression, emotion, and personal experience in producing art. In Romanticism, the "natural" is privileged over the conventional or the artificial.

**Rondeau:**  a fifteen-line poem, generally octosyllabic, with only two rhymes throughout its three stanzas, and an unrhymed refrain at the end of the ninth and fifteenth lines, repeating part of the opening line.

**Sarcasm:**  See *irony*.

**Satire:**  literary work designed to make fun of or seriously criticize its subject. According to many literary theories of the Renaissance and neoclassical periods, the ridicule through satire of a certain sort of behavior may function for the reader or audience as a corrective of such behavior.

**Scansion:**   the formal analysis of patterns of rhythm and rhyme in poetry. Each line of verse will have a certain number of fairly regular "beats" consisting of alternating stressed and unstressed syllables. To "scan" a poem is to count the beats in each line, to mark stressed and unstressed syllables and indicate their combination into "feet," to note pauses, and to identify rhyme schemes with letters of the alphabet.

**Scheme:**   See *figures of speech*.

**Schools:**   In the sixteenth and seventeenth centuries the different forms of school in England included Cathedral schools (often founded with a view to the education of members of the choir); grammar schools (often founded by towns or by guilds, and teaching a much broader curriculum than the modern sense of "grammar" might suggest, private schools, operated by private individuals out of private residences; and public schools, which (like the private schools and the grammar schools) operated independent of any church authority, but unlike the grammar schools and private schools were organized as independent charities, and often offered free education. Over the centuries certain of these public schools, while remaining not-for-profit institutions, began to accept fee-paying students and to adopt standards that made them more and more exclusive. In the eighteenth and nineteenth century attendance at such prestigious public boarding schools as Eton, Westminster, and Winchester had become almost exclusively the preserve of the upper classes; by the nineteenth century such "public" schools were the equivalent of private schools in North America. Though a few girls attended some early grammar schools, the greater part of this educational system was for boys only. Though a number of individuals of earlier periods were concerned to increase the number of private schools for girls, the movement to create a parallel girls' system of public schools and grammar schools dates from the later nineteenth century.

**Septet:**   a stanza containing seven lines.

**Serf:**   in the medieval period, a person of unfree status, typically engaged in working the land.

**Sestet:**   a six-line stanza that forms the second grouping of lines in an Italian / Petrarchan sonnet, following the octave. See *sonnet* and *sestina*.

**Sestina:**   an elaborate unrhymed poem with six 6-line stanzas and a 3-line envoy.

**Shire:**   originally a multiple estate; since the late medieval period a larger territory forming an administrative unit—also referred to as a county.

**Simile:**   a *figure of speech* (a trope) which makes an explicit comparison between a particular object and another object or idea that is similar in some (often unexpected) way. A simile always uses "like" or "as" to signal the connection. Compare with *metaphor* above.

**Sonnet:**   a highly structured lyric poem, which normally has fourteen lines of iambic pentameter. We can distinguish four major variations of the sonnet.

   **Italian/Petrarchan:**   named for the 14th-century Italian poet Petrarch, has an octave rhyming *abbaabba*, and a sestet rhyming *cdecde*, or *cdcdcd* (other arrangements are possible here). Usually, a turn in argument takes place between octave and sestet.

**Miltonic:**  developed by Milton and similar to the Petrarchan in rhyme scheme, but eliminating the turn after the octave, thus giving greater unity to the poem's structure of thought.

**Shakespearean:**  often called the English sonnet, this form has three quatrains and a couplet. The quatrains rhyme internally but do not interlock: *abab cdcd efef gg*. The turn may occur after the second quatrain, but is usually revealed in the final couplet. Shakespeare's sonnets are the best-known examples of this form.

**Spenserian:**  after Edmund Spenser, who developed the form in his sonnet cycle *Amoretti*. This sonnet form has three quatrains linked through interlocking rhyme, and a separately rhyming couplet: *abab bcbc cdcd ee*.

**Speaker:**  in the late medieval period, a member of the Commons in Parliament who spoke on behalf of that entire group. (The Commons first elected a Speaker in 1376.) In later eras the role of Speaker became one of chairing debates in the House of Commons and arbitrating disputes over matters of procedure.

**Spenserian Stanza:**  a nine-line stanza, with eight iambic pentameters and a concluding alexandrine, rhyming *ababbcbcc*.

**Spondee:**  a metrical foot containing two strong stressed syllables: // (e.g., blind mouths).

**Sprung Rhythm:**  a modern variation of accentual verse, created by the English poet Gerard Manley Hopkins, in which rhythms are determined largely by the number of strong stresses in a line, without regard to the number of unstressed syllables. Hopkins felt that sprung rhythm more closely approximated the natural rhythms of speech than did conventional poetry.

**Stanza:**  any lines of verse that are grouped together in a poem and separated from other similarly-structured groups by a space. In metrical poetry, stanzas share metrical and rhyming patterns; however, stanzas may also be formed on the basis of thought, as in irregular odes. Conventional stanza forms include the *tercet*, the *quatrain*, *rhyme royal*, the *Spenserian stanza*, the *ballad stanza*, and *ottava rima*.

**Stream of Consciousness:**  narrative technique that attempts to convey in prose fiction a sense of the progression of the full range of thoughts and sensations occurring within a character's mind. Twentieth-century pioneers in the use of the stream of consciousness technique include Dorothy Richardson, Virginia Woolf, and James Joyce.

**Stress:**  See *accent*.

**Strophe:**  the first stanza in a Pindaric ode. This is followed by an *antistrophe* (see above), which presents the same metrical pattern and rhyme scheme, and finally by an *epode*, differing in meter from the preceding stanzas. Upon completion of this "triad," the entire sequence can recur. *Strophe* may also describe a stanza or other subdivision in other kinds of poem.

**Sublime:**  a concept, most popular in eighteenth-century England, of the qualities of grandeur, power, and awe that may be inherent in or produced by undomesticated nature or great art. The sublime was thought of as higher and loftier than something that is merely beautiful.

**Subplot:**  a line of story that is subordinate to the main storyline of a narrative. (Note that properly speaking a subplot is a category of story material, not of plot.)

**Substitution:**  a deliberate change from the dominant pattern of stresses in a line of verse to create emphasis or variation. Thus the first line of Shakespeare's sonnet "'Shall I compare thee to a summer's day?' is decidedly iambic in meter (x / x / x / x / x /), whereas the second line substitutes a trochee (/ x) in the opening foot: "Thou art more lovely and more temperate."

**Subtext:**  implied or suggested meaning of a passage of text, or of an entire work.

**Syllabic Verse:**  poetry in which the length of a line is measured solely by the number of syllables, regardless of accents or patterns of stress.

**Syllable:**  vocal sound or group of sounds forming a unit of speech; a syllable may be formed with a single effort of articulation. Some syllables consist of a single phoneme (e.g., the word *I*, or the first syllable in the word *u*-ni-ty) but others may be made up of several phonemes (as with one-syllable words such as *lengths*, *splurged*, and *through*). By contrast, the much shorter words *ago*, *any*, and *open* each have two syllables.

**Symbol:**  a word, image, or idea that represents something more, or other, than for what it at first appears to stand. Like metaphor, the symbol extends meaning; but while the tenor and vehicle of metaphor are bound in a specific relationship, a symbol may have a range of connotations. For example, the image of a rose may call forth associations of love, passion, transience, fragility, youth and beauty, among others. Depending upon the context, such an image could be interpreted in a variety of ways, as in Blake's lyric, "The Sick Rose." Though this power of symbolic representation characterizes all language, poetry most particularly endows the concrete imagery evoked through language with a larger meaning. Such meaning is implied rather than explicitly stated; indeed, much of the power of symbolic language lies in the reader's ability to make meaningful sense of it.

**Syncope:**  in poetry, the dropping of a letter or syllable from the middle of a word, as in "trav'ler." Such a contraction allows a line to stay within a metrical scheme. See also *catalexis* and *elision*.

**Synecdoche:**  a kind of *metonymy* in which a writer substitutes the name of a part of something to signify the whole: for example, "sail" for ship or "hand" for a member of the ship's crew.

**Tercet:**  a group, or stanza, of three lines, often linked by an interlocking rhyme scheme as in *terza rima*. See also *triplet*.

**Terza Rima:**  an arrangement of tercets interlocked by a rhyme scheme of *aba bcb cdc ded*, etc., and ending with a couplet that rhymes with the second-last line of the final tercet (for example, *efe*, *ff*). See, for example, Percy Shelley's "Ode to the West Wind."

**Tetrameter:**  a line of poetry containing four metrical feet.

**Theme:**  the governing idea of a discourse, conveyed through the development of the subject, and through the recurrence of certain words, sounds, or metrical patterns. See also *motif*.

**Third-Person Narrative:**  See *narrative perspective*.

**Tone:**   the writer's attitude toward a given subject or audience, as expressed though an authorial persona or "voice." Tone can be projected through particular choices of wording, imagery, figures of speech, and rhythmic devices. Compare *mood*.

**Tories:**   See *Political Parties*.

**Tragedy:**   in the traditional definition originating in discussions of ancient Greek drama, a serious narrative recounting the downfall of the protagonist. More loosely, the term has been applied to a wide variety of literary forms in which the tone is predominantly a dark one and the narrative does not end happily.

**Transcendentalism:**   a philosophical movement that influenced such Victorian writers as Thomas Carlyle and Robert Browning. Also a mode of Romantic thought, Transcendentalism places the supernatural and the natural within one great Unity and believes that each individual person embodies aspects of the divine.

**Trimeter:**   a line of poetry containing three metrical feet.

**Triolet:**   a French form in which the first line appears three times in a poem of only eight lines. The first line is repeated at lines 4 and 7; the second line is repeated in line 8. The triolet has only two rhymes: *abaaabab*.

**Triple Foot:**   poetic foot of three syllables. The possible varieties of triple foot are the anapest (in which two unstressed syllables are followed by a stressed syllable), the dactyl (in which a stressed syllable is followed by two unstressed lines), and the mollossus (in which all three syllables are stressed equally). English poetry tends to use duple rhythms far more frequently than triple rhythms.

**Triplet:**   a group of three lines with the same end-rhyme, much used by eighteenth-century poets to vary or punctuate the flow of couplets. See also *tercet*.

**Trivium:**   group of three academic subjects (dialectic, grammar, and rhetoric) that were part of the university curriculum in the Middle Ages. Their study precedes that of the more advanced subjects of the *quadrivium*.

**Trochee:**   a metrical foot containing one strong stress followed by one weak stress: / x (heaven, lover).

**Trope:**   any figure of speech that plays on our understandings of words to extend, alter, or transform "literal" meaning. Common tropes include *metaphor*, *simile*, *personification*, *hyperbole*, *metonymy*, *oxymoron*, *synecdoche*, and *irony*. See also *figures of speech*, above.

**Turn** (Italian "volta"):   the point in a *sonnet* where the mood or argument changes. The turn may occur between the octave and sestet, i.e., after the eighth line, or in the final couplet, depending on the kind of sonnet.

**Unities:**   Many literary theorists of the late sixteenth through late eighteenth centuries held that a play should ideally be presented as representing a single place, and confining the action to a single day and a single dominant event. They disapproved of plots involving gaps or long periods of time, shifts in place, or subplots. These concepts, which came to be referred to as the unities of space, time, and action, were based on a misreading of classical authorities (principally of Aristotle).

*Vers de societé*:    French: literally, "verse about society." The term originated with poetry written by aristocrats and upper-middle-class poets that specifically disavows the ambition of creating "high art" while treating the concerns of their own group in verse forms that demonstrate a high degree of formal control (e.g., artful rhymes, surprising turns of diction).

*Vers libre* (French):    See *free verse* above.

Verse:    a general term for works of poetry, usually referring to poems that incorporate some kind of metrical structure. The term may also describe a line of poetry, though more frequently it is applied to a stanza.

Villanelle:    a poem usually consisting of 19 lines, with five 3-line stanzas (tercets) rhyming *aba*, and a concluding quatrain rhyming *abaa*. The first and third lines of the first tercet are repeated at fixed intervals throughout the rest of the poem. See, for example, Dylan Thomas's "Do Not Go Gentle Into That Good Night."

Whigs:    See *Political Parties*.

Workhouse:    public institution in which the poor were provided with a minimal level of sustenance and with lodging in exchange for work performed. Early workhouses were typically administered by individual parishes. In 1834 a unified system covering all of England and Wales was put into effect.

Zeugma:    a *figure of speech* (trope) in which one word links or "yokes" two others in the same sentence, often to comic or ironic effect. For example, a verb may govern two objects, as in Pope's line "Or stain her honour, or her new brocade."

# Permissions Acknowledgments

**Achebe, Chinua**. "The Sacrificial Egg," from GIRLS AT WAR AND OTHER STORIES. New York: Anchor, 1990. Copyright © 1972, 1973 by Chinua Achebe. Used by permission of Doubleday, a division of Random House, Inc., of the Emma Sweeney Agency and of Harold Ober Associates Incorporated; "An Image of Africa," from HOPES AND IMPEDIMENTS. New York: Anchor, 1990. Copyright © 1988 by Chinua Achebe. Used by permission of Doubleday, a division of Random House, Inc. and of the Emma Sweeney Agency.

**Aiken, Conrad**. "Diverse Realists." Originally printed in *The Dial*, 8 November, 1917.

**Allain, Marie-Françoise**. Excerpts from THE OTHER MAN: CONVERSATIONS WITH GRAHAM GREENE. Trans. from the French by Guido Waldman. London: The Bodley Head, 1983. English translation copyright © 1983 by the Bodley Head and Simon and Schuster. Reprinted by permission of The Random House Group Ltd. and Simon and Schuster.

**Alvi, Moniza**. "And If," from CARRYING MY WIFE. Northumberland: Bloodaxe Books, 2000; "How the World Split in Two," from HOW THE STONE FOUND ITS VOICE. Northumberland: Bloodaxe Books, 2005. Copyright © Bloodaxe Books.

**Armitage, Simon**. "The English" and "It Could Be You," from THE UNIVERSAL HOME DOCTOR. London: Faber, 2002. Reprinted by permission of Faber and Faber Ltd.

**Armstrong, J.A.** "Another Reply to Flanders Fields," from THE BEST LOVED POEMS OF THE AMERICAN PEOPLE. Ed. Hazel Felleman. New York: Doubleday, 1936.

**Atwood, Margaret**. "Further Arrivals," "Death of a Young Son by Drowning," "The Immigrants," "Later in Belleville: Career," "Thoughts From Underground," "Daguerreotype Taken in Old Age" and "A Bus Along St. Clair: December," from THE JOURNALS OF SUSANNA MOODIE. Toronto: Oxford University Press, 1970. Copyright © Oxford University Press Canada 1973, 1976. Reprinted by permission of the publisher and of Houghton Mifflin Company. All rights reserved; "We Are Hard" and "You Fit into Me," from POWER POLITICS. Toronto: House of Anansi Press, 1996. Copyright © 1971, 1996 by Margaret Atwood. Reprinted by permission of the publisher; "*The Handmaid's Tale* and *Oryx and Crake* in Context." PMLA, 119.3 (2004): 513-517. Reprinted by permission of Margaret Atwood. Originally published in PMLA, copyright © 2004 by O.W. Toad Ltd.

**Auden, W. H.** "O What is that Sound," from COLLECTED POEMS. New York: Vintage, 1991. Copyright © by W.H. Auden 1951; "At Last Our Secret is Out" and excerpts from "The Sea and The Mirror," from COLLECTED POEMS. New York: Vintage, 1991. Copyright © 1976 by Edward Mendelson, William Meredith and Monroe K. Spears, Executors of the Estate of W.H. Auden; "Stop All The Clocks," "Spain 1937," "Lullaby," "As I Walked Out One Evening," "Musée des Beaux Arts," "In Memory of W.B. Yeats" and "September 1, 1939," from COLLECTED POEMS. New York: Vintage, 1991. Copyright © by W.H. Auden 1940 and renewed 1968. Reprinted by permission of Faber and Faber Ltd; "The Shield of Achilles," from COLLECTED POEMS. New York: Vintage, 1991. Copyright © by W.H. Auden 1937 and renewed 1965; "The Truest Poet is the Most

Feigning," from COLLECTED POEMS. New York: Vintage, 1991. Copyright © by W.H. Auden 1954; "Writing," from THE DYER'S HAND AND OTHER ESSAYS. London: Faber, 1975. Copyright © by W.H. Auden 1962. Used by permission of Random House Inc.

Beckett, Samuel. "Whoroscope," from COLLECTED POEMS IN ENGLISH AND FRENCH. New York: Grove/Atlantic, 1977. Copyright © 1977 by Samuel Beckett; Excerpts from "Texts for Nothing," and "The Calmative," from STORIES AND TEXTS FOR NOTHING. New York: Grove/Atlantic, 1967. Copyright © 1967 by Samuel Beckett; "Imagination Dead Imagine," from FIRST LOVE AND OTHER SHORTS. New York: Grove/Atlantic, 1966. Copyright © 1966 by Samuel Beckett; "Krapp's Last Tape," from THE COLLECTED SHORTER PLAYS OF SAMUEL BECKETT. New York: Grove/Atlantic, 1984. Copyright © by Samuel Beckett 1958; "Dante ... Bruno . Vico .. Joyce," from DISJECTA. New York: Grove/Atlantic, 1984. Copyright © 1961 by Samuel Beckett.

Boland, Eavan. "9. Night Feed" and "Listen. This is the Noise of Myth," from AN ORIGIN LIKE WATER: COLLECTED POEMS 1967-1987. New York: W.W. Norton & Company, 1996. Copyright © 1996 by Eavan Boland. Reprinted by permission of the publisher and of Carcanet Press Limited; "Anna Liffey," from IN A TIME OF VIOLENCE. New York: W.W. Norton & Company, 1994. Copyright 1994 by Eavan Boland. Reprinted by permission of the publisher and of Carcanet Press Limited; "II. Against Love Poetry," from AGAINST LOVE POETRY: POEMS. New York: W.W. Norton & Company, 2001. Copyright © 2001 by Eavan Boland. Used by permission of the publisher and of Carcanet Press Limited.

Bowen, Elizabeth. "Oh Madam...," from THE COLLECTED STORIES OF ELIZABETH BOWEN. London: Jonathan Cape, 1980. Reproduced by permission of Curtis Brown Group Ltd., London on behalf of the Estate of Elizabeth Bowen, Copyright © Elizabeth Bowen 1941.

Breeze, Jean 'Binta'. "earth cries," from THE ARRIVAL OF BRIGHTEYE & OTHER POEMS. Northumberland: Bloodaxe, 2000. Copyright © Bloodaxe Books.

Byatt, A.S. "The July Ghost," from SUGAR AND OTHER STORIES. New York: Simon & Schuster, 1987. Reprinted by permission of Sll/sterling Lord Literistic, Inc., Copyright © 1986 by Antonia Byatt.

Campbell, David. "Men in Green," from SELECTED POEMS. Sydney: Angus and Robertson, 1968. Reprinted by kind of permission of Judy Campbell.

Cannan, May Wedderburn. Excerpts from GREY GHOSTS AND VOICE. Kineton: The Roundwood Press, 1976.

Carrington, Leonora. "The Debutante," from LA DAME OVALE. Paris: GLM, 1939. Copyright © 2006 Leonora Carrington / Artists Rights Society (ARS), New York.

Carter, Angela. "The Bloody Chamber," from THE BLOODY CHAMBER AND OTHER STORIES. New York: Penguin, 1993. Reproduced by permission of the author c/o Rogers, Coleridge & White Ltd., 20 Powis Mews, London W11 1JN, Copyright © 1979 by Angela Carter.

**Chapman, Graham, et al.** "Dead Parrot Sketch" and "Pet Conversion," from MONTY PYTHONS FLYING CIRCUS: JUST THE WORDS, VOL. ONE. London: Methuen, 1999. Copyright © Python (Monty) Pictures Ltd, 1989; "Dirty Hungarian Phrasebook" and "Spam," from MONTY PYTHONS FLYING CIRCUS: JUST THE WORDS, VOL. TWO. London: Methuen, 1999. Copyright © Python (Monty) Pictures Ltd, 1989.

**Charles, Hughie, and Ross Parker.** "We'll Meet Again." Words and Music by Hughie Charles and Ross Parker. Copyright © 1939 (Renewed) by Irwin Dash Music Co., Ltd. All Rights for the Western Hemisphere controlled by Music Sales Corporation (ASCAP). International copyright secured. All right reserved. Reprinted by permission.

**Churchill, Caryl.** TOP GIRLS. London: Methuen, 1982. This play is fully protected by copyright. All rights reserved. All enquiries concerning the rights for professional or amateur stage productions must be made to: Casarotto Ramsay & Associates Ltd. 60-66 Wardour Street London, W1V 4ND. Tel: (0) 20 7287 4450. Fax: (0) 20 7287 9128. Email: agents@casarotto.uk.com. Website: www.casarotto.uk.com.

**Cunard, Nancy.** Excerpts from "Jamaica – The Negro Island" and "The White Man's Duty: An Analysis of the Colonial Question in Light of the Atlantic Charter," from ESSAYS ON RACE AND EMPIRE. Ed. Maureen Moynagh. Peterborough: Broadview, 2002. Reprinted by permission of A.R.A. Hobson.

**Dabydeen, David.** "Slave Song," "Coolie Odyssey," "Preface" and "Turner I-VI," from TURNER: NEW AND SELECTED POEMS. Leeds: Peepal, 2002. Copyright © David Dabydeen 1995, 2002.

**Doolittle, Hilda (HD).** "Oread" and "The Pool," from COLLECTED POEMS, 1912-1944. New York: New Directions, 1983. Copyright © 1982 by The Estate of Hilda Doolittle. Reprinted by permission of the publisher.

**Douglas, Keith.** "Vergissmeinnicht," from THE COMPLETE POEMS. London: Faber, 2000. Copyright © 1978, 1998 by the Estate of Keith Douglas. Reprinted by permission of Faber and Faber Ltd, an affiliate of Farrar, Straus and Giroux, LLC.

**Duffy, Carol Ann.** "Stealing," from SELLING MANHATTAN. London: Anvil Press Poetry, 1988; "Adultery," "The Good Teachers," "Drunk" and "Mean Time," from MEAN TIME. London: Anvil Press Poetry, 1993. Reprinted by permission of the publisher; "Wish" "Mrs. Lazarus," from THE WORLD'S WIFE. London: Faber, 1999. Reprinted by permission of Macmillan, London, UK; "Rapture," from RAPTURE. London: Picador, 2005. Reprinted by permission of Macmillan, London, UK.

**Eliot, T.S.** "Journey of the Magi," "Marina" and "Burnt Norton," from COMPLETE POEMS AND PLAYS, 1909-1950. New York: Harcourt, 1952. Reprinted by permission of Faber and Faber Ltd.

**Ellis, Havelock.** "Sexual Inversion," from STUDIES IN THE PSYCHOLOGY OF SEX: VOLUME 2. Philadelphia: F.A. Davis, 1918. Reprinted by permission of the publisher.

**Evaristo, Bernardine.** Excerpts from LARA. Reproduced by permission of Curtis Brown Group Ltd., London on behalf of Bernardine Evaristo. Copyright © Bernardine Evaristo, 1997.

**Fenton, James**. "A German Requiem," from THE MEMORY OF WAR. Edinburgh: Salamander, 1980. Reprinted by permission of PFD on behalf of James Fenton.

**Fitzgerald, Penelope**. "The Axe," from THE TIMES ANTHOLOGY OF GHOST STORIES. London: Jonathan Cape, 1975. Used by permission of the Random House Group Limited.

**Flint, F.S.** "Imagisme." Originally published in *Poetry Magazine*, March 1913.

**Forrest-Thomson, Veronica**. "Identikit" and "Phrase-Book," from COLLECTED POEMS AND TRANSLATIONS. Lewes, East Sussex: Allardyce, Barnett, 1990. Copyright © Jonathan Culler and the Estate of Veronica-Forrest Thomson 1990 and Allardyce, Barnett, Publishers 1990. Reprinted by permission of Allardyce, Barnett Publishers.

**Forster, E.M.** "The Road from Colonus," from THE COLLECTED TALES OF E.M. FORSTER. New York: Knopf, 1947. Copyright © Alfred A. Knopf, a division of Random House Inc., 1947. Used by permission of publisher and of The Provost and Scholars of King's College, Cambridge and The Society of Authors as the Literary Representatives of the Estate of E.M. Forster; "What I Believe," from TWO CHEERS FOR DEMOCRACY. New York: Harcourt, 1951. Copyright © 1951 by E.M. Forster and renewed 1979 by Donald Parry. Reprinted by permission of Harcourt Inc., of The Provost and Scholars of King's College, Cambridge and of The Society of Authors as the Literary Representatives of the Estate of E.M. Forster; Excerpts from "Terminal Note," from MAURICE. Toronto: Macmillan, 1971. Copyright © 1971 by the trustees of the late E.M. Forster. Used by permission of W.W. Norton & Company, Inc., and by The Provost and Scholars of King's College, Cambridge and The Society of Authors as the Literary Representatives of the Estate of E.M. Forster.

**Graves, Robert**. "The Cool Web," "Down, Wanton, Down!" and "Recalling War," from COMPLETE POEMS IN ONE VOLUME. Ed. Patrick Quinn. Manchester: Carcanet, 2000. Reprinted by permission of the publisher; Excerpts from GOODBYE TO ALL THAT. New York: Doubleday, 1929.

**Greene, Graham**. "The Basement Room," from COLLECTED STORIES. New York: Penguin Books, 1992. Reprinted by permission of David Higham Associates; "Preface," from THE FALLEN IDOL. London: Penguin, 1992. Copyright © 1950 by Graham Greene. Reprinted by permission of International Creative Management, Inc.

**Gunn, Thom**. "The Wound," "Tamer and Hawk," "To His Cynical Mistress," "The Hug" and "The Missing," from COLLECTED POEMS. New York: Farrar, Straus & Giroux, 1995. Copyright © 1994 by Thom Gunn. All poems reprinted by permission of the publisher and of Faber and Faber Ltd.

**Harrison, Tony**. "Them & [uz]" and "t'Ark," from SELECTED POEMS. London: Penguin, 1987. Copyright © Tony Harrison; Excerpts from "v.," from v. Northumberland: Bloodaxe Books, 1985. Copyright © Bloodaxe Books; "Sonnets for August 1945 (I)," from v. AND OTHER POEMS. New York: Farrar, Straus & Giroux, 1990.

**Harsnet, David**. "Art," from LEGION. London, Faber, 2005. Reprinted by permission of Faber and Faber Ltd.

& White., 20 Powis Mews, London W11 1JN and of Scribner, an imprint of Simon and Schuster Adult Publishing Group.

**Larkin, Phillip.** "Church Going," from THE LESS DECEIVED. Yorkshire: Marvel Press, 1955; "Days," "Dockery and Son," "Annus Mirabilis," "High Window," "This Be The Verse," "Vers de Société," "The Old Fools" and "Aubade," from COLLECTED POEMS. London: Faber, 2003. Copyright © 1988, 2003 by the Estate of Philip Larkin. Reprinted by permission of Faber and Faber Ltd and of Farrar, Straus & Giroux, LLC.

**Lawrence, D.H.** "Tortoise Shout" and "Bavarian Gentians," from THE COMPLETE POEMS OF D.H. LAWRENCE. Eds. Vivian De Sola Pinto and Warren Roberts. New York: Penguin, 1964. Reproduced by permission of Pollinger Limited and the proprietor; "Snake," from BIRDS, BEASTS AND FLOWERS: POEMS BY D.H. LAWRENCE. New York: Haskell House Publishers Ltd., 1974. Reproduced by permission of Pollinger Limited and the proprietor; "The Hopi Snake Dance," from MORNINGS IN MEXICO AND ETRUSCAN PLACES. London: Martin Secker, 1927. Reproduced by permission of Pollinger Limited and the proprietor; "Why the Novel Matters," from PHOENIX: THE POSTHUMOUS PAPERS OF D.H. LAWRENCE. Ed. Edward McDonald. London: William Heinemann Ltd., 1961. Reproduced by permission of Pollinger Limited and the proprietor.

**Lehmann, John.** Excerpts from "Foreword," from PENGUIN NEW WRITING NO. 5. Middlesex: Penguin, 1941. Reprinted by permission of David Higham Associates.

**LePan, Douglas.** "Below Monte Cassino" and "The Haystack," from WEATHERING IT: COMPLETE POEMS 1948-1987. Toronto: McClelland and Stewart, 1987. Copyright © 1987 The Estate of Douglas LePan. (Don LePan, literary executor, c/o Broadview Press); "Personality of the Poet: Some Recollections of T.S. Eliot," from BRIGHT GLASS OF MEMORY. Toronto: McGraw Hill, 1979. Copyright © 1979 The Estate of Douglas LePan. (Don LePan, literary executor, c/o Broadview Press).

**Lessing, Doris.** "To Room Nineteen," from A MAN AND TWO WOMEN. New York: Simon and Schuster, 1984. Copyright © 1963 Doris Lessing. Reprinted by kind permission of Jonathan Clowes Ltd., London, on behalf of Doris Lessing; Excerpts from "Preface," from THE GOLDEN NOTEBOOK. New York: Simon and Schuster, 1962. Copyright © 1972 by Doris Lessing. Reprinted by kind permission of Jonathan Clowes Ltd., London, on behalf of Doris Lessing.

**Lewis, Gwyneth.** "Mother Tongue," from CHAOTIC ANGELS. Northumberland: Bloodaxe Books, 2005. Copyright © Bloodaxe Books.

**Loy, Mina.** "Three Moments in Paris – One O'Clock at Night" and "Love Songs 1, 2 and 3," from THE LAST LUNAR BAEDEKER. Highlands: Jargon, 1982. Copyright © 1982 by The Jargon Society. Reprinted by permission of Roger L. Conover, Mina Loy's editor and literary executor.

**McEwan, Ian.** "Last Day of Summer," from FIRST LOVE, LAST RIGHTS. London: Jonathan Cape, 1975. Copyright © 1975 Ian McEwan. Reproduced by permission of the author, c/o Rogers, Coleridge & White Ltd., 20 Powis Mews, London W11 1JN.

**McGuckian, Medbh.** "Slips" and "The Sofa," from THE FLOWER MASTER AND OTHER POEMS. Loughcrew: The Gallery Press, 1993. Reprinted by kind permission of the author and of

**Orwell, George.** Excerpts from HOMAGE TO CATALONIA. New York: Harvest, 1969. Copyright © 1937 by George Orwell, 1952 and renewed 1980 by Sonia Brownell Orwell. Reprinted by permission of the publisher and Bill Hamilton as the Literary Executor of the Estate of the Late Sonia Brownell Orwell and Martin Secker & Warburg Ltd; "Politics and the English Language" and "Shooting an Elephant," from SHOOTING AN ELEPHANT AND OTHER ESSAYS. New York: Harvest, 1984. Copyright © 1936 and 1946 respectively by George Orwell, 1950 by the publisher, and renewed 1979 by Sonia Brownell Orwell. Reprinted by permission of the publisher and Bill Hamilton as the Literary Executor of the Estate of the Late Sonia Brownell Orwell and Martin Secker & Warburg Ltd; Excerpts from THE ROAD TO WIGAN PIER. New York: Harvest, 1972. Copyright © 1936 by George Orwell, and 1997 by the Estate of Sonia B. Orwell. Reprinted by permission of the publisher and Bill Hamilton as the Literary Executor of the Estate of the Late Sonia Brownell Orwell and Martin Secker & Warburg Ltd.; Excerpts from "Anti-Semitism in Britain," from SUCH, SUCH WERE THE JOYS. New York: Harcourt, 1953. Copyright © 1945 by Sonia Brownell Orwell and renewed 1973 by Sonia Pitt-Rivers. Reprinted by permission of Harcourt, Inc; Excerpts from THE COLLECTED ESSAYS, JOURNALISM AND LETTERS OF GEORGE ORWELL, VOLUME 1: 1920-1940. Ed. Sonia Orwell and Ian Angus. New York: Harvest, 1971. Copyright © 1968 by Sonia Brownell Orwell and renewed 1996 by Mark Hamilton. Reprinted by permission of Harcourt Inc.

**Osborne, John.** Excerpts from "A Better Class of Person: An Autobiography Vol. 1," from LOOKING BACK. London: Faber, 1999. Reprinted by kind permission of Gordon Dickerson.

**O'Sullivan, Maggie.** Excerpts from "Starlings," from HOUSE OF SHAMAN. London: Reality Street, 1993. Reprinted by permission of Reality Street Editions, 63 All Saints Street, Hastings, East Sussex TN34 3BN, www.realitystreet.co.uk.

**Oswald, Alice.** "Wedding," from THE THING IN THE GAP-STONE STILE. London: Faber, 1994. Reprinted by permission of PFD on behalf of Alice Oswald; "Woods, Etc.," from WOODS, ETC. New York: Oxford University Press, 1996. Reprinted by permission of PFD on behalf of Alice Oswald.

**Owen, Wilfred.** Excerpts from WILFRED OWEN: THE COLLECTED LETTERS. New York: Oxford University Press, 1967. Reprinted by permission of the publisher.

**Page, P.K.** "The Stenographers," "The Landlady," "Ecce Homo," "Stories of Snow," "Young Girls," "After Rain," "Nursing Home," "Planet Earth," and excerpts from "Address at Simon Fraser," from THE HIDDEN ROOM (TWO VOLS). Erin, Ontario: Porcupine's Quill, 1997. Copyright © 1997 by P.K. Page; "Calgary," from HAND LUGGAGE (A MEMOIR IN VERSE). Erin, Ontario: Porcupine's Quill, 2006. Copyright © 2006 by P.K. Page.

**Palmer, Vance.** "The Farmer Remembers the Somme," from THE PENGUIN BOOK OF AUSTRALIAN VERSE. Victoria: Penguin, 1972.

**Pinter, Harold.** "The Homecoming," from PLAYS: THREE. London: Methuen, 1978. Reprinted by permission of Faber and Faber Ltd.

**Pound, Ezra.** "In a Station of the Metro," "Alba" and "L'Art 1910," from PERSONAE. London: Elkin Mathews, 1909. Copyright © 1926 by Ezra Pound. Reprinted by permission of New Directions

Publishing Corp;  Excerpts from "A Few Don'ts," from "A Retrospect," from THE LITERARY ESSAYS OF EZRA POUND. New York: New Directions, 1954. Copyright © 1935 by Ezra Pound. Reprinted by permission of the publisher; Excerpts from "Vorticism.," from GAUDIER-BRZESKA: A MEMOIR. London: Bodley Head, 1916. Copyright © 1980 by New Directions Publishing Corp. Reprinted by permission of New Directions Publishing Corp; "Drunken Helots and Mr. Eliot." Originally published in *The Egoist*, June 1917. Copyright © 1926 by Ezra Pound. Reprinted by permission of New Directions Publishing Corp.

**Raine, Craig**. "A Martian Sends a Postcard Home," from A MARTIAN SENDS A POSTCARD HOME. Oxford: Oxford University Press, 1979. Copyright © 1979 by Craig Raine.

**Raworth, Tom**. "Out of a Sudden," from CLEAN AND WELL LIT. New York: Roof Books, 1996; "Looking For Language," from COLLECTED POEMS. Manchester: Carcanet, 2003. Reprinted by permission of the publisher.

**Reed, Henry**. "I: Naming of Parts," from LESSONS OF WAR. New York: Chilmark Press, 1970. Reprinted by kind permission of The Estate of Henry Reed.

**Rhys, Jean**. "Let Them Call it Jazz," from TIGERS ARE BETTER - LOOKING. London: Penguin, 1972. Copyright © Jean Rhys 1972.

**Richardson, Dorothy**. "About Punctuation." Originally published in *The Adelphi*, 1 April, 1924. Reprinted by permission of Paterson Marsh Ltd on behalf of The Estate of Dorothy Richardson; "Journey to Paradise," from JOURNEY TO PARADISE. London: Virago, 1989. By permission of Paterson Marsh Ltd on behalf of The Estate of Dorothy Richardson; "Foreword," from PILGRIMAGE. London: Virago, 1979. By permission of Paterson Marsh Ltd on behalf of The Estate of Dorothy Richardson.

**Ritchie, Charles**. Excerpts from THE SIREN YEARS: A CANADIAN DIPLOMAT ABROAD 1937-1945. Toronto: McClelland & Stewart, 2001. Used by permission of the publisher.

**Roberts, Robert**. Excerpts from THE CLASSIC SLUM. London: Penguin, 1990. Reprinted by kind permission of Mr. G. Roberts.

**Rushdie, Salman**. "Is Nothing Sacred?," from IMAGINARY HOMELANDS. New York: Viking, 1991. Copyright © Salman Rushdie 1991. Used by permission of Viking Penguin, a division of Penguin Group (USA) Inc.

**Sassoon, Siegfried**. "They," "Glory of Women" and "Everyone Sang," from COLLECTED POEMS OF SIEGFRIED SASSOON. London: Faber, 1961. Copyright © 1918, 1920 by EP Dutton. Copyright © 1936, 1946, 1947, 1948 by Siegfried Sassoon. Used by kind permission of George Sassoon and Viking Penguin, a division of Penguin Group (USA) Inc; Excerpts from "Part II," from MEMOIRS OF AN INFANTRY OFFICER. London: Faber, 1930. Copyright © Siegfried Sassoon by kind permission of George Sassoon.

**Shaw, Bernard**. "Mrs. Warren's Profession," from PLAYS UNPLEASANT. London: Penguin, 1988. The Society of Authors on behalf of the Estate of Bernard Shaw, Copyright © 1898, 1913, 1926, 1930, 1933, 1941 by George Bernard Shaw. Copyright © 1905 Brentano's. Copyright © 1957 by

Excerpts from "Introduction," from A VISION. New York: Macmillan, 1983. Reprinted with permission of Scribner, an imprint of Simon & Schuster Adult Publishing Group, copyright © 1937 by W.B. Yeats; copyright renewed © 1965 by Bertha Georgie Yeats and Anne Butler Yeats.

## PICTURE CREDITS

Cover: © 1961 Estate of Vanessa Bell courtesy Henrietta Garnett. Color Insert: "Workshop," by Wyndham Lewis, The Tate Gallery, London/Art Resource, NY. Reprinted by permission of Art Resource."Kendal Street," by Sirkka-Liisa Konttinen, 1969. Reprinted by permission. Page XXXVII: Getty Images. Page XL: Getty Images. Page XLI: Getty Images. Page XLII: Wide World Photos. Page XLIII: Penguin Books, 1938. Page XLIX: Getty Images. Page L: (top right) Getty Images. Page LI: Getty Images. Page LII: Getty Images. Page LVII: Getty Images. LIX: United Press International. LX: *Brave New World* by Aldous Huxley, published by Chatto & Windus, 1932. Reprinted by permission of The Random House Group Ltd. Page LXI: Random House, Inc. Page 1: Reproduced by permission of the National Portrait Gallery, London. Page 48: Reproduced by permission of the National Portrait Gallery, London. Page 93: Reproduced by permission of the National Portrait Gallery, London. Page 98: Reproduced by permission of the National Portrait Gallery, London. Page 101: Reproduced by permission of the National Portrait Gallery, London. Page 105: Reproduced by permission of the National Portrait Gallery, London. Page 107: Reproduced by permission of the National Portrait Gallery, London. Page 111: Reproduced by permission of the National Portrait Gallery, London. Page 144: Reproduced by permission of the National Portrait Gallery, London. Page 188: Portrait by Lisa Brawn. Page 201: Portrait by Lisa Brawn. Page 213: Reproduced by permission of the National Portrait Gallery, London. Page 285: Reproduced by permission of the National Portrait Gallery, London. Page 287: Sylvia Beach Papers. Manuscripts Division. Department of Rare Books and Special Collections. Princeton University Library. Page 376: Reproduced by permission of the National Portrait Gallery, London. Page 414: Getty Images. Page 424: Reproduced by permission of the National Portrait Gallery, London. Page 442: Reproduced by permission of the National Portrait Gallery, London. Page 479: Les Demoiselles d'Avignon, 1907. By Pablo Picasso. © Picasso Estate / SODRAC (2006). Page 499: Copyright © Paul Joyce / National Portrait Gallery, London. Reproduced by permission of the National Portrait Gallery, London. Page 510: Reproduced by permission of the David Jones Trust. Page 515: Photo by Peter Stark. Page 517: Portrait by Lisa Brawn. Page 527: Portrait by Lisa Brawn. Page 532: Copyright © estate of Felix H. Man / National Portrait Gallery, London. Reproduced by permission of the National Portrait Gallery, London. Page 551: Portrait by Lisa Brawn. Page 573: Reproduced by permission of the National Portrait Gallery, London. Page 589: Crown Copyright. Page 618: Getty Images. Page 620: The Press Association. Page 622 (both images): Getty Images. Page 627: Getty Images. Page 634: Image courtesy of Marion Kalter. Page 638: Reproduced by permission of the National Portrait Gallery, London. Page 657: Reproduced by permission of the National Portrait Gallery, London. Page 661: Portrait by Terry Milligan, reproduced by permission of Lorien Milligan. Page 666: Photo coutrsy of Barbara Pedrick. Reprinted by permission of The Porcupine's Quill. Page 669: Photo courtesy of Jonny Baker. Page 675: Photograph by Jillian Edelstein, Camera Press London. Page 681: Photograph by Yousuf Karsh, Camera Press London. Page 698: Portrait by Lisa Brawn. Page 705: Portrait by Lisa Brawn. Page 730: Photo courtesy of the artist Fergus Greer. Page 734: Photo – Mark Gerson. Page 765: Portrait by Lisa Brawn. Page 769: Photograph by Collections/Fay Godwin. Page 786: Getty Images. Page 799: Getty Images. Page 805: Photo courtesy of Don Hamerman. Page 814: Reproduced by permission of the National Portrait Gallery, London. Page 819: © The Nobel Foundation. Reprinted by permission. Page 834: Photo by Derek Shapton. Page 852: With friendly permission by Unionsverlag. Page 859: Reproduced by permission of the National Portrait Gallery, London. Page 866: © Jess Atwood Gibson. Page 877: Courtesy of Michael Ondaatji and Trident Media. Page 833: Photo – Mark Gerson. Page 914: Reproduced by permission of the National Portrait Gallery, London. Page 952: Portrait by Lisa Brawn. Page 981: Portrait by Lisa Brawn. Page 990: Photo courtesy of Neil Wilder/www.wilderwilder.net. Page 999: Reproduced by permission of the National Portrait Gallery, London. Page 1004: Portrait by Lisa Brawn. Page 1012: Portrait by Lisa Brawn. Page 1020: With kind permission of David Dabydeen. Page 1027: Reprinted by permission of Anvil Press Poetry.  Page 1087: Reproduced by permission of the National Portrait Gallery, London. Page 1057: Reproduced by permission of the National Portrait Gallery, London. Page 1065: Portrait by Lisa Brawn.

The publisher has endeavored to contact rights holders of all copyright material and would appreciate receiving any information as to errors or omissions.

# Index of First Lines

# INDEX OF AUTHORS AND TITLES